The Logic of
International Relations

The Logic of International Relations

Seventh Edition

Walter S. Jones
Long Island University

HarperCollins*Publishers*

Sponsoring Editor: Lauren Silverman
Project Editor: Melonie Parnes
Design and Cover Coordinator: Peter Noa
Text and Cover Design: Merlin Communications, Inc.
Cover Illustration: Slanina Computer Design
Photo Research: Mira Schachne
Production: Willie Lane/Sunaina Sehwani
Compositor: BookMasters, Inc.
Printer and Binder: R. R. Donnelley & Sons, Company
Cover Printer: Lehigh Press, Inc.

The Logic of International Relations, Seventh Edition

Library of Congress Cataloging-in-Publication Data

Jones, Walter S., 1938–
    The logic of international relations / Walter S. Jones. — 7th ed.
        p.   cm.
    Includes index.
    ISBN 0–67–352034–X
    1. International relations.   I. Title.
JX1395.J66   1991
327—dc20   90–23432
                                                                             CIP

91 92 93 94 9 8 7 6 5 4 3 2 1

To Sally and Steven, Doug, and Sarah,
whose generation may have the final opportunity
to answer the question, "Will man survive?"

And to the memory of Leo Gross (1903–1990)
Gentleman, mentor, scholar, inspiration.

Brief Contents

Detailed Contents

Preface

The task of revising a lengthy and comprehensive text in international relations for the period 1988–1990 has been both exhilarating and frustrating. So swift has been the pace of change in Europe, Asia, Central America, Africa, and the Soviet Union itself that each writing session has begun with a revision of its predecessor. Revisions continued right up to the last moment, even into page proofs, in an effort to explicate in as current a fashion as possible the rapid evolution of the world order. When the sixth edition of *The Logic of International Relations* was completed in 1987, *glasnost* had only recently invaded the world's political lexicon and *perestroika* had yet to come. Today, while new troubles have replaced old, the world order is vastly transformed.

When work on the seventh edition commenced, the principal objectives were to update political, military, and economic content; to condense historical materials; and to continue to clarify the perceptual components of the global system. Shortly the mandate changed: This was to be "the first post-Cold War text in international relations." But the daily news provided ample evidence that although Soviet, American, and European perceptions might have evolved at unprecedented rates, there are countless international transactions that are outside the boundaries of the historic Cold War standoff. Hence while I have attempted in this edition to demonstrate the causes and consequences of the Cold War's demise, I have not attempted to paint a sweepingly new view of the global order. The new crisis in the Persian Gulf and the Arabian Peninsula, the continuing problems of starvation, refugees, child deaths, arms sales, petroleum costs, excess urbanization, debt, trade and payment imbalances, and the alarming acceleration of global environmental deterioration all remind us that the end of the Cold War is not one with the end of history; and while it alters some aspects of world order, it does not freeze time. A first—or second or third or *nth*—post-Cold War text in international relations may deal with extraordinary changes in superpower relations, yet be faced by scores of less constructive trends in world politics and economics with which to deal.

In preparing this edition, I have enjoyed and benefited from the generosity of many colleagues throughout the country. Professor Michael Haas of the University of Hawaii compiled his notes on the sixth edition into a most enlightening chapter-by-chapter critique with scores of suggestions. Professor Lawrence J. Finkelstein of Northern Illinois University did much the same, then followed with carefully detailed suggestions, bibliographic references that I had overlooked, and some tightly woven arguments that I hope have strengthened the chapters on international law and organization. Professor Richard W. Fox of Nassau Community College (New York) came forward with suggestions and margin notes pointing to a number of nuances of organization, content, and style. Professor James Satterwhite of Bluffton College pointed out flaws and errors and offered additional suggestions. The original manuscript for the seventh edition was reviewed by Professor Brinton Rowdybush of College of Wooster with the most exemplary thoroughness consisting of countless margin notes and several pages of suggestions.

I want also to acknowledge the role of the readers and the professors who have used previous editions of *The Logic of International Relations*. It is clear that the message of this book—that an effective understanding of contemporary international relations requires a method that is both interdisciplinary and multinational—has reached many thousands of young people throughout the English-speaking world. These students have been alerted to the need to view world politics through more than a single set of national lenses. Should the post-Cold War world be one of less confrontational national ideologies, this lesson shall be no less important. That the international relations professoriate and its students should turn to this book for this message is the author's everlasting reward.

My friends and new colleagues at Channel 12, Long Island's cable news channel, assisted me through their questions in formulating my views and analyses of many issues. Their more than 50 invitations of my live comments between May 1989 and October 1990 on China, the Soviet Union, East and West Europe, the American invasion of Panama, the Iraq-Kuwait crisis and the subsequent military and diplomatic events, and the United Nations and American foreign policy in general were most timely in the preparation of this volume. I express my appreciation particularly to Glenn Fishkin, Carol Silva, Roma Torre, and Lea Tyrrell.

Perhaps the least enviable contributors to this book are the people at Harper-Collins who, in the midst of receiving this and other manuscripts from Scott, Foresman Company, were faced with unusually early deadlines. Only the skill of Lauren Silverman, Melonie Parnes, Richard Smith and the loyal phalanx of anonymous designers, editors, and artists behind them could have produced this volume on schedule.

Aside from those who contributed to this work by way of their knowledge and expertise, there are many others who did so through the more subtle yet invaluable gifts of buoying my strength and perseverance as I attempted to balance writing in a time of unprecedented change with the daily vicissitudes of an academic vice presidency. Their special contributions are their friendship and good humor, and their concern for my exhaustion. The list of their names is long, but at the top are Gail Allan, Betty Bruce, Denis Eichhorn, Melodee Gandia, Nancy Nakashian, Gale Stevens-Haynes, David Steinberg, and George Sutton. I owe a special note of appreciation to Ellen McHugh, whose hard work and patented brand of humor lightened my burden regularly. On a list of one is Barbara Lott Jones, who lived with this work at home and sometimes on her computer. Her immersion in her public relations business compensated for the many hours and weekends of foregone personal time entailed in a work of this magnitude, but her support in so many ways never flagged. The security and happiness of all these people gives me hope that *The Logic of International Relations* might make some small contribution to understanding and global stability.

For any shortcomings and imperfections that might have survived all of this assistance, the author alone is responsible.

W. S. J.

Introduction

There are several questions of style and organization in the book that may at first seem odd and will be misleading without explanation. The book begins, in the first five chapters, with an analysis of the world outlooks of five principal "actors" in the contemporary international system: the Soviet Union, the United States, the major Western allies, China and a composite of the Third World. It begins with an examination of how each point of view is influenced by concepts, values, national interests and ideologies, rather than a statement of universal laws and regularities describing all actors, as is done in most texts. This emphasis on *perceptual analysis* is based on the belief that differences in national goals and perceptions are the origin of the two overarching conflicts of our time: the dispute between East and West and the conflict between North and South.

For the fullest appreciation of the differences among perceptions of the international system, this book uses an experimental method of presentation. Instead of taking a detached, objective, "scientific" perspective and looking at each actor's view critically, it tries to step into each nation's shoes to look at the world from its own point of view. This is an exercise in role-playing, or more nearly exactly, in role-writing, imagining first the outlook of a Soviet citizen, then seeing the world from an American point of view, then from that of an ally of the United States, then as a Chinese communist and finally from a synthesized Third World perspective. This differs greatly from the usual approach of newspapers, histories and most of our sources of information, which stand above their subjects as "neutral and objective" observers. The task of understanding viewpoints that differ profoundly from our own is so difficult that it is necessary temporarily to suspend judgment the better to appreciate the perspective of the other. To judge is to be separate from. This book uses the Stanislawski theory of method acting: the reader will try temporarily to *be* the figure he/she wishes to understand.

A few reservations and caveats about the experiment at this point. First, the various perspectives are presented in a mixture of original texts and the words of the author acting as an intermediary organizing the original texts for an American audience. This provides some flavor of the original, while permitting a quicker pace than would be possible with full texts.

Second, the book concentrates on idealized pictures of each actor, emphasizing values and professed beliefs. There is a danger here in mistaking mere rhetoric for the actual motives; we know that speechwriters often use idealistic disguises for less lofty goals, such as the pursuit of power. The differences between nations are undoubtedly exaggerated when only ideals are presented, but they would be understated if, like most introductory texts, this one concentrated instead on universal modes of behavior that ignore critical differences between actors. In a sense, then, this book errs on the side of principles, drawing caricatures that highlight the unique and defining features rather than a completely proportioned portrait.

Third, the author concedes that it is partly artificial to speak of *the* perceptual system of the United States or of any other party, particularly that of the greatly varied Third World states. Within each national actor there are elites with differences of opinion regarding the national interest, the optimal course of strategy and other issues. This book tries in each case to develop a characterization that subsumes these differences, at least as far as the dominant elites are concerned. Yet the analysis gives less importance to dissenting opinions within each national actor that have not in the post-war period influenced policy directly or substantially. For example, in the American case the analysis centers mainly on anticommunist perspective that in fact guided policy from 1948 through 1988, and only in passing does it review various revisionist challenges to the dominant outlook. In other words, the analysis focuses on various orthodoxies, not on minority views or factions that have been consistently out of power.

Fourth, one feature of the presentation may be especially controversial. Considerable attention is given to internal political features and to problems of the various actors that shape their external outlooks. Conventional analysis draws a fairly sharp distinction between domestic politics and foreign policy, but many international relations specialists are finding this rigid boundary a hinderance to understanding the roots of international behavior. To a considerable degree, the foreign actions of nations are continuations of essentially domestic processes and demands, and certainly international perceptions cannot be separated entirely from the broader value base that gives rise to them. This explains the emphasis on domestic matters at key points.

Fifth, the analysis presented here takes the nation-state to be the principal actor in international affairs. To some extent this is no longer accurate, as international organizations and some less formal transnational phenomena rise in importance. These newer actors are treated at length in the latter half of this volume. Their importance notwithstanding, the key actors are still nation-states and their official bureaucracies, accounting for perhaps 80 percent of real power in international relations. The first two parts of the book, comprising eleven of the book's eighteen chapters, stress these national actors over others.

Sixth, since the publication of the first edition of *The Logic of International Relations* in 1974, the role and character of the Cold War changed entirely.

For about half the life of this book, détente between the Soviet Union and the United States and the relaxation of Sino-American tensions reduced the probability of serious confrontation, except between China and the Soviet Union. From 1980 to 1988, however, détente failed as a regulator of Soviet-American relations, and the decade was marked by mutual suspicion, accelerated arms production and angry rhetoric. The new wave of American conservatism coincided with the revival of Soviet adventurism (as in Afghanistan) and tightening of the Soviet grip on Eastern Europe (as in Poland), so that the celebrated period of détente seemed only to have been a brief interlude in the Cold War. Then, unexpectedly, the pace of global events accelerated, and by the autumn of 1990 the Cold War was history. Following the opening of the Berlin Wall, East and West Germany were unified as one within the North Atlantic Treaty Organization (NATO), terminating in a single stroke both World War II and the Cold War. Communism failed throughout Eastern Europe, and even the Kremlin announced plans to convert from a centrally-planned economy to a market economy. New agreements were reached on severe reduction of Soviet and American troop strengths in Europe. Mikhail Gorbachev was awarded the 1990 Nobel Prize for Peace for canceling Soviet domination of Eastern Europe. For the first time in history, the Soviet and American ambassadors stood as allies in the United Nations Security Council in efforts to control hostilities in the Arabian Peninsula resulting from Iraq's annexation of Kuwait by force, and its threat to do the same to Saudi Arabia.

As the Cold War abated change occurred in other parts of the world with equally unprecedented speed. In Africa, Namibia became a sovereign nation after 70 years of South African domination, nearly half of them in defiance of the United Nations and the International Court of Justice. In South Africa itself, a new government took dramatic steps to eliminate *apartheid,* the constitutional policy of racial separation under which the minority white population (about 5 million) ruled over the majority black population of approximately 25 million. Steps included the release of political prisoners, including Nelson Mandela, who had been the incarcerated symbol of black nationalism for decades. They also included the desegregation of public facilities including rest rooms, swimming pools, and transportation vehicles. Moreover, Cuba removed its troops from Angola after more than a decade of military support to the communist element in a bloody civil war.

In Central America, the Nicaraguan civil war ended and a Washington-backed anti-Sandinista government was elected, leaving Fidel Castro of Cuba the only self-appointed head of state in the hemisphere. In Asia, Soviet troops were removed from Afghanistan with a public acknowledgement from the Kremlin that its involvement there had been ''immoral.'' So ended the Soviet Union's Vietnam, though not the brutal civil war of Afghanistan. Cambodia continued to struggle toward internal peace. China, after years of peaceful progress, resorted to political oppression initiated by a military attack on peaceful, democratic protestors in Tiananmen Square in Beijing. The new internal politics of China forestalled the reestablishment of relations with the Soviet Union and set back considerably China's economic and political relations with the United States, Japan and Europe. The two Koreas had their first ministerial discussions, raising hopes of eventual reunification. And China, in a bold challenge to its neighbor and friend North Korea, on whose behalf China had intervened in the Korean War 40 years earlier, entered into a formal trade agreement with South Korea.

These are but a few examples of the remarkable progress made in world politics in the period 1987 through 1990. Whether or not they portend a massive transformation of the world order as has been predicted by such luminaries as President George Bush is for time to tell. We are reminded, after all, that new problems can replace the old, as is so dramatically illustrated by Iraq's military adventures in the Arabian Peninsula and the world's reaction to it. Similarly, there are old problems that remain despite the end of the Cold War and progress made elsewhere: The Arab-Israel-PLO issues are a case in point. The lesson, nonetheless, is both simple and profound: There has been no peacetime era in modern history in which such sweeping change in global politics has occurred at such a rapid rate. And a few examples will show that the global economy has contributed to the pace: (1) in this same time period the United States has gone from being the world's largest creditor nation to the largest debtor; (2) as the Soviet Union and Eastern Europe transform from socialist to market-driven economies, Western Europe speeds toward full economic union in 1992 with the establishment of a new monetary system; and (3) world-wide recognition that much of the Third World's accumulated international debt can never be repaid has resulted in the application of a limited program of debt reduction by discounting, lightening the burden on some Third World debtors, but forcing many banks, including several in the United States, to transfer reserves to cover unpaid obligations. In the most far-reaching instance, President Bush canceled more than $6 billion of Egyptian debt in return for Cairo's participation in the multinational deterrence force in Saudi Arabia. Although this book does not claim that these events have created an entirely new world order, it does attempt to demonstrate the interaction of these political and economic phenomena with various national perceptions and their impact on the contemporary global order.

And finally, a word about the political implications of perceptual analysis. It has been said that this method tends to be forgiving of sins, and that it views each actor in the sympathetic light of its own values and experiences. Ultimately, it is charged, each actor is free of responsibility, each the victim of respective misperceptions. The author concedes that an agnostic analysis of positions, giving the internal logic of each case and avoiding absolute external judgments, may introduce greater moral ambiguities than fixing a single position from which to assess all the alternative views. These dilemmas of relativism and ambiguity are inherent in international relations, and it is necessary to leave the comforts of one's own belief system in order to understand other, equally compelling contributions to global coexistence. Relations between nations are in their very nature a meeting place of divergent perceptions.

PART I

The Logic of National Perceptions

CHAPTER 1

The Soviet Perspective

For Soviet citizens accustomed to orthodoxy, political monopoly of the Communist Party, an economic system of central distribution, and a system of compliance dominated by KGB intrusion in personal lives and armed suppression of democratic movements, change is everywhere. The *glasnost* (access to information) and *perestroika* (restructuring) that Mikhail Gorbachev ushered in, in the short space of two years, has resulted in sweeping changes in politics, the economy, and the machinery of state and foreign policy. Witness a few salient events of 1989 and 1990:

- Goal miners strike for improved working conditions and wages, and Gorbachev himself is dispatched from Moscow to urge them back to work. Earlier, persuasion would have been an armed phenomenon.
- Ethnic strife bordering on civil war erupts in four of the fifteen constituent republics of the Soviet Union, and in only one instance do Soviet troops play even a small part. And, contrary to custom, their role was largely passive.
- Both the Communist Party and the government are restructured so as to transfer power out of the party and into the government. And where merger of party and government once ruled the Soviet Union with monopoly power, multiple political parties arise. Some of the most powerful figures in Soviet politics publicly break with the Communist Party.
- Lithuania declares political independence, establishes its own constitution, and declares the supremacy of its law over that of Moscow. The Kremlin's response is entirely economic (temporarily cutting off supplies of industrial and domestic fuels), and agrees to discuss a procedure and date for final independence on the sole condition that Lithuania suspend its declaration.
- The Russian Republic, the largest and parent unit of the union, declares the supremacy of its law with little response from the central government.

- The Soviet Union stands idly by while one Eastern European public after another topples its communist government and, in many instances, requests the withdrawal of Soviet troops. Even more surprisingly, once the issue of Polish borders is settled, the Kremlin agrees to the reunification of East and West Germany, acceding to the West's demand that membership in the North Atlantic Treaty Organization (NATO) be a condition.
- When Iraq invades and conquers Kuwait, the Soviet Foreign Minister and the American Secretary of State meet in Moscow to issue a joint communiqué condemning Baghdad's actions, and vote together in the United Nations Security Council on an American resolution calling for the imposition of global and comprehensive economic sanctions. This follows upon Moscow's public declaration that it will discontinue all arms shipments to Iraq, one of the Kremlin's largest arms customers.
- Freedom of religion, for over 70 years considered "the opiate of the masses," is restored pursuant to President Gorbechev's personal promise to Pope John Paul.

In every aspect of life, change is the dominant theme in the Soviet Union; and it is a theme that carries over into the Kremlin's external policies, commitments and behavior. The new recognition of the failure of Marxism-Leninism as both a political and an economic system affects daily living, individual and national aspirations, and the relations of the Soviet Union virtually throughout the world. The changing relations with Europe, both East and West, have opened the way to the commercial credits, loans, and West Germany's offer to build housing in the Soviet Union for military personnel returning from Eastern Europe. The Berlin Wall, for 40 years the principal symbolic chain in the Iron Curtain, is now a tourist attraction through which both travel and commerce now pass unhindered.

Changing relations with the United States have opened the way to unprecedented reductions of military personnel and arms, both conventional and nuclear, in Europe. Although much work remains, the stage is now unquestionably set for sharp reductions in war-making potential consistent with the diminished threat of conflict. The United States has agreed to more liberal trading relations, and has held out the promise of most-favored-nation status (most beneficial terms of trade offered to any trading partner) to the Soviet Union once there are assurances of the self-determination of the peoples in the constituent republics. And the Kremlin has ceased to charge the United States with being an imperialist power. When American forces invaded Panama in order to force Manuel Noriega from power, the Soviet Union mildly branded the action an aggression but, in a departure from habit, declined to call it "imperialist aggression."

Together with its new global outlook, the severe economic conditions of the Soviet Union compelled it to look differently upon the Third World, too. In barely two years it withdrew its troops from Afghanistan and publicly declared its policy there to have been "immoral," announced its intention to reduce its military and economic aid to Cuba, removed its hand from the power distribution of the Middle East except in conjunction with the United States and others in the Iraq-Kuwait war, and discontinued all apparent efforts to support anti-American governments or challenges in Central America, South America and the Caribbean. Its effort to normalize relations with China, for years considered by Soviet orthodoxy to be a deviant communist power, was thwarted by global public opinion following the Chinese massacre of freedom demonstrators in Tiananmen Square in Beijing.

After three-quarters of a century of heavy-handed politics led in succession by Lenin, Stalin, Khrushchev and Brezhnev, the turn in political methods introduced by Gorbachev borders on the astonishing even for the most forward-looking Soviet observer. Gone swiftly and suddenly are absolute control of the economy, the insistence on the Eastern European security buffer zone against NATOs threat, the dominant notion of capitalist encirclement that for so long justified enslavement as an instrument of survival, military glorification, and the omnipresence of the state police. So abrupt and pervasive are these changes that they can be understood only against the backdrop of the traditional Marxist-Leninist orthodoxy and the long-standing Soviet Cold War global perspective.

The classical Soviet point of view had two core themes: a theme of a Russian nation, with a long history of goals and conflicts before communism, and a communist theme based on a universal ideology, a system of beliefs and values purporting to apply equally to all countries. The revolutionaries of 1917 were probably motivated more by communist ideology than by Russian nationalism; one of their first acts was to sign away large portions of Russia (containing one-third of its population and three-quarters of its iron ore) in a very unfavorable peace treaty with Germany at Brest-Litovsk to preserve a kernel, however reduced in size, for the world's first communist state. Russian national interests were subordinated to the communist ideological goal of establishing a revolutionary base.

In recent years, the mixture of goals shifted to a greater emphasis on national interests and a reduction of communism's universal goals. More attention is given to the problems of Russian society and the demands of the Russian people and less to world revolution. To understand the Soviet view, it is necessary to see the basic tenets of communist ideology as intertwined with the historical interests of the Russian nation.

Communist ideology introduces a unique analysis of the basic behavioral laws that underlie the spectrum of human relations and explains in an orderly way the otherwise unintelligible complexities of society. Karl Marx and Friedrich Engels provided the basic analysis of capitalism and the state, and Vladimir Lenin, using Marx's "objective truth," contributed the main analysis of the international system.

Fundamentals of Communism

Economic Determinism

Marxist-Leninist philosophy holds that the foundation of society is the economic system and the social relationships it produces. Josef Stalin said, "The basis is the economic system. . . . The superstructure consists of the political, legal, religious, artistic, philosophical views of society, and the political, legal, and other institutions corresponding to them.'' Communism is thus a branch of the materialist school of philosophy.

What distinguishes Marxism-Leninism as a materialist philosophy is its conception of class relations as the root of social interaction. In *The Communist Manifesto* Marx declared:

> The history of all human society, past and present, has been the history of class struggles.
>
> Freeman and slave, patrician and plebeian, baron and serf, guild-burgess and journeyman—in a word, oppressor and oppressed—stood in sharp opposition each to the other.

This theory holds that in every organized society, one class controls the ownership of the means of production, and it uses political authority and all-powerful institutions to maintain this control. The ownership class extracts surpluses produced by the laboring masses. Society is a pyramid in which the broad working class at the bottom produces wealth for the privileged elite at the top.

Feudalism and Capitalism

This principle is seen in the feudal pattern of agriculture in which ownership of land was concentrated in the hands of a small nobility, the lords, for whose benefit it was worked by impoverished peasants. The laborers lived in shanties on a minimum subsistence, sustaining themselves from disaster to disaster. The lord lived in a baronial mansion at leisure, enjoying his daily diet of sport and cultivation of the arts. The landlords were not, of course, chosen by God; they achieved their position initially by conquests, foreclosure on usurious loans, and royal grants, and they passed on their control through inheritance. Government was intertwined with feudal landownership: The lords gave a portion of their wealth and power to support the state, and the state used its physical force to guarantee the rights of property—that is, the position of the lords. The whole system was sanctified by the church, the "opiate of the masses."

Industry, the second and more modern form of production, displaced feudalism. A new class of owners was created, the capitalists, whose interests were tied not to land but to factories. In the capitalist mode, the bourgeoisie monopolizes control of machinery, assembly lines, and other modern means of production plus a financial infrastructure. Now the labor power of the workers itself has become a commodity, to be sold in the market to the highest bidder. By maintaining a surplus labor force—the pool of the unemployed—the price of labor (wages) is depressed. The industrial workers become proletarians where before they were serfs. The emergence of the capitalist mode of production shifts the center of power from landlords to industry. After a period of struggle, the bourgeoisie seizes the reins of state from the landed gentry. Now the power of the state is used to provide infrastructure and supports for capitalist manufacture, trade, and finance. This is not to suggest that feudalism disappears altogether; even today, in certain less developed outposts of the imperial world, landlords collect rents of 60 percent or more of the workers' wages. But the controlling interests of the free market industrial state are the capitalists.

Origins of the State

Economic exploitation creates political relations in society. "The state," Engels wrote, "has not existed from all eternity. There have been societies that did without it, that had no conception of the state and state power. At a certain stage of economic development which was necessarily bound up with the cleavage of society into classes, the state became a necessity owing to this cleavage."[1] Lenin added, "History shows that the state as a special apparatus for coercing people arose only wherever and whenever there appeared a division of society into classes, that is, a division into groups of people some of whom are permanently in a position to appropriate the labor of others."[2] The state, he concluded, "is an organ of class rule."[3]

Social Controls

This is not to suggest that the physical might of the state is the only (or even main) means whereby the elite protects its position. No social system, however oppressive, habitually uses force when there are less expensive and more efficient means of control available.

Coercion is the most visible form of control, but it is the least reliable. It requires vigilance and an elaborate network of enforcing agents who themselves are loyal to the system, and it raises a constant danger of rebellion. A social system that is forced to fall back on extensive coercion is on the point of collapse.

More efficient than coercion are market controls, meaning a structure of material rewards keyed to positive behavior—carrot in place of stick. Capitalism, for example, is superior as a form of exploitation to slavery, because now the workers have the illusion of free choice. Their victimization is masked by what appear to be impersonal market forces, rather than naked threats by identifiable enemies.

But the most effective form of behavioral control is neither coercion nor the market, because both of these depend on external regulation of the individual. Normative controls work through education and social training to produce a set of norms and to identify expectations that act as internal regulators of

---

[1]Friedrich Engels, "Origin of the Family, Private Property, and the State," in *Selected Works of Marx and Engels* (Moscow: Foreign Languages Publishing House, 1951), vol. 2, p. 239.
[2]Lenin "The State" (1919), in *Selected Works* (London: Lawrence & Wishart, 1939), vol. 2, p. 644.
[3]Lenin, "State and Revolution," in *Selected Works* (New York: International Publishers, 1943), vol. 7, p. 9.

The sunset of the Cold War: President Ronald Reagan, President-elect George Bush, and Mikhail Gorbachev, then Chairman of the Soviet Communist Party, bid farewell to the Cold War in the shadow of the Statue of Liberty, 1988.
Source: Reuters/Bettman

behavior. Individual consciousness is patterned to fit the desired social model. False consciousness exists when deceptive morals, ideologies, and religions are used to mask injustice behind a façade of legitimacy and legality. Individuals are betrayed by their own education, and they come to revere the very institutions that exploit them.

In general, normative social controls, supported by a structure of market rewards for cooperative behavior, are capitalism's first line of defense. Only in the last resort is brute force on the part of the state necessary. Control by the state ensures the smooth operation of all three forms of control. Public law and administration are thus extensions of the relations of production.

The Meaning of Revolution

Marxism prescribes a revolutionary solution to the problem of class rule. The aroused proletariat rips the instruments of control from the bourgeoisie and uses the state apparatus to seize the means of production, thus changing the entire basis of social relations. "Expropriation of the expropriators" gives land to the peasants and factories to the workers. A certain amount of violence may be necessary, because the ruling class will not give over its position voluntarily, but this is nothing next to the much greater violence of the everyday capitalist system. As Nikita Khrushchev said, "The use or nonuse of violence in the transition of socialism depends on the resistance of the exploiters, on whether the exploiting class itself resorts to violence, rather than on the proletariat." Communism does not romanticize violence, but it regards pacifism as bourgeois sentimentality. No matter how many crumbs the ruling class may let drop from its overloaded tables, the capitalist system will always rest on foundations of injustice and suffering, and it must be overthrown.[4]

Marxism regards revolution as both desirable and inevitable. History is progressive, and each epoch represents an inevitable advance from the preceding period. Capitalism itself outdates all previous forms of social order; no poet could compose an ode to capitalism as flowery as Marx's celebration of its accomplishments. But capitalism rests on class exploitation, so although it is necessary and progressive, it is also unjust. Eventually, it produces the seeds of its own destruction. Mature capitalism is increasingly monopolistic and insatiable in its profit hunger. Eventually, a point is reached at which the economy is saturated with enterprises, and the relentless search for investment opportunities drives the weaker capitalists back into the proletariat. The competition of the workers becomes more severe, driving wages down; and the misery of the proletariat grows.

Capitalism, which began as a progressive force leading humanity to the possibility of fulfilling all human needs through industry, becomes an obstacle to the next step. The army of the unemployed grows, production cannot be consumed, rates of profit fall, general desperation prevails. Capitalism has created

---

[4]Robert C. Tucker, *The Marxian Revolutionary Idea* (New York: Norton, 1969).

the machinery to satisfy human needs, but it cannot use this machinery rationally. It is driven by its inner dynamic to amplify its contradictions until only revolution can rationalize society again.

Soviet faith in the inevitable march of history from its capitalist phase to socialism is unchanged from the early days of Leninism. In 1982, in a speech commemorating the sixtieth anniversary of the founding of the Soviet Union (dated not from the 1917 revolution but from the close of the unionizing civil war in 1922), Yuri Andropov noted that

> The imperialists have not given up the schemes of economic war against the socialist countries, of interfering in their internal affairs in the hope of eroding their social system, and are trying to win military superiority over the USSR, over all the countries of the socialist community. Of course, these plans are sure to fail. It is not given to anyone to turn back the course of historical development. Attempts to "strangle" socialism failed even when the Soviet state was still getting on its feet and was the only socialist country in the world. So surely nothing will come out of it now.[5]

Despite the presumed inevitable results of historical development, Marx's prediction that capitalism would collapse of its own weight has not yet been fulfilled. Although he apparently expected the collapse of advanced capitalist states by 1900, these centers have become progressively more secure. Meanwhile, revolution has occurred in the Soviet Union, China, Cuba, North Korea, and Vietnam, none of which conformed to the Marxist premise that mature capitalism must precede communism. How has this paradox occurred? In the Soviet view, the answer lies in the subtle ways in which capitalism manipulates the international system.

Lenin's View of the International System

Lenin extended Marx's analysis of society to a conception of international relations. Capitalism saved itself, according to Lenin, by reaching the stage of imperialism in which international dynamics temporarily ameliorate the conflicts at home. Borrowing from the English economist John A. Hobson, Lenin showed that capitalism depends not only on oppression within the borders of the home state but also on the external oppression of whole peoples in other parts of the international system. Lenin called this the "internationalization of the class system."

Searching for the Highest Rate of Return   One imperial drive given particular emphasis in Lenin's analysis is the search for the highest rate of return on

---

[5]Yuri Andropov, "Sixty Years of the USSR," December 12, 1982. English translation from *Moscow News*, no. 52, 1982, and reprinted in Martin Ebon, *The Andropov File: The Life and Ideas of Yuri Andropov, General Secretary of the Communist Party of the USSR* (New York: McGraw-Hill, 1983), pp. 249–264, at pp. 259–260.

capital. In the advanced stage of development, the centers of capital become saturated with investment, and the rate of return on new investment is relatively low. Less developed portions of the world still have not had production raised to its full level of exploitive efficiency, so new capital realizes a higher rate of return. Capitalists, therefore, compete with one another for investment opportunities and concomitant spheres of influence around the world. Imperialism is, in this model, mainly a search for high-return investment opportunities for surplus capital.

Searching for Markets Another factor cited by theorists of imperialism to explain the international nature of capitalism is the search for markets for surplus production. The capitalist system of production rests on a fundamental inefficiency in distribution. The workers must be paid less than the full value of their product if the capitalist is to retain a large share of production for profits. But this means that the workers are unable to buy all that they produce. Other markets must be found for the surplus products. So in addition to providing investment opportunities, colonies and spheres of influence can provide captive markets. This can be seen in many historical cases of colonial empires.

Controlling Raw Materials A third reason for the internationalization of capitalism is the need to control the richest sources of raw materials wherever they exist. Monopoly capital minimizes the costs of production by suppressing wages and by developing the cheapest sources of supply. Thus the bounties of nature located in the undeveloped world are important prizes for international capital.

In this way, the international class system reduces the poor nations of the world to the status of suppliers of raw materials and cheap labor, as well as captive centers of foreign investment and import dependency. The colonies must not be permitted to develop on their own, free of foreign control, but rather are kept as dependent subsystems in the empire of capital. As in the home system of exploitation, the capitalists reinforce their international position with a preponderance of physical might. Controlling the government of their own states, they use its power to secure their own positions. Naturally, this international system of exploitation is disguised by legal and moral principles that give a veneer of legitimacy to the capitalists' plundering. Much of international law, for example, was written by the imperial states to protect their position; an example is the Treaty of Berlin (1885) in which the European powers delineated the future legal borders within Africa.

The Growth of Imperialism During the earlier period of this international system of exploitation, capitalists were very crude in competing with one another for the most profitable prizes. In the days of colonialism, the capitalist states actually fought wars over who was to benefit from which subjugations. In the resulting colonies, bourgeois functionaries developed a political system and an infrastructure (rails, ports, and so on) conducive to profitable investment.

In later years, this system has (with exceptions) become more subtle and durable. Direct control offended the national spirit of the subject peoples, so international capital has relinquished formal colonialism. Titular control has been passed on to the national bourgeoisie, a native class of capitalists comprising a subsystem of the international system. The native bourgeoisie are co-opted by giving them a small share in the profits of national exploitation (for example, the royalties from a mining investment). There is a pleasant illusion of self-determination. In case of trouble, the imperialists can use their overwhelming position in the international economic system to deny markets to any subject state that refuses to comply (the boycott of Cuban sugar by the United States, for instance), and the national bourgeoisie can be relied on to put the recalcitrant former colony back on course. Occasionally, it is necessary to use direct force to stop a revolution by those who see through this delusional system. In these and other ways, neocolonialism preserves and even extends the imperial system while giving the Third World a false sense of independence.

The development of the imperial system gives capitalism a temporary reprieve, postponing its inevitable collapse. A portion of the gains of imperialism has been passed along to the organized workers in the centers of capital, raising their living standard and thus preventing an alliance with the unemployed. This, combined with the promotion of racism and ethnic divisions, has enabled the ruling class to forestall revolution. In the poor countries, however, the class basis of the international system is only too visible. Hence, the paradox that revolution seems to be ripest where capitalism is least mature. Stalin explained this phenomenon in *The Foundations of Leninism:*

> Formerly, it was the accepted thing to speak of the existence or absence of objective conditions for the proletarian revolution in individual countries, or, to be more precise, in one or another developed country. Now this point of view is no longer adequate. Now we must speak of the existence of objective conditions for the revolution in the entire system of world imperialist economy as an integral unit. . . .
>
> Where will the revolution begin? . . .
>
> Where industry is more developed, where the proletariat constitutes the majority, where there is more culture, where there is more democracy—that was the reply given formerly.
>
> No, objects the Leninist theory of revolution (imperialism); *not necessarily where industry is more developed,* and so forth. The front of capital will be pierced where the chain of imperialism is weakest. . . .[6]

Revolution may come first in the most progressive states of the underdeveloped world, and the centers of capital may be the last, rather than the first, to fall. But eventually communism will be universal.

---

[6]Josef Stalin, *The Foundations of Leninism* (New York: International Publishers, 1931).

The State Withers Away

What form will communism take after the revolution against capitalism succeeds? Marx and Engels were not very specific on this critical question. Because of this ambiguity, it has been possible for Trotskyists and other so-called independent socialists in Western countries to build an anti-Soviet propaganda campaign that accuses the Soviet state of betraying the revolution and even of being non-Marxist.

One point in this anti-Soviet line is based on Engels's prediction in his *Anti-Duhring* that after the victory of the socialist revolution, the state would wither away and be replaced by a society without coercion. Obviously the Soviet state has not disappeared. But Engels's formula had in view the victory of socialism in all countries or in most countries. The reality of today is that socialism is surrounded by a hostile capitalist encirclement, so the country "of the victorious revolution must not weaken but must in every way strengthen its state, the state organs, the organs of the intelligence service, the army, if that country does not want to be smashed by the capitalist encirclement."[7] Stalin knew that the old Russia was repeatedly beaten by foreign enemies—the French and English in the Crimean War (1856), the Japanese in 1905, the Germans in 1917—precisely because of its political and industrial backwardness. The new Russia would have to use the most modern and practical means to ensure the survival of the first communist advances in a still-capitalist world and to protect the Russian nation.

Democracy

Western critics have always accused the Soviet Union of suppressing democratic principles by not adopting the Euro-American concept of electoral democracy based on the ideas of John Locke and Jean Jacques Rousseau. But in the classical Soviet view, bourgeois elections were regarded as part of the state apparatus of capitalism. Even if balloting were conducted without deceit, and a decision made by a voting majority, the outcome could not correspond to the objective interests of the masses anyway. False consciousness, perpetuated by class control of the mass media and the educational system, blinds the voters. Pious electoral candidates, most of whom are leading capitalists, further obscure the issue, often by using a false demonology of the communist threat to stir up fears. Marxist-Leninists always rejected this as a meaningless version of democracy.

In this same classical view, real people's or workers' democracy emphasized the objective nature of the social system rather than the mechanics of the formal decision process. It was insisted that work is available to all in the Soviet Union, and that slums, poverty, and chronic alcoholism, which are so much the hallmark of the so-called democracies of the West, did not exist. The critical question of Marxism-Leninism is whether a social system, especially in its

---

[7]Josef Stalin, "Reply to Comrades," *Pravda*, August 2, 1950.

ownership of the means of production, can serve the interests of the masses. The meaning of social justice, in this view, is not a spurious procedural question, but one of real outcomes—of substance rather than process.

This classical version of the Marxist-Leninist understanding of democracy underwent a radical change in 1989 and 1990. Then, under the inspiration of *glasnost* (access to information) and *perestroika* (restructuring), introduced by Mikhail Gorbachev, contested elections to the Soviet parliament were permitted, although only members of the Communist Party of the Soviet Union (CPSU) were allowed to compete. Only months later, following the fall of one communist government after another in Eastern Europe and even the disbanding of some of Eastern Europe's strongest communist parties, Gorbachev persuaded the Central Committee of the CPSU voluntarily to abandon the party's 72-year monopoly on political power, opening for the first time since the Bolshevik revolution of 1917 the possibility of a pluralism of ideas within the party and even the possibility of a multiparty political system. To some, these changes were overdue reforms; to others they were necessities brought on by a lightening-fast series of events not only in Eastern Europe but inside the Soviet Union itself. These included labor unrest among miners, ethnic unrest in several of the constituent republics, civil war between Armenians and Azerbaijanis that required armed Soviet intervention, and the threat of secession by Lithuania, Latvia, and Estonia. V. A. Medvedev, the ideological secretary of the party, called for democratic reforms portended by events in Eastern Europe and by the failure of the Soviet economy, saying that "during the decades of distortions and stagnation, such a critical mass of explosive material has accumulated that further delay could have resulted in a shock of enormous strength." He added that in order to prevent a catastrophe, it was necessary "to transform the impending explosion into a controlled reaction."[8] And Western interpreters reported Gorbachev himself as having urged the Central Committee to permit a multiparty system to usher in a "normal democracy."

Six months before the formal consideration of multiple political parties, the CPSU had discussed its future goals and structure. During the debate, Gorbachev stated:

> The [communist] party cannot gain authority by decree. No mighty decree or decision can do this now. Our authority was acquired at the first stage of *perestroika* by having offered society the policy of *perestroika*. And society trusted the party, supported it and followed it. Today authority can be won only by the decisive and consistent carrying out of the policy of *perestroika*. There is not nor will there be any other way for the party to win authority. If someone thinks otherwise this is unrealistic, comrades.
>
>   . . . .
>
> If *perestroika* is a revolution—and we agreed that it is—and if it means profound changes in attitudes toward property, the status of the individual, the basics of the political system and the spiritual realm, and if it is to transform the people into a force of change in society, then how can all of this take place quietly and smoothly?

---

[8]As quoted in *The New York Times*, February 7, 1990, p. 1.

And do we really need to be overcome with panic when the revolutionary processes have become a reality? We have caused them by our policy.

. . . .

The restructuring processes that have unfurled today are enveloping all realms of our life. They are revealing much unusual and much that is sometimes hard to accept. This is generating additional tension. But that is what these revolutionary years are all about! We must understand all of this and act like a revolutionary party. Otherwise forces will appear which, seeing that the party is lagging behind, will try to seize the initiative. This is already happening.[9]

Just six months later, Gorbachev asked the Central Committee of the CPSU to accept the fact that political pluralism already existed, and to permit the free exercise of multiparty politics free of the CPSU's constitutional power monopoly.

Diplomacy

Leninism also has its own view of making foreign policy, one that prevails in the Soviet view yet today. Unlike the pre-Soviet Russians who formulated foreign policy in secret forums and without consultation with the masses, Lenin's new international policy required a "new socialist diplomacy" that was

. . . destined to break down the wall which the exploiters had always carefully raised between foreign policy and the mass of working people, and thus to turn the masses from a mere object of foreign policy into a force actively influencing international affairs in their own interests. The birth itself of socialist foreign policy made it immediately possible to move crucial international problems out of the secrecy of closed tsarist offices into the street, which the bourgeoisie so completely scorned, and bring them within reach of the workers and all working people. This was a thoroughly class, thoroughly Party-type kind of change. For the first time, it enabled the masses effectively to influence politics. . . .

In contrast, however, nonsocialist diplomacy continues to be conducted beyond the reach of working people.

What is Washington busy with now? One hysterical propaganda campaign after another. First the public is told of a "Soviet military threat." Then it is sold a bill of goods on the subject of the USA "lagging behind" the USSR strategically. People are also either being intimidated with tales of "international terrorism" or told cock-and-bull stories regarding the events in Poland, Central America and South and Southeast Asia. All this has its own logic, of course: the imperialists are able to indulge in creating new weapons of mass destruction only as a result of deceiving the masses.[10]

---

[9]As quoted in *The New York Times,* July 23, 1989, p. 16.

[10]Yuri Andropov, "Leninism: A Source of Inexhaustible Revolutionary Energy and Creativity of the Masses," April 22, 1982, in English translation by the Soviet press service, Novosti, and printed in the Soviet press on May 15, 1982. Reprinted in Martin Ebon, *The Andropov File,* pp. 224–238, at p. 235. A different translation of the same address appears in Y. V. Andropov, *Speeches and Writings* (New York: Pergamon Press, 1983), pp. 216–234, particularly pp. 228–

Russian National Interests

We have seen in a selective discussion of key issues in Soviet ideology that communist thought is an analytical scheme of universal applicability adapted to the specific situation of the first communist regime. This adaptation imposed on Marxism-Leninism compelling issues of Russian national interest, since defense of Russia became the essence of defending communism. Stalin intertwined national and ideological imperatives in 1927 when he defined a revolutionary as "he who without arguments, unconditionally, openly and honestly . . . is ready to defend and strengthen the USSR, since the USSR is the first proletarian, revolutionary state in the world." Moreover, "to advance the revolutionary movement is impossible without defending the USSR."[11] Thus, an historic accident married communism to the international position and national interests of a particular country.

Marx and Engels had been skeptical of nationalism and predicted its early demise as the interests of both the workers and the capitalists were internationalized. Polish and French workers would be united against capitalists of the two countries; and class, rather than nationality, would survive as the critical line of division. In this view, nationalism is nothing more than a false consciousness dividing the proletariat.

But the First World War convinced Lenin that communist ideology would have to adjust to the continued potency of the national idea. The workers of every country dropped all pretense of proletarian internationalism when war broke out, and marched blindly behind the various national flags. The Second International in 1907 had called upon all European socialist parties and trade unions to resist an international conflict, which would serve none but competing capitalist interests. But grand expectations of worker solidarity were shattered in the summer of 1914 when not a single major socialist party in Europe opposed war, and the German Social Democratic party, the leading Marxist group, voted unanimously for government war credits. The lesson for Lenin was that communism must join with nationalism rather than oppose it.[12] The power of this merger became visible 30 years later when communist parties emerged from the Second World War leading patriotic resistance movements in China, Indochina, Yugoslavia, Greece, and elsewhere.

The Russian revolutionaries of 1917 found themselves at the head not just of a nationalist movement but of a national state. They were an opposition party whose entire organization and philosophy had been geared to destructive action, suddenly in a position of responsibility rather than insurgency. Not just grand principles but physical Soviet realities had to be dealt with.

---

229. There the final sentence appears as follows: "There is a logic, albeit perverted, in this propaganda: indeed, to advertise weapons of mass destruction and to prod the world to war the imperialists have to deceive the masses."

[11]Josef Stalin, "The International Situation and the Defense of the USSR" (August 1, 1927), *Sochineniya* (Moscow: Gospolitizdat, 1949), vol. 10, p. 61.

[12]Adam B. Ulam, *Expansion and Coexistence: The History of Soviet Foreign Policy 1917–67* (New York: Praeger, 1968), pp. 13, 18–19, 24–25.

The first national issue was the challenge of unifying the vast Soviet land mass and the diverse peoples of the Soviet state into a cohesive nation under effective administration from Moscow. This would entail giant logistical difficulties under the best of conditions. In Russia, it was compounded by vexing nationalities problems, from oriental minorities in the maritime provinces to Ukrainian separatism on the European border, with the Turkic peoples of Central Asia in between. "Russification" of the nationalities of the Caucasus and the Baltic littoral had resisted the best efforts of the tsars. The first vital necessity imposed on the communist government was the amalgamation and federation of many separate pieces into a Union of Soviet Socialist Republics.[13] By the time the process was completed, the USSR consisted of 16 such republics, with the Russian Soviet Federal Socialist Republic (RSFSR) comprising almost 90 percent of the land mass. The other 15 formed an almost continuous rim of incorporated territories beginning in the northwest at the Finnish border to the deep south of the Soviet Union, interrupted only by the Black and Caspian seas. (See Figure 1-1.)

Another condition imposed on the Soviet government was the necessity to insulate the state from excessive economic, cultural, and military penetration by the expansionist powers of Western Europe. From 1917 to 1940, the communists used an economic policy of autarky, a political policy of limited intercourse, and a strategic policy designed to equilibrate a European balance of power. Some Western observers dismissed these defensive maneuvers as Stalinist paranoia overlaid onto a traditional Russian xenophobia,[14] but the same actions can also be seen as a realistic response to a distinct external threat.

Another part of the historic Russian policy that preceded communism but has been continued is the pursuit of influence in critical border areas: Poland, the Balkans, the Bosporus and Dardanelles straits, Manchuria, Finland, and elsewhere. The value of these policies is economic, strategic, and even cultural (pan-Slavism), in addition to the impetus given by communist ideology. Indeed, it is argued by some that the whole modern Soviet policy is nothing more than a continuation of the imperialism of the tsars, even in North Korea, Afghanistan, and Mongolia.[15] The Balkan wars, the Crimean War, the Russo-Japanese War—all anticipated the broad pattern of Soviet policy in later years, except that Soviet leadership has succeeded, where the tsars failed, in achieving influence in Eastern Europe. Winston Churchill said that Soviet policy is "a riddle wrapped in a mystery inside an enigma. . . . But . . . the key is Russian national interest."[16]

The relative position of various national interests and ideological goals in Soviet foreign policy changes over time. But it surely cannot be said that the

---

[13]For a thorough, current study of the contemporary consequences, see Basile Kerblay, *Modern Soviet Society* (New York: Pantheon Books, 1983), particularly Chapters 2, 8–9.

[14]Basil Dmytryshyn, *USSR: A Concise History* (New York: Scribner's, 1965), pp. 143–153, 200–207, 247–259.

[15]Tsarist and communist imperialism are compared in Michael Karpovitch, "Russian Imperialism or Communist Aggression," *The New Leader,* June 4, 1951, p. 18.

[16]Winston Churchill, *The Gathering Storm* (Boston: Houghton Mifflin, 1948), p. 449.

Figure 1–1 The Soviet Union's unruly republics.

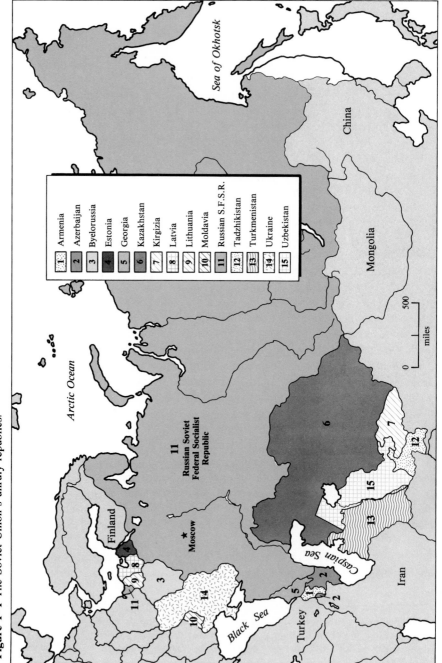

After *Time*, January 22, 1990, p. 32.

USSR is little more than a conspiracy disguised as a state. Indeed, it is probable that Russian national demands have overshadowed questions of communist principle, particularly in more recent years.

The Soviet Revolution and the International System

The interplay of national and ideological themes in Russian policy can be seen in the Soviet interpretation of major events in international relations since 1917.

The First World War and the Russian Revolution

Until 1917, capitalist countries controlled the entire international system. All regions not part of the advanced capitalist world were dominated, directly or indirectly, by it and exploited as subject markets and sources of raw materials. The capital-exporting countries divided the world among themselves, and periodic readjustments, sometimes involving wars, occurred. Russians call the First World War the Imperialist War because they see it as having been a struggle among rival imperialists for the most desirable spoils.

The capitalist countries understood from the outset that the Bolshevik Revolution of 1917 posed a threat to their international system. Britain, France, the United States, and other imperialist powers sent an international army to join domestic counterrevolutionaries (the ''White'' armies) in a struggle that lasted from 1917 to 1921. (The United States played a relatively minor role, sending 14,000 troops and suffering 1000 casualties. The intervention is relatively unknown to Americans today, although it is well remembered by Russians.) For a while, the tides of battle gave the imperial powers hope of preventing Russia's defection from the capitalist world, but the Red armies finally prevailed, and revolution was secured. From the outset, therefore, the hostility of the capitalist world to socialism was manifest. But could it have been otherwise, when the very existence of the Soviet Union would encourage other revolutionary movements?

The capitalists did succeed in preventing other revolutions for many years by a combination of clever anti-Soviet propaganda and the repression of revolutionary movements. The Soviet Union was an island in a hostile sea and, as such, needed to spend huge portions of its resources on its defenses. Nonetheless, great progress was made from 1917 to 1940 in developing a revolutionary society, and in rebuilding the Soviet economy from the ravages of the First World War.

The Second World War

The second great European war erupted when a particularly virulent form of imperialism took hold in Germany, a late starter in the imperialist division of the world. Its leadership was determined to extend its hegemony at the expense of the other capitalist states, making war inevitable. The lunatic Adolf

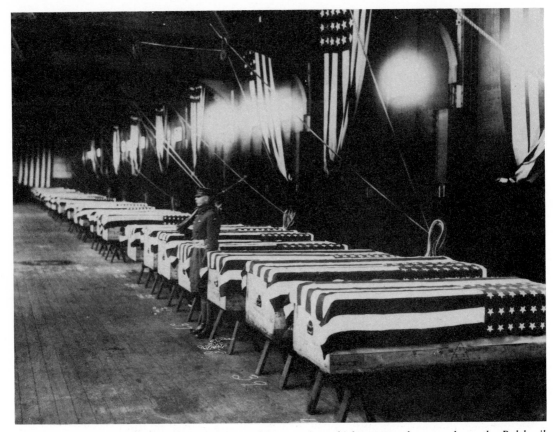

America's participation in the 1918–1919 War of Intervention which attempted to overthrow the Bolshevik regime is now virtually forgotten in the US—though it is well remembered in the USSR. Here, the bodies of 111 American soldiers killed in Russia lie on the army piers at Hoboken, New Jersey. About 1000 Americans died in the war, early martyrs in the struggle against communism.
Source: AP/Wide World

Hitler also proposed to lead a holy war against communism—that is, against the Soviet Union. The German-Italian-Japanese Anti-Comintern Pact led some of the Western powers to flirt briefly with the idea of neutrality, to turn Hitler east and let the Nazis and communists bleed each other dry. Harry S Truman, then a US senator, said on the occasion of the Nazi invasion of Russia, "If we see that Germany is winning we ought to help Russia and if Russia is winning we ought to help Germany and in that way let them kill as many as possible."[17] But Hitler's expansionist aims forced the other capitalist states into a wartime alliance with the Soviet Union. The United States and Britain, still deeply anticommunist and dedicated to the overthrow of the Soviet government, temporarily suspended this goal to deal with the more immediate danger of fascist Germany.

---

[17]*The New York Times*, June 24, 1941.

The Western powers did succeed, however, in shifting most of the burden of the European war to the Soviet Union. The great victory over fascism was paid for by Russian blood and by the heroic efforts of the Soviet people, while the capitalist allies delayed opening the second front on the West until 1944. Of the 22 million Allied lives lost in the war, an estimated 20 million were Soviet. The United States, by comparison, although it made an important financial and military contribution, lost only 300,000 (1.5 percent of the Soviet loss). The Nazi invaders destroyed and plundered more than 1100 Russian villages and towns, razing many, whereas the Western Allies suffered only minor damage. Many historians hold that the Soviet Union came very close to defeating the Germans single-handedly. Churchill said that Russia's fighting men "did the main work of tearing the guts out of the German army."

The Origins of the Cold War

These great human and material sacrifices did bring some gains for Soviet revolutionary and national interests after the war. The Red armies were decisive in liberating a number of countries from fascist occupation in 1945–1946, particularly in Eastern Europe. Following the war, socialist governments were established with Soviet aid in Poland, Hungary, Bulgaria, Czechoslovakia, Romania, Albania, and the Soviet-occupied sector of (East) Germany. Other communist movements, with lesser amounts of Soviet aid, established socialist regimes in Yugoslavia and China. Within three years of the war's end, the Soviet Union had moved from isolation in a world of capitalist powers to partnership and leadership in a communist bloc comprising half the world's population! Thus, the anticommunist fanaticism of the fascists had a reverse effect in the long term.

As in 1917, the Western capitalist powers wasted no time developing a propaganda offensive against socialist gains. The establishment of communist governments in Eastern Europe was characterized as Soviet imperialism, whereas the restoration of capitalist forms in the West European countries was, of course, portrayed as the will of the people. The imperialists demanded that the financiers and landlords be returned to their "proper" position in the East European states, including even East Germany. The Soviet Union, it would seem, was expected to reproduce exactly the conditions that led to the two world wars and then sit back politely and wait for the next invasion. Instead, the Soviet Union committed itself to the establishment of a new order in Eastern Europe in cooperation with its new allies. The peoples of the communist world were not deceived by Western propaganda, although the Western governments did succeed in reinforcing the false anticommunist perceptions of their own peoples in some cases.

By 1950, the new imperialist North Atlantic Treaty Organization (NATO) alliance system was developed against the Soviet Union and its allies. More than 50 hostile military bases were constructed by the Americans around the Soviet periphery, reinforced by the American lead in the development of atomic weapons. This capitalist encirclement forced the socialist states to spend an inordinately large portion of their productive efforts on defensive capabilities to prevent imperialist adventures. The following interpretation of the origins of the Cold War was offered by Konstantin Chernenko, who served as General Secretary of the Soviet Communist Party in 1984 and 1985:

> In pursuit of world supremacy, the U.S. ruling circles openly declared that their aims could be achieved only from a position of strength, and waged the so-called cold war. At their initiative the aggressive bloc of imperialist countries was formed in 1949 under the name of . . . (NATO). On a scale hitherto unknown, the United States expanded the arms race and began to step up the production of atomic, thermonuclear, bacteriological weapons and other types of mass destruction weapons. American military bases, targeted on the USSR and other socialist countries, were being quickly set up; new military blocs were formed. . . .
>
> The Communist Party of the Soviet Union (CPSU) and the Soviet government could not ignore the dangerous course of American imperialism, which had the atomic weapons at its disposal, and openly proclaimed its intention to achieve the "rolling back" of socialism. We had constantly to build up the USSR's defense capability. The fact that the Soviet Union came into possession of atomic, and later thermonuclear, weapons, and mastered the production of intercontinental missiles, which put an end to U.S. atomic blackmail, is of immense principled significance.[18]

It is ironic that the imperialists have managed to convince some people that the Soviet Union has aggressive designs, when it is the Americans who keep their bases far from home on the borders of the Soviet heartland, and not the other way around! Leonid Brezhnev, General Secretary of the Communist Party of the Soviet Union, protested on March 30, 1971:

> The peoples will not be deceived by the attempts to ascribe to the Soviet Union intentions which are alien to it. We declare with a full sense of responsibility: we have no territorial claims on anyone whatsoever, we threaten no one, and have no intention of attacking anyone, we stand for the free and independent development of all nations. But let no one, for his part, try to talk to us in terms of ultimatums and strength.[19]

In the less-developed portions of the world still under their control, the imperialists have intensified their exploitation of Afro-Asian and Latin American peoples and resources. These poorer countries have, in most cases, been given technical independence, but they remain under the control of neoimperialism through reactionary puppet governments, military interventions, and the manipulation of international markets. Within the capitalist countries, privileged segments of the working class have been given a small share in the wealth extracted from the Third World to buy their complicity in the imperial system.

The Soviet view finds the capitalist countries aggressive and the revolutionary countries defensive. The revolutionary movement is strong, but its final victory is postponed by the might of the imperialists. The Soviet Union has

---

[18]Excerpt from a book in Victor Pribytkov, *Soviet-U.S. Relations: The Selected Writings and Speeches of Konstantin U. Chernenko* (New York: Praeger, 1984), pp. 127–162, at p. 140.

[19]M. Gribanov, *Security for Europe* (Moscow: Novosti Press Agency, 1972), p. 19. Originally stated at Twenty-fourth Congress of the Communist Party of the Soviet Union.

assumed the burden of defending the revolutionary advances that have been gained against imperialist reaction, while giving extensive aid to advance new anti-imperialist movements where they develop. The world system thus consists of an imperialist bloc led by the United States, a socialist bloc led by the USSR, and the Third World nations at various stages of development toward socialism but in many cases still dominated by the imperialists.

The Soviet Defense Perimeter

Despite the "grand alliance" under which the Soviet Union and the Western allies conducted the Second World War, it was clear to the Soviet government that the fall of fascism would be followed by a resumption of anticommunist and anti-Soviet policy in the West. Fear of capitalist encirclement dominated Josef Stalin's thinking as the fighting wore to a close; thus, Soviet troops were positioned for a post-war occupation that would provide a permanent defense perimeter around the Eastern European boundary. In the diplomatic agreements that followed, the Soviets achieved a strong position in East Germany, Poland, Hungary, Czechoslovakia, Bulgaria, and Romania while independent but friendly communist governments were developing farther east to Yugoslavia and Albania.

To meet the Western threat posed by the formation of NATO, the Kremlin established the Warsaw Pact as a counterbalancing alliance. Simultaneously, like the United States, it used its strength as the dominant partner in alliance to support Eastern European governments sympathetic to Soviet foreign policy both by developing the centrally planned production and distribution system of Council for Mutual Economic Assistance (COMECON) and by using forceful intervention where necessary to suppress Western-inspired antirevolutionary activities. In 1968, on the occasion of a Warsaw Pact invasion of Czechoslavakia to put down a West-leaning liberalization movement led by Alexander Dubcek, Leonid Brezhnev pronounced a full rationale for such actions. Known as the Brezhnev Doctrine and often likened to the Monroe Doctrine under which the United States frequently intervened in Latin America and the Caribbean, this rationale posited that the security and welfare of the socialist commonwealth of Eastern Europe (part of worldwide proletarian internationalism) is superior to the needs of a single member. Although the 1968 invasion was the last of its kind (Polish martial law was sufficient to restore order to Poland during Solidarity's liberalization movement in 1980), the Brezhnev Doctrine remained a cornerstone of intra-alliance policy for more than two decades.

But that, too, fell to *perestroika* and *glasnost* in the era of Mikhail Gorbachev's reforms. In 1989, as one communist government after another fell in Eastern Europe—in East Germany, Poland, Hungary, Czechoslovakia, and Romania—Soviet troops were unmoved; and after hints that he had no intention of invoking the Brezhnev Doctrine, Gorbachev openly called upon the Polish communist government to release its grip on power and to permit political self-determination. Shortly thereafter, he explicitly renounced the Brezhnev Doctrine, and with that renunciation, enabled Eastern Europeans to strike out on their own paths of government and economics. As communist loyalists and militant reformers in Romania fought a brief but brutal civil war, Gorbachev even let it be known that he might intervene with Soviet troops on behalf of the reform movement, although intervention never occurred.

The immediate future of the defense perimeter is filled with questions. The reunification of the two Germanys and the inclusion of the new Germany in NATO, together with the Soviet agreement to remove all troops from Poland and Hungary in 1990 and 1991, leaves the perimeter speckled with holes and devoid of much of its reason for existing. Moreover, President Gorbachev has offered the view that with the end of the Cold War, both NATO and the Warsaw Pact will evolve into political rather than military alliances. This suggests that in Soviet strategic thinking, the need for the perimeter no longer exists and is as obsolete as the Warsaw Pact itself. From the American perspective, the end of the Soviet occupation of Eastern Europe has become more important temporarily than new agreements on nuclear arms. But paradoxically, because NATO is such an important instrument for American foreign policy in dealing with allies, a weakened Warsaw Pact is welcomed in Soviet-American relations, but diminishes an important instrument in trans-Atlantic relations.

This lingering problem notwithstanding, Gorbachev's program for the 1990s is to establish a "common European home" free of menacing military alliances and marked by self-determination in Eastern Europe. And this concept, in the words of one Soviet analyst, "means decomposition of the empire, in our own interest."[20]

The Soviet View of the United States

In the traditional, pre-Gorbachev Soviet perspective, the United States was always the greatest threat to the Soviet Union among the capitalist powers. The early years of the Cold War were followed by the establishment of American military and economic hegemony aimed not only at the establishment of an American Century but also at the containment of the Soviet Union and the spread of socialist revolution. America as the world's policeman, guardian of a global *pax Americana,* was an unmistakable threat both to Soviet security and to Marxism-Leninism throughout the world. The Soviet view of America, then, is the driving force of Moscow's foreign policy and has a magnitude of importance second only to that of the imperatives of ideology.

American Economic Imperialism

From the Soviet perspective, the United States is uniquely important to modern imperialism. American foreign investors play critical roles in the economies of more than 75 foreign nations. The gross value of goods and services produced in foreign countries by American-owned facilities is over $60 billion per year. If we consider US enterprises abroad as an aggregate, they would comprise the fourth largest country in the world, with a gross annual product

---

[20]As quoted in *The New York Times,* November 30, 1989, p. A20.

larger than that of any country except the United States itself, Japan, or the Soviet Union.[21] Some large American firms alone dwarf the national economies in which they operate.

From the Marxist perspective, the transnational corporation is the ultimately mature form of monopoly capitalism. The year 1982 is particularly illustrative of the consequences of transnational business activity, because it was a year of deep recession for the entire economy of the Western world. In that year, several of the largest American corporations producing abroad had total sales of $20 billion or more each. Exxon's sales, for example, rose to more than $97 billion, and both General Motors' and Mobil Oil's rose to $60 billion. Together, the 15 largest of these corporations had sales of $570 billion. This amount was almost a quarter of the American gross domestic product for the year, and more strikingly, it was 21 percent of the gross domestic product of all the developing countries combined for the year.

The imperialistic effect of this variety of business activity is particularly marked in the developing world.[22] These corporations control the terms of trade and the volume of exports, as well as labor movements. In addition, they determine the modernity of the economic infrastructure, control local politics, and, in general, establish the economic destinies of the developing peoples. Hence, the transnational corporations control the developing economies, both through their activities in the host state and through the terms of trade with which they conduct business between the home state and the host state. Approximately one-half of all American exports go to developing countries at terms of trade that keep the developing countries in constant debt to the United States. This debt is covered by loans from American banks and increases by as much as 20 percent each year. In many of those countries, the debt now equals as much as 60 percent of their annual gross domestic product, and in some of them, the annual debt service is over 10 percent of their gross domestic product and is as much as 40 percent of the value of their total exports. This relationship, accordingly, is a debt trap for the developing countries. From the Soviet perspective, "the siphoning off of financial resources from the developing countries in connection with their external debt is the most cynical and parasitic form of neocolonialist plunder and is an important element of the system of neocolonialist exploitation."[23]

For some small countries, the operations and decisions of one or two large private investors are more important to national welfare than are the decisions of the highest domestic political officials, resulting in external control. The lust for overseas investments exists mainly because American investments in less-developed countries return, according to Marxist computations, higher rates of profit than is normal within the home countries of the capitalists. This

---

[21]Leo Model, "The Politics of Private Foreign Investment," *Foreign Affairs,* July 1967, pp. 640–641.
[22]Y. Stepanov, "The TNCs in the Strategy for Imperialist Expansion," *International Affairs* (Moscow), December 1985, pp. 68–76.
[23]A. Shitnikov and G. Markov, "The West's 'Debt Trap' for the Developing Countries," *International Affairs* (Moscow), August 1985, pp. 35–43, at p. 39.

is, of course, a boon to the Americans, but a disastrous drain of wealth from the poor countries. United States investments in Latin America, for example, totaled less than $4 billion from 1950 to 1965. The returns on these investments that went back to the United States during this period were over $11 billion, almost three times as much.[24] For many individual countries, the outflow of profits to the United States is two to four times as great as is the inflow of investment from the United States every year. This is one crude indicator of the exploitative character of the system of American economic dominance.

The highly favorable economic position of the American capitalists is secured and advanced by military force, just as the earlier imperialists used conquests and invasions to gain and protect a foothold for economic penetration. The United States protects its traders and investors by maintaining American armed forces in no fewer than 64 countries, truly a record in the history of empires. Naturally the hundreds of bases that are involved are rationalized in terms of protecting these countries from Soviet imperialism and internal subversion, the American euphemisms for revolution. The American world system reaches farther and deeper than has any previous imperial system in history, approximating a truly worldwide system of military, political, and economic control.[25]

The United States has achieved this dominant position by pushing aside older imperial systems and also by extending the range of the imperial system beyond its former reach, partly as a result of the two world wars. The United States entered each of these wars only after the other major capitalist powers were already weakened, and it emerged with the most nearly intact economy. Meanwhile, it exacted colonial and other enriching concessions from its allies and defeated enemies. Indeed, it even went so far as partly to colonize the European countries themselves. Of course, the Europeans are not quite as helpless as are some Third World states, and they are attempting to counterbalance the weight of American economic power by developing institutions to defend their own interests.

In addition to assuming the colonial enterprises of the older capitalist states, the United States has also deepened its penetration of the world market areas that were formerly not fully exploited. This is reflected in the spread of foreign branches of United States banks all over the world. Table 1–1 shows how bank branches have grown and how this growth is due partly to a great increase in the number of countries in which United States financial institutions operate. Sometimes the subject governments do not resist the invasion but, rather, welcome it. This is partly because of the control exerted on these governments but also because of the poverty of such countries from long years of exploitation. As a result of the extraction of capital from them over many years, they are not able to develop enterprises of their own and consequently

---

[24]V. Panov, *The Economic Weapons of Neo-Colonialism* (Moscow: Novosti Press Agency, 1972).
[25]N. Simonia, *The Third World and the Struggle for Economic Independence* (Moscow: Novosti Press Agency, 1972).

Table 1–1 US bank branches outside the United States.

	1918	1939	1950	1955	1960	1967	1975
Number of branches	61	89	95	111	124	298	732
Number of countries	16	22	24	26	33	55	NA

Source: Through 1967, Harry Magdoff, *The Age of Imperialism* (New York: Monthly Review Press, 1969), p. 56. Copyright © by Harry Magdoff and reprinted with permission of Monthly Review Press. For 1975, Andrew F. Brimmer and Frederick R. Dahl, "The Growth of US Banking Abroad," *Journal of Finance*, May 1975, pp. 341–363.

depend on outside aid. This makes them vulnerable to American firms looking for profitable investment, and, of course, it makes the future of these countries even more dependent on foreign influence.

Owing to these patterns of investment and ownership of foreign production, the American role in the world imperial system is huge and growing. American capitalist imperialism dominates the economic and political order in many countries, often with substantially negative effects in the dominated countries.

We turn now to a second Soviet proposition, that this imperialist behavior is rooted in the nature of American capitalism. This theory that imperialism is caused by capitalism distinguishes the socialist view from other critiques of American foreign policy. American liberals, for example, also tend to see US foreign policy in a critical light but trace its failings to excessive anticommunist zeal or to misperceptions of the objective situation in other countries, rather than to the basic nature of capitalism. If capitalism inherently tends to be imperialistic, the problem of imperialism will be more difficult to solve within a capitalistic framework than if the cause of imperialism is the more superficial issue of mistaken policies. Thus, the relationship between capitalism and imperialism is a critical difference between socialist views of American imperialism and other theories.[26]

In the Leninist view, there are three needs that make capitalism externalize itself to imperialism: (1) the need for raw materials, (2) the thirst for captive export markets, and especially (3) the search for secure, high-yield foreign investment opportunities. All three of these dynamics operate in the American case.

Raw Materials The huge American industrial apparatus consumes immense quantities of imported raw materials without which it would suffer a severe decline. Although the United States was a net exporter of raw materials until 1920, since that year it has been increasingly dependent on imports, including reliance on foreign sources of vital petroleum fuels. Sixty-two industrial raw materials are listed by the Department of Defense as strategic and critical materials crucial to the warmaking ability of the United States, of which more than half of the annual consumption must be imported. For most of these materials, more than 80 percent of the supply is imported. It is obviously in the

---

[26]This critical distinction is developed in Robert Tucker, *American Foreign Policy and the Radical Left* (Baltimore: Johns Hopkins University Press, 1971).

interest of American capitalism to secure these foreign sources of supply and to control the cheapest sources of raw materials. Both goals are served by American political-military domination of the supplier countries.

Profits and Foreign Markets   Serious as it is, the raw-material issue is a relatively small point compared with the other two themes of the Leninist analysis: the issues of controlling foreign markets and investment opportunities. The very profits of American firms are tied closely to the control of other countries. To assess this proposition, consider the relative magnitude of foreign sales by American producers compared with sales within the United States. Taking the total of exports and sales abroad by American-owned enterprises located outside the United States, the foreign market is equal to approximately 25 percent of the total output of US-owned farms, factories, and mines, and a somewhat higher percentage of profits.[27] (Furthermore, while in 1961 American manufacturers exported $15 billion in goods and foreign affiliates of American industries sold $25 billion in goods, in 1970, the values increased to $35 billion in exports from the United States and $90 billion for sales by foreign affiliates. Thus, in that decade, exports increased by 133 percent, while the sales of foreign affiliates skyrocketed by almost 400 percent.[28])

A brief look at annual performance (see Table 1–2) reveals the extent to which American manufacturers rely on foreign markets. In 1988, America's 15 leading export corporations produced a total of $524 billion in goods, of which they exported $65 billion or 12.4 percent. Compare this to 1982, when the top 50 exporters (as compared with 15 in 1988) produced goods valued at $629 billion and exported $59 billion, or barely 10 percent. A look at specific industries is even more revealing. In 1988, when the American automobile industry was widely believed to be crumbling under the weight of Japanese and European competition, the big three American automakers all ranked in the top six as exporters measured by value of exports. In the computer industry, where Japanese competition was also widely feared, IBM, Digital, Hewlett Packard, and UNISYS all ranked in the top 15 as exporters. The two largest manufacturers of commercial aircraft, Boeing and McDonnell Douglas, make the list annually.

Table 1–3 looks at the phenomenon of foreign-market dependence in a slightly different way, ranking exporters not by value of exports, but by the percentage of total goods exported. This ranking demonstrates that of the top 15 American manufacturers, exports comprise between 16.1 percent and 46.3 percent of total goods produced. The table shows that 46.3 percent of everything (measured in value rather than volume) built by Boeing is sold outside the United States. From the Soviet perspective, this represents extraordinary evidence of the imperialism of American industry and of the international linking of capitalist interests.

---

[27] Harry Magdoff, *The Age of Imperialism* (New York: Monthly Review Press, 1969), pp. 173–202, especially pp. 177–178.

[28] "The Multinational Corporation and the World Economy," Committee on Finance, US Senate, 1973, p. 12.

Table 1–2 Fifteen leading American exporters ranked by dependence on foreign markets, 1988, in billions of US dollars.

Rank as Exporter by Value	Company	Total Export Sales	Total Sales	Percentage of Total Exported
1	General Motors	$9.4 billion	$121.1 billion	7.8
2	Ford Motor	8.8	92.4	9.5
3	Boeing	7.8	17.0	46.3
4	General Electric	5.7	49.4	11.6
5	IBM	5.0	60.0	8.3
6	Chrysler Motors	4.3	35.5	12.2
7	E. I. duPont de Nemours	4.2	32.5	12.9
8	McDonnell Douglas	3.5	15.1	23.0
9	Caterpillar	2.9	10.4	28.1
10	United Technologies	2.8	18.1	15.8
11	Eastman Kodak	2.3	17.0	13.5
12	Digital	2.1	11.5	18.2
13	Hewlett Packard	2.1	9.8	21.0
14	UNISYS	2.0	9.9	20.3
15	Philip Morris	1.9	25.9	7.2

Source: "America's Fifty Biggest Exporters," *Fortune*, July 17, 1989, pp. 50–51.

Table 1–3 Fifteen leading American exporters ranked by percentage dependence on foreign markets, 1988.

Rank by Exports as Percentage of Total Sales	Company	Percentage of Total Sales Exported
1	Boeing	46.3
2	Minnesota Mining/Manufacturing	32.3
3	Compaq Computer	29.6
4	Caterpillar	28.1
5	McDonnell Douglas	23.0
6	Motorola	21.1
7	Hewlett Packard	21.0
8	UNISYS	20.3
9	Ethyl	20.0
10	FMC	19.7
11	Digital	18.2
12	Hoechst Celanese	17.0
13	General Dynamics	16.7
14	Union Carbide	16.7
15	Combustion Engineering	16.1

Source: "America's Fifty Biggest Exporters," *Fortune*, July 17, 1989, pp. 50–51.

Foreign Investment Opportunities   But in the socialist view, even these figures understate the linkages between American imperialism and the class interest of capitalists. An important additional point is the concentration of foreign interests compared with the domestic American economy. Only about 50 firms control more than half of all US foreign investments; fewer than 200 control more than 80 percent. Thus, the foreign operations of American capital are far more monopolistic than are the domestic operations: The largest and most powerful corporations tend to have a disproportionate interest in the foreign market.

From the socialist perspective, this is significant because concentrated economic interests are better organized and more influential politically than are dispersed economic interests. Thus, a large industry that is concentrated, such as the General Electric Company, has more influence than does a large industry that is dispersed, such as retail drugstores, even though the total sales of all retail drugstores may be larger than those of General Electric. The huge concentration of power in the foreign investment and export sectors gives added weight to these interests.

The Military-Industrial Complex

Another link between imperialism and the interests of capitalism is the military-industrial complex, even though it serves a domestic rather than a foreign market. Military spending comprises another 10 percent of the profits of capitalism and, again, more for large firms than small ones. In addition, a large percentage of the US labor force is involved in defense production. If we add defense to exports and foreign investments and count only the largest firms, we may estimate that the world structure accounts for 35 to 40 percent of the profits of the top capitalist interests. The proposition is demonstrated: There is a clear linkage between capitalism as a socioeconomic system and the tendency to imperialism seen in American foreign policy.

How does this connection between the economic sectors of capitalism and the political policies of the US government operate? There are both direct and indirect linkages. By studying the personal backgrounds, career origins, and bureaucratic job cycles of the 234 top American foreign-policy decision makers from 1944 through 1960, the years in which the American empire absorbed the older imperial structures and became the dominant force in the world system, it can be shown that a relatively small number of individuals circulated among the top policy bureaus during these years. Moreover, about 60 percent of these came from big-business, investment, and major law firm backgrounds.[29] There is an equally impressive circulation of personnel between the armed services and the top defense-supply firms. For example, more than 2000 retired officers above the rank of colonel or naval captain are now in executive positions with the largest defense corporations. One linkage between imperialism and capitalism is the shared interests of the top capitalists and key government officials in the United States.

---

[29]Gabriel Kolko, *The Roots of American Foreign Policy* (Boston: Beacon Press, 1969), pp. 16–26.

Another link is the influence that foreign-oriented capitalists are believed to exercise within the Congress and the American public. The Pentagon alone commanded in 1968 a force of 6140 public relations officers assigned to sell the armed services' point of view around the world. Of these, 339 were legislative liaison lobbyists assigned to the US Congress. In addition, the private defense firms, the exporters, and the foreign-investment interests all had lobbying and public relations operations of their own, including sophisticated Washington law firms to exercise influence with members of Congress.

But these are only the structural linkages of the military-industrial complex. The real menace is the purposes for which the complex exists and the goals for which it takes responsibility in imperialist foreign policy. The principle of these goals is maintenance of the myth that socialism is a menace to capitalism through the might of the Soviet Union. This overlooks the fact that traditional bourgeois governmental institutions throughout the capitalist world are approaching collapse under their own weight as capitalism advances toward full maturation and then destruction. Meanwhile, capitalist institutions profit from the fear of war. These profits are reinvested in the war machine of imperialism, promoting yet newer generations of the arms race. In this way, the economies and foreign policies of the imperial states become fused with militarism which, according to Marx, is the ultimate expression of capitalism.[30]

The military-industrial complex has yet another goal, namely, the advancement of an international arms race so costly that the Soviet Union will be able to equal the arms expenditures of the imperialists only at the expense of other economic priorities. In this way the military-industrial complex is an instrument of international economic warfare designed to strangle socialism. At the same time, in capitalist economic theory, the stimulus of the arms race becomes the basis for sustained economic growth, even though vast increases in military budgets have been unable to offset damaging economic cycles and massive unemployment. Given these arguments, the following is revealed:

> . . . . for all the might and influence of the US military-industrial complex and its vested interest in a militaristic course being pursued, the arms race is not the result of the monopoly activity of this economic and socio-political grouping, as bourgeois-liberal critics of militarism often try to prove. Many facts show that *modern militarism and its specific creation—the arms race—is the product of the entire socio-economic system of imperialism, primarily its most developed and most reactionary component—American imperialism.*[31]

Although Americans vigorously deny the existence of a military-industrial complex and insist that the economy is unreliant on huge military spending, the Soviet government finds satisfaction in occasional statements from the United States that firmly demonstrate their own view. One of these occurred at the time at which the president of the military contractor Tracor resigned. The following is an American journalist's interpretation.

---

[30]E. Kuzmin, ''Traditional Bourgeois Institutions of Power in Deepening Crisis,'' *International Affairs* (Moscow), August 1985, pp. 61–69.

[31]Y. Katasonov, ''Socio-Economic Factors of the Arms Race,'' *International Affairs* (Moscow), January 1985, pp. 39–47, at p. 47.

Retired Adm. Bobby R. Inman, whose military career included a stint at the helm of the National Security Agency, resigned as head of Tracor Holdings, Inc., conceding that even his years as a master spy didn't alert him to the impending end of the Cold War and its devastating effect on the highly leveraged defense contractor.

"I never foresaw in the most optimistic forecasts the pace at which change has taken place in Eastern Europe," Mr. Inman said in an interview. "I'm elated to see it all unravel on that side [of the Iron Curtain] from the personal point of view, but from the investor's point of view, it isn't good news."[32]

To suggestions that the Soviet Union, too, might have a military-industrial complex, there are stern denials. When the leading Soviet expert on the United States was asked about the "Soviet military-industrial complex . . . which also plays a decisive role in the arms race," he replied:

> You should not try to create a symmetry where the situation is very different. Besides, to have a good arms race, you really need just one military-industrial complex.

The Soviet Union does, of course, have a defense industry and modern armed forces.

> But our defense industry does not operate for profit and thus lacks the expansionist drive that characterizes the arms industry of the West. Besides, our economy does not need the booster of military spending that has been turned on more than once in the West to tackle the problem of insufficient demand in the economy.[33]

This statement is consistent with the historic Soviet view that Western arms policy is linked directly to economic imperialism and the inherent weaknesses of capitalism.

American Militarism and Anti-Soviet Hysteria

Until 1988, the Soviet view of the United States changed little. Because of Washington's loss of world military superiority, the changing role of the Third World, the deterioration of American control over the Western allies, and political changes in the United States affecting the conduct of foreign relations, the United States, following the demise of détente, became increasingly militaristic. This was evidenced not only in military budgets and propaganda, but also in Washington's international behavior as well.

This militarism was built on the myth of a Soviet threat or of a global Soviet military buildup, a myth created in Washington with the assistance of the defense industries, the Pentagon, the government bureaucracy, the academic community, and the news media. "They thrive and prosper on the phantom of the 'Soviet threat.' They always take good care to nurture it when it

---

[32]Michael Allen, *The Wall Street Journal,* December 27, 1989, p. B4.
[33]Statement by Georgi Arbatov, in Georgi Arbatov and Willem Oltmans, *The Soviet Viewpoint* (New York: Dodd, Mead, 1983), pp. 110–111.

gets too worn out through heavy use."[34] It is the work of Americans "who simply longed to be provoked and were desperately searching for a pretext" for resumption of the Cold War.[35] Then, having created the fable, these elements doubled spending on weapons of mass destruction and threatened all socialist and Third World peoples with annihilation. For both economic and imperial purposes, the United States was determined to regain military superiority over the Soviet Union, the motherland of socialism, which is increasingly surrounded by the threat of Western aggression, now with the assistance of two huge and powerful Asian allies: Japan and China.

Washington's allies were almost as much the victims of this policy as the Soviet Union. Much of the anti-Soviet hysteria emanating from Washington was designed to perpetuate fears of the Soviet Union among the allies in order to gain control of Western European, Japanese, and Chinese foreign policies. By tactics of fear, the United States attempted to generate the energy that its policy lacked virtually everywhere except in North America. Ample evidence was supplied in 1983 during the European debate about deployment of new American Pershing II and Cruise missiles. When the issue of the necessity of the weapons was raised, one senior State Department official declared that the principal issue at hand was not strategic parity with Soviet SS-20 missiles but "alliance management."[36]

The improvement of Sino-American relations prior to 1989 was a deliberate provocation of the Soviet Union by both the United States and China. It resulted in closing the ring around the Soviet Union and requiring that Moscow revise its targeting strategy in the Pacific. It was a major contributor to the deterioration of détente. While Americans were busily concocting stories about Soviet expansionism, the new military and diplomatic policies of the United States that included China and Western Europe as well as a strategy of limited nuclear war, provoked the Kremlin into new defensive strategies in such places as Afghanistan. All Soviet ventures were defensive in nature and "extraneous" to the context of détente; hence it was American policy that led to its demise.[37]

The militant tone of the Reagan administration at the time of the deployment of new missiles in Europe impelled Yuri Andropov to release a statement on Soviet-American relations in which he wrote:

> In their striving to justify in some way their dangerous, inhuman policies, the same people pile heaps of slander on the Soviet Union, on socialism as a social system, with the tone being set by the President of the United States himself.

[34]Arbatov and Oltmans, *The Soviet Viewpoint*, p. 107.

[35]Georgi Arbatov, "A Soviet Commentary," in Arthur Macy Cox, *Russian Roulette: The Superpower Game* (New York: Times Books, 1982), pp. 182–183.

[36]Richard Burt, *Time*, December 5, 1983, p. 29. The complete statement: "The purpose of this whole exercise is maximum political advantage. It's not arms control we're engaged in, it's alliance management."

[37]For specific comments, see Georgi Arbatov, "A Soviet Commentary," in Cox, *Russian Roulette*, pp. 173–199; and Arbatov and Oltmans, *The Soviet Viewpoint*, especially pp. 62, 86, 104, 107, 167, 178.

> One must say bluntly—it is an unattractive sight when, with a view to smearing the Soviet people, leaders of such a country as the United States resort to what almost amounts to obscenities alternating with hypocritical preaching about morals and humanism.[38]

Two weeks later, another attack was made on the Reagan administration. This one acknowledged that although all American presidents are elected on the basis of their connections with the economic elite and oligarchy, Ronald Reagan in particular "was pushed upward by a group of 'the powers that be,' who discovered in him a cynical demagogue and obedient apostle of big business." It declared that "a policy of madness is gaining the upper hand" in Washington, one exceeding a mere "flurry of great-power messianism" to "an obsession with attaining world domination. . . ."[39] At about the same time Andropov's successor, Konstantin Chernenko, described American foreign policy as "bellicose, great power, and extremely egoistic. . . ."[40]

The third succession of power took place in early 1985 when Mikhail Gorbachev succeeded Konstantin Chernenko. Just weeks earlier, Ronald Reagan began his second term as President of United States. Even as the two prepared for the Geneva summit later that year—the first between Soviet and American leaders in nearly seven years—American rhetoric continued at a high pitch. As Washington and the Kremlin exchanged rejections of each other's arms reduction proposals, the Soviet Union stood firm on the position that no progress could be made unless the United States abandoned its effort to militarize outer space by way of the Strategic Defense Initiative (the "Star Wars" program of antimissile defenses in space). The United States, in return, declared repeatedly that no matter what compromises the Kremlin might be willing to make on other matters, the SDI would proceed. In an interview with *Time* magazine, Gorbachev charged that the Reagan position was "truly a case of driving in nails, snipping off the heads and then expecting everyone to pull them out with their teeth!"[41]

More important, however, was Gorbachev's general assessment of the prospects for progressive arms diplomacy with Washington. He offered two interpretations of the possible American goals:

> On the one hand, the impression is that of some kind of confusion or uncertainty in Washington. The only explanation for this I can see is anxiety lest our initiatives wreck the version about the Soviet Union being the "focus of evil" and the source of universal danger, on which, strictly speaking, the entire arms race policy is pivoted. On the other hand, the impression is one of a lack of a sense of

---

[38]Yuri Andropov, "Text of Soviet Statement on Relations with U.S.," *The New York Times*, September 29, 1983, p. A14. The text was released by Tass on the preceding day.

[39]Alexander Yakovlev, "The Harsh Soviet Line on Reagan," The *Washington Post*, October 16, 1983, p. B5. The author is director of the Soviet Institute of World Economics and International Relations.

[40]From a speech in Pribytkov, *Soviet-U.S. Relations*, pp. 120–124, at p. 123.

[41]Taken from the Soviet translation in *International Affairs* (Moscow), October 1985, pp. 3–16, at p. 11.

responsibility for the destinies of the world. And this, frankly speaking, gives rise again and again to the question whether it is at all possible in such an atmosphere to conduct business in a normal way and to build rational relations between countries.[42]

Months later, after the Geneva summit and in the midst of a distinct bilateral rhetorical deterioration, Gorbachev informed the Twenty-seventh Congress of the Soviet Communist party that serious progress on arms control and other international issues with the United States was complicated by the fact that during the Reagan administration, the United States suffered from "social senility" that "augments its recklessness" in world affairs.[43]

But American imperialism and militarism cannot stop the imperturbable march of history. In the seven decades since the Soviet revolution, three main phases of the transition from capitalism to socialism have already taken place. The first was the revolution, an event that established the Soviet socialist state as a counterweight to capitalist-imperialist domination. The second was the defeat of the fascist forces and the destruction of fascism during the Second World War, although with the assistance of capitalist countries. And third, during the 1970s, imperialism lost it superiority over socialism, with the establishment of Soviet-American military parity.[44] Thus is formed a platform from which the Soviet promotes mature global socialism without fear of military domination by the reactionary forces of capitalism and imperialism.

This is the theory of American imperialism and militarism long espoused by Soviet observers and socialists around the world. The United States was the dominant power in the global system of imperialism that exercises control almost everywhere outside the communist world. Domination takes military, political, and economic forms and is motivated by interests that are rooted in American capitalism. Thus, Lenin's perception that capitalism tends to produce imperialism because of foreign investment dynamics, the need for export outlets, and the search for cheap sources of raw materials describes, in the traditional Soviet view, the reality of American behavior. The theory of American capitalist imperialism was not just a rhetorical device employed by Soviet propaganda but a real analysis of America's role in the world shared by Soviet communists and other observers who consider themselves anti-imperialistic.

The era of *glasnost* and *perestroika* brought considerable change to these long-standing views. Mikhail Gorbachev's vision of world peace, Soviet political and economic modernization, and improved Soviet-American relations began to materialize before the end of the Reagan presidency. The most dramatic steps were the withdrawal of Soviet troops from Afghanistan, a Soviet admission that Soviet military participation there had been "immoral," and a Soviet-American agreement to dismantle all intermediate-range nuclear forces in Europe. They also agreed to mutual visits for on-site inspection of the re-

---

[42]*International Affairs* (Moscow), October 1985, p. 4.

[43]Quoted in *Christian Science Monitor*, February 26, 1986, p. 28.

[44]V. Zagladin, "World Balance of Forces and the Development of International Relations," *International Affairs* (Moscow), March 1985, pp. 65–74.

moval and destruction of the weapons. As President Reagan left office, he dropped the rhetoric of the Soviet Union as "the evil empire" and began to refer instead to "my friend Gorby."

In 1989, even before the dramatic independence movement in Eastern Europe, the Soviet Union declared publicly that it no longer anticipated military action from NATO. In an unprecedented appearance before the House Armed Services Committee of the US Congress, Marshal Sergei Akhromeyev, Gorbachev's foremost military adviser, testified in part as follows:

> Here in the United States and in my country, Americans now and then put this question: "Do you really believe that the United States and NATO intend to unleash a warfare against the U.S.S.R. and the Warsaw Treaty Organization member countries?"
>
> I am personally convinced that neither the United States nor its allies intend today to unleash a warfare against the U.S.S.R. and its allies. I openly make this kind of statement in my country. We are telling our people that the tensions in the world, and war danger, have diminished. And this has been the result of positive changes in the relations between the U.S.S.R. and the U.S.
>
> We are convinced that political means to achieve national security will predominate in the 1990's, while the role of military means must decrease. The U.S.S.R. intends to work to this end in the 1990's. This course was approved by the body of our supreme power, the Congress of the People's Deputies of the U.S.S.R.[45]

Under these circumstances, it is the new Soviet view that NATO and the Warsaw Pact can be disbanded or become merely political alliances in which military might has withered, with the Warsaw Pact stripped of the power to intervene in the domestic political affairs of its members.[46]

The Soviet View of Western Europe

Europe is the most immediate geopolitical issue in Soviet foreign policy. The Soviet Union has been subjected to three major invasions from the West in the past 150 years—twice from Germany. Any Soviet government would have as a paramount interest the question of European security and defense. Today these traditional issues are compounded because three of the world's six nuclear powers (USSR, Britain, and France) are European, and the line of division between the capitalist and socialist worlds runs right through the heart of Europe. On the Western side of the line of demarcation, the NATO alliance members maintain armed forces in excess of 5 million troops organized in 24 divisions, armed with 7200 nuclear warheads and an abundance of conventional air, sea, and land matériel. On the communist side of the line, the War-

---

[45]*The New York Times*, July 31, 1989, p. A15.
[46]For quotations and analysis, see "Gorbachev's Hope for Future: 'A Common European Home,'" *The New York Times*, November 30, 1989, pp. 1 and A20.

saw Pact nations maintain a defensive shield (see Figure 1–2). All the world's largest economies (except Japan) are engaged in this massive confrontation of forces in Central Europe. Quite naturally, the issue of security in Europe looms large in the Soviet view.

From the beginning in 1949, the Soviet foreign ministry objected to the formation of the NATO alliance. The Soviet government favored an all-European security conference to conclude a nonaggression, collective security treaty instead of constructing two opposed systems of alliances. Signatories to the treaty would pledge themselves to refrain from attacking one another and renounce the threat and use of force. Hostile coalitions would be prohibited,

Figure 1–2 The Soviet perspective: Eastern Europe seen as a buffer for Soviet Defense.

and in the case of an armed attack on one or several of the signatories, the others would regard this as an attack on themselves and would render the necessary military aid. This system would be maintained by forming political and military consultative committees.

The Western states consistently rejected this proposal, doubting Soviet intentions and, in the Soviet view, preferring to maintain the network of hostile and aggressive alliances in the hope of restoring capitalism in Eastern Europe, or at least preventing the further spread of revolutionary movements. Thus, the socialist states were forced to form the Warsaw Pact counteralliance in their own defense. The defensive nature of the Warsaw Pact organization is shown by the provision that in case of the discontinuance of the North Atlantic (Western) alliance, the pact would be invalidated automatically. Thus, according to the Soviet view, the responsibility for the system of Cold War alliances lies with the West.

To accomplish the key goal of preventing an attack from the West in the absence of a European security system, three critical imperatives dominated Soviet strategic thinking until 1989:

1. Governments sympathetic to the USSR and socialist in orientation had to be maintained in the belt of Eastern European countries that lies between the Soviet heartland and the powerful countries of Western Europe, especially Germany. In the West, these East European states were considered a buffer zone of satellite states.
2. Germany, the most powerful and historically the most aggressive country of Europe, responsible for the terrible suffering and depredations of the war, must be neutralized as a threat. Preserving the division of Germany into East and West is a necessary and expedient means of reducing the German threat. A government sympathetic to the USSR must be maintained in the East.
3. The military powers of the West European countries must be counterbalanced by the military power of the USSR and the East European countries. This is the mission of the Warsaw Pact.

Soviet policy after the Second World War achieved all three of its aims in Europe. As an outcome of the war, Poland, Czechoslovakia, Hungary, Romania, Albania, Yugoslavia, and Bulgaria all became communist countries, most of them reliable allies against the possibilities of a Western invasion. The strategic location of Czechoslovakia, through which there is direct access to Soviet territory from West Germany, helps explain why the Soviet Union invaded that country in 1968 rather than risk its move out of the Soviet camp and into a friendly relationship with West Germany. Such an alteration in position would have jeopardized the entire Soviet–Eastern European defense system.

The problem of an immensely powerful Germany, once so threatening, has been reduced by partition and by the Soviet-American agreement at Helsinki in 1975, which recognizes as permanent the post–Second World War boundaries. The division of Germany into two zones, originally a by-product of a 1945 military convenience, had become a reality prior to Helsinki. The USSR could not have allowed the zone under its influence to rejoin the western half while West Germany maintains a capitalist social system and an alliance with imperialism. In addition, the Soviet Union strenuously opposes nuclear development in West Germany. An aggressive West Germany armed with atomic bombs could have nightmarish consequences not only for the Soviet Union but also for Poland, Czechoslovakia, and other East European countries.

Finally, to secure control in Eastern Europe and to counterbalance NATO, Soviet and other communist forces were maintained at levels superior to Western ground forces. Communist divisions in Central Europe have outnumbered those of the NATO countries since the Second World War. Although the West considered this a menace to the capitalist international order, in Moscow it was seen as a simple necessity for preserving the socialist commonwealth.

In recent years, several issues outstanding in the postwar division of Europe have been settled. First in order among them has been the conclusion of a treaty between the Soviet Union and West Germany in 1970, paving the way for the solution of all outstanding questions between these two crucial countries. The realistic *Ostpolitik* of West Germany has created the possibility of an acceptance of the de facto situation in Europe as the basis for new relations in this region. In particular, Germany accepted the Oder-Neisse line as Poland's western border with East Germany and recognized the permanence of the two Germanies. The two signatories also pledged themselves to refrain from the use or threat of force and to guide their relations by the principles of the United Nations Charter.

The treaty was followed a year later (1971) by the signing of a four-power agreement on West Berlin by France, the United States, Great Britain, and the Soviet Union. The agreement detailed a basis for relations between that city and West and East Germany, prohibited the use of force, and resolved many technical issues that had been barriers to the relaxation of tensions and the opening of borders for the freer passage of visitors. Although this agreement did not satisfy all sides, it did lay a realistic basis for the improvement of relations, bypassing the insistence on absolute principles that always leads to an impasse. Thus, some of the key issues in Central Europe have been resolved by political moderation.

The Soviet Union had paralleled this peace offensive with a renewed call for a general European Security Conference. In 1966, at a conference in Bucharest, Romania, the Soviet Union and six other socialist countries proposed the holding of an all-European conference on security and cooperation. It aimed at expanding nondiscriminatory East-West trade and at reducing military tension in Europe by gradual dissolution of military blocs, dismantling of foreign bases, withdrawal of foreign troops, and renunciation of the use of force.

At a subsequent meeting in Budapest in 1970, this proposal was expanded to emphasize economic, scientific, and environmental issues with a view to promoting political cooperation among the European states. And most significantly, the Budapest Memorandum proposed the establishment of a permanent all-European political body to deal with questions of security and cooperation. The European Security Conference held in Madrid in 1980 was sabotaged by American insistence on attacking the human rights record of the Soviet Union. The conference met periodically through 1981 and 1982, although the opposing sides were deadlocked over security issues. Both Western condemnation of Soviet behavior in Afghanistan and Poland, and NATO's determination to deploy new theater nuclear weapons that jeopardize the security of the Soviet missile force from a first nuclear strike contributed to the impasse. The conference concluded at the end of 1983 with a call for a first-phase European Disarmament Conference, which convened in Stockholm early in 1984. Although there was little significant progress on regional disarmament, attention was focused increasingly on the process of confidence building in Europe. This was an effort to determine the social, political, and economic bases for Pan-European peace as a precursor to the removal of strategic arms.

Before the severe breakdown of relations in the 1980s, however, there was an eight-year period that promised a thaw in Soviet-American relations, despite differences over Soviet policy in Africa and generally over the subject of human rights. From the Soviet perspective, the thaw rested on several bases. From a strategic point of view, increased fear of Chinese strength on the Asian borders was an incentive to more peaceful relations in Europe (although, paradoxically, improved relations between Beijing and Washington resulted in renewed suspicions in the Kremlin of American motives). Second, the phenomenon of Eurocommunism further loosened the economic dependence of Eastern Europe on the Soviet Union. It opened both intergovernmental (official) and transnational (popular and unofficial) avenues to improved relations between Eastern Europe and the countries of the European Common Market, thus greatly strengthening the potential for international trade balances among the Eastern European countries. Third, and a matter of utmost importance to Soviet planners in all areas pertaining to economic modernization, agricultural production, and military preparedness, Moscow increasingly recognized its need for access to the superior technological capabilities of the United States, Japan, and Western Europe. Although American critics of technological trade with the Soviet Union argued that it merely strengthened the military potential of their country's principal adversary, the Soviets, in acknowledging that the gap between the two countries could be closed through such trade, recognized that its continuation depended on moderation in their foreign policy.

Détente and Its Demise

A popular attitude prevailed from the end of the Vietnam War through the 1970s that fundamental changes in East-West attitudes had called a halt to the Cold War. This attitude was expressed as *détente* and was seen by both East and West as a promising new foundation for foreign policy. But in the Soviet view, the specific conditions and political assumptions of détente, as applied to American diplomacy and to American political expectations, was unreasonable, one-sided, and generally unfair. Détente, after all, was only one characteristic of complex international dynamics subject to change at all times and places. Therefore, in the Soviet view, the playing out of competing interests is a natural part of international politics and should be allowed to continue without the fearful assumption that every Soviet-American competition will result in a severe deterioration of relations between the two great capitals. Thus, while Americans were quick to assume that every new Soviet move was a threat to détente, Soviet planners argued instead that détente was "the art of tradeoffs between competitors, not an arrangement whereby new friends solemnly swear to end the contest.'' Far from being an agreement to preserve a status quo or a particular world power distribution, détente was a theory of international politics that enabled the Soviet Union to pursue its interests without direct military involvement in areas of specific American dominance, to the end that the Soviet Union might fulfill its goals of full superpower status. The Kremlin regarded détente not as a set of global rules preventing the acquisition of its goals but ensuring the peaceful evolution of a world order in which every important international issue would require Soviet participation.[47]

However it was interpreted in the West, détente did not survive the 1970s. Increasing Western hostility to the Soviet Union and its internal and external policies made it clear that the West understood détente to apply restraint to Soviet pursuit of great power interests. Examples abound: American destruction of the socialist regime of Chile; constant American attacks on the human rights policies of the Soviet Union; NATO charges of aggressive Warsaw Pact intentions in Europe; reconstruction of Sino-American relations as a form of tacit aggression against the Soviet Union by both Washington and Beijing; continued American intrusion in the affairs of the Eastern bloc by condemnation of Soviet actions in Poland, together with American economic retaliation; American plans to deploy an MX missile system, a major variant of the nuclear arms race threatening its stability; failure of the United States to ratify the SALT II treaty; emphasis in American nuclear targeting on countervalue strategy (aimed at population and industrial centers); deployment of highly accurate Cruise and Pershing II missiles in Western Europe; inflammatory rhetoric of the Reagan administration accusing the Soviet Union of planning military superiority designed to enslave the world; and so on. The militarism and anti-Soviet hysteria of the United States, together with the expanded threat of nuclear war following the deployment of new American weapons, struck the Soviet Union as signs of hostility, not of an enlightened Western attitude called détente, which provided assurances of great power, peace, and freedom of action in areas not directly under the control of one another. Détente had been merely a ruse under which the West perpetuated the Cold War.[48] In such an environment, it was necessary for the Kremlin to discontinue the Intermediate-range Nuclear Forces (INF) talks regarding Europe and the Strategic Arms Reduction Talks (START) on intercontinental nuclear weapons. Although the Soviets longed for the return of détente and normalization of relations with the United States, their moves were based on the

> gaping discrepancy between U.S. policy and today's realities. Officials in Washington have forgotten, or simply do not want to remember, that successful talks on arms limitation and the very prevention of nuclear war call for normal relations, relations of peaceful coexistence and détente between countries with dif-

[47]Dimitri K. Simes, ''Détente, Russian-Style,'' *Foreign Policy,* Fall 1978, pp. 47–62.

[48]John Lewis Gaddis, ''The Rise, Fall and Future of Détente,'' *Foreign Affairs,* Winter 1983–1984, pp. 354–377. Gaddis presents the revisionist interpretation that détente from the American viewpoint was not a new strategy ''but a means of updating and reinvigorating containment.''

ferent social systems. . . . One cannot count on the preservation of peace, or on the success of the negotiations, while at the same time unleashing a wholesale political war against the socialist countries, spurring on the arms race, and fanning hatred and mistrust of the Soviet Union.[49]

As we have seen in the case of the Soviet perception of the United States, the era of *glasnost* and *perestroika* brought sharp changes to the perception of Western Europe as well. The Kremlin's willingness to permit its Eastern European empire to dissolve in the Kremlin's own economic interest, its willingness to permit NATO and the Warsaw Pact to evolve into political alliances, its apparent eagerness to denounce the Brezhnev Doctrine, all in favor of a "common European home," indicate a revolutionary revision of the official attitude toward Western Europe. Caught between a foundering economy and a restive public eager to enjoy the benefits of modern living, as do Western Europeans, and willing to come to terms with the capitalist powers even at the expense of the Marxist-Leninist notion that capitalism is imperialism, the CPSU has set a course toward the West. No longer fearing capitalist encirclement or military invasion because of its own strength and vision, the Kremlin now seeks full partnership in the global economy toward which an expanded economic relationship with an undivided Europe will follow Germany's 1990 reunification.

There are, of course, military complications to all this. NATO and Western nuclear arms will not disappear over night. These issues are addressed in Part II, "The Logic of Power."

The Soviet View of China

The persistent conflict between the Soviet Union and China has grown in importance to the Soviet world outlook until recently, contributing to the desire for reduced tensions in Europe. This antagonism is a very old issue, predating communism in the two countries. The historical fact of an expansionist Russia relentlessly pressing eastward has naturally brought conflict between two giants who share a 6000-mile border. The issues dividing the USSR and China today include both ideological questions and historical national interests that would conflict regardless of ideology.

National Border Disputes

The border may be separated into three general regions of conflict.

Western Region   In the western region, the 1850-mile border between Soviet Central Asia and China's Sinkiang Province divides homogeneous ethnic minorities (Uighurs, Tadzhiks, Kazaks) whose movements do not always observe the legal boundaries. China conducts its atomic testing and some atomic pro-

---

[49]Georgi Arbatov, in Arbatov and Oltmans, *The Soviet Viewpoint*, p. 86.

duction in Sinkiang, raising other special issues. The most serious problem from the Soviet point of view is that China controls the Ili Valley gateway to Turkestan, making the protection of Soviet Central Asia militarily difficult. This Great Gateway of the Nations—the Dzungarian Gates—was the route through which the hordes of Genghis Khan invaded Europe, and it has long been a problem of Russian (and later Soviet) defense.

Eastern Region   In the eastern region, the 2300-mile border separating the Soviet maritime regions and Pacific ports from Chinese Manchuria is a special problem. These Soviet Far Eastern assets are vital commercial and military links, but they are logistically remote from the Soviet heartland and are difficult to defend. On the Chinese side of the border is the main Manchurian industrial region, which confers logistical advantages. China's claims for revisions of the existing line of demarcation, based on historical issues, would bring Chinese power right up to the city limits of Khabarovsk and in other ways substantially weaken the Soviet position. Therefore, the Soviet Union insists on the principle of sanctity of treaties and denies the ambitious Chinese claims.

Central Region   In the remaining region, the 2650-mile Chinese border with Outer Mongolia, the issue is not border delineation or strategic balance but the question of control over Outer Mongolia itself. This quasi-independent nation is now under Soviet influence. China asserts a historical right to suzerainty—a claim that the Soviets regard as pure troublemaking.

This 6000-mile border cannot be directly defended mile by mile, so defense depends on a system of mutual threats and general military preparations. Hundreds of thousands of troops are deployed on each side. Several skirmishes resulting in deaths occurred during the late 1960s and the early 1970s, and pessimistic predictions speak forebodingly of the potential for much larger encounters.

The potential for military conflict reaches beyond the common boundary of the two giant powers. For almost 20 years they have competed for Mongolia, now in the Soviet orbit, and for as long they have nervously watched each other's interests, maneuvers, and investments in India, Pakistan, and Bangladesh. During the Vietnam War, Peking and Moscow competed for dominant influence over Hanoi, with Ho Chi Minh playing a coy game of accepting the assistance of both without succumbing to the control of either. There were unconfirmed reports, however, that Soviet goods bound for the North Vietnamese war effort were being held up on railroad sidings in China, in order that the dominant military aid might be thought to be from China.

More recently, continental Asian events have taken a number of peculiar turns. First, Japan has reached formal peace with both China and the Soviet Union. Second, Beijing and Washington have exchanged diplomatic recognitions, putting an end to a bitter mutual antipathy and the sponsoring of wars through their surrogates; and the rapprochement of China with the West has improved China's conventional military potential as well as its political-military relations with NATO on the Soviet western front. Third, and of most immediate apparent value, China invaded Vietnam as an act of punitive aggression for Hanoi's conquest of Cambodia.

In an effort to offset this apparent Chinese advantage in the competition among the nonnuclear areas of Asia, the Soviet Union has moved naval vessels into Cam Rahn Bay, a huge naval facility built by and for the use of the US Navy during the Vietnam War. Furthermore, the military relationship among China, NATO, and Japan has called for an increase in Soviet vigilance throughout the North Pacific; Soviet air, naval, submarine, intelligence, and communications activities have been expanded there, particularly in the Soviet-held islands north of Japan. These are not aggressive moves, in the Soviet view, but the necessary defensive consequence of a new and ever more threatening form of encirclement by imperial and ideologically revisionist forces. Indeed, Konstantin Chernenko, before rising to be General Secretary of the Soviet Communist Party, observed that "the cause of international security has quite a few adversaries. These are, above all, the forces of imperialism and they have accomplices—dictatorial regimes, military juntas, and Beijing's hegemony seekers."[50]

Ideological Disputes

In addition to this conflict of national interests, there are key ideological issues in dispute between the two communist giants. Since the death of Stalin in 1953, Chinese propaganda has portrayed the Soviet Union as a center of new social imperialism just as abhorrent as that of the Western capitalists. China has called for "alternative paths to socialism" in the communist bloc, in which the central determination of bloc policy by the Soviet Union would be ended in favor of a concept of self-determination by each country. China even laid claim to the mantle of ideological leadership, portraying Mao-Tse-tung as a contemporary and coequal of Lenin, while the present Soviet leadership is seen as a gang of bureaucratic hacks. Chinese propaganda has made virulent attacks of all kinds on the intentions and integrity of the Soviet Communist party. The Soviets regard the Chinese charge that the broadening of Soviet interests to Afghanistan and other areas in the Third World represents the establishment of social imperialism as a particularly repugnant ideological diversion. Pure Marxism-Leninism reserves the charge of imperialism for capitalists and other fascists.

The Soviets rejected these claims as irresponsible, ill founded, and motivated by wild ambition. Both alternative paths and Chinese leadership are invalidated by the simple reality that only Soviet might, backed up by the huge Soviet economy, can in fact defend the revolutionary states from capitalist encirclement and promote revolutionary gains in the Third World.

In addition, the alternative-paths-to-socialism slogan causes disunity in the socialist camp and creates a false idea of relativism. The Soviets have never denied that revolutionary principles must adjust to the special conditions in

---

[50]Chernenko in a speech to the Communist party of Cuba, 1980, in Pribykov, *Soviet-U.S. Relations,* pp. 87–89, at p. 87.

each country, but they firmly reject the extreme go-it-alone lengths to which this idea is carried by China. The ideal form is collective determination of bloc policy by international party congresses, as practiced since 1945 and even earlier. The Soviet Union does not propose to rule by arbitrary and unilateral fiat, but neither does it propose to allow purely national interests within the bloc to rise above the collective interests of the bloc as a whole. The Brezhnev Doctrine, pronounced in 1968 in justification of the Warsaw Pact countries' invasion and occupation of a liberalizing Czechoslovakia, reaffirmed the primacy of the collective socialist good over the particular interests of any single country within the camp. United, the socialist world will prosper; but divided, it will fall to hostile capitalist encirclement. This maxim was complicated by Beijing's improved ties with governments of Eastern Europe, thus accelerating the erosion of socialist solidarity.

The Soviet Union itself, it was argued, must be the first among equals. The USSR was the first revolutionary state and spawned the others. The Soviet Communist party is the direct heir of Lenin and is ideologically and materially the best prepared for the leadership position. Thus, the Soviets rejected the ideological as well as the territorial claims of the Chinese adventurists and increasingly hold them responsible for the deterioration of the proletarian internationalism, both by undermining Soviet superiority and by making threatening accommodations with the West. In fact, it was not until 1982, when the Soviet Union was concerned with the Western orientation of Chinese foreign policy, that the Kremlin acknowledged for the first time that China is a socialist state; but it did so with a stern reminder that socialist China's dangerous leanings toward the capitalist and imperialist West were intrinsically damaging to the cause of global socialism.

The deterioration of détente with the West occurred simultaneously with major changes in China and in Chinese foreign policy. The death of Mao Tsetung in 1976 brought enormous changes to Chinese relations with the West, with obvious implications for Soviet foreign policy. But the emergence of a new Chinese political outlook did not have direct benefits for the Kremlin and did not ease the necessity for vigilance on the Eastern front. Thus the new Chinese diplomacy presented a triple cost to the Soviet Union.

1. The Chinese connection with the West and with its economic, technological, and military capabilities increased the Chinese threat in Soviet policy.
2. The opening of China to new ideas and new modes of diplomacy and commerce threatened to erode Moscow's position as the unchallenged pinnacle of proletarian internationalism, as China worked out new relations with Eastern Europe.
3. The new Chinese leadership took fewer steps to improve relations with the Kremlin than with Washington and the other NATO capitals.

Hence, while the West was largely freed of the burden of countering Chinese foreign policy in Asia and elsewhere, the burden for the Soviet Union multiplied:

These circumstances have important implications for Moscow's global diplomacy, particularly on control of strategic arms. Growing Sino-American accord

Source: Drawing by Ross; © 1990, The New Yorker Magazine, Inc.

and the increasing nuclear capability of China combine to raise the eventual threat of a serious challenge to the Soviet Union in a part of the world where it is at a geo-political disadvantage. As a result, arms control talks with the United States cannot be limited to Soviet-American parity, but must take into account the special imperative of China in Soviet strategic policy. While, therefore, Washington is willing to negotiate only over arms equality, the Soviets must be concerned about equal security. In this way the China problem complicates Soviet diplomatic strategy elsewhere.[51]

More recently, however, Sino-Soviet relations have thawed. The Chinese policy of equidistance—maintaining a safe distance from both the Soviet Union and the United States but dealing with each—has diminished the Westward drift feared by the Kremlin. The military stability of Asia, except in Cambodia, has reduced the threat of increasing Chinese regional power. And the American preoccupation with Japanese economic domination has reduced the alliancelike behavior of Washington and Beijing. Although its troops remain at the Sino-Soviet border, these changes have enabled the Kremlin to view as less likely any serious military confrontation with China.

---

[51]Dan L. Strode, "Arms Control and Sino-Soviet Relations," *ORBIS*, Spring 1984, pp. 163–188.

And, once again, enter *glasnost* and *perestroika*. Under these banners the Soviet Union has desired to improve relations not only with the West, but with China as well. Exploratory trade talks were conducted during the early days of the Soviet-American thaw in 1988, and in 1989 the talks culminated with Mikhail Gorbachev's historic visit to Beijing. This was the first visit ever made by the top-ranking Soviet official to China in the history of the Chinese revolution, and might have had historic consequences had other events not intervened. Using the presence of the world press in Beijing to cover the Gorbachev visit, dissident Chinese students demonstrated for freedom of the press and protested government corruption. The situation remained tense throughout Gorbachev's visit and turned to violence after his departure, although the press was still present to record the bloody events. Because the Chinese reaction was to turn inward and forsake at least temporarily Beijing's international goals, and because Gorbachev's policy is to align with progressive tolerance rather than repressive reactionism, the talks were informally discontinued.

Conclusion

The classical Soviet point of view was a combination of Russian national interests and communist ideological principles. The international system was seen as largely unjust and threatening to the Soviet Union, whose main role was to defend itself and its allies and to combat international injustice.

The dominant theme in this view was the theory of imperialism. Capitalism, which is still the social system in most of the advanced and powerful countries, was seen as supported by class exploitation, and imperialism was seen as simply the international expression of this exploitation. Imperialism was capitalist class exploitation across national boundaries. Capitalist systems needed empires to provide (1) raw materials, (2) markets for domestic exports, and (3) high returns on investments. These drives led the imperialist states to dominate the poorer countries.

The communist countries defected from this international class system. As the first and strongest socialist state, the USSR was the natural leader. The military might of the imperialists was such that direct challenge to the imperial system was not possible. But it was the obligation of the USSR to defend the communist states that already existed from capitalist-inspired counter-revolution or invasion and, insofar as is possible, to help other countries on the path to revolution.

As the leading imperialist power, the United States had a special role in the international system. It controlled more than half of the imperialist system of exploitation and was immensely powerful militarily. It maintained a vast network of alliances designed at the minimum to keep control of all countries not already communist and possibly even "to roll back communism" (that is, recapture the liberated countries for the imperial system). The United States was also important in that it was most skillful in hiding its true position behind moral and ideological disguises that befuddle many non-Marxists.

The capitalist world encircled socialism, and only the Soviet shield protected and advanced the world revolutionary movement. Yet a dissident faction within the socialist camp, led by China, divided and disunified revolutionary states and created an internal opposition to the Soviet leadership. Only the solidity of the Warsaw bloc in Eastern Europe prevented renewed aggression from the capitalist world. The unity of the socialist commonwealth stood above the claims of factions within individual countries. Chinese adventurism was opposed at every point, and the solidarity of the revolutionary world was maintained. Only in this way could the final victory of socialism be achieved over the long run.

This classical view is undergoing extraordinarily rapid change, having evolved more in 24 months from late 1988 through late 1990 than most national perspectives change in decades. In part out of economic necessity, in part out of uncontrollable external events, and in part out of genuine reform, the combined policies of *glasnost* (access to information) and *perestroika* (restructuring) introduced by Mikhail Gorbachev have led to a remarkable transformation of national perception. From communist power monopoly to the consideration of multiparty politics; from the Brezhnev Doctrine to the self-determination of national peoples in Eastern Europe; from a hard-line balance of nuclear terror to rapid reduction in arms; from a planned regional production and distribution system to a quest for full partnership in the global economy—by all these rapid changes the Soviet view of the world and its competing actors has evolved very recently. The goal now is to make fruitful accommodations with capitalist powers, to transform from a fortress Europe to a common European home including the United States as a cultural extension of Europe, with full knowledge that to achieve these, the Soviet Union must "decompose" its Eastern European empire for its own sake.

CHAPTER 2

The American Perspective

Ironically, for much of the last three decades, it has been easier for many Americans to entertain a friendly picture of the Soviet or the Chinese view than to appreciate the role of an official of their own country. Particularly in the wake of the twin calamities of Vietnam and Watergate, together with the fall and rise of Cold War rhetoric, before 1988, there was a willingness to look closely at the communist side, a willingness that made the shortcomings of their own country seem all the more glaring.

During the 1980s, however, a revised view of the American role in world affairs developed. Growing awareness of the Soviet military strength after a decade of curtailed military sentiment at home called into question the adequacy of national preparedness in a manner unknown since the 1930s, and the presidential elections of 1980, 1984, and 1988, as well as the congressional elections of 1982 and 1986, seemed to be, among other things, a repudiation of post–Vietnam War foreign policy and a call for a new national outlook. President Ronald Reagan called for a renewed vigilance against Soviet expansionism with its threat to democratic principles the world over and against the efforts of the Third World to command world events in a way that could diminish the standard of living in the United States. A wave of conservatism and patriotism swept the country, as much among young people as among their elders. With the major exception of student reaction against compulsory registration for Selective Service (although the actual draft did not exist), most youthful political activity leaned sharply toward conservative policy proposals, both domestic and international.

Radical change occurred only in and after 1988. President Reagan departed from the White House on a tide of public sentiment driven principally by vast improvement in relations with the Soviet Union as the result of three summits in a short period of time. George Bush, running on a conservative platform and turning toward the political center only as the campaign ground to a close, defeated Michael Dukakis by a huge margin in both popular votes and states, and swept into the White House amid unprecedented optimism that the Cold War might be on the wane. Soviet leader Mikhail Gorbachev's popularity among Americans gave the president more room for diplomatic initiatives than any of his recent predecessors had enjoyed, and the two took full advantage at a Malta summit (1989), which they concluded with the friendliest and most forward-looking joint press conference ever held between Soviet and American leaders. The 1990s opened with a broad sense among Americans that the Cold War had passed into history, and the willingness of the Kremlin to permit political and economic self-determination throughout Eastern Europe in exchange for full partnership in the global economy was interpreted as the dawn of a new era. True, conservatives tended to credit the success of containment and tough stands on arms reduction with this sudden transformation of world events, whereas liberals inclined toward the theory that Gorbachev's bold initiatives through *glasnost* and *perestroika* had actually opened the doors to peace. Via whichever route, however, by 1990 the American world view had changed dramatically, and political discourse shifted almost suddenly from containment and arms races to priorities for "cutting up the peace dividend."

In these changes of view, perceptual analysis need not imply that a particular outlook is correct and another incorrect—only that when attitudes toward world perspective change, there is a strong internal logic consistent with the evidence when it is ordered in a certain, even if changed, way.

Rebuttal to the Theory of American Economic Imperialism

Throughout the years since World War II, one obstacle to improved relations between the United States and the major communist governments has been the contention of the latter that the United States is pursuing a design of world economic imperialism and hegemony. Although this claim is heard infrequently from post-Maoist China and more frequently from the post-détente Soviet Union, this is a basic ideological difference between East and West that guides perceptions and obstructs peaceful relations. According to neo-Leninist critics, the mature phase of capitalism is characterized by a saturation of the domestic market with surplus capital and by overproduction. The maintenance of the profit structure depends on the penetration of foreign markets for high-yield investment opportunities, export outlets, and secure sources of the cheapest raw materials. For the United States, the necessary expansion has been justified behind a disguise of anticommunism and defense of the Free World. This is said to explain the basic dynamic of US Cold War policy and domination of much of the Third World. The neo-Leninist analysis, presented at length in the preceding chapter, is rejected by orthodox theorists on the following factual grounds:

1. **Foreign investment profits are not higher.** Over the past 20 years, American manufacturing investments at home have returned a profit slightly higher than have in-

vestments abroad. It is false, therefore, to argue that American capital is being driven from the domestic market to foreign markets for higher profit.

2. **American capitalism does not depend on foreign markets.** It is true that American foreign investments total in value more than do the national economies of all but the United States itself, Japan, and the Soviet Union. But these foreign assets are only a fraction of the book value of American corporations. In most industries, exports account for less than 10 percent of total sales, although a few industries depend heavily on sales abroad: computers, aerospace, and farm machinery in particular.

3. **American capitalism does not depend on exploitation of the Third World.** Less-developed countries are only a small portion of the market for US foreign investment and exports, and they are gradually declining in importance except with respect to arms. American capital increasingly finds it more profitable to invest in developed countries than in underdeveloped areas, in large part because of the differences in political stability and, therefore, the safety of investments. It is not plausible to argue that American capitalism needs to dominate small countries or to retard their growth.

4. **Vietnam cannot be explained as economic imperialism.** The natural resources and market value of Vietnam or all of Southeast Asia could not begin to repay the costs of war: $150 billion, ten years of war, and 50,000 American lives. The rice, tungsten, teak, and small offshore oil deposits of Indochina are relatively minor in value. American policy in Vietnam cannot be explained by the imperatives of capitalism. The stock market averages, which Leninists would have predicted to rise with the war, instead fell sharply, indicating that Vietnam was not good for business.

5. **There is not a clearly defined capitalist ruling class in America.** The neo-Leninist theory assumes that major multinational corporations are owned and managed by a small, definable class with vast influence in the American political process. In truth, the means of production are widely owned, including millions of successful small businesses. Even the large industries have widely dispersed ownership through shareholding. Sixty-seven percent of Americans—about 140 million people—own stocks directly or indirectly (through pension funds, insurance companies, and other collective institutional investors). Thirty-five million Americans own shares directly in the stock markets. Although there are some very large stockholders as well, to some degree America has achieved "people's capitalism." There is not a sharp line between rich and poor.

   Moreover, the rich/poor division is just one way of slicing the pie in pluralistic democracy. Catholics are sometimes opposed to Protestants, men to women, black to white, Irish to Italian, farmer to worker, young to old, urban to rural, North to South, and hawk to dove among other divisions. Each conflict crosscuts the others, and instead of immutably opposed permanent classes, pluralism offers shifting coalitions and factions. Government is not the permanent agent of one class, but an arbiter standing above the various divisions, favoring first one, then another.

6. **Economic interests do not determine American foreign policy.** Even if the neo-Leninist can demonstrate that America profits from a foreign market, it does not follow that policy toward that country is guided by material gain. In general, security interests and ideological principles tend to override limited economic gains in the determination of foreign policy, according to the orthodox view. If, like many

Table 2–1 American banks among the world's 50 largest commercial banks, 1989.

Name	Headquarters	Rank in Top 50
Citicorp	New York	12
Chase Manhattan	New York	37
Bankamerica	San Francisco	38
J. P. Morgan	New York	49

Source: Fortune, July 31, 1989, p. 286.

neo-Leninists, we discount Soviet imperialism as an official mythology created by American propaganda, we must rely on exotic explanations such as economic determinism to explain American policy. But if we accept the reality of the Soviet threat, the primacy of security interests in determining US policy is apparent. The theory of American economic imperialism is, in the dominant American view, a tired set of worn shibboleths to be mouthed without conviction by Soviet speech makers on state occasions.[1]

7. **The count of American bank branches abroad, even in the Third World, is a valueless exercise for two reasons.** First, there are only four American entries among the world's 50 largest commercial banks, and three of them are in the lowest third. And among the foremost 25, only one is American: Citicorp of New York ranks twelfth globally (see Table 2–1). Moreover, in 1989, Citicorp's assets totaled about $208 billion, whereas those of Dai-Ichi Kangyo Bank of Tokyo, the world's richest, rose to about $380 billion. Among the top 25, Japan controls the list with 17 entries (see Table 2–2); and although all four American banks in the top 50 have assets totaling $584 billion, the top five of Japan's alone have assets totaling over $1.4 trillion. Oddly, the Beijing-based Bank of China ranks number 26 in the world, well ahead of all American banks except Citicorp.

Second, it may be that American banks have devoted a disproportionate share of their assets to Third World investments; however, recent history has demonstrated plentifully that Third World investments are not necessarily lucrative investments at all. As indicated in Chapter 14 "International Monetary Exchange," many American banks have lost great sums owing to the chronic inability of Third World countries to service their debts. By 1990, under the Brady Plan of debt restructuring, many of these banks were attempting to discount these debts in order to collect anything at all, and many were transferring current reserves into special accounts for future offset of losses.

8. **The extent of American direct and portfolio investment abroad is no measure of imperialism unless it is matched to foreign investment in the United States.** Once again, recent history reveals that if both sides of the issue are examined, then the United States is not the imperialist, but the imperialized. By early 1990 (see Chapter 14 for details), the net foreign investment position of the United States— that is, value of American investments abroad against the value of foreign investments in the United States—was in deficit by almost $600 billion.

---

[1]This analysis borrows heavily from Robert W. Tucker, *The Radical Left and American Foreign Policy* (Baltimore: Johns Hopkins University Press, 1971), especially pp. 124–138.

Table 2–2 National distribution of the world's 25 largest commercial banks, 1989.

Country	Number of Banks in Top 25
Japan	17
France	4
Britain	2
West Germany	1
United States	1

Source: Fortune, July 31, 1989, p. 286.

From the American perspective, these facts and figures dispel the Leninist claim that American capitalism is intrinsically imperialistic. Indeed, in an age in which computerized communications and the international flow of money have built a single global economy out of what was once an unrelated string of national economies, the classical notion of imperialism by a single national force is obsolete.

Roots of the American World View

Whereas Marxist thought begins with a theory of class conflict and revolution, the American traditional world view turns on questions of political freedom and tyranny. Freedom—understood as self-determination, majority rule, and the right of dissent—is the highest goal in the hierarchy of core values. ''Give me liberty or give me death,'' demanded Patrick Henry. When Americans evaluate other social systems, the first questions they ask usually concern the degree of freedom of speech and religion, the right to vote, and tolerance of dissent. Political and religious liberty are put above economic well-being and questions of economic justice.

The relative unconcern of Americans for class injustices, compared with those of other peoples, has been credited to the lack of a feudal experience. Absentee landlordism and other abuses of feudalism left in many other countries a bitter heritage of class conflict, which was much less pronounced here.[2] The promise of open land beyond the frontier before 1900 made America a land of opportunity where wealth was the direct reward for hard work and poverty the punishment for laziness or stupidity.[3] The early settlers who came to the New World sought not class revolution but religious tolerance (for example, Puritans, Mennonites) and economic opportunity. Capitalism itself demanded a free market, entrepreneurial liberty, and political self-determination, at least for the commercial classes.

---

[2]The importance of a nonfeudal past is explored by Louis Hartz in *The Liberal Tradition in America* (New York: Harcourt Brace and World, 1955).

[3]The significance of the frontier is explored in Frederick Jackson Turner, *The Frontier in American History* (New York: Henry A. Holt, 1920). See also David Potter, *People of Plenty* (Chicago: University of Chicago Press, 1954).

These origins were consistent with the evolution of a philosophy of the social contract. In this theory, the state is constituted by freely consenting individuals to protect the security and advance the common interests of society. Government "derives its just powers from the consent of the governed," in Thomas Jefferson's words. Revolution is justified not in terms of class upheaval but as a legitimate response to political tyranny.

The principal danger to liberty is the inherent tendency of government to expand without limitation and to extinguish the rights of citizens. Power corrupts, and absolute power corrupts absolutely. Tyranny is averted, and governmental power is limited in the United States by constitutional restraints, majority rule, guaranteed minority rights, checks and balances among 80,000 separately elected governmental units, and the separation of executive, legislative, and judicial powers. Power is at every point balanced against power: civilian control of the military, judicial oversight of the constitutionality of legislative and executive actions, state versus federal authority, direct election of high officials, and other checks. The obsession of the entire design is eternal vigilance against despotism.

The American Image of International Relations

The problem of defending freedom against tyrannical tendencies exists not just within individual societies but in international relations as well. The parallel to individual freedom in international society is the principle of national independence and self-determination, and the parallel to infringement of individual rights is the violation of territorial sovereignty and foreign interference in the internal affairs of a free nation. Civil freedom is threatened when uncontrolled authority expands to tyranny. International freedom is threatened when one nation or coalition undertakes to extend its power to the domination of others. In both cases, injustice begins when one power center upsets the natural balance of forces and seeks an unwarranted expansion.

Historically, internal and external tyranny have been linked in the American view. Democratic governments and free peoples are thought to be naturally peace loving, whereas tyrannies and dictatorships have an innate tendency to expand beyond their own borders to make demands on their neighbors. An unchecked tyranny in one country is soon a danger to the entire world.

The Image of the Aggressor

The image of the International Aggressor is an important component of the American belief system. (An image is a simplified representation of reality that serves as a mental ordering device.) The Aggressor is a bully who employs military threats and actions to subdue weaker states and to seize from them any assets he wishes. He is immune to normal considerations of justice and regards international law and morality as mere sentimentality. His appetite for expansion is insatiable, especially when motivated by a messianic ideology, and success in one conquest does not appease him but whets his appetite for more. He is cunning in the use of propaganda to conceal his intentions, and he regards agreements and treaties as mere expedients rather than obligations.

The only restraint that the Aggressor truly respects is physical opposition. If the world is to be ruled by reason and not by force, and if weak members of the international community are not to be left at the mercy of the strong, it is the special responsibility of the larger democratic states to oppose international lawlessness. The United States in particular is obligated by its vast resources and its historic ideals to play a role of leadership in guaranteeing minimum standards of international behavior.

The dominant theme of American diplomatic history during the twentieth century has been the search for an appropriate role. On the one side are the ideals of the American people and the perceived problems of the international system; on the other side are the limits of American commitment to external affairs. Repeatedly, the United States has been called on to respond to aggression in other parts of the world, but the American people have continued to find the role of world policeman unnatural.

Aggression in the Twentieth Century

Before the First World War, the United States was relatively uninvolved on the world stage. Although potentially powerful, it was insulated from foreign conflicts by vast oceans on both shores, and the dominant position of the United States in the Western Hemisphere ensured safety within this zone. Moreover, the global system from 1815 until 1914 was relatively stable and rarely called for active American military participation. The major European states that dominated the world system pursued essentially conservative policies of maintaining the status quo (although redistributive goals were pursued in relation to colonial issues), and the security of American interests was hardly affected by the tides of world politics.

American foreign policy during this period had three cornerstones:

1. **Isolationism:** nonentanglement in the complex web of European military alliances and intrigues. These were perceived as having little consequence for Americans.
2. **The Monroe Doctrine:** an insistence on European nonintervention in the Western Hemisphere, in effect declaring Latin America as the United States' sphere of influence.
3. **Commercial expansion:** full participation in free international trade and access to world markets while avoiding foreign conflicts.

In general, these principles asserted for the United States a major role as a world economic actor but a minor role in world political and military affairs.

This relatively harmonious world was thoroughly upset in 1914 with the outbreak of the First World War. For the first time since 1815, a major power seemed bent on fundamental redistribution and alteration of the European balance, with vast consequences for the rest of the world. Within months, most of the big powers and their allies and colonies were drawn into the complex struggle, and a variety of regional antagonisms separate from the main issues

"On the Threshold!"
Source: Copyright Gale, *Los Angeles Times*, reprinted by permission.

were added to the conflict. The United States, protected by geographic position from the main issues and confused by the morass of charges and countercharges, claims and counterclaims, stayed out of the war for three years.

But as the war progressed, America's early neutrality and isolationist attitude gave way to growing hostility toward Germany and an increasing sympathy to the Allies, especially Britain. Ties of language and custom with England, as well as strong commercial links, made true neutrality impossible. Moreover, the struggle was increasingly viewed as a deeply moral issue of democracy and decency (England) versus dictatorship and barbarism (Germany). This image of the German Aggressor was promoted by British propaganda and was taken up by President Woodrow Wilson to build public support for entry into the war on the Allied side. When German submarines began sinking American commercial vessels with civilian passengers aboard, American opinion was enraged, and the image of the Aggressor was driven deep into the public consciousness. President Wilson's memorable war message on April 2, 1917, spoke directly to the key themes in the image. The war was caused by an attempt at territorial expansion by tyrants.

> We have no quarrel with the German people. . . . It was not upon their impulse that their government acted. . . . It was a war determined as wars used to be determined upon in the old, unhappy days when peoples were nowhere consulted

by their rulers and wars were provoked and waged in the interest of dynasties or of little groups of ambitious men who were accustomed to use their fellow men as pawns or tools.

The United States had tried to stand apart, Wilson declared, but had discovered to its sorrow that it could not escape the responsibility to oppose massive aggression.

A steadfast concern for peace can never be maintained except by a partnership of democratic nations. We are glad . . . to fight thus for the ultimate peace of the world and for the liberation of its peoples, the German peoples included; for the rights of nations great and small and the privilege of men everywhere to choose their own way of life and of obedience. . . . America is privileged to spend her blood and her might for the principles that gave her birth and happiness and the peace which she has treasured. . . . The world must be made safe for democracy.

The United States would fight not for narrow national interests but for the restoration of an international system based on principles of justice and non-aggression.

We have no selfish ends to serve. We desire no conquest, no dominion. We seek no indemnities for ourselves, no material compensation for the sacrifices we shall freely make. We are but one of the champions of mankind.[4]

This break with historic isolationism signified for the United States the beginning of an active role in the defense of Western democracy.

The 1919 Settlement

The leadership's approach to the Peace Conference after the German defeat in 1918 provides further clues to the operation of the Aggressor image in the American world view. Wilsonian thought traced the origins of German external aggression to roots of internal tyranny, so the first task was to redesign the German political order. The Weimar Constitution, which was drafted largely by Americans and which borrowed heavily from Anglo-American constitutional experience, projected for Germany a model democratic system eliminating all traces of autocratic rule. Combined with a compulsory program of disarmament and industrial limitation, it seemed to guarantee that Germany would never again attempt aggressive expansion.

On the international level, the Wilsonian design was to seek new systematic guarantees against potential future threats to stability. The idea of collective security was founded in the institutional form of the League of Nations (precursor to the United Nations). In effect, this modeled future international relations on the principle of an alliance of major powers permanently committed to oppose aggression. Unfortunately, the League had little success in fulfilling

---

[4]Woodrow Wilson, *War Message*, 65th Cong., 1st sess., Senate document no. 5 (Washington D.C.: US Government Printing Office, 1971), pp. 3–8.

these goals when new threats to international peace developed. Domestic political opposition and a resurgence of isolationism prevented the United States from actively supporting the League in the way that Wilson had designed. Moreover, the major powers were not, in most cases, able to agree on joint policy toward expansionary movements, and it became clear that opposition to aggression on grounds of principle was less important to most leaders than was the pursuit of more narrowly conceived national interests. The dream of collective security evaporated, and international relations reverted to the more familiar pattern of power politics from which, in fact, it had never varied.

The Second World War

Within 15 years of victory in the Great War, three new Aggressors moved to subdue new victims. First, in a mounting series of crises, militant Japan seized control of the crucial Manchurian industrial region of China in 1931. In 1933, Adolf Hitler used the ill-conceived emergency-powers clause of the Weimar Constitution to overthrow the German Republic and establish the fanatical and aggressive Third Reich dictatorship. In 1935, Benito Mussolini led Fascist Italy into a war of conquest in Ethiopia. In 1935, Hitler remilitarized the Rhineland in preparation for war. In 1937, Japan extended its movement in China with an eye to total conquest.

President Franklin D. Roosevelt warned the American people in 1937 that "the epidemic of world lawlessness is spreading," but Americans remained firmly isolationist. Reluctance to get involved was based on retrospective doubts about the First World War, including scandalous revelations about the activities of munitions profiteers and British propagandists in promoting the earlier war policy. A January 1937 poll showed that 64 percent of Americans questioned thought that it had been a mistake to enter the previous war. Many Americans resolved not to be trumpeted into foreign troubles a second time. The Neutrality Act of 1937 formalized this attitude in law.

Critical events in the deepening European crisis began in 1938. The German *Anschluss* absorbed Austria into Germany in March, signaling the opening of military advances in Europe. The democratic powers stood by, helplessly making indignant statements. When Hitler subsequently demanded that Czechoslovakia surrender the Sudetenland on the grounds that its population was German speaking, the war alarm sounded across the continent. Czechoslovakia counted on its defensive alliances with France and Russia, while Hitler confidently expected that the Allies would balk at war.

In September the United States requested, and Hitler and Mussolini agreed to, a big-power crisis conference at Munich. Included were the two fascist leaders and the premiers of Britain and France (but not of the Soviet Union), who met to discuss the Czech crisis and how war might be averted. At Munich the democratic leaders took Hitler at his word that he would make no further demands if given the Sudetenland, and the Allies abandoned Czechoslovakia to its fate. Prime Minister Neville Chamberlain returned to London with the wishful declaration that he had achieved "peace in our time," on the grounds of Hitler's promise that this was "the last territorial claim which I have to make in Europe.'' These are now remembered as some of the most tragic statements in diplomatic history.

The Munich sellout is universally cited as a classic case of appeasing an aggressor. The futility of this policy was immediately apparent when Hitler absorbed the remains of Czechoslovakia and went on to the invasion of Poland, which finally triggered British and French resistance. Many historians believe, in the light of the documents that have since become available, that the Allies could have stopped Hitler at the Sudetenland before he captured the Czech munitions industry. This might have deterred further expansionary moves. An additional cost of appeasement was the stimulus it gave to Soviet fears that the Allies were trying to turn Hitler east at Soviet expense, a perception that led to the infamous Hitler-Stalin nonaggression pact, which temporarily took Russia out of the antifascist alliance. Americans took from this bitter experience a deep skepticism about appeasers who would compromise with aggressors (a practice subsequently known as ''Munich-mindedness'').

As German armies rolled over Denmark, Norway, Belgium, Holland, Luxembourg, and finally France, and as the nightmare of Nazi rule was extended across the continent, American isolationist feeling began to give way to alarm. President Roosevelt reported to the American people that even the security of the United States itself was not absolutely guaranteed.

> Armed defense of democratic existence is now being gallantly waged in four continents. If that defense fails, all the population and all the resources of Europe, Asia, Africa and Australasia will be dominated by the conquerors. Let us remember that the total of those populations and their resources in those four continents greatly exceeds the sum total of the population and the resources of the whole of the Western Hemisphere many times over.

Roosevelt asserted that beyond considerations of domestic security, ''We know that enduring peace cannot be bought at the cost of other people's freedom.'' What was truly at issue was the ability of a tyrannical movement to commit aggression against other people at will.

> Every realist knows that the democratic way of life is at this moment being directly assailed in every part of the world—assailed either by arms, or by secret spreading of poisonous propaganda by those who seek to destroy unity and promote discord in nations that are still at peace.
>
> During sixteen long months this assault has blotted out the whole pattern of democratic life in an appalling number of independent nations, great and small. The assailants are still on the march, threatening other nations, great and small.[5]

The American people did not fully throw off the philosophy of isolationism and enter the struggle against fascist aggression until the Japanese surprise attack on the American naval and air base at Pearl Harbor, Hawaii, on December 7, 1941. The purpose of the attack was to immobilize American defenses against Japanese seizures of American, British, and Dutch possessions in the

---

[5]*Congressional Record*, vol. 87, January 6, 1941, p. 46.

Far East, but many Americans perceived the event as a step toward a move on Hawaii or even California. An enraged public gave overwhelming support to a declaration of war against Germany as well as Japan. But once in the war, broad principles of an allied defense against aggression took precedence over purely national concerns. For example, a frequent poll question during the war was, "If Hitler offered peace now to all countries on the basis of not going further but of leaving matters as they now are, would you favor or oppose such a peace?" Support for peace on these terms was generally below 20 percent. In many concrete ways, American war conduct manifested a broad commitment to principles of nonaggression and universal self-determination, rather than a pure concern with American self-interest.

The 1945 Settlement

Following the war, the United States and its allies once again set about to secure the future international system. The German and Japanese political systems were redesigned by occupation authorities along modern democratic principles, and the United Nations was founded to reestablish the machinery of collective security that had failed in the League of Nations. Americans took the lead in proposing a reformation of the world system; more than half of the respondents in several polls favored the idea of a world government with the power to control the armed forces of all nations, including the United States. The United States joined the United Nations immediately (whereas it had stayed out of the League) and was from the beginning one of its most active and supportive members.

The greatest shift in American policy, then, was a strategic reorientation from isolationism to a permanent commitment to world responsibilities. In contrast with the almost complete disarmament after 1918, demobilization after 1945 left a standing army of more than a million and a global network of active American military bases. Americans had concluded from the experience of "coming to Europe's rescue" in two world wars that a position of responsibility in world politics was an inescapable obligation of the most powerful democracy, and that the interests of world stability and American security would be best served by involvement rather than by isolation.

This shift in perception characterized mass opinion as well as the views of policymakers. In various polls on isolationism since 1949, between two-thirds and four-fifths of respondents have favored the option of an active international role for the United States, working closely with other nations rather than taking an independent position. However, when the question is posed in the form, "Has this country gone too far in concerning itself with problems in other parts of the world?", opinion is more evenly divided.[6] It appears that the United States should, in the majority view, play an active role in defense of certain interests and principles but should not attempt to be "policeman of the world." National exhaustion over the Vietnam War served to deepen this sentiment.

---

[6]See John E. Mueller, *War, Presidents, and Public Opinion* (New York: Wiley, 1973), p. 110.

Several points should be made about the terms under which the United States entered the world arena between 1914 and 1945. The tragic course of world history during these four decades convinced Americans that Europe had failed in its stewardship of world order. Twice the New World had been forced to rescue the Old from its own contradictions. The United States entered the world arena flushed with tremendous success at home in building the world's most dynamic economic and political entity and bursting with ideas for international reform. It had emerged from the two wars as the only major actor that had not been subjected to invasion, humiliating occupation, or the terror of aerial bombardment. The decisive role of its power in the two victories reinforced a sense of invincibility, built on the innate optimism of a people who had little experience with tragedy. America based its new image of "leader of the free world" on this foundation of pride and self-confidence.

It has been argued that the unique innocence Americans brought to international politics has been a liability as well as an advantage. An optimistic people has a tendency to reduce burdensome complexities to simplistic explanations and easy formulas, and Americans have often compressed their understanding of difficult issues into purified political and moral principles.[7] Not every conflict can be understood as a struggle between good and evil. In particular, the tendency to interpret the motivations of all adversaries through the lens of the Aggressor theory may distort reality and lead to false solutions. This is especially dangerous when America's response is founded on the anti-appeasement principle of countering perceived aggression by a strong willingness to use force. The twin problems of accurately defining threats to the peace and formulating an appropriate response by the United States reached a more acute stage as the shape of the postwar world emerged from the fog of the battle against the Axis imperialists.

Origins of the Cold War

The settlement of 1945 that ended the violence of the Second World War created at the same time the basis of the Cold War. The United States and the Soviet Union ceased to be allies in the common struggle against fascism and initiated a prolonged competition for the political mastery of Europe, Asia, and the world. There are profound differences of opinion among informed Americans about the origins of the Cold War, and alternative interpretations greatly affect the understanding of many other issues.[8]

---

[7] Henry Kissinger, *American Foreign Policy* (New York: Norton, 1969), for example.

[8] Studies of the origins of the Cold War abound. Among the most thorough full-length studies that represent a spectrum of viewpoints ranging from strongly pro-American to equally strongly critical of the United States are these: Herbert Feis, *From Trust to Terror* (New York: Norton, 1970); Denna F. Fleming, *The Cold War and Its Origins* (Garden City, N.Y.: Doubleday, 1961), two vols.; John Lewis Gaddis, *The United States and the Origins of the Cold War* (New York: Columbia University Press, 1972); David Horowitz, *Free World Colossus* (New York: Hill and Wang, 1965); Vojtech Mastny, *Russia's Road to the Cold War* (New York: Columbia University Press, 1979); Hugh Seton-Watson, *Neither Peace nor War* (New York: Praeger, 1960); Martin J. Sherwin, *A World Destroyed* (New York: Random House, 1973); Ronald Steele, *Pax Americana* (New York: Viking, 1967); and Daniel Yergin, *Shattered Peace* (Boston: Houghton Mifflin, 1977).

The alliance with the Soviet Union against Hitler was undertaken by the United States out of necessity. Before 1941, a deep-seated suspicion of Stalin and Soviet communism had severely restricted commercial and political relations with the USSR. These fears were amplified during the decade before the war by reports of massive purges in Moscow, the virtual extermination of several million farmers of the kulak class, and other denials of human rights. Soviet foreign behavior was typified in the American mind by subversive activities of the Comintern that seemed to threaten the democratic states, by the hated Hitler-Stalin nonaggression pact, and by a brutal attack on tiny Finland.

But the wartime alliance of necessity, once undertaken, generated a warmth between the two peoples. There was a new respect in the United States for the deep commitment of the Russians to their struggle against fascism. Some American officials projected a new era of cooperation between dissimilar but friendly societies after the war, including cooperation in guaranteeing collective security through the Security Council of the United Nations. Other possible contingencies in relations with the USSR were not thoroughly examined by Washington before the end of the war, and little realistic and systematic planning was done for the design of the postwar world beyond the United Nations. In Moscow, however, some fateful and extensive decisions were being taken on postwar policy and actions. This difference was later to produce deep American shock at Soviet designs.

Some joint discussion of the postwar liberation took place at the Teheran, Yalta, and Potsdam conferences. The three Big Powers—the United States, the USSR, and Britain—agreed on several essentials. The Nazi war machine would be destroyed by Soviet armies moving from the east and American and British forces moving from the west. Temporarily, each of the Allies would be responsible for establishing civil order in the territories liberated by its forces, pending the assumed restoration of self-determination and free elections. Eventually, the occupation forces would withdraw, and the various nations would resume their independent lives.

It was understood that as a matter of simple realism, the Soviets could not be expected to tolerate potentially hostile alliances along their borders again and that the new East European governments would have to respect this principle in their foreign affairs. An informal understanding provided this formula to guide political development during the transitional period:

Romania	90 percent Soviet
Bulgaria	80 percent Soviet
Hungary	50/50 Soviet/West
Yugoslavia	50/50 Soviet/West
Greece	90 percent British

It was also understood that the Western European countries, including France and Italy, would not be under Soviet influence but that Soviet security needs would have a large say in Poland and Czechoslovakia. Germany, the most serious problem, would be divided into four zones—under American, Soviet, British and French control—disarmed, and eventually reunified after pacification and political reconstruction. Additional understandings applied to Korea, Japan, and other countries and to the United Nations.

What was not intended in these agreements, and was definitely not anticipated in the West, was that the Soviets would leave the Red armies permanently in control of the Eastern European states, creating a satellite chain linked by virtual puppet governments. Americans were outraged by the naked use of Soviet power to create colonies. In Poland, for example, the Soviets shocked world opinion by abetting in the extermination of antifascist but noncommunist freedom fighters and, after they were destroyed, putting in their place an all-communist government reporting directly to Moscow. In Czechoslovakia, a democratic coalition of communists and noncommunist leftist parties was destroyed by a Moscow-ordered communist coup. In Germany, the Soviet zone of occupation was converted into a permanent puppet state, and the agreed goal of reunification was scuttled. The idea of free elections was forgotten. ''Across Europe,'' Winston Churchill declared to the American people at Fulton, Missouri, on March 5, 1946,

> from Stettin in the Baltic to Trieste in the Adriatic, an Iron Curtain has descended across the continent. Behind that line lie all the capitals of the ancient states of central and eastern Europe. Warsaw, Berlin, Prague, Vienna, Budapest, Belgrade, Bucharest, and Sofia, all these famous cities and populations around them. . . . The Communist parties, which were very small in all these eastern states of Europe, have been raised to prominence and power far beyond their numbers and are seeking everywhere to obtain totalitarian control. Police governments are prevailing in nearly every case.[9]

Even more alarming was what was perceived as the effort by the Soviet Union to push this Iron Curtain forward and bring additional lands under communist control. Subversive activities were encouraged in France and Italy; claims were advanced against Iran; the communist-controlled Viet Minh moved against French control in Indochina; threats were made against Turkey; and an insurgent movement was mounted in Malaya. In China, the communists reopened their struggle against the Kuomintang government.

Throughout the world, insurgent parties fomented disorder and revolution in the name of communism. Many in the West concluded that the USSR sought not just security on its frontiers but expansion everywhere, and possibly even mastery of the earth.[10] Dissenters argued that not every revolutionary event could be traced to a conspiratorial command center in Moscow.

The Truman Doctrine

The case that finally produced a crisis atmosphere in Washington was that of Greece. There, the retreating Germans had destroyed railways, ports, bridges,

---

[9]*The New York Times,* March 6, 1946, p. 4.
[10]See, for example, Elliot Goodman, *The Soviet Design for a World State* (New York: Columbia University Press, 1960).

communications facilities, and the network of orderly civil administration. More than a thousand villages were burned. By 1947, a majority of children tested were tubercular. In this atmosphere, rival communist and monarchist factions of the former antifascist resistance were locked in civil war. It was believed in Washington, although there were dissenters, that Stalin had given the go-ahead signal to the insurgents and that Soviet arms were flowing freely to the communist side in violation of the understanding that Greece was to be under Western influence.

This crisis had special significance for the assessment of Soviet intentions. If indeed this were a Soviet move against Greece, Russian expansionary goals evidently included political issues quite remote from critical zones of national defense. Stalin seemed to have in mind ambitious plans for the destruction of capitalism, in disregard of his agreements. On the other hand, some continued to see the Soviet Union pursuing essentially defensive goals or, at worst, regional expansion along the familiar lines of tsarist imperialism, rather than a truly global power grab in the name of communism. A great debate about Soviet motives and a search for the wisest response began in the United States.

The dominant school of thought, given its classic expression in the "containment" philosophy of diplomat and scholar George Kennan, was that Soviet policy served ideological imperatives demanding global struggle and opposition to capitalism. He explained:

> Of the original ideology, nothing has been officially junked. . . . The first . . . concept is the innate antagonism between capitalism and socialism. . . . It means that there can never be on Moscow's side any sincere assumption of a community of aims between the Soviet Union and powers which are regarded as capitalist.

The responsibility to oppose this policy of limitless conflict fell to the United States which, Kennan said, must base its actions on the principle of containing Soviet power within its existing boundaries until internal changes within the Soviet leadership produced an abandonment of aggressive intentions.

> The Soviet pressure against the free institutions of the Western World is something that can be contained by the adroit and vigilant application of counterforce at a series of constantly shifting geographical and political points, corresponding to the shifts and maneuvres of Soviet policy.[11]

This point of view was shared by President Harry S Truman, who incorporated it in his enunciation of the Truman Doctrine on March 12, 1947. His speech made the analogy between communist aggression and the Nazi aggression that preceded it: The "fundamental issue" in the war with Germany and Japan had been "the creation of conditions in which . . . nations . . . will be able to work out a way of life free from coercion." Now, once again, we had

---

[11]George Kennan (writing under the pseudonym "Mr. X"), "The Sources of Soviet Conduct," *Foreign Affairs*, July 1947.

to be "willing to help free people to maintain their free institutions and their national integrity against aggressive movements that seek to impose upon them totalitarian regimes." Note the themes of aggressive dictatorship versus peaceful democracy in the following passage from Truman's address:

> The peoples of a number of countries of the world have recently had totalitarian regimes forced upon them against their will. . . . At the present moment in world history nearly every nation must choose between alternative ways of life. The choice is too often not a free one.
>
> One way of life is based upon the will of the majority, and is distinguished by free institutions, representative government, free elections, guarantees of individual liberty, freedom of speech and religion and freedom from political oppression.
>
> The second way of life is based upon the will of a minority forcibly imposed upon the majority. It relies upon terror and oppression, a controlled press and radio, fixed elections and the suppression of personal freedom.
>
> I believe that it must be the policy of the United States to support peoples who are resisting attempted subjugation by armed minorities or by outside pressures.
>
> I believe that we must assist free peoples to work out their own destinies in their own way.[12]

Note also that the United States will "support peoples who are resisting attempted subjugation by armed minorities." This suggests intervention against aggression even when the rebels are nationals of the same country, blurring the distinction between international aggression and civil war.

Critiques of the Truman Doctrine

The Truman-Kennan perspective was criticized from several camps. The "realist" school, headed by Hans Morgenthau, accused it of sentimentalism and moralism. The containment strategy was justified

> not primarily in terms of the traditional American interest in the maintenance of the European balance of power, but in terms of a universal moral principle. This principle is derived from the assumption that the issue between the United States and the Soviet Union . . . must be defined in terms of "alternative ways of life" . . . [and] proclaims the defense of free, democratic nations everywhere in the world against "direct or indirect aggression." . . . Thus the Truman Doctrine transformed a concrete interest of the U.S. in a geographically defined part of the world into a moral principle of worldwide validity, to be applied regardless of the limits of American interest and of American power. . . . As a guide to political action, it is the victim, as all moral principles must be, of two congenital political weaknesses: the inability to distinguish between what is desirable and what is possible, and the inability to distinguish between what is desirable and what is essential.[13]

---

[12]*Congressional Record*, vol. 93, March 12, 1947, pp. 1999–2000.
[13]Hans J. Morgenthau, *In Defense of the National Interest* (New York: Knopf, 1950), pp. 120–121.

Journalist Walter Lippmann, another realist, called the Truman Doctrine "a strategic monstrosity" that could not succeed in changing the situation in Eastern Europe. "No state in Eastern Europe can be independent of the Kremlin as long as the Red Army is within it and around it," he wrote. And the Red army would remain as long as Russia was threatened with hostile encirclement across the military line of division in Western Europe. "The presence of these non-European armies in the continent of Europe perpetuates the division," he continued. The wise course of American response would be to offer the Soviets a mutual withdrawal, US forces to leave the Western sector and Soviet forces to return to the USSR. "If the Red Army is in Russia, and not on the Elbe . . . the power of the Russian imperialists to realize their ambitions will have been reduced decisively." The containment policy was seen as having exactly the opposite effect and therefore as an incorrect response to Soviet expansion.[14]

The "liberation" school of dissenters, headed by John Foster Dulles, who later became secretary of state to Republican President Dwight David Eisenhower, took a position opposite to the realists. Dulles objected that containment was a passive policy that always left open the question, "Which of us will be the next victim?" It projected for the United States a static political role, allowing the Kremlin to determine the place and terms of conflict. "Ours are treadmill policies which, at best, might perhaps keep us in the same place until we drop exhausted." It was a law of history that "the dynamic prevails over the static," and the correct response to Soviet imperialism was not mere defense but an active offense. We could not just contain communism at its present boundaries but had to carry the struggle across the Iron Curtain to pursue the liberation of captive nations that have already fallen to Soviet imperialism.[15]

The third and final major school of dissent may be called, in the parlance of later Vietnam debate, the "dove school." Climaxing in the unsuccessful 1948 presidential drive of former Secretary of Agriculture Henry A. Wallace, the doves argued that the containment policy itself endangered peace and provoked the very Soviet posture that it deplored. Wallace asserted that "a great part of our conflict with Russia is the normal conflict between two strong and sovereign nations and can be solved in normal ways. . . . When Britain competes for resources, we settle our differences as friends. When Russia competes for them, we sound a fire alarm and thank God for the atom bomb. Why?" Wallace argued for cooperation in the United Nations rather than a worldwide anticommunist military crusade. He predicted that containment would force the United States to support dictators everywhere in the name of defense: "Every fascist dictator will know that he has money in our bank. . . . Free-

---

[14]Walter Lippmann, *The Cold War* (New York: Harper and Row, 1947), p. 61. See also Ronald Steel, *Walter Lippmann and the American Century* (Boston: Atlantic-Little, Brown, 1980), chap. 34.

[15]John Foster Dulles, "A Policy of Liberation," *Life,* May 19, 1952, pp. 147–148. See also Townsend Hoopes, *The Devil and John Foster Dulles* (Boston: Atlantic-Little, Brown, 1973), chap. 13.

dom, in whose name Americans have died, will become a catchword for reaction."[16]

A similar view was argued by Robert A. Taft, the leading conservative of the time, who objected to the North Atlantic Alliance as "a treaty by which one nation undertakes to arm half the world against the other half," and predicted that "this treaty . . . means inevitably an arms race." Taft, like the doves, feared that "if Russia sees itself ringed gradually by so-called defensive arms, from Norway and Denmark to Turkey and Greece . . . it may decide that the arming of Europe, regardless of its present purpose, looks like an attack upon Russia."[17]

The "containment" and "liberation" schools portray the Soviet Union largely in terms of the Aggressor, whereas "realist" and "dove" schools of thought take a more limited view of the threat posed by communism. The magnitude of the Soviet threat has been a question of fierce controversy among American scholars and Kremlinologists. Inferences about Soviet motives have ranged from a portrayal of designs for world domination[18] to the view of a defensive Soviet Union acting more in fear of the West than in pursuit of an autonomous hegemonial will.[19]

The majority of Americans followed President Truman's lead in taking the hard line. A Gallup poll asked, "As you hear and read about Russia these days, do you believe Russia is trying to build herself up to be the ruling power of the world, or do you think Russia is just building up protection against being attacked in another way?" In June 1946, just after Churchill's Iron Curtain speech, 58 percent favored the "ruling power" interpretation, as opposed to 29 percent for the "protection" interpretation. By November 1950, after the adoption of the Truman Doctrine and the onset of the Korean War, 81 percent favored the "ruling power" theory, as opposed to only 9 percent for the "protection" theory. In January of 1948, 83 percent of Americans favored stopping all trade with Russia. The ratification of the NATO pact "to stop Soviet expansionism" was endorsed by 67 percent. Late in 1954, *Time* magazine defined the communist idea of coexistence as "a period of deceptive docility while gathering strength for a new assault."[20] Clearly, the great debate had been won by the containment theorists.

Deepening Hostility

Hostility between the United States and the Soviet Union deepened after the promulgation of the Truman Doctrine and the establishment of the North Atlantic Treaty. A constant stream of negative headlines concerning events in the communist world reinforced and strengthened the convictions of the contain-

---

[16]Speech by Henry A. Wallace at Madison Square Garden, New York City, on March 31, 1947, printed in *Congressional Record*, 80th Cong., 1st sess., Appendix, pp. A1572–A1573.
[17]Speech by Robert A. Taft, *Congressional Record*, 81st Cong., 1st sess., pp. 9208–9210.
[18]Goodman, *The Soviet Design for a World State*.
[19]Fleming, *The Cold War and Its Origins*.
[20]*Time*, November 8, 1954.

ment model. The Soviets suppressed liberalization movements in East Germany in 1953, in Hungary in 1956, and in Czechoslovakia in 1968, to mention only the large-scale coercive actions. Oppression against captive peoples was also perceived in China's forcible annexation of Tibet and Soviet policy toward non-Russian minorities within the USSR. These negative impressions were confirmed by millions of refugees who voted with their feet by fleeing communism to seek new homes in the Free World. Three million left East Germany for the West (prompting the construction of the Berlin Wall to stop the outflow); 180,000 left Hungary in 1956; and 500,000 came to the United States from Cuba. Even relatives of the ruling elite, including Josef Stalin's own daughter and Fidel Castro's sister, defected to the democratic world. Some of these migrants were motivated by economic considerations (foreign workers also came to Germany from Italy and Greece, without apparent political motivation, and more Puerto Ricans than Cubans have come to the United States), but many others described themselves as political refugees and reported their former countries to be hostile to basic human rights. It appeared to the majority of Americans that these outer signs were the tip of an iceberg of repression and that the communists retained power only through the massive use of police coercion.

In addition to political repression, Americans saw the Soviet Union impose a system of economic imperialism on its captive nations after 1945. While the United States poured billions of dollars in Marshall Plan aid into the devastated economies of former allies and enemies, restoring Europe and Japan to economic health, the Soviet Union milked approximately $20 billion out of its zone of occupation, through four devices:

1. Billions of dollars in war reparations were assessed against East Germany, Hungary, and Romania.

2. A special price system was imposed for trade within the communist bloc, characterized by high prices for Soviet goods and low prices for exports by satellite nations. One result was losses to Poland of about $500 million in discounted coal exports to the USSR between 1946 and 1956.

3. Joint stock companies were established as a highly exploitive form of Soviet foreign investment in East European economies. Former German firms were expropriated by Russia under the Administration for Soviet Property Abroad, and their value was counted as Moscow's investment against which fair returns to Russia were calculated. Joint stock companies of this and other types transferred additional billions of dollars in value to the USSR.

4. Interdependence of production was forced on the satellite economies, restricting their trade with the West and giving priority to Soviet deliveries. Raw-material dependency is illustrated by the case of Poland, which, in 1957, imported from the USSR 100 percent of its oil, 70 percent of its iron ore, 78 percent of its nickel, and 67 percent of its cotton. From 1945 through 1956, exploitation of Eastern Europe was ruthless, although economic relations were more nearly equal after 1956.[21]

---

[21]Zbigniew Brzezinski, *The Soviet Bloc* (Cambridge, Mass.: Harvard University Press, 1967), pp. 124–128, 282–287, 376. See also Paul Marer, "The Political Economy of Soviet Relations with

The Continuity of Policy: Korea and Vietnam

For 25 years, American policy remained firm and unvarying in its opposition to what was perceived as communist aggression. Isolationist impulses were suppressed, and the most extensive commitments ever undertaken by a single power were honored. The essential continuity of the policy can be seen in a comparison of statements in the Korean and Vietnam wars, separated by a span of 15 years.

President Truman explained the problem in Korea to the American people in bleak terms in a radio address in April of 1951:

> The Communists in the Kremlin are engaged in a monstrous conspiracy to stamp out freedom all over the world. . . . The whole Communist imperialism is back of the attack on peace in the Far East.

Truman said that American strategy was based on the lessons of dealing with communist aggression:

> In the simplest terms, what we are trying to do in Korea is this: we are trying to prevent a third world war. . . . If [the Free World] had followed the right policies in the 1930's—if the free countries had acted together to crush the aggression of the dictators, and if they had acted in the beginning, when the aggression was small—there probably would have been no World War II. If history taught us anything, it is that aggression anywhere in the world is a threat to peace everywhere in the world.[22]

Strikingly parallel themes were later used to explain the necessity for American military intervention in Vietnam. A 1965 State Department White Paper portrayed that struggle as a typical attempt at communist aggression:

> South Vietnam is fighting for its life against a brutal campaign of terror and armed attack inspired, directed, supplied, and controlled by the Communist regime in Hanoi. . . . Aggression has been loosed against an independent people who want to make their way in peace and freedom.[23]

President Richard M. Nixon said in 1969:

> If Hanoi were to succeed in taking over South Vietnam by force—even after the power of the United States had been engaged—it would greatly strengthen those leaders who scorn negotiation, who advocate aggression, who minimize the risks of confrontation. It would bring peace now, but it would enormously increase the danger of a bigger war later.[24]

Comecon,'' in Steven Rosen and James Kurth, eds., *Testing the Theory of Economic Imperialism* (Lexington, Mass.: D. C. Heath, 1974).

[22]*The New York Times,* April 17, 1951.

[23]US Department of State, *Aggression from the North: The Record of North Vietnam's Campaign to Conquer South Vietnam* (Washington, D.C.: US Government Printing Office, 1965).

[24]"Address to the Nation on Vietnam," May 14, 1969. See *The Public Papers of the Presidents of the United States: Richard M. Nixon, 1969,* pp. 369–375, at pp. 370–371.

In both wars American policy was based on four basic propositions: (1) that conflict is due to communist aggression against the Free World; (2) that communist expansion cannot be appeased and must be stopped by force, if necessary; (3) that as leader of the Free World, the United States is obligated to serve as a counterweight to communist aggression; and (4) that fighting a small war now will prevent a larger one later. This was the stern formulation of American foreign policy ideals from 1947 to approximately 1970.

America's Post-Vietnam World View

The withdrawal of American troops from Vietnam in 1973 signaled the end of an age of US foreign policy. To be sure, the event itself was uncharacteristic of Washington's policy since the enunciation of the Truman Doctrine. But the abandonment by the Nixon administration of the costly anticommunist crusade in Asia gave larger meaning to the event: The United States was engaged in a major reassessment of its foreign commitments, of its place in the international system, and of the means that it would invoke henceforth to influence significant international events. It seems irrational that the immense investment of lives, resources, and political fortunes in Vietnam in the name of freedom should suddenly have been overturned in favor of a unilateral withdrawal that would inevitably lead to reunification of North and South Vietnam under a communist flag. Quite clearly, such a decision could have been made only in the context of other changes in the American world view.

In fact, many converging perceptions and policy shifts rendered the American departure logical. First, the communist bloc had come to be seen as having several (although not necessarily equal) competing centers of power rather than a unified command center in Moscow. In particular, the growing Sino-Soviet dispute had alerted the West after 1960 to China's independence from the Soviet yoke, and the competition between Moscow and Beijing over the policy of North Vietnam during the war served to strengthen the American expectation of a deeper rift between the two communist giants after its conclusion. Thus, the prevailing image of communism shifted from the fearful monolithic one to a more differentiated theory of polycentrism, which implied the possibility for Americans of exploiting a more fluid international political scene by dealing with different factions of the splintered communist world. This same view led President Nixon to begin the process of normalization of relations with China, a policy consummated by formal diplomatic recognition in 1979 by President Jimmy Carter.

Second, some amelioration now seemed to moderate the relentless hostility of Soviet actions. After 50 years of revolution and rapid economic growth and 20 years after the death of Stalin, the Soviet Union had grown soft and somewhat more satisfied with its own position in the world. The dominant elites in Moscow clearly favored coexistence with the West and minimizing the risks of war. Like the American government, Moscow was under continuing pressure from various industrial, regional, and consumer interests to hold down defense spending. The hawk group in the Politburo was on the decline, and new possibilities for cooperation with the West were open.

Third, the Cold War itself had come to be waged in less strident ideological terms. Whereas attention to communist events in the early years had been highly selective, concentrating on negative news, later impressions included positive achievement in the USSR, China, and the East European states. Some observers saw a gradual process of convergence between the two economic systems, with the Soviets instituting managerial reforms (''Liebermanism'') and loosening other tendencies toward free enterprise, while the capitalist states accepted increased government planning and participation in their economies. Also, increased awareness of continuing injustices in the West itself, such as the suppression of black people in the United States, weakened the moral righteousness of anticommunism.

Many people had come to see the problem of dealing with the USSR as a practical balance-of-power issue instead of a battle between the forces of light and the forces of darkness. A less moralistic foreign policy permitted a more pragmatic exploration of options. As perceptions of the USSR shifted from the image of Aggressor to one of more complex, less dangerous patterns of motivation, cooperative proposals were less vulnerable to charges of appeasement by domestic opponents.

In this atmosphere, the United States was able to open a new phase in its dealings with the communist world during the 1970s, particularly after its withdrawal from Vietnam. The reversal of 25 years of hostile relations with China is only one pertinent example. In addition, several major agreements on arms control and political settlements were reached with the Soviet Union, notably the strategic arms limitation agreements (SALT I and SALT II, the latter of which was not ratified by the United States Senate), the interim agreement on arms limitation and human rights at Vladivostok, and the long-awaited settlement of the German borders, a problem remaining from the collapse of Nazi Germany in 1945. Western European trade with Eastern Europe had already increased tenfold during the 1960s, but in the 1970s the volume continued to climb, particularly with the emergence of Eurocommunism. Trade between the United States and the Soviet Union increased as well, and American firms and corporations based in the territories of American allies entered into agreements with Moscow to establish production plants in the Soviet Union. Trade agreements blossomed for shipment to the USSR of American computers and other state-of-the-art technological materials, many of which were known to have immediate use in military development and application.

Sino-American trade grew from nothing to a thriving exchange (the first Chinese ship to visit an American port since 1949 arrived in early 1979). The Coca-Cola Company was even invited by the Chinese to establish a bottling facility on Chinese territory. Because of the improved atmosphere that made possible all these and other changes, American officials began trumpeting, in the mid-1970s, that the Cold War was over. This, of course, could not be taken literally, since over $400 billion in defense expenditure continued annually by the Soviet Union and the United States alone as they glared, even if more tolerantly, at each other across military lines the world over. But it seemed clear, nevertheless, that by the time of the American withdrawal from

Vietnam, a new era of de-escalation was in progress, however gradual and interrupted. The revised international climate, and particularly the consequences for Soviet-American relations, ushered in the era of détente.

Like most significant changes in political relations, détente did not occupy a fixed period of time, having had no precise beginning and no identifiable end. Rather, it comprised a stretch of time marked more by evolving attitudes than by dates and events. Although not dated with the American withdrawal from Vietnam, it was surely permitted by the spirit in which that withdrawal occurred; and while not brought to a close by any single incident, it was extinguished by a gradual loss of American confidence in the fidelity of new Soviet attitudes toward world politics. One American observer interpreted détente as a loss of consensus on the basic anticommunist goals of American foreign policy.[25] Another summarized the history of détente as a self-imposed public mood in the United States resulting from exhaustion over Vietnam, loss of confidence in the morality and judgment of American leadership, discontent over global responsibilities, and skepticism over activities undertaken in the name of national defense. Under these circumstances a charitable view of the Soviet Union was preferred to the tough-minded decisions and policies that the United States needed to take to maintain its vigilance against the Soviet challenge.[26] Détente, therefore, came and went with attitude, not with events and landmark years. Unlike peace and war, which have precise anniversaries to celebrate, conflicts such as the Cold War and times of tranquil confidence such as détente do not.

In 1975, then, it might have seemed that détente was a solid and reliable foundation for American foreign policy and arms limitation, but the next year revealed its transparency. The Soviet-Cuban intervention in Angola on behalf of communist independence forces raised fresh questions about Soviet expansionist aims. Still aching from the Vietnam experience, the nation debated its response. A bitter battle raged between President Gerald Ford and Secretary of State Henry Kissinger, on the one hand, and Congress on the other, over whether or not the United States should intervene indirectly by assisting noncommunist forces in the struggle for independence from Portuguese colonialism. The rancor of the battle, which Congress won by denying supporting funds for an indirect counterintervention, threw a dark shadow over détente and severely embarrassed the president in the presidential primaries and election of 1976. Ford declared the word *détente* to have been removed from the American political lexicon; Secretary Kissinger countered with the prediction that long-term improvement in Soviet-American relations would soon revive the word and the concept. Indeed, despite upheavals of faith, *détente* was not long out of use.

Despite the lingering sentiment of détente, however, a succession of events gradually eroded American faith. During the last two and one-half years of the 1970s, American officials saw troubling evidence that the Soviet Union intended to exploit détente to its political and economic advantage, while still

---

[25]George Quester, "Consensus Lost," *Foreign Policy,* no. 40, Fall 1980, pp. 18–32.
[26]Dimitri K. Simes, "The Anti-Soviet Brigade," *Foreign Policy,* no. 37, Winter 1979–1980, pp. 28–42, especially pp. 28–29.

pursuing familiar, ideologically inspired ends and enforcing familiar forms of domestic oppression. The principal evidence was threefold. First, Moscow had vastly increased its military capabilities by every measure: annual cost, deployment of new weapons systems, increase in size of armed forces, and so on. Moreover, contrary to a common Western perception, most of the buildup of the most modern arms was not along the Chinese front but in Central Europe. Second, in spite of its agreement at Vladivostok to curb its assault on political dissenters, the Soviet government continued to impose brutal punishment on those who were publicly critical of its policies. And third, the pattern of Soviet arms sales indicated to American observers that Moscow was intent on disrupting the global balance of forces and the regional balances in the Middle East, Africa, and Europe; on extending its naval forces to areas of Western interest; and on sponsoring armed communist revolution in Central America and the Caribbean. These observations reawakened concern about the long-range intentions of Soviet foreign policy and about the trustworthiness of Soviet commitment to détente.

Specifically, the strategic buildup was seen by Western skeptics as evidence that the Soviet Union was intent on maintaining a level of tension in Europe aimed at preventing economic ties between the Eastern and the Western sectors from eroding Moscow's economic, military, and ideological stranglehold on its Warsaw Pact allies. The maintenance of continental tension was a way for the Soviet Union to prevent any deterioration in the regional socialist commonwealth. The arms transfer policy of the Soviets, in turn, was seen as a means of preparing to exploit tactical situations—not for random advantage but as a means of developing and expanding the number of socialist centers in the world. Together, they would eventually integrate into a larger socialist commonwealth. A study of official Soviet statements regarding the ideological foundations of foreign policy by an American observer was summarized as follows:

> The growing ''organic'' relationships with the socialist commonwealth are represented as a ''law-governed'' process; this process is ''organically'' linked with ''proletarian internationalism''; ''proletarian internationalism'' is ''organically'' combined with ''peaceful coexistence''; and ''peaceful coexistence,'' defined as a product of the changed balance of forces, is ''organically'' tied to the ideological struggle between social systems. Thus, the processes that are effecting the triumph of socialism over capitalism are functionally interconnected; a change in one structural relationship produces change in the others.[27]

Détente, then, had become a camouflage for a subtle, ideologically inspired renewal of determination to alter the international system in such a way as to promote the triumph of socialism over capitalism, to bring an end to the American era, and to reinforce Moscow as the center of a worldwide socialist commonwealth. Another observer concluded from similar evidence that while the strategic policy of the Kremlin was to instill fear of its power everywhere,

---

[27]R. Judson Mitchell, ''A New Brezhnev Doctrine: The Restructuring of International Relations,'' *World Politics,* April 1978, pp. 366–390.

its diplomatic practice was an act of seduction designed to persuade others that Moscow had accepted its role in the contemporary world order and had abandoned aspirations for a Soviet world state.[28]

The turn of the decade demolished détente, and optimistic claims of the Cold War's demise were replaced everywhere in the West by declarations that it had been revived. The first indicative event occurred in the waning days of 1979, when the Soviet Union invaded Afghanistan in support of a communist government and expelled the foreign press. Thereafter, Soviet troops put down dissent and unrest with brutal force. Meanwhile, as events in the Persian Gulf rose from tepid to boiling, Soviet troops moved ever closer to the Iranian border, arousing fears of expanding Soviet activity, intervention in a revolutionary Iran, and direct great-power confrontation over the Gulf area. This event, coupled with redoubled Soviet arms development and an increasingly bellicose tone regarding the American role in Western Europe, seemed testimony to the four-year-old view that détente had expired and to the persistent view of some that the Cold War had never ended.

Intrabloc events of 1980–1981 added further to this grave interpretation. During the summer of 1980, Polish labor became restive over wages, conditions of work, and food prices. As the country went onto strict meat rationing, the unrest grew into the first organized labor strike in Poland since the establishment of the Soviet bloc after the Second World War. The shipyard strike at Gdansk resulted not only in major concessions (at least on paper) regarding the right of Polish laborers to organize in unions outside government control; it also resulted in the Kremlin's removal of the Polish leadership. Moreover, Warsaw Pact troop maneuvers and scantily veiled Soviet threats to strikers, particularly as unrest moved to other industries and other parts of Poland, brought back memories of forceful Soviet interventions in East Germany (1953), Hungary (1956), and Czechoslovakia (1968). The West waited to see if Polish dissent would be crushed in the name of a unified Socialist commonwealth. The United States applied economic sanctions against Poland, verbally encouraged the Solidarity movement, and repeatedly condemned both the Polish and Soviet governments. Although the dissent was not forcefully crushed, countless political activists were incarcerated, and the threat of force was ever present. Lech Walesa, leader of the movement, was unable to leave the country to receive his Nobel Peace Prize in 1983 for fear that he would not be permitted to return. At Walesa's urging, the United States began easing sanctions more than a year after the discontinuation of martial law, since more harm was being done to Polish citizens than to the intransigent government.

With hawks now seemingly in control of Soviet policy, fear was rampant in the West that a struggle for power within the Kremlin might touch off an irresponsible, politically inspired military adventure somewhere other than in Afghanistan or Poland. Secretary of State Edmund Muskie reported after a meeting of the NATO foreign ministers that the allies were united as they had

---

[28]Kenneth L. Adelman, ''Fear, Seduction and Growing Soviet Strength,'' *ORBIS*, Winter 1978, pp. 743–765.

not been for decades, even after the OPEC petroleum embargo of 1973–1974. Policies of rearmament dominated the American presidential and congressional campaigns of 1980. If the outcome of the elections was unclear on other issues, it was certain that on the matter of American military status the election spoke with historic voice: détente was dead, the Cold War had returned, and once again the United States must multiply its arms development effort in face of the Soviet challenge.[29] A congressional study made public before President Ronald Reagan's inauguration estimated that the effort to catch the Soviets in both conventional and strategic military potential might take as much as eight years and $80 billion. Despite the magnitude of the estimate, the American taxpayers were quietly resigned to the need. And SALT II, withdrawn from the Senate's ratification process by President Jimmy Carter ostensibly as a protest of Soviet behavior but probably because of fear that the Soviet-wary Senate would reject it, was declared by the Reagan administration to be defeatist and void in its negotiated form.[30]

Leonid Brezhnev's death in 1982 was followed by a peaceful succession that brought to power Yuri Andropov, former director of the dreaded KGB, the Soviet secret police. Andropov had already been the target of much Western criticism, for it was he who had initiated the policy whereby KGB psychiatrists declared political dissenters emotionally unfit and then had them committed to mental hospitals as a form of imprisonment. He had also been the Soviet ambassador to Hungary during the forceful suppression of revolt there in 1956.[31] He was no friend of the West, and the Reagan administration greeted his rise to power with unabashed verbal attacks on Soviet intentions around the world. Within a year, much of which Andropov spent in illness and away from public life, the USSR had walked out of all arms negotiations; both the Soviet Union and the United States had deployed new-generation missiles in Europe; and Soviet-American relations were at their lowest point since the height of the Cold War in the 1950s. American condemnation of continued Soviet policies in Poland (despite the formal lifting of martial law) and in Afghanistan, together with proof that the Kremlin was providing arms to the leftist government of Nicaragua and the rebels in El Salvador, fueled the revived image of the Soviets as the Aggressor. The shooting down of a civilian Korean airliner in 1983 was seen as a statement of the inhumane Soviet character; and a brief American invasion of Grenada to depose a leftist government and rid the population of communist influence was an announcement of Wash-

---

[29]In an apparent epitaph to détente, Aleksandr Solzhenitsyn, the expatriate Russian Nobel Laureaute, wrote that "even after Afghanistan the Soviet leaders will be only too happy to restore détente to the status quo ante—an opportunity for them to purchase all that they require in between acts of aggression." See "Misconceptions About Russia Are a Threat to America," *Foreign Affairs,* Spring 1980, pp. 597–834, at p. 807.

[30]For a representative spectrum of American positions on the SALT II agreement concerning both international strategic and domestic political questions, see the five-article section entitled "SALT and Beyond," in *Foreign Policy,* Summer 1979, pp. 49–123.

[31]Martin Ebon, *The Andropov File* (New York: McGraw-Hill, 1983), chap. 6, "The Hungarian Connection," chronicles Andropov's "duplicity" during this episode but holds open the possibility that Andropov attempted to prevent military intervention.

ington's intention that it would no longer take a passive position on Soviet interferences in the inter-American community. It was, in fact, in this context that the Reagan Doctrine was enunciated, under which the United States would use economic and military aid to attempt to win back countries and peoples previously taken over by communist power.

Soviet behavior from 1976 through the mid-1980s persuaded many Americans that the USSR was no longer the revolutionary center of Marxism-Leninism but an expansionist empire in the classic tradition. Suffering from political, ideological, economic, and agricultural failure and eager to establish political, regional, and strategic security, the Soviet Union was poised to expand everywhere and anywhere Western vigilance was perceived as unsteady.[32] In the words of a former secretary of defense:

> The Soviets' extraordinary misinterpretation of the American character and . . . style poses a question which deserves careful examination and may provide a long-term and perhaps tragic theme for superpower relations. Are the moods of the superpowers, reflecting both longer-term and more recent experiences as well as their internal political dynamics, so out-of-phase with one another that they preclude simultaneity in seeking a modus vivendi? The question has become increasingly pressing, as the visible American willingness to reach a long-term accommodation during the 1970s was aborted as a consequence of the Soviets' deep-seated impulses never to flag in the quest for marginal advantages. By the end of the 1970s, the Soviets had managed to dispel much of the American goodwill (and a fair amount of naïveté as well). The American anger continued, indeed expanded, during the 1980s—at just the point that the Soviets might have been prepared to accept longer-term accommodation. These contraptual fluctuations in mood may turn out to be the most permanent feature of these 40 years of superpower relations.[33]

The challenge of the latter half of the 1980s, then, was to resolve these asynchronous mood swings between the superpowers.

Three major portents converged in 1985 to give an optimistic opening to this period. First, President Reagan was elected for the second time, by an overwhelming margin and with a new determination to bring distinction to his administration in superpower relations and a noticeable reduction in his verbal ideological fervor. Second, Soviet power passed to Mikhail Gorbachev after the brief periods of rule by Yuri Andropov and Konstantin Chernenko, each of whom died in office. With Gorbachev, the succession from Leonid Brezhnev was finally complete. And third, nuclear arms negotiations resumed in earnest.

Ever since the death of Josef Stalin in 1953, Westerners have been fascinated by the political consequences of power succession in the Soviet Union. This fascination was particularly pronounced with Gorbachev. At 54 years, he

---

[32]Edward N. Luttwak, *The Grand Strategy of the Soviet Union* (New York: St. Martin's Press, 1983), especially chaps. 5 and 6.

[33]James Schlesinger, "The Eagle and the Bear," *Foreign Affairs,* Summer 1985, pp. 937–961, at pp. 939–940.

was the youngest Soviet leader ever. Unlike his predecessors and most of his potential challengers, he was born after the October Revolution and was not rooted politically in the Russo-Japanese War, the First World War, or the Russian revolution. He was trained as a lawyer, admitted at an early age to the Communist party, and advanced in rank quickly, largely with the help of Nikita Khrushchev. Thus, he is a man separate from the generation that came to power as a consequence of Stalin's purges of the 1930s. From the beginning, Americans viewed him as a different type of Soviet leader, not bombastic and boastful as Khrushchev or dour and sinister as Brezhnev. Instead, he seemed

"I hear Communism is dead."

Source: Drawing by Weber; © 1989, The New Yorker Magazine, Inc.

to be friendly, open, frank, relatively stylish—almost a Western-style politi-
cian. His manner earned credibility, and while there was a great deal of speculation in the early months about what kind of leader he would be, from the
start the tone in the United States was optimistic.

Even President Reagan, who throughout the first four years in office had
maintained an unbroken record of rhetorical hostility toward the Soviet Union,
treated Gorbachev differently. By the time of his second inauguration and his
State of the Union Address in 1986, it was well known in the West that the
Soviet economy was in far worse condition than had previously been believed.
The combination of this knowledge and a gamble that Gorbachev would conduct Soviet affairs differently apparently prompted the president to adopt a
markedly modified tone:

> The United States and the Soviet Union are not alike; we are two equal and
> competing Superpowers divided only by a difference in our ''systems.'' The
> United States is a free and open society, a democracy in which a free press and
> free speech flourish. The people of the Soviet Union live in a closed dictatorship
> in which democratic freedoms are denied. Their leaders do not respond to the
> will of the people; their decisions are not determined by public debate or dissent;
> they proclaim, and pursue, the goal of Leninist ''revolution.''
>
> And so the tensions between us reflect differences that cannot be washed
> away. But the future is not predetermined. Knowing this, and truly desiring to
> make the differences between us smaller and more manageable, the United
> States continues to pursue progress in all aspects of our relationship with the
> Soviet Union.
>
> Our Administration seeks to ensure that this relationship remains peaceful. We
> want restraint to be the Soviet leadership's most realistic option and will see to it
> that our freedoms and those of our Allies are protected.
>
> We seek a secure future at all levels of arms, particularly nuclear forces,
> through agreements that are equitable and verifiable. The soundness of our pro-
> posals, our renewed military strength, and our bipartisan determination to assure
> a strong deterrent create incentives for the Soviet Union to negotiate seriously.
>
> We can move toward a better, more cooperative working relationship with the
> Soviet Union if the Soviet leadership is willing. This will require full Soviet
> compliance with the letter and spirit of both past and future agreements.
>
> . . . I . . . hope to see greater communication and broader contact between
> our peoples. I am optimistic that if the Soviet leadership is willing to meet us
> halfway, we will be able to put our relations on a more cooperative footing in
> 1986.[34]

This tone was rewarded by a rapid series of events which, by the time of the
summit in the United States in 1988, had persuaded most Americans that this
time the Cold War really *was* over. These events included among others:

* Gorbachev's distancing himself from the military by downgrading the political
  staff of the defense minister

---

[34]State of the Union Address, February 4, 1986, in the *US Department of State Bulletin*, April
1986, pp. 25–29, at p. 27.

- Gorbachev's speech before the General Assembly of the United Nations in which he promised improved cooperation, announcing his intention to make up most unpaid Soviet contributions (excluding notably those for the Korean War and peacekeeping operations prior to 1967)
- The Soviet-American arms agreement in which all intermediate-range nuclear forces (INF) were not only removed from the European theater, but destroyed under witness of officers from one another's armed services
- Real reductions in Soviet defense spending
- The complete withdrawal of Soviet troops from Afghanistan, where for nine years the Kremlin had been engaged in what Americans were fond of calling "the Soviets' Vietnam"
- Gorbachev's reversal of a five-year Soviet insistence that strategic arms reduction talks could proceed only if the United States would abandon the Strategic Defense Initiative (SDI, or "Star Wars")
- Gorbachev's announcement of unilateral troop withdrawals from Eastern Europe without requiring concessions of the United States or NATO, followed later by an agreement on much deeper bilateral cuts

With the effect of all this activity working on the peace-loving imaginations of Americans, President George Bush entered the White House faced with one of the most extraordinary contradictions in American foreign policy in the century: on the one hand, the promise of greatly improved Soviet-American relations, and even a close to the Cold War; but, on the other hand, despite its vast power, the United States was insolvent. The combination of huge annual budget and trade deficits and a net investment position of more than $350 billion deficit, including a national debt increasingly funded by the foreign purchase of US Treasury securities, created an unprecedented contradiction between US power, on the one hand, and its insolvency on the other.[35] (American insolvency is covered in detail in Chapter 14, "International Monetary Exchange.")

By 1988, Gorbachev was heralded virtually throughout the world as foremost among contemporary statesmen and stateswomen. Prior to 1988, for example, no Soviet leader or citizen had ever been listed among the ten most popular men or most popular women by Americans in the Gallup poll, but in 1988 Gorbachev broke onto the list as number eight. A year later, after George Bush had been elected president but before his inauguration, Gorbachev jumped to number two behind only Ronald Reagan, who ranked first for eight consecutive years. In 1989, a West German poll indicated that Gorbachev was more widely respected even than the popular Chancellor Helmut Kohl. In the same year, after his historic visit to the Vatican in which Gorbachev pledged to Pope John Paul II the restoration of religious freedom in the Soviet Union, the American Council of Churches adopted Gorbachev as its man of the year. And

---

[35]Several writers have addressed this so-called Lippmann Gap, referring to the dictum of the late columnist Walter Lippmann that "[f]oreign policy consists in bringing into balance . . . the nation's commitments and the nation's power." See as examples Samuel P. Huntington, "Coping with the Lippmann Gap," *Foreign Affairs*, America and the World 1987/88 edition, pp. 453–477, and James Chace, "A New Grand Strategy," *Foreign Policy*, Spring 1989, pp. 3–25.

Time magazine, breaking from a tradition of more than 60 years, passed over its man or woman of the year contest and selected Mikhail Gorbachev as Man of the Decade, to the great consternation of American conservatives who had pegged Ronald Reagan for a similar celebration. One poll among Americans indicated that by a substantial margin, for the first time Americans thought economic war with Japan a greater possibility than armed hostilities with the Soviet Union.

Americans approved not only of Gorbachev, but of his policies as well. The Gallup poll reported that 65 percent of those asked thought that at the end of 1988, the USSR was "undergoing major changes," whereas only 28 percent thought that there were no basic changes, only a new leader. At the same time, however, 76 percent thought peaceful coexistence with the Soviet Union more than likely than before, with only 16 percent thinking that relations would continue to deteriorate.[36] Six months later, 65 percent thought that *perestroika* would ultimately succeed (only 21 percent thought it would not); 61 percent agreed that social and economic changes in the USSR would "come about peacefully," and 66 percent thought that *glasnost* would continue. In this same poll, 60 percent feared that if efforts to change the economy did not succeed within "the next few years," Gorbachev would be replaced.[37]

His popularity in the West notwithstanding, Gorbachev found a growing gap between his foreign policy successes and the many problems of the Soviet Union and of proletarian internationalism. His pronouncement in 1985 of *perestroika,* designed to reform the domestic economic system, had little initial success. This was followed, then, by the announcement of *glasnost,* under which Gorbachev appealed to the "creative intelligensia" to join him in pressuring the proletariat in order to energize the state and economy. As an incentive, he offered freedom of expression (*glasnost* is interpreted in the West as freedom of access to information), and as a symbol of his sincerity, released the celebrated scientist and dissident Andrei Sakharov from political imprisonment. This was a popular move both at home and abroad, but it could not mask the reality that *glasnost* unleashed a fury of attack on the Soviet system, and illuminated the fact that the successes the Soviet Union might have had in economic or security matters were at one with its history of criminal suppression of the people.[38]

In the United States, admiration of Gorbachev turned to empathy and support in 1989 and 1990 when events quickened to a dizzying pace. Indeed, the pace was so great that books, papers, and even newspaper articles were obsolete before they even appeared on the stands. As the dominoes of the Soviet world began to fall in East Germany, Hungary, Poland, Czechoslovakia, Romania, and Bulgaria, Americans admired Gorbachev's restraint and his renunciation of the Brezhnev Doctrine, abandoning the old Soviet impulse to

---

[36]*Gallup Report,* January 1989.
[37]*Gallup Report,* June 1989.
[38]This passage follows closely that of Z., "To the Stalin Mausoleum," *Daedalus,* Winter 1990, pp. 295–344. A briefer version of this paper written under the pseudonym Z. appeared in *The New York Times,* January 4, 1990, p. A23 under the title "The Soviets' Last Crisis."

Source: Reprinted with special permission of King Features Syndicate.

quell dissent forcefully and wishing Eastern Europeans well in their self-determination. When Lithuania, Estonia, and Latvia began moving toward secession, Americans were torn between historical recollection that these are "captive nations" celebrated annually as part of Cold War ritual, and hope that Gorbachev's reforms would not fall victim to conservative reactionism resulting from disintegration of the Soviet Union itself. And when the Soviet government found it necessary to intervene militarily in the brief civil war between Azerbaijanis and Armenians, Americans were as sorrowful about the implications for *glasnost* as they were over the carnage. The White House, the State Department, the Defense Department, the Congress, and the press all exercised self-restraint.

Meanwhile, a visit by Secretary of State James Baker to Moscow resulted in optimism that a 1990 summit would bring major progress in strategic arms reduction, and informal agreement was reached on major bilateral reductions in ground forces in Europe, apparently by an American equity formula that had previously been rejected by the Kremlin. Less than a week later in Ottawa, Canada, representatives of the United States, the USSR, NATO, the Warsaw Pact, and the two Germanys met. From that meeting emerged a formal agreement to reduce Soviet and American forces in Europe to 195,000 each except that the United States might, at its option, retain 30,000 more provided that they be in Britain and southern Europe, far from the NATO-Warsaw Pact boundary. In addition, the meeting produced an agreement on a two-step process for the reunification of the two Germanys. There followed a

Baltic Freedom Day, 1986

Proclamation 5501. June 12, 1986
By the President of the United States of America

A Proclamation

The United States was born in a War of Independence against an oppressive rule. We stood up for inalienable rights given by God and declared that governments that systematically violate those rights lose their claim to legitimacy.

It is a tragedy of our time that many peoples continue to live under the brutal totalitarian rule of the Soviet empire. We will expose the inhumanity of the oppressors and speak out on behalf of the oppressed. We will denounce tyranny and champion the cause of its victims.

Baltic Freedom Day provides these opportunities. On this day, we observe the anniversary of the callous and treacherous subjugation of three independent and freedom-loving states. Forty-six years ago, invading Soviet armies, in collusion with the Nazi regime, overran and occupied the Republics of Estonia, Latvia, and Lithuania. Through police-state tactics, the occupation and subjugation continue. Soviet outrages against these peoples have included massive deportations from their native soil to concentration camps in Siberia and elsewhere. At the same time masses of Russians have been uprooted from their homes and relocated in the Baltic nations in an effort to eradicate the cultural and ethnic heritage of the Baltic peoples. Against all recognized principles of international law, justice, and humanity, the Soviets have continued their domination over Lithuania, Latvia, and Estonia. The United States has never recognized their forced incorporation into the U.S.S.R. It is illegal, indefensible, and iniquitous.

We are engaged in a very real struggle to focus the world's attention on one of the gravest wrongs of our age—the stubborn and contemptuous Soviet disregard for the sovereignty of independent nations and the rights of oppressed peoples. As evidence, we hold up its first victims—the heroic Baltic nations we honor today. To do less is to acquiesce in injustice and to betray our heritage as champions of human freedom.

As a Nation, we are the standard-bearers of freedom and a beacon of hope to the oppressed. Ours is the mission of the prophet Isaiah, "to bind up the brokenhearted, proclaim liberty to the captives, and the opening of the prison to them that are bound."

The Congress of the United States, by Senate Joint Resolution 271, has designated June 14, 1986, as "Baltic Freedom Day" and authorized and requested the President to issue a proclamation in observance of this event.

Now, Therefore, I, Ronald Reagan, President of the United States of America, do hereby proclaim June 14, 1986, as Baltic Freedom Day. I call upon the people of the United States to observe this day with appropriate remembrances and ceremonies and to reaffirm their commitment to the principles of liberty and self-determination for all peoples.

In Witness Whereof, I have hereunto set my hand this twelfth day of June, in the year of our Lord nineteen hundred and eighty-six, and of the Independence of the United States of America the two hundred and tenth.

Ronald Reagan

Source: Weekly Compilation of Presidential Documents, June 16, 1986, pp. 791–792.

series of "four plus two meetings" (a reference to the four occupying powers—United States, Soviet Union, Britain and France—and the two Germanys). Here the parties settled three main issues: (1) the speed and process for the economic and political reunification; (2) settlement and guarantee of the Polish borders with Germany; and (3) the thorny question of the eastern sector's relationship to the Warsaw Pact and/or NATO. After a few months of insisting that a reunified Germany be neutral, Gorbachev finally accepted the Western view that all of Germany be a member of NATO. By mid-1990, the East German currency had been replaced by the West German mark, and all parties were urging rapid political integration in an effort to meet the 1992 goal of economic union of the European Community. Reunification: October 1990.

Americans were surprised by Soviet acquiescence on both the conventional arms issue and the matter of German reunification, particularly the concession on NATO membership. While most credited the record speed to *perestroika* and to Mikhail Gorbachev, others looked deeper. Up-to-date information indicated that the long-standing prediction of the economic collapse of the Soviet Union was actually close at hand, and many reasoned that the Kremlin simply could not afford to maintain Cold War-level troop commitments in Eastern Europe. Furthermore, the access of the Western press to previously closed meetings of the CPSU had enabled the West to know that the party was prepared to witness the "decomposition" of the empire as the price of domestic economic survival. In addition, as these events unfolded, political unrest within the Soviet Union and the move toward secession among a few of the constituent republics required the full attention of the Soviet leadership. So while Americans generally celebrated their victory in the Cold War, they also looked sympathetically at Mikhail Gorbachev at a time at which his international popularity belied his political peril at home.

Americans were also dazzled by Gorbachev's political maneuvers. Contested elections were allowed for seats in the parliamentary body of the Soviet government, the National Congress of People's Deputies, to which substantial power was transferred. Open debate and political criticism, for the first time televised domestically and open to the foreign press, became standard in a matter of months. Even the meetings of the Central Committee of the Communist Party of the Soviet Union were opened, and the world was treated to fresh quotations regarding such revolutionary declarations as the "decomposition" of the empire for the sake of Soviet economic security and the voluntary sacrifice of political power monopoly in favor of political pluralism and multiparty politics.

All this Americans ascribed to the skill of Gorbachev's second Soviet revolution of the twentieth century. But because the USSR was fraught with such tremendous problems, concern grew that Gorbachev might not survive regressive pressures from the remaining Kruschevites and Brezhnevites. The stock market had a momentary panic when it was reported in early 1990, apparently inaccurately, that Gorbachev had offered his resignation to the Central Committee of the CPSU. In fact, he emerged from the committee meetings stronger than ever personally, but still beset with problems. He was informed by his colleagues that time was running out: If *perestroika* did not begin to work

Source: Drawing by Lorenz; © 1990 The New Yorker Magazine, Inc.

soon, either the state or the reform movement would be in severe difficulty simply because *glasnost* had set in motion events that had either to succeed in the short run or be reversed before the state collapses. Under any prior Soviet leadership, Americans would have opted for failure; but for Gorbachev's reforms and vision of peace and prosperity, they strengthened their resolve. Even the Defense Department did its part by announcing that it would continue its attempt to strip $80 billion from the defense budget in the next five years.

But aside from Americans' affection for Gorbachev personally, what was the real state of Soviet-American relations at the opening of the 1990s? The popular notion was that the Cold War had ended. President Bush was cautious not to overstate the claim, and the Department of Defense, while attempting to reduce its budget, did so only in small amounts and in selected areas, arguing that although the Kremlin is removing ground troops from Eastern Europe, it continues to build up its strategic forces.

Opinion about the future of the East-West ideological dispute varied considerably. Many Americans credited Ronald Reagan's hard line on arms and other matters as having forced Gorbachev to reform. Others cited the heroism of Gorbachev. Structured analysis took a somewhat different course. One widely acclaimed paper, written by a State Department policy planner, proclaimed "The End of History."

What we may be witnessing is not just the end of the cold war, or the passing of a particular period of postwar history, but the end of history as such: that is, the end point of mankind's ideological evolution and the universalization of Western liberal democracy as the final form of human government.[39]

This self-congratulatory view was overshadowed only six months later with the publication of a lengthy paper, reprinted in *The New York Times* in a briefer version but for a broader, worldwide audience. The author, whose name is unknown (leading to speculation that he or she is highly placed in American policy circles), argues that Gorbachev's supposed reforms are not reforms at all, but a fundamental critique of "the very basis of Soviet order and the historic matrix of what until now was called 'developed' . . . socialism." What we are seeing now, says the author, is the failure of economic *perestroika* alongside "the runaway success of *glasnost* and the progress of democratization and popular politicization."

> The false problem of how to restructure Leninism is now giving way to the real problem of how to dismantle the system, how to effect at last an exit from communism. *Perestroika* is not a solution, but a transition to this exit. . . . [C]ommunism is not reforming itself, it is disintegrating.

The author concludes that the Soviet government cannot produce a communist system that is economically efficient and, at the same time, democratic; nor can it bring about a transition from a party-state with a planned economy to a democratic, free-market system. The only help the West can render is to assist Gorbachev in reducing the arms burden to concentrate on the domestic economy, and to work with him in establishing parallel market operations and free trade zones in order to ease the transition into the future.[40]

Such careful analysis notwithstanding, Americans rejoice with *Time* magazine following the Central Committee of the CPSU's agreement to sacrifice its 72-year stranglehold on political power by permitting multiple parties. "*Starting Over*: Gorbachev turns his back to Lenin."[41]

The United States and the Third World

Although much of the American world perspective centers on its relations with the two communist giants and on its allies, the Third World, too, plays an increasingly important role. Much of the Northern Hemisphere (including China) is industrially and economically underdeveloped, as is most of the Southern Hemisphere (excluding Australia and New Zealand). Prior to 1945, most of the Third World peoples lived in the imperial possessions of the European powers, but their emancipation through the processes of the United Nations, particularly after 1960, has made them independently governed.

---

[39]Francis Fukuyama, "The End of History," *National Interest,* Summer 1989.
[40]Z., "To the Stalin Mausoleum," *Daedalus,* Winter 1990.
[41]*Time,* cover, February 19, 1990.

They comprise nearly 70 percent of the world's population yet produce less than 10 percent of its goods; they have the most rapidly growing populations; and they have rising expectations regarding their global status and their share of the world's economic wealth. These factors together result in their having a major voice in global politics.

In the early postwar years, the United States selflessly supported both the independence and economic aspirations of the Third World. From 1950 to the present, American taxpayers have given scores of billions of dollars for the improvement of nutrition, transportation, health, population control, agricultural development, industrial development, education, and the like in areas of the world with which they are unfamiliar. This generosity was motivated in part by humane concern and in part as ideological competition with the Soviet Union, a competition in which both Washington and Moscow attempted to secure the loyalty of these peoples as they became politically independent.

Although the United States continues, both on its own and through international organizations, to provide considerable assistance to the Third World, the American attitude toward such foreign aid has shifted. Americans have grown weary of the waste and corruption to which their aid has been subjected. The revelations of crime and corruption that emerged from the Marcos flight from the Philippines were, to many Americans, conclusive evidence of the untrustworthiness of aid recipients.

Furthermore, Americans have tired of giving funds to peoples who have rejected American principles in favor of authoritarian governments, often socialist and anti-American. To charges of American neoimperialism, the response is that the failures of development are not attributable to American principles or American aid but to socialism, excessive urbanization, corruption, and civil disorder.[42] And that governments receiving American funds in turn should condemn the United States' relationship with Israel or its determination to prevent the spread of socialism in Latin America is a reprehensible contradiction. At the United Nations, the frequency with which the United States has voted with the majority has declined steadily, demonstrating that the political voice of the Third World has steered the organization away from the course of pro-Western democracy upon which it had embarked before these lands became independent.

Whereas Third World peoples often regard American economic policy and the activities of its transnational corporations as imperialistic, Americans hold the view that without American public aid and private capital, these peoples would still be impoverished, unemployed, and generally backward. Indeed, Taiwan and South Korea, two Third World countries that attracted large amounts of American investment and huge sums of American foreign assistance in the early Cold War years, now enjoy the highest standards of living anywhere in the non-oil-producing Third World. The New International Economic Order, declared by the United Nations as a result of the political coali-

---

[42]Norman Gall, ''The Four Horsemen Ride Again,'' *Forbes*, July 28, 1986, pp. 95–103. Gall labels these four items the ''four horsemen of the development apocalypse.''

tion of the Third World governments, is accepted by the United States in principle but is feared nonetheless as an instrument capable of disrupting free trade in favor of preferential treatment of the poor nations. A new economic order in which the recipient states are habitually unable to pay their monetary debts, affecting negatively both the trade and the payments balances of the United States, is a difficult economic order for accounting-conscious America to understand. The economic demands of the Third World are regarded by Americans as unending, unreasonable, nonreciprocal, unruly, and a costly burden for the United States, both politically and economically.

If the politics of the Third World in general causes discomfort for Americans, the economics of the oil-producing members is particularly irritating. Since the coming of age of the Organization of Petroleum Exporting Countries (OPEC) in 1973, American consumers of oil and petroleum products have been at the economic mercy of a handful of states, some radical in their demand that the industrialized West pay the social and economic costs of modernization, and some more moderate. Together, however, they raised the cost of imported oil by a multiple of almost ten, which caused domestic prices to skyrocket, the cost of industrial production to rise, severe inflation, and a tremendously disruptive redistribution of foreign currency reserves. And to add insult to injury, on most critical issues of world politics, particularly those pertaining to the Middle East, most of these governments are the outspoken opponents of American policy.

During the 1980s, the United States retaliated against this uneven relationship. It announced its withdrawal from the United Nations Educational, Social, and Cultural Organization (UNESCO) in protest of that agency's anti-Westernism. It increased its support to antigovernment forces in Nicaragua and to the pro-American government of El Salvador, despite that government's poor record on matters pertaining to human rights. It forcefully rid Grenada of communism and pro-Soviet influences. (''In Grenada,'' declared President Reagan during a celebration honoring the completion of the third year of his presidency, ''we set a people free.'' President Bush made similar claims after an invasion of Panama that resulted in removing Manuel Noriega from power, which he had held by terror even after free elections had designated a new government.) Congress passed legislation preventing the release of financial aid to communist-dominated countries, and the Reagan administration used its voting strength in the World Bank to prevent an increase in the bank's maximum authorization for loans to the Third World. And in a rare breach of inter-American solidarity on a matter involving an external party, President Reagan broke from neutrality and openly assisted Britain in nonmilitary ways against Argentina in the Falkland Islands War. He also ordered the bombing of Libya in retaliation for the latter's state-sponsored terrorism in the Middle East and Western Europe.

The resurgence of American self-awareness as a global power has resulted in a more assertive attitude toward those parts of the Third World that were once Western oriented but have subsequently turned socialist, for example, Nicaragua, Afghanistan, Mozambique, Ethiopia, and Grenada. Observing that many of the insurgency movements in the Third World now are anticommunist rather than communist, Washington has adopted a new attitude toward economic assistance to rebellion, its premise being that communism in the Third World is reversible. In what has come to be known informally as the Reagan Doctrine, the administration and the Congress are increasingly willing to lend assistance, not to aid the defense against communism, but to take the offensive in hope of its reversal. This is done on the premise that the use of force, and assistance in the use of force, against tyranny is intrinsically moral.[43] But the practical consequence of this policy was for half a decade a statement to the Soviet Union about the reassertion of American power in the Third World at a time when the Kremlin was reassessing its geographically independent policy concerning the developing countries. Early in the Gorbachev era, the Soviets realized that the cost of supporting virtually every leftist movement without a virtual guarantee of subsequent allegiance to Moscow was intolerable. With the maturation of *glasnost,* an East-West deemphasis of arms and the urgency of addressing Soviet economic modernization, Soviet-American confrontations in the Third World are diminishing rapidly. With the Red army out of Afghanistan and Cuban troops out of Angola, the only remaining points of contention are Soviet military aid to Nicaragua (and from Nicaragua to El Salvador) and Cuba.

The United States and the Global Economy

As the United States emerged from isolation in the 1930s, it took the first steps toward becoming the world's dominant economic power. In order to strengthen the prewar and wartime economies and Britain and France, Washington entered into a set of agreements to strengthen the British pound and the French franc in the world market. Second, through the Lend-Lease Act, the United States vowed to provide military products to the Allies even before Japan's attack on Pearl Harbor (December 7, 1941) and American entry into the war. Billions of dollars in trucks, tanks, arms, personnel carriers, planes, ammunition, and so on went to Britain, France, China, the Soviet Union, and others under this plan. And because combat never extended to North America, American industrial might was greatly advanced by the war; ground fighting and aerial bombing had virtually destroyed the industrial capabilities of Britain, France, the Soviet Union, Japan, Italy, Germany, and China.

At war's end, therefore, the United States was at an industrial and economic crest. The transformation to a peacetime economy was assisted by the huge need for industrial products abroad. A further boost was provided by the Cold War. Fearful of potential Soviet aggression and concerned that the destitution of Western Europeans might lead to a surge of socialist sentiment, the Congress appropriated $14 billion for the European Recovery Plan, often referred to as the Marshall Plan. The purpose of these funds was to rebuild the Euro-

---

[43]Stephen S. Rosenfeld, ''The Guns of July,'' *Foreign Affairs,* Spring 1986, pp. 698–714.

pean consumer economies and thereby strengthen their constitutional governments. Meanwhile, American investors began a long period of direct
investment in Europe in order both to manufacture and sell goods in the recovering economies. The Cold War and the Korean War (1950–1953) illuminated
the importance of maintaining a mixed wartime-peacetime economy, so government funds were poured into the defense industry even as private investment multiplied. American industrial wealth soared.

America also went to the aid of the vanquished. Although the postwar occupation of both Japan and Germany was to have been long and to have resulted in militarily weak states, American strategic thinking changed radically
with the onset of the Cold War. When communist forces won the Chinese civil
war, and when only seven months later North Korea invaded the south, the
military importance of Japan changed entirely. When the division of Europe
was completed by the establishment of NATO and the Warsaw Pact, the need
for an industrially and militarily (though nonnuclear) strong West Germany
became urgent. Through investment and aid (including Marshall Plan aid to
West Germany), the former enemies were rebuilt.

In the intervening years, the American position has been reversed. Now in
place of large balance-of-trade surpluses is a chronic, annual deficit in the
vicinity of $150 billion. American goods ranging from food to pharmaceuticals
are excluded from Japan, and trade with Western Europe becomes more difficult. In order to support its annual budget deficit of $60 to $100 billion, the
US Treasury Department sells bonds, now bought in increasing amounts by
overseas rather than domestic investors. Moreover, the net investment position
of the United States (the balance of American investment abroad and foreign
investments in the United States) has fallen from a large surplus to nearly a
$600 billion deficit in 1990. More and more Americans feel victimized by the
economic system constructed largely on postwar American policy and money.
Traditionally given to the philosophy of free trade, Americans now see free
trade as tilted against them and are more inclined toward protectionism and
retaliatory trade policies. ''Free trade is fair trade,'' Ronald Reagan said often.
In its law and its foreign economic policy, a major goal of the United States
today is to alter the international trading regime in order to bring the table
back to level.

Japan

From the American standpoint, the reconstruction of Japan was a magnificent
success that backfired terribly. Japan became economically self-sufficient—
except for its extraordinary reliance on foreign energy sources—and began
quickly to compete in global markets. Today Japan enjoys a huge annual balance of trade surplus, much of it at the expense of the United States. This
results from twin facts: Americans have huge appetites for Japanese manufactures, particularly automobiles and electronics, while Japanese law and public
policy make it very difficult for American goods to penetrate the Japanese
market. In the United States this is seen as a grossly uneven economic rela-

tionship leading to repeated demands for protectionism (policies to limit Japanese imports), to threats of trade war and difficult trade negotiations designed to open Japan to American goods.

The economic contest is complicated by the cost of Japanese security, too much of which is borne by American taxpayers. The United States has repeatedly asked the Japanese to review their fraction of this "burden sharing," and one government commission after another has done so. But only once was there an agreement to raise the Japanese share, and the amount had virtually no effect on the budget of the US Department of Defense.

By the late 1980s, yet another source of trouble entered the relationship: Japanese interests began to multiply their investments in the United States. Although some kinds of direct investment had been going on for years—the popular Honda Accord, for example, had been built in Ohio for several years—investment now turned in new directions including schools and colleges, recreational facilities, entertainment empires, huge urban properties, and US Treasury securities. The magnitude of these purchases gave rise to worry about the "selling off" of America, and inspired one humorist to declare that Americans need no longer fear that they will be driven out by Soviet communists, but that they will be evicted by Japanese. By 1989, public opinion polls indicated that the threat of economic warfare with Japan had greatly surpassed that of armed conflict with the Soviet Union.

The European Community

Since 1954, Western Europe has been in the process of creating a single, multinational economy (see Chapter 17, "International Integration and Transnational Participation," for details). The European Economic Community (EEC) was created by six states (West Germany, France, Italy, Belgium, Luxumbourg and The Netherlands), and its membership now numbers 12. (Britain, Ireland, and Denmark were first admitted, then Spain and Portugal and finally Greece.) Today the community comprises a population greater than that of the United States and the largest capitalist market in the world. West Germany, like Japan, rebuilt after the Second World War largely with American funds, has the second strongest industrial economy in the world following only Japan.

As the Community has developed, its own industries have satisfied more and more of its consumer demand, reducing relative need for American goods. Simultaneously, its industrial overcapacity has enabled it to exceed the United States in world markets. Hence, as with Japan, each new success of the community is seen as a threat to the global commercial position of the United States.

The approach of 1992, the year in which full economic union among the 12 is to occur, is of particular concern to Americans. There is fear that the community may evolve into a "fortress Europe" from which American goods will be excluded. Already threats of trade war have been exchanged. Some American corporations are responding to fear by increasing their direct investment within the community in order "to get behind" the tariff barriers—to produce goods within the community and sell them there so that they will not have to be imported across exorbitantly expensive tariff barriers. The collapse of Soviet power in Eastern Europe; the October 1990 reunification of Germany; and potentially rich investment opportunities in Hungary, Poland, and Czechoslovakia hold open the possibility that the community's reach may be extended, as do the interests of Austria and Switzerland and the Nordic states. In all this, Americans see both difficulties trading in Europe and greater competition in other world markets.

U.S. Agenda after the Cold War

The convergence of two exceedingly important events—the end of the Cold War and the troubling new conditions of global economic competition—have shocked American foreign policy to its roots. According to one observer, with the end of the Cold War "The guiding assumption of American foreign policy has fallen apart."[44] If, indeed, the Cold War is over, and if Soviet-American competition in the Third World dissolves as rapidly as has the military stand-off in Europe, then clearly the agenda of American foreign policy in the future is its place in the global economy.

Conclusion

The twentieth century has seen a radical alteration in the world position of the United States. It entered the epoch clinging to isolation but was forced twice in 25 years to intervene in critical European conflicts that threatened world stability. After 1945, with American influence and prestige still intact among the noncommunist Allies, an obligation was accepted to play a permanent international role. Thus, America twice went to war against spreading communism, once in Korea and once in Vietnam. The close of the latter conflict occurred in a global environment that seemed a portent to improving relations between the communist and noncommunist worlds. The détente that followed ended in bitter disappointment for Americans. Despite the momentary promise of peace after the Vietnam War, the persistent confrontation of NATO and the Warsaw Pact, together with nagging problems in Central America and the Middle East, perpetuated the dominant theme of military modernization on foreign policy debate.

The 1980s brought the most remarkable spectrum of hopes and rhetoric. The decade began with the Soviet Union's occupying Afghanistan and with martial law in Poland imposed on a liberalization movement. Soviet strength virtually throughout the world—in Europe, Asia, the Pacific, Africa, Central America, and the Caribbean—seemed ominous to Americans. The Reagan administration committed the nation to an extravagant but, to the majority, necessary arms program based on the continuing threat of the Soviet Union as the "evil

---

[44]Walter LaFeber, *Chronicle of Higher Education,* January 3, 1990, p. A11.

empire.'' Meanwhile, relations with China were normalized, as new, forward-looking leadership welcomed foreign investment and commerce as methods of rapid economic development. On the economic front, a worldwide recession was followed by a recovery throughout the West and Japan that increased global trading competition, much to the detriment of the United States and its balance of trade.

By the close of the decade, attention had shifted almost entirely from national security to economic competition. There was a widespread feeling that the Cold War had ended with the demise of Soviet power in Eastern Europe and the urgent need of the Soviet leadership to address itself to the domestic economy. What just a few years earlier had been ''the evil empire'' was an empire no more, having stood by and watched all of Eastern Europe elect self-determination and having been rocked by the civil strife and secession movements within several of the constituent republics of the Soviet Union itself. *Perestroika* and *glasnost,* the companion programs of the Gorbachev government, were seen as dramatic Westward shifts of political philosophy—not mere alterations of rhetoric, but genuine reestablishment of the principles of rule, the exercise of power, and relationship between the government and the population. The decision of the CPSU to permit power to migrate from the party to the Congress of People's Deputies, together with its willingness to give up its monopoly and permit the rise of multiple competing parties, added to the sense among Americans that liberal democracy had triumphed in the Soviet Union over a failed and brutal experiment of 73 years. Many Americans credited this to US foreign policy, others to the revolutionary and visionary Gorbachev. Either way, the Berlin Wall was gone; agreements had been reached on troop reductions in Europe; Germany was soon reunified; communist governments had toppled throughout Eastern Europe; and national security had been replaced by the nation's economic woes as the first item on the agenda.

Those difficulties focused on Japan, Western Europe, and the Third World. The huge and chronic trade deficit with respect to Japan, the fear of a fortress Europe shutting out American firms and American goods after economic union in 1992, and the Third World's trio of problems—need for financial aid, demand for preferential trading status, and staggering debt—all weighed heavily on Americans who, for a half-century, have been accustomed to economic domination and uninterrupted enrichment. As security imperatives diminished, the national agenda turned to the American position in international commerce. The era of the United States as world policeman was over; now Americans were not content to be a declining power.

CHAPTER 3

The Perspectives of America's Major Allies

The concept of a mulitparty balance in world politics, together with the reality of the burgeoning importance of the nonmilitary components of power, calls for a review of the international perspectives of those modern industrial nations that contribute independently to the world balance. To achieve this balance they must remain free from foreign economic and military domination. These two conditions—modernity and autonomy—typify some of America's principal allies, particularly Japan, the European Community countries, and Canada. Each of these countries has achieved a high level of industrial activity, a major competitive position in world economic affairs and a sophisticated security system. Yet in both military and economic relations, each is intertwined with the interests and capabilities of the United States. There is a delicate balance between independent decision making and domination from Washington and Wall Street. For each, accordingly, a world view is colored as much by the ambivalence of relations with closest friend as by the fear of potential enemies.

Japan

A paradox of forces shapes the Japanese world view. On the one hand, Japan is intensely nationalistic and has a proud history of cultural continuity and empire. Yet on the other hand, Japan removed itself entirely from world affairs from 1640 to 1854, when it was "opened" by threat of force by the American fleet of Commodore Matthew C. Perry. After the First World War, Japan was humiliated by the refusal of the Western powers to include in the Covenant of the League of Nations a declaration of racial equality. In 1945, under relentless firebombing and two atomic attacks, Japan was forced into surrender; and after six years of occupation by American troops, a peace treaty was arranged at the price of a series of military and economic agreements that compromised Japan's self-determination.

Yet despite these restraints, in the years since the Second World War, Japan had undergone a remarkable economic recovery that survived even the severe world economic fluctuations of the 1970s and early 1980s. At present rates of growth this small nation, which fits a population half that of United States into a territorial mass only the size of Montana, may well exceed the gross national product (GNP) of the United States in the 1990s. But to understand the unique elements of the Japanese world view, it is necessary first to examine the evolution of modern Japan.

The Opening of Japan

Like China, Japan fell into the covetous orbit of American Manifest Destiny in the nineteenth century. As the China trade multiplied after 1844, American merchants eyed Japan as an additional source of Oriental goods and as a supply station and refuge that would minimize the hazards of the long Pacific journey. Already Americans had absorbed the idea of this new land, and it had inspired their missionary zeal: Popular tales about the Japanese treatment of shipwrecked sailors had prompted some Americans to brand the Japanese enemies of humankind. After two unsuccessful diplomatic efforts, in the wake of expansionism in the Mexican War and the acquisition of the Pacific coast, American nationalism and the idea of "opening" Japan converged. The departure of Perry's squadron was appropriately festive to the anticipated results, for it was to mark the first time Americans would deal directly with the Japanese since the Napoleonic Wars, during which a few Americans had carried on the trickle of Dutch trade that Japan permitted. (Ironically, one of the sites of that trade was Nagasaki, the second of the two cities destroyed a century later by America's atomic bombs.)

In 1854, the Japanese entered reluctantly into a treaty with the United States, seeing it as an opportunity to learn industrial science. If the commercial treaty opened the door to Japan, the immediate evolution of Japanese-American relations propped it wide. For by 1858, although Japan had gained few concessions, Americans had acquired most-favored-nation status (granting automatic improvement of trading conditions if Japan were to offer more liberal terms to any other party), the right of extraterritoriality (Americans charged with crimes in Japan were to be tried in American courts by American laws), and the rights to teach Western religions and to establish religious institutions. As was the case in early Sino-American relations, then, the principal mark of these early dealings with the West was imbalance: Japan was assigned the obligations, while America gained the lucrative and enviable benefits.

Japanese Expansionism

As exploitative as the American presence might have been, it was not pervasive. As Japan became more aware of the industrial revolution elsewhere and commenced its own modernization, it was free to conduct its own foreign policy (except as its external interests were limited by its trade treaties with Washington and other capitals). Hence, despite a watchful eye from America, Japan was able to begin, in the last decade of the century, a quest for its own empire. Control of Korea, long an object of competition among China, Japan, and Russia, prompted the Sino-Japanese War of 1894–1895, a war that Japan won because of its superior arms and modernization. Although Chinese interests were uprooted from Korea and Taiwan (Formosa), Japanese acquisitions on the Asian mainland were seized by Russia with the assistance of France and Germany. It was clear that if Japan were to achieve status as the dominant modern Asian state, the influence of the Western states within the region would have to be restricted.

Peace was but a lull, as the Russo-Japanese War (1904–1905) ensued, largely over competing claims to Manchuria and Korea. Again, however, a Western state's policy was to dominate the outcome. Having acquired the Philippines in 1898, the United States hoped that Asia and the Pacific would be stabilized by a Russo-Japanese stalemate. In view of Russia's apparent edge, President Theodore Roosevelt's policy was to encourage Japan to limit the Russian successes by dangling postwar rewards. But when Japan won decisive land and sea battles and appeared ready to seize eastern Siberia, Roosevelt saw urgent need for a peace that would ensure the stalemate, as war apparently could not. While giving his assent in the Taft-Katsura Agreement of 1905 to Japanese control of Korea, Roosevelt urged moderation of Tokyo's other expectations of indemnification. He did not force these compromises on Japan; however, popular and editorial opinion in that country focused dissatisfaction with the peace treaty on America: US policy seemed to have betrayed the Japanese victory. The flames of hostility were fanned by frequent reports of anti-Japanese racial violence in California and by American policies that excluded Asian immigrants. With Russia vanquished and China quieted by Western colonialism, redress of grievances with the United States became the focal point of Japanese politics.[1]

The tenuous understanding that was achieved through a visit of the American fleet (painted white) to Japanese ports and through executive agreements concerning immigration and mutual respect for Pacific territories was broken by the First World War. When at the war's outset Germany vacated its China holdings, Japan moved swiftly to occupy them. Shortly thereafter, Tokyo issued to China the Twenty-one Demands (1915), which sought to enlarge Japan's influence throughout China. Because wartime diplomacy did little to resolve these issues, their persistence accentuated the mutual distrust. At the Paris Peace Conference, Japan—its economy vibrant, its navy among the world's most modern, and its national spirit running high—attached the China issue to a demand that the Covenant of the League of Nations include a declaration of racial equality. Without it Japan would not bow to President Wood-

[1]Raymond A. Esthus, *Theodore Roosevelt and Japan* (Seattle: University of Washington Press, 1966); Howard K. Beale, *Theodore Roosevelt and the Rise of America to World Power* (Baltimore: Johns Hopkins University Press, 1956), particularly chap. 5; and Charles E. Neu, *An Uncertain Friendship* (Cambridge, Mass.: Harvard University Press, 1967).

row Wilson's demand for a timetable for the return of Germany's former holdings to China. For their part, some European states rich in colonial holdings throughout the nonwhite world rejected Japan's demand. Western resistance prevailed, leaving the China question unresolved but, worse, leaving the Japanese more convinced than before of the untrustworthiness of Western intentions.

The breakdown of trust was recorded also in a division of Japanese opinion concerning the country's role in the postwar world. The civilian government and conservative elements readily subscribed to the Washington Treaties of 1922, which sought a permanent balance of interests in China and a restriction on naval armaments. But to expansionists and the military, naval arms limitation and the new diplomatic regime for China constituted surrender to a Western design to regulate Japan's influence in Asia. The military slowly became virtually self-governing, and by 1931 the government denied that troops were moving into Manchuria even while the army was using a minor (and deliberately provoked) skirmish at Mukden as the pretext for a massive invasion of Manchuria and eventually of China, Asia, and the Pacific. To the expansionists this was a policy born of having been denied, through habitual Western interferences, the prizes of conquest in 1885, 1905, and 1918. Consistent with this thinking were the decisions to withdraw from the League of Nations, to create the Greater East Asian Co-Prosperity Sphere, and to join the Axis Alliance (1940) with Germany and Italy. These moves were additionally encouraged by the imperfections of American neutrality and its tendency to favor China, and Washington's economic sanctions against Japan. Prevention, then, or at least delay, of American intervention in the Asian war necessitated the Japanese attack on the American fleet at Pearl Harbor, Hawaii, on December 7, 1941.[2]

The horrors of the Second World War in the Pacific reached their climax with several events that apparently were indicative of Western attitudes toward the Orient. On the tactical front, as an alternative to invasion, the United States chose to firebomb Japanese population centers, a policy facilitated by the discovery of napalm (jellied gasoline); even worse, it used the only two atomic bombs in existence to devastate the industrial cities of Hiroshima and Nagasaki. Two political decisions also stand out in Japanese memories. First, at the Potsdam (Berlin) Conference, held a scant three weeks prior to the war's end, it was decided to force Japan into unconditional surrender and to reject an offer of surrender that had as its sole condition the preservation of the tradition of the emperor's sovereignty. (This condition was subsequently accepted, but only after two atomic bombings.) Second, the Soviet Union declared war on Japan on the day of the second atomic attack, giving Moscow five days of belligerency and almost no combat, but a claim to reparations despite five years of formal Soviet-Japanese nonbelligerency.

To the Japanese, the firebombings were an unnecessary and heinous attack on innocent civilian populations. These and the atomic bombings were wholly unnecessary in view of the offer to surrender on a single cultural condition.

---

[2]Herbert Feis, *The Road to Pearl Harbor* (Princeton, N.J.: Princeton University Press, 1950.)

Because there was no strategic value to the use of atomic bombs, Japan already having reached virtual submission, these attacks are taken as evidence of the American intention to pulverize Japanese society or to demonstrate American strength to the Soviet Union at great and indiscriminate cost. The opportunism of the Soviet Union was seen with equal suspicion.

One haunting question pervades all of these arguments: Would the Second World War have concluded in this manner had Caucasian rather than Oriental lives been at stake, Western civilization rather than Asian?

During the occupation that followed, the Japanese were faced not only with national reconstruction, but also with the need for a revitalization of self-esteem under a victor whose intentions they did not trust even in good times.

The American Occupation

The prevailing international climate when Japan embarked on its program of restoration was one of utter turmoil. All Europe was in tatters; China was in the middle of a civil war; and the Soviet-American wartime rapport had broken down. Japan had to accept the United States as the sole occupying power, despite the intentions of the Allies to have a multilateral policy. It also had to acknowledge General Douglas MacArthur as the Supreme Commander of the Allied Powers in the Pacific, even though he personified the Allied conquest of Japan.

The Japanese were still less pleased with the American estimate that nearly a quarter-century would be needed to achieve the objectives of occupation: democratization, industrial restoration at a level below war potential, land reform and agricultural self-sufficiency, and the purging of war criminals and imperialists. Remarkably, nearly all these had been achieved, or set in irreversible motion, in little more than three years. Within that time, MacArthur had authorized the drafting of a new constitution, and by the end of 1948, he and others were publicly calling for an expeditious termination of the occupation.

Although the Japanese attributed the speed to their own forbearance as much as to American policy, they recognized that a prolonged occupation, if not oppressive, might be preferable to speedy independence. The Cold War was under way; Korean reunification talks between Moscow and Washington had broken down; and the ideological future of Asia seemed written in the forthcoming victory of Chinese communism over the Kuomintang (the Chinese Nationalist party). Independence would mean dealing with the Soviet Union, balancing the interests of two Chinas, accommodating American economic and military might when its right of intrusion was no longer acknowledged, and surviving on industries that would be long on productive capacity but short on raw materials and energy sources. Now was scarcely a propitious time for new Asian ventures.

Again, however, the decision escaped the Japanese, as occurrences within months of Mao's victory and the Korean War altered Japan's place in the American world scheme. No longer did the United States look upon Japan as a pastoral and self-sufficient island kingdom but, rather, as a powerful, industrialized, and strategically located ally; an atomic fortress and haven for Amer-

Ruins of Nagasaki after the atomic bombing in August 1945.
Source: John Bennewitz/Black Star.

ican investments; and a center of operations for American manipulation of Asian power. The cover of United Nations legitimacy in Korea could not conceal the fact that in its decision to contain communism in Asia, Washington had summarily transformed the purposes, the timing, and the consequences of the Japan occupation.[3]

The Pacific Treaties and Japanese Prosperity

Amidst these new circumstances, John Foster Dulles, later Secretary of State, began to negotiate the Pacific Treaties of 1951. Dulles's zealous anticommunism, heightened by events in China and Korea, seemed to ensure a revised

---

[3]Frederick S. Dunn, *Peace-Making and Settlement with Japan* (Princeton, N.J.: Princeton University Press, 1963).

role for Japan; his insistence on a "peace of reconciliation" rather than a "peace of retribution"[4] created a cordial negotiating environment. It was clear from the beginning, however, that within the framework of reconciliation, the United States would seek to acquire Cold War access to Japanese territory and would insist on including Japan in a growing chain of anticommunist alliances. The peace of reconciliation would have to facilitate Washington's Cold War strategies.

Of the four Pacific Treaties that resulted from Dulles's diplomacy, two pertained directly to Japan. (The other two linked the Philippines, Australia, and New Zealand to American alliances. Both the Soviet government and the Chinese government of Mao were excluded from the Pacific Treaties.) In the Peace Treaty, Japan was obliged to sacrifice virtually all territories acquired since 1895 and to enter into reparations negotiations with those Allied governments whose territories had been occupied by Japanese troops between 1931 and 1945. More important, however, were the clauses that prepared for Japan's inclusion in the American security system. As a consequence of these, the Security Treaty went into effect simultaneously with the Peace Treaty.

In the early years of these agreements, great benefits accrued to Japan. Because of American willingness to bear the cost of Japan's security, the share of GNP that would have normally have gone to defense was invested instead in economic growth, leading to annual growth rates until 1981 of twice those of other industrial states. In fact, for the period 1960 to 1981, Japan's average annual growth in GNP per capita was 3.3 times the combined average of the United States, Canada, Britain, France, and West Germany. (The growth was reduced to about the same level of those states by the recession of 1981–1983.) In terms of GNP (as contrasted with GNP per capita), Japan's productivity multiplied 12 times between 1950 and 1976, whereas the GNP of the United States multiplied only 2.3 times and that of Western Europe about 3 times.

Equally important, however, is the growth of Japan's industrial sector, since Japan's exports emphasize automotive and electronics manufactures. As Table 3–1 indicates, in the 1980s Japan's annual rate of growth in the industrial sector declined to 4.9 percent as against 8.5 percent for the preceding 15 years. But compare it with the average performance of Japan's principal industrial partners, which fell from an annual average of 2.4 percent growth in the early period to a bare 1.6 percent in the 1980s. In the early period, then, Japan's industrial economy grew 3.5 times faster than did the average of the others; and in the 1980s, the comparative figure is 3.1 times.

Meanwhile, the favorable trade and payments balances that accompanied this seemingly miraculous recovery from the Second World War enabled the Japanese yen to share the spotlight with the German mark as the most valuable

---

[4]As a young man, Dulles had been a member of the American Peace Commission at the Paris talks leading to the Treaty of Versailles. He came away from the conference with the conviction that the peace would not last because it was punitive, thus forming the basis for his later strategy of negotiating a Japanese peace treaty based on reconciliation rather than retribution. See Townsend Hoopes, *The Devil and John Foster Dulles* (Boston: Atlantic-Little, Brown, 1973), especially chaps. 2 and 7.

Table 3–1 Comparison of average annual growth rates in the industrial sector, 1965–1980 and 1980–1987, for Japan and principal trading partners, in percentages.

	1965–1980	1980–1987
Japan	8.5%	4.9%
United States	1.7 ⎫	2.9 ⎫
Britain	−0.5 ⎪	1.8 ⎪
France	4.3 ⎬ 2.4% = Avg.	−0.1 ⎬ 1.6% = Avg.
Canada	3.5 ⎪	3.0 ⎪
West Germany	2.8 ⎭	0.4 ⎭
Ratio	8.5/2.4 = 3.5%	4.9/1.6 = 3.1%

Source: World Bank, *World Development Report 1989*, from table 2, pp.166–167.

and desirable currency in the world. By all measures except military might, therefore, Japan's status as a major power has been taken for granted for one and a half decades.[5]

Despite these remarkable evidences of redevelopment, however, not all was well in the early and intermediate phases of Japan's return to principal power status. For even as the Japanese economy surged upward, external events imposed other burdens, many of which collided with the Japanese urge for more self-determined foreign policies.

Resolving the Legacies of War

Although Japan's security was assured by the treaties, there remained many issues of fundamental importance to Japan's postwar redevelopment, some of which led to occasional disruptions in its relations with Washington. Among the most important was working out an effective economic relationship with China under communist control. China's need for industrial goods and Japan's need for raw materials and markets would create a remarkable trading partnership. Yet, as Japan's ability to promote this relationship matured, American's obsession with the isolation of China resulted in pressure against massive Japanese trading with China. The Japanese interpreted this not only as an interference with national decision making but also as an affront to national economic growth. They also viewed it as an American effort to use the isolation of China as an instrument for restricting Japanese competition with American manufacturers. Furthermore, it was seen as a cause of unnecessary delay in normalizing the international relations of Asia, a delay from which Japan might suffer and for which it might be held responsible.

In view of the extreme sensitivities of the China–Japan–United States triangle prior to Washington's reassessment of its Asian policy, Japan was not free to establish diplomatic relations or to conduct full economic activity with

---

[5]For example, see Herman Kahn, *The Emerging Japanese Superstate: Challenge and Response* (Englewood Cliffs, N.J.: Prentice-Hall, 1971); Nobutaka Ike, *Japan: The New Superstate* (San Francisco: Freeman, 1973); and Frank Gibney, *Japan: The Fragile Super Power*, rev. ed. (New York: Norton, 1979).

China until 1971 and 1972.[6] But then the volume of Sino-Japanese trade quickly jumped over the billion-dollar level and grew steadily, crossing the $10 billion mark in 1981. The high point of $21.3 billion occurred in 1985, then settled back to $16.5 billion in 1987. The trade consists principally of Japanese exports of steel, machinery, and other industrial products, and Japanese imports of oil, coal, and other natural resources from China. Today, Japan's trade with and investments in China lead those of all other nations, and the two have also entered into a joint oil exploration agreement in the Pacific.

The changing Chinese global perspective has influenced the strategic relationship between the two Asian powers. During the period of closest Sino-American relations (1976–1980), Japanese and Chinese anti-Soviet strategies were coordinated; but as the Chinese have embarked more recently on a policy of improved relations with both the United States and the Soviet Union, with dependence on neither, the openness of the relationship has diminished. China's century-long fear of Japanese military power also contributes to skepticism regarding the value of too-close collaboration on military matters. Nonetheless, the Japanese need for fuel and the Chinese need for technology transfer for military-related manufacturing leaves open the possibility of closer cooperation in the future.

A second issue of postwar importance to Japan was the settlement of the Okinawa question. Of the many territorial questions left over from the Second World War, none has been more symbolic to the Japanese than Okinawa. Even after conclusion of the Pacific Treaties, this large territory, regarded by the Japanese as a virtually a fifth home island, remained in American control, continuing as a major center for conventional and nuclear military strategies. Washington persistently rejected the growing demand for the reversion of Okinawa to Japanese sovereignty, particularly as the Vietnam War underscored the importance of Okinawa to American strategy. The question was further complicated in the Senate by powerful interests that insisted on restricting Japanese textile exports to the United States as a condition for the reversion of Okinawa. Finally in 1972, amid global trade negotiations, the American reassessment of its policy in Vietnam and normalization of relations with China, Okinawa was returned to Japan by treaty, subject to American rights under the Mutual Security Treaty of 1950.

Yet another issue critical to the reestablishment of full sovereignty and an independent foreign policy pertained to the American military bases. Under the terms of the Security Treaty, the United States was allowed to maintain military bases throughout Japan. These bases were a source of particular resentment. They were viewed as remnants of the occupation, as symbolic of something less than sovereignty for Japan, and as a potential danger to Japan should the enemies of the United States take retaliatory action. Most annoying to the Japanese was the continued use of their ports and territorial waters for servicing the nuclear submarine fleet, a presence that the bomb-conscious population detested. Successful efforts to negotiate the removal of nuclear

---

[6]Chae-Jin Lee, "The Making of the Sino-Japanese Peace and Friendship Treaty," *Pacific Affairs*, Fall 1979, pp. 420–445.

weapons from the home islands, and the requirement that the Japanese government be afforded the right of "prior consent" for the combat use of American bases on the home islands, only partially allayed national dissatisfactions. A succession of American-oriented governments desperately sought compromise on these issues lest popular demand weaken the government and lead to a movement for national rearmament. With increasing fretfulness, a Japan restored to economic power and revitalized in national purpose reached for ways to effect its role in a world where the most troubling restraints were perceived as emanating from its closest partner.

As Washington and Tokyo struggled to bring these issues to peaceful conclusions, the Americanization of the Vietnam War intruded upon their relations. The enlarged military presence of the United States in Asia (1964–1973) brought new strains to Japan's foreign policy and to its internal politics. Although the government tacitly supported the American commitment in Vietnam, the war became increasingly unpopular among the Japanese. In particular, it accentuated fears of Japanese involvement should excesses of American strategy (such as B-52 launchings from Okinawa) result in retaliatory actions. The war also hardened the American position on the Okinawa issue, just as the balance-of-payments deterioration suffered by the United States during the war heightened American intolerance of Japan's export capability. Finally, to the extent that American involvement was motivated by the desire to isolate China and to contain its influence, the war threatened to prolong the restrictions on Sino-Japanese trade. Underlying all these fears, however, was a prevailing apprehension that through its policy in Southeast Asia, the United States was attempting the adjust the Asian power distribution in directions that would measure the benefits to the United States partly by the costs to Japan.

Japan from Recovery to World Stature: The Many Obstacles

From a century and a quarter of relations with the West, the Japanese learned that international decisions concerning Asia tend to be made less by coordinated diplomacy than by the rush of events. Not inconsistently, then, just when the opportunity for consideration of Asian issues seemed possible in the diminished fighting in Southeast Asia, the Japanese found new disrupting problems. At a time when an independent role for Japan in Asian and world politics might have evolved, many of the basic assumptions on which Japan had built its political and economic policies were subverted.

The Nixon Doctrine In its search for methods of face-saving withdrawal from Vietnam, President Richard M. Nixon's administration considered noninterventionary paths to Western-oriented political stability in the underindustrialized world. The Nixon Doctrine was first proclaimed during 1970.[7]

---

[7]Richard M. Nixon, *US Foreign Policy for the 1970s,* report to the Congress by the President of the United States, February 25, 1971.

Although its full meaning was never aired, in essence it meant that the United States would no longer intervene in civil or regional wars but would provide arms and military information to help governments meet insurrections. The reaffirmation of the Japanese-American Security Treaty exempts Japan from the terms of the doctrine; yet its simple utterance nevertheless brought crisis to the issue of Japanese defense. What might the result be for the security of Asia and the Pacific? Would it now be necessary for Japan to undertake a major remilitarization? Despite the formal status of the Security Treaty, did the Nixon Doctrine and the American withdrawal from Southeast Asia portend reduced reliability in the Japanese-American security relation? Should Japan become a nuclear power?[8]

Regional events have compounded these problems. The rapid changes in Southeast Asia from 1973 to 1975—particularly, full American withdrawal and the exclusion of Western-oriented governments and factions from South Vietnam, Laos, and Cambodia—opened a potential sphere of influence to which the Japanese government and investors quickly responded. These opportunities seem offset, however, by the jeopardy to regional stability created by the precarious Soviet-American-Chinese triangle and by the entry of India into the exclusive circle of nuclear powers (1974). At a time when the reliability of the American nuclear umbrella was in doubt, competitive ventures on an Asian continent between two regional nuclear powers (India and China) accentuated the urgency of whether Japan should "go nuclear." Long a heated issue in domestic politics between those who abhor nuclear strategy and those who consider it the only fruitful path to foreign policy independent of the United States, this topic was renewed by the Indian development.[9] It was not settled until 1976, when the Japanese government signed the Nuclear Non-Proliferation Treaty, a multilateral treaty prohibiting the spread of nuclear weapons by its signatories.

The First Nixon Shock   Events quickened in 1971 after President Nixon announced his intention to visit China the following winter. This decision, made without consulting Tokyo, took the Japanese by complete surprise. They could not comprehend even the remote possibility of Sino-American détente prior to complete resolution of the Southeast Asian war; and neither could they avoid suspicions about American motives in attempting to normalize relations with China while at the same time forbidding Japan to modernize its relations, particularly with regard to trade. To make matters worse, if the United States ceased isolating China and enacted the Nixon Doctrine simultaneously, were the imperatives for Japanese security multiplied? Were the concurrent changes of the security and political relations of Asia cumulative, in the sense that the natural trading partnership between China and Japan might produce new forms

---

[8]For a detailed consideration of the Nixon Doctrine's implications for Japan, see Robert E. Osgood, *The Weary and the Wary: US and Japanese Security Policies in Transition* (Baltimore: Johns Hopkins University Press, 1972).

[9]Frank C. Langdon, "Japanese Reactions to India's Nuclear Explosion," *Pacific Affairs,* Summer 1975, pp. 173–180.

of conflict? Once the national shock over the president's announcement had been digested, an anxiety of substantial change in Asia took root, one introduced unilaterally by the United States. The path to independent policy, so vivid only a few years earlier, now became cluttered by unforeseen, unknown, and menacing complications.

The Second Nixon Shock Scarcely a month after the China-visit announcement, the Nixon administration took steps to correct what it perceived to be the causes of economic recession. Among other things, to reduce foreign competition in the United States, the government imposed for 90 days an additional tariff of 10 percent on all imported goods, with certain exceptions for less-developed countries and specially protected commodities. The Japanese interpreted this as an attempt to force a revaluation of their currency—a long-held objective in Washington—and as an assault on Japanese-built automobiles. A measure of the shock wave is that in 1970 US-Japanese trade was valued at $10 billion and had grown in 1973 to $19 billion. In all its trading history, only with Canada had the United States previously done an excess of $10 billion business in a single year. Furthermore, for Japan the larger share of the total amount was in exports, enabling it to maintain an enviable balance-of-trade surplus. Yet another measure was the immediate effect of unemployment in the Japanese automotive industry.

By this act the United States had directly and boldly intervened in Japan's domestic and international economic policies as a reprisal for success and had restricted Japan's ability to compete in the world's large industrial markets. Japan's postwar economic renaissance, supported by the United States as a way of controlling the Asian power distribution during the Korean War and the Cold War, had now become too competitive. Once again, by unilateral American decision, the setting in which Japan would have to design its regional and world roles was fraught with the uncertainty of altered assumptions.

The Petroleum Crisis Japan's economic stability was now subject to new pressures. Caught in global recession and inflation, forced by Washington to revalue their currency in a direction injurious to their prosperity, and once again conscious of their vulnerability to foreign economic decisions, the Japanese also saw domestic capital flow out to lucrative investment opportunities elsewhere. As a result of all these factors, they watched their remarkable growth rate slide toward zero and their enviable payments surplus begin to dwindle.

Before effective changes could be made, in 1973 the Organization of Petroleum Exporting Countries (OPEC) threatened Japan with an oil embargo unless it either discontinued its relations and trading policy with Israel or offered technological assistance to the OPEC members. Even after the embargo threat was withdrawn on the basis of an oil-for-technology agreement, the price of oil continued to rise to an intolerably high level, forcing Japan to petition the United States for a collective diplomatic offensive by the oil-consuming countries.

Table 3–2 Comparative energy consumption and production.

	World Rank as Energy Consumer	World Rank as Energy Producer
US	1	1
USSR	2	2
China	3	4
Japan	4	23
West Germany	5	12
UK	6	9
Canada	7	6
France	8	22
Poland	9	7
India	10	16

Source: United Nations Statistical Yearbook, 1981.

But the humiliation did not terminate with this new reliance on Washington. Nor did the danger end with removal of the embargo threat, for the Japanese have always been acutely aware of their dependence on external sources of raw materials and fuels. In the 1970s, with their economy the world's fastest growing, there could be no substitute for long-range certainty of stable fuel resources. After all, as early as 1972 it had been estimated that by 1985 Japan's annual consumption of energy would equal 40 percent of the total world use in 1970. In keeping with this prediction, the government had made plans for a twentyfold increase in electrical generation from nuclear fuels. It was also exploring for oil with South Korea and Taiwan, arranging for petroleum exploration in Siberia under contract with the Soviet Union, and forging joint exploration arrangements with Canada and China.

In the meantime, there was a growing gap between Japan's position as a producer of energy and its rank as a consumer, as Table 3–2 indicates. By 1976, Japan had become the world's sixth largest consumer of fuel per capita and the fourth largest in gross national consumption, while the country ranked only as the twenty-third largest producer, earning that position only by virtue of nuclear fuel development. Even today, nearly three-quarters of all energy burned in Japan is oil, approximately 80 percent of which is imported from the Middle East. Thus, fluctuations of supply occasioned by OPEC or by disruptive events in the Middle East (for example, war between Israel and the Arab states, the curtailment of exports from Iran, and the like) are particularly threatening to Japan.

Japan's immediate response to the increased oil price was to expand its industrial exports to the Middle East. Unable to compete with the United States and Europe in arms sales, however, Japan's ability to offset the rising price of oil was limited. Although it was able to increase the value of its exports to the region by more than five times in 1974, the first full year after the crisis commenced, the increased cost of petroleum importation, together with Japan's rising oil demand, resulted in a trade deficit with the Middle East of more than

$11 billion, larger than that of any other state, and an increase of 320 percent over the preceding year.[10]

Still, the problem worsens. From 1973 to 1982, the price of OPEC petroleum increased by more than 1000 percent. The revolution in Iran (1978–1979) resulted in a temporary discontinuation of oil exportation and in competitive bidding for Iranian oil, which pushed the price above OPEC levels. The war between Iran and Iraq that began in 1980 was catastrophic for Iranian oil fields, pipelines, and refining facilities, thus increasing the burden on Japan to find alternative sources of oil and substitute fuels. By early 1981, Japan was purchasing coal mines in West Virginia, negotiating with Canada for a $5 billion purchase of coal for its steel industries over a 15-year period, investing in petroleum exploration in Canada's Beaufort Sea, and considering a coal liquification plant with Canada.

The Middle Eastern events of 1978–1980, resulting in what the Japanese call the second petroleum crisis, resulted in both a reduction in volume and a 60 percent increase in price. The response was Japan's first detailed and coordinated energy policy, based not only on revised estimates of imports but also on conservation, increased reliance on nuclear fuel, and increased diversification of international sources of energy.[11]

Contemporary Japan: The Security Dilemma

One of the recurring themes of Japanese policy and of Japanese-American relations is that of burden sharing regarding the cost of Japan's security. In one respect, this is an economic matter: Because the United States has carried the economic burden of Japan's defense against aggression, the Japanese have had more funds available for capital investment and economic growth, the results of which have substantially altered the respective roles of the United States and Japan in the global economy. In another respect, it is a contradiction between the lingering Japanese notion of its role in the world, on the one hand, and the strategic realities of the Pacific, on the other.

Throughout the 1960s and 1970s, Washington repeatedly asked Tokyo to assume a larger share of the defense burden. Successive presidents and Congresses appealed to Tokyo but were generally met by conservatism driven by the Japanese notion that beyond the modest forces needed to protect the home islands against conventional invasions, it was unable to shoulder the burden of defense. And although local defense is a prerogative and responsibility of any government, the limitation of Japan's strategic reach to the East Asian region, together with its constitutional prohibition on the development of nuclear defenses, places natural limits on its defense expenditures. As a consequence, in 1976, after a full and formal study of the nation's defense needs, the Japanese Diet (parliament) adopted a policy limiting the defense budget to 1.0 percent

---

[10]Atef Sultan, "Japan Sells Hard to Make Up Oil Deficit," *Middle East Economic Digest,* December 5, 1975, pp. 5–9, 29–30.

[11]P. N. Nemetz, I. Vertinsky, and P. Vertinsky, "Japan's Energy Policy at the Crossroads," *Pacific Affairs,* Winter 1984–1985, pp. 553–576.

of its annual GNP. Because the GNP grew each year, the actual expenditure in the years immediately following adoption of the policy rose by as much as 9.0 percent.

In the years of Soviet-American détente, Washington's objection to this policy was occasional and mild. But as détente diminished and American defense spending started to mount with the first Reagan budget, demands for a larger share of the Japanese contribution to Asian security began to swell. In 1982, Washington formally asked Tokyo to raise its defense budget to 2.0 percent of its GNP, a twofold increase over the established limit. The Japanese were not entirely unprepared for this request. In 1979, a Comprehensive National Security Study Group proposed a 25.0 percent annual increase in defense expenditures to create an effective ''denial force.'' But minimal attention was paid to this recommendation because its authorship had been dominated by a group of so-called military realists who played only a small part in the broader national security debate. In 1980, however, events shed a more urgent light on the situation. As a result of a rapid Soviet military investment in the Pacific, particularly in the islands north of the home islands occupied by Soviet forces since the end of World War II, Prime Minister Yasuhiro Nakasone declared his intention to build defense forces sufficient to deny Soviet submarines passage through the four vital straits of Japan. Moscow, already angered by the Sino-Japanese Treaty of Peace and Friendship, countered with a threat of consequences worse than Hiroshima and Nagasaki. By 1983, as the Soviet force deployment altered both the nuclear and conventional balances in East Asia, by including SS-20 missiles, Backfire bombers, and a greatly expanded submarine fleet, Nakasone was able to promise President Ronald Reagan during a visit to Washington that he would create of Japan ''an unsinkable battleship'' in the Pacific.[12]

Not until 1986 did sentiment begin to rise once again for breaching the established barrier. In that year, the Japan Defense Agency released a study of the Soviet defense buildup in the region, showing the following increases over the ten-year period:

	1976	1986
SS-20 missiles	0	162
Backfire bombers	0	85
Divisions	31	41
Armed forces	300,000	370,000
Combat aircraft	2,030	2,390
Naval forces (vessels)	755	840

---

[12]For differing and representative views of the Japanese defense debate as it has evolved since 1980, see Joseph M. Ha and John Guinasso, ''Japan's Rearmament Dilemma: The Paradox of Recovery,'' *Pacific Affairs,* Summer 1980, pp. 245–268; Taketsugu Tsurutani, ''Japan's Security, Defense Responsibilities, and Capabilities,'' *ORBIS,* Spring 1981, pp. 89–106; and Frank Langdon, ''The Security Debate in Japan,'' *Pacific Affairs,* Fall 1985, pp. 397–410.

The study limited naval forces to ships of 1.25 million tons or more, and the increases during the decade were reported to include the most modern aircraft carriers, nuclear missile cruisers, and missile destroyers in the Soviet fleet worldwide.

In order to counter this potential threat, the study called for an annual military budget of 1.038 percent for the period 1986 through 1990, for a total five-year increase of $92 billion (American value). The purposes of the plan as proposed were three: (1) to improve Japan's ability to defend its air space, to protect its vital sea lanes, and to improve its ability to engage in combat in coastal waters and beyond; (2) to improve Japan's C^3I capabilities (communications, command, control, and intelligence) by such measures as the improved use of intelligence satellites; and (3) to improve Japan's ability to engage in sustained armed conflict. To meet these goals, the study called for four categories of expansion over a five-year period:

	1986	1990
Fighter aircraft	306	320
Tanks	1146	1205
Submarines	14	16
Antisubmarine patrol aircraft	76	100

Although these goals and sums are modest by Soviet and American standards, they are huge when measured against recent Japanese experience and its national vision of the necessities of security.[13] And the debate is far from conclusive, as military realism has yet to set its roots deep in Japanese society. One critic summarized for many the more conservative sentiment: "For the Japanese people, putting brakes on the expansion of their own country's military power has become Japan's international responsibility and thus a standard for national conduct."[14] At the time of writing, the extraordinary events of Eastern Europe and of Soviet-American affairs had not reached to Asia, so it was uncertain how the decisive changes in bilateral Cold War military strategies might affect the Japanese view of military expenditure.

Contemporary Japan: The Problems of Economic Success

If the cost of defense burden sharing is one of the nagging issues of Japanese-American relations, then its twin is constant friction over the differing views of these two wealthy friends on the global economy and their respective posi-

---

[13]For a review of the Japan Defense Agency White Paper and the statistical source for these passages, see Chūma Kiyokufu, "The 1986–90 Defense Plan: Does It Go Too Far?" *Japan Quarterly,* January–March 1986, pp. 13–18; and Bruce Roscoe, "Menace from Moscow," *Far Eastern Economic Review,* August 21, 1986, pp. 38–39.

[14]Odawara Atsushi, "No Tampering With the Brakes on Military Expansion," *Japan Quarterly,* July–September 1985, pp. 248–254, at pp. 248–249.

tions in it. From the American perspective, the long-term willingness to sponsor Japan's defense has given the Japanese an advantage in industrial and technological development that now has resulted in huge American balance-of-trade deficits in its economic relations with Japan, deficits that are deepened by unfair and discriminatory economic practices that limit the sale of American goods in Japan. From the Japanese perspective, the national trade advantages result from enlightened management, improving worker productivity, wise and profitable investment, and a healthy relationship between the private sector and the government, particularly as represented by the powerful Ministry of International Trade and Industry (MITI). Another view holds that the imbalance results from unrealistically high dollar values, particularly in the postrecession years of the 1980s. Still another view holds that the imbalance is an inadvertent consequence of Reaganomics, a policy of the first Reagan administration designed to reduce taxes in order to encourage greater capital accumulation in the private sector for industrial development. One Japanese observer sees the 1981 tax reductions as having created an economically damaging federal deficit requiring more dollars from a small revenue to be used for national debt service. At the same time, says this analyst, increased capital investment occurred at the expense of the savings rate. This in turn produced a huge demand for consumer goods that could not be met by domestic industry, with a sharp increase in imports and in the resulting trade imbalance.[15] A fourth view attempts to explode the myth that the Japanese economy continues to grow at a rate similar to that in the years following World War II. That study shows that although the Japanese GNP grew at an annual rate of about 10 percent from 1950 to 1973, between 1974 and 1984 the rate dropped to 3.6 percent, leaving a considerably smaller gap in the respective growth rates of the United States and Japan.[16] Table 3–3 compares several different economic indicators for the United States and Japan for the periods 1965–1980 and 1980–1987. The closing of the gap in most of these categories tells the Japanese that American complaints about industrial investment advantage are unfounded.

When any country considers its economic position, it must look beyond a single trading partner. And as Americans complain about their trade with Japan, the Japanese are well aware that the United States has trade deficits with others of its trading partners, as well. Table 3–4 compares Japanese-American trade with US trade with other industrialized partners. From these data, the Japanese conclude that to target Japan for special policies, exclusions, or retaliations is unwarranted. It is undeniably true that the largest part of the US trade deficit results from its trade with Japan. Nonetheless, it is equally true that American consumers prefer to purchase Japanese goods than the goods of any other country; and it is equally true that with the other six of the largest American trading partners, American imports exceed exports. The problem,

---

[15]Iida Tsuneo, "What Japan Can't Do About Trade Friction," *Japan Quarterly,* July–September 1986, pp. 252–255.

[16]Edward J. Lincoln, "Disentangling the Mess in US-Japan Economic Relations," *Brookings Review,* Fall 1985, pp. 22–27.

Table 3–3 Average annual growth rates 1965–1980 and 1980–1987 for the United States and Japan in selected categories.

Category	1965–1980		1980–1987	
	Japan (%)	US (%)	Japan (%)	US (%)
GDP	6.3	2.7	3.8	3.1
Industry	8.5	1.7	4.9	2.9
Manufacturing	9.4	6.7	2.5	3.9
Services	5.2	3.1	3.4	3.0

Source: World Development Report 1989, table 2, pp. 166–167.
Notes: (1) This table uses gross domestic product (GDP) rather than GNP, so it includes only goods and services produced at home and excludes all those produced by transnational affiliates; (2) manufacturing is a subset of industry and is separately reported because it is largely manufacturing output that has fueled the Japanese growth.

Table 3–4 Direction of US trade, 1987, in billions of US dollars.

Rank as US Trade Partner	US Imports	US Exports	US Balance	US Ratio Imports:Exports
1. Canada	$71.5 billion	$57.4 billion	($ 14.1 billion)	1:2
2. Japan	88.1	28.2	(59.9)	3:1
3. W. Germany	28.0	11.7	(16.3)	2:4
4. Mexico	20.5	14.6	(5.9)	1:4
5. UK	18.0	14.1	(3.9)	1:3
6. France	11.2	7.9	(3.3)	1:4
7. Brazil	8.4	4.0	(4.4)	2:1

Source: International Monetary Fund, *Direction of Trade Statistics Yearbook*, 1988, pp. 406–407.

therefore, is in the American competitive position, and the magnitude of the portion that is Japanese is no more than that.

In assessing their economic growth and trading success with other nations, the Japanese also compare themselves with the most rapidly expanding economies of Asia, and they find themselves lagging behind badly. Table 3–5 shows these comparative positions. Furthermore, while Washington looks to Tokyo as the source of most of its problems in global industrial trade, there also have been serious infractions of international trading practices in places such as South Korea and Taiwan, infractions for which the United States would more readily accuse Japan than the others.

One sympathetic American observer attempted to put the issues in perspective:

> It is easier to accept such explanations as Japan's industrial plants were devastated by a world war, and it could therefore build modern facilities; Japan copied Western technology; Japanese companies undersell American ones because they dump goods . . . ; Japanese companies succeed because they are subsidized and protected by their government; Japanese workers receive low salaries; Japanese

Table 3–5 Comparison of average annual industrial growth rates for Japan and developing Asian economies, 1965–1980 and 1980–1987.

	1965–1980 (%)	1980–1987 (%)
Japan	8.5	4.9
Malaysia	NA	5.8
South Korea	16.5	10.8
Singapore	11.9	4.0
Indonesia	11.9	2.1
Pakistan	6.4	9.1
India	4.0	7.2
	Avg. = 10.1	Avg. = 6.5
Ratios	8.5/10.1 = 0.84	4.9/6.5 = 0.75

Source: World Bank, *World Development Report 1989*, table 2, pp. 166–167. Unfortunately, this source does not report similar figures for Taiwan or Hong Kong.

companies exporting to the United States violate antitrust and customs regulations.

It is more comfortable to overlook Japan's continued modernization decades after rebuilding from World War II, its effective organization, its genius in adapting technology, its patience in marketing, its disciplined work force. It is more comfortable not to ask how its businessmen could remain so zealous in selling goods in America if they were basically selling below cost. It is disquieting to admit that the Japanese have beaten us [Americans] in economic competition because of their superior planning, organization, and effort.[17]

In this age of extreme sensitivity to conditions of the global economy and persistent official and popular talk of import restrictions, however, a more commonly encountered attitude reflects the words of John Connally, a former governor of Texas and secretary of the treasury. In an early speech to test his popularity for a run at the Republican nomination for president in 1980, he warned that unless the Japanese open their markets more to American goods, they should "be prepared to sit on the Yokohama docks in [their] Toyotas and [their] little Datsuns and watch [their] own little portable TV sets because we have all of them we need."[18]

The Japanese are proudly aware of the statistical evidence from which this American attitude stems. Since 1970, the Japanese trade position with respect to the United States has improved steadily. Table 3–6 indicates that at the

---

[17]Ezra F. Vogel, *Japan as Number One: Lessons for America* (Cambridge, Mass.: Harvard University Press, 1979), pp. 225–226. See also James C. Abegglen and Thomas H. Hout, "Facing Up to the Trade Gap With Japan," *Foreign Affairs*, Fall 1978, pp. 146–168; Richard Tanner Pascale and Anthony G. Athos, *The Art of Japanese Management* (New York: Simon & Schuster, 1981); William Ouchi, *Theory Z: How American Business Can Meet the Japanese Challenge* (Reading, Mass.: Addison-Wesley, 1981); and Edson W. Spencer, "Japan: Stimulus or Scapegoat?" *Foreign Affairs*, Fall 1983, pp. 123–137.

[18]Speech in Jacksonville, Fla., on April 27, 1979, as quoted in the *Christian Science Monitor*, May 2, 1979, p. 7.

beginning of the 1970s, the Japanese trade surplus with the United States (a measure of the relationship between imports and exports) was barely $3.2 billion. It was on the rise when the petroleum crisis intervened, after which (in 1976) a steep increase became the annual trend. In 1982, the total American trade deficit (excess of imports over exports) reached $31.7 billion, of which Japan accounted for precisely half. In the mid-1980s, the American trade deficit rose catastrophically, as did its deficit with respect to Japan. Of the total American deficit of $148 billion in 1986, $54 billion was attributed to an excess of imports from Japan, accounting for 36.5 percent of the total. As Table 3–6 indicates, however, in 1988 and 1989 Japanese exports to the United States rose less quickly that did the imports from the United States. From the Japanese perspective, this is ample evidence that they are doing everything feasible to open their import markets to American goods, despite the persistent charge from the United States of unfair and uneven trade.

Table 3–6 Japan's trade with the United States, 1971–1989, expressed in billions of US dollars.

	Japanese Imports from US	Japanese Exports to US	Total Value	Japanese Balance
1971	$ 4.1 billion	$ 7.3 billion	$ 11.4 billion	$ 3.2 billion
1972	5.0	9.1	14.1	4.1
1973	8.3	9.7	18.0	1.4
1974	10.7	12.3	23.0	1.6
1975	9.6	11.3	20.9	1.7
1976	10.1	15.5	25.6	5.4
1977	10.5	18.6	29.1	8.1
1978	12.9	24.5	37.4	11.6
1979	17.6	26.2	43.8	8.6
1980	20.8	30.7	51.5	9.9
1981	21.8	37.6	58.4	15.8
1982	21.0	37.7	58.7	16.7
1983	21.9	41.2	63.1	19.3
1984	23.6	57.1	80.7	33.5
1985	22.6	68.8	81.4	46.2
1986	26.9	81.9	108.8	55.0
1987	28.2	84.6	112.8	56.4
1988	37.1	89.8	126.9	52.6
1989	49.3	92.9	142.2	43.6

Note: For 1989, the figures are based on projections from the actual performance reported by the US government for the first three fiscal quarters.
Sources: This information is available in a variety of places, most importantly, the US Department of Commerce, *Survey of Current Business* (monthly), *The Economic Report of the President* (annual), *The Statistical Abstract of the United States* (annual), and the International Monetary Fund, *Direction of Trade Yearbook* (annual).

The deliberate policy effort to open Japan's import markets and the policy of opening Japan to foreign investment are two of the measures taken to address American complaints about uneven trade. The growing price-consciousness of the Japanese, who are accustomed to pay for a watermelon what Americans pay for a bicycle, is forcing policymakers to more liberal import policies. Yet, as the Japanese attitude about global trade evolves, a realistic sense of bilateral responsibility endures.

Some foreign criticism of Japan's lack of market openness, its free riding on the global economy, and its lack of defense consciousness is justified; and the Japanese are aware of these problems. They are endeavoring to change their practices at a speed and in ways compatible with Japan's broader national interests. But the Japanese have their own frustrations with the way America operates in the global economy. For example, much of the trade imbalance between America and Japan has been caused by the U.S. fiscal deficit, the overexpansion in domestic consumer demand, and the insistence . . . that an overvalued dollar is indicative of a strong America. It is unreasonable to call upon Japan alone to redress the imbalance. Even Americans recognize that this "credit card mentality" of sustaining the domestic economy by borrowing abroad cannot last forever.[19]

Japan, then, is willing to make policy concessions to the United States, but the problem cannot be resolved until Washington is willing to do likewise.

The emphasis in Japanese-American economic diplomacy is now clearly on Japanese imports from the United States. The improvement in the balance of imports and exports at the end of the 1980s indicates clearly that as Japan's markets open to American goods, there will be less reason for American resentment over Japan's economic triumphs. In the 1990 round of negotiations, the United States sought agreements on supercomputers, earth satellites, wood and wood products, telecommunications equipment, construction services, pharmaceuticals, and agricultural products, all of which the US government wishes to be able to market in Japan. In addition, talks included reform of Japanese land-use policies, its merchandise distribution system, and its government procurement processes that prevent foreign interests from selling directly to the Japanese government. The urgency of these talks was underscored by the fact that the Trade Act of 1988 requires the president of the United States to commence retaliatory policies against Japan if progress is not made. At the time of writing, these talks were just about to begin.[20]

Meanwhile, Japanese capital continued to sink more deeply into the economies of the world, just as Japanese goods became more and more evident. Japan's foreign investment in 1970 totaled about $3.3 billion and by 1979 had grown to about $31 billion, a tenfold increase. By 1985, it was estimated that

---

[19]Saburo Okita, "Japan's Quiet Strength," *Foreign Policy,* Summer 1989, pp. 128–145, at p. 132.
[20]This follows closely but not precisely "Carla Hills, Trade Warrior," *Business Week,* January 22, 1990, pp. 50–55.

Japan's net overseas assets reached $120 billion, with a projection of $556 billion by 1995. Approximately half of the annual increase in these assets is in North America.[21]

Matters are further complicated by Japan's awareness that the very success of its economy creates regional problems. Japan's status as the dominant economic power of Asia cannot go unnoticed by its neighbors, who will eventually compete for its markets and who are already aware of the political costs of Japan's burgeoning private investment in Asia and the Pacific.[22] Furthermore, it may be in their interests to restrict the availability of fuel to Japan. This raises still a new security imperative in view of Japan's dependence on Middle Eastern oil; it could require more than a fivefold increase in naval strength to defend their 7500-mile sea journey from source to home.[23]

The Japanese world view, then, is that of a nation that is developed economically but remains highly dependent on the resources, markets, and stable economic policies of others in order to prosper. Most especially, the view is shaped by having arrived at the threshold of world power status at a time when the power distribution is changing rapidly and the conditions of security on which Japanese economic growth has been predicated are in upheaval. As a result, the national role remains undefined, and national politics is a battleground for decisions about changes in economic and military policies.

Western Europe

Until half a century ago, world politics was Eurocentric. Europe was the center of the Industrial Revolution, home of the world's great financial capitals, site of the principal military and political rivalries, and the metropole from which vast empires were directed. Much of the world's population outside Europe, in Africa and Asia, was under European domination; and still more did Australia, North America, the Caribbean, and the Near East owe allegiance to one or other of the European powers. Even the American role in the First World War, an intense but transitory plunge into global politics, did little to alter the fundamental structure of international politics. By refusing to join the League of Nations, the United States handed back the management of international affairs to the European governments. Neither could the defeat of Germany and the realignment of old empires change the fact that world politics revolved around Europe.

But the First World War set in motion certain inexorable trends. First, it gave Americans an external vision that they had not previously had (although,

---

[21]Nigel Holloway, "Building on Empire," *Far Eastern Economic Review,* September 4, 1986, pp. 59–60; and Bruce Roscoe, "Japan Picks Winners to Hurdle the Fences," *Far Eastern Economic Review,* September 4, 1986, pp. 60–61.

[22]Jon Halliday and Gavan McCormack, *Japanese Imperialism Today* (New York: Monthly Review Press, 1973).

[23]Jay B. Sorenson, "Japan: The Dilemmas of Security," *Asian Affairs,* July–August 1975, pp. 363–370.

in general their reaction was one of withdrawal). Still, the war demands on American industry produced a most modern and productive economy. Second, Russia's participation in the war ended with the Bolshevik Revolution in 1917, which gave birth to the Soviet Union and brought the Communist party to power. With a government dedicated to the transformation of a feudal society, massive industrialization, and the defense of state against capitalist encirclement, the Soviet Union meant change for Europe and the world. Third, in settling the issues involved in the First World War, it was broadly acknowledged that imperialism and colonialism were major causes of war. The doctrine of national self-determination emerged and foretold the eventual collapse of the European empires.

In a real sense, then, the First World War launched many of the forces that the Second concluded. The Second World War left continental Europe in ruins, but American industry had grown to unprecedented capability, as it had supplied all the allies including the Soviet Union since 1941. Similarly, although Western Europe depended on the United States for reconstruction, the Soviet Union and the Eastern European states began recovery on their own. Together, these events rearranged the international power distribution so that virtually all effective power was clustered around either the United States or the Soviet Union. Europe was cordoned into the Soviet-allied Eastern sector and the American-allied Western sector. World politics was no longer Eurocentric but bipolar, a configuration in which, far from being the pivotal point of global relations, Western Europe was an object of conflict between the two giants.

From this unaccustomed position, Western Europe looked to the United States for both defense and economic regeneration, objectives in which the United States readily assisted. Apart from America's European roots and heritage, the Cold War confrontation with the Soviet Union dictated that the United States act to preserve democratic polities and free-market economies wherever possible, particularly in Western Europe. This policy, although always expressed in ideological terms, had the firm support of American merchants and manufacturers (whose production surplus cried out for external markets) and of American labor (which equally needed external buyers to maintain full employment). The investment community lent its support, too, on the grounds that a reconstructed Europe would borrow American capital and that a Western Europe staunchly defended from the menace of Soviet invasion would be a safe place for investment. Basic American Cold War foreign policies, enunciated from 1947 through 1949, arose out of the ideological threat and from the convergence of all these interests and were aimed at the reconstruction of Europe. These included the European Recovery Plan (the Marshall Plan) of 1947, in which Washington committed almost $15 billion to Western Europe's revitalization; the Truman Doctrine (1947), which proclaimed Washington's intention to resist the territorial advance of communism and on which the containment policy was based; and the institutionalization of European-American defense in the North Atlantic Treaty Organization (NATO) in 1949. Each of these moves presupposed a prolonged threat of Soviet aggression.

During the era of Europe's recovery and of agreement on the imminence of the Soviet threat, the cooperation forged by the Marshall Plan and NATO was constructive. But as Europe neared full restoration and as the threat of war abated by the late 1950s, trans-Atlantic strains began to develop. Most of these occurred in the economic sphere, although there was a loss of harmony on security matters as well. Most important in both categories, however, was the uniting of Europe, a process of economic consolidation for more successful competition with the United States and a revitalized Japan. As the states of Western Europe grew more interdependent after 1958, they asserted greater independence of the United States. American efforts to maintain the tenor of the trans-Atlantic partnership after the restoration of Western Europe fueled the potential conflict among allies.

The Uniting of Europe

When the European Recovery Plan was launched in 1947, the United States encouraged common economic planning among the aid recipients. The strategy for designing grant requests was for the European governments to study their common needs, design a policy among them, and submit a joint proposal to Washington. This was the beginning of cooperative economic planning, an idea that took firm root by 1958. At that time, the economies of the region were rapidly fulfilling their recovery expectations, and the fear of invasion from Eastern Europe seemed remote. Now, however, while their individual economies were thriving (although not all equally), they realized their inability to compete with the United States. The American postwar starting point enabled the United States to outrace Europe in the production of goods that sold better even in European markets than did European goods. Another reason for the noncompetitive position of the Europeans was that their national economies were too small to encourage the most efficient production. Furthermore, Europe was slow to develop its own capital market, and American money for multiplication of production facilities was scarce in this period, though it later became so abundant that its value dropped drastically. For all these reasons and more, the states of Western Europe seized upon the idea of a supranational economy, in which the economic needs of the group would supersede those of any single state and in which trade among members would be facilitated while the entry of foreign goods would become more difficult.[24]

The European Community (EC) is composed of several constituent organizations, each designated a "community." Principal among these are the European Economic Community (EEC), the European Coal and Steel Community

---

[24]For a review of the historical passage from cooperation to competition with an essentially European perspective, see Ernst H. van der Beugel, *From Marshall Aid to Atlantic Partnership* (Amsterdam: Elsevier, 1966); and Henry A. Kissinger, *The Troubled Partnership: A Re-Appraisal of the Atlantic Alliance* (New York: McGraw-Hill, 1965). For a study of European alternative strategies for effective global competition, see Alastair Buchan, *Europe's Future, Europe's Choices: Models of Western Europe in the 1970's* (New York: Columbia University Press, 1969). For an American interpretation sympathetic to the European, see Richard J. Barnet, *The Alliance* (New York: Simon & Schuster, 1983).

(ECSC), and the European Atomic Energy Commission (EURATOM). This text will use EC to refer to the larger community and EEC to identify the economic subsystem alone.

Because of its traditional reluctance to enter continental affairs and in part its unwillingness to join a French-inspired venture, the British government elected to take its own course. Hence, as the EEC (or European Common Market) was established by six European states, the British set up the competing European Free Trade Area (EFTA). Together the Common Market and the EFTA included virtually all of industrial Western Europe. The EEC, with its larger industrial potential and its greater demand for industrial goods (particularly as EFTA became weakened by the declining British economy), was measurably the more successful of the two and, accordingly, the one that tended to widen further the trans-Atlantic division. France blocked Britain's attempt to leave EFTA and join the EEC in 1963 because of President Charles de Gaulle's fervent desire ''to de-Americanize'' Europe, a goal that he deemed unattainable if Britain were to enter while retaining its special relationship with the United States. It was not until 1973 that Britain joined the EEC, together with Denmark and Ireland, leaving EFTA divided but increasing the EEC from The Six to The Nine. Together, the enlarged Economic Community had a GNP of over $1 trillion, which was equivalent to 83 percent of the United States' GNP. In the next three years, although the GNP of the EEC continued to grow, it dropped to 78 percent of the United States' GNP. In the years following, however, and with the addition of Greece to the community in 1981, the economic performance of the EC grew steadily in comparison with the United States. With Greece contributing only $43 billion to the economic performance of the community, the total community GNP reached a level of 95 percent of that of the United States. With the increase to a membership of 12, the EC begins to approximate the GNP of the United States. The latest comprehensive figures are for 1987 (see Table 3–7), and they indicate that the 12 members of the EC had an aggregate GNP in 1987 equal to 92 percent of that of the United States.

Beyond these raw facts lies a single compelling conclusion: Acting in concert, the member states of the EC comprise one of the most productive, and therefore most powerful and influential, actors on the international stage. Despite their individual problems, their disparities, their separate national identities, and the disagreements among them, it is as a composite whole rather than as individual states that they play a critical role in contemporary international relations. Together, they are working to restore Western Europe as a principal world center rather than an area of Soviet-American competition or a handmaiden of American foreign policy. It is the world perspective of this ''United States of Europe'' that we will explore here.

One point merits emphasis. It cannot be said that on all issues there is a definable ''Western European world view''; rather, there is a French world view, a German world view, and so on. One French observer put it this way:

> In order to do a better job of analyzing the relations between Western Europe and the United States, one has to consider successively the dialogues between

Table 3–7 Comparison of economic performances of the United States and the EEC, 1987.

Country	GNP, 1987 (billions)
Belgium	$ 138.5
Denmark	97.5
France	846.9
Greece	45.9
Ireland	25.6
Italy	632.1
Luxembourg	6.2
Netherlands	213.5
Portugal	33.4
Spain	284.0
United Kingdon	666.7
West Germany	1129.9
Total EC	4120.2
United States	4488.5

Source: Statistical Abstract of the United States, 1989, p. 823.

Bonn and Washington, London and Washington, Paris and Washington, all of which differ from one another. More precisely, it is desirable to separate two problems: (a) the attitude of the American government toward the European Community, or more generally, the effort to create a European unity; and (b) the attitude of the American government toward the different European governments in respect to the various problems posed. *There is no global dialogue taking place between Europe as an entity and the United States.*[25]

But although, indeed, there may be no such dialogue at present, the issue at question here is somewhat different. Our concern is not with the unique national differences in relations with the United States, but with the common effort to establish an economic and security community from which to compete more effectively in global economic relations and to reduce security dependence on Washington. Hence, the focus of this analysis is on the compound force rather than on the individual member states.

European-American Trade

The prime economic rationale underlying the EC is the theory of customs union, which seeks to expand trade among the members by eliminating tariffs and other trade barriers among them and to guard against foreign imports by setting a common trade policy toward nonmembers. Through this device, the

[25]Raymond Aron, "Europe and the United States: The Relations Between Europeans and Americans," in David S. Landes, ed., *Western Europe: The Trials of Partnership* (Lexington, Mass.: Lexington Books, 1977), p. 27. Emphasis added.

EC pursues economic stimulation by capturing a larger share of the European market and by generating investment capital for expanding production for external competition. The central objective is improved competitive position, although it was evident from the start that such competition would eventually run afoul of the American economic nationalism. This was accepted by Europe as a natural extension of the cooperative recovery assisted earlier by the United States.

While Europeans looked forward to trade equality with the United States and to the profitability of their customs union, Americans were quickly awakened to their potential losses. In a preventive step, Congress passed the Trade Expansion Act of 1962, which authorized the executive branch to negotiate sweeping tariff reductions. To Europe the objective was self-evident: Americans, concerned that the toddling EC might erode their lucrative export surplus, were searching for ways to reduce its competitive position. Because of these negotiations and despite dire American predictions of trade loss, the composite EEC trade balance for any typical year shows a slight deficit, with only Germany turning up a significant surplus. For the remainder of the community, the trading relationship with the United States is stable, with only France showing a trend toward deepening deficit.

Europeans consider American efforts to manipulate the EC's trade balance, and particularly to undermine Germany's surplus, to be retaliations for Europe's success. This was especially pronounced in 1971, when the United States increased import tariffs by 10 percent in an attempt at economic stabilization. Because they considered this an assault on European competition and on the value of German currency, the EC economic ministers jointly labeled the tariff increase a step short of an American declaration of trade warfare. They pledged that if the new and illegal tariff were not discontinued within 90 days, they would respond by increasing the barriers to American trade in Europe. A multilateral agreement on changes in currency valuations averted a showdown. The near-crisis demonstrated, nevertheless, the awareness by Europeans and Americans of the degree of damage that each can inflict upon the other in international trade.

By the middle of the 1980s, exchanges of threats of trade retaliation and trade warfare were common, not only between the United States and Western Europe, but also between the two of them and Japan. Just as it became common knowledge that the unity of the Japanese-American alliance was endangered by economic discord, so too did it become widely known and accepted that the Atlantic Alliance was wracked with discontent over both economic issues and the cost of security burden sharing. The United States and the EC exchanged threats of trade retaliation over agricultural products, cotton, wines, many industrial goods, and even commercial jet aircraft, with respect to which the United States charged the EC governments with subsidizing aircraft parts in such a way as to make Europe-built craft a better bargain to American air carriers than were those built in the United States. These factors led one American to observe that in the present decade, ''Alliance governments are more anxious to defend their economic autonomy than to pay their share of collective defense burdens.''

Specifically, the trans-Atlantic economic acrimony centers on six elements:

1. The growing use of trade restrictions by governments in efforts to protect domestic industries from foreign competition within the domestic market.
2. The growing use of export subsidies by governments in order to promote domestic employment and to expand the export sector by reducing the apparent cost of production.
3. Frequent manipulation of domestic interest rates and adjustment of currency exchange rates in order to reduce domestic inflation and to make exported goods more attractive abroad by making them less expensive in comparison with similar goods produced in the host economy.
4. The emergence of national industrial policies in which the government becomes a "partner" in phasing out failing industries and in sponsoring new ones, in order to overcome in the world's markets those goods produced entirely by private investment in competitor economies.
5. Disagreement over the value of trade with the Soviet Union and Eastern European countries, with some (for example, the United States) attempting to use trade limitations as a means of political leverage, and others (for example, the EC) looking past ideological factors to trade as a means of expanding domestic employment and balancing trade performance.
6. The use of individualized national policies to take maximum short-term advantage of trade with the Third World, whereas others have preferred taking less advantage while awaiting effective international management of the North-South trading axis.[26]

Despite the growth of conservative political influences in Britain, France, West Germany, and, to a lesser degree, Italy and Spain, the EC governments were unanimous in their separation from the Reagan government on the view that the evil character of the Soviet Union should determine the economic segregation of West from East. This, together with other American tendencies to disregard the European world view, was viewed broadly by Europeans as America's newfound unilateralism. By the end of 1985, fully 300 individual pieces of protectionist (trade restriction) legislation were before the Congress. But as evidence of the growing bilateral tendency toward reciprocal—even retaliatory—trade restraint, an OECD study showed that the amount of American industrial imports subjected to trade restriction rose from 6 percent in 1980 to 13 percent in 1983. In the same period, the amount of industrial imports subjected to trade restraint by the EEC rose from 11 percent to 15 percent.[27]

Contrary to public perception, European-American trade competition is not limited to industrial produce. Particularly during the 1980–1983 recession, when world industrial trade dropped steadily and the American balance of

---

[26]Adapted from Walter Goldstein, "Economic Discord in the Atlantic Alliance," in Robert J. Jackson, ed., *Continuity of Discord: Crises and Responses in the Atlantic Community* (New York: Praeger, 1985), pp. 183–199.

[27]Thierry de Montbrial, "The European Dimension," *Foreign Affairs,* America and the World 1985 issue, pp. 499–514.

trade fell dangerously, competition in agricultural trade eroded the spirit of partnership. As wheat prices fell and stocks accumulated, particularly in the United States, European grain exports doubled. The increase resulted in part from the Soviet preference for European grain (after the United States broke an agreement and embargoed grain to the Soviet Union in response to the Afghanistan and Poland events) and in part from a disagreement between the EEC and Washington on the interpretation of certain export provisions oɪ agreements resulting from the 1979 Tokyo round of negotiations of the General Agreement on Tariffs and Trade.[28] This type of disagreement is likely to recur as the EEC seeks a diversified export base and as the United States relies increasingly on agricultural exports to balance its trade against superior competition in industrial goods from Europe and Japan.

Increasingly two specific factors dominate the economic discussion between the EC and the United States. The first, one that has been accumulating importance for a decade, is the twin trade and budgetary deficits of the United States. Although Americans complain that their trade deficit with respect to the EC results from uneven and, therefore, unfair trading practices in Europe, Western Europeans find the problem in the inability of the United States to control its budgetary deficit. The United States lives beyond its means, and its apparent prosperity and prolonged recovery from the recession of the early 1980s is masked by its borrowing abroad and by the insatiable appetite of Americans for European and Japanese goods. The American trade deficit, then, is not a result of unfair practices abroad, but of fiscal mismanagement in the United States.

The second of these factors dates to 1954, when the process of European economic integration began. The end of 1992 has been set as the date for completion of the union, although many important principles were unsettled at the beginning of 1990, such as the use of a single currency, changes in principles of transnational investment, and others. As the date of union approaches, Western Europeans fear that Americans will blame them increasingly for their international economic problems: that America's shortcomings will be laid to Western Europe's successes. Because the problem lies really with American fiscal management and with "paying the bill for the Reagan years," the prospective consequences of this misunderstanding on the American part are daunting to Western Europeans. The latter would prefer to see union of The Twelve as ushering in not new and bigger barriers to trade, but a "competitive revolution."[29]

The unknown element is the economic direction and fate of the Eastern European nations freed in the 1989–90 from the planned production and distribution of the COMECON, virtually all of which was designed to benefit the Soviet Union as the defender of the socialist commonwealth of the region and of proletarian internationalism universally. On the one hand, these economies

---

[28]Nicholas Butler, "The Ploughshares War Between Europe and America," *Foreign Affairs,* Fall 1983, pp. 105–122.

[29]George Taucher, "1992: A Competitive Revolution," *European Affairs,* Winter 1989, pp. 53–60.

Source: © Van Howell.

are backward and failing fast. On the other hand, they contain inestimable opportunity for reconstruction and development. Will Western European union give the EC a competitive edge here? What combination of private investment and government aid will stimulate these economies? Will the union eventually spread eastward? As central Europe for 45 years was the security preoccupation of the West, today, both by itself and because of the coincidence of its liberation with Western European economic union in 1992, it is the subject of economic and political-economic conjecturing.

From the European perspective, trade difficulties are but part of the economic discord with the United States. The other issue that fogs the route to full and equal competition is the American ownership of European production through direct foreign investment.

American Direct Investment in Europe

The uniting of Europe commenced at a time when American investors were seeking external opportunities and when, in an effort to improve efficiency, industries were becoming multinational. Because the maturation of European customs unions threatened their exports, American manufacturers wished to get behind the tariff barriers presented by EFTA and the EC, by buying and building plants in European nations as foreign subsidiaries. These would manufacture goods primarily for sale in Europe. Such goods, although bringing profit to American corporations, would be free of import duties in European markets. Subsequent increases in productivity would be financed not from fresh American capital but from profit, the remainder of which would be repatriated and thereby removed from the European economy. The initial investment in this trend, recorded as capital leaving the United States, rose to such heights that the American balance of payments, already adversely affected by military commitment in Vietnam, slipped into severe deficit. President Lyndon B. Johnson responded by introducing a voluntary restraints program in which American firms were requested to moderate their foreign capital expenditures. But despite these pleas, by 1967 American firms controlled nearly 8000 foreign subsidiaries, of which nearly half were in the EFTA and EC countries.[30] Of these, two-thirds were in Britain, France, Germany, and Italy. The continuing outflow of capital for this purpose resulted in the imposition of mandatory controls in 1968.[31]

Table 3–8 demonstrates the volume of direct American investment in the combined EC economy. Measured by the extent to which America's total world direct investment is located in the EC, the facts are even more striking: In 1970, American direct investment in the EC totaled 27 percent of the world-

Table 3–8 American direct investment (total book value) in the EC, 1960–1988.

Year	US$ (billions)
1960	5.9
1965	11.4
1970	20.1
1973	31.3
1978	56.0
1982	77.7
1984	78.9
1988	126.5

Source: Statistical Abstract of the United States for 1975, 1977, 1979, 1981, 1982/83, and 1986; and *Survey of Current Business*, August 1988. For the years prior to 1973, the original six members and Britain are used. Denmark and Ireland are added in 1973, Greece in 1982, and Spain and Portugal in 1988.

---

[30]Raymond Vernon, *Sovereignty at Bay: The Multinational Spread of US Enterprises* (New York: Basic Books, 1971), p. 141.

[31]US Department of Commerce, *The Multinational Corporations: Studies in US Foreign Investment,* 1972.

wide amount; by 1978, the fraction had risen to 33 percent, and by 1988 to 39 percent ($126.5 billion out of a global total of $326.9 billion). From the European perspective, in an age in which the net American investment position fell into deficit (more American assets owned by non-Americans than foreign interests held by Americans), US investors were striking it rich through their direct investments within the EC.

The prevalence of American capital and the extensive American ownership of European production led to severe disenchantment among those Europeans who previously expected effective competition with the United States both inside Europe and out. Some called upon Europeans to restore their own economic destiny by adopting American managerial techniques.[32] Others, such as President de Gaulle, insisted that the only path to effective competition was the "de-Americanization of Europe." Although this theme was not universally espoused among the EC members, it was widely felt that continued American domination of European capital and production not only deferred equal competition but actually placed Europe in a position of dependency and colonization. This made a double blow of American retaliations for Europe's success. Furthermore, because American firms effectively penetrated the customs union and thus prevented European firms from dominating their own markets, the latter's share of European markets may be too small to stimulate the most efficient production. As a result, the regional idea rapidly gave way to corporate demands for globalization of European industries. Thus, more and more European industries, which were previously considered the foundations of regional integration, are going multinational instead.[33]

By 1990, just two years prior to the expectation of full union among the Twelve, the facts surrounding these arguments had evolved considerably. Combined, the EC states comprised a larger population and a larger internal market than the United States. Furthermore, the presence of American industrial subsidiaries helped reduce unemployment throughout Europe. And as the cost of production in the United States led many corporations to depend on their external subsidiaries, Europe now counted among its exports many goods that previously were made in the United States. Add to these the net improvement in public tax revenues from Americans producing in Europe, the favorable balance of trade in the EC with respect to the United States, and the speed with which Western Europeans, particularly British, Dutch, and French, were buying assets in the United States, including US Treasury securities, real estate, and industrial subsidiaries. By 1990, then, European fears of American direct investment had dwindled to almost nothing, as the net investment position of the EC improved against that of the United States.

Noneconomic Strains

In addition to persisting economic matters, which ensure that the Euro-American relationship will always be one as much of competition as of coop-

[32]J. J. Servan-Schreiber, *The American Challenge* (New York: Avon Books, 1968).
[33]Raymond Vernon et al., *Big Business and the State: Changing Relations in Western Europe* (Cambridge, Mass.: Harvard University Press, 1974).

eration, there are a number of underlying issues in the relationship that lead to doubt and occasional disruption. One of these involved the natural tension between the United States as a trans-Atlantic power and the United States as a global power. Europeans have frequently objected to non-European American foreign policies that are inconsistent with Europe's aims in the world or that are undertaken at risk to the trans-Atlantic community without consultation with the European partners.

Occasionally, this "fitful rush toward global unilateralism," as one European calls it, strikes directly at the partnership with considerable cost to the European interest.[34] The most outstanding example was the effort of President Ronald Reagan to prevent the construction of a gas pipeline from Siberia to Europe, through which the European governments would have bought millions of dollars worth of natural gas annually. When the Europeans themselves refused under American pressure to discontinue the contract with the Soviet Union, President Reagan attempted to thwart their desires by threatening with prosecution any American firm or European-based affiliate of any American firm that participated in any way in the sale, planning or installation of parts of the pipeline. The United States argued over a ten-month period in 1981 and 1982 that it opposed the pipeline because it did not want European economic and military strategies to become dependent on a source of fuel that could be discontinued at any time. The Europeans, however, responded that the policy was inspired by an inappropriate attempt on the part of the Reagan administration to couple Europe's fuel needs with the American effort to impose economic sanctions on the Soviet Union for its use of martial law in Poland to crush the independent Solidarity labor movement. The matter was settled in favor of the European view after nearly a year of discontent and in the context of larger trade issues involving European steel exports.

Largest among the causes of European-American discord, however, was the widening gap on interpreting Soviet foreign policy, particularly in Europe. While the United States engaged in an endless barrage of rhetoric about Soviet intentions of global conquest, Europeans took the view that although the Soviet Union was more powerful than a decade ago, its influence had actually waned.[35] In a rare break from President Reagan's policies, British Prime Minister Margaret Thatcher said in 1984 that the West must do more to secure the confidence of the Kremlin on matters of arms competition and control, even while Washington blamed the discontinuation of three different arms negotiations on the Soviets.

By 1984, the difference between the dominant European view of the Soviet Union and that of the Reagan administration was so great that many Europeans were questioning the capability of American foreign policy to adjust to world realities. The issue was sufficiently serious to merit the extensive quotation of one British writer. Noting that there were two views of the American under-

---

[34]Josef Joffe, "Europe and America: The Politics of Resentment (cont'd)," *Foreign Affairs,* America and the World 1982 issue, pp. 567–590, at p. 567.

[35]For a detailed analysis, see Jonathan Steele, *Soviet Power: The Kremlin's Foreign Policy—Brezhnev to Andropov* (New York: Simon & Schuster, 1983). Steele is a British news correspondent.

standing of Soviet policy, he rejected the first, namely, that after a decade of weakness and humiliation, America is now preparing to stall the spread of Soviet influence.

> The other view is shared to a greater or lesser extent by much of the rest of mankind. . . . It is that the Reagan Administration has vastly overreacted to the Soviet threat, thereby distorting the American (and hence the world) economy, quickening the arms race, warping its own judgment about events in the Third World, and further debasing the language of international intercourse with feverish rhetoric. A subsidiary charge, laid principally by Europeans, Canadians and many Latin Americans, is that in a desperate desire to rediscover "leadership," the United States under Reagan has reverted to its world unilateral habits, resenting and ignoring, when it deigns to notice, the independent views and interests of its friends and allies.
>
> It is in my experience almost impossible to convey even to the most experienced Americans just how deeply rooted and widely spread the critical view has become. It is, however, worth recalling . . . that a devastating but entirely reputable opinion poll taken in January [1983] . . . showed that no less than 70 percent of the British lacked any confidence in the judgment of the American Administration. This did not mean that they were neutralist or soft on communism or anything of the kind; on the contrary, their answers to another question proved that they were overwhelmingly in favor of NATO. It simply showed that they did not trust President Reagan and gave him no credit for successful leadership. Similar polls have been taken in other European countries, but the appearance of these sentiments in Britain, the most solid and phlegmatic member of the Alliance, may legitimately be regarded as a measure of the chasm that lies between current American perceptions of the world and the world's perception of America.[36]

Such a broad critique of American attitudes was symbolic of the deterioration of trust between Europe and the United States, an erosion that found its way not only into economic matters but into commonly held security matters as well. From the European perspective, NATO continued to play its original role of forming the first line of defense against any Soviet threat, but it was also the focal point of divergent notions about strategies, arms control, troop deployments, military appropriations, defense burden sharing, and a host of other issues that lie at the interface of military strategy and the politics of alliance. Most distressing of all was the possibility that in preparing for a limited nuclear war "both winnable and survivable," the Pentagon might have been basing its nuclear strategy on the unspoken premise of using Western Europe as a line of defense for the United States. (The actual issues of nuclear and conventional forces in NATO are discussed in Chapters 10 and 11.)

All this evolved with exceptional speed in the latter half of the 1980s. Despite their disdain for President Reagan's unilateral announcement at the hast-

---

[36]From David Watt, "As a European Saw It," reprinted by permission from *Foreign Affairs*, America and the World 1983 issue, pp. 521–532, at pp. 521–522. Copyright 1983 by the Council on Foreign Relations, Inc.

ily planned Reykjavik summit with Gorbachev in 1986, a declaration made in consultation with European leaders, most heralded the removal of the INFs the following year. They rejoiced in Gorbachev's announcement in a speech at the United Nations of unilateral troop reductions in Eastern Europe. And they watched with awe Gorbachev's willingness to permit virtually all of Eastern Europe to abandon (and in the case of Romania, overthrow) communist rule and launch processes of both political and economic liberalism. To a large extent, while Americans proclaimed 1989 the year in which Ronald Reagan won the Cold War, Western Europeans took the view that the arms buildup and the rhetoric of the first Reagan administration had actually revitalized a dormant Cold War, and that the vision of Gorbachev and the spirit of Eastern European peoples had simply called off the Cold War.

The European Community and Trans-Atlantic Defense

If the emphasis of the EC is on regionalism, then the underlying postulate of the Western security system is Atlanticism. And if the United States relates to the EC in the economic sphere as an overbearing competitor, then it presents itself to the European members of NATO as a dominant partner, unsure of its objectives but resistant to change in its stature. As in the economic sphere, the community members acknowledge their reliance on the United States but deplore the political and economic consequences of imbalance. Is American control of trans-Atlantic defense policy an instrument for preventing a marked alteration of political and economic relations? Is it a means by which Washington and its economic interests pursue economic Atlanticism as an alternative to effective competition from a united Europe? Is European integration feasible in the presence of a NATO as presently structured? Is NATO integrative of Atlanticism but disintegrative of Europeanism?

Despite the clear European dilemma on the security issue, however, there is among the NATO partners considerable fragmentation of perception. Until 1990, all suffered a degree of anxiety concerning the acknowledged superiority of the Warsaw Pact's conventional forces, although Germany and France were more alarmed about the growing nuclear threat posed by the strategic competition of the USSR and the United States. During the 1970s, Washington pressed the Europeans for a redistribution of the costs of the alliance, calling for a greater European contribution so that the United States might diminish its burden. With the onset of the 1980s, Washington saw a need for allies on both sides of the Atlantic to increase their commitments, and talk in the Senate of a reduced American share vanished until 1987. At that time, in view of the increased reliance of American policy on intermediate-range missiles and dissatisfaction over the refusal of the European allies to increase their contributions to cost burden sharing in NATO, the United States once again debated the removal of 100,000 troops from Europe. Removal of those troops and their dependents would have had severe consequences for some of the European economies and would have widened still further the gap between NATO's conventional forces and those of the Warsaw Pact nations.

Nevertheless, Europeans continued to differ in their attitudes toward the imminence of danger from the East. The more liberal elements argued that the Soviet Union's demands for a stable European balance had been satiated by 1980 and that the NATO deployment of Pershing II and land-based cruise missiles beginning at the end of 1983 was a destabilizing event that called for further Soviet deployments. The more conservative, on the other hand, argued that the Soviet Union had been quietly building its strike forces in order to exploit any weakness in Western defenses. To these people, Soviet deployments following the arrival of the first new American missiles were evidence of aggressive Soviet intentions for both conventional and nuclear superiority across the East-West border of Europe. The Kremlin's refusal to continue the Strategic Arms Reduction Talks (START), the INF Talks, and the Mutual Balanced Force Reduction Talks (MBFR) at the end of 1983 was seen by the conservative camp as further evidence of Soviet intentions to secure superiority.

Of these two positions, the former was dominant in Europe and the latter in the United States. The difference between them went beyond simple disagreement. That the views should have emerged into prominence during the debate over the new missile deployments indicates fundamentally different premises for the nuclear weapons of NATO. One European observer put it this way:

> In the past, Europeans had tended to view nuclear weapons both as a means of last resort and as an alternative to expensive conventional defense. The United States, on the other hand, had increasingly come to regard nuclear weapons as an integral part of the military effort, designed to provide a spectrum of deterrence across the range of conceivable military contingencies. Both of these approaches were challenged by the missile controversy, and their contradictions revealed: in Europe, the unreasonably high dependence on nuclear weapons for defense; in the United States, the impermissible slide from deterring to contemplating fighting a nuclear war.[37]

But beyond questions of strategy are matters of dependence. Throughout NATO's history, the European partners have felt themselves subject to American strategy, command, and equipment decisions. In response, the French in 1965 removed themselves from the NATO integrated command (although not from the organization itself) and ordered NATO headquarters and all military personnel and equipment not under the command of the French government removed from French soil. More typically, however, NATO members have attempted to resolve cooperatively the dilemma of Atlanticism and Europeanism. Within Europe, for example, both Britain and France have undertaken independent nuclear policies, each premised not on the thought of destroying a potential enemy but on that of developing the capability to inflict intolerable harm: a policy of minimal deterrence.[38] These national developments resulted

---

[37]Christopher Bertram, "Europe and America in 1983," *Foreign Affairs*, America and the World 1983 issue, pp. 616–631, at pp. 628–629.

[38]For a study that indicates a probably illegal association of the United States with the French

in public debate about the creation of an Anglo-French deterrent, a prospective policy of combining British and French nuclear capabilities under a planning system that will reduce the dependence on American strategy. Furthermore, the Eurogroup within NATO continues to press collectively for a greater European voice in the strategic planning of NATO, an effort designed to take maximum advantage of the American commitment while minimizing European servitude to Washington's objectives for the alliance. None of these efforts, though, can deal effectively with a confrontation with the conventional military strength of the Warsaw Pact without American participation. Americans, then, ask the question, "How much longer must we bear the cost of Western Europe's defense even while suffering from increasingly effective European economic competition?" Simultaneously, Western Europeans are asking, "How can we reduce our reliance on the United States without emasculating the alliance to the point at which the balance of forces across all of Europe is irreparably damaged? And how can we promote Europeanism without eroding Atlanticism to the point of inviting American retaliation and coercion?" To Americans, the costs of NATO are unevenly divided because they carry the bulk of the economic burden. But Western Europeans have always believed that they themselves have assumed the social and political costs of the reliance on Washington. As long as the costs are perceived and measured differently, the tension between Atlanticism and Europeanism will persist, and the Western European perception of the global system will continue to focus more nervously on the dangers imposed by its closest non-European friend than on any anticipated threat within Europe.

Quite obviously, even before 1990 the choice was never between NATO and no NATO, but between a security alliance fraught with conflict or one in which the costs of alliance were tolerable to all parties in military, political, and economic terms. In the words of one European, "The Western Europeans, suffering from perceived U.S. heavy-handedness, want a safety net and not a straitjacket."[39] By 1990, however, this was not only perfectly clear, but doubly important. For in that year, as the collapse of communist governments throughout Eastern Europe reduced the Warsaw Pact to shambles and the Soviets agreed that a reunified Germany might be a member of NATO, the future of NATO itself came into question. Is NATO now an obsolete security system? To some in both Western Europe and the United States, the question was premature. Others, thinking along the lines of Mikhail Gorbachev, assumed that the alliance would retain its political purposes despite its decline as a security system. Many Europeans, conscious of the degree of political might wielded by Washington through NATO, preferred to think along lines drawn by an earlier American observer: Without the constant threat of a unifying enemy, NATO is incapable of sustained purpose.[40] Still others feared that the United

---

nuclear forces (*force de frappe*), see Richard H. Ullman, "The Covert French Connection," *Foreign Policy,* Summer, 1989, pp. 3–33.

[39]Peter Bender, "The Superpower Squeeze," *Foreign Policy,* Winter 1986–87, pp. 98–113.

[40]George Ball, "Europe Without a Unifying Adversary," in G. R. Urban, ed., *Détente* (New York: Universe Books, 1976), pp. 229–242.

". . . Look out for partial clearing in Poland with scattered uprisings across the Baltic states . . . further south, continued flash floods of humanity rush from East Germany clear across Czechoslovakia and Hungary into Austria with expected highs in the thousands and a 35 percent chance of continued glasnost. . ."
Source: © Walt Handelsman/The Times Picayune/Tribune Media Services.

States would cling to NATO after the demise of its security value because of the political objective of what Americans called "alliance management."[41]

Western Europe After the Cold War

Western Europeans consider themselves to be on the threshold of a great adventure in a time at which the forces of history permit bold, imaginative policies. The completion of economic union in 1992, together with the liberation of virtually all of Eastern Europe, seems to return Europe's destiny to Europeans after for nearly half a century in which Europe lay between the two great poles of a Soviet-American world structure. NATO and the Warsaw Pact seem to be on the verge of extinction; the preservation of the Soviet state in the Gorbachev era has virtually removed the threat of war in Central Europe; economic issues have replaced security in dominance of the political agenda; and the insolvency of the United States calls for a reduction of its reliance on foreign policy through alliance management. They are determined that the final take-off of the EC will not be delayed by the remnants of the Cold War, by

[41]Although this was not a new expression, it was given more urgent meaning in 1983. At that time, one US government official declared that American pressure on Europe for the installation of new nuclear weapons was "not for security at all, but for alliance management." See Richard A. Burt, *Time*, December 5, 1983, p. 29. For a study of this notion, see Lawrence Freedman, "Managing Alliances," *Foreign Policy*, Summer 1988, pp. 65–85.

The Berlin Wall, for 28 years the symbol of a divided Europe, becomes a festive gathering place for East and West Berliners as the two Germanys moved toward unification, 1990.
Source: © 1989 Burnett/Contact Press Images.

the legacy of an outmoded NATO, or by the reluctance of the United States to alter the bases of its foreign policy in an age of revolutionary peaceful change based on economic competition rather than military confrontation.

Canada

If there is one indicator to differentiate the relationship of the United States with Japan and Western Europe from that with Canada, it is proximity. Like its Asian and European counterparts, Canada shares an extensive economy and security relationship with the United States. But that relationship has the added features of a 3000-mile undefended border and a long tradition of intimate economic cooperation. Although until the end of the Second World War Canadian economic and political relations were closely tied to the United Kingdom, the predominance of the American economy since the war and the aggressive diffusion of American capital have reversed this course. At present, the trading relation between Canada and the United States reaches an annual value exceeding that of any other bilateral economic relation in history ($167 billion in 1989); such has been the case for over a decade.

Canada's total economic capacity at present ranks ninth in the world by GNP and thirteenth by GNP per capita. Also, its capacity is increasing because of its vast mineral reserves. Supporting a population of only 24 million

(10 percent that of the United States and only 20 percent that of Japan) in one of the world's largest territorial masses will enable Canada to preserve its natural resources longer than most nation-states can, although at the present rates of extraction the petroleum and natural gas reserves (those presently known) will have been depleted within 25 years.

But despite these apparent foundations for national autonomy, the geographical closeness of the United States has fostered a pattern of investment, trade, and managerial control leading to what some call partnership and others label a colonial relationship. Still others are tempted to refer to an integrated Canadian-American economy, although such an observation ignores the asymmetry of benefits. The conditions that surround the effort to establish full economic, cultural, and political sovereignty out of this lopsided partnership govern the Canadian world perspective.

Domestic Influences Affecting the Canadian World View

Canadian domestic politics is divided along several firmly drawn lines. Most significant among them is the ethnic distinction between the dominant Anglo-Canadians and the French-Canadians, who are concentrated in Quebec Province. Although French-Canadians consider themselves a nation within a nation, only at the extreme is French-Canadian nationalism separatist. They are deeply persuaded that as a minority they have been exploited and oppressed by the English. Nevertheless, in their external outlook they are concerned for Canada's economic independence from the United States. As a self-proclaimed oppressed minority, they were unusually sympathetic to young Americans who emigrated to Canada rather than serve in the armed forces in Vietnam and whose criticism of American foreign policy and of the American establishment accentuated the appetite for Canadian autonomy even more than for Quebec's secession.

For their part, the Anglo-Canadians have been slower to recognize the costs of economic ties to the United States, having for so long depended on American capital for industrialization. Those who inhabit the industrial heartland, however, which for the most part is centered close to the American industrial complexes along the Great Lakes, have developed a new self-consciousness regarding managerial control and are now eager to establish full Canadian economic sovereignty by reducing American ownership of the nation's industry. It is this geographic distinction that forms the second line of division among Canadians in determining their world outlook.

A third important line of difference in Canadian politics is that between the continentalists and the nationalists. The continentalists have resolved in their minds the partner/colony debate by declaring their preference for an economy integrated with that of the United States for the maximum profit of Canada. This view is now held most notably by mineral exporters who find that national pricing systems put them at a disadvantage with respect to profits that can be earned in the United States, and among those who reside at the industrial fringes, who believe that national investment policies favor the industrial heartland and retard the economic development of their own regions.

The nationalists, however—the growing number of Canadians who believe that American investment and ownership have already exceeded the desirable level—avidly support policies drawn to safeguard Canada from further encroachment, policies that will reduce American industrial ownership of Canada. It is principally the convergence of this sentiment among the Anglo-Canadians who comprise the new entrepreneurial class (and who yearn for national scientific and technological development) with the more traditional French-Canadian nationalism that had led to the now widely recognized new era in Canadian-American relations.[42] The new Anglo-Canadian nationalists, who are amply and vigorously represented in government, particularly deplore the deleterious effects on Canada of American legal control over foreign subsidiaries in Canada. The government recognizes this problem of extraterritorial control as a political intrusion more costly than mere foreign ownership.[43] It is with these thoughts in mind that the nationalists have sharpened their focus of the Canadian world view on the economic relationship with the United States. Nonetheless, "ambivalance concerning the choice of a proper balance between autonomy and integration has been a recurrent feature of Canadian foreign policy."[44] Ecological, security, and cultural problems follow next, in that order.

As has been indicated, the trading relationship between Canada and the United States is the world's largest. Trade with the United States consistently comprises two-thirds of all Canadian trade. Table 3–9 indicates both the volume and the growth in this trade, together with the evolution of Canada's trade surplus. Most particularly, note the years 1982 through 1986. In 1982, the Canadian surplus doubled and nearly doubled again by 1986. In that year, the Canadian surplus accounted for 15 percent of the total US trade deficit. It was about this time that Washington began pressing Canada for a new free-trade agreement, and at which Canadians began to increase their imports from the United States. From 1986 through 1989, Canada's exports to the United States increased by approximately $20 billion while imports from the United States grew by $34 billion, thus gradually reducing the Canadian surplus in this trading relationship.

Even before the disparity in Canadian-American trade became so great, the Canadian advantage was not without high costs. In the long run, perhaps the greatest cost will prove to be the premature depletion of natural resources. More immediately, however, Canadians are concerned with the American political and corporate controls to which their economy is susceptible. In the

---

[42]Robert Gilpin, "Integration and Disintegration on the North American Continent," *International Organization,* vol. 28, 1974, pp. 851–1874. See also John Sloan Dickey, "Canada Independent," *Foreign Affairs,* July 1972, pp. 684–1699; and Gerald F. Rutan, "Stresses and Fractures in Canadian-American Relations. The Emergence of a New Environment," *ORBIS,* vol. 18, Summer 1974, pp. 582–593.

[43]"Foreign Ownership and the Structure of Canadian Industry: A Report of the Task Force on the Structure of Canadian Industry," January 1968, pp. 310–345.

[44]Michael B. Dolan, Brian Tomlin, and Harald von Reikhoff, "Integration and Autonomy in Canadian–United States Relations, 1963–1972," *Canadian Journal of Political Science,* June 1982, pp. 331–363, at p. 332.

Table 3–9 Canadian-American trade, 1969–1989, and the Canadian balance, all in billions of US dollars.

	Canadian Imports	Canadian Exports	Total Value	Canadian Balance
1969	$ 9.5 billion	$ 9.8 billion	$ 19.3 billion	$ 0.3 billion
1973	16.5	17.1	33.6	0.6
1977	25.8	29.6	55.4	3.8
1978	28.4	33.5	61.9	5.1
1979	33.1	38.1	71.2	5.0
1980	35.4	41.5	76.9	6.1
1981	39.6	46.4	86.0	6.8
1982	33.7	46.5	80.2	12.8
1983	38.2	52.1	90.3	13.9
1984	46.5	66.5	113.0	20.0
1985	47.3	69.0	116.3	21.7
1986	45.3	68.0	113.3	22.7
1987	57.4	71.5	128.9	14.2
1988	71.7	81.4	153.1	9.7
1989	79.1	88.4	167.5	9.3

Note: On this chart, the figures for 1989 are based on actual performance through three fiscal quarters and projection of the fourth.
Sources: Statistical information on annual trade is found in a variety of sources including *Direction of Trade Yearbook, The Economic Report of the President* and, for most recent information, *Survey of Current Business.*

automobile industry, for example, stimulation of production occurred only as a result of an Auto Pact (1965), in which Canada sacrificed tariff revenues in return for anticipated employment benefits and lower consumer prices. But employment has been subject to economic fluctuations in the United States and to the decisions of the multinational auto companies to relocate production. Furthermore, subsequent investment has come largely from profit, rather than from fresh capital flowing from the United States. At the intergovernmental level, in order to minimize Canada's trade surplus with respect to the United States, American policy on automobile trade ensures that in this single commodity, Canada will have a fluctuating deficit. Finally, Canadians fear that in their efforts to negotiate conditions that will enhance the industrial sector, they may be forced by Washington into a continental policy in natural resources that will both accelerate the depletion of reserves and further erode national autonomy.

Thus, behind the Canadian trade surplus lurk the dangers of extreme reliance on a single partner for both import and export markets and the problems of external investment and foreign industrial ownership that give rise to these external controls. Furthermore, because Canada's trade base is small compared with those of the United States, Japan, and Western Europe, it is unusually vulnerable to world trends toward protectionism (tariffs and other barriers to trade that governments use to protect their domestic economies against imported goods). For this reason, Canada attempted throughout the 1970s to expand trade relations with the Third World and to play a vigorous part in the frequent multilateral trade negotiations in order to encourage free international trade.[45]

Direct Private Investment

During the lengthy period of British influence in the Canadian economy, private investment was mostly of the portfolio type—that is, the purchase of stocks and bonds on securities markets. As the era of American domination began, however, with investments rising from approximately $5 billion to $25 billion in 20 years, the pattern shifted from portfolio investment to the purchase of Canadian firms and mineral deposits and the construction of foreign subsidiaries of American firms. In the immediate postwar years and in the early years (1955–1965) of intense Canadian industrial development, government planning took for granted that this direct private investment was profitable. It brought needed managerial skills as well as capital into the country; it hastened industrialization and the ability to exploit natural resource reserves; it created profit and increased employment; and it generated public revenue as well as export surpluses. The rapid and sustained increases in the GNP and in per capita income seemed testimony to the wisdom of an open policy on direct private investment from the United States.

As Canadian economic nationalism began to rise, however, this policy was reappraised. Between 1964 and 1967, for example, Canadians who thought there was enough American capital in their economy rose from 46 percent to 67 percent of those questioned. Clearly the population was aware of how much the partnership with the United States was decaying into colonial subordination. Table 3–10 dramatizes the basis for this fear. By 1972, only 37 percent of Canadians polled felt that they shared with the United States an economic partnership, whereas 34 percent felt that they had become colonized. Only 34 percent felt that dependence on the United States was good for

Table 3–10 Foreign and American ownership of selected Canadian industries, 1971.

Industry	% Foreign Ownership	% American Ownership
Iron mining	86.2	85.8
Petroleum refining	99.9	72.0
Oil and gas wells	82.6	65.0

Source: Adapted from 1967 Report of Corporations and Labour Unions Return Act as quoted in the Report of the Standing Committee on External Affairs and National Defense, on investigation into Canada-US relations ("The Wahn Report") and as produced in Malcolm Levin and Christine Sylvester, *Foreign Ownership* (Don Mills, Ontario: General Publishing, 1972), p. 74.

---

[45]See statement of the Honorable Don Jamieson, Secretary of State for External Affairs, on February 5, 1979, entitled "A Canadian View of the Multilateral Trade Negotiations" (Ottawa: Ministry of External Affairs), paper no. 79/3.

Table 3–11 Direct American investment in Canada, 1970–1988, expressed in billions of US dollars.

	1970	*1978*	*1985*	*1988*
US worldwide investment	$75.5	$168.1	$232.7	$326.9
US investment in Canada	$21.0	$ 37.3	46.4	61.2
Canada investment as percentage of American worldwide investment	28%	22%	20%	18.7%

Source: Statistical Abstract of the United States, 1979 and 1982/1983; for 1985 and 1989, US Department of Commerce, *Survey of Current Business,* August 1986 and August 1989.

Canada; 53 percent thought it bad.[46] Table 3–11 summarizes direct American investment in Canada. It shows that while Canadian investments were becoming a smaller fraction of worldwide American investment, American ownership of Canadian industry actually doubled in value during the early 1980s.

After decades of satisfaction with the profitability of American investment, national preoccupation turned to the sordid side. The Gray Task Force in 1972 focused as much on the costs of dependence as on its benefits. In a marked departure from traditional assumptions, the Gray Report concluded that most of the profit accrued to Canada was actually drawn not from American investment capital but from the American corporations' ability to exploit Canadian resources.[47] If this is the case, then the wise course for Canada is to distinguish between investment policy as a capital venture and foreign ownership, and thereafter to restrict foreign direct investment to a level below 50 percent ownership or control. As early as 1970, a plurality (although not a majority) of Canadians polled reported that they would approve a policy of restricting American ownership to 49 percent in any industry even if it meant a reduction in the national standard of living!

The Gray Report was followed only months later by an extensive government report on Canadian relations with the United States, entitled *Options for the Future,* a statement on foreign affairs by Mitchell Sharp, minister for external affairs.[48] Major portions of this report dealt with the question of whether asymmetrical interdependence with the United States automatically threatened Canada's economic sovereignty. For both trade and investment policies, the report suggested that Canada should measure permissible relations in

[46]For an extensive statistical study of Canadian attitudes toward American domination, see John H. Sigler and Dennis Goresky, "Public Opinion on United States–Canadian Relations," *International Organization,* vol. 28, 1974, pp. 637–668. For a briefer survey pertaining specifically to attitudes on foreign investment, refer to John Fayerweather, *Foreign Investment in Canada: Prospects for National Policy* (White Plains, N.Y.: International Arts and Sciences Press, 1973), pp. 13–72.

[47]Gray Task Force Report, *Foreign Direct Investment in Canada* (Ottawa: Information Canada, 1972).

[48]Published as a special issue of *International Perspectives* (Ottawa: Information Canada, Autumn, 1972).

how they would benefit Canada and Canadians. Thereafter, Parliament entertained a variety of proposals for screening investments by foreign sources in accordance with the requirement that a project strengthen the Canadian economy without further deteriorating national control over economic activity. Recognizing that excessive nationalism might damage the economy by repelling useful investments, the government sought a policy that would run a delicate line between destructive nationalism and equally destructive continentalism.

Efforts at reducing the amount of foreign (and particularly American) ownership had resulted, by 1979, in a decline to 28.5 percent ownership by foreign investors of all Canadian industry. Of the total, 75 percent continued to be American owned.

In autumn 1984, however, Canada's politics took a sharp conservative turn. After more than a decade of liberal dominance, the Progressive Conservative party and Prime Minister Brian Mulroney took the reins of government, committed to the notions of free trade with the United States and a return to more open policies with respect to American direct private investment in Canadian industry. The conservative American press hailed Mulroney's accession to power as the occasion of returning Canada from economic isolation and cheered him for not being "a prisoner of the out-dated, semi-socialist ideas that infected so many of his predecessors." Said the same source, "Smart U.S. businessmen and investors smell opportunity."[49]

Despite their common ideological orientations, the Mulroney-Reagan relationship did not get off to a fast start. It was fully two years before President Reagan conceded to Mulroney's insistence on taking serious bilateral initiatives on the acid rain problem; Canadians were offended by Reagan's decision to withdraw from the Alaska oil pipeline project after Ottawa had made an enormous financial commitment to it; and US-Canadian relations continued to falter on Washington's insistence that Canada make a larger contribution to the cost of the NATO alliance. But the March 1986 summit meeting in Washington successfully subordinated all other issues to the future of the North American economic relationship as talk of free trade negotiations filled the presses of both countries. While the conservative press supported Mulroney's initiatives, the more liberal press labeled the free-trade issue "Mulroney's panacea," arguing that such a policy would damage Canadian independence as an economic partner of the United States.[50]

Although both Mulroney and Reagan were committed to completion of a free-trade treaty, the path was strewn with obstacles. Protectionist interests in the Senate resulted twice in the imposition of excessive tariffs on Canadian goods (largely on wood products), offending Mulroney as well as his backers. Domestic politics also plagued the Canadian side, most particularly in the in-

---

[49]Edwin A. Finn, Jr., and Richard C. Morais, "Good Neighbors Again," *Forbes,* May 19, 1986, pp. 130–134. The cover proclaims: "Canada—Open for Business Again."

[50]See, for example, Michael Peterman, "Mulroney's Panacea," *Journal of Canadian Studies,* Spring 1986, pp. 3–4. This is a dissenting editorial on the notion that free trade with the United States is necessarily good for Canada.

stance in which the province of Ontario insisted on the right to veto any final treaty if it were harmful to the province. And while the acid rain problem remained, an old fisheries issue was resolved. The Canadian election campaign of 1988 centered to a large degree on the free-trade issue, with the basic positions essentially unchanged: Conservatives supported it on the grounds of potential growth in Canadian exports to the United States, and liberals rejected it on grounds that natural resources would be depleted by free trade and that Canadian independence would be sacrificed. The election became a referendum on the free-trade issue, and the conservatives prevailed by a substantial margin.

Natural Resources

Canada's richness in natural resources permits a favorable trade balance with the United States. Although fuel products (including uranium) comprise the bulk of such resources, Canada is also plentiful in ore deposits. The United States is the largest customer, to the extent that by exporting half of its annual gas and oil production, Canada fulfills about 6 percent of the total American demand.

In an era of fuel shortages and gloomy predictions about exhaustion of resources, it would seem that it is the United States that is dependent on Canada in this regard, and on the surface this is accurate. In 1971, however, prior to the concerted effort to "Canadianize" the economy, the mining and refining industries were largely under foreign ownership in general, and American in particular, as is indicated by Table 3–10. Thereafter, with the combined effects of the Canadianization program and a National Energy Program designed to protect national fuel reserves in the wake of the 1973–1974 OPEC embargo, the percentage of domestic control began to increase. Consequently, by 1979, approximately 63 percent (as compared with 83 percent in 1971) of the oil and gas industry was under foreign control, 47 percent (as contrasted with 65 percent earlier) in American hands.[51]

But from the Canadian perspective, the statistics portray only a fraction of the story. Under foreign control, the profit from these enterprises contributes little to the Canadian economy but is repatriated to the United States. Moreover, the rate of production is determined less by Canadian public policy than by American demand and American corporate decisions. Of paramount importance is the tendency of Canadian fuel production to become enmeshed in American foreign policy. The OPEC threat of a total oil embargo as a lever on Israeli-American relations in 1973 heightened Washington's interest in a continental oil policy that would formally subordinate Canadian national policy to joint Canadian-American determination. The growing demand for fuel in the United States, the steady increase of OPEC petroleum prices, and the increased reliance of the United States on external sources of fuel (both petroleum and natural gas) in the remaining years of the 1970s made the attractiveness of Canada's riches even greater. Coupled with gradual depletion

---

[51]Jock A. Finlayson and David G. Haglund, "Oil Politics and Canada–United States Relations," *Political Science Quarterly*, Summer 1984, pp. 271–283.

of Canada's reserves, such overtures continue to threaten Canadian autonomy, despite the fact that Canada's annual export volume of fuel to the United States is declining steadily, while its volume to Japan increases.

Canadian international affairs are centered on another natural resource as well: its fishing industry. Long an exporter of fish and other edible products of the sea, this portion of the Canadian economy was subjected to disruption as a consequence of extending the country's territorial waters to 200 miles in 1977. The United States did likewise (despite its customary objection to the 200-mile limit by other governments), and this change in policy gave rise to a fisheries dispute between Canada and the United States concerning (1) the establishment of their common border in the sea and (2) the rights of their respective fishing fleets in the disputed waters until such time as the border issue might be settled. Differing attitudes toward this issue led to a deep rift in relations until the matter was resolved in early 1979, a settlement that the Secretary of State for External Affairs labeled "an auspicious and promising development in Canada/USA relations."[52]

Added to its concern for preserving its natural resources is Canada's long-standing determination to avoid environmental pollution. It is particularly concerned about the consequences of acid raid, precipitation that brings with it airborne industrial pollutants that have a number of negative chemical influences on the environment. These include stunting wheat and grain growth and killing all fish stocks in fresh water ponds and lakes. Because ecological pollution knows nothing of national boundaries, Canadians continue to be concerned about the continental consequences of Washington's failure to attack the acid rain problem; and the Trudeau administration was openly critical of President Reagan in 1984 when he rejected all overtures, both domestic and international, to include in his budget message to Congress a fund for dealing with the problem. Mulroney felt similarly rebuffed in 1985 when his first summit meeting with Reagan failed to produce results other than reiteration of the claim by the United States that more research was needed before Washington could participate in a continental program to attack the problem.

The 1986 Mulroney-Reagan summit was preceded by the release of several reports in each country regarding acid rain. A report of the US National Academy of Sciences certified earlier claims that artificial pollutants, principally sulfur dioxide emissions, have caused the acidification of many streams and lakes in the eastern United States (see Figure 3–1). A report of the Office of Technology Assessment of the Congress cited evidence that half of the lakes in the eastern 23 states are seriously affected, many possibly beyond correction. Because these findings confirmed earlier Canadian claims about the magnitude of the problem, President Reagan went to the summit prepared to announce Washington's willingness to form a bilateral control commission and to undertake with private industry a five-year, $5 billion program to develop the technology to clean the emission of certain industries and utilities.[53] Although

---

[52]See statement by the Honorable Don Jamieson, "An Auspicious Development in Canada/USA Relations" (Ottawa: Ministry of Foreign Affairs, 1979), paper no. 79/4.

[53]For a summary written from the Canadian perspective, see *Canada Today/d'aujourd'hui* (Summit '86), vol. 17, no. 2, 1986, pp. 12–13.

Figure 3-1 Acid rain sensitivity in the United States and Canada. The dotted sections are low in natural buffers and particularly sensitive to acidic precipitation.

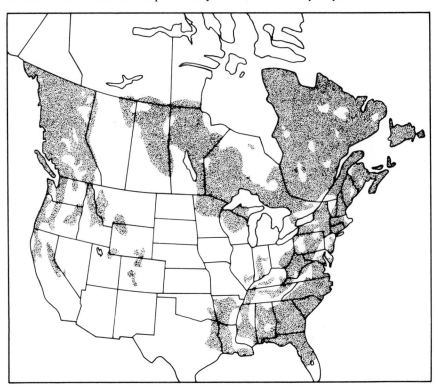

From *Canada Today / d'aujourd'hui* (Summit '86), vol. 17, no. 2, 1986, p. 12. Reprinted by permission.

these agreements were made, American funds were not appropriated, so the diplomatic problem was not solved in the Reagan years. Because of the importance of the free-trade issue in 1988, the acid rain issue remained secondary in the election campaign.

Security

Although the principal Canadian-American links are currently economic, they were originally forged around the need for a continental defense policy during the Second World War. That partnership was epitomized by including Canada in the Hyde Park Declaration of 1941, which agreed on a common production effort between the United States and Britain to meet wartime industrial and munitions needs. Later, Canada became an active member of NATO, although it declined to participate in the Inter-American Treaty of Mutual Assistance, the military wing of the Organization of American States. The continental radar defense system, NORAD, is a joint Canadian-American undertaking of long standing, as are several bilateral defense planning boards.

Despite this cooperation in common security matters, Canada has steadfastly refused to endorse American defense strategy in its entirety. Ottawa was one of the first Western capitals to break with Washington over both Korea and Vietnam; it sold wheat to China and the Soviet Union during the era of containment; it opened diplomatic relations with China during the Vietnam War (although at a point at which this act probably facilitated American withdrawal from Southeast Asia and aided Sino-American normalization); and while reducing its commitment to NATO, Canada became one of the the main contributors to the United Nations' armed peacekeeping expeditions. It is evident that one of the central tenets of Canadian defense policy is to distinguish between Canadian-American relations on continental and extracontinental matters.

This independent attitude results not simply from a different ideological view of the world or from disavowal of a global role. It rises, rather, from the will to conduct foreign policies from which Canada will prosper without the constraints of the American world view. It assumes that transnational economic relations are more effective governors of the international system than are ideological confrontations and arms races. This attitude has enabled the Canadian government to reduce military expenditures over the last decade both in absolute number of dollars and as a percentage of GNP. Built into this policy is the realization that threats to Canadian security are extremely remote. Canada grows less responsive to what it considers excessive sensitivity in the United States to apparent threats to the security of North America and to the common economic interests of the United States and Canada.

During the 1980s, Canadian-American relations encountered unprecedented strain. The anti-Soviet rhetoric of the United States and the escalation of the strategic arms race during the Reagan years made Canadians suspicious of the purported good will of the United States in global relations. A public opinion poll taken in mid-1983 by the Canadian Institute of International Affairs revealed that while 51 percent of those polled continued to regard the Soviet Union as the principal threat to world peace, fully 21 percent had come to regard the United States as a greater danger.

A somewhat more specific source of friction arose in 1983 over American testing of air-launched cruise missiles over Canadian territory. An initial agreement had been sought by the Carter administration but it was not finalized until 1982. From mid-1983 to early 1984, when for the first time the missiles were transported across Canada fixed to the wings of an American bomber, public opinion rose in opposition to the tests. More than half of the Canadians polled on the tests opposed them.[54] Court efforts to prevent the flight failed, and despite a great public outcry, the first flight was made in March 1984. These are strategic arms rather than theater arms, and Canadians

---

[54]For a review of the principal issues afflicting Canadian-American relations during the Reagan years—economic, ecological and military—see Adam Bromke and Kim Richard Nossal, "Tensions in Canada's Foreign Policy," *Foreign Affairs,* Winter 1983–1984, pp. 335–353. The public opinion polls referred to here are cited in the Bromke-Nossal article. For a more extensive study, one that bridges the eras of liberalism (1970s) and conservatism (1980s) in Canadian foreign relations, see Stephen Clarkson, *Canada and the Reagan Challenge: Crisis in the Canadian-American Relationship* (Ottawa: Canadian Institute for Foreign Policy, 1982).

are aware that in the event of a nuclear confrontation between the Soviet Union and the United States, the cruise missiles will be launched against Soviet targets from American aircraft in Canadian air space.

Canadian concern about the strategic arms race was symbolized by Prime Minister Pierre Trudeau's trip to all the world's principal capitals during late 1983 and early 1984 seeking to stimulate new arms reduction talks and to secure commitments from heads of state on the principles for reducing tensions surrounding the arms race. Trudeau's visit to Washington was particularly disconcerting to him and to Canadians in general, for it was widely felt—and corroborated by the American press—that his efforts had been rebuffed tactlessly by the American president.

Washington's disregard for Trudeau's peace initiative and his international liberalism in general made doubly sweet the conservative victory in 1984 that brought Brian Mulroney to power. Quickly, consistent with his pledge to improve US-Canadian relations, Mulroney reviewed Canada's defense policies. This resulted in an agreement to carry 12 percent of the cost of NORAD, to modernize the Canadian contribution to NATO in West Germany, and to commit Can$180 billion to defense in the next 15 years, an actual increase of about $2 billion annually after inflation.[55]

As one of the world's most productive states, Canada has all the ingredients of an independent and prosperous foreign policy and of continued national economic growth and autonomy. At present, however, neither of these goals is held in the tight control of Canadian decision makers, inasmuch as the resources and production facilities on which each relies are controlled by foreign interests, mostly American. Because this degree of external control raises the specter of foreign interference, the Canadian world view is one that is especially wary of the motives, needs, and machinations of its neighbor to the south, a neighbor that is friendly but rapacious; tolerant but ambitious beyond its means; libertarian in philosophy but determined that the foundations of its global supremacy will not be eroded. It is because Canada is so closely tied to those foundations and because its quest for autonomy is perceived by the United States to contribute to its erosion that the Canadian perspective of the international system is tinted by a growing sense of association with the dependent middle-ranking powers. Also, there is a commensurate sense of separation from the United States to the extent that Washington insists on those modes of interdependence that prevent Canada from achieving a full sense of autonomy in a world that it finds otherwise comfortably peaceful.

Conclusion

In a world of nuclear superpowers and economic upheaval caused by the new roles of the mineral-rich states, it is understandable that the American student

---

[55]On this and other Mulroney initiatives covered in this section, see Adam Bromke and Kim Richard Nossal, "A Turning Point in the U.S.-Canadian Relations," *Foreign Affairs*, Fall 1987, pp. 150–169.

of international affairs should fail to recognize the diversity of outlook to be found even among those states that are most interdependent. It is not the purpose of this chapter to argue that the Western alliance system is in imminent danger of collapse or that the foundations of cooperation within it have deteriorated beyond repair. It is intended to demonstrate, rather, that the volume of political and economic transaction that occurs among the Western allies in North America, Western Europe, and Asia creates internal problems, difficulties that are not related to attitudes concerning the Soviet Union or China or the Third World. Close mutual identity fertilizes inequalities, stimulates demands, and breeds resistance. As the conditions of world order enable America's industrial allies to reduce their dependence on Washington, they find themselves facing an ally that, through military and economic preponderance, attempts to forestall changes that would advantage its allies but disadvantage itself. Because their own global perspectives differ vastly from those of the United States, these allies struggle to avoid subordination to American foreign policy.

CHAPTER 4

The Chinese Perspective

National perceptions are not permanent. Just as events of the late 1970s brought about a reassessment of the American world position, so too did the Chinese attitude undergo major changes. From 1950 to 1976, the Chinese perspective was a product of Maoism, that is, of the leadership, domestic policies, and foreign policies of Chairman Mao Tse-tung. With the death of Mao and the emergence of national leadership with a broader view of China's position in the world, new tolerances and aspirations developed, resulting in a marked revision of Chinese perceptions. But as evidence that old ideas die hard, in 1989 there occurred a partial reversal, the duration of which has yet to be determined. Thousands of students demanding freedom of the press and exposure of corruption in government, used the global press coverage given to the historic visit of Soviet President Mikhail Gorbachev to Beijing as an opportunity to mount massive demonstrations in Tiananmen Square; and following Gorbachev's departure, units of the Red army were ordered to fire on the crowd. The Chinese government branded the demonstrators "antirevolutionary hooligans" led on by foreign, anti-Chinese forces, and after clearing the square, set about on a nationwide sweep to arrest the leaders and restore ideological purity.

Nevertheless, for the most part, the world perspective of the People's Republic is based on a fusion of two great forces: a national force developed out of China's long history, and an ideological force of Marxism-Leninism-Maoism. Both elements must contribute to an analysis of contemporary policy and outlook. The national force is a consequence of a continuous political experience spanning 2000 years. But the infusion of communist ideology has modified and reshaped China's self-perception and the image of the country in the outer world. Perhaps the historical force accounts for three-quarters of the national perspective and the ideology of communism for most of the remainder.

China's history falls broadly into three periods: (1) the long classical epoch of imperial greatness (the "Middle Kingdom"), (2) a century of degradation and Western domination from 1840 to 1945, and (3) the modern period of national revolution and rebirth. It is impossible to understand China today without at least a general comprehension of these three periods.

The Middle Kingdom Period: Classical China

Classical China was a vast empire comparable to the great Roman Empire in the West but enduring over a longer historical period. Most of the people under the direct sovereignty of the Middle Kingdom were ethnic Chinese (that is, Han Chinese), but this included a multitude of regional, cultural, religious, and linguistic differences. Chinese were as different from one another as the European peoples were, and their integration into a single political unit was one of the great feats of early social engineering that is still not completely understood.

One factor behind this system of central government may have been that for its survival China requires a huge irrigation network to control the twin problems of flooding and drought that are characteristic of its rivers. The basic requirements of agricultural production depend on rigorous social controls to ensure the orderly development of hydraulic works over the territory. Because of their mutual water needs, the diverse lands of China joined politically.

This is not to suggest that China was a fully integrated society. Local potentates known as warlords wielded great power in their regions throughout Chinese history, and during long periods the emperor ruled only at their discretion. When the imperial center was weak, the warlords carved out zones of control and reduced the emperor to a powerless figurehead dependent on the warlord armies. Only when the imperial court was strong, free of corruption, and skillful in building necessary coalitions, could the power of the warlords be reduced and the central government truly able to rule. In a sense, the empire was a syndicate of local organizations; tension always existed between the central and regional powers.

The authority of the emperor was legitimized by the belief that he ruled by divine sanction as the Son of Heaven occupying the celestial throne. Emperors were dethroned throughout Chinese history, but this was explained by the convention that they had lost the mandate of heaven, as evidenced by the success of their enemies, and the divine sanction had therefore passed to the new rulers.

The officially encouraged culture of China was essentially conservative. It emphasized the Confucian virtues of obedience and filial piety, a system of moral obligations guiding all social behavior. Individuals derived identity mainly as members of the nuclear family or community and through other group identities. Within these units every individual had some importance; outside them the individual was nothing.

The educational system emphasized knowledge of the classic writings. It was more concerned with the development of values than with the acquisition of functional knowledge; and advancement in society, to the extent that it depended on education, stemmed more from command of the ancient texts than from expertise.

All segments of Chinese thought, even reformist and revolutionary, were portrayed as conservative and restorative of the principles in the venerated classics. Reforms were rationalized as reinterpretation of the great books, said to be more consistent with the original intentions of the texts than with existing practices (comparable to the US Supreme Court's stimulation of social change by reinterpretation of the Constitution). This system of reverence for the classical texts served as a stabilizing element in Chinese history. It encouraged a profound respect for literacy; scholar/administrators were revered and powerful men, and the inventor of writing was deified. The nation was guided by the accumulated wisdom of a thousand years.

The Chinese believed themselves to be the center of world civilization, having relatively little contact with other peoples except weak states on the periphery of the empire. Many of these were periodically conquered by China during expansionist phases, only to regain independence when the warlord struggles reduced the emperor's ability to exercise control in the outlying regions. (This expansion and contraction of China over time make it difficult to define today exactly what the boundaries of the classical kingdom were. China's proper historical borders, over which there is now so much contention, depend on the historical dates chosen as the base years.)

Under the tribute system, the rulers of the peripheral societies kept themselves in power by acknowledging the superiority of the Chinese emperor, sending gifts and offerings of homage. These gifts were not significant in economic terms, but they reinforced the Chinese national self-image as the Middle Kingdom at the center of known civilization. Non-Chinese were regarded as barbarians. A new envoy would arrive with a caravan of gifts for the emperor, kneel before the Son of Heaven three times in the act of *kowtow,* and present the tribute. This ritual set the tone for the entire relationship between China and other peoples, one not of equality but of dominance and submission. China saw little need for the outside world and therefore sent forth few explorers, traders, or conquerors.

The Century of Humiliation: The Meeting with the West

This stable, conservative and self-confident Chinese society was in for a rude awakening when it came into contact with the dynamic societies of Europe and North America. The Chinese were very poorly prepared for this experience, and the shock of it reverberates even today.

The first Europeans came to China to spread Christianity and to find trading opportunities. Both the Christians and the merchants discovered that their arrival stirred relatively little interest. In other parts of the world, explorers had been revered as gods or at least as men of extraordinary power and inventiveness, but in China they were received as envoys from inferior civilizations. Early Chinese maps portray entities called England, France, America, Portugal, and so on as small islands on the fringes of a world with a huge China at the center. The advanced products of Europe that so dazzled other peoples were received unexcitedly in China. The Son of Heaven wrote to the king of England in 1793:

> The virtue and prestige of the Celestial Dynasty having spread far and wide, the kings of myriad nations come by land and sea with all sorts of precious things. Consequently, there is nothing we lack, as your principal envoy and others have themselves observed. We have never set much store on strange or ingenious objects, nor do we need any more of your country's manufacturers.[1]

Christian missionaries were tolerated but were regarded as a nuisance.

China may not have been much interested in the Europeans, but the Westerners coveted China. By 1715, the British had established the first commercial base at Canton, and they were soon joined by French, Dutch, and American traders who, under close Chinese control, were confined to tiny enclaves and hampered by travel and other restrictions. Europeans were required to deal exclusively with a government trade monopoly, and Chinese were forbidden to teach them languages. The traders grew increasingly unhappy with these restrictions, and energetic representations were made to the emperor, but to no avail.

Perhaps the most serious problem to the traders was the relative lack of interest in Western products. To buy from China they had to sell in exchange something that the Chinese wanted. The Europeans discovered that there was one major marketable product. Its nature, and the fact that its open sale was encouraged, may surprise the modern reader: The product was opium.

Opium had been known in China for many years, but as in Europe and America, its sale and use were prohibited. Before the Europeans stimulated the trade, opium addiction was a minor problem, partly because Chinese cultural traditions discouraged personal hedonism and antisocial behavior. But after the European trade reached its peak, in some communities as much as 50 percent of the population was addicted. The imperial government tried repeatedly to stop this traffic by decree, but with little effect. In 1729, at the time of the first decree, importation was approximately 200 chests of pure opium per year. By 1830, this had grown to about 19,000 chests, and by 1838 to 30,000. European persistence joined with ineffective decrees and corruption among Chinese officials to encourage growth of the drug trade.

The Opium War

The encounter of China with the West culminated in the Opium War in 1839, when a serious effort was finally made to halt the corrupt trade. A Chinese official named Lin Tse-hsu, commissioned to control the contraband, ringed the commercial enclave at Canton with troops, seized $11 million worth of

---

[1]Quoted in John K. Fairbank and Ssu-yu Teng, eds., *China's Response to the West: A Documentary Survey* (Cambridge, Mass.: Harvard University Press, 1954), p. 19.

opium, and drove the drug traffic out of Canton altogether. The British government, construing this as aggressive interference with freedom of international trade, promptly initiated a battle that resulted in the destruction of the Chinese forts at Canton and the signing of the Treaty of Nanking in 1842. In military terms China's losses were minor. But a handful of barbarians employing the mere gadgetry of their inferior civilizations had been able to humble the great Chinese empire. As one Chinese official said at the time to the British, "Except for your ships being solid, your gunfire fierce, and your rockets powerful, what other abilities have you?"[2]

The Opium War was the first in a long series of national defeats that lasted from 1840 to 1945, the Century of Humiliation. During this hundred years the power of the celestial throne was destroyed, and China found itself increasingly the victim of external enemies—Europe and Japan—and internal dissolution—the warlords.

In the Treaty of Nanking (1842), China was forced to give Hong Kong to Britain in perpetuity, to reopen Canton and the opium trade, to pay $21 million in reparations (a huge amount, equivalent to the American federal budget at the time) and, most important of all in the long run, to give four more treaty ports to the Europeans. Treaty ports were put under the direct control of the Europeans; they were extraterritorial, meaning that even civil laws were to be enforced by European courts. (In Cushing's Treaty of 1844, the United States was granted similar rights.) These unequal treaties led to many insults, including the lax treatment of Europeans convicted of crimes against Chinese and even a sign in a park in Shanghai prohibiting Chinese and dogs.

China went into steady decline after the Opium War. In 1858, there was another skirmish in which British, French, American, and Russian negotiators, backed by 30 gunboats and 3000 troops, forced open 11 more ports to trade. Worse, they demanded for the first time access to the interior, meaning penetration from the coastal areas into the vast heartland. Now all of China would be open.

The T'aip'ing Rebellion

Another step in the decline was the T'aip'ing Rebellion, a civil war that occurred during the same years as the American Civil War, 1861 to 1865. In the American war about 400,000 died; in China the losses were closer to 20 million. The rebellion was a mass uprising led by a zealous Chinese Christian who had been converted by a missionary and believed that God whispered to him at night to redeem the nation. The T'aip'ings favored communal forms of social organization and production, a kind of peasant communism before Marx.

At first the Europeans looked with interest on the rebellion, thinking that its avowedly Christian leadership might have beneficial results. With European neutrality, the rebels almost succeeded in destroying the Manchu Dynasty. But

---

[2]Quoted in John Stoessinger, *Nations in Darkness* (New York: Random House, 1971), p. 14.

late in the struggle, the Western governments concluded that the fanatical zeal of the T'aip'ings might make them more difficult to deal with than were the corrupt officials of the imperial court, and so they aided the emperor in putting down the rebels. The war ended with the imperial government weakened, the peasant movement destroyed, and the Europeans strengthened. The very power of the Manchu Dynasty to survive thereafter depended directly on the Europeans.

Chinese society entered a period of self-criticism. How could China prevent total colonization by Europe? The policy of clinging to the great traditions and refusing to acknowledge the inevitability of change had failed. China had scorned Western technology, but a handful of foreigners had reduced China to submission. This point was driven home in 1894 when Japan, which had met the Western challenge by adopting Western economic and industrial values, seized the peninsula of Korea from China. In a mere quarter-century Japan had modernized its economic and military capacities while China had declined. The contrast was particularly humiliating.

Only with the victory of Chinese communism in 1949 can the control of China from the outside be said to have ended. But even during the latter half of the subjugation period there were significant attempts at national self-assertion.

The Boxer Rebellion

The first attempt at self-assertion was the Boxer Rebellion in 1900. The Japanese victory over China (1894–1895), the spread of European commercial exploitation, and the growth of Christianity outraged national sensibilities, and some nationalists believed that the only recourse was a popular uprising against the white devils. In 1900, large numbers of young patriots joined in a rebellion by the Society of Harmonious Fists, otherwise known as the Boxers. Attacks on converts to Christianity, on missionaries, and especially on Euro-

The 5-yuan bill of the Kuomintang government, dated 1935, is printed in English on one side, demonstrating the dominant position of foreign business in the Chinese economy.

pean commercial and industrial interests aroused the Europeans to resistance. Here was a struggle between the Chinese, who felt that they were defending national independence, and the Europeans, who thought they were defending the rights of free trade and protecting their citizens. The Chinese were enraged by the unceasing advances of foreign profiteers and missionaries. The Europeans were enraged by the assassination of the German minister and other wanton acts of violence against Western civilians and their Chinese friends. The United States demanded "speedy suppression of these rioters, the restoration of order, the punishment of the criminals and the derelict officials, and prompt compensation for the property destroyed."[3]

The Boxer Rebellion was counterproductive, stimulating foreign exploitation rather than stopping it. An eight-nation European force crushed the rebellion and looted the city of Peking. The collaboration of the Chinese government with the Boxers destroyed the remnants of foreign cooperation. Westerners now proposed the wholesale dismemberment of China into spheres of influence under the control of the various European powers. But the British and the Americans were opposed to the spheres of influence concept and insisted on the open door, under which there would be freedom of trade in all parts of China—that is, everybody would share equally in the exploitation of China. Instead of outright colonization, France, Germany, Great Britain, Japan, and the United States shared in the profits of carving up China and controlling many of its railroads, ports, and mines, and of dominating its foreign trade.

Sun Yat-sen and the Republic of China

These external incursions combined with internal rebellion and corruption to produce a period of self-criticism in China toward the close of the nineteenth century. The rebellion of the Boxers failed, but the revolutionary spirit spread and deepened. In 1911, a nationalist rebellion by followers of Dr. Sun Yat-sen, the father of modern China, succeeded in overthrowing the Manchu Dynasty, which by then had become thoroughly discredited. But the revolutionaries had seized a rump government. Real power went to the warlords, who filled the vacuum created by a weak center. Sun Yat-sen was quickly replaced by the most powerful of the warlords, Yuan Shih-k'ai, who suppressed Sun's Nationalist party, the Kuomintang (KMT). Sun fled the country, the party went underground, and the ideals of 1911 were temporarily defeated.

The Russian Revolution in 1917 revived the cause of Chinese nationalism. When European revolutions failed to materialize and Russia found itself an island in a hostile capitalist sea, the Soviet leaders looked with great interest to the possibility of a friendly China. In 1922, the Russians offered Sun Yat-sen substantial aid for his Kuomintang. The Russians conceded that "the conditions necessary for the establishment of either socialism or communism do not exist in China." In exchange, Sun admitted the Chinese Communist party into the Kuomintang. Russian aid reawakened hopes of national rebirth.

---

[3]Quoted in Edmund Clubb, *Twentieth-Century China* (New York: Columbia University Press, 1964), p. 27.

Sun Yat-sen's death in 1925 occasioned the rise of a powerful new figure in the leadership of the Kuomintang: Chiang Kai-shek. Chiang was later to lead the most corrupt elements in China in their struggle to cling to power, but in this early period he was an important figure in the Chinese nationalist movement.

Chiang Kai-shek

Chiang organized and led a military campaign to break the power of the warlords in order to reunite China and to set it on a path to national development. In the Northern Expedition, Chiang's armies swept the country and destroyed or absorbed the power of the warlords. With the success of the Northern Expedition, a major step had been taken in the reunification of China.

Chiang rewarded the communists for their participation in a united front against the warlords by turning on them in the middle of one quiet night in 1927, having them dragged from their beds and shot in the streets. He did not want any competitors for power in the system of personal control he was to create. In one sweep, the membership of the Chinese Communist Party was reduced from 50,000 to 10,000.

The Rise of Mao and the Communist Party

In 1928, a new figure emerged, a previously minor functionary named Mao Tse-tung. In five years of difficult organizing (1928–1933), he built a party of 300,000 and a Red army to oppose Chiang's Kuomintang. However, Mao's forces were no match for the huge Kuomintang, and in 1933, 400,000 KMT troops killed 60,000 Red soldiers, still another defeat for revolution in China. The surviving elements of the Red army made the famous Long March across China to sanctuary in the mountains. No ordinary retreat, the Long March was a 6000-mile forced march by 90,000 men and women, taking more than a year while they evaded KMT harassment on all sides. It is one of the great feats of military history and is celebrated in poems and operas throughout China today.

But successful evasion of KMT troops by the communists contributed little to expelling foreign influences. While the struggle between opposing Chinese forces unfolded, foreign interests continued their rape of China. In 1931, Japanese troops invaded Manchuria by way of Korea (which Japan controlled as a result of the Russo-Japanese War of 1904–1905) and in so doing achieved a foothold for further expansion through the so-called Greater East Asia Co-Prosperity Sphere, the Japanese term for their empire in Asia and the Pacific. Meanwhile, the Soviet Union, hostile to the peasant foundation of Chinese communism—pure Marxism preaches communism developing through the strength of the proletariat in industrial economies—doubted that the conditions for effective revolution existed in China. As a result, it was considered more important to limit the growth of Japanese interests in China than to influence the outcome of the Chinese civil war. Right up until World War II, therefore, Soviet aid, in the form of money, aircraft, advisers, and provisions, was directed to the Nationalists (KMT).

The conclusion of the war meant little more than the removal of Japan as a threat to China, since disorder and administrative chaos followed the Japanese withdrawal. The Soviet Union, expecting the restoration of effective KMT control, lost no time in looting the industrial wealth of Manchuria abandoned by the Japanese. Whole factories were transported to Soviet territory. The Kremlin urged the Chinese communists to join a coalition with the KMT as the only available means of gaining access to a portion of political power. This coincided with the American view, as expressed in the mission of General George C. Marshall, that further struggle between the Nationalist and Communist parties would be useless and fratricidal and that a coalition should be structured to speed national recovery.

By this time, however, the communists had hopes of an independent strategy. Mao knew that the administrative structure of the KMT had been shattered by the war and that popular support for Chiang had evaporated. Over the course of the nearly half-century-long struggle to free China from foreign control, national society had in fact disintegrated.[4] Furthermore, the communists had emerged from the world war in many areas as heroes of the anti-Japanese resistance. The seeming selflessness and patriotism of the communist forces in wartime were contrasted in the public mind with the image of the Kuomintang as a self-seeking party of corrupt officials and landowners clinging to their own position in society. When the communists entered a village, they turned all land over to the peasants. When the KMT reentered, their initial act was often land repossession. The difference was not lost on the peasants.

In the civil war that raged from 1945 to 1949, the position of the KMT steadily declined. Whole divisions of Chiang's soldiers, including officers, deserted to the Red army. To the end, the Russians continued to write off the communist cause as hopeless and continued their relationship with Chiang. But the fierce determination of Mao's forces led to the final rout of the KMT in 1949. Chiang fled with the remnants of his army to the island of Taiwan (Formosa), subdued the people of that island when they resisted, and established a new but much-reduced dominion behind the shield of the US Seventh Fleet, which since 1950 has protected the KMT from attack from the mainland. In the view of mainland Chinese, this US act was an unjustified intervention denying the Chinese people the right to complete their own revolution and preserving the insulting fiction of a rump government in exile. Nevertheless, with the flight of the KMT the Century of Humiliation was concluded, and China was reborn as a free and self-determined nation.

Modern China: Rebirth and Revolution

The world outlook of Communist China since 1949 has been deeply influenced by this history. Unlike the Soviet Union or the United States and its

---

[4]James E. Sheridan, *China in Disintegration: The Republican Era in Chinese History, 1912–1949* (New York: Free Press, 1975).

principal allies, China's soul has been seared by exploitation, humiliation, and oppression. The last remnant of the seemingly endless waves of foreign conquerors passed through China within the memory of the current generation of leaders. The difference between the sturdily independent and self-sufficient China of today and the previously pathetic and degenerate China is obvious even to its enemies. Without exaggeration, the absolutely overriding consideration of Chinese foreign and domestic policy has been the restoration and preservation of China as a powerful and independent nation invulnerable to external conquest and domination. This goal has required both objective and subjective changes, including the revival of self-confidence. But until the conclusion of the Vietnam War, and until the 1970s were nearly concluded, there was no disagreement among modern Chinese leaders concerning the paramount necessities of national defense and self-sufficiency. The enemies of China had to be kept at bay; and doing so meant deflecting the threats from the world's two most powerful and imperialistic countries: the United States and the Soviet Union.

In the ideological flexibility that followed Mao's death, the Chinese approach to world affairs changed substantially and evolved rapidly. Between 1974 and 1977, for example, China adopted a "three-world" theory of global politics in which the three worlds were defined differently than they are in the classic three-world concept of industrialized West, Soviet bloc, and developing world. In the Chinese theory, the first world is the imperial world of the Soviet Union and the United States; the second is composed of all other developed states; and the third world is the developing nations, with China as the inspirational leader. By 1978, however, as Sino-Soviet relations reached their lowest point and relations with the United States and the NATO countries improved rapidly, the Chinese world view became much more Western oriented. The objective of this shift was to unite with all anti-Soviet countries against the social-imperialist, an ideological adaptation in which the Chinese accepted the notion that even some socialist countries can have imperial ways. The early 1980s, which brought signs of a Sino-Soviet thaw and increasingly strained Sino-American relations, also saw the Chinese world view as becoming one of self-reliance and neutralism on East-West relations.[5]

This rapid evolution of the Chinese world view is a result of both domestic and international affairs. On the domestic front, three forces shape Chinese international attitudes. The first is that in recent years, internal Chinese politics has taken a conservative turn which has resulted in the reshaping of domestic institutions along a traditional Soviet-type line. Some critics have gone so far as to refer to this development as the Sovietization of Chinese politics, a reference to form rather than substance. The second force is a desire to avoid dependence on the West, a possibility that appeared distinct at a time when the lure of Western technology seemed to be the correct answer to the Soviet mil-

---

[5]Herbert S. Yee, "The Three World Theory and Post-Mao China's Global Strategy," *International Affairs* (London), Spring 1983. One Chinese author ascribes the invention of this theory to Mao Tse-tung. See Huan Xiang, "On Sino-U.S. Relations," *Foreign Affairs*, Fall 1981, pp. 35–53, at pp. 35–36. The author is vice-president of the Chinese Academy of Social Sciences.

itary buildup in the Pacific. Third, relaxation of tensions with the Soviet Union is essential to the regional environment needed for China to succeed in its long-term four modernizations policy, a policy calling for the gradual modernization of agriculture, defense, science, and technology.[6]

The international stimuli to a rapidly evolving world view are even more complex. They include the Chinese leadership of the Third World, a status that confronts China with disparate expectations; continued Soviet military expansion in Asia and the Pacific; an evolving economic and military relationship with Japan as well as with the United States and Western Europe; and anxieties over the political relationship with the United States, a relationship strained by the refusal of the United States to discontinue arms sales to Taiwan by the Reagan administration and, subsequently, American condemnation of the use of arms in Tienanmen Square in 1989 by the Bush administration. A major confrontation may have been avoided when, in 1990, the Senate upheld by a narrow vote President Bush's veto of a bill offering Chinese students in the United States permanent sanctuary.

Under these combined internal and international circumstances, the current Chinese leadership has chosen a path away from the pro-West, anti-Soviet coalition of the period between 1978 and 1981. Instead, it crafted a policy of balanced relations with the Soviet Union and other communist states (particularly the hard-line North Koreans and East Germans) on the one hand, and the United States and Western Europe, on the other hand. Meanwhile, its political and economic relations with Japan improved greatly. It is one of the great ironies of modern history that the setback caused by the events in Tienanmen Square in 1989 occurred during and immediately after Mikhail Gorbachev's visit, an occasion on which China had hoped to launch a new chapter in Sino-Soviet relations in its quest for virtually worldwide diplomatic and economic relations. If ideological imperatives were carefully balanced with economic goals before June 1989, domestic ideological consistency won at least temporarily over global economic relations.

Throughout this evolution, however, the intensely nationalistic outlook of the Chinese communist leadership has dictated an emphasis on defensive, China-centered priorities in international relations. We can infer the following hierarchy of priorities in the formulation of Chinese foreign policy since 1949:

1. Defense against external military attack or domination
2. Reintegration of outlying and alienated territories (particularly Tibet, Sinkiang, and Inner Mongolia; see Figure 4–1)
3. Incorporation of Taiwan in the national administrative structure
4. Prevention of foreign nonmilitary interference in Chinese domestic affairs
5. Reestablishment of international respect, and the achievement of a leading role in regional and international affairs

Each of these principles requires brief elaboration.

---

[6]Edmund Lee (a pseudonym), ''Beijing's Balancing Act,'' *Foreign Policy,* Summer 1983, pp. 27–46.

Figure 4–1 China and Soviet Union, showing disputed territories.

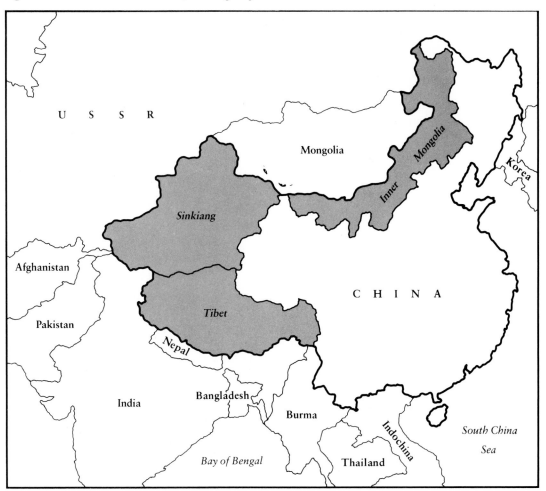

National Defense

Defense of national territory and national values is, of course, the primary concern of any state. To the extent that a state feels that its territorial integrity is threatened, this concern becomes even greater. Since 1949 and until recently, China has perceived itself as threatened by either the United States or the Soviet Union and sometimes by both. Furthermore, China's geopolitical characteristics add to its concern about national defense. The 6000-mile land border separating China and the Soviet Union (including Soviet-influenced Outer Mongolia) is the world's longest hostile border and is considered indefensible mile by mile. On the east, the Chinese navy cannot defend the seaward approaches on the Yellow Sea, the East and South China seas, or the Straits of Taiwan. Even the Indian borders on the southwest demand extensive defensive preparations. Under these circumstances, China must rely for its defense on primitive nuclear deterrence and on the reluctance of its opponents to undertake an invasion. It is not difficult to understand the obsession of China's leadership with security and defensive preparations.

The Chinese economy has made impressive strides since 1949, but they are inadequate to support simultaneously the technological demands of modern warfare (including significant nuclear and missile capability) and a rising standard of living. China has found it difficult even to sustain a major industrial effort, largely because of bottlenecks in supplies of energy and transportation. Wars abroad, limited as they were, had a devastating impact on the modernization plans of the late 1970s and early 1980s, as the February 1979 punitive war against the Vietnamese demonstrated. This test of the economic strength underlying China's military power spotlighted its glaring weaknesses and its inability to sustain a major war effort.

Despite spending as large a fraction of its GNP on defense as does West Germany, China's defense capability lags behind. Its air force is small in comparison with those of the United States and the Soviet Union and cannot begin to meet even the level of technological sophistication of hostile forces in Taiwan. The navy is insignificant by comparison; and the nuclear arsenal, while a real threat in regional combat and perhaps to some Soviet targets, is small in contrast with those of the United States and the USSR and lacks the array of delivery methods on which the latter two have built their deterrence policies.

China did test a submarine-launched ballistic missile in late 1982, one with a range appropriate to Soviet targets in Asia and the Pacific. The test enabled the Chinese to boast that they are now able ''to enter the ranks of advanced nations in sophistication of national defense technology while being backward in economic modernization.''[7] In fact, however, while it is the ultimate goal of the Chinese to be self-sufficient in military technology, at present it is dependent principally on Western supply. By 1982, the United States alone had approved export licenses related to air defense radar equipment, transport helicopters, instrumentation for testing jet engines, communications systems, computing equipment, integrated circuits, submarine tracking systems, range-finding instruments, and tank engines.

The huge population and extensive territory of China, together with the resource potential of the territory, have not yet been marshaled into modern military and economic capabilities. China is looking to the West to compensate for some of these deficiencies, not only through military technology and equipment, but also through military relationships that some have been tempted to consider incipient alliances. In fact, however, while an arms-trade relationship did develop in the 1980s, the flexible Chinese world view makes such a relationship a temporary expedient. In 1983 the Chinese rejected Secretary of Defense Caspar Weinberger's proposal on the exchange of military missions; and in 1984, during his state visit to the United States, Premier Zhao Ziyang (Chao Tzu-yang) announced that China has no intention of entering into an alliance with Washington.

---

[7]Beijing Radio, as quoted in William T. Tow, ''Sino-Japanese Security Cooperation: Evaluation and Prospects,'' *Pacific Affairs*, Spring 1983, pp. 51–83, at p. 55.

Reintegration of Outlying and Alienated Territories

During the Century of Humiliation, huge slices of Chinese territory were lost to hostile powers, as indicated in Table 4–1, through a series of unequal treaties. Despite early renunciation of these treaties by the Mao government and demands for return of these territories, more modern Chinese territorial concern focuses on the outlying and alienated areas within the current Chinese territory. Of particular concern are Tibet, Sinkiang, and Inner Mongolia.

The dynastic history of China and the longevity of its civilization conceal the fact that like most large nations, China has a number of national minorities within its population. These are particularly evident in the outlying and border areas of the territory where distance from the governmental and cultural centers of China has resulted in the preservation of diverse languages, cultures, and national identities. Although small in numbers as part of the nation of a billion, these peoples occupy vast regions that could impose major new demands on Chinese defense and economic development if their inhabitants were to achieve independence from or incorporation into other nations. The increasing number of Soviet-oriented Uigurs in Sinkiang, the province in which China has its most important nuclear weapons facilities, poses a constant threat to China's territorial integrity and defense modernization. Tibet, forcefully reincorporated in 1950, is subject to repeated rebellion in favor of national autonomy. For fully 40 years, China has maintained a policy of intimidation, heavy-handedness, and great national chauvinism toward these minorities.

Table 4–1 Historic losses of Chinese territory.

Territory	Recipient	Year
1. Northeast Frontier Agency; Assam	Britain	after 1820
2. Left Bank of Amur River	Russia	1858
3. Maritime Territory	Russia	1860
4. Tashkent Region	Russia	1864
5. Bhutan	Britain	1865
6. Sakhalin	Russia-Japan	after 1875
7. Ryukyu Islands	Japan	1879
8. Indochina	France	1885
9. Siam (now Thailand)	Independence	1885
10. Burma	Britain	1886
11. Sino-Burmese Frontier Region	Britain	1886
12. Sikkim	Britain	1889
13. Taiwan and the Pescadores	Japan	1895
14. Malaya	Britain	1895
15. Korea	Japan	1895 and 1905
16. Ladakh	Britain	1896
17. Nepal	Britain	1898

China has not yet succeeded in integrating all its diverse cultures into the dominant Han culture. This is no less true of the Soviet Union and the United States; but in China's case, divergences of national identity have direct territorial corollaries, making the reintegration of these peoples and territories an urgent priority.

The Reincorporation of Taiwan

The reincorporation of Taiwan is a special issue, different from all other territorial demands. In this case, both the People's Republic government and the Kuomintang government on Taiwan insist that the island is rightly a province of China (although some of the native Taiwanese, who comprise 85 percent of the island's population, demand national independence). The point at issue has been the larger one: Which party is the rightful ruler of China, of which Taiwan is a part? The Nationalists on Taiwan have refused to concede to demands for reincorporation, and for several years following the Korean War annually reaffirmed their intention to retake the mainland, by force if necessary. A combination of reason, dependence on the guarantee against communist conquest provided by the US Navy, and the futility of the mission all contributed to the emptiness of this threat. Nevertheless, despite the vast changes in the international politics of Asia in recent years, together with sharply changed Sino-American relations, Beijing continues to regard the issue of Taiwan as one of the paramount challenges for Chinese policy in the future.

"Hey . . . talking about imperialism . . ."
Source: © Behrendt (*Het Parool*, Amsterdam)/Rothco

During the period of Sino-American normalization (1972–1978) and the early phases of formal diplomatic relations (1979–present), the Taiwan issue has repeatedly upset the bilateral relationship. From the Chinese perspective, despite the good intentions of formal declarations, the United States continues on a course of duplicity on which it treats Taiwan as a separate state in political, economic, and military policies while formally acknowledging that it is part of a single China over which the Chinese Communist party holds sovereignty. In the Chinese view, American obligations are inscribed in three documents:

1. **The Shanghai Communiqué,** the formal joint statement that concluded President Richard Nixon's historic visit to China in 1972. In it the parties agreed that there is but one China, including Taiwan, and that the Beijing government is its sole governing authority. On the strength of this Washington agreed to eventual military withdrawal.[8]

2. **The Joint Communiqué on the Establishment of Diplomatic Relations** immediately preceding full diplomatic exchange on January 1, 1979.[9] Once again, the principle of one China including Taiwan was declared, as was acknowledgment of Beijing's exclusive governing right. Nonetheless, "Within this context, the people of the United States will maintain cultural, commercial and other unofficial relations with the people of Taiwan." This language indicated that formal diplomatic exchange with Taiwan would be discontinued, as would the old military alliance.[10] President Jimmy Carter, in an effort to keep faith with these goals, abrogated the Mutual Defense Treaty, an act upheld by the Supreme Court as within presidential power in a lawsuit brought by angry members of the Senate. The president also asked Congress for legislation outlining the terms under which informal relations with Taiwan would be maintained. The result was the Taiwan Relations Act of 1979 which, in the Chinese view, embodies the duplicity of American foreign policy. While the act established a private institute to deal with Taiwan in the absence of formal diplomatic relations, it also preserved all US rights that existed prior to the full recognition of Beijing including the right of the United States to provide Taiwan with "such defense articles and defense services as may be necessary to enable Taiwan to maintain a sufficient self-defense capability."[11] The affront occasioned by

---

[8]For the official text of the Shanghai Communiqué, see *US Department of State Bulletin,* March 20, 1972, pp. 435–438; and *Peking Review,* March 3, 1972, pp. 4–5. The latter is an English translation of the Chinese text but contains no significant variations that might have led to a misunderstanding of intent.

[9]For the official text of the Joint Communiqué on the Establishment of Diplomatic Relations, see *Weekly Compilation of Presidential Documents,* December 18, 1978, pp. 2264–2265. Although recognition did not take place until January 1, 1979, President Carter read the communiqué to the nation during a news conference on December 15, with the result that its publication bears an early date.

[10]For a careful study of the implications of the communiqué on American relations with both China and Taiwan, see John W. Carver, "Arms Sales, the Taiwan Question, and Sino-U.S. Relations," *ORBIS,* Winter 1983, pp. 999–1035.

[11]For a brief history of the Taiwan Relations Act by one of its sponsors, see Jacob K. Javits, "Congress and Foreign Relations: The Taiwan Relations Act," *Foreign Affairs,* Fall 1981, pp.

the act itself was doubled when, during the first term of Ronald Reagan's presidency, the United States resumed arms sales to Taiwan.

3. **The US-China Joint Communiqué of August 17, 1982,** which followed nine months of negotiations set off by the new arms sales to Taiwan. Once again, the United States pledged its support for a single China governed exclusively by Beijing, and repeated its intention "gradually" and "over a period of time" unspecified in the agreement to discontinue an independent military relationship with Taiwan.[12]

From the Chinese perspective, the prospects for an eventual solution to the Taiwan problem of Chinese sovereignty have brightened in recent years. In 1981, Beijing released a statement of principles for the reincorporation of separated territories, including Hong Kong and Taiwan. One of these is the principle of one China with two systems, a guarantee that reincorporated territories will be permitted to retain their social and economic systems. This is intended as a pledge that reunification will not be followed by forced communization. Moreover, although China has not made a declaration that it will not use force to bring about reunification, it has reduced to five circumstances the potential use of force: a declaration of independence by Taiwan; the development by Taiwan of nuclear weapons; a diplomatic drift on the part of Taiwan toward the Soviet Union; Taiwan's loss of internal control through succession in leadership of social pluralism; and Taiwan's failure to discuss the reunification issue for an intolerably long period.[13]

A second bright spot from the viewpoint of China is the 1984 Anglo-Chinese agreement on the reunification of Hong Kong with China in 1997, with a guarantee to retain Hong Kong's social and economic systems.[14] Beijing hopes to use this as a model to demonstrate to the KMT that it is serious about its reunification principles. Indeed, Beijing has gone even beyond the Hong Kong example by assuring Taiwan that after reunification, it would be permitted to keep its separate local government, to retain its self-defense forces, and to undertake a limited independent international role. It has not said whether or not it would permit Taiwan to import arms.

As these events unfolded, China and Taiwan have adopted a revised rhetorical tone with each other. In 1985, for example, during a commemoration of the fortieth anniversary of the end of the Second World War, a spokesperson for the Chinese Communist party publicly acknowledged the fruitful coopera-

---

54–62. Senator Javits was the senior Republican on the Senate Foreign Relations Committee when the act was passed. For the full text of the Taiwan Relations Act, see *Congressional Record* (House Proceedings), March 26, 1979, pp. 6254–6256.

[12]For the full text of the August 1982 communiqué, see *US Department of State Bulletin,* October 1982, p. 20. For a review of other irritating episodes in this problem, see Zi Zhongyun and Zhuang Qubing, "Sino-U.S. Relations: Opportunities and Potential Crisis," *Beijing Review,* October 14, 1985, pp. 21–24.

[13]This summary of the current Chinese position on reunification is taken from Guo-cang Huan, "Taiwan: A View from Beijing," *Foreign Affairs,* Summer 1985, pp. 1064–1080.

[14]For a text of the agreement and an interpretive article, see "Joint Sino-British Declaration on Hong Kong," *Beijing Review,* October 1, 1984, pp. 14–15, i–xx.

tion of the party and the KMT against Japanese aggression.[15] Less than a year later, China and Taiwan had their first political meeting in the history of their division. The occasion was Taiwan's desire to secure the return of a Boeing 747 cargo plane that had fallen into the hands of the Chinese government after its pilot had fled to the mainland for political asylum. The discussions resulted in an agreement under which the Chinese released the plane; more important, they marked Taiwan's first departure from its principle of no contact with the government in Beijing. Indeed, after concluding the Anglo-Chinese agreement on the future of Hong Kong, Beijing launched a comprehensive effort to increase contacts with Taiwan. Out of this came $2 billion in annual trade through the ports of Tokyo, Hong Kong, and Singapore.

Nature also played its part. In early 1988, Chang Ching-kuo, son of Chiang Kai-shek (the KMT leader who lost the civil war in China and fled to Taiwan in 1950 to establish the rival Republic of China) and president of the Republic of China for 13 years, died and left his unfulfilled term of office to Lee Teng-hui. This event is important particularly because although Lee had sat in the inner circle of the KMT for several years, unlike his predecessors, he is a native-born Taiwanese, the first to head the government of the Republic. Time will determine the meaning of this event for Beijing-Taipei relations and, indeed, for the triangular relations among Beijing, Taipei, and Washington. For while the passage of power to Taiwan natives and away from the heirs of the Chinese civil war might soften Beijing's attitude on reunification, that same passage of power brought on Taiwanese demands for self-determination.[16]

Preventing External Nonmilitary Interference

Nonmilitary interference has been easier to achieve than the reincorporation of Taiwan will be. The traditional foreign interests were simply evicted after the revolution from their commercial and industrial positions. Foreign investments were expropriated, including, for example, $196 million in American holdings and larger amounts for other countries. Most remaining foreign residents were pressured to leave the country, and a deliberate policy of national isolation was adopted, a reaction in part to the isolation being imposed on China by the West.

There were some important exceptions to this curtailment of external interference, particularly involving the Soviet Union and India. Soviet leaders took advantage of China's weakness immediately after the civil war to demand certain concessions in exchange for Soviet aid. These included the so-called mixed companies to develop Chinese oil and mineral resources, airlines, railroads, and other facilities. These gave Soviet personnel direct influence over and access to internal Chinese affairs. One form of Soviet behavior particularly disturbing to the Chinese was the covert support of Uigur separatist elements in Sinkiang. After 1955, the joint stock companies were phased out, but

---

[15]Wu Jingsheng, "Reassessing the War in China," *Beijing Review,* August 12, 1985, pp. 13–22.
[16]Selig S. Harrison, "Taiwan After Chiang Ching-kuo," *Foreign Affairs,* Spring 1988, pp. 790–808.

subversive activities in remote regions were more difficult to uproot, particularly during the darkest years of Sino-Soviet relations.

China perceives India to have interfered in Chinese internal affairs with regard to Tibet. One of the first acts of the People's Liberation Army after the revolution was the repossession of Tibet on October 7, 1950. India, part of whose territory abuts Tibet, refused to recognize Chinese suzerainty and gave various forms of covert aid to Tibetan autonomists. In April of 1954, the Indian government seemed to recognize the Chinese claim in an agreement referring to "the Tibet region of China," but this did not settle the issue. In 1958, Prime Minister Nehru of India announced, and then under Chinese pressure canceled, a visit to Tibet to symbolize support for Tibetan nationalists. This was one element sparking a Tibetan revolt against China in 1959, a revolt quickly suppressed by the Chinese authorities at a cost of 65,000 Tibetan lives. India is known to have allowed the shipment of supplies to the Tibetan guerrillas, and various dissident Tibetan elements fled to India after the revolt. In these ways, India has supported Tibet against China.

The issue of Indian interference is complicated by territorial issues on the remote Indo-Tibetan border in the Himalayan mountains. This region is so desolate that it might seem to be of little interest to anyone. But a Chinese arterial road in Tibet passes through a portion of the area that each claims. Indian claims rest on a Sino-Indian treaty of nineteenth-century vintage. China views this document as an unequal treaty of a bygone era, without legal or moral force today, and rests its own claims on historical boundaries. This dispute led to a brief but bitter Sino-Indian border war in 1962, which resulted in a reaffirmation of the Chinese claims. Despite the remoteness of the territory, however, the dispute continues.

China's Search for Renewed International Respect

The search for international respect has been substantially rewarded in recent years. Although the Chinese were eager to improve relations with the West and interpreted the 1972 visit to China of President Richard Nixon, a confirmed anticommunist and rabid Sinophobe, as a sign that their country could no longer be ignored and isolated and that their achievements had at last gained the acknowledgment and respect of the world. The seating of the Chinese delegation in the Security Council of the United Nations in place of the "Republic of China" delegation institutionalized the new great power image. Finally, the establishment of formal diplomatic relations with almost every major capitalist state, including the United States—for fully 30 years the chief impediment to China's drive for international respect and often its open enemy—culminated a patient and persistent quest for acceptance in the international community. By the end of 1985, China enjoyed diplomatic relations with 130 states, representing virtually every form of government on the spectrum, from communist to right-wing dictatorship.

China characterizes its own global role as that of the anti-imperialist supporter of Third World revolutionary movements. In this view, the world's subjugated peoples must go through two stages to free themselves from domination and oppression, the stages of national and social revolution. National revolution is the overthrow of colonialism and foreign control over territory and resources, including the economic mechanisms of neoimperialism. Social revolution means a change in class ownership of the means of production, taking control from the landlords and capitalists and giving it to the workers and peasants.

A pragmatic assessment of the Third World's attitude toward large state intervention, as well as China's own lack of military and economic resources, makes it unusual for China to intervene in the affairs of other states except through verbal exhortation. Indeed, the official position of the Chinese government on intervention, even on behalf of revolution, purports to be purely Marxist, whereas the Soviet turn to social imperialism is a dreaded departure from Marxism-Leninism. In the Chinese view,

> No Marxist would ever hesitate to state that communism will inevitably replace capitalism. . . . But Marxists also believe that it is entirely up to the people of a country to choose their own social system and it is futile for any outside force to try to do that on their behalf. Marxists always stand for peaceful coexistence among countries with different social systems; they do not stand for an "export of revolution." Particularly, they are opposed to any aggression or expansion carried out in the name of "revolution" or of "supporting revolution," and are opposed to the use of force or any attempt to use force as a means to settle differences arising from the difference of social systems and interests.[17]

The denial of aggressive intentions is central not only to Chinese diplomacy, but also to its fundamental notion of its own development. In the Chinese view, peace and economic development are interdependent. On the one hand, progress in development cannot be suspended in order to build military might. On the other hand, however, a strong China contributes to "the growth of the world's forces for peace."[18] On this basis China rejects its own growth as a hegemonic power, even regionally. One of the Eight Principles of China's diplomacy is "never seeking hegemony or succumbing to the pressure of hegemonism."[19] Furthermore, it is a fundamental tenet of Chinese foreign policy that the Third World movement has forever changed global politics to the extent that hegemonism cannot occur. According to Premier Zhao Ziyang (Chao Tzu-yang),

> A fundamental change has taken place in the pattern of post-war international relations owing to the rise of the Third World and the development of the Nonaligned movement. The days when a few big powers could dominate the world are gone once and for all.[20]

---

[17]Huan Xiang, "On Sino-U.S. Relations," *Foreign Affairs,* Fall 1981, pp. 38–39.
[18]See the text of the Seventh Five-Year Plan in China, *Beijing Review,* October 7, 1985, pp. vi–xxiv, particularly p. xxiii.
[19]From "Eight Principles for China's Diplomacy," a speech by General Secretary Hu Yaobang, excerpted in *Beijing Review,* October 21, 1985, p. 7.
[20]Speech to the United Nations General Assembly on October 24, 1985, reproduced in *Beijing Review,* November 4, 1985, pp. 15–17, at p. 16.

Relations with the United States

From the communist victory in 1949 through 1970, China and the United States regarded each other as implacable enemies. Although Americans saw the triumph of the Red army as the loss of China leading to a sweep of Red hordes across Asia, the revolution represented to the Chinese a rebirth. With the expectation that the political revolution would be followed by a comprehensive social and economic revolution, China saw an opportunity to rid the land of foreign influences (including nationalist influences, seen as foreign dominated) and a chance to build a modern society on pure socialist principles. America's aid to Chiang Kai-shek, both economic and military (the latter in the form of intervention by the US Seventh Fleet), confirmed China's fears of the hostile intentions of the West. Why, except to defeat communism and to restore Chinese nationalism, would Americans want to support this corrupt vestige of the past?

Misperceptions and hostilities were magnified by the Korean War. The United States considered the invasion of South Korea by North Korea in June 1950 as an act of international aggression inspired and planned by Beijing and Moscow; however, China played a minimal role even when American forces drove the Northern forces out of the South and began the conquest of the North. As American troops approached the Yalu River and, therefore, Chinese Manchurian territory, China's restraint in face of America's anticommunist adventure gave way. In late November, with the American Seventh Division within striking distance of Manchuria and General Douglas MacArthur publicly advocating attack across the Yalu, China responded with 200,000 counterattacking troops, driving the Americans back and producing an eventual standoff. In return for this act of Chinese self-defense, the American government arranged for the United Nations to brand China an "aggressor against the United Nations." Continued threats of American attack, even with atomic weapons, drove home to Beijing the urgency with which America wished to rid Asia of communism and China of its hard-won victory over the corrupt and aged KMT. Moreover, the Korean experience, both before and after the Chinese military response, underscored the extent to which the United Nations had become an instrument of American power rather than an independent and objective instrument for the regulation of international order.

American hostility was further confirmed to the Chinese by Washington's opposition to legitimate revolutionary aspirations in Indochina. As early as 1949, America had given financial aid to France in order to secure its colonial hold on Indochina, liberated in 1945 from Japanese conquest, and to oppose the patriotic forces led by the Viet Minh. When the French effort collapsed at the bloody battle of Dienbienphu in 1954, the United States moved to replace France as the dominant foreign power in Indochina, even though this had not previously been an area of American interest or involvement. A puppet government of former French collaborators was devised, and American military and financial assistance was used to put a new face on colonialism in the region. Opposition to supposed Chinese influence in Hanoi provided the rationale for the new American policy, because China still labored under the label of "aggressor," and thus Indochina became another base for the American encirclement of China. From South Vietnam, a creature almost exclusively of American policy, anti-Chinese influences were extended to Thailand and Cambodia (now Kampuchea), with each of which China had previously enjoyed fairly good relations. Here again the United States demonstrated its hostile intentions by supporting corrupt and oppressive regimes that declared themselves to be the enemies of China.

By the mid-1950s, everywhere the Chinese looked they found the United States in alliance with anti-Chinese forces—Indonesia, Malaysia, the Philippines, Taiwan, Korea, Vietnam, Laos, Cambodia, Thailand, and India—all far from the continental United States and clearly not traditional areas of American concern or deployment. In no manner could its security be construed to depend on these distant activities. Yet the United States invested vast sums and spent scores of thousands of lives to secure political satellites on the Asian periphery, just as the British, Germans, Japanese, and French had acted to subdue local populations in earlier periods.

From 1949 to the close of the Vietnam War, while Americans visualized hordes of aggressive, mindless, and doctrinaire Chinese, Chinese publications depicted a China encircled by hostile American troops poised to strike at the heart of the Chinese homeland. Although Washington intervened repeatedly (indeed, continuously) in Asian affairs remote from American interests but adjacent to those of China, Beijing established no foreign military bases and undertook no aggression. Who, then, was truly the aggressor?

Despite this deeply troubled history, the Sino-American thaw that began in 1971 and progressed in earnest after 1976, has led to the near-elimination of political invective between these two nations. Both have much to gain from the newer and warmer relationship, not least among the benefits the growth of trade (Chinese natural resources for American industrial and technological goods), peaceful participation in the regional and global balances, a common front against the threat of Soviet aggression, and the general stability of peaceful diplomatic relations. America's restrained reaction to China's invasion of Vietnam in 1979 gives some indication of the degree to which Washington is now willing to accept an independent Chinese role in the regional balance, yet it also indicated the limits beyond which it is not willing to permit China to roam. And from that attempt on the part of China to teach Vietnam a lesson, China learned something of itself: It lacks the military strength and the industrial power to extend its power even a few hundred miles beyond its own borders. China's power, then, is still limited by a variety of vital internal and external factors that peace with America and nuclear power status alone cannot overcome.

Thus, while asserting itself as a major regional power, China's principal attention is focused on economic development. Beginning with the Four Modernizations Plan in 1978 (modernization of agriculture, industry, technology, and defense), China's economic growth has been quite remarkable. And with a growing tolerance of free enterprise, as evidenced in its free-trade zones and invitation to external development capital, it is clear that ideological changes are part of that development. Peaceful diplomatic relations with the United States also are crucial to this growth. The United States has grown to third among China's trading partners, following Japan and Hong Kong, reaching

Replicas of the Statue of Liberty flourished throughout China in the spring of 1989 as the Red Army swept Tiananmen Square (Beijing) of protesters for democratic changes and then conducted a nation-wide search for the rebellious leaders.
Source: AP/Wide World

$7.8 billion in total value in 1987. Similarly, Americans are the largest investors in China. In 1986, the two completed an agreement by which the United States will supply nuclear fuel and technology to the growth of the Chinese electrical industry, with appropriate safeguards against the conversion of these resources into military uses.

Because of the growing Chinese dependence on the United States for economic expansion, its fears of American military action have been replaced by nervousness over the reliability of the United States as an economic partner. Particularly thorny in Sino-American relations is the growing threat of trade protectionism in the United States. Should textiles alone be subjected to import controls, China would lose millions of dollars annually, and its trade deficit with respect to the United States (already accumulated to over $1 billion), would mount.

Chinese leaders are well aware that American interest in Chinese modernization is partly strategic and partly economic. On the one hand, in the waning years of the Cold War, sound relations among the United States, China, and Japan are an indispensible counterweight to Soviet expansion in Asia and the Pacific. And yet, on the other hand, the growing trade tension between Washington and Tokyo, together with the anticipated post-Cold War drive of the United States to reassert itself as the world's principal commercial power, makes China an ever more important export market for the Americans. The Chinese objected repeatedly to the bellicose tone of President Reagan's foreign policies in Asia and with respect to the socialist Third World, and look with hope for improved relations with the Bush administration. Among the signs for which they look is the discontinuation of American arms exports to Taiwan and the repeal of economic sanctions imposed by Washington after the shooting of counterrevolutionaries in Tiananmen Square in 1989. By early 1990, they were pleased that the president's National Security Adviser had made two trips to Beijing (the first of them not revealed to the public until after the second), and that the US Senate had upheld President Bush's veto of a congressional act to grant permanent sanctuary to Chinese students in the United States.

China will not, however, adopt a policy of improved relations with the United States at any price. It has made it clear that there will be no military alliance between the two despite growing ties, and the historic visit of Mikhail Gorbachev to Beijing in 1989 dramatized China's willingness to establish détente with Moscow. In fact, because breaking Soviet and American hegemonism is one of the roots of Chinese foreign policy, strong and reliable relations with both Washington and Moscow is a long-term goal. In the meanwhile, Beijing has adopted a policy of equidistance in which it avails itself of the best relations available with each of the superpowers but will neither ally with nor succumb to the pressure of either. Premier Zhao Ziyang (Chao Tzu-yang) declared this principle succinctly when addressing the Sixth National People's Congress in 1985:

> We take a principled stand in handling our relations with the United States and
> the Soviet Union. We will not refrain from improving relations with them be-

cause we oppose their hegemonism, nor will we give up our antihegemonist stand because we want to improve relations with them, nor will we try to improve our relations with one of them at the expense of the other.[21]

Relations with the Soviet Union

Mao Tse-tung hoped that the final victory of the Red army in 1949 would attract Soviet assistance, despite the skepticism with which the Kremlin viewed Chinese communism from its origins in the 1920s through the civil war and expulsion of the KMT. Even the Soviet raids on Manchuria's industrial regions in the years immediately following the Japanese surrender did not dampen the expectation of Soviet aid. Indeed, a victorious Peking hoped that the Soviets might consider reparations for their part in the dismantling of Manchuria and for the other benefits that the Yalta Conference conceded to the Soviet Union at China's expense.

Accordingly, Mao made an unprecedented three-month visit to Moscow in December 1949, immediately after his victory. In a prolonged and dramatic series of negotiations, he presented the Chinese case to the Soviet leadership. Surely this was an epic development in the history of the communist movement: There stood Mao Tse-tung and Josef Stalin, at the pinnacle of power in two of the world's great nations, celebrating the greatest revolutionary achievement since 1917. Surely between them they could adjust the seemingly trivial issues dividing natural allies?

On the basis of what is now known, it can be said that the conflicts between China and the Soviet Union were a great deal more profound than the Western world realized at the time and that boundary conflicts were overlaid by substantial ideological disagreements. Stalin greeted Mao as an architect of revolution accepting the homage of a follower from a minor province. Nikita Krushchev later revealed that Stalin had treated his guest in a domineering and demeaning manner, refusing to respond seriously to the rightfulness of Chinese demands.

Stalin took as given the primacy of the Soviet Communist party in the world communist movement and seemed to expect China to fall in faithfully behind the Soviet advance guard. He regarded loyalty to the Soviet party as the cardinal obligation of communists everywhere, because defense of revolution required first of all international solidarity and discipline. The requirements of the socialist bloc as a whole stood above the demands of individual countries. The Soviet Union was the source of all revolutionary inspiration, as well as the sword and shield against the threatening capitalist world. Furthermore, Mao was reminded of his great debt to the Soviet Union during the war. In Mao's view, this aid had gone principally to the KMT for use against the Communist party.

Mao left Moscow with a very discouraging package. On only one territorial issue was there any concession by Stalin—a phased return of Port Arthur,

---

[21]Speech reprinted in *Beijing Review*, May 21, 1985, pp. 17–20, at p. 19.

The Chinese Red Army sweeps Tiananmen Square in Beijing of thousands of protesters for democratic changes, spring 1989.
Source: © Franklin/Magnum

acquired in 1945. On the issue of economic aid, the Russians pledged only $300 million for five years in high-interest loans, less than the United States gave to France to support the war in Indochina. Other assistance included joint Sino-Soviet companies for the exploitation of oil and mineral resources, with

Soviet control of 51 percent of the stock. These terms were scarcely fraternal expressions of support.

This all must have been highly objectionable to the Chinese leader. The Soviet contribution to revolutionary success in China had been minimal—in fact, Soviet support flowed mainly to Chiang Kia-shek until the very end of the civil war. Had the Chinese party leadership accepted the advice of Stalin in 1945 to forgo revolutionary struggle during the years of Chiang's greatest weakness (after the Japanese collapse), there might never have been a communist victory. Now the Soviet Union demanded the right to dictate the future course of action for a regime that it did not create and, in fact, came very close to opposing. At the time, however, the Chinese leadership had little choice but to submit to the Soviet will, for the West, with a few exceptions, had adopted a policy of isolating China. In spite of the tensions, which deepened over the years, the Chinese continue to acknowledge the support of the Soviets during the crucial early years of the People's Republic, even though the extent of Soviet assistance was disappointing at the time.

Sino-Soviet relations deteriorated during the 1950s as the Chinese pursued a course that, in their judgment, was more suitable to the culture and preindustrial economy of the state, although it was inconsistent with Soviet wishes. The Chinese resented the reluctance of the Kremlin to supply more aid. Eventually, Chinese departures from the Soviet model of industrialization, which required extensive purchases of heavy machinery, became more pronounced. The sharp turn toward the Maoist model of economic development, which emphasized the role of human labor and agriculture, accentuated the ideological rift with the Kremlin. Mao perceived the Soviet reaction as evidence of a desire to oppose his Great Leap Forward and rapid communization, assuming that the Soviets feared that China would become too powerful a rival in the communist world. Twice Mao tested Soviet friendship, once by confrontation with the United States in the Taiwan Straits (1958) and once in a Sino-Indian border dispute (1962). In each case, the Soviets declined to assist the Chinese. Withdrawing all their technicians, leaving half-finished industrial plants, and taking home all spare parts for Soviet-built military and industrial equipment, the Soviets added fuel to the fire by tearing up the Sino-Soviet nuclear sharing agreement and then by signing the Nuclear Test Ban Treaty of 1963. The latter of these two acts was interpreted by the Chinese as a Soviet effort to deny them membership in the coveted nuclear club of major powers. The tension between the two intensified steadily and in 1963 erupted in open dispute. From that time to the present, their relationship until recently has been one of bitter enmity. The Chinese looked on aghast as, in 1968, the Soviet Union invaded Czechoslovakia and declared in the Brezhnev Doctrine that the interests of the socialist commonwealth are greater than those of any of its individual members. It was undoubtedly this event, coupled with border conflicts with the Soviet Union and the United States' reassessment of its Asian policy during the waning years of the Vietnam War, that led China to reconsider its relationship with the other old enemy, the United States.

If China's relations with the United States are fairly described as normalization with thorny episodes, then Sino-Soviet relations may be considered as an intermittent thaw and can be dated to approximately 1976. In that year,

General Secretary Leonid Brezhnev declared for the first time that the Soviet Union would be willing to base its relations with China on the principle of peaceful coexistence, a term previously used for describing relations between the Soviet bloc and the West. This signaled an acknowledgment of China as an independent socialist force in global politics. It was not until six years later that the Soviet leader openly suggested the beginning of border talks with China, presumably in an effort (1982) to exploit the temporary deterioration of Sino-American relations that resulted from the Taiwan arms-sale crisis. There followed an exchange of official visits, the beginning of serious trade in 1983, and a very rapid diminution of rhetorical zeal between the parties. With its new pragmatic attitude toward the superpowers, China now looks forward to improved relations with the Soviet Union as a further stimulus to domestic economic development. Had antirevolutionary student demonstrations not called for armed eradication immediately after Mikhail Gorbachev's 1989 visit, and had the demonstrations during the visit not diverted the attention of the world press from Sino-Soviet relations, a giant step might have been taken. Two major obstacles to improved relations have already been eliminated: the presence of Soviet troops in Afghanistan, removed in 1989 after 12 years of combat; and removal of the Soviet-supported Vietnamese occupation of Cambodia where, according to the late Soviet Communist Party General Secretary Konstantin Chernenko, the people had "overthrown the fanatical regime of Maoist puppets."[22] Although Soviet troops and intermediate-range ballistic missiles are still stationed at the Sino-Soviet border, a sharp reduction in tensions during the Gorbachev era of *glasnost* and *perestroika* raises hopes that this obstacle, too, might soon be gone.

The collapse of Soviet control in Eastern Europe in 1989 and 1990 both relieves and complicates China's policy. On the one hand, Gorbachev's renunciation of the Brezhnev Doctrine and his willing acknowledgment of the right of self-determination throughout the area suggests that the Soviet Union is no longer a "social imperialist," a label long applied to the Kremlin by Beijing. But on the other hand, growing Soviet tolerance of anticommunist forces in Eastern Europe and the threat of social and political dissolution within several integral parts of the Soviet Union itself—Lithuania, Latvia, Estonia, Azerbaijan, Moldavia, Armenia—have upset China's relations with many of its close friends. The world's comparison of Gorbachev's heroic liberalism with Beijing's use of military force within the city in 1989 embarrasses the Chinese leadership. How comforting it must have been for the Chinese when Soviet military force was called out to quell civil war and a pro-Iranian secessionist movement in Azerbaijan in 1990.

Relations with Japan

Japan is one of the powers that benefited most from China's subjugation during the Century of Humiliation. The invasions and conquests of 1894, 1931,

---

[22]From a speech reproduced in Victor Pribytkov, ed., *Soviet-U.S. Relations: The Selected Writings and Speeches of Konstantin U. Chernenko* (New York: Praeger, 1984), pp. 64–69, at p. 66.

and the Second World War brought to China the harshest consequences of Japanese militarism, and many living Chinese remember well the cruel behavior of the Japanese army. Chinese fears were not completely erased by the defeat of Japan in 1945. A prolonged boom has moved the Japanese economy to the third position among industrial powers, behind the United States and the USSR, but well ahead of China.

During most of the period when the United States isolated China, both the Beijing and Tokyo governments wished to establish normal trade relations. The Japanese need for raw materials, particularly fuels and ores, is historical and urgent (and was a major reason for Japanese militarism in the 1930s). For its part, China was in severe need of industrial goods to assist the Great Leap Forward, aid that came from the Soviet Union in too-small a volume and at too-high a political price. Yet until the Sino-American thaw, Tokyo's military association with Washington was an ever-present threat of a resurgence of Japanese imperialism. More recently, as the Chinese have begun to appreciate the values of an American presence in Asia, the military alliance between Japan and the United States is viewed as an assurance that Japan will not undertake militaristic imperialism. The American nuclear umbrella, which enables Japan to honor the commitments of its postwar constitution to foresake a nuclear military capacity, helps ensure that a healthy trading relationship with Japan will not deteriorate into an imbalance that might invite conquest.

That Japan is the principal economic investor in China is regarded as almost entirely beneficial to the latter's economic development. Thus, in the Chinese view, Japan has moved from the position of imperial conqueror to one of natural and accessible trading partner, and part of the Western alliance that protects China against Soviet aggression.

In recent years, trade with Japan has increased dramatically. Japan now receives 16 percent of China's exports, and 23 percent of China's imports come from Japan. In absolute numbers the trade is still small: Although Japan accounts for nearly 20 percent of China's external trade, China accounts for only a little more than 1 percent of Japan's. Nevertheless, the central position that economic development plays in China's plans for the decade, together with the peaceful but uncertain relationship of China and the United States and the wary improvements of Sino-Soviet relations, almost ensures that Japan and China will develop a gradual economic interdependence.

Conclusion

Perhaps the most abiding characteristic of the international political system is its dynamism—the constant change of relative positions, aims, and national values and expectations. We have seen that in this century the Soviet Union has emerged from tsarism to vibrant socialism. The United States has risen from isolation to a position of world dominance, from which contemporary events and changes are forcing its reluctant retreat. America's principal allies (with the exception of Canada, which has grown steadily in international prominence even while holding off American economic encroachments) have gone through the turmoils of two global wars, near-total economic destruction, and, in the cases of Germany and Japan, thorough rebuilding after military occupation. They have by now established themselves as major competitors of the United States, although heavily dependent on Washington for defense and national security.

The impact of the twentieth century on China has been equally profound. Because of bitter memories of the Century of Humiliation and fears of hostile encirclement, the Chinese international perspective has, until recently, been entirely one of defense. Even today that perspective is largely defensive. To the Chinese, the international system seems to be fraught with dangers of imperialism, whether from capitalist nations hostile to the Chinese Revolution or from a Soviet government self-selected as the exclusive heir to Karl Marx's socialist doctrine and embittered by China's notion of separate centers of socialism. Wherever practicable, China has promoted revolutionary trends elsewhere and has supported anti-imperialist forces. But only with the opening of massive trade and diplomatic relations with Japan and the United States has China begun to extend itself into the international system, and it has done so in a new global environment in which complex political and economic forces have made it possible for the country to face the rest of the world less defensively.

Through it all, China adheres closely to the view that each people must struggle for its own national and social liberation for the final defeat of imperialism and for global implementation of the Five Principles of Peaceful Coexistence. To play an effective part, China has reaffirmed its determination to undergo rapid and thorough economic modernization and to exert increasing influence over the power distribution of Asia, both among the Asian states and with respect to external superpower influence over Asian affairs. The irony in China's case is that its economic and military modernization has become remarkably dependent on the capitalist world, particularly on the wealth of the United States and Japan. Furthermore, since 1976, the course of modern Chinese foreign policy was based principally on cultivating the friendship of the United States. Now, however, confident of the future and freed from a brief bout with anti-Soviet fever, Beijing has opted for a flexible policy with the superpowers, one that mixes fear with confidence, ideology with pragmatism, and a vision of the future with a keen awareness of the Century of Humiliation. By Beijing's own choice and by the world's reaction to the 1989 event in Tiananmen Square, China has turned internally once again. When the political and diplomatic wounds heal, China will resume its economic development and pursue its policy of equidistance.

CHAPTER 5

The Third World Perspective

Traditionally, the study of international relations has focused almost exclusively on those actors examined in the preceding chapters. As complex as diplomacy has always been, the criteria for selecting important international aspects of it for discussion, and for describing the structure dynamics of international policies, were few in number. Principal actors were those countries that participated in high politics, those that contributed significantly to the world's military balance, those that were capable of bringing force to bear upon interstate relations, those that were part of critical communications flows throughout the world, and those that were most productive and deeply involved in world economic transactions. Other areas of the globe, most of them formerly colonized, were at the disposal of the major actors, who exploited their territories, their riches, and their peoples in order to compete more effectively among the privileged few.

The realignment of world politics after the Second World War did not occur exclusively through ideological issues. Unmistakably, the postwar collapse of relations between the Soviet world and the West, although viewed by different parties as having been caused by different factors, led to an East-West confrontation which still threatens to erupt in nuclear war. But at the same time, the emancipation of the formerly colonized peoples of Africa, Asia, the Middle East, South and Central America, the Caribbean, and the South Pacific began to foretell a second major conflict of contemporary international relations: the North-South confrontation. In contrast with the ideological and military foundations of the East-West crisis, the North-South confrontation evolved principally over economic issues and secondarily over political and human rights issues.

At the simplest level, the North-South crisis is a result of the imbalance between the wealthy industrialized countries of the Northern Hemisphere and the impoverished, underindustrialized peoples of the Southern Hemisphere. It developed during the early Cold War years, when newly independent countries wished to avoid embroilment in political controversy between the West (the First World) and the East (the Second World) and produced a loose coalition of economically deprived states, held together only by bonds of newness and poverty. The members of this group came to be known in the 1950s as the nonaligned states, or the less-developed countries (LDCs). Although they comprise more than half the global population and their populations increase at a rate considerably above those of the industrialized states, their composite industrial production is less than a third of America's or Western Europe's. Per capita incomes throughout the Third World (except in a few oil-rich countries) are a small fraction of those of the United States and Europe and are rising at slower rates. Moreover, the gap between the rich and the poor is not closing but widening.

When we speak of poverty in the Third World, it should be distinguished from deprivation in the industrialized nations. The poverty of American cities, for example, harsh though it is, is softened by many features not found in the slums of the developing countries: hot and cold running water, sewers and toilets, electrical appliances, a diversified diet including at least occasional meat, and even automobiles. By contrast, hundreds of thousands of people in Calcutta, including whole families, live, sleep, and die in streets and doorways, literally competing with rats for food. Poverty in the United States is dramatic if we compare it with the wealth of the majority of Americans, but the American poor would be considered very fortunate by most of the peoples of the developing countries.

Although the common theme among the Third World countries is the struggle for development, within this unifying focus we must recognize broad differences among the more than 110 nations that comprise the group. First, although poverty was originally their most notable similarity, deep cleavages have occurred among the relations of Third World countries. No longer are all of them poor; indeed, the tiny country of Qatar has the world's highest per capita income. Kuwait and the United Arab Emirates follow closely. All of this is attributable to the huge international demand for oil and to the success of the Organization of Petroleum Exporting Countries (OPEC) in sharply raising the world price. Other oil-exporting countries of the Third World enjoy great national riches too. Nevertheless, the Third World is understood to consist of countries ranging in national wealth from utter poverty and infant industrialization (such as Bangladesh, Pakistan, India, and Sri Lanka) to substantial national wealth, still accompanied by underindustrialization (such as the OPEC nations).

Other useful distinctions in avoiding the misperception that all Third World countries are alike include the following:

Resources The poor countries vary greatly in the natural resources with which they are endowed. Some, like the Sudan, lack many raw materials and are hampered in their development by the relative barrenness of the earth itself. Others, like Nigeria, are richly endowed with the blessings of nature and need only to find the social and political means to utilize their gifts.

Population   Less-developed countries also vary in the concentration of their human populations. Some are teemingly overpopulated; tiny Java (Indonesia) has more than one-third the population of the United States. Others are sparsely populated; oil-rich Libya is almost empty; and Tanzania cultivates only one-third of its arable land. Some are largely urban societies, concentrated in and dominated by the cities. Others are agricultural societies or even nomadic wandering cultures. Some are huge in territory, such as India and Brazil. Others are countries of postage-stamp dimensions, such as El Salvador, Lebanon, and Gabon.

Ethnic Divisions   Third World countries differ greatly in their ethnic composition and in the unity or diversity of their peoples. Some, such as Chile, have relatively homogeneous populations. Others are sharply divided into two or three ethnic groups among whom there may be deep conflicts; for example, the struggle in Nigeria between the Ibo and the Hausa and Yoruba erupted into civil war in the late 1960s. Others are composed of a multiplicity of peoples held together by slender threads of common interest. An example is India, whose people speak the following languages: Hindi, Urdu, Bengali, Punjabi, Tamil, Kannada, and Telugu, as well as many dialects. So incomprehensible are these to one another that the national tongue is English, the former colonial language. Thus, some Third World peoples are highly unified and ready to face national economic problems, whereas others face sharp ethnic divisions that consume much of the national energy.

Political Histories   The nations of the Third World also have very different political histories. Some were colonies until recently (for example, Morocco, Kenya), and others have not been subjected to direct foreign control for many centuries (Thailand). Some are ancient countries (Iran) that have existed as political entities longer than the United States has; others are new political creations recently formed by colonial masters for their own administrative convenience (Nigeria) or new federations of formerly separate peoples (Malaysia).

Modernizing and Traditional Cultures   Some peoples hew closely to ancient traditions, have a low consciousness of nationalism, and are concerned mainly with age-old problems of village and religious life. In other societies, the traditional order is under challenge by a modernizing elite; some variety of participatory revolution is under way; and national identities are superseding antiquated principles of social organization. Literacy rates vary widely in developing countries.

Governments   Governmental types include traditional ruling elites and monarchies, elected regimes on the Western democratic model, military juntas that have come to power by coup d'état, and revolutionary movements.

Economies Economies vary from those highly dependent on imports and exports (Chile) to others for which foreign trade is relatively secondary (India); from societies in which income is distributed very unequally (Saudi Arabia) to highly egalitarian cases (Cuba); from primarily agrarian (Sri Lanka) to substantially industrial (Singapore); from stagnation (Afghanistan) to rapid growth (Brazil); from capitalist (Argentina) to socialist (Vietnam); and along many other dimensions.

These distinctions are overshadowed in significance, however, by the impact on world politics found in the evolution of the Third World's collective diplomatic voice. Once only representative of a loose coalition of noncompetitive states dominated and exploited by the industrial powers, the voice of the Third World has grown in both volume and tone. Despite the differences that characterize the members, unity within diversity has enabled the LDCs to impose significant change on the structure of international politics and on the nonmilitary power relations of states (and more recently with the massive expenditure on armaments by some Third World states, such as Cuba and Syria, even the military relations of larger states). It is because of the awakening of the South to its political and economic potential, and because of the inappropriateness of military solutions to North-South issues, that the traditional measures of international power relations have deteriorated, that the structural characteristics of the postwar world have changed, and that the diplomatic practices of a power-oriented world have been found wanting in North-South relations.

For almost half of its 40 years, the evolution of Third World politics was gradual, conservative, and largely unrewarding, owing equally to disarray and the successful resistance of the industrial states. Despite major declarations of solidarity at Bandung (Indonesia) in 1955, at Cairo (Egypt) in 1962, and at the first three meetings of the United Nations Conference on Trade and Development (UNCTAD) in 1964, 1968, and 1972, new inspiration came to the Third World movement only in 1973 when political and economic events converged. At a summit conference of nonaligned governments in Algiers, a concerted effort was launched to bring to fruition the economic agenda of the UNCTAD, and a specific program of action for developing a New International Economic Order was launched. Later in the year, renewed warfare between Israel and its Arab adversaries resulted in an oil embargo on the Western supporters of Israel, dramatizing for the first time the potential economic and political powers of the Third World.

With the resulting control of world oil prices by OPEC, and more particularly by its Arab members, the Third World was able to force its economic agenda on the United Nations in the form of the Sixth Special Session of the General Assembly, which formally launched the New International Economic Order. There followed two vacuous attempts by the industrialized states to wrest back the initiative, one the Seventh Special Session (1975) and the other the Conference on International Economic Cooperation, a two-year (1975–1977) attempt to bring control to North-South economic relations while promoting the rate of the South's development. The 1979 meeting of UNCTAD in Manila, at which the LDCs specifically requested action to restructure their international debts, to stabilize fluctuating world prices in a number of commodities that they exported, and to reduce tariff barriers among the industrial states, resulted in little progress. In the half-decade following the 1973 petroleum crisis, the structural capacity to deal with North-South issues had changed markedly, but progress was infinitely slow. Nevertheless, it is broadly recognized that the 1973–1975 phase of the Third World's evolution as a political force was typified by two dramatic changes: (1) the formulation of a unified position on international economic issues with respect to the industrial countries and (2) the determination to transform this united position and the perceived collective economic power of the Third World countries into an instrument of political pressure for the implementation of a New International Economic Order. Most important, the diplomacy of the Third World from the Algiers summit through the Sixth Special Session of the General Assembly is of crucial importance because it succeeded, for the first time, in politicizing the development issue.[1]

The North-South Dialogue

The reaction of the industrialized states to this new development in the Third World's status was one of resistance. The United States and many of its major Western trading partners initially refused to participate in preparations for the Sixth Special Session and, upon its conclusion, declared their intent not to participate in some of the outcomes. To the Third World this reaction was confirmation that the industrial powers had participated in the Sixth Special Session principally as a means of breaking the solidarity that OPEC had wrought, and their resolve was strengthened to benefit from OPEC politics and to forge other cartels that might add to the pressure on the wealthy states.

This mood, which dominated both the Sixth Special Session and the Paris planning sessions for the Seventh Special Session, was broken by a sharp reversal on the part of the United States. In an address prior to the Seventh Special Session, Secretary of State Henry Kissinger announced that the United States was "prepared to engage in a constructive dialogue and to work cooperatively" on issues pertaining to the New International Economic Order.[2] This new tone dominated opening statements at the Seventh Special Session, and the industrial states announced their intention to "turn away from confrontation" and approach the New International Economic Order with conciliation and in a mood of responsiveness to the initiatives of the Third World. The North-South Dialogue had commenced.

---

[1] Karl P. Sauvant, "Toward the New International Economic Order," in Karl P. Sauvant and Hajo Hasenpflug, eds., *The New International Economic Order: Confrontation or Cooperation Between North and South?* (Boulder, Colo.: Westview, 1977), pp. 3–19.

[2] "Address by the Honorable Henry A. Kissinger, Secretary of State, before the Kansas City International Relations Council, Missouri, May 13, 1975," in *Issues at the Special Session of the 1975 U.N. General Assembly* (Washington, D.C.: US Government Printing Office, 1975). A more detailed background can be found in Catherine B. Gwin, "The Seventh Special Session: Toward a New Phase of Relations Between the Developed and the Developing States?" in Sauvant and Hasenpflug, eds., *The New International Economic Order*, pp. 97–117.

The Seventh Special Session, the first phase of the North-South Dialogue, concluded in a carefully negotiated agenda for action, principally addressing problems of international trade and transfer of resources and technology. Because UNCTAD is the principal forum of the Third World, the responsibility fell to UNCTAD to transform that compromise into an agenda for economic action. As its first step, UNCTAD prepared a summary statement, "Trade and Development Issues in the Context of a New International Economic Order," from which we summarize the content of the North-South Dialogue as follows:

I. *An Economic Security System for Developing Countries*

    a. Integrated Programme for Commodities—commodity market stabilization and price stabilization for the primary exports of the developing states.

    b. Improved Compensatory Financing Facilities—adaptation of the International Monetary Fund or establishment of a substitute organization to supervise stabilization agreements and provide compensatory export shortfalls resulting from international market instability.

    c. Debt Relief—improved mechanisms of channeling capital to the Third World and for reducing the indebtedness that hinders development.

II. *Changing the Structure of International Economic Relations*

    a. Reducing the Economic Dependence of the Developing Countries—expanding trade in manufactures, strengthening the technological base of the Third World, and establishing a marketing and distribution system for primary commodities.

    b. Strengthening Trade and Economic Cooperation Among Developing Countries—reorientation of development strategy to one of collective self-reliance rather than dependence on the developed states, including thorough development of new international machinery.

    c. Global Management of Resources—including the establishment of new rules of international trade, reform of the international monetary system, and the development of strategies for the rational use of resources.[3]

UNCTAD, then, had by the end of the 1970s set an agenda designed to promote trade expansion, improve economic cooperation among developing states, restructure international debts, and promote economic integration among the developing states in support of collective self-reliance.

The months and years that followed UNCTAD V (the Manila Conference), however, were among the most difficult in the history of the Third World. Deteriorating political relations between the United States and the Soviet Union had both political and economic repercussions in the Third World. China had set out on a new diplomatic course with a broader focus than just the Third World. Worldwide economic stagnation and recession resulted in deepening unemployment, a sharp drop in export prices, and inflation of import costs. The need to assume additional debt added to the weight of the

---

[3]*Trade and Development Issues in the Context of a New International Economic Order* (UNCTAD/OSG/L/Rev.1), February 1976, pp. 8–33. Reprinted with minor adaptations from Sauvant and Hasenpflug, eds., *The New International Economic Order*, pp. 39–62.

Volcano of discontent.
Source: Drawing by Eugene Mihaesco.

Third World's short-term and long-term burdens. And instability in oil prices widened the economic gap not only between the industrialized world and the developing world, but between the oil-producing and the oil-importing members of the Third World as well.

In some nations, the reversal of growth patterns was so serious that the question of survival was foremost. At the urging of the Third World, the United Nations marked the beginning of the third Development Decade with a Conference on the Least Developed Countries. At this conference, a program of action for the survival of 31 states totaling 220 million people (later increased to 36 countries) was established.[4] Special aid projects were designated for

Afghanistan	Lao People's Democratic Republic
Bangladesh	Lesotho

---

[4]For a review of the conference, see Thomas G. Weiss, ''The U.N. Conference on the Least Developed Nations,'' *International Affairs* (London), Autumn 1983; and Thomas G. Weiss and Anthony Jennings, *More for the Least?* (Lexington, Mass.: D. C. Heath, 1983).

Benin	Malawi
Bhutan	Maldives
Botswana	Mali
Burundi	Nepal
Cape Verde	Niger
Central African Republic	Rwanda
Chad	Samoa
Cameroon	Sao Tome and Principe
Democratic Yemen	Sierra Leone
Djibouti	Somalia
Equatorial Guinea	Sudan
Ethiopia	Togo
Gambia	Uganda
Guinea	United Republic of Tanzania
Guinea-Bissau	Upper Volta
Haiti	Yemen Arab Republic

Only a year earlier, an Independent Commission on International Development Issues, chaired by former West German Chancellor Willy Brandt, had issued a report entitled *North-South: A Program for Survival*. The report had noted that the conditions at the turn of the decade were such as to demand not simply more international aid, but ". . . new structures. What is now on the agenda is a rearrangement of international relations, the building of a new order and a new kind of comprehensive approach to the problems of development."[5]

But the deepening worldwide recession in the early 1980s resulted in a collapse in commodity prices for the Third World's exports. Between 1980 and 1982, the total loss is estimated to have been approximately $21 billion. Furthermore, recession and unemployment in the industrialized West promoted demands of protectionism, that is, government policies designed to protect domestic products from price competition with imported products. From the Third World's perspective, the entire postwar trend toward free trade was not only in jeopardy but was also being adjusted by the industrialized world in violation of its own principles enunciated through the General Agreement on Tariffs and Trade, to the severe detriment of the Third World.

It was against this background that UNCTAD VI convened at Belgrade, Yugoslavia, in mid-1983. In preparation for the conference, the Third World held two preliminary meetings: the Group of Seventy-Seven, which speaks for 125 developing nations, met in Argentina; and the 101 politically nonaligned nations met in India. Together, these groups hoped that UNCTAD VI would produce guarantees against further protectionism among the developed countries,

---

[5]*North-South: A Program for Survival*, The Report of the Independent Commission on International Development Issues Under the Chairmanship of Willy Brandt (Cambridge, Mass.: MIT Press, 1980), p. 18. In 1982, the commission reconvened to review its findings and recommendations, and published a subsequent report, *Common Crisis—North-South: Cooperation for World Recovery* (Cambridge, Mass.: MIT Press, 1983). The commission found that since its first report, world economic conditions had worsened to the extent that emergency measures were needed to avoid such consequences as mass starvation.

activate a number of commodity price agreements as well as a Commodity Fund to support sagging commodity prices on the world market, and double the aid of the developed countries to the 36 least developed. But opinion between the North and the South was sharply divided, and the Third World left the conference with little satisfaction. Particularly, they found that on many issues, although other industrialized countries abstained from voting, the United States cast the sole negative vote. UNCTAD VI produced little of value for the Third World.

In 1986, the United Nations turned its attention to Africa by holding a Special General Assembly Session on Africa. This was brought on by a concern over both the inclining militarization of Africa and the extreme slowness of economic development aggravated by widespread famine and the flow of political refugees. The session resulted in the adoption of a Programme of Action for African Recovery and Development for the years 1986 to 1990, founded on the assumption that ''a stagnant and perpetually backward Africa is not in the interests of the international community.'' The plan called for $128 billion in investment in Africa, $46 billion from external sources, and the remainder from the mobilization and reallocation of indigenous resources. The emphasis on agricultural development, with approximately $57 billion earmarked for immediate agricultural actions, $60 billion to agricultural support (for example, transportation, communication, distribution systems), $3.5 billion for drought control (including harnessing water resources and reforestation), and the remainder, $7 billion, to human resources in the form of training and improved working conditions.[6]

Behind the politics of international economic development lies the key question in any analysis of the Third World: What are the causes and cures of underdevelopment? Why are some countries impoverished and others enjoy high standards of living? There are two sharply conflicting causal theories of underdevelopment. The conventional theory, favored in the Western countries and the less-developed countries closely associated with the West (such as Brazil or Indonesia), blames poverty on internal conditions within the poor countries that prevent them from achieving the advances accomplished by the developed countries. The radical theory, favored by revolutionary thinkers and the more militant voices in the Third World (such as Cuba and Libya), blames poverty on international conditions of exploitation of the poor countries by the developed nations. The conventional theory sees the rich countries trying to help the poor lift themselves up by the bootstraps; the radical theory sees the rich countries profiting at the expense of the poor through foreign investment and trade.

The Conventional Theory of Development

According to the conventional theory, the process of economic growth and development in the LDCs has been arrested because of low rates of productiv-

---

[6]*United Nations Chronicle*, August 1986, pp. 7–14.

ity combined with high levels of social waste and inefficiency. The Western standard of living is high because modern high-technology workers produce a great deal in eight hours. Conversely, LDC workers produce less, although they labor longer hours, because they work inefficiently with primitive tools and methods. For example, the American farm laborer works, on the average, more than one hundred acres, whereas the LDC farmer averages less than three acres. Furthermore, the American squeezes two or three times as much annual yield out of each acre by using advanced methods of fertilization, irrigation, and scientific farming. The result is that the American farmer is able to feed about 50 people; the LDC farm worker feeds fewer than two. The higher rate of agricultural productivity in the Western countries allows a surplus to be invested in industrial development, whereas retarded agricultural production in less-developed countries slows economic growth and drains the labor force.

Western workers are more productive, not because of image or superior genes, but simply because they have machinery and automation to multiply the results of their labor. US production consumes about 22,000 pounds of coal equivalent energy annually per capita; in India the comparable figure is 380 pounds per capita. Western productivity is based on using artificial means to multiply the efficiency of human workers.

The LDCs cannot match the mechanization of the West because of a shortage of capital. It is estimated that the average American worker is supported by $30,000 worth of capital equipment in addition to a substantial investment in education ("human capital") and economic infrastructure (roads, railroads, telephones, harbors, and so on). The most basic question for the conventional theorists, then, is how and where the LDCs can raise the capital necessary to increase productivity so as to lift themselves from the cycle of poverty.

The basic source of capital for all economies is production itself. Capital is a surplus of production, a portion that is not exhausted by personal consumption but saved and invested. If 200 bushels of wheat are produced by a peasant family and only 100 are immediately needed to sustain the lives of the producers, the other 100 can be sold or traded for tools and tractors (capital goods) that would enable the family to increase its production, say to 300 bushels, the next year. The second year, perhaps 150 of the 300 bushels could be converted into "producer's goods"—that is, invested—to raise production still higher in the third year. Thus, the theory of self-sustaining growth holds that eventually a point is reached when productivity gains become normal as a result of constantly increasing investment. Under these circumstances, it becomes possible to achieve permanently expanding capitalization and also rising personal consumption.

The problem, according to the conventional theorist, is that economies reach this point of "takeoff" to self-sustaining growth only under conditions of rapid capital accumulation. But most of the LDCs have been able to achieve only modest rates of saving and investment because of poverty itself and various forms of waste and inefficiency. Even when surpluses might be generated, they tend to be squandered on unnecessary forms of consumption rather than on growth-oriented investment. Five kinds of waste significantly retard development: (1) runaway population growth, (2) excessive urbanization, (3) excessive military expenditures, (4) needless luxury consumption, (5) official corruption, and (6) management inefficiency.

Wastes that Retard Development

Population Growth   Populations are growing much faster in the LDCs than in the developed countries (see Table 5–1). Developed countries grew by less than 1 percent per year during the 1980s; Africa grew by 2.9 percent annually, and Latin America by 2.3 percent. It is estimated that by the turn of the century Latin America's population will have reached 495,000—triple its population a half-century earlier.

The LDCs have twice as much of their population under ten years of age as do the developed countries. Because infants and young children consume but do not produce, they act as a drain on economic growth. It is estimated that a country with a 3 percent population growth rate must invest 6 percent of its production each year just to keep up with the increase, without achieving any expansion of per capita income.

There is a tragic irony in the growth performance of the Third World. Even in those years in which the economic growth rates of the developing countries outran those of the industrial economies, population growth exceeded economic growth. Thus, the combined burdens of population growth and external debt deprive economic growth of its development value.

Why is the population explosion occurring in the Third World? The cause is not, as many people believe, an increase in the birthrate; this has remained relatively stable. Rather, a decline in the death rate has been achieved by improved public health, medicine, and nutrition. Historically, the richer countries have compensated for the longer life expectancy by cutting the birthrate more or less correspondingly, and their average family size tends to be considerably smaller than that of the developing world's. The LDCs are caught in a difficult transition point: Life expectancy is rising rapidly, and birthrates are dropping very slowly. As a result, their population growth is much more rapid than it

Table 5–1 Where population is growing the fastest.

	Population (millions)			Annual Growth Rate
	1950	1970	1977	1980–1985
Latin America	165	283	414	2.3%
Africa	224	361	572	2.9
Asia	1,376	2,102	2,866	1.5
North America	166	227	266	0.9
Soviet Union	180	242	281	1.0
Europe	392	459	493	0.3

Source: United Nations Demographic Yearbook, 1986.

once was, far exceeding the population growth of the industrialized countries. Pertinent comparisons are shown in Table 5–2.

Efforts by some LDCs to solve this problem through birth control and family planning have not, on the whole, made a great impact. Many peoples consider large families a blessing, have religious objections to birth control, or are culturally ill suited to the regular use of birth control methods. Some novel approaches have had a limited success. In India, the payment of a small reward (less than $5) has induced men who already have several children to undergo voluntary sterilization. In China, the government has long urged young people to postpone marriage and childbearing until they reach 25 or 30 years of age. More recently, however, the population control program in China has been combined with the ideology of heroic work effort and has produced a national system in which cohabitation and personal sexual practices are matters of public interest.

Various medical innovations may achieve real breakthroughs in controlling the population growth of the Third World. Among these are oral contraception for men and chemical agents that prevent conception even if taken several hours after insemination. Meanwhile, in many countries the population growth is not being arrested, and one result is continued economic stagnation and declining per capita gross national product (GNP).

Excessive Urbanization　A generation ago, all the world's principal population centers were in the industrialized countries. New York, Tokyo, London, Paris, Rome, and Moscow led the list. Gradually, however, through both disparate birthrates in the developed and less-developed worlds and migration phenomena, other names began to appear on the list: Cairo, Mexico City, Rio de Janeiro, and Buenos Aires are examples. Today the United Nations estimates that by the turn of the century, all but three of the world's largest cities will be in the underindustrialized world. Mexico City, already in 1986 the most populous city with 18.1 million inhabitants, will have grown to 26.3 million.

This marked urbanization of Third World populations is a major obstacle to economic and social development. As urban populations grow, they require a variety of public services, including health care, education, water, waste removal, and economic security. These can be provided only through economic

Table 5–2 Comparative population trends between industrialized and developing countries, 1965–2000.

	Average Size of Household			Birthrate (per 1000 population)		
	1965	*1980*	*2000*	*1965*	*1980*	*2000*
Industrialized	3.5	3.1	2.6	17.9	15.6	14.9
Developing	5.2	5.0	4.1	38.4	29.4	24.3

Source: UN Chronicle, November 1982, p. 36.

growth followed by either central planning (socialism) or capital accumulation and taxation (economic liberalism). If the population outpaces economic growth, neither route will be available. The alternatives are reduced, therefore, to inadequate development and progress at the cost of external debt.

Urbanization in the Third World runs afoul of these alternatives. International debt is accumulating in Third World countries not only for agricultural and industrial development but also for development of the basic economic infrastructure, water and waste facilities, technical training, health care, and population control. And although most cities in the developed world contain a combination of extreme wealth and hopeless poverty and squalor, those of the Third World are among the products of our greatest inhumanity. Self-sufficiency of the urban poor is a more distant goal even than for the rural poor who, in presence of fertile soil and seasonal rains, are able at least to survive. Furthermore, the urban impoverished are much more exposed to environment-related disease, crimes of violence, inequities of justice, and social predators. The risks are greater for women and children than for healthy men.

Thus, the burdens of urbanization compound the phenomenon of economic development, by which economic growth rates in absolute terms are rendered fruitless. If the benefits of growth must be squandered on public assistance, an overburdened criminal justice system, indigent medical care, and the like, they cannot be used either for centrally planned economic advancement or for capital accumulation, investment, and taxation. They find their way into neither the public nor the private economy, and apparent economic gains are lost in a self-fulfilling system of declining economic capabilities.

Excessive Military Expenditure   A third form of waste that erodes the small increases in production that the developing countries are able to achieve is military expenditure. Many developing countries spend large portions of their scarce resources on the maintenance of armed forces. From 1973 through 1982, for example, the oil-producing developing countries spent approximately $360 billion on military policy; the nonoil group spent an additional $374 billion. Together, their total military bill for the decade was $734 billion. In susbsequent years, the total commitment to military spending diminished somewhat. The reduced power of OPEC, the reduction in the worldwide demand for oil, and the general disruption in world prices resulting from the recession forced down oil prices. Among the results were reduced income among the oil exporters and, in fact, a shift from enormous balance-of-trade surpluses to significant deficits. For the nonoil producers, high fuel prices together with lower prices for their exports forced similar reductions in public budgets. In each case, arms imports were in the affected sectors, and spending went down in both current and constant dollars.

The years between 1973 and 1982 represents OPEC's ascendency, a period in which Western industrialized nations eagerly provided arms to the Third World, particularly to the oil-producing members, in return for steady supplies of petroleum. The major shift in the arms supply occurred after the oil crisis in the West during the winter of 1973–1974. During the nine years between

1965 and 1973, the Third World purchased a total of $25 billion in arms from abroad; in the succeeding nine years (1974 to 1982), this figure jumped to $76.2 billion, a threefold increase. Similarly, in the earlier period, the greatest annual amount of arms purchased was $3.7 billion (in 1971 and again in 1973); in the latter period, the highest was $11.2 billion (1978). From 1984 to 1988, 15 nations supplied the Third World with a record $115 billion in weapons, ranging annually from a low of $21 billion and a high of $28 billion. The five largest suppliers among the 15 were the Soviet Union, the United States, France, Britain, and China. Table 5–3 demonstrates their contributions to this supply. The largest single reason for the major increase in arms trade with the Third World during this period was the Iran-Iraq War. The Soviet war in Afghanistan and instability in Central America, Africa, the Middle East, and Southeast Asia, and persistent tension between Pakistan and India accounted for much of the remainder.

Military expenditures in the Third World have been increasing since 1974 more rapidly than has its general economic growth. The consequence is that an expanding share of national income is lavished on armaments, so military costs are a severe drain on its economic growth potential. In addition, the Third World countries together expend two to three times as much for modern arms annually as they receive in foreign nonmilitary assistance. Although many have attempted to recover some of the losses incurred by military expenditure by assigning troops to economic development projects, it is generally acknowledged that the excessive and costly arms buildup among the developing countries is a luxurious indulgence undertaken at an immense loss for their social and economic development.

The cost of maintaining the Soviet-American strategic arms race so dominates the thinking about world military expenditures that the cost of arming the Third World is often overlooked. But for advocates of the conventional theory of development, the military costs of the Third World are every bit as wasteful as is the balance of terror. Critics of American arms expenditure are fond of reciting the number of hospitals, schools, modern farms, medical discoveries, and social programs that could be supported by the money spent on a new generation of missiles. Those who subscribe to the conventional theory of development are equally quick to point out that were it not for the military investment in the Third World over the last decade, social and economic de-

Table 5–3 Principal arms suppliers to the Third World, 1984–1988, in billions of US dollars at 1985 constant dollars.

	1984	1985	1986	1987	1988	Total
USSR	$7.4 billion	$8.6 billion	$9.1 billion	$11.7 billion	$9.0 billion	$45.8 billion
US	4.9	4.0	4.8	6.2	3.5	23.4
France	3.3	3.7	3.4	2.6	1.7	14.7
China	1.2	1.0	1.3	2.2	2.0	7.7
Britain	1.1	0.8	1.4	1.7	1.5	6.5

Source: SIPRI Yearbook 1989, p. 198.

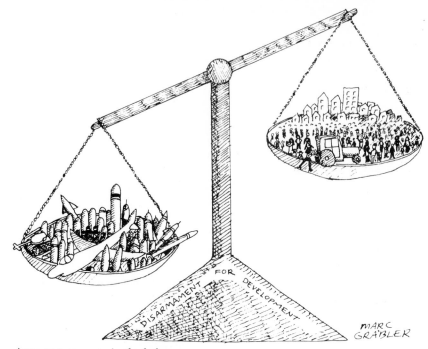

Arms and economy in the balance.
Source: Copyright Marc Grabler, *UN Chonicle*

velopment could have been accelerated immeasurably. It seems ironic to these commentators that so much should be wasted on arms, only to have the same governments coming back to the Western capitals and to the United Nations and its aid agencies requesting still more funds for development.

But those who associate the cost of armaments with forgone development opportunities look beyond the military expenditures of the Third World and concentrate on the world's total commitment to arms. Willy Brandt, for example, former West German Chancellor and now advocate for international reform, equates idle arms stockpiles with nuclear war itself, with respect to development. ''[T]he ever increasing accumulation of destructive machinery would come to be seen as even more perverse [than war itself]—an arsenal which kills people even without being used because it eats up the money without which people are condemned to death through starvation.''[7] Although not a new rallying call, the Brandt declaration has formed the basis of a number of studies on the reallocation of national and international resources from arms to development. One such study, conducted under the auspices of the United Nations, projects the availability of additional funds for international economic development from 1980 to 2000 using two major indices: per-year baseline contributions to development by industrialized countries and additional contributions resulting from the reduction in military expense commitments.

---

[7]Willy Brandt, *Peace and Development* (London: The Third World Foundation, 1985).

Figure 5–1 Potential added investment in Third World development through reduction in worldwide arms expenditures, 1970–2000.

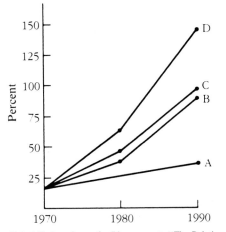

From United Nations Centre for Disarmament, "The Relationship Between Disarmament and Development," 1983, p. 94.

In Figure 5–1, line A results from a linear projection from 1980 to 2000, with the industrialized countries making a standard contribution of 0.35 percent of their annual GNP to Third World development. Line B makes a similar projection, this time factoring in an additional 15 percent contribution throughout the 1980s and an additional 25 percent contribution throughout the 1990s resulting from the reduction in arms spending. Line C deals only with baseline (pre-arms-reduction) contributions, but using a figure of 0.7 percent of annual GNP throughout the 1980s and 1.0 percent throughout the 1990s. Finally, line D uses the baseline assumptions of line C but then adds contributions resulting from 15 percent arms reductions in the 1980s and 25 percent in the 1990s. Because the values are based on 1970 (not adjusted for inflation or changes in currency values), the magnitude of the differences is difficult to appreciate. Nonetheless, the essence of the argument is that as one moves from the minimal assumption of line A to the maximal assumption of line D, the value of investment in Third World development multiplies by a factor of approximately 12.[8]

Luxury Consumption In many poor countries, the abysmal poverty of the masses contrasts sharply with the astronomical wealth of a handful of landlords, maharajas, princes, or industrial barons. The stratification (unequal dis-

[8]For a careful econometric analysis of the impact of the Third World's own expenditures on armaments on its development, see Saadet Deger, *Military Expenditure in Third World Countries: The Economic Effects* (London: Routledge and Kegan Paul, 1986).

tribution) of wealth is much sharper in the LDCs than in the wealthy nations. For example, in Colombia the top 5 percent of the population gets 42 percent of the income. (In the United States, the top 5 percent of the population gets 16 percent of the income.) In more than half the developing countries, less than 10 percent of farms have over half the cultivable acreage. In general, the percentage distribution of income is less equitable in the LDCs.

It might be thought that concentrations of wealth could be invested in economic development. But the rich throw away much of this potential through luxury spending on automobiles and baronial estates instead of putting it to developmental purposes. The wealthy classes in the Third World tend to emulate privileged Americans and Europeans. In addition, some send sizable amounts abroad to avoid taxes and possible confiscation. The "Swiss-banks" factor is said to have drained more than $3 billion out of Latin America alone in unauthorized outflows during the 1960s. Keeping this money at home for useful investment could have replaced about one-third of foreign aid.

But not all luxury expenditures are by individuals. Often in the past, poor nations used their precious funds to create false impressions of their economic condition. Sometimes in the name of religion—as in massive temples and shrines—and sometimes in more secular forms—such as massive public works projects that were of secondary value to society—these choices severely strained public budgets. Perhaps the most striking example is in the Ivory Coast, where a Christian leader of a non-Christian people has squandered hundreds of millions of dollars to construct a full-size equivalent of the Vatican in the African desert. More recently, international aid projects, both intergovernmental and through international organizations, have sought to prevent this

Waste in the Third World: The Yamoussoukro basilica rises in the open land of the Ivory Coast at a cost of more than $200 million.
Source: Bruce Iverson/TIME Magazine

sort of waste by monitoring the uses of domestic public revenues as a condition of providing external assistance. The recipients often regard this as an unwarranted interference in domestic affairs, but to the conventional theory of development, this is neither more nor less than a prudent control on the distribution of scarce resources.

Official Corruption   Luxury spending by individuals often crosses over into corruption and abuse of public authority. Although this is by no means a creature of the Third World (for example, the repeated revelations of corporate theft against the US government by way of fraudulent charges in defense contracts, or the frequency of federal indictments for violations of the securities and exchange laws of the United States), the scarcity of wealth means that corruption will have a much deeper consequence for a developing economy. In the United States, more than 90 percent of the taxes that are due (after loopholes) are successfully collected, but some LDCs have an actual collection rate below 50 percent. The state treasury—one of the main instruments of development—is thus depleted by tax evasion. In addition, allotments from the treasury are eroded by the corruption of project administrators at every level. A flood of resources put into the pipeline at one end can come out the other end reduced to a trickle. Sometimes corruption takes the form of ''legitimate'' expenditures such as luxury cars for officials and inflated expense accounts.

Another form of waste that we may list under corruption is lavish expenditure on prestige projects whose only function is to satisfy the needs of the ruling elites. Examples include opulent presidential palaces and ostentatious airports used only by the rich and other relatively private luxuries. Taken together, these various forms of corruption are a significant drain on the process of capital accumulation.

The two most exceptional instances of public corruption and its consequences for developing economies have occurred in lands greatly favored by American foreign military and economic aid. They involve the Shah of Iran and President Ferdinand Marcos of the Philippines. Each was a close ally of American diplomatic and military policy, and each received billions of dollars from the United States in military and economic development aid. Each eventually fell ignominiously at the hand of revolutionary public opinion, the shah to a fundamentalist revolution and Marcos to exile after having attempted to rig a presidential election that he had lost to the wife of his assassinated political rival. After the shah's fall, Iranian officials claimed that fully $24 billion of public funds, most of it US aid, had been exported by the shah, most of it to the United States, for his own wealth. And upon the fall of Marcos, revelation followed revelation regarding Marcos's property holdings in the United States and elsewhere, Swiss bank accounts, lavish shopping sprees, political favoritism in the use of aid funds, and so on, all totaling many billions of dollars. One can but wonder how different might be both the politics and the economies of these two countries had corruption not so dramatically intervened in investment capital.

Management Inefficiency The management of a thriving economy is an enormously complex affair both economically and politically. In addition to tax revenue, economic managers must arrange for finance, negotiate loans at tolerable interest rates, marshal human resources, establish priorities, create infrastructures, train personnel for industrial functions, make judgments about risks and probable profits, induce investments from internal and external sources, ensure economic efficiency and productivity, and perform thousands of other integrated functions. Modern economies are far too complicated to be guided by an "invisible hand" or other self-regulator. Instead, countless well-trained specialists are needed both for creation and coordination. Just as a musician must know the scales before sight-reading Beethoven, so must a growing economy develop around trained and dedicated specialists. In realizing this, the developing countries have for the past four decades sent their most promising young scientists and managers to the industrialized world for education and training. Many of these have gone either to the United States or Western Europe for training in capitalist economics or to the Soviet Union for training in socialist economics. The objective is to improve the speed and efficiency of economic development without incurring additional dependence on or interference by foreign interests.

The long-range costs of inefficient planning and economic implementation are illustrated dramatically in the spending binge carried on by the OPEC countries from 1974 to 1978. During that time, they spent more than $400 billion on development projects, and Western observers estimate that more than half of it may have been wasted.

> Immediate social and political consequences of rapid development were already evident: inflation, unsound organization, an excessive building boom, a large influx of foreigners, an adverse impact on agriculture and traditional industries and often a lopsided distribution of wealth. These problems, in turn, led to a weakening of established social and political values, accompanied by disappointment and resentment.[9]

Foreign Economic Assistance

As we have seen, the LDCs are typically low-income agrarian societies that devote the greater portion of their economic activity to subsistence production. Industrial development and agricultural mechanization are the keys to economic expansion, but these are inhibited by a shortage of capital rooted in low productivity. The small capital surpluses that do accumulate are depleted by population growth, excessive urbanization, military expenditures, luxury consumption, corruption, and inefficient management. This basic solution, in the conventional view, is to find new sources of capital and to use more effectively the capital that is available.

---

[9]Quoted from Robert Stobaugh and Daniel Yergin, "Energy: An Emergency Telescoped," *Foreign Affairs*, America and the World 1979 issue, pp. 562–595, at pp. 564–565.

While LDCs are suffering from a scarcity of capital and technology, these assets exist in surplus in the developed countries. Can the rich states, at reasonable cost to themselves, stimulate the systems of the poor states by injecting economic nutrients at critical points? Can we devise an effective means of capital transfer to prime the pump of development, without making unreasonable demands on the benevolence of the prosperous peoples? Four forms of assistance from the developed nations to the LDCs have dominated the theory and practice of the conventional view: (1) foreign aid, (2) foreign trade, (3) foreign direct investment, and (4) technical assistance.

Foreign Aid   Foreign aid is a transfer of publicly held or publicly guaranteed resources to one or more developing countries, either in the form of direct funding or in commodities and goods subsidized by the donor country. It can take the form of outright grants or of long-term, low-interest loans. It may come directly from a single country (called bilateral aid) or from an international organization or other funding consortium that has use of the funds of several donor states (called multilateral aid). When loans are involved, they may be made on a short-term basis (usually for not more than one year), on an intermediate basis (usually for one to ten years), or for the long term (ten or more years, usually 25 but sometimes as long as 40 years). Because of the length of time for repayment and the favorable interest rates, developing countries usually prefer long-term loans to the others.

When the United Nations initiated the first Development Decade (1960–1970), it was hoped that the developed countries might eventually raise their international assistance to a level of 1 percent of GNP per year. Later, when UNCTAD became the major economic voice of the Third World, the goal was scaled down to a more modest 0.7 percent. Among the principal Western lenders, however, only the Netherlands and Sweden had ever exceeded a full percentage of GNP through 1981, and only the Netherlands, Sweden, and Norway had crossed the 0.7 percent mark in the ten-year average. Table 5–4 shows the performances of several principal industrialized nations with respect to the internationally established goals.

By 1970, after having given more than $125 billion in bilateral economic and military assistance since the Second World War, plus substantial amounts of Food for Peace and multilateral aid, the American willingness to contribute had declined. An increased awareness of unanswered social needs within the United States has led to demands by Congress and the public that US resources be used to solve domestic problems first. Aid appropriations are a favorite target of the taxpayer revolt. In addition, some liberals have begun to oppose foreign assistance as a potential foot in the door for American interventionism, and conservatives are offended by hostility toward the United States among the more than 75 developing countries that have shared this largesse. Some US economists have come to see aid as a worn-out formula that doesn't work. Billions of dollars were poured into the Alliance for Progress in Latin America, for example, without achieving the decisive development breakthrough that had been promised by President Kennedy. In general, the American disillusionment with aid makes unlikely the expansion of giving by

Third World famine: Victims of civil war and starvation in Mozambique.
Source: William Campbell/TIME Magazine

the United States. Furthermore, the collapse of communist governments in Eastern Europe in 1989 and 1990, on the eve of Western European economic unity in 1992, raised serious issues about the ability of the West and Japan to supply enough development capital to spur a sharp economic recovery and conversion to market economies. Because the US Congress was faced with deficit reduction at the time, there was little prospect of additional aid appropriations. As this book went to press, the plan in Washington was to address

Table 5–4 International aid by principal suppliers with respect to the original UNDP goal and the revised UNCTAD goal, expressed in percentage of GNP for maximum annual contribution and average annual contribution, 1971–1981.

	Maximum Annual		Ten-Year Average	
United Arab Emirates	11.9			
Saudi Arabia	8.2			
Kuwait	8.2		6.8	United Arab Emirates
Netherlands	1.0		6.6	Saudi Arabia
Sweden	1.0	UNDP Goal (1%)	5.0	Kuwait
Norway	0.9		0.9	Netherlands
France	0.7		0.9	Sweden
		UNCTAD Goal	0.8	Norway
West Germany	0.5	(0.7%)	0.6	France
United Kingdom	0.5		0.5	Canada
Canada	0.5		0.5	Australia
Australia	0.5		0.4	West Germany
United States	0.3		0.4	United Kingdom
Japan	0.3		0.2	United States
Italy	0.2		0.2	Japan
			0.1	Italy

Source: World Bank, *World Development Report, 1983.*

the needs of Eastern Europe by redirecting aid currently given to the five principal recipients in the Third World.

As the figures demonstrate, however, other industrialized countries and the oil-exporting countries of the Third World have entered where the United States has tended to retreat. Some experts have argued that the OPEC countries have become lenders principally as a means of offsetting Western charges that OPEC's price increases between 1973 and 1983 had a more devastating impact on Third World development than did any Western policy, because the non-oil-producing Third World countries were faced with the same increases as were the industrial giants. Moreover, while the industrial trading partners had industrial produce with which to balance (or at least partially balance) their international trade and capital accounts, the non-oil-developing countries were driven further into debt by OPEC policies. Much of OPEC's lending policy was designed to ease this burden and was in the form of petroleum subsidies.

Worldwide economic recession and OPEC's loss of grip on the international petroleum market, each of which occurred in the early 1980s, resulted in rather sharp declines in foreign assistance by both the Western industrialized countries and the Middle East oil producers. This is evident in that in 1984, the flow of new public and publicly guaranteed capital to the Third World was almost 10 percent below what it had been in 1979, and moreover, 1984 was a recovery year.

Unfortunately, increases by all donors will not be sufficient to meet the capital needs of the LDCs during the rest of this century. Some economists believe that the LDCs could usefully absorb five or ten times as much outside capital as will be available. But the present prospect is a general decline in the significance of foreign aid, despite population and growth needs.

Needless to say, not all capital that flows to the Third World comes from governments and international organizations. Huge volumes also come from banks and other financial institutions of the wealthier states. Although this is not technically "foreign aid," it nonetheless complicates the external financial dealings of virtually all Third World governments. On the one hand, it provides substantial amounts of investment capital, thus contributing to the rate of development. On the other hand, however, it multiplies problems of repayment and debt service. In the last decade, many Third World governments have been forced into a debt cycle in which they have had to borrow more in order to meet their repayment schedules, only to find their obligations increased. Many have entered into agreements to reschedule repayment, and some have defaulted. Because of the frequency and intensity of these problems, the reduction of Third World debt is now one of the central issues of the global political economy. The problem itself and the many efforts to address it are covered in detail in Chapter 14.

Foreign Trade It is for more than poetic reasons that foreign aid and foreign trade are considered by the conventional view of development to be the principal ingredients of modernization. Because self-sufficiency is impossible in most economies, the acquisition of foreign sources of goods (imports) and foreign markets for the export of products are essential elements in economic expansion.

More specifically, foreign trade plays several important roles in a developing economy, one of which relates directly to foreign aid. Aid, which in effect is the temporary importation of money, brings new debt, both in the form of principal that must be repaid either gradually or at some distant point and in the form of interest. Hence, every dollar borrowed represents a dollar plus in the debt column. Because domestic sources of public revenue are scarce in the developing economies, profit from the export of products is the safest route to repayment of debt (debt service). Export trade, then, is an important source of new capital. The certainty of export markets is also important in determining the volume of a product that will be produced, a factor that, in turn, determines the selling price of the item in both domestic and foreign markets. The price, for its part, helps determine the ability of the product to compete in world markets. Finally, export trade is essential in maintaining the developing economy's trade balance. While accumulating a capital debt by borrowing foreign money, a developing economy cannot afford also to amass a trade deficit, a situation in which the value of its imports exceeds the value of its exports. Part of a development strategy, therefore, must be the manufacture of products for export in sufficient quantities and at competitive prices so that the sale of goods in world markets will at least equal in value the goods that are imported.

Although export potential is an extremely complicated issue, it can be simplified as depending primarily on (1) annual production growth and (2) production growth per capita. The first is straight forward: Is the country able to increase annually the amount it produces? The second is more complicated, because it relates production growth to population and domestic consumption. If, for example, a population remains stable and production grows, then more goods ought to be available for export. If, on the other hand, production remains the same and the population grows, then the per capita production has declined; and if domestic consumption simply remained the same per capita, there would be less available for export.

Statistical data indicate that through the 1970s and 1980s, Third World aggregate production grew somewhat faster than did that of the industrialized nations. Figure 5–2 shows that only in 1984 did the industrialized countries enjoy an aggregate advantage in growth over the developing nations. More striking is the performance of the non-oil-developing nations, which lagged by only half a percent behind the entire Third World (held up by the huge oil export profits of the mid-1970s) for the decade of the 1970s, but which outraced both the industrialized nations and combined oil and nonoil Third World countries throughout the 1980s.

Figure 5–2 Annual percentages of production growth comparing the industrialized world, the aggregate Third World, and the non-oil Third World, 1971–1989.

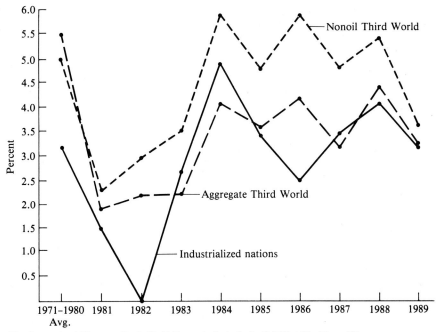

After International Monetary Fund, *World Economic Outlook*, April 1989, table A1, p. 125.

But production alone tells only part of the story. When population increases are factored into the equation, we find that the value of production growth in the Third World from an export perspective is quite different. Figure 5–3 demonstrates that the aggregate Third World—the oil-exporting and the nonoil combined—had a poorer per capita growth performance in the 1980s than did the industrialized countries. Oddly, however, it was the decline in exports that depressed the aggregate, for the curve representing the nonoil Third World in the 1980s shows that its members fared on annual average somewhat better than the industrialized countries.

Thus far we have looked only at export potential by comparing Third World annual production and per capita production growth rates with those of the industrialized world. But potential itself does not measure real growth or contraction in the ability of production to provide investment capital. The two issues that measure the transformation of potential to real gain (or loss) are (1) relation of exports to imports and (2) terms of trade. Clearly, if the value of exports exceeds that of imports, there is a real capital gain when exports increase. If, on the other hand, the relationship of export value to import value is reversed, then only huge increases in exports will overcome the difference. Moreover, if price fluctuations alter the value of imports, exports, or both,

Figure 5–3 Annual percentage growth in per capita gross domestic product in the Third World and per capita gross national product for the industrialized world, 1971–1989. Because the goal of this graph is to show availability of exports, the comparison of gross domestic product in one instance with gross national product in the other is not inconsistent. In the Third World, virtually all production is domestic, so despite conflicting expressions, the graph compares aggregate export potential.

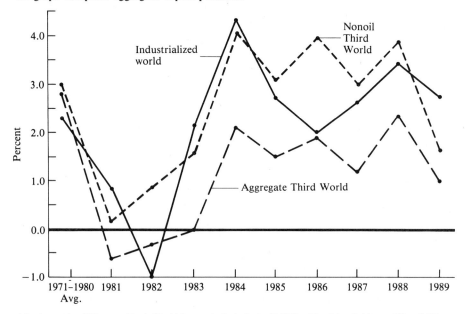

After International Monetary Fund, *World Economic Outlook*, April 1989, tables A4 and A6, pp. 129 and 131.

then changes in volume may or may not compensate for changes in value. The terms-of-trade issue (price fluctuation) is left to the next section. Note, however, Table 5–5, which shows the annual change in export and import volumes for the Third World from 1971 to 1989 as well as the tabulated net difference. In 1983–1988, the aggregate Third World made trading progress as measured by volume.

From the conventional viewpoint, the remaining test of progress is the exported goods themselves: Does change and diversity of exports away from primary products (fuels, minerals, and agricultural goods) toward manufactured goods and semimanufactures indicate progress as defined by modernity rather than volume? First, let us clear away the petroleum question. During the 1970s, the price of Third World (OPEC) oil skyrocketed, but over the period of the decade the amount exported did not. And in the 1980s, there were wild fluctuations in both price and volume because of periodic efforts to fix price to production quotas. But there is another side to this issue, namely, that from 1975 to 1989, the non-oil-producing Third World began to consume more petroleum as it modernized its economic infrastructure and aimed at industrial diversification. In 1981, for example, the amount of oil exported by Third World countries declined by almost 14 percent, yet the amount imported by non-oil-producing Third World trading partners increased by almost 23 percent.

In categories of export, Figure 5–4 shows that relative stability in agricultural exports from the Third World is offset to a large extent by marked volatility and inconsistency in export of minerals. But annual growth in manufactured goods, although inconsistent, is generally in a positive direction. This seems to indicate that the Third World is gradually moving away from reliance on primary products that are subject to wild fluctuation of both demand (volume) and price in world markets, and toward manufactured goods with respect to which prices are more nearly stable.

Table 5–5 Annual growth (or decline) in export and import volume, together with net change, 1971–1989, for the aggregate Third World.

	Export Volume (%)	Import Volume (%)	Net Change (%)
1971–1980 avg.	3.6	8.1	−4.5
1981	−5.3	8.2	−13.5
1982	−6.6	−3.5	−3.1
1983	1.9	−2.7	4.6
1984	7.1	2.5	4.6
1985	0.9	−0.6	1.5
1986	9.2	−4.0	13.2
1987	10.6	5.9	4.7
1988	11.0	10.2	0.8
1989	5.5	5.6	−0.1

Source: International Monetary Fund, *World Economic Outlook*, April 1989, tables A24 and A25, pp. 150 and 151.

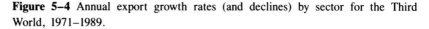

Figure 5–4 Annual export growth rates (and declines) by sector for the Third World, 1971–1989.

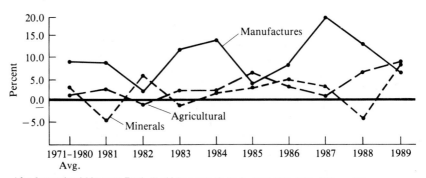

After International Monetary Fund, *World Economic Outlook*, April 1989, table A24, p. 150.

Foreign Direct Investment Because the flow of governmental foreign aid is not on the recommended scale, conventional theorists look for other forms of capital transfers from the developed to the less-developed states. Long-term private investment by profit-seeking firms offers the greatest possibility of expanded resource flow. Billions of dollars move every day through the money markets of the United States, Western Europe, and Japan, and if even a fraction were directed to the Third World, the effect would be substantial. But the share of global foreign investment going to developing countries has in fact been declining as the wealthy nations focus their trade and investment increasingly on one another. The problem for the conventional approach is to attract new interest from global business to invest in the developing countries.

This positive attitude toward foreign capital, advocated by Western-oriented governments such as Indonesia, Brazil, and Taiwan, is directly opposed to the radical ideology of states like Libya and Cuba, which depict foreign investment as a form of neocolonialism. Even the Western-oriented states share some fear of multinational giants such as General Motors, whose annual global sales dwarf the GNPs of more than 110 countries. But conventional theorists argue that controlled foreign investment is a proven stimulus to rapid growth, as demonstrated in South Korea, Brazil, Nigeria, and other countries. To attract more foreign investment, many countries maintain public relations offices and consulates in the major capital centers (New York, London, Paris, and Tokyo, for instance) and publish advertisements and lavish inserts in the world financial press (such as *The Wall Street Journal* and *Fortune*) singing the praises of investment in their economies.

Advocates of increased foreign investment enumerate the following advantages of foreign capital:[10]

1. **Jobs.** Most positions created by foreign firms go to indigenous workers. For example, US multinational enterprises operating in the developing countries employ more than 3 million locals, as against only 25,000 American nationals located abroad.

---

[10]Roberto Campos, ''Economic Policy and Political Myths,'' in Paul E. Sigmund, ed., *The Ideologies of the Developing Nations* (New York: Praeger, 1967), pp. 418–424.

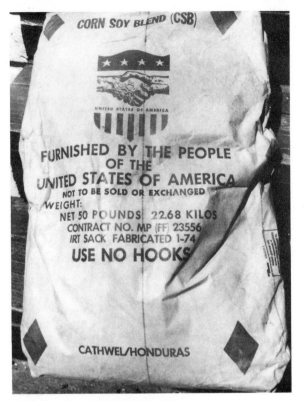

Western aid—simple humanitarianism, or a worn-out for-
mula that doesn't work?
Source: U.S. Agency for International Development.

2. **Technology.** The foreign firm brings the most advanced methods and technologies, acting as an agent for the transfer of new knowledge. This spills over to local sub-contractors as production is integrated in the local economy.

3. **Import substitution.** Foreign investment often helps the balance of payments of the LDC by enabling it to produce for itself what it once imported.

4. **Market access.** The foreign firm brings international market connections conducive to a continued inflow of capital and the expansion of export opportunities.

5. **Efficiency.** The profit incentive is keyed to cost reduction and the maximum use of resources. The foreign investor has a natural motive and the managerial skills to organize local people and information in the most cost-effective and productive way.

6. **Demonstration effect.** Local enterprises may be induced to utilize the techniques and management ideas of the efficient foreign branch to maintain their competitive position.

7. **Planning.** International investors are in an excellent position to assess the comparative advantages of local production in world markets, and they may aid in the identification of ideal lead sectors for planned national economic development.[11]

[11]Harry G. Johnson, "The Multinational Corporation as an Agency of Economic Development," in Barbara Ward, Lenore D'Anjou, and J. D. Runnalls, eds., *The Widening Gap* (New York:

For all these reasons, the politically more conservative voices in the Third World reject the isolationist course of a closed door to Western capitalism.

Technical Assistance   A fourth form of international aid to the developing countries is technical assistance. Most of the world's research and development is conducted in the rich countries. If the results of technological advances are not to be confined to the privileged peoples, and if the benefits of scientific discovery are to be shared by all of humanity, a means must be found to facilitate what has been called the transnational migration of knowledge. Examples of technical assistance include the Atoms for Peace Program, under which the United States has given small atomic reactors and fissionable materials to more than 50 countries to promote peaceful applications of nuclear technology; the arid zone research program, under which the United States supports research on desalinization of sea water by advanced means; and most significant of all, scientific advantages in agriculture known collectively as the Green Revolution, which brings to developing nations modern cultivation techniques and new seed strains that make possible a dramatic increase in farm productivity.

Using the new methods of the Green Revolution, the output of grain cereals (rice, corn, wheat) can be multiplied without any expansion of acreage or the labor force. For example, high-yielding dwarf variety wheat, pioneered in Mexico, has a genetic potential double or triple that of the best yielders among older, tall-strawed varieties.[12] With American help, this advance has been introduced, along with the necessary supporting improvements in fertilizer, insecticides, weed killers, irrigation, and machinery, on the Indian subcontinent.

The results have been spectacular. India increased its wheat production by 80 percent in four years, Pakistan by 60 percent in two. These two nations have long been known as major food-deficit sufferers, dependent on charitable imports. Now they are approaching not only self-sufficiency but even surplus and a capacity for export.

A similar advance in high-yielding dwarf variety rice, IR8, has ended the Philippines' historic dependence on rice imports. Transfer of the Philippine advances to Sri Lanka increased the latter's production by 26 percent in three years. Many other countries are benefiting from these hybrid grains, including Afghanistan, Burma, Indonesia, Iran, Laos, Malaysia, Morocco, Nepal, Tunisia, Turkey, and Vietnam.[13] It is also known that the Green Revolution is finding its way into the communist world.

These impressive achievements have vast political and economic consequences. A few years ago, leading demographers were predicting a global food crisis caused by population expansion. It is not clear whether this problem is

---

Columbia University Press, 1971), pp. 242–251.

[12]Norman Borlaug, "The Green Revolution, Peace, and Humanity," *Population Research Bulletin,* selection no. 35, January 1971.

[13]Lester Brown, "The Social Impact of the Green Revolution," *International Conciliation,* no. 581, January 1971.

now solved or only postponed, but the present trend seems to be toward food self-sufficiency. This trend will reduce external dependence and relieve balance-of-payments problems. Internally, productivity increases may support advances in industrialization. Many of the now advanced nations squeezed their surpluses out of agriculture to finance industrial development, and we can expect this pattern to be repeated in the LDCs. Thus, the Green Revolution may promote a more dynamic political and economic prospect for the developing countries.

There are, however, some costs that must be accounted for in the balance sheet of the Green Revolution. The intensive use of chemical fertilizers and insecticides raises ecological issues that are now familiar in the wealthier nations. Fish and wildlife are endangered, and the runoff carries excessive nutrients and poisons to the oceans, whose ability to sustain pollution is not infinite. The vulnerability of the new strains to disease requires increasing dosages of insecticide, with the long-term danger that new insect varieties will develop that are resistant to all known poisons.

There are also social problems associated with the Green Revolution. Advanced agriculture is based on the substitution of capital for labor to pay for machines, seeds, fertilizer, insecticides, and irrigation systems. As agriculture becomes capital intensive rather than labor intensive, small farmers are squeezed out. Agricultural employment may be reduced as productivity increases. Thus, the effect of the Green Revolution is to widen class disparities rather than to narrow them, increasing the characteristic problem noted earlier in regard to stratification. The initial beneficiaries of the Green Revolution may be the already prosperous rather than the suffering poor. But advocates of the conventional theory argue that the flood of benefits will inevitably trickle down to the lower classes and that the solution to maldistribution effects is rational planning by governments rather than forgoing the possibilities of the new approach.

The benefits of technical assistance are not limited, of course, to the agricultural sector. In industry, computers and advanced electronic equipment have been transferred to the developing countries to improve productivity and to expand industrial potential. Computers have also been introduced to improve managerial efficiency and education. Advances in chemical technology have enabled many of the oil-rich developing countries to improve their own refining capabilities, thus permitting them to deliver finished products rather than crude oil to industrial consumers.

Furthermore, both governments and international organizations such as the United Nations make technical experts available to the developing countries. Faced with technical problems in management, industry, finance, or agriculture, developing countries can call upon foreign personnel from foreign agencies for assistance. These persons are part of the network by which technology is gradually transferred to the Third World from the industrialized centers of the world.

The technological revolution, a product of a handful of industrialized countries, holds two benefits for the underindustrialized nations. First, it provides the instruments of technology to improve management, manufacturing, communications, transportation, and the like. Second, because of wages that are relatively lower than those in the industrialized countries, the manufacture of technological goods offers opportunities for employment in parts of the Third World in which political stability invites foreign plant construction. Indeed, this has become such a serious problem that many technology corporations in the United States, Japan, and Western Europe import virtually all their own manufactures, thus depriving their domestic labor forces of countless job opportunities.

These two phenomena together—the use of technological products for economic development and the employment of vast numbers of persons in the manufacture of technological devices—comprise the phenomenon known as technology transfer. Not surprisingly, outside Eastern Europe the principal technology exporters are Japan, West Germany, the United States, Italy, Britain, and France. Together, in 1970, they exported to the Middle East alone some $2.2 billion in technology; by 1982 this amount had risen to $42 billion, distributed as follows:[14]

Japan	23 percent of total
West Germany	22
United States	20
Italy	14
France	9
Britain	9

But the greatest impact of technology on economic development has not occurred in the Middle East; rather, it has occurred in Singapore, Indonesia, Hong Kong, Taiwan, and South Korea. In all of these countries, per capita incomes are rising fast; exports are improving at rates considerably above those of the rest of the world; and trade surpluses with such nations as the United States are beginning to sound alarms of protectionism similar to that in regard to Japan's trade surplus.

The Radical Theory of Development

The radical theory of development disagrees fundamentally with the foregoing view regarding both the causes and cures of underdevelopment. To the conventional theorist, the cause is internal inefficiency, and the cure is outside help from the developed states. To the radical, the cause is international exploitation by exactly these developed "friends," and the cure is a fundamental change of international relations between the poor and the rich. Indeed, the very medicine proposed by the conventional theorist—technical assistance, foreign investment, trade, and aid—is considered the root of the disease by the radical, for whom investment, trade, and aid are extractive mechanisms that systematically siphon away the wealth of the developing countries.

---

[14]US Congress, Office of Technology Assessment, *OTA Report Brief,* "Technology Transfer to the Middle East," September 1984.

The two schools disagree on basic assumptions regarding the global inequality of life. To the conventional theorist, the rich are ahead of the poor because of dedicated effort and managerial skills. To the radical, the Western peoples achieved their advantage, "not by the laws of the market, but by a particular sequence of world conquest and land occupation."[15] It follows from the conventional view that when the poor make up the gap in productive skills (with the help of foreign aid and so on), the economic gap will close. It follows from the radical view that only cutting the international relationship will end the unjust division of the world's wealth.

The conventional view posits an essential similarity between the development problems of the poor today and the problems successfully mastered by the now rich states in earlier periods. It says in effect, "Just as the United States and Europe developed yesterday and Japan and Mexico are developing today, so will you, the late starters, develop tomorrow." Development is portrayed as a linear process in which every economy passes through certain known stages of economic growth.[16]

Radical analysis rejects this portrayal of the developing countries. The economies of the big capitalist states started as largely autonomous markets under domestic control, although international trade and investment were conducted within careful limits. The economies of the Third World, however, enter the modern development epoch as mere subsystems of global capitalism, having long ago been penetrated by foreign interests and been made economic satellites of the dominant states of the North. The global system consists of a "center"—Europe, America, and Japan—and a "periphery"—the dependent economies of Latin America, Africa, and Asia. The basic economic institutions of the dependencies were formed in response to the insistent demands of the industrial world, rather than in relation to local needs and interests. The typical dependency economy is geared to the export of commodities needed by the industrial center and the import of products from the center. This is known as the pattern of foreign-oriented development, in which external rather than domestic influences shape the society, economy, and political structure.

What produced this lopsided and unnatural development, so heavily dependent on foreign interests? In the earliest period, it was caused by massive raw material hunger on the part of the industrial nations. The underdeveloped regions, subdued and controlled by the superior military force of the center, were reduced to being cheap suppliers of raw materials, useful mainly for their wells or mines or tea or rubber. Cuba became a sugar plantation, Bolivia a

---

[15]See Ward, D'Anjou, and Runnalls, eds., *The Widening Gap,* pp. 152–164, where the two views are eloquently contrasted. For major expressions of the radical theory, see Samir Amin, *Unequal Development* (New York: Monthly Review Press, 1976); and Paul Baran and Paul Sweezy, *Monopoly Capital* (New York: Monthly Review Press, 1966). See also Barbara Ward, *The Radical Economic World View* (New York: Basic Books, 1979). Gunnar Myrdal, *Against the Stream: Critical Essays on Economics* (New York: Vintage, 1972), presents some challenging critiques of the conventional theory of development.

[16]Walt W. Rostow, *The Stages of Economic Growth* (London: Cambridge University Press, 1960), is the standard source for this view.

tin mine, the Arab world an oil field, Southeast Asia a rubber plantation, Gabon (in Barbara Ward's phrase) ''a faint appendage to a mineral deposit.'' In many cases, local impulses to produce industrial goods for home consumption were quelled by the dominant foreigners, as the dependency was needed as a secure market for exactly these products from the center. Thus, foreign domination served to channel economic activity into a high degree of forced specialization.

In most of the developing nations, one main export item accounts for a much higher portion of foreign sales, unlike the export pattern in the rich nations. Thus, it is fair to say that the typical developing country is a one- or two-product exporter, whereas the typical developed nation has a diversified economy. Venezuela exports 90 percent oil; Colombia depends on coffee; Cuba has not escaped sugar dependence; and two-thirds of Chilean exports are copper. Should the mineral be exhausted (as is happening in Bolivia) or a cheaper source be found for the national product (such as the seabed), or should changing consumer preferences reduce demand, dependent economies could be destroyed. In other words, highly specialized economies are dangerously subject to the vicissitudes of the world market.

The Terms-of-Trade Problem

Despite the growth in the Third World's manufactured exports, the export commodities in which the LDCs specialize tend to be primary products—minerals, fuels, and crops taken more or less directly from the earth, with minimal processing. This commodity composition of trade adversely affects developing economies. One reason is the tendency of primary product export prices to fluctuate substantially and sometimes extremely in the world market. Colombian coffee, for example, earned $7 in 1977 but fell to $3 in 1981. In the same interval, cocoa fell from over $5 to below $2. More significantly, while primary product export prices are dropping, industrial product import prices tend to rise rather steadily. In fact, a study done by the World Bank shows that when the export prices of a large sample of agricultural and mining (excluding oil) products are measured against the rising cost of industrial imports, the commodity prices of exports from the Third World were actually lower in 1982 than at any time since the end of the Second World War. When large portions of an economic activity and a labor force are tied to export products that are so unstable in the world market, wild boom-and-bust cycles may result that are socially hazardous and detrimental to orderly economic development. Furthermore, it is this kind of price decay with respect to industrial products that Third World economists consider an intrinsic inequality in trade between the industrialized world and the Third World.[17]

---

[17]Two classics developing this view from different perspectives are the United Nations Conference on Trade and Development, *Towards a New Trade Policy for Development* (1964), universally known as the Prebisch Report; and Arghiri Emmanuel, *Unequal Exchange: The Imperialism of International Trade* (New York: Monthly Review Press, 1972).

The relationship between world prices for primary products and those for industrial products is at the heart of the terms-of-trade problem for the developing economies. Defined as export value divided by import value, terms of trade becomes a measure of the extent to which international trade assists in the development of a national economy. On balance, the developing countries conduct their most disadvantageous trade with the developed market economies because in the terms of that trade, Third World primary products are exported at unstable and declining world prices, whereas industrial produce is imported at stable and increasing prices. Nonetheless, trade with the developed market economies continues to be a larger part of the aggregate trade of the Third World, thus annually accentuating the terms-of-trade dilemma. As a consequence, billions of dollars have been drained out of the developing world simply by loss of value relative to industrial goods. It is significant that this drain results not from explicit imperialism or exploitation but, rather, from the quiet operation of market laws seemingly beyond anyone's control—so called objective world market prices.

One might reasonably expect that as industrialization increases in the Third World, dependence on primary commodities would abate and terms of trade improve. In fact, however, despite the efforts made at industrializing the Third World, few of its members have increased by more than a small percentage the portion of total production that is not related to primary products. The structure of production is such that only a handful of developing countries have manufacturing sectors that, as a percentage of total production, are equal to those of the 15 largest industrialized market economies (greater than 20 percent of total production). They are listed in Table 5–6.

Elsewhere in the Third World, agricultural and mining products continue to be the principal focuses of economic development. And even in the countries listed, a comparison of industrial sectors to those of the largest market economies is possible only in part because with the technological revolution and the growing service sectors in the West, industrial productivity is actually falling.

Table 5–6 Principal industrialized nations of the Third World measured by manufacturing as a percentage of annual gross domestic product.

Argentina	Philippines
Brazil	Republic of Korea
China	Singapore
Hong Kong	South Africa
India	Thailand
Jamaica	Turkey
Mauritius	Uruguay
Mexico	Venezuela
Nicaragua	Sambia
Peru	Zimbabwe

Source: World Development Report 1989, adapted from table 2, pp. 166–167.

Productivity Increases   The terms-of-trade factor puts the poor states in a position that cannot be compared with that of the rich states in an earlier period. The now advanced states achieved rapid increases in productivity during their "takeoff" stage, and these are regarded as the key to their success. But today, the primary price decay erodes productivity gains. Malaysia, for example, increased its rubber exports almost 25 percent from 1960 to 1968—from 850,000 to 1.1 million tons—while significantly reducing its plantation labor force. This is a notable gain in productivity. But its income from rubber sales declined by about 33 percent during these years as prices fell. In effect, productivity increases were passed along to foreign consumers in the form of lower prices, rather than to Malaysian workers in the form of higher wages and living standards. The terms-of-trade problem can be a treadmill on which it is necessary to run faster and faster just to stand still.

Inelastic Demand   Explanations of this phenomenon are based on the disadvantages of primary products against those of finished goods. One is the relative inelasticity of demand for primary goods—only so many bananas will be consumed no matter how many are produced, tending to reduce prices after the market is saturated.

Unorganized Labor   Another factor is the position of labor in the Third World compared with that of the industrial countries. Workers in the advanced states are relatively well organized into trade unions and can command a share of the gains from productivity increases. The comparative weakness of labor organizations in the Third World, however, allows productivity gains to be taken by management in the form of profits or to be passed on to consumers in the form of lower prices. Productivity gains in the center are taken at home, but productivity gains in the periphery tend to flow away—to the center—in the form of lower prices or in profits remitted to foreign owners. The deck is stacked in favor of the already developed world, and mere productivity advances of the type advocated by the conventional theorists will not change the unfavorable rules.

The Radical View of Foreign Investment

Although the conventional theorist views the multinational corporation as an agency for the transfer of capital and technology for the betterment of the developing countries, the radical theorist sees it as an instrument of foreign control extracting exorbitant profits. US investment, for example, increases its capital annually in both the developed and the developing worlds. However, the annual earnings yielded to American investors in the LDCs greatly exceed in percentage the annual yield from investments in the developed world, as is demonstrated in Table 5–7. Typically, the margin of earnings on investments in the Third World runs between 30 percent and 300 percent higher than in the industrialized nations, with the greatest advantages in the primary products. Even in 1985, when, as the table indicates, investments in the developed economies yielded a higher percentage return than did those in the Third World,

Table 5–7 Annual American earnings as a percentage of investment in developed and developing countries, 1970–1985, expressed in billions of US dollars.

	American Investments in Industrialized Countries			American Investments in Developing Countries		
	Investment	Earnings	% Earnings/ Investments	Investments	Earnings	% Earnings/ Investments
1970	51.8	4.6	9	19.2	2.9	15
1974	82.9	10.4	13	19.5	7.9	40
1977	108.0	6.0	6	33.7	7.8	21
1979	137.9	24.4	18	47.8	12.7	27
1980	158.2	24.6	16	53.2	11.9	22
1982	154.4	11.6	8	48.1	8.8	18
1983	155.7	13.8	9	45.8	5.7	12
1984	157.5	14.1	9	50.1	6.9	14
1985	172.8	26.7	15	54.5	7.4	14
1987	232.7	45.9	20	70.7	12.5	18
1988	245.5	38.2	16	76.8	13.9	18

Source: For 1970–1979, *Statistical Abstract of the United States, 1980,* table 1529, p. 865; for 1980–1985, *Statistical Abstract of the United States, 1987,* table 1395, p. 782; for 1987 and 1988, *Survey of Current Business,* August 1989, pp. 62–64.

there is an explanation. In that year, American banks suffered a loss of $1.1 billion on debt rescheduling by Third World governments unable to meet their annual repayment obligations. When this is added back to the total investment earnings, the aggregate investments in the Third World yielded a 16 percent profit, as contrasted with a 15 percent profit in the developed economies.

In the radical theory of development, these findings indicate an accelerated rate of economic penetration and exploitation of the Third World by the developed nations in the guise of direct private investment. Because earnings gained on these investments are returned to the industrialized economies rather than left as investment funds in the Third World, American and other Western investors are actually decapitalizing the underdeveloped economies.

Multinational firms use several devices to evade legal restrictions on excess profits. For example, one foreign subsidiary of a multinational conglomerate typically buys some of its intermediate components from other branches of the same parent located in other countries. The internal "prices" of such sales may be manipulated by the parent for optimal bookkeeping results, taking losses in one subsidiary in which profits are restricted and showing them in another in which they are not. Other devices include the manipulation of royalties, management fees, and other internally negotiated "costs." The multinational enterprise has a variety of options to remit profits without defying legal limits.

Another objection to foreign capital is its effect on the social and class structure of the host society. The foreign firm is at first typically an isolated enclave of modern economics in a sea of underdevelopment, but eventually a network of subcontractors extends the patterns of dependency outside the company gates. Often the multinational guest dwarfs all local enterprises. The sales revenue of the United Fruit Company, for example, exceeds the entire national budgets of countries such as Panama, Nicaragua, Honduras, Guatemala, and El Salvador. The pure economic power of such an entity opens the doors of the middle and even the top strata of the official bureaucracy and creates at the same time a dependent class of local merchants and bankers. In addition, the foreign firm develops a special relationship with certain privileged sections of the labor force, sometimes by paying wages slightly above the depressed local rates. US firms in northern Mexico, for example, are able to pay 75 cents an hour, which is more than three times the local average but at the same time less than a fifth of the rate in nearby southern Texas. Local workers are co-opted by the competition for these prized jobs. In effect, foreign capital creates satellite classes whose interests are tied to the *dependencia* syndrome.

Objections to Foreign Aid

It may seem surprising that even foreign aid is regarded with suspicion in the radical theory. If we concede that dependence on foreign capital and primary product exports is disadvantageous, wouldn't it seem to follow that aid as a form of capital transfer would give the recipient some relief?

There are several objections to this view. First, most foreign aid consists not of simple grants but of interest-bearing loans that must be repaid. The typical LDC runs a chronic payments deficit because of the unfavorable balance of trade and the drain of excess profits to foreign firms. Borrowing foreign aid to make up the gap in current bills leads to mounting indebtedness and simply defers the day of reckoning, accumulating losses to be repaid in some future golden age. Borrowing from Peter to pay Paul (or "rolling over" the debt) does not break the pattern of dependency but reinforces and perpetuates it. Table 5–8 shows the growth of debt payments throughout the 1980s and the International Monetary Funds estimate for 1990, distinguishing between amortization payment (amount due on principal) and payment of interest for each year, together with the total annual payment. The figures are all expressed in relation to the value of goods and services exported in the same years. For example, in 1988, the Third World as a whole faced interest payments equal to 83 percent of their total combined exports for the same year, and interests on principal equal to another 88 percent of exports. In sum, therefore, these countries combined owed in cash on debt 171 percent of the value of everything they expected to export in the same year. To the radical theorist, then, the conventional theory errs greatly in stipulating that foreign aid provides the investment capital with which to expand per capita gross domestic product in order to export more and convert a positive trade balance into new investment capital. To the radical theorist, aid begets not capital but additional debt and deeper dependence on the industrialized sources of funds.

This analysis is limited to the radical theory's evaluation of foreign assistance as a means of accumulating development capital. There are many other

Table 5–8 Annual Third World debt service as a percentage function of exports, 1981–1990.

Year	Amortization Payment Due (%)	Interest Due (%)	Total Annual Payment Due (%)
1981	58.5	68.4	127.0
1982	61.2	78.8	140.1
1983	51.1	73.8	124.9
1984	58.4	82.5	140.8
1985	63.3	81.4	144.7
1986	73.1	77.0	150.1
1987	85.6	72.0	157.6
1988	88.0	83.3	171.3
1989	85.0	97.7	182.7
1990	87.4	97.8	185.2

Source: International Monetary Fund, *World Economic Outlook,* April 1989, table A49, p. 196.

aspects of the debt of the Third World, and those are examined in detail in Chapter 14.

Alternative Futures

Throughout the last quarter-century, the debate regarding international economic development has been conducted principally between the traditionalists (whose analyses focus on modernization strategies) and the radicals (who prefer to concentrate on the intrinsic characteristics of the international system that perpetuate dependency). More recently, however, a number of scholars have suggested new approaches to the problem. One, for example, has noted that neither of the two dominant theories can explain the late development of some countries because economic advancement is not necessarily tied exclusively to economic factors. This observation leads to the conclusion that disparate paths to development must consider such local sociological factors as traditions, motives, attitudes, and religious influences on traditionalism and modernism.[18]

A second effort at expanding the debate beyond the two dominant theories begins with the premise that in each developing state, class formation, capital formation, and the formalization of state authority take place at different times and at different paces. Furthermore, contemporary conditions render some of these states authoritarian, others nationalistic, and some dependent on external economies or even now in decline. The conclusion is that social interests and state policies influence dependency situations in order to multiply development possibilities and to create a variety of patterns of change explicable by

---

[18]Ogura Mitsuo, "The Sociology of Development and Issues Surrounding Late Development," *International Studies Quarterly,* December 1982, pp. 596–625, trans. David Olson.

neither the traditional theory nor the dependency theory.[19]

Still a third observation notes that in addition to the world's economic center and its periphery, there exists a semiperiphery of Third World states that are already fairly industrialized or are industrializing rapidly. For these states, development is led by manufactured exports rather than by agricultural or other primary export products. As a result, there are different paths to development that are not recognized by either of the dominant theories of economic development.[20]

Nonetheless, if reliance on foreign investment and aid is rejected as a solution to the development problem of the Third World, what are the alternatives? A majority of developing peoples now live under governments socialist in nature, but what does this mean to international relations beyond the symbolic hostility to capitalism?

A number of development models exist, and we will examine some of them. It is important to point out, however, that as the ideological solidarity of the Third World begins to crack significantly, there is less urgency among the developing countries to emulate the growth principles of model countries. There has arisen a new individualism among the Third World countries that defies the adoption of existing models and calls instead for individual development efforts that seem peculiar to the political cultures of the countries themselves. Nonetheless, certain models do appear still to contain a wealth of proven experience from which individual efforts might draw.

The Chinese Model

Some voices in the developing countries, such as the ruling party in Tanzania and the Maoist groups in Latin America, cite values in the Chinese experience for other poor countries. Before the communists took power, the industrial and commercial sectors of the Chinese economy were thoroughly penetrated by foreign influence, to the extent that paper and metal currency was printed in English on one side. As late as 1935, foreigners controlled 95 percent of China's iron, three-quarters of its coal, half its textile production, and most of its shipping, public utilities, banking, insurance, and trade. Most industrial workers were employed by foreign firms, and the Chinese social structure showed many of the typical symptoms of what we now call the dependency syndrome. The corrective steps taken by the communists after 1949 were harsh, but they succeeded in cutting the ties of dependency and putting China on a self-reliant path of rapid development. China in effect virtually sealed its borders to capitalist trade and investment and adopted an economic policy of isolation and autarky for 20 years.

---

[19]Michael Bratton, "Patterns of Development and Underdevelopment: Toward a Comparison," *International Studies Quarterly,* September 1982, pp. 333–372.

[20]James A Caporaso, "Industrialization in the Periphery: The Evolving Global Division of Labor," *International Studies Quarterly,* September 1981, pp. 347–384. The author emphasizes Argentina, Mexico, South Korea, Singapore, Portugal, Brazil, Hong Kong, the Philippines, and Spain. Note similarity to text accompanying Table 5–6 in this chapter.

Could the Chinese example of the closed door and almost total self-reliance be imitated by other developing countries? Probably not. China is a world in itself, a nation of over a billion people providing a huge internal market with diversified resources and productive potentials. The 30 LDCs of sub-Saharan Africa taken together have less than 25 percent of this population base; individually, most developing countries are much smaller. Most economists agree that the cost of isolationism to a small country would be a substantially reduced rate of growth, if not economic collapse. Moreover, China itself found that isolation was not an effective route to economic modernization, and in the decade preceding its retrenchment following the forceful termination of a democratic movement (Tiananmen Square, Beijing, in 1989), China deliberately conducted a broad international economic policy designed to speed economic growth.

Regional Integration

Another solution open to small nations is that of forming regional economic groups to consolidate the economics of several neighboring states into one large entity. Present experiments in economic integration among developing countries include the East African Common Market, the Arab Common Market, the Central American Common Market, and the Latin American Free Trade Association. Degrees of integration range from the free-trade area (where tariffs on trade among members are eliminated), through the customs union (where a common external tariff is added to the free-trade area) to the common market (where labor and capital as well as goods and services are permitted to move freely). Later steps in economic integration may include monetary union (a common currency), the merger of tax systems, and finally a single national budget including a shared defense budget. Each stage of economic integration has political costs as well as benefits, and inevitably some elites will gain from a merger while others will lose. The success of developing nations in achieving regional integration is partly a function of the relative strengths of these forces.

Another obstacle to regional economic integration is the fear that the costs and benefits of cooperation will be distributed unequally. Experience has shown that without special preferential measures favoring the less-developed members of a group, the benefits of integration are likely to be concentrated in the more advanced countries, while a disproportionate share of the costs will be borne by the less advanced ones. In theory, this inequality could be relieved by asymmetrical tariff policies providing a higher degree of protection for a prolonged transition period for the less-developed states, as well as directly subsidizing their development in key sectors. But in practice, even the more advanced members of a regional grouping tend to experience developmental strains, and national priorities rather than mutual interests tend to prevail. Moreover, the economic systems of neighboring states may have a limited potential for integration. States whose previous economic development was geared to the export of highly specialized products to the developed countries may find difficult the expansion of trade with fellow developing countries. The noncomplementarity of developing economies explains their tendency to concentrate the volume of trade on distant, more advanced partners rather than on their neighbors.

Another obstacle to integration is the national pride of newly independent countries and the mutual hostility of some adjoining states. Integration requires a sacrifice of unrestricted autonomy in favor of joint decision making, and this in turn requires mutual trust and a willingness to accept a shared fate.[21] Many developing countries, especially those that gained independence within the past two decades, seem to prefer a go-it-alone strategy. Indeed, intra-African economic integration has declined rather than increased since the collapse of the colonial empires, and dependence on the center paradoxically has increased. During the colonial period, integration was forced on diverse neighbors by their European masters, such as the French-imposed West African Customs Union and the Equatorial African Customs Union. Britain established a common market, a common currency, and common railways and other services in the East African colonies of Kenya, Uganda, and Tanganyika. Since independence, however, these cooperative arrangements have been largely dismantled. The lines of commerce and communication from most developing nations thus flow not to their neighbors but to the nations of the center, like spokes to a hub.[22]

Commodity Producer Cartels

In reality, many developing countries seem destined to play the role of primary product exporters for years to come, given all the obstacles to radical alternatives such as the closed door or regionalization. Means of stepping up the pace of economic development will have to be found within the present framework of commodity specialization. For this reason, some leaders of exporting countries are looking for progress in the formation of agreements among producers of primary products to regulate and improve the prices of their commodities.

The outstanding example of success for such producer groups is OPEC, which succeeded in raising the world price of crude oil more than 900 percent between 1973 and 1982. Petroleum exporters with large populations, such as Nigeria and Indonesia, suddenly had the capital resources to finance development at a greatly expanded pace. Exporters with small populations, such as Saudi Arabia, Kuwait, and the United Arab Emirates, not only could afford rags-to-riches luxuries at home but also were able to accumulate huge and unprecedented financial surpluses with which to influence other countries, even the great powers. The entire world watched as Saudi Arabia, once de-

---

[21]D. C. Mead, "The Distribution of Gains in Customs Unions between Developing Countries," *Kyklos,* vol. 21, pp. 713–734; R. F. Mikesell, "The Theory of Common Market as Applied to Regional Arrangements among Developing Countries," in R. F. Harrod and D. C. Hague, eds., *International Trade Theory in a Developing World* (New York: Macmillan, 1963), pp. 205–229.

[22]Dharam P. Ghai, "Perspectives on Future Economic Prospects and Problems in Africa," in Jagdish Bhagwati, ed., *Economics and World Order* (New York: Macmillan, 1972), pp. 265–266.

scribed as "rushing madly from the eleventh century into the twelfth," banked a $30 billion surplus in one year, while Great Britain, on whose empire the sun was never to set, was at its feet.

Oil is, of course, a very special commodity in international trade. It is the lifeblood of modern industrial society, and as the world becomes more wary of the dangers of nuclear substitutes, access to oil becomes a more precious foundation of economic growth than ever. Any substantial halt in oil flows could render prostrate the great industrial economies of the West and particularly of Japan, which is almost totally dependent on imported oil. Western Europe and the United States are only relatively less dependent on international sources of oil. From 1973 to 1980, American dependence on OPEC alone increased nearly threefold, and the uncertainty of supply from Iran following the Iranian revolution in 1978–1979 increased American reliance on the more radical members of OPEC. By mid-1979, it was an open secret in Washington that achieving diplomatic leverage over OPEC had become the first priority of American foreign economic policy. More than ever before it was realized that a renewed oil embargo would be a uniquely potent weapon against the industrial West in forcing the North-South Dialogue back to confrontation.

The monetary value of oil in international trade is a second noteworthy attribute of this unique resource. The revenue from trade in oil makes minuscule that of all other raw materials and fuels combined, and oil trade has a more profound impact on the balances of payments of the industrial states than do all other forms of trade, industrial and agricultural. From the West's vantage point, the balance-of-trade issue is magnified by the small population bases of some of the OPEC states, which removes the necessity for large import volumes that might otherwise offset some of the surplus from oil exports. As a result, Saudi Arabia increased its international currency reserves 5000 percent between 1970 and 1981 (and Kuwait and the United Arab Emirates had increases of 2400 and 3500 percent, respectively). For purposes of comparison, during the same period the American increase was 800 percent, the same as Japan's, and France and West Germany showed increases of 1000 and 600 percent, respectively. Meanwhile, the annual trade balances of the principal industrial oil consumers went into deeper deficit. In the United States, for example, oil imports alone added $10 billion to the trade deficit of 1979 and $14 billion more in 1980.

It is not necessary to expand on these numerical evidences of OPEC's power to demonstrate that the pattern of dependency between the North and the South, at least insofar as fuel was concerned during the glory days of OPEC, was reversed with enormous significance for multilateral diplomacy and international relations in general. Furthermore, the OPEC experience seemed to demonstrate that a Third World cartel in a primary product badly needed by the industrial economies of the West and Japan would be a most advantageous route to economic development.

Yet despite the unique opportunity presented by oil for the formation of a cartel, it was never certain that even OPEC could sustain its strong position in the world economy. Historic ethnic and religious conflicts among the principal Arab members were the early challenges to unity. Later came disagreements on pricing and production policies, with the more radical members arguing for steep increases in price and reduction in production. Such a policy would have brought rapid capital accumulation and postponement of the eventual exhaustion of supply. Meanwhile, the moderate members, conscious of the impact of pricing policies on the industrial economies and, therefore, on the world economy, argued for modest price increases and careful controls over production in individual member states.

External crises mingled with internal conflict as the 1980s approached. The Iranians held wholly new attitudes toward the world after their revolution. The war between Iran and Iraq threatened the security of the Middle East as well as the steady, peaceful oil export commerce out of the Persian Gulf through the Strait of Hormuz to the open sea. (A military closure of the strait would have prevented oil exports from Iran, Iraq, Katar, Bahrain, Kuwait, and the United Arab Emirates and forced Saudi Arabia to transfer all its export oil from its rich eastern fields to the Red Sea.) The Soviet invasion of Afghanistan added a dimension of insecurity and uncertainty, as did the constant threat of war among Lebanon, Syria, Israel, and the Palestine Liberation Organization. Finally, the world economic recession, generally regarded as the worst in 50 years, upset international trade and the global flow of capital.

In the presence of these external influences, matched internally by disagreement on price and production policies, OPEC lost control of the world petroleum market. Market gluts appeared where severe shortages had existed previously, and once again the price of oil began to drop. Although there was temporary stability during 1981 and 1982, the OPEC meeting of early 1983 was fraught with disagreement. The unity forged a decade earlier around the theme of common policy in the interest of rapid economic and social development had evaporated. As Figure 5–5 demonstrates, the price of oil per barrel fell sharply in 1985 and 1986 before reaching essential stability thereafter. In 1983, the International Monetary Fund had estimated that each 10 percent reduction in price would cost the OPEC countries about $18 billion in profits,[23] so the decline from $28 per barrel to $9 meant a loss of some $36 billion in 1986 and recovery of less than half of that in 1987 prior to another decline.

Nevertheless, to the extent that OPEC has succeeded in advancing its goals, the question remains whether the cartel experience can be duplicated by producer groups in other primary commodities. Members of the Intergovernmental Committee of Copper Exporting Countries, the Union of Banana Exporting Countries, the International Tin Council, and at least a dozen other commodity groups hope so, but professional observers disagree on their prospects. Five conditions determine whether a cartel will be durable and effective.[24]

1. **Price elasticity of demand.** Demand must be relatively unresponsive to price. If a commodity is important to consumers, and substitutes for it are not readily available, then price increases can be imposed without a severe loss of sales. This is the

---

[23]International Monetary Fund, *World Economic Outlook, 1983*, from table 69, p. 238.
[24]Adapted from Steven D. Krasner, "Oil Is the Exception," *Foreign Policy*, Spring 1974, pp. 68–90.

Figure 5–5 Average petroleum prices, 1984–1989 in US dollars. The Arabian Peninsula crisis that began with Iraq's annexation of Kuwait in 1990 drove the price of oil to approximately $40 per barrel by October 1, 1990.

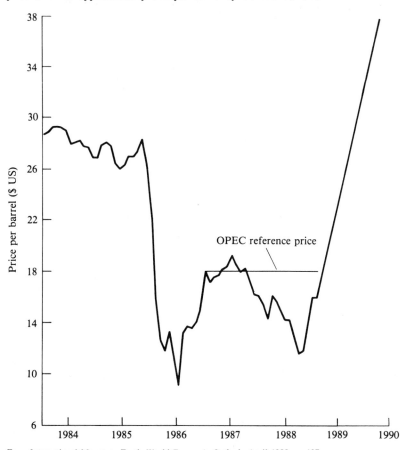

From International Monetary Fund, *World Economic Outlook*, April 1989, p. 107.

case with oil, and it is also believed to be true of minerals such as copper and aluminum and some foods such as coffee. Other products, such as natural rubber and bananas, have a more elastic demand and cannot increase in price without also curtailing sales.

2. **Limited number of producers.** A relatively small number of producers controlling a relatively large share of total world exports in a commodity is ideal for collusion. This condition is met by at least eight major commodities in which the top four LDC producers account for over half of world exports. Moreover, there must be high barriers to entry against new producers—that is, it must be difficult for new competitors to break into a market by underselling the cartel price. This also is true for many commodities, whether because of the limits of raw material sources, climatic and soil conditions, the start-up costs of production, or other factors.

3. **Shared experience of producers.** Producing states must be aware of their interdependence and be willing to cooperate and act as a limited economic coalition. This

condition also is met by producers of several commodities, although in other cases the necessary basis of shared values is less evident.

4. **Consumer resistance.** The probability that a cartel will be successful will be reduced if consumers are organized for effective resistance. In the petroleum market, the position of the major oil companies is believed to have facilitated collusion among the exporting countries. But other commodity markets lack such middlemen, and the probability of resistance may be higher.

5. **Ability to take a long-term perspective.** A cartel member must be prepared to accept short-term costs for long-term gains. The market may contract severely as buyers resist the inflated price and draw down their inventories. The oil-exporting states were in a good position to curtail production, as they could live for some time on the substantial capital reserves previously accumulated. Also, the production of oil is not labor intensive, and relatively few workers were idled by the deliberate slow-down. Countries with small financial reserves and high proportions of the labor force dependent on export production are in a poor position to pay the short-term costs of cartelization. The temptation to cheat may be irresistible to the poorer cartel members, who will be able to take advantage of the situation by price shaving. In no other commodity are producing countries in as strong a position to accept short-term costs as in oil.

Is cartelization of other primary commodities, then, probable or improbable? The evidence is ambiguous, but some Western observers believe that the developed world will face "one, two, many OPECs,"[25] and some Third World leaders believe that this is the first opportunity for the developing countries truly to redress the global inequalities between rich and poor. Advanced states are being forced to consider a range of defensive measures to protect themselves from price gouging by cartels. Some have proposed expanding buffer stockpiles and diversifying sources of supply of primary commodities as measures to prepare for economic warfare. Consumer coalitions would be constructed to oppose the producer cartels. In the extreme case of economic strangulation of the industrial states by a hypothetical long-term oil embargo, some have raised the possibility of direct military intervention to ensure access to supplies and possibly to reduce prices if they were to reach dangerous levels.

Others reject this economic warfare model and call for cooperation between the producing and the consuming states to raise the income of the primary producers with minimum disruption to the international economy. Third World spokespersons particularly believe that the global redistribution of wealth is long overdue and that increases in prices of exports of developing countries will be a principal means of achieving this. They reject the charge that the new price of oil is artificially high; rather, it was the old price that was artificially low. The rich countries have become used to a terms-of-trade structure that must be changed, and they are finding the transition painful. Americans have become accustomed to a situation in which their standard of living, measured

---

[25]See especially C. Fred Bergsten, "The Threat from the Third World," *Foreign Policy,* Summer 1973; and his "The Threat is Real," *Foreign Policy,* Spring 1974.

in per capita GNP, is 23 times that of developing countries. Now the developing world has an effective means of changing this balance of wealth, admittedly at some cost to the developing world, and they are unmoved by the cries that "you're bankrupting us."

The Soviet Union may be expected to support the Third World on this issue. The USSR is the world's leading producer of petroleum and is a fairly substantial exporter to East and West European countries as well. The change in the price of oil achieved by OPEC resulted in direct gains to the USSR of about $2 billion per year in export earnings, partly at the expense of the East European communist states. The Soviet Union is a major primary product exporter, and it would be strengthened by further revision in the terms of trade, while the NATO allies and Japan are the world's major raw materials importers.

The United States is in a less favorable position but still is better situated than Europe or Japan. The United States imports about 15 percent of the critical industrial materials it consumes, compared with about 75 percent for Europe and Japan. And although the absolute volume of imports is high, dependence is concentrated on other developed countries rather than on Third World sources. The leading suppliers of nonfuel raw materials to America are Canada, Australia, Zimbabwe, South Africa, and Brazil. As commodity power becomes more important to international relations, the United States can be expected to upgrade its alliance with these states. For only a few minerals— notably bauxite (aluminum), manganese, tin, and natural rubber—is the supply significantly centered in the Third World, and for these, alternative sources of supply and substitute materials are available at some cost of transportation. Moreover, the United States is itself the leading exporter of another category of primary commodities: wheat and other grains. As the world's breadbasket, the United States has gained substantially from the inflation of world food prices. Indeed, increased agricultural export revenues almost canceled out the increased costs of imported oil in the US balance of payments for the first two years after the 1973 oil embargo. Since then, however, the more rapid increase in petroleum prices than in agricultural and industrial exports has contributed dramatically to American deficits in international trade and payments, revealing that at least in the short run, America is no less vulnerable to resource warfare than are other industrial states.

Conclusion

This exploration of the radical and conventional theories of underdevelopment has revealed some of the theoretical and practical issues that underlie the North-South Dialogue and the perspective of Third World nations on the contemporary international system. Emancipated and free from imperialism, this huge portion of the earth's population remains enslaved by a poverty unimaginable in comparison with even the lowliest standards of the industrialized world. Although formal colonization may no longer exist, the economic control of the Third World by the economic tentacles of the developed world is everywhere true, and by their exploitation of Third World resources and populations they perpetuate the gap between wealthy and poor. International machinery and a generation of imaginative economic policy planning may have changed the characteristics and statistics of national subordination, but the basic stratification of the world's nations and peoples is relatively unchanged.

However, the demand for national emancipation that led to the coalition known as the Third World has been followed by a revolution of rising expectation—in economics, in human rights, and in social development. Modern communications, rising levels of literacy, and increased individual contacts of Third World individuals with the industrial world (through formal education and employment in multinational corporations, in particular) have stimulated an appetite for better standards of living and release from a system of international oppression. Neither socialism nor capitalism has provided an adequate formula for dealing with national economic issues or with international economic issues that so crucially affect the developing nation. And the governments of neither capitalist nor socialist nations have provided political initiatives to reverse the spiral of dependence, debt, and subordination. Only the power of OPEC has risen from the Third World with a loud enough voice to have been heard as a challenge to the prevailing norms of the international political economy. From the viewpoint of the developing states, therefore, the North-South Dialogue either will usher in a new era of cooperation between rich and poor for the implementation of a new international economic order, or it will have been an interlude between two different eras of international politics. The first is characterized by dependence of the South on the North; the second is marked by relentless economic warfare as the advanced industrial civilizations try desperately to obtain the primary products on which their own well-being depends.

CHAPTER 6

Perceptions in World Politics

W e have reviewed the perceptual frames of five of the major actors (or groups of actors) in today's international system—the Soviet Union, the United States, America's principal allies, China, and the Third World. Until *glasnost*, the dominant Soviet view was that of a world divided into two innately hostile camps of capitalism and socialism, itself the protector of the socialist camp, and the United States the world headquarters of antirevolutionary reaction and imperialism. And until the substantial thaw in world politics in recent years, Americans generally saw Soviet communism as an inherently expansionist totalitarian ideology threatening to engulf the weaker nations of the Free World, which were protected only by the umbrella of American power. Washington's allies perceived themselves to be threatened less by the communist menace than by subordination to the United States as modern economic colonies rapidly becoming a threat to American economic dominance. The Chinese, recently driven within by domestic political events after a decade of rapid modernization and evolving global political and economic policies, saw the Soviet-American Cold War as a thin disguise for two competing imperialisms, both trying behind masks of protective benevolence to expand their domination. Insistent that the events of June 1989 did nothing to interrupt China's path to modernization, Beijing leaders continue to see China as the true home of peoples' revolutions and as a model for national development in a world of equals without superpowers. And because Marxism-Leninism-Maoism posits that the state will eventually wither away, so too will interstate relations, leaving behind a world of equal peoples in mature global socialism. The Third World countries, hungry for economic as well as political independence, are occupied less with these East-West conflicts than with the undiminished North-South conflict of colonialism, economic dependency, and an international environment hostile to the development of the small powers.

Each of these perceptual outlooks supports itself with an array of data and historical analyses. Each seems to its proponents so well supported by facts that it needs no further substantiation. Each perceptual system regards the others as inaccurate and dishonest. Proponents of the other points of view are victims of misperception or are dissimulators who know the truth but for ulterior motives pretend to have a different perception. In short, laypersons and national policymakers believe their own perceptual systems to be true and those of opponents to be at least partly false.

How is it possible for each perceptual system to resist change when confronted with contradictory information? Why don't the leaders of the world sit down and iron out their differences, correct one another's misperceptions, and resolve at least the portion of their conflicts that is rooted in misunderstanding? Why don't they get down to the facts and replace all this confusion with an understanding of reality?

To answer these questions, it will help to understand some of the propositions in the theory of international perceptions—propositions adapted from social psychology and applied to the study of international relations.

Facts

In everyday life, we generally assume that our understanding of reality flows directly from that reality itself. It is common sense that certain things are facts whereas the opposite assertions are not and that if we can ascertain the facts, certain conclusions will follow. The purpose of information gathering, for both the scientist and the decision maker, is to determine the facts from which knowledge of reality can be drawn.

Perceptual theorists do not accept this simple conception of knowledge. To them, knowledge has a subjective as well as an objective component: The facts do not speak for themselves but are given meaning by each interpreter from his or her own analytical point of view. The conclusion that follows from facts depends on the interpretation that is given to the facts.

Furthermore, facts do not spring from reality but are, rather, particular pieces of information from reality that are selected by an observer as having importance, while other pieces of information are rejected as lacking importance. "Reality" consists of an infinite amount of potential information, from which only a tiny part is taken as a set of facts. For example, in writing the history of a particular war, the historian must select only a small portion of the available data to report. Millions of individuals are involved in billions and trillions of acts; billions of decisions are made by participants; the patterns of interaction are beyond imagination. The historian must select from all this a few pieces of information that seem, summarily, to describe the interactions and succinctly explain their causes. Students of history and historiography know only too well that the facts do not speak for themselves.

Social science summarizes this view of facts in a terse definition: A fact is but a peculiar ordering of reality according to a theoretic interest.[1] That is, the facts themselves are imposed on reality by the observer, rather than the other way around; and the very nature of the facts themselves depends on the questions the observer chooses to ask. Because each perceptual system asks its own questions, observers of divergent viewpoints naturally arrive at different answers or facts.

To illustrate: From the Soviet point of view, data on the profit structure of American corporations are the body of facts that one must have to understand the international system; from the American point of view, it is off the point entirely. Someone given 20 minutes to explain the Cold War who spends 15 on the nature of American investments will be regarded by a Soviet listener as having given "the facts," but by an American as having evaded them. To the American listener, the real facts have to do with Soviet aggression and American response, and examples of this kind of Soviet behavior will be pertinent. "Facts" are thus subjectively defined and are themselves a phenomenon of perceptions. Perceptions cannot be corrected when confronted with facts if the facts themselves are perceptions.

Values, Beliefs, and Cognitions

Perceptual theorists distinguish among three components of perception: values, beliefs, and cognitions. A value is a preference for one state of reality over another. For example, health is better than illness; green is prettier than blue. Values do not specify what is but, rather, what ought to be. Values assign a relative worth to objects and conditions.

A belief is a conviction that a description of reality is true, proven, or known. Often it is based on prior reception of information from the environment ("I have learned that . . ."), but it is not the same as the data themselves. It is an analytical proposition that relates individual pieces of data into a "proven" pattern. For example, democratic governments are less warlike than totalitarian governments; imperialism is the mature phase of monopoly capitalism. A belief is not the same as a value. One might believe that communism brings a higher rate of economic growth and that capitalism has a better record of protecting individual freedoms. Given these beliefs, one must decide whether capitalism or communism is better according to one's own values. Which is worth more, economic growth or personal liberties?

A cognition is data or information received from the environment; for example, Russia is selling war planes to Syria. Cognitions are key elements in establishing perceptual systems and in changing those systems. The concept of changing national perceptions refers to introducing cognitions that will revise beliefs and values. If we held a conference between the major Cold War actors to iron out their differences and misperceptions, our purpose would be to in-

[1]See David Easton, *The Political System* (New York: Knopf, 1953).

fluence perceptions by introducing new information. We would try to change stubborn beliefs and values that cause conflict by confronting each side with new cognitive data.

Unfortunately, it has been found in a variety of studies that at all levels of human behavior, deeply held values and beliefs are highly resistant to change through new cognition. Social psychological research supports a theory of cognitive dissonance. Briefly stated, this theory holds that when a deeply held value or belief is contradicted by a new message from the environment (a dissonant cognition), the message (fact, cognition) will be rejected and the value or belief retained. This may not take the form of outright rejection of the discrepant message; rather, it may take the alternative form of reinterpretation of the datum to make it consistent with existing belief. But the effect is the same: the individual's value and belief system protects itself from external alteration.[2]

We might relate this phenomenon to the idea of an economy of thought. It is very "expensive" to carry about in one's head all the information supporting one view and its opposite. Mental economy requires that we have a filtering system to fit a single reality to our preconceptions so that we are not constantly revising our basic perceptual systems, with all the readaptation and adjustment that that would require. Political organizations choose as their leaders individuals with known points of view that concur reliably with those of the membership. If national leaders were relatively free to revise their perceptual frameworks, they would not be reliable. Hence, the rigidity and predictability of the leadership's perceptual system is an asset to the group. The leader should not be quicker to change than are his or her constituents.

The constituents, on the other side, must not be overly vulnerable to perceptual change from external influences. If foreign leaders could appeal over the head of a national leader to his or her own constituents, they might manipulate these persons to their own advantage. For this and other reasons, it is functional for each nation to have its own system of authorities, public officials who determine the overall national interest with regard to other nations. These same public officials play a major role in channeling the cognitions that reach their publics. Many studies have shown that individuals will accept or reject the same information depending on whether it comes from a positive or negative prestige source. Thus, constituents choose their leaders partly for the relative inflexibility of their perceptual systems, and the leaders process incoming information in such a way as to maintain the existing perceptual system of the constituents. The national belief system is thus stable and resistant to change.[3]

---

[2]See Leon Festinger, *The Theory of Cognitive Dissonance* (Stanford, Calif.: Stanford University Press, 1962).

[3]Compare Herbert Kelman, ed., *International Behavior: A Social Psychological Analysis* (New York: Holt, Rinehart and Winston, 1965), especially "The Effects of Events on National and International Images" by Karl Deutsch and Richard Merritt; Ole Holsti, "The Belief System and National Images," *Journal of Conflict Resolution*, vol. 6, 1962, pp. 244–252; Kenneth Boulding, *The Image* (New York: Harper & Row, 1960); Robert Jervis, *The Logic of Images in International*

For all these reasons, we can safely assume that national perceptual frameworks will usually survive challenges from other nations and new experiences. They may make superficial or cosmetic improvements to adjust to new realities at times, but fundamental change is a long-term process. The vehicle of national policy is steered by looking in the rearview mirror; nations are influenced more by where they have been than by where they are going. For over a quarter of a century the United States continued to respond to the failure of isolationism and the ill wisdom of Munich. Soviet policy continues to be obsessed with the territorial invasions of two world wars and with a threadbare theory of capitalism that is now over a century old. China's policy has, until very recently, been shaped by recollections of the Century of Humiliation. The Third World's concept of colonialism has scarcely evolved. Hardened perceptions, because of the conviction with which they are held and the information shaping for which they are used, are major obstacles to political progress.

Selective Perception in Big-Power Intervention

We have seen that international events are selectively perceived by key actors and that every reality has multiple meanings depending on the nationality and political orientation of the perceiver. This principle can be seen sharply in a comparison of two big-power interventions in the middle 1960s: American military intervention in the Dominican Republic and Soviet military intervention in Czechoslovakia.

The United States sent 25,000 marines into the Dominican Republic in the spring of 1965 to prevent that country from shifting leftward; three years later, the Soviet Union initiated a military invasion of Czechoslovakia to forestall that country's drift toward political liberalism. The Dominican Republic is in the traditional American sphere of influence in the Caribbean, and Czechoslovakia is a key element of the traditional Soviet sphere in Eastern Europe. Thus, to many outside observers, the two events were a clear demonstration of the dual-imperialism philosophy of the superpowers, dividing the world between them and intervening freely in the affairs of lesser states in their respective hegemonies. But to the superpowers themselves, these events had very different meanings; each justified its own behavior as different in kind from the lawless intervention of the other. Perceptual analysis provides a key to understanding these two cases.

The Dominican Republic, 1965

The Dominican crisis arose from a conflict between a right-wing military government and a rebellion by supporters of ousted civilian president Juan Bosch. Bosch had been the first freely elected president in 38 years following a long

---

Relations (Princeton, N.J.: Princeton University Press, 1971); and also by Jervis, *Perception and Misperception in International Politics* (Princeton, N.J.: Princeton University Press, 1976).

period of dictatorship, but he was evicted from office by a military coup after only nine months. The crisis of 1965 erupted when a constitutionalist movement attempted to restore him to office and to remove the generals. American officials on the scene and in Washington viewed the rebellion as a communist conspiracy using the good name of Bosch as a mere convenience, although this characterization was disputed by many observers. President Lyndon B. Johnson felt obligated to dispatch the marines to Santo Domingo to prevent another Cuba from arising in the Caribbean.

By what right, we may ask, did the United States intervene in what were manifestly the internal affairs of the Dominican Republic, regardless of how American officials might have felt about events there? It was conceded that the rebellion itself was composed entirely of Dominican citizens, making the American action a foreign intervention in a civil war. This accusation had an important effect on America's self-image, because the United States considers itself a strict adherent to the principle of nonintervention in the internal affairs of other countries, as codified in the United Nations Charter, the Charter of the Organization of American States, and elsewhere in international law.

American officials responded that although all the rebels were indeed Dominican, the rebellion was nonetheless part of the international communist conspiracy and was, in the words of the legal adviser to the State Department, "an attempt by a conspiratorial group inspired from the outside to seize control by force" and was thus "an assault upon the independence and integrity" of the Dominican Republic.[4] It follows that American intervention was justified to protect the Dominican people from domination by a hostile, external political force.

The Soviet reaction to the American intervention was swift and indignant and accorded with the strong reactions of many noncommunist governments. Soviet Ambassador N. T. Fedorenko said at the United Nations on May 1, 1965, "There can be no justification for the invasion of the territory of a sovereign state by the United States armed forces, . . . a cynical violation of the elementary norms of international law." Fedorenko specifically rejected one argument in defense of the American action: the assertion that intervention was justified by the principles of the Inter-American System as enunciated by the Organization of American States (OAS). This United States–dominated organization had passed several resolutions that affirmed and validated the American contention that communism was inherently a foreign threat to Western hemispheric nations, and on several occasions the OAS had endorsed American military interventions in Latin American countries to oppose developments believed to be communist inspired.

The Soviet spokesperson objected that this American position amounted to a belief that

> the right to decide the fate of the Dominican Republic rests only partly with the people of that country and partly with their neighbors. . . . Such statements are

---

[4]Statement of Leonard C. Meeker, "Legal Basis for United States Action in the Dominican Republic," reprinted in Abram Chayes, Thomas Ehrlich, and Andreas F. Lowenfeld, *International Legal Process*, vol. 2 (Boston: Little, Brown, 1969), p. 1182.

incompatible with the obligations of the United States under the United Nations Charter, which prohibits any interference in the internal affairs of other countries . . . . The question of internal organization and regime is purely an internal affair of the Dominican people themselves and they alone . . . have the right to decide it without any pressure or interference from outside.

The United States, Fedorenko insisted, cannot act in Latin America ''as if it was [*sic*] in its own private domain, . . . as if it were a question of Alabama or Mississippi.''[5] Thus, the United States had invoked certain regional principles that allegedly superseded the usual rule of noninterference, while the Soviet Union rejected these claims and stood firmly on traditional international law and standards of decent behavior.

Three years later, these positions were exactly reversed, and the diplomats of the two countries demonstrated an extraordinary rhetorical dexterity in reversing roles and taking opposite parts in the case of the Soviet invasion of Czechoslovakia. This time it was the Soviet Union that asserted a special regional right to intervene in the internal affairs of a sovereign country, and the United States that was outraged at the naked display of international gangsterism.

Czechoslovakia, 1968

The crisis in Czechoslovakia materialized when the government headed by Alexander Dubĉek began to move its domestic and foreign policies in directions that differed in basic orientation from the philosophy of the Soviet Union, leader of the Warsaw Pact nations. Just as the United States had feared another Fidel Castro in the Dominican Republic, the USSR came to fear another Tito in Czechoslovakia. (This is a reference to Marshall Josip Tito, the long-time maverick leader of communist Yugoslavia, who had advanced the notion of ''separate roads to socialism,'' a theoretical threat to Soviet monopoly over the political philosophy of the Eastern bloc.) This might constitute an independent communist regime that could not be counted on to contribute to regional stability and that might ally itself with hostile extraregional powers (that is, NATO). To prevent this, several hundred thousand troops of the Soviet Union and other Warsaw Pact nations entered Prague in August 1968 to dismantle and replace the Dubĉek government.

American officials, reflecting opinion in most of the world, labeled the Soviet action an outrage. Secretary of State Dean Rusk insisted that a small country is entitled to live its own life without having the will of a dominant neighbor forced upon it. American spokespersons portrayed the Czech events as a plain act of foreign interference, comparable to the Nazi invasion of Czechoslovakia in 1938.

The defense of the Soviet action began with the proposition that the Dubĉek government had become a conscious or unconscious agent of capitalist imperialism. Antisocialist forces were seeking to sever Czechoslovakia from the socialist commonwealth. And although these antisocialist forces were Czecho-

---

[5]Fedorenko's remarks as reprinted in Thomas M. Franck and Edward Wiesband, *Word Politics* (New York: Oxford University Press, 1972), pp. 97–102.

slovak nationals, giving the conflict the appearance of an internal affair, Russia claimed to possess "irrefutable data concerning ties between the internal reaction in Czechoslovakia and the outside world," according to Soviet UN representative Jacob Malik.[6]

Furthermore, *Pravda* argued that the Czech government was responsible "not just to its own people, but also to all the socialist countries." Czechoslovakia occupies a crucial geopolitical position in the European balance of power, and "weakening of any of the links in the world system of socialism directly affects all the socialist countries, which cannot look indifferently upon this."[7] In effect the Soviet argument invoked the very same regional right to intervene that it had rejected in the Dominican case.

American spokespersons were equally inconsistent. Officials rejected most strenuously the assertion that there are special rules within the socialist commonwealth that supersede the universal principle of noninterference, even though the United States had asserted precisely such a special relationship for the OAS in the Dominican case. "No matter what the intimacy of one country with another," a United States delegate at the United Nations argued, "neither may claim a right to invade the territory of its friend."[8] And yet the American nations could, in this view, determine that no more communist governments would be tolerated in the Western Hemisphere, even if such governments were established by purely internal processes.

Thus, the two superpowers sharply reversed their positions to accord with policy considerations. The Soviet Union rejected the idea that "the right to decide the fate of the Dominican Republic rests only partly with the people of that country and partly with their neighbors" but at the same time asserted that the Czech government "is responsible not just to its own people but to all the socialist countries." The United States asserted that the OAS, as the institutional expression of the Inter-American system, could make determinations regarding the internal movement of members toward a communist government, but the Warsaw Pact bloc could not exercise the same rights in the name of the socialist commonwealth.

Conflicting Perceptions

Underlying these disagreements of principle are critical differences in political perception. American officials see the Inter-American system as a free association of self-determined nations, whereas the socialist commonwealth is a mere collection of satellites and puppets of the USSR. Soviet officials, on the other hand, see the OAS as a formal historical expression of American imperialism in Latin America, whereas the socialist commonwealth is an alliance of

---

[6]UN Security Council, Doc. S/PV 1441, August 21, 1968, p. 32.

[7]*Pravda* statement reprinted in *The New York Times*, September 27, 1968, p. 3.

[8]Statement of the US representative to the UN Special Committee on the Principles of International Law on Legal Aspects of the Invasion and Occupation of Czechoslovakia, September 12, 1968, in *US Department of State Bulletin*, vol. 59, October 14, 1968, p. 394.

The USSR in Czechoslovakia, 1968.
Source: AP/Wide World

progressive states under the leadership of the USSR. Thus, even if detailed cognitions of the two events were identical, interpretation would involve conflicting sets of prior contextual beliefs and values. To Americans, a shift toward communism would be a loss of freedom; Soviets would see a progressive and even inevitable development. However, Americans regarded the liberal movement of the Prague regime away from Soviet-style orthodoxy as progressive and hopeful, but Soviet observers saw it as regression toward capitalism. Officials of the two countries would reject the contention that their positions in the two cases were contradictory.

Each side could also defend its actions by pointing to certain factual differences that favor a given perception. The Soviet intervention interrupted the otherwise peaceful evolution of Czechoslovakia, whereas the smaller US force helped end a fratricidal civil war that was already under way. The US intervention was followed by reasonably free elections, but the Soviet intervention was followed by continued repression. On the other side, there is a pattern of US economic domination in the Dominican Republic, whereas economic relations in Eastern Europe actually favor Czechoslovakia over the USSR. Also, Czechoslovakia is vital to the Soviet defense network, but the Dominican

Republic is a minor matter for the United States—raising the argument that the Soviet intervention might have been the more justifiable in the name of necessity.

Facts of this sort can be raised to justify the rationalization of either side that its case is different. Unflattering parallels can be rejected by either side, and the perceptual framework can remain invulnerable to empirical or logical refutation. This comparison of two cases shows that an intelligent perceptual structure is highly resistant to change, even in the face of direct contradiction.[9]

These two examples, although a quarter-century old and somewhat remote from contemporary events, are particularly illustrative of the problem of conflicting perceptions. Not only did the United States and the Soviet Union fail to understand each other in these instances, but each failed to recognize the contradictions of its own logic.

Although not all such perceptual contradictions reveal themselves with such clarity as in these events, recent history is filled with evidences of perceptual confusion. In 1980, for example, while the Iranian government was holding American hostages in retaliation for American support of the brutalities of the ousted shah, that same government invoked international law against Iraq for behavior that contributed eventually to war between the two. Remarkable reversals in logic are also seen in the respective Soviet and American attitudes toward the Americanization of the Vietnam War and the Soviet Union's long and equally costly war in Afghanistan.

Soviet and American perceptions of the downing of Korean Airlines Flight 007 in 1983 constitute a similar example. From the American viewpoint, the craft was an easily identifiable civilian plane, characterized by its size, by the peculiar bulb superstructure of the Boeing 747 design, and by its commercial markings. To have shot it down with inadequate attempts to land it safely, even though it had strayed accidentally over Soviet territory in the Pacific, was a wanton act of disrespect for human life and unmistakable evidence of the savagery and barbarity of Soviet leaders. From the Soviet viewpoint, it was a craft that had crossed paths with a known American reconnaissance craft and then flown deliberately over Soviet territory on an act of espionage, conducted under cover of civilian markings. Any subsequent use of crowded civilian airliners to conduct intelligence missions in Soviet airspace would meet a similar fate. And any Soviet military personnel who might be reprimanded or punished as a result of the event would be singled out not for having permitted firing on the craft, but for having delayed firing until almost after the craft had escaped Soviet air space. If there were any savages or barbarians involved in the incident, they were the South Korean and American officials who had subjected hundreds of civilian passengers to the dangers of international intrigue.

---

[9]For an extended comparison of the Dominican and Czechoslovak interventions, including thorough documentary citations, see Franck and Wiesband, *Word Politics*. For other comments, together with a comprehensive treatment of the roles of doctrines and perceptions in the management of international crisis, see Friedrich V. Kratochwil, *International Order and Foreign Policy: A Theoretical Sketch of Post-War International Politics* (Boulder, Colo.: Westview Press, 1978).

Special Problems of Superpower Perceptions

Because of the enormous and unprecedented ability of the superpowers to influence world events, through both modern communications technologies and their political influence, perceptions and misperceptions among the leaders of the Soviet Union and the United States are especially important to world order. Virtually every day, through either formal diplomacy or public statement, Washington and the Kremlin exchange ideas on a broad variety of subjects with potentially far-reaching consequences. As we have seen, these changes may be fraught with imprecision and are not, therefore, conducive to effective and progressive decision making. Clarity of ideas, precision of communication, and reciprocity in the development of trust are among the requisite ingredients of global stability; and a bilateral superpower environment of distrust, hardened through the years against penetration by demystified facts, is not a reliable basis for progress. Thus, it is important that we dwell for a moment on the special problems of the perceptions and misperceptions of the United States and Soviet Union.

Many Americans are sympathetic to the idea that the leaders of other countries tend to look at the world through ideological lenses that create perceptual distortion, but they reject the view that such an analysis can be applied with equal validity to the American case. Is it not true, they ask, that the United States has a free press in which diverse opinions and outlooks are represented? Virtually every point of view, no matter how silly or outrageous, has its own publication in the fantastic array of printed materials available. This contrasts sharply with the situation in the communist countries and in most of the Third World, where available information sources tend to be monopolized by the political party in power and only a single point of view is available. It would seem that the free market of ideas in the United States would make Americans less vulnerable to self-deceptions and rigid ideological distortions.

There is ample justification for this expectation, and it must be conceded that American policy mistakes are freely criticized at home as well as abroad, whereas dissent in some other countries is partially or completely suppressed. Alternative perceptions and policies are openly discussed within the domestic political structure of the United States, and misperceptions are quickly pointed out by domestic critics. Thus, the mechanisms of potential self-correction seem to operate much more effectively in America.

At the same time, it is undeniable that certain crucial American misperceptions have managed to persist over very long periods of time, despite the repeated efforts at correction by intelligent and responsible dissenters. For example, the American image of China as a satellite of the Soviet Union dominated the ideas of foreign policy decision makers until at least 1960, long after this misperception should have been adjusted by available information. Dissenters who questioned the orthodox point of view in the early years after the Chinese revolution had their patriotism and loyalty to the American anticommunist cause vigorously challenged; only the bravest voices were willing to continue their dissent from the official mythology. That other pictures of China could be obtained in small dissenting magazines and publications is in-

"The other side?"
Source: From *Herblock's State of the Union* (Simon & Schuster, 1972)

teresting but not particularly meaningful. The dominant misperception was reinforced by all the major publications and the broadcast media—information
that supported the official view. The free market of ideas is not a guarantee
against false orthodoxies and misperceptions, although it does help keep alive
varying points of view.

Another hazard of the American self-perception is the easy assumption
made in this country that what Americans think is typical of world opinion.
The people of the United States, like people elsewhere, are prone to the delu-
sion that when an opinion prevails among everyone they know, it is equally
popular elsewhere. Americans are particularly subject to this error, because of
their view of themselves as the leaders of the Free World. Samplings of public
opinion in different countries show, however, that the particular outlook of
America is not universally popular and that there are many issues on which
American public opinion is inconsistent with opinion abroad. For example, the
Gallup organization conducted an 11-nation public-opinion poll in November
1967 on United States policy in Vietnam (see Figure 6–1). It found that outside the United States the military escalation policy was almost universally
unpopular; within the United States, however, the majority of opinion favored
even greater escalation. In 9 of the 11 Free World countries polled, American
withdrawal was overwhelmingly the favored opinion, but in the United States,
53 percent favored even greater escalation and only 31 percent favored withdrawal. On this issue, apparently, the American people isolated themselves
from world opinion and deluded themselves that they were the shield of the

Figure 6–1 Eleven-nation Gallup poll on Vietnam.

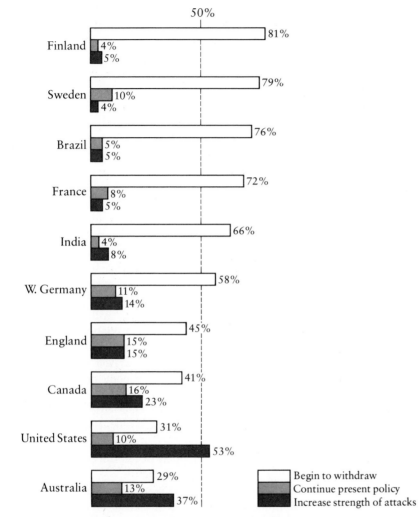

From Gallup Opinion Index, no. 29; November 1967. Reprinted by permission.

Free World. It is reasonable to conclude that Americans, despite a remarkable free press and apparent good intentions, are no less prone to errors and misperceptions than are other peoples and that they as much as others should listen carefully to the opinions of both acknowledged friends and apparent enemies.

Moreover, although Americans regard other political cultures as ideological, they fail to recognize that much of the domestic backdrop of their own foreign policy is ideologically motivated. They consider their ideology simply as democratic, and they dismiss skepticism concerning it. American foreign policy is virtuous, and dissent is un-American. Indeed, despite the health of the American two-party political system, the pages of the nation's diplomatic history are dotted with theories of foreign policy that call for either bipartisanship or nonpartisanship, that declare that politics stops at the water's edge, or that the best politics of foreign policy is no politics. In the effort to depoliticize foreign policy, particularly during periods of war or other national crisis, episodes of messianism are not uncommon. In his first detailed report to the American public on the two atomic bombings of Japan in 1945, for example, President Harry S Truman invoked heavenly authority:

> We must constitute ourselves trustees of this new force—to prevent its misuse, and to turn it into channels of service to mankind.
>
> It is an awful responsibility which has come to us.
>
> We thank God that it has come to us, instead of to our enemies; and we pray that He may guide us to use it in His ways and for His purposes.[10]

Over 40 years later, President Ronald Reagan declared, "I have always believed that this anointed land was set apart in an uncommon way, that a divine plan placed this great continent between the oceans to be found by people from every corner of the earth who had a special love of faith and freedom." And ". . . we are enjoined by scripture and the Lord Jesus to oppose [the evil empire of the Soviet Union] with all our might." Any American foreign policy, however ill conceived or inhumane and however offensive to international law, is justified by heavenly decree.[11]

An analysis of this phenomenon less spiritual in tone deals with the ethos of the American vision of its world role. Because in foreign relations all states seek to express their cultural uniqueness and reinforce identity, foreign policy in general and security policy in particular tend to be derived in part from whatever myths and ahistorical perceptions thrive in the body politic. In the case of the United States, those myths spring from a moral sense of historical separation from the banal politics of Europe, from a unique vision of a bountiful New World, and from a sense of moral exceptionalism. Hence, Americans see foreign policy in terms of the good and the evil (as in democracy and naziism or democracy and communism) and in goals of reformism (leading to internationalist foreign policy) or self-conscious isolation.[12]

The consequences of foreign policy based on this assumption are themselves threats to a stable world order, because it exempts American policy from the rule of self-restraint. Constitutional guarantees of freedom of expression and free press are thus crucially important balances to official doxology.

The problems of Soviet perceptions and misperceptions are equally complex. In a world in which the superpowers daily fling invective back and forth, it is not enough to label the Kremlin anti-West or anticapitalist. It does not suffice to conclude that the Soviet Union is, in former President Reagan's

---

[10]"Radio Report to the American People on the Potsdam Conference," August 9, 1945. See *Public Papers of the Presidents of the United States: Harry S Truman, 1945*, pp. 203–214, at p. 213.

[11]For a review of the contemporary consequences of this kind of foreign policy thinking, see Arthur Schlesinger, Jr., "Foreign Policy and the American Character," *Foreign Affairs*, Fall 1983, pp. 1–16.

[12]Michael Vlahos, "The End of America's Postwar Ethos," *Foreign Affairs*, Summer 1988, pp. 1091–1107.

words, "an evil empire" or to determine in one's mind whether capitalist encirclement is a Western aggression against the East or a defensive reaction to the Kremlin's avowed intent to overtake the West. At issue is nothing less than a set of presumptions about world politics that evolve from Marxism-Leninism that differ totally from those that have come to the West from the Renaissance and the Enlightenment. Although Soviet leaders may not appeal to God, they do turn in a form of secular faith to the Marxist-Leninist precepts regarding socialism, the world revolution, the dictatorship of the proletariat, the inevitable decline and destruction of capitalism, and notions of democracy that center on economic equality rather than political liberty. On the occasion of General Secretary Konstantin Chernenko's death in 1985, the Communist party and the Soviet government released a joint letter to the Soviet people in which they proclaimed that

> The CPSU is equipped with the immortal revolutionary doctrine of Marxism-Leninism. It is unswervingly following the path charted by Lenin and will never deviate from that path.
>
> The party will continue to pursue its course toward the all-around perfection of developed socialism. . . . The party has always regarded dedication to Marxism-Leninism . . . and proletarian socialist internationalism as the supreme spiritual values of the Soviet people.[13]

It is against this background that Soviet images were formed for virtually the entire life of the Soviet state. Long before 1917, Marx observed that materialism is a vital expression of capitalism. Given two Western invasions in less than a half-century and post–World War II capitalist encirclement, the nuclear arms race and the European military balance evolved not from transient political differences but from the necessity of capitalism to express and defend itself against historical inevitability through the economics of military arms. Moreover, as arms policy demonstrates its inability alone to adjust the course of history, in the view of General Secretary Mikhail Gorbachev in 1985, "the practical actions of imperialism, especially United States imperialism, ever more clearly elucidate [a policy] of social revenge on the basis of achieving military superiority over socialism."[14] The American target, then, is seen not as the Soviet territory or leadership but as the future itself.

Soviet ideology is not a mere instrument of foreign policy. It is, rather, a scientific instrument that shapes and guides the world revolution. Indeed, the supremacy of socialism in world affairs is its objective ability through scientific substantiation and theoretical elaboration to understand the forces of history and the world revolution against imperialism. It is by these techniques that the inevitability of history is revealed, and it is these revelations that

---

[13]Letter reproduced in *International Affairs* (Moscow), April 1985, pp. 12–14, at p. 13.

[14]General Secretary Mikhail Gorbachev in an address to the Plenum of the Communist party of the Soviet Union preparing for the Twenty-Seventh Congress, quoted in *The New York Times*, October 16, 1985, p. D17. For the full text in English translation, see Mikhail S. Gorbachev, *The Coming Century of Peace* (New York: Richardson and Steirman, 1986), pp. 280–293.

guide policymaking so as to advance the world revolution rather than permit the imperialist forces to retard it. [15]

Because Soviet ideology is a scientific instrument for the interpretation and adjustment of social forces, it follows that the perceptions of Soviet leaders will be formed not by what the West says it is but by what Marxism-Leninism determines it to be. Consequently, Western diplomacy, strategic policy, arms negotiation tactics, activities in the Third World, and so forth are not seen as isolated political events but as parts of a fabric of antisocialist aggression and antirevolutionary reaction. Doctrine anoints Soviet actions as the advancement of the irreversible forces of history, but Western policies are shaped by political orientation into an aggressive though fruitless effort to postpone the inevitable victory of peoples free from state oppression and imperialism.

Despite their tenacious character, it is not true, of course, that perceptions never change, even among the world's principal powers. Americans did eventually sacrifice the notion that all socialism is militaristic communism of Soviet origin, just as they abandoned the idea that China in communist control could never be dealt with. Indeed, in the last three years substantial perceptual shifts have occurred in Soviet-American relations. Gorbachev's *perestroika*, the internal restructuring that has allowed relatively free voting, public criticism of the party and government, and the partial capitalization of the economy, has lent unprecedented flexibility to the Soviet view of the world economy. Similarly, Gorbachev's *glasnost*, a policy of openness and cooperation with the West, has ushered in new opportunities for trade and control of nuclear, conventional, and chemical armaments. His visit to the United States in 1988 was welcomed as warmly by Americans as a state visit from any of America's principal allies. Indeed, one public opinion poll demonstrated shortly thereafter that Americans consider more serious the economic threat from Japan than the Soviet military threat. So although public perceptions evolve slowly and often fitfully, even in societies guaranteed intellectual freedom, they do nonetheless adjust to modern conditions; and, indeed, without those adjustments, at first unilateral and then bilateral and even multilateral, the global political system cannot progress peacefully.

Conclusion

We live in a world of nations created in response to revolutionary ideals that inspired the founders and continue to motivate subsequent generations. The Pilgrim Fathers, the early Bolsheviks, the Chinese Maoists, and the various inspirational heroes of the Third World countries all bequeathed to their followers a special sense of creative mission and a feeling of obligation to carry forward the advances of their revolution. Today, like the missionaries of more religious times, each nation sends forth its young people into the outside

---

[15]See, as an example, N. Kapchenko, "The Peace Potential of Soviet Foreign Policy," *International Affairs* (Moscow), July 1985, p. 86.

world to convert the heathen and spread the gospel. This messianic spirit can be a constructive and energizing force, but when it is overlaid by misperceptions and self-delusions it can become a dangerous basis for international relations. In the incisive words of one observer, the following is the image of ideological warfare in the modern world:

> The claim to universality which inspires the moral code of one particular group is incompatible with the identical claim of another group; the world has room for only one, and the other must yield or be destroyed. Thus, carrying their idols before them, the nationalistic masses of our time meet in the international arena, each group convinced that it executes the mandate of history, that it does for humanity what it seems to do for itself, and that it fulfills a sacred mission ordained by Providence, however defined.[16]

But ideology is not the sole basis of international transaction. Nothing has eroded the state's monopoly over information more than modern communications technology; and the speed with which diverse peoples change in other places has greatly diminished the ability of governments to hold their peoples ideological captives. The Soviet government yields peacefully to the demands of coal miners after the most widespread labor unrest in Soviet history. People all over the world observe Chinese troops open fire on unarmed students in Tiananmen Square rather than acknowledge demands of democratic reform. The US Congress concedes to the wishes of five Central American presidents on the dissolution of the Nicaraguan anticommunist *contras* as the price of peace in that region. These and scores of other major changes, all enacted on an uncensored global stage, have direct consequences for international stability not merely because of their factual contents, but because of their capacity to invade the communications monopolies of governments, and thereafter to call into question tired political orthodoxies and launch the gradual process of mass perceptual transformation.

---

[16]Hans Morgenthau, *Politics Among Nations,* 4th ed. (New York: Knopf, 1967), p. 249.

PART II

The Logic of Power

CHAPTER 7

Power

The previous chapters have been concerned with values, perceptions, and goals of key actors in the contemporary international system. This section focuses on the instruments of foreign policy and the ways that systems of international relations constrain states in their goals. We will move from the level of actors to that of systems and interrelationships.

The Nature of Power

What is power in international relations? We may define it broadly as the ability of an actor on the international stage to use tangible and intangible resources and assets in such a way as to influence the outcomes of international events to its own satisfaction. This definition points out some of the important features in the relationship of influence among actors. First, power is the means by which international actors deal with one another. It implies possession, but specifically a collection of possessions to create an ability. Second, power is not a natural political attribute but a product of material (tangible) and behavioral (intangible) resources, each of which has its unique place in the totality of the actor's power. Third, power is a means for achieving influence over other actors who are competing for outcomes favorable to their objectives. And fourth, the rational use of power is an attempt to shape the outcome of international events in a way that will maintain or improve the actor's satisfaction with the international political environment. The derived satisfaction is normally a measure of the degree to which the influential policymaking elite of a nation perceives its needs and objectives to be served by the prevailing international norms.

These characteristics of power suggest others. It is important, for example, to think of power as having an instrumental character. Power is a means to an end, an instrument for achieving objectives. But the possession of power will be meaningless if its application is unable to bring about results that enhance the wielder's self-interest. Furthermore, one must consider the relative character of power. When two states compete over an international objective, their abilities to exert power may be roughly equal (a symmetrical power relationship) or severely unequal (an asymmetrical power relationship). Thus, it is important when assessing power to ask, "Powerful relative to whom or to what?" We know, for example, that in 1935 Italy was sufficiently powerful to overrun Ethiopia; its First World War weapons quickly subdued a primitive society. But the same Italian armed forces were virtually impotent in the face of the modern Allied assault eight years later.

More modern military examples have dramatized still another peculiarity of power: The use of power may have diminishing returns. In South Vietnam, for example, the United States used virtually all military means short of nuclear warfare to bring about a North Vietnamese withdrawal. Yet for all its firepower, it failed to achieve its objective. The North Vietnamese and Viet Cong, infinitely less powerful militarily, were able to seize upon national will and deteriorating support for the war in the United States and elsewhere to achieve politically what they could not achieve militarily: governmental self-determination and the expulsion of American force. The diminishing returns of American firepower, together with the superior intangible resources that the North Vietnamese were able to utilize, redressed the apparent asymmetry of their relationship. Some forms of power are impotent indeed!

But vivid as such military examples may be, not all power relationships are measured in armaments. In fact, it should be said categorically that power is not force, and the ability to exert power is not limited to forceful situations. Indeed, international actors exercise their power unceasingly; yet rarely, given the huge volume of international transactions, do they resort to force. Although the frequency of forceful operations may tempt us to think otherwise, the use of force in international relations is an aberration of the normal power relations between states. Force should be thought of as residing at the extreme end of a continuum of choices available to a nation when its agents want to manipulate the outcomes of events.

At the other extreme of that continuum is persuasion, or the achievement of influence by the power of reason. Regrettably, it is appropriate only in those international situations in which two actors have a close similarity of objective, or in which one asks but a small alteration in the policy of another in an event that is not crucial to the latter. Beyond this rare case, the achievement of influence depends on the relative availability of positive and negative sanctions to affect the behavior of the other party. When the sanctions are positive, they may be regarded as rewards or inducements to concur in a particular policy. One government, for example, may offer a major trading concession to another in exchange for its support on an issue. When such enticements fail, the same government may resort to negative sanctions, to punishments or deprivations, to alter the course of another state's policy. It may threaten to rupture diplomatic relations, to discontinue trade, or to carry out any of countless other deprivations. Or in situations crucial to its satisfaction, an actor can threaten or use force. Force, then, is the result of an escalation in the power relationship between actors.

The choice of any of these methods of power depends on several factors in the relationship of the parties. Foremost is the importance of the outcome. A government will not threaten nuclear war over small issues or issues of marginal importance. In addition, the choice of methods depends in part on the access that one actor has to another. Specifically, if the relationship is one in which there is a general agreement on the composition of international satisfaction, then persuasion and rewards will normally be adequate. Equally important, however, is the degree of similarity in the respective interpretations of the specific issue. For example, since the Second World War, the United States and Britain have enjoyed an extraordinarily high degree of mutuality on general issues of international satisfaction. Yet they broke sharply over the British role in the Suez War of 1956, an occasion on which the United States resorted to diplomatic embarrassment—public withholding of concurrence— in order to alter the course of British policy. In some cases the problem has another dimension, one in which one government is simply unable to reach another. This was particularly true in the Cold War years when in order to exert power over America's allies, the Soviet Union had to contend with American responses, and in trying to reach the governments of Eastern Europe the United States was faced with Soviet counteractions.

In all of these situations, it may be concluded that one actor has power over the other when it enjoys a superior power position relative to the issue at hand, although not necessarily an asymmetrical advantage on all issues. In all cases, diplomatic effectiveness is linked to the capabilities that underlie policy. In cases of ultimate confrontation, it is linked to the state's military capabilities.

The Ingredients of Power Potential

Studies of power in international relations recognize that power is a mixture of capabilities derived from both domestic sources and international activities. Furthermore, such studies recognize that power comes from three sources: natural, sociopsychological, and synthetic. The importance of each varies according to the type of international transaction and to the choice of power exercise that has been selected as a matter of national policy. Needless to say, the greater the degree of conflict and the more coercive the intentions, the more intricate will be the combination of power ingredients brought to bear.

Natural Sources of Power

Among the natural sources of power, geography is one of the more important. Decades ago geography was widely regarded as the most important single ingredient of power, although this theory has faded considerably in the era of jet and missile warfare. Nevertheless, geography and territorial position are among the most enduring determinants of national power. They determine the extent of the land mass, which affects both the ease (size) and the difficulty (length of hostile borders) of national defense. The vast extent of the Russian land mass frustrated and devoured invading armies throughout history, causing the defeat of Napoleon in 1812 and of Hitler nearly 150 years later. But just as sheer size can multiply the defensive capabilities of a state and reduce its vulnerability to enemies, so too can lengthy borders be detrimental to strategic planning and military costs. Both China and the Soviet Union, for example, which share the world's longest border, are acutely aware of the additional costliness the border presents. Similarly Israel, surrounded by boundaries easily traversed by hostile tanks and infantry and further weakened by its tiny size, is severely hindered in national defense by the natural aspects of geography. In contrast, Switzerland is safeguarded against land invasion by mountain barriers, and the United States is protected by 3000 miles of ocean on the east and 6000 on the west, which separate it from major potential antagonists. (The Pearl Harbor Memorial is, of course, an ever-present reminder that Hawaii is the exception.)

It has been demonstrated that the frequency of wars correlates with the number of borders a nation shares, an observation that has led to the theory of geographic opportunity.[1] It was once fashionable in the study of international relations to search for simple geopolitical laws that delineated national power for all time. Three prominent examples are:

1. Sir Halford Mackinder's heartland formula in 1904: "He who rules Eastern Europe commands the Heartland of Eurasia; who rules the Heartland commands the World Island of Europe, Asia, and Africa; and who rules the World Island commands the World."[2]
2. The dictum of Alfred T. Mahan, an American theorist of the late nineteenth century, that control of the seas is decisive in the global balance.[3]
3. Attempts to explain the sweep of Russian imperialism as a search for warm-water ports open in winter.

Although while there can be no doubt of the importance of seapower, warm-water ports, and control of Eastern Europe, efforts to derive immutable geopolitical laws from specific historical instances are prey to fallacy. No monocausal theory can account for the richness of military and political geography. This is not, however, to deny the importance of special geopolitical assets such as the Suez and Panama canals, the Persian Gulf, the Straits of Gibraltar, the Dardanelles, and the Straits of Malacca and Hormuz.

But even geographic features of power are not limited in their significance to security. Just as warm-water ports may house major naval facilities, so too do they facilitate international trade, support oceanic and suboceanic research,

---

[1]James Paul Wesley, "Frequency of Wars and Geographical Opportunity," *Journal of Conflict Resolution,* vol. 6, no. 4, December 1962, pp. 387–389.

[2]Sir Halford Mackinder, *Democratic Ideals and Reality* (New York: Henry A. Holt, 1919), p. 150.

[3]Alfred T. Mahan, *The Influence of Sea Power upon History* (Boston: Little, Brown, 1890).

and provide other services vital to national enrichment. By the same token, territorial size not only figures in the equation of national defense but also determines in part the resources that will sustain a population at peace and contribute to the national economic well-being. Any of these factors may play a major role in national cohesiveness, the stature of the nation in the international community, and in general, the satisfaction of the population with international events and its ability to foster that satisfaction.

As suggested in the discussion of geography, a second critical component of power is natural resources. Relative endowments of natural resources and raw materials may affect the power of a nation significantly, although here again we should not assume an inflexible connection. There is no doubt that plentiful natural resources have helped create the superpower status of the United States and the Soviet Union and may someday do the same for China and Brazil. Nations rich in raw materials are less dependent on the outside world and hence less vulnerable to negative sanctions (blockade, boycott, and so on). And they are better able to apply both positive and negative sanctions to opponents; the wealth conferred by natural resources may be held out as a reward, or it may be withheld as a form of persuasive deprivation. Ultimately, it may be used to expand the military potential of the state: the highest negative sanctioning (warmaking) capability.

An extraordinarily instructive example of the ability of natural resources to affect world politics, even to the point of altering its course, is found in the recent policies of the underindustrialized oil-producing states. From 1973 to 1983, through rapid and very large increases in the price of crude petroleum, and by acting collectively through the Organization of Petroleum Exporting Countries (OPEC), most of them accumulated such huge trade surpluses and reserves of foreign currencies (''petrodollars'') that they were able to finance rapid development and to throw the international monetary system into upheaval, loosening its former imperialistic patterns. In addition, the coincidence of these events with Arab-Israeli war in 1973, enabled the Arab members of OPEC to use the threat of oil embargo and the actual reduction of petroleum exports as an instrument to force many industrialized states to alter their political and economic policies in the region.

Yet, these observations do not offset the fact that many poorly endowed nations are powerful and many richly endowed countries are weak. Japan, for example, imports most of its critical raw materials and yet has been one of the most important economic and military powers of the twentieth century; Indonesia, with huge reserves of minerals, has played an insignificant role on the world stage. A nation that effectively mobilizes its economic and industrial capacities may adjust to a scarcity of raw materials by importing primary products and exporting finished goods. Critical strategic materials can be stockpiled against the possibility of war-time blockade, and natural and synthetic substitutes can be devised in case of shortages.

Quite aside from the warmaking capability that natural resources may impart, such richness is a vital part of national power. It is not because petroleum enables the OPEC members to wage war, for example, that they were able to adjust the global power distribution by cooperative oil export policies.

It is the need of the industrialized world for those riches that led to the adjustment of international trading relations and the accelerated economic development. The sheer volume of international trade in raw materials dramatizes the amount of dependence that drives it. Also, it indicates the extent to which abundance in natural resources can enhance the ability of a state to influence other parties and, finally, to influence the outcomes of international events without overt force. Only in extreme cases for the need of sanctioning capability are natural resources correlated to military preparedness.

A third natural component of power is population.[4] In general, large populations are capable of a variety of social functions and services. They are able to promote industrial vitality, make maximum use of resources, and support large military components. Yet there are major exceptions to the rule that size and power are directly correlated. Indonesia, for example, with 152 million people, cannot be ranked in modernity and power with West Germany (62 million), nor can India (676 million) be imagined above Japan (118 million). Table 7–1 reveals the disparity between population size and economic modernity as a measure of power. The contribution of population to power depends not exclusively on size but on the social, economic, and psychological consequences of size as well. Among these qualitative factors are level of technical skill, productivity per capita, level of social and political development, and effective coordination of human and material resources. Unskilled, starving, and ineffectively governed populations such as that of India cannot marshal into effective power their other resources. China, where population size has traditionally been a barrier to the modernization of power potential, has only now begun to coordinate its human resources to the point of turning them toward effective development of the state.

Social and Psychological Components of Power

Just as national population size has significance for power, so too do the images, attitudes, and expectations of peoples. Among the most critical is national self-image, which contributes acutely to the concept of the role that the nation ought to play. Ideas, even when perverse, govern foreign policy in large measure. Such slogans, for example, as "White Man's Burden," "Manifest Destiny," and "World Policeman" not only express a mood about national expectation but also form a social framework in which national policy is set. Such policies may be a manifestation more of mood than of rational choice.

Images of others are an equally important part of the policymaking framework. When national peoples hold the governments and peoples of other nation-states in high regard, their attitudes toward foreign relations reflect tolerance and forbearance; when they view the second party with mistrust, suspicion, and fear, their expectations about foreign policy are reactive at best. Social-psychological research has amply demonstrated that demands on foreign

---

[4] For a good general theoretical background, see Katherine Organski and A. F. K. Organski, *Population and World Power* (New York: Oxford University Press, 1960).

Table 7–1 Disparity between population and economic modernity as measure of power.

	Population		Gross National Product		
World Rank	*Population (millions)*		*World Rank*	*GNP (US$ billions)*	*GNP/capita (US$)*
1	1,104	China	7	375.5	342
2	797	India	12	190.5	248
3	284	USSR	2	2,129.0	7,635
4	246	US	1	3,887.0	16,240
5	175	Indonesia	23	83.5	483
6	144	Brazil	11	213.8	1,527
7	123	Japan	3	1,319.0	10,920
8	105	Bangladesh	49	14.5	143
9	105	Nigeria	26	77.0	749
10	105	Pakistan	40	36.3	367
11	83	Mexico	14	168.1	2,139
13	61	W. Germany	4	629.9	10,320
14	59	Philippines	43	30.3	520
15	57	UK	6	446.2	7,882
16	57	Italy	8	355.1	6,216
17	56	France	5	492.8	8,932
24	42	So. Korea	22	86.6	2,110
25	39	Poland	10	238.0	6,398
28	32	Argentina	27	69.4	2,287
30	26	Canada	9	335.4	13,220

To be read this way: India ranks second in the world in total population with 797 million people, yet it ranks only twelfth in GNP ($190.5 billion) and has a per capita annual income of only $248. Canada, in contrast, ranks thirtieth in population with 26 million people, yet ranks ninth in GNP ($335.4 billion) and has an annual per capita income of $13,220.

Note: The data source for national income is imperfect. The *Statistical Abstract* provides data for only 63 countries, although it covers the principal economies. However, it excludes such countries as Saudi Arabia with a high GNP, and Kuwait, which has one of the highest per capita incomes in the world. Hence, the rank numbers in this table probably vary by one or two below approximately the tenth GNP rank.

Source: For population, *UN Statistical Papers*, "Population and Vital Statistics Report: Data Available as of 1 July, 1989," using the last official estimate for each country; for GNP and GNP per capita, *Statistical Abstract of the United States, 1989*, p. 822.

policy stem significantly from perception and from attitudes that peoples hold toward others.

All these images are products of political socialization, the process by which the individual acquires political attitudes. And just as national peoples prepare through fear, affection, and propaganda to trust some governments and distrust others, so too do they prepare themselves to measure the potential impacts of international events. Political information is also measured against these ingrained mind sets that socialization provides, giving rise to images of situations. Not all events are crises, and not all evoke severe responses. The reaction to an event is a product of the immediacy of the event's consequences.

If an event touches closely on the interests of an individual and threatens to have some immediate impact, the reaction will be pronounced; if it and its probable consequences seem remote, the reaction will be muted. Clearly, when a salient event is initiated by a national actor whose intentions are feared or distrusted, the tendency of an opposing government to prepare a forceful response is understandable. Similarly, in such circumstances the sociopsychological mood of the body politic is elevated, with the result that great pressure is placed on foreign policy. An adventurous response may be tolerated. This is all a result of the mental and emotional interpretation of information.

Political socialization is a continuous process, although ideas that are firmly fixed are difficult to erase or even alter. Nevertheless, it is not uncommon for events to change in significance. In the United States, for example, it seemed likely that the enmity toward China, firmly established in 1950, would take decades or even generations to reverse. Yet a single presidential visit to China unleashed a remarkable groundswell of reversed opinion, with the result that normalization of relations was able to commence in a matter of only months. In another familiar case, the American attitude toward continued warfare in Southeast Asia turned around sharply between 1968 and 1972, to the point that there was public demand to discontinue the American involvement without having achieved even minimal objectives. Policymaking in Washington could not for long resist this new element in the opinion structure and was forced to implement a policy of withdrawal, a policy that only a few months earlier had been officially regarded as defeatist and treacherous. It became clear to major decision makers that the ability of the government to exert power was limited by the political consequences of resocialization, by the political meaning of a new national mood about the war.

All these images of self and others contribute to yet another component of power: public support and cohesion. Support of government and popular unity are critical morale factors in national power. Internal divisions consume political and military resources needed to secure domestic cohesion, and they pose the danger of a fifth column—a domestic faction unifying itself with a foreign enemy. For example, some Ukrainian separatists joined the Nazi invaders of the Soviet Union in the hope of liberation from Russian domination. A relatively unified population such as Israel's, on the other hand, is capable of great exertions.

Unity does not necessarily indicate how democratic a government is. It is not consistently true that democratic regimes have enjoyed more popular support in foreign affairs than have authoritarian governments. Germans rallied behind Hitler from 1936 to 1945, whereas the French were on the whole less unified in support of their democracy in the prewar years. The popularity of a government is difficult to measure from the outside—for example, the Castro government of Cuba is considered highly popular by some observers and highly unpopular by others. What counts in conflict is the effective disposition of the population to mobilize resources and undertake sacrifices proportionate to the perceived importance of the outcome. Thus, unity and public will are the indispensable catalysts for transforming potential power into useful power.

Final among the social determinants of power is leadership. The quality of leadership is the most unpredictable component of national power. Leadership orchestrates the other components, defines goals in a realizable manner, and determines the path of strategy.[5]

China exemplifies the extent to which a change in leadership alone can mobilize the other latent energies and capacities of a nation, transforming it from the weak victim of a succession of international predators to a self-sufficient power able to exercise considerable influence in foreign affairs. The same population with the same territory and endowment of natural resources can be weak and disunited or strong and dynamic, depending on the quality of leadership.

Sometimes the rise of a unique individual at a particular moment catalyzes other historical forces to change the trend of events. Napoleon, Bismarck, Hitler, Franklin Roosevelt, de Gaulle, Lenin, Castro, Gandhi, Churchill, Mao— these were visionary and sometimes charismatic leaders who changed the equation of international power and the course of international history. Some believe that the role of the individual hero in history has been falsely glamorized and overstated and that events are decided more by systematic factors in national capability than by such idiosyncratic elements as individual personalities. And yet who does not believe that an incredible determination on the part of the British people to resist, in a bleak hour when Britain stood alone, was roused by Winston Churchill's defiance: "We shall fight on the beaches, we shall fight on the landing grounds, we shall fight in the fields and in the streets, we shall fight in the hills; we will never surrender." Leadership cannot create power out of air but can dip into untapped reserves of national creative energy. Sometimes a single statesperson makes the difference.

The Synthetic Components of Power

In addition to the natural and sociopsychological determinants of power, there are some that are synthetic. These involve the skillful use of human and other resources in such a way as to coordinate, develop, and ready the state to put its power into motion. Most important are industrial capacity and military preparedness.

Industrial capacity is virtually synonymous with major-power status in the twentieth century. Modern war requires both a sophisticated manufacturing capability and huge economic resources. The victory of the Allied powers in the Second World War, for example, may be traced to the ability of Soviet and American assembly lines to turn out artillery pieces, tanks, and aircraft in

---

[5]Substantial scholarship exists on the extent to which leadership personality determines the selection of strategies (including war/no-war decisions). See particularly Harold D. Lasswell, *Psychopathology and Politics* (Chicago: University of Chicago Press, 1930) and *Power and Personality* (New York: Norton, 1948); and a quantitative study by Lloyd S. Etheredge, *A World of Men: The Private Sources of American Foreign Policy* (Cambridge, Mass.: MIT Press, 1978).

Table 7–2 Ten principal military powers by expenditure, 1988.

	Military Expenditure (US$ billions)	Rank in GNP
US	267.8	1
USSR	260.0	2
France	29.1	5
W. Germ.	28.2	4
UK	26.1	6
Japan	21.6	3
Italy	15.2	8
Saudi Arabia	15.0	< 10
China	11.0	7
India	8.8	12

Source: For military expenditure, *SIPRI Yearbook, 1989*, pp. 183–187, expressed in constant dollars and exchange rates based on 1986 US values. (Soviet and Chinese figures are SIPRI estimates and have a high degree of uncertainty. American intelligence sources place Soviet military expenditures as much as 50 percent higher.) For GNP, *Statistical Abstract of the United States, 1989*, p. 822. See the source note to Table 7–1 on the limitations of this list for an explanation of Saudi Arabia.

greater numbers than the German and Japanese factories. The economic costs are staggering: The individual American soldier today is supported by annual equipment expenditures of almost $45,000; American outlays in Vietnam averaged several hundred thousand dollars for each communist soldier killed. Modern warfare is mechanized, expensive, and technologically complex, and the ranking of nations by gross national product (GNP) approximates closely their ranking in military power[6] (see Table 7–2).

Quantitative studies of power and capability have tended to confirm the importance of industrial capacity as the single most important determinant of power.[7] One found that the wealthier state or coalition won 31 of 39 international wars from 1815 to 1945, suggesting that an advantage in industrial capacity brings victory in four of five cases.[8] This reduces the warmaking function from heroic exploits of brave men to mundane statistical comparisons among the number of ironworkers, ballbearing output, efficiency of the airframe industry, and so forth. Military might today depends as much on the managers and engineers as on the generals.

---

[6]Indeed, one study found that lay people's perceptions regarding the power rankings of nations correlate highly with GNP—people expect rich nations to be stronger. Norman Alcock and Alan Newcombe, "The Perception of National Power," *Journal of Conflict Resolution*, vol. 14, no. 3, November 1970, pp. 335–343.

[7]F. Clifford German, "A Tentative Evaluation of World Power," *Journal of Conflict Resolution*, vol. 4, no. 1, March 1960, pp. 138–144; Rudolph Rummel, "Indicators of Cross-National and International Patterns," *American Political Science Review*, vol. 68, no. 1, March 1969, pp. 127–147; Bruce Russett, *International Regions and the International System* (Chicago: Rand McNally, 1967); and Harvey Starr, *War Coalitions* (Lexington, Mass.: D. C. Heath, 1973).

[8]Steven Rosen, "War Power and the Willingness to Suffer," in Bruce Russett, ed., *Peace, War, and Numbers* (Beverly Hills, Calif.: Sage, 1972), pp. 176–178.

The power of population . . . Public calisthenics are an integral part of the Chinese civil defense program.
Source: Dennis Brack / Black Star

We have identified several elements of national power potential: geography, natural resources, industrial capacity, population, governmental support, and the quality of leadership. All are important, but industrial capacity is the outstanding economic variable, and the quality of leadership is the most important political factor. Each state has a certain innate capacity to exercise influence on the world stage, and leadership determines the extent and purposes for which this capacity will be used.

Power and the Role of War

The exercise of power takes many forms in international relations. Economic rewards and punishments may be used to elicit favorable responses from other nations. Cultural influence may be extended through the transfer of products, mass media, student exchanges, and published materials. Public opinion in other countries can be influenced through direct propaganda efforts such as the Voice of America and the large foreign radio transmission programs of the Soviet Union, Egypt, and other states. The international sale of armaments provides the exporter with a variety of positive and negative sanctioning powers, as shipments can be expanded or withheld. Power within international organizations and alliances may take the form of skillful lobbying and bargaining. Influence operates by various means, and it should not be assumed that the exercise of power most often involves the application of physical force. Most typically, force is used when one actor, unable to compromise on the outcome of an issue, perceives that it must deprive the opponent of alternative solutions.

Still, force tends to have overriding importance in international relations. Arab states may attempt to revise their borders with Israel through diplomatic persuasion, propaganda, economic sanctions, and a host of other means, but in territorial conflicts, war is often the ultimate means. Especially in the international arena, where institutional means of conflict resolution are still at a low level of development and peace-enforcing authority is weak, the potential influence of an actor is critically dependent on its capacity to wage war in the regions where its values are deeply engaged.

We may conceptualize war as a distribution mechanism making allocations of scarce goods to competing parties The two sides make mutually exclusive claims to a given position or resource (such as a piece of territory or control of the instruments of state), and war decides who is to get what. The decision rule that operates in making a settlement is to award to each side a share of the disputed values that corresponds to its relative war power. War establishes a ratio of power between the contestants, and political bargaining allocates the prize according to this formula.

It is crucial, therefore, to understand the nature of power in war. The factors of power potential are translated into effective war power in terms of two specific warmaking capabilities: strength, meaning the ability to impose sanctions or to destroy the assets of the adversary, and cost tolerance, meaning the willingness to tolerate deprivation or the destruction that the enemy imposes on one's own assets. Our relative power in war is a function of my willingness to tolerate the harm that you are able to impose, versus your willingness to tolerate the harm that I am able to impose. Thus, the power to win wars is based on political as well as military factors.

Cost Tolerance

The visible side of war is the mutual imposition of negative sanctions by two parties, tempting the observer to view the power relationship mainly as a function of relative strength. But the critical role of cost tolerance cannot be overlooked. A party inferior in strength and yet superior in cost tolerance may paradoxically be more powerful than a strong opponent less willing to suffer. This was precisely the case in Vietnam, where the physical might of the United States vastly exceeded that of the communists, yet the total power equation was nearly even or tilted to the weaker side. Ho Chi Minh predicted, "In the end the Americans will kill ten patriots for every American who dies, but it is they who will tire first." This was also the model in Algeria, where the deep commitment of the nationalists enabled them to withstand the immense power of France longer than the less committed French were willing to accept much lower costs delivered to them by the Algerians. A study of 40 wars found that almost half of them were won by the party that suffered more.[9]

Revolutionary strategists who see themselves fighting the might of global imperialism have put special emphasis on the idea that courageous hearts can compensate for the opponents' superior strength. The power of the anti-imperialists is their willingness to die; Arab commandos call themselves *fedayeen*—"the sacrificers." Chinese strategists, too, emphasize the military importance of revolutionary commitment and determination, and an Irish revolutionist said, "It is a question which can last longer, the whip or the back."

This image of war is one of torture. The victims are on the table, and the question is whether their will can be broken by torment. Sometimes the victims' resistance is actually stiffened by their suffering. German terror bombing of London had such a reverse effect—"the stimulus of blows."[10] A more recent example is the American bombing of North Vietnam:

> So far from terrorizing and disrupting the people the bombings seem to me to have stimulated and consolidated them. By the nature of the attacks so far, civilian casualties have not been very great, but they have been enough to provide the government of the Vietnam Republic with the most totally unchallengeable propaganda they could ever have dreamed of. A nation of peasants and manual workers who might have felt restive or dissatisfied under the stress of totalitarian conditions had been obliged to forget their differences in the common sense of resistance and self-defense. From the moment the US dropped its first bomb on the North of Vietnam, she welded the nation together unshakeably.[11]

The revolutionary's conviction that the will to resist can overcome immense disparities in material strength is often questioned by orthodox strategists. To a claim that communist cost tolerance in Vietnam was a bottomless pit, for example, Henry Kissinger is said to have replied, "Every pit has a bottom." Although it is evident that in their devotion to a cause the revolutionaries may survive overwhelming odds, it is clear that Kissinger is also right: More often than not, the weaker party will yield. The nation with a superior industrial capacity starts with a long lead in war power.

Starting and Ending Wars

Overrating your own power means relatively underrating your opponent. In the First World War, for example, both the French and the Germans expected quick victories within a matter of weeks; both were disappointed. In Vietnam, each side long believed that the other would eventually yield, so that victory was purely a matter of time. The communists seemed to have in mind the example of Algeria or their own victory over the French in Vietnam, whereas

---

[9]Rosen, "War Power and the Willingness to Suffer."

[10]Arnold Toynbee, *A Study of History* (London: Oxford University Press, 1934), vol. 2, pp. 100–112.

[11]James Cameron, *Here Is Your Enemy* (New York: Holt, Rinehart and Winston, 1966), p. 66.

the Americans based their policy on the model of postwar Greece and Malaya, where guerrillas had been defeated.

We noted earlier that the function of a war settlement is to allocate values in proportion to war power. Because the two parties have different pictures of the power ratio in advance of the fighting, they propose different settlements to each other. Each considers that the other is offering too little. The Americans reasoned in Vietnam, "Why should we accept a communist-dominated coalition government when they will be unable to force one on the battlefield?" The communists reasoned, "Why should we give up our political goals as the Americans demand when the trend of battle is sure to favor us?" The disparity in power perceptions ensures conflicting political demands.

Some theorists have argued that were it not for the disparity in power perceptions it would not be necessary to fight wars at all. Having a common assessment of the power ratio, the parties could simulate the war decision by

A rebellious Sikh instructs a small child on the handling of a pistol during occupation of an Indian holy place, 1988.
Source: AP/Wide World

making the same settlement in advance, without the bloodshed.[12] Both sides would be favored by avoiding violence if the same distribution could be achieved without it. Some parties might fight anyway without expecting victory, in despair at the alternatives or in "confident hope of a miracle," or at least to make it expensive for the aggressor; but in most cases, rational decision makers would make the settlement without pointless violence.

The poverty of this theory is evident: It is seldom possible to predict the outcome with confidence. Opinions will differ about what resources the enemy has, what resources the enemy will use, how much outside help each side will get, whether the enemy will tolerate a given level of costs, exactly what the enemy intends to do, and which of several conflicting statistical estimates is correct. It is undoubtedly true that "the most effective prerequisite for preventing struggle, the exact knowledge of the comparative strength of the two parties, is very often obtainable only by the actual fighting out of the conflict."[13] Unfortunately, "No medium of exchange [can] be devised which [will] bear the same relation to estimates of fighting power as monetary metals do to estimates of economic value."[14] War itself must sometimes resolve diverse perceptions of the power ratio.

Wars end when the parties arrive at a common picture of their relative power and a common assessment of appropriate settlement claims. There is negotiating on these questions within each nation as well as between nations. Internal debate may split between "superpatriots," who want to fight on for national honor regardless of the odds, and "traitors," who are accused of being overly eager to throw in the towel and surrender. Leaders making peace on less than perfect terms must sell both the settlement and their version of the battlefield situation to their own people.

One of the functions of international mediation is to help national leaders find domestic support for imperfect settlements. When a significant portion of the politically active population believes that the war situation is not as dire as claimed by the leadership, and/or that the leadership is making a needlessly unfavorable settlement, the basis may be molded for a later political reaction against the settlement. One of Hitler's main appeals was the claim that the nation had been sold out in 1918 and his demand that the Versailles treaty be repudiated as a document of shame. A stable settlement means that the agreement, however unfavorable, must be accepted as realistic.

Some kinds of conflict lend themselves to settlement more readily than do others. In pre-Napoleonic wars, common symbols were available as manifestations of potency visible to both sides—for example, possession of a specific fortress or strategic position. When one side gained possession of these symbols, it was clear to leaders and followers on both sides that the issue was

---

[12]See, for example, Raymond Mack and Richard Snyder, "An Analysis of Social Conflict," *Journal of Conflict Resolution*, vol. 1, no. 2, June 1957, p. 217.

[13]Georg Simmel, "The Sociology of Conflict," *American Journal of Sociology*, vol. 9, January 1904, pp. 490–525.

[14]Harold D. Lasswell, "Compromise," in *Encyclopedia of the Social Sciences*, vol. 4 (New York: Macmillan, 1930), p. 148.

concluded.[15] In modern war, struggle engages whole societies, and victory and defeat are not so clearly marked. The victor is the side that wins the last battle, but which battle is the last is not so obvious. One exception to this problem might be a nuclear war, in which the conclusion would be only too decisive.

Wars end when mutual rejection of claims is not worth the costs of continued fighting to either side, in light of the available strategic estimates. As the power estimates of the two sides become congruent, their offers of settlement converge. In Vietnam, the United States at first offered the Vietcong a deal that amounted to its dissolution as a political force, and the Vietcong offered to preside over the dismemberment of the Saigon regime. As the two sides' optimistic hopes of decisive victory were frustrated, they came closer together.

The immediate function of war, then, is to provide empirical evidence to adjust divergent assessments of relative power in order to permit the parties to develop similar perceptions of reality on which to base a settlement. The purpose of fighting is not ordinarily to destroy an opponent completely (the "Carthaginian peace") or to deprive it of residual strength and render it helpless and defenseless. Wars seldom go this far. It is not usually necessary to destroy an opponent to change its opinion or values or to cancel its objectives. The Second World War, which was fought to an unconditional surrender, is a notable exception.

Wars begin with a determination on the part of each group to convince the opponent of its version of the power ratio. The ideal strategic goal in war is to bring the enemy's power estimate to the point at which it will agree to the settlement that one seeks. Full victory is obtained by one side if it can bring the other's perception all the way around to its view. Typically, however, there

---

[15]See Lewis Coser, "The Termination of Conflict," *Journal of Conflict Resolution,* vol. 5, no. 2, December 1961, pp. 347–353. Many of the ideas in this chapter were developed in this seminal article. See also Anatol Rapoport's introduction to Karl von Clausewitz, *On War* (Baltimore: Penguin, 1968), p. 19.

is a process of mutual adjustment and compromise, where neither side can completely enforce its version of reality. Thus, the terms of settlement resulting from a negotiated peace will inscribe the power ratio for the moment, and whether or not those terms will be able to maintain the peace over time will depend on both their accuracy and the subsequent evolution of the power ratio between the parties.

Measuring War Power

How do we determine which of two adversaries is the more powerful? How is it possible, given the complexities of the power relationship, to say that one nation is a major power and another weak? How can decision makers reasonably estimate their national power potential in relation to a certain opponent, to chart a strategic course in the face of many uncertainties? One observer noted that in war "all action must . . . be planned in a mere twilight, which . . . like the effect of fog or moonshine, gives to things exaggerated dimensions and an unnatural appearance."[16] Systematic planning requires reasonably reliable bases on which to estimate the probabilities that a given course of action will have a predictable outcome. How can national leadership measure the balance of war power and plan accordingly?

There are many inherent uncertainties and difficulties in assigning specific weights to the various factors in war power, particularly in advance of actual fighting. The cost tolerance factor is wholly psychological and subjective, and there is no empirical referent simply visible to both parties by which the willingness to endure negative sanctions can be estimated reliably in advance.

Even purely physical capabilities in war are exceedingly difficult to estimate. Simple magnitudes of hardware must be assessed. How many X-type tanks equal a Y piece of artillery, and under what conditions of development? Obviously, opinions will vary. Even the gross defense expenditures of an opponent may be difficult to estimate. It has been shown, for instance, that different methods of computation by reliable analysts yield estimates of Soviet defense expenditures as a percentage of US defense expenditures ranging from 28 percent to more than 100 percent for the same year.[17] Still more difficult to estimate is the skill a nation can show in the use of its available forces.

The age of the computer and the availability of quantitative techniques for measuring social and political phenomena have resulted in repeated efforts to give a precise answer to the question, "What is the probable outcome of a war between State A and State B?" Far more than a scholar's game, this quest has been a statesperson's obsession; during the early years of involvement in Vietnam, Secretary of Defense Robert McNamara employed a battery of computer techniques and highly trained quantitative social scientists in an attempt to measure the probable outcomes of alternative strategies for victory in limited

---

[16]Karl von Clausewitz, *On War* (Baltimore: Penguin 1968), p. 189; originally published in 1832.
[17]Lynn Turgeon, "The Enigma of Soviet Defense Expenditures," *Journal of Conflict Resolution*, vol. 8, no. 2, June 1964, pp. 116–120.

war. Although the attempts at prediction all failed miserably, the drive for new and better answers continues.

The most common starting point in compiling measurable and comparable indices is the relative GNP of the involved parties. These give rough measures of the economic capacity of states to wage war, but careful scrutiny of results shows that the economic data alone are not enough. Recently it has been argued that the measurement of probable outcomes must rest not only on a variety of economic data but also on data expressing the level of political development of each participant, on the ground that economic and political development do not necessarily occur at the same pace. Hence, a country with evidence of economic growth might still lack the political capability to organize its human and other resources for war. In addition to economic comparability, any prediction of probable outcomes must include a measure of the capacity of the political system of each combatant to fulfill the demands of its own constituents and the different and special demands that are imposed on it by the international political environment.

The measurement of the internal factors involves quantitative evidence of governmental ability to exert as much control as possible on the population in order to achieve international objectives. To give mathematical order to the relative strengths of enemies, the internal component of power must be tabulated. A suggested formula is

$$\text{internal component of power} = \frac{\text{gross national product}}{\text{population}} \times (\text{population}) \times (\text{tax effort})$$

where the tax effort is the computed relation of the tax capacity of the economy (based on GNP) and the willingness of the government to exert pressure to extract enough to wage war effectively. It is also suggested that the external component of power be expressed as

$$(\text{foreign aid accumulated}) \times (\text{tax effort of the recipient})$$

The total measurable power of the state, then, should be the sum of these two formulae, and by tabulating these indices for two or more combatants, a rough measurement of probable outcome should emerge.[18]

Efforts to measure only the tangible frustrate attempts to measure power comprehensively, however, and undoubtedly explain the limitation of McNamara's effort to measure comparability of the potential to win. Power, in addition to being relative, is situationally specific and cannot be divorced from purpose.[19] Thus, in addition to measuring tangible capability, any successful formula must include not only perceptions but motivations as well. Apparently

---

[18]A. F. K. Organski and Jacek Kugler, "Davids and Goliaths: Predicting the Outcomes of International Wars," *Comparative Political Studies,* July 1978, pp. 141–180.

[19]David A. Baldwin, "Power Analysis and World Politics: New Trends Versus Old Tendencies," *World Politics,* January 1979, pp. 161–194. Baldwin summarized several studies of power comparability, critiqued their weaknesses, and identified their valuable contributions.

with these warnings in mind, another researcher attempted to measure both the physical and the motivational elements of power, this time using the formula:

$$P_p = (C + E + M) \times (S + W)$$

where P_p is perceived power; C is the critical mass of population and territory; E and M are economic and military capabilities, respectively; S is strategic purposes; and W is the will to pursue national strategies. Simply stated, power is the product of physical and psychological capabilities. A 1975 study assessed each of these and produced a global assessment of real power capability. Despite the superior physical position of the United States, the behavioral determination of the Soviet Union at that time not to be subordinated to the United States gave the Kremlin a decided edge in real power (by an index nearly twice that of the United States).[20] Despite the American military buildup during the Reagan years, it is probable that the moderation of the Soviet world view in the *perestroika/glasnost* era and the contemporary American foreign policy priorities have reduced the gap between the two. And if alliances rather than single superpowers are taken into consideration, the result is probably even greater convergence. Powerlessness of the Eastern bloc and the growing tendency toward Western European independence of Washington as full economic integration approaches in 1992 both diminish the tendency toward East-West military hostilities and increase the emphasis on economy-related foreign policies and mutual toleration.

If the present power ratio between two parties is not easily measured, the projection of trends to predict probable future power relations is even more difficult to make. To assess present and future conditions, each party must make complex calculations based on arbitrary assumptions. Policy must be planned on the basis of perceptions of present factors and expectations of the future. The result is a highly conjectural process of reasoning in which it is necessary to rely on "guesstimates" at critical points to reach general and usable conclusions on which to base policy. How do you weigh the imponderables? Referring to the final decision to attack Pearl Harbor, the Japanese war minister said, "Once in a while it is necessary for one to close one's eyes and jump from the stage of the Kiyomizu Temple."[21] The Japanese

> went to war with a beautifully complex plan of attack but without a clear answer to the single question of how they were going to win. There was, to be sure, the expectation that the U.S. would shortly decide that the costs of defeating Japan were not worth the gains and would therefore seek a compromise peace. But the Japanese did not give this critical hypothesis any real analysis. It was a hope nourished from despair at the alternatives.[22]

---

[20]Ray S. Cline, *World Power Assessment: A Calculus of Strategic Drift* (Washington, D.C.: Georgetown University, Center for Strategic and International Studies, 1975).

[21]Quoted in Stanford Studies in International Conflict and Integration, *Annual Report to the Ford Foundation* (Stanford, Calif.: Stanford University Press, 1961), p. 4.

[22]Warner Schilling, "Surprise Attack, Death, and War," *Journal of Conflict Resolution*, vol. 9, no. 3, September 1965, p. 389.

At each stage of strategic analysis, opinions diverge over whether optimistic or pessimistic assessments are warranted. Alternative pictures of any situation confront decision makers with a range of power ratios from which they must choose. Should President Lyndon B. Johnson have listened to the Joint Chiefs of Staff in 1965, who told him that the communists could be defeated in Vietnam within two years, or to the CIA, which gave him a much gloomier prediction?

Research findings are highly contradictory about whether statespersons generally decide on optimistic estimates or darker ones. One study found that social groups tend to overrate themselves and underrate their opponents,[23] but another found quite the opposite: that the "armed services inevitably overstate the military capabilities of the opponent."[24] Still a third study found that aggressors sometimes recognize the potential superiority of their opponents, perceiving this edge more clearly than do the defenders, but take the risk that it will not be effective.[25] The inconclusiveness of this evidence underscores the subjective component in framing assumptions about going to war.

It is likely that a full study of strategic planning in past wars would show that decision makers tended to use optimistic rather than pessimistic assumptions if both were based on equally plausible information. Effective leadership will concede critical objectives only when there is no reasonable hope of successful struggle. The rational strategy for mobilizing public will and forging national unity is to use the more optimistic estimates, provided that they are equiprobable with pessimistic alternatives.

Sometimes, of course, the use of hopeful estimates is mere grasping at straws. When the overwhelmingly superior Athenians demanded that the Melians surrender during the Peloponnesian War (431–404 B.C.), the Melians chose to resist.

> We know that the fortune of war is sometimes more impartial than the disproportion of numbers might lead one to suppose; to submit is to give ourselves over to despair, while action still preserves for us a hope that we may stand erect.[26]

It was an unfortunate decision. The Melians were easily defeated; the men all put to death; the women and children taken as slaves.

Another example of the grasping-at-straws syndrome was the reasoning of a Spanish commander about to sail with the Armada to its defeat at the hands of the British navy, a defeat that destroyed Spain as a global power (1588):

---

[23]Bernard Bass and George Dunteman, "Biases in the Evaluation of One's Own Group, Its Allies, and Opponents," *Journal of Conflict Resolution*, vol. 7, no. 1, March 1963, pp. 16–20.

[24]Samuel Huntington, "Arms Races," in Carl Friedrich and Seymour Harris, eds., *Public Policy 1958* (Cambridge, Mass.: Harvard University Press, 1958). "In 1914, for instance, the Germans estimated the French Army to have 121,000 more men than the German Army, the French estimated the German Army to have 134,000 more men than the French Army, but both parties agreed in their estimates of the military forces of third parties."

[25]Bruce Russett, "The Calculus of Deterrence," *Journal of Conflict Resolution*, vol. 7, no. 2, June 1963, p. 97.

[26]Thucydides, *The Peloponnesian War* (New York: Modern Library, 1951), pp. 330–337.

It is well known that we fight in God's cause. So when we meet the English, God will surely arrange matters so that we can grapple and board them, either by sending some strange freak of weather, or more likely, just by depriving the English of their wits. If we come to close quarters, Spanish valor and Spanish steel—and the great mass of soldiers we shall have on board—will make our victory certain. But unless God helps us by making a miracle, the English, who have faster guns and handier ships than ours, and many more long-range guns, and who know their advantage as well as we do, will never close with us at all, but stand aloof and blow us to pieces with their culverins, without our being able to do them any serious hurt. . . . So we are sailing against England in the confident hope of a miracle.[27]

Such was a very unfortunate line of thought.

These are the extreme cases. Ordinarily, optimistic planning is based not on wild fancy but on seemingly reasonable estimates, such as the expectation of the Joint Chiefs in 1965 that the North Vietnamese could not withstand strategic bombing or the deployment of a half-million well-armed American troops. Doubters may offer gloomier projections, but they cannot prove their case over the optimists. The final decision is always in some measure a leap of faith. Hitler bet that the British and French would not intervene over Czechoslovakia; he was right. Secretary of State Dean Acheson and President Harry S Truman bet that the Chinese would not intervene in Korea; they were wrong. Certainty is much easier looking back than for the decision maker forced to rely on advance projections!

Avoiding War

In our discussion of power, we have given primary emphasis to the threat or use of force as a means of influence. The dilemma is that nations continue to find military capabilities useful and necessary instruments of diplomatic action (as evidenced by constantly expanding defense budgets in many countries and the frequency of war as demonstrated in Table 7–3), even while technological changes make the use of violence ever-more horrible and cataclysmic. In ancient and medieval warfare, a battle might rage all morning between two mercenary armies, pause, and then resume with equal ferocity in the afternoon, leaving at the end of the day losses of perhaps twenty men and a donkey. In trench warfare, on the other hand, the gain or loss of a few hundred yards may cost ten thousand lives. This form of fighting accounts for the dramatic increase in casualties in conventional warfare during the first quarter of the present century (see Figure 7–1). Modern nuclear warfare has the potential to tower above these numbers, as exemplified in the 100,000 deaths that resulted from the atomic bombings of Hiroshima and Nagasaki in 1945. Recent advances in both explosive might and delivery accuracy would enable a missile-

---

[27]Quoted in Bernard Brodie and Fawn Brodie, *From Crossbow to H-bomb* (New York: Dell, 1962), pp. 67–68.

Table 7–3 Civil and international wars, 106, from 1945 to 1990, with starting dates.

Syria—Lebanon	1945	Northern Ireland	1969
Indonesia	1945	Ethiopia (Eritrea)	1970
China	1945	Cambodia	1971
Malaya	1945	Bangladesh—Kashmir	1971
Indochina	1946	Burundi	1972
Greece	1946	Israel—Arab states	1973
Madagascar	1947	Iraq (Kurdish)	1974
India—Pakistan	1947	Cyprus	1974
Kashmir	1947	Angola	1975
Philippines	1948	Timor—Indonesia	1975
Israel—Arab states	1948	Lebanon	1975
Hyderabad	1948	Spanish Morocco	1976
Burma	1948	Somalia—Ethiopia	1977
Korea	1950	Ethiopia (Eritrea)	1977
Taiwan	1950	Syria—Lebanon	1977
Tibet	1950	Libya—Egypt	1977
Kenya	1952	Iran	1978
Guatemala	1954	Nicaragua	1978
Algeria	1954	Vietnam—Laos	1978
Sudan	1955	Chad	1978
Cyprus	1955	Zaire	1978
Sinai	1956	Rhodesia (Zimbabwe)	1978
Hungary	1956	N. Yemen—S. Yemen	1979
Suez	1956	Uganda—Tanzania	1979
Lebanon	1958	China—Vietnam	1979
Cuba	1958	Vietnam—Kampuchea	1979
Vietnam	1959	Nicaragua	1979
Himalayas	1959	South Africa—Angola	1979
Rwanda	1959	USSR—Afghanistan	1980
Laos	1959	Iran—Iraq	1980
Congo	1960	El Salvador	1980
Colombia	1960	Peru	1980
Cuba (Bay of Pigs)	1961	W. Sahara	1981
Goa	1961	Britain—Argentina	
Angola	1961	(Falkland Islands)	1982
Yemen	1962	Israel—Syria—PLO	
West New Guinea	1962	(in Lebanon)	1982
Portuguese Guinea	1962	South Africa	1982
Algeria—Morocco	1963	Sudan	1982
Cyprus	1963	Seychelles	1982
Malaysia	1963	Kampuchea—Thailand	1983
Somalia—Kenya	1963	Sri Lanka	1983
Zanzibar	1964	US—Grenada	1983
Thailand	1964	Sudan—Libya	1983
Mozambique	1964	Mozambique	1984
Dominican Republic	1965	Turkey—Iraq (Kurdish)	1984
India—Pakistan	1965	India (Sikh)	1986
Indonesia	1965	Mozambique—Zimbabwe	1986
Biafra	1966	Colombia	1989
Israel—Arab states	1967	Panama	1989
Czechoslovakia	1968	Romania	1989
Malaysia	1969	USSR (Azerbaijan)	1990
El Salvador	1969	Liberia	1990
Chad	1969	Iraq—Kuwait	1990

Figure 7–1 War casualties in Europe, 1500–1925.

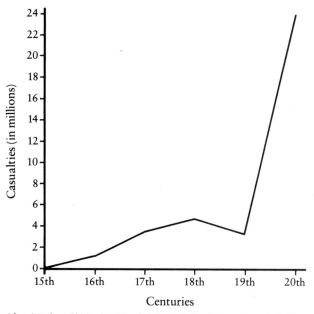

After data from Pitirim Sorokin, *Social and Cultural Dynamics*, vol. 3 (New York: Bedminster Press, 1962), originally published in 1937.

launched thermonuclear war targeted to major population centers to kill millions of people instantly. Indeed, one of the great complications in predicting conflict behavior in the modern era results from the fact that fundamental arms developments that once took up to 500 years may now take only five years.[28] As a consequence, managers of power must be concerned not only with emnities and magnitudes, but also with all the destabilizing effects of rapid strategic change.

Clearly, controls must be established over the use of force, both to prevent the outbreak of war and to limit the scope and intensity of struggle once begun. International relations scholars look to three basic ideas for the control of power in the next hundred years:

1. War prevention through regional and global balances of power between quarreling states, so that resorting to war is made unprofitable, even though disagreements continue.

2. War prevention by balance of terror, a variant of the balance-of-power concept, in which technologically developed adversaries have the capability for mutually as-

---

[28]Herman Kahn, *On Thermonuclear War* (Princeton, N.J.: Princeton University Press, 1960). There is, of course, a limit to this rate of change. Today, although there may be no end of technically achievable ideas for war and defense, the level of sophistication of these ideas requires substantial time for implementation. The same factor multiplies the cost of each successive generation of weapons. It is estimated, for example, that the deployment of the American Strategic Defense Initiative (the so-called Star Wars defense system in space) will take a minimum of 30 years and will rise to a cost equal to one-third of the current GNP.

sured destruction through finely targeted instantaneous warfare. Aggression is deterred by the certainty of intolerably destructive retaliation.

3. War prevention by further institutionalization of mediation and other means for the nonviolent resolution of international conflict, ultimately including a central peacekeeping authority and the disarming of nation-states.

Because the first two ideas address the practical problem of deterrence in a world of heavily armed states acting autonomously in their respective interests, most contemporary scholars and diplomats consider them the most realistic options for the foreseeable future. Although inordinately expensive and consuming vast amounts of natural resources, these ideas respond to the decentralized and hostile environment in which political differences are acted out. Replacing this model of international relations with one built on intergovernmental institutions capable of establishing and enforcing an equitable distribution of values in the manner now served by war and deterrence is a process long held in infancy. To some observers it is an impossible dream. To others, who look beyond unstable peace to the survival of humankind and the betterment of its condition, it is the endurance of the nation-state system that is the impossible dream. The system of individual nation-states means precariously balancing 50 or more nuclear powers deeply divided by ideological, territorial, and economic conflicts. If, since the Second World War, national

Army Medical Examiner: "At last a perfect soldier!"
Source: Antiwar cartoon by Robert Minor, 1915, reproduced in Stephen Becker,
Comic Art in America (New York: Simon & Schuster, 1959).

governments have given us two new wars per year, why must one presume that the costly pursuit of peace through competition is superior to the quest for peace through cooperation?

We will next explore war and peace through the balance-of-power and the balance-of-terror approaches. Part IV of this book will consider the quest for peace and stability through political transformation of the international system.

CHAPTER 8

The Balance of Power

Historians, diplomats, and students of international relations often assert that the only way to keep peace is through a careful "balance of power." What do we mean by this commonly used expression? It connotes not only military and deterrent capabilities but also the entire structure of power and influence that governs the relations of states. Balance of power is concerned, therefore, not solely with the ability of states to threaten their neighbors or to dissuade others from planned policies; rather, it encompasses all the political capabilities of states—coercive and pacific—by which the delicate balance of conflict without war is maintained.

Meanings of "Balance of Power"

Among lay persons and scholars alike, the expression "balance of power" has many uses. Consider four uses in these sentences:

1. There is a balance of power between India and Pakistan.
2. The balance of power favors the United States.
3. The balance of power has shifted in favor of Israel.
4. Britain was the crucial actor in the nineteenth-century balance-of-power system.

Clearly, there are several different meanings here. The first statement implies that equilibrium exists between two parties. Further, the relations of the respective parties with outside states, particularly the nuclear superpowers, are nearly equal, thus preventing the occurrence of disequilibrium by the unilateral addition of external strength. In short, the equilibrium in the relations between India and Pakistan exists because neither has significantly more power

Figure 8–1 (a) Two-part equilibrium. (b) Equilibrium maintenance.

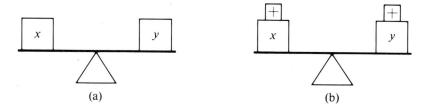

or influence; neither can distort the balance. Figure 8–1(a) shows the situation that exists; (b) shows the maintenance of equilibrium by the equal use of influence upon outside states.

The second statement carries a sharply different implication. To say that the balance favors one party over the other is to introduce a disequilibrium. Although this meaning is most frequently used to describe the balance of military forces, in its broadest usage it says that the United States holds the upper hand over some other party and is able to rely on greater military, diplomatic, and other resources. Throughout most of the Cold War, for example, the United States and the Soviet Union, although perhaps not absolutely equal in military potential (the United States probably always had superior military technology), had practical equivalence. Yet the United States had a vast edge in influence and in ability to work its will with economic resources. Hence, despite mutual superiority in arms and a balance of terror, the balance of power has traditionally favored the United States. Balance of power defined as disequilibrium is diagramed in Figure 8–2.

Now consider the third sentence: The balance of power has shifted in favor of Israel. This sentence connotes either a shift from equilibrium to disequilibrium or a shift in predominance from one party to the other. Acquisition of a new weapons system by Israel might have a major impact on the Middle Eastern balance, as might a change in the country's stature by a diplomatic victory. Recognition by West Germany, for example, improved Israel's access to military and industrial goods and gave it a new and powerful friend. Similarly, although the 1967 Israel-Arab War was preceded by regional equilibrium, Israel's victory significantly upset military and political relations both in the Middle East and among the major powers, who had to apply their influences anew to reestablish equilibrium. Figure 8–3 depicts the two patterns of a shift in balance.

Figure 8–2 (a) Disequilibrium favoring *y*. (b) Disequilibrium favoring *x*.

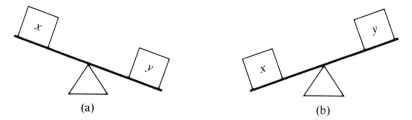

Figure 8–3 (a) Equilibrium shift to disequilibrium. (b) Disequilibrium shift to opposite disequilibrium.

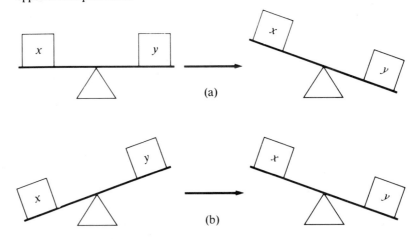

(a)

(b)

The fourth statement implies still a different meaning, which cannot be illustrated by the simple balance beam. The balance-of-power system was a specific historical event in a Eurocentric world from the nineteenth century to the outbreak of the First World War. In that system, states behaved in certain ways (described next), with one state conserving its influence solely to maintain equilibrium.

In summary, then, in place of a concise definition of "balance of power" we may say that it is a concept of many meanings, particularly equilibrium, disequilibrium, and shifts in dominance, as well as a particular historical systemic principle. This chapter will examine the various ideas behind the term. It is particularly concerned with balance as a system of keeping peace.[1]

Balance of Power as an Analytical Device

In the preceding chapter we explored a number of characteristics of power in international relations. Before we begin to examine the concept of the balance of power, the student is reminded of some of these features:

1. In international relations, the potential for conflict is permanent.
2. In international relations, power is permanent, and so the objective of a balance is not to eliminate power but to control and manage it for peaceful purposes.
3. Power is not an absolute entity but is quantitatively relative to the power of others.
4. Power is achievable by the aggregation of natural, sociopsychological, and synthetic resources.

---

[1]For thorough discussions of the several, and often confusing, meanings of "balance of power," see Inis L. Claude, Jr., *Power in International Relations* (New York: Random House, 1962), particularly part 1; and Ernst B. Haas, "The Balance of Power: Prescription, Concept, or Propaganda?" *World Politics,* vol. 5, 1953, pp. 442–477. A third useful source is Hans J. Morgenthau, *Politics Among Nations,* 4th ed. (New York: Knopf, 1967), pp. 161–163.

5. Except in abnormal circumstances, the acquisition of power is for the achievement of subsequent objectives. Power is, then, an instrument of the state rather than a self-standing possession of the state.

In light of these observations, the balance of power can be presented as an analytical concept for exploring the practical effects of equilibrium and disequilibrium in world politics and for assessing the consequences of power shifts. It becomes an analytical device rather than a form of advocacy, prescribing no particular model(s) for world peace. Instead, it searches out the conditions of order and disorder in international relations, concentrating on the sources and consequences of balance and imbalance.

The role that a state plays in a global or regional balance of power is determined by its capabilities and intentions (see Chapter 7). In its external relations, a government makes what are presumably rational and calculated determinations of the costs and benefits of specific policies as related to specific objectives. From these formulae it sets the course of foreign policy, and by them it determines the state's role in the balance of power. "Will we attempt to enlarge our power, or are our present interests served in the international system by the power that we presently command?" "Do our relations with a neighbor require that we alter the existing balance?" Or, "Is our neighbor altering the balance to our detriment, and must we, therefore, increase our power potential?"

This distinction between power and power potential is an important one in the balance-of-power concept. Many states have considerable potential power but have little effect on global or regional balances. Thus, the balance-of-power theory must take into account the stages of power readiness. The possession of adequate resources of power is potential power. When these are developed, coordinated, and supplied with the will to use power, then the state possesses mobilized power. And when the developed resources are applied to actual situations, the state commands active power (or kinetic power).

The lowest stage of readiness (potential power) gives to a state little more than a passive role in the balance of power. More powerful states are only minimally moved by the actions of the potentially powerful. Such a state, in turn, must acquiesce in the prevailing norms of the international system (since it is ill prepared to alter them), must tie itself to the objectives and means of a more powerful state, or must mobilize its power to play an active part in the balance.

Command of mobilized power, in contrast, enables the state to be a major actor. Such a status compels other contestants to assess the relativity of power, the possibility of overbearing coalitions, and the potential for sudden changes in the balance or redistribution of influence or major unilateral technological advances. The balance of power is concerned mainly with the balance of mobilized power.

Force—the extreme utilization of mobilized power—is used to alter the power balance drastically and rapidly. A state may wish to correct a disequilibrium by force or to upset a power balance to the advantage of its own objectives. Perhaps the most illustrative use of active power in the balance-of-power theory is the preemptive war. This is warfare in which State *A* anticipates an attack by State *B*. Rather than wait for an orderly escalation of hostilities, *A* destroys *B*'s capability before *B* has a chance to start the fighting. *A* has preempted *B* by an anticipatory attack depriving *B* of altering the balance of power, and in the course of affairs may have done so itself. Israel's purpose in attacking Arab military airfields in 1967 was preemptive. This means that Israel's intentions were not aggressive and not designed to aggrandize national territory, nor to alter the balance in Israel's favor. Rather, Israel wanted to strike at Egypt and Syria in a selective manner so as to destroy their capability to alter the balance at a moment when Israel anticipated attacks from the Arab states.

Preventive war has similar balance-of-power connotations. This is a type of selective attack undertaken against an enemy state considerably before that state has effective military potential. Long before China was a nuclear power, for example, people throughout the West, perhaps even in the Soviet Union, openly mused on the efficacy of preventive attacks on Chinese installations to delay its nuclear development and prolong its weakness. Japan's attack on Pearl Harbor in 1941 was a different type of preventive war, conducted to deprive the United States of retaliatory strength as Japan contemplated further territorial quests in Asia and the Pacific. Israel's attack on an Iraqi nuclear plant in 1981 was designed to prevent its regional enemy from developing nuclear weapons. The only real difference between preemptive and preventive war is the time element; the effects for the balance of power are identical.

In the traditional study of international relations, it was assumed that the balance of power was determined exclusively by military relativities. More modern concepts of international relations, in contrast, recognize that relative military preparedness is not the sole determinant of the balance of power. The tendency now is to distinguish between military power, on the one hand, and the overall ability to command international influence, on the other. Thus, a major component of the balance of power is economic potential.

Modern Japan is a case in point. Since the end of the Second World War, Japan has not been a significant military power. Its defense is firmly tied to American strategic policy, although in the Vietnam era that policy often offended Japan's sense of security. Despite this military inferiority, Japan has resumed major-power status by virtue of its enormous economic revitalization. Even without military power, its regional influence is growing apace, based on its bilateral economic relations and on its ability to lead Asia and the Pacific in international development programs.

Western Europe is another illustrative case. The rapidly changing technology of war has outpaced the ability of even the most industrialized Western European states to compete alone. Economically, it is their collective activity and production that give the European states a major world role, rather than their individual efforts. Despite the continued European reliance on the trans-Atlantic security arrangement, Western Europe has achieved major-power status through its ability to compete in world trade. Thus, one can go farther than to say that Western Europe plays a major role in the global power balance.

One can conclude that through economic restoration, these states acquired a role in the global balance by using their resources to force change in it.

The Middle Eastern example of forced change in the global power balance through nonmilitary action between 1973 and 1983 is more recent and more striking, principally because its impact was registered in a much shorter time than in the case of either Japan or Western Europe. By deciding to profit from oil in the same way that Western commercial interests had done previously and by tying their oil export policy to political objectives concerning Israel, the Middle Eastern oil-producing states were able to force changes in the foreign policies of virtually all Western industrialized countries and Japan. While still developing industrially, their vast petrodollar reserves substantially affected economic relations throughout the nonsocialist world. And the threat of a petroleum boycott, which the oil-producing states' new wealth afforded them, was sufficiently menacing to Japan, Western Europe, and the United States that it was one of the most fruitful instruments of foreign policy available anywhere. Consequently, this capability forced a change in the regional and global power balances virtually without a military component. The weakening of the Organization of Petroleum Exporting Countries (OPEC) in 1981 and its near-collapse in 1983–1985 deprived its members of their former advantage, but without a redistribution of global wealth similar to that in the pre-OPEC period. In 1986, OPEC tried once again to control daily output in order to reconstruct its former political advantage; but four years and several attempts later, although it had succeeded in elevating the world petroleum price once again (but not to 1975 levels), it had failed to recapture its coveted political power.

Having now considered the fundamental issues of equilibrium, disequilibrium, and change in balance of power theory, we will turn to some alternative structural models.

Structural Models of Balance of Power

Although balance-of-power theory does not prescribe a preferred model of global or regional stability, it does facilitate description of the principal power configurations that have existed in the past 150 years. The theory also enables us to demonstrate graphically the power relations of major states and groups of states, whether their relation is global in interaction or limited to a region of the world.

These models are of no greater value than to depict roughly power configurations that have existed in the past. They attempt to freeze time in the sense of describing relations in fixed position, rather than to explain the dynamic flow of relations among international actors. In this sense, these models are static; and they are as artificial as is a tinker-toy model of a molecule that demonstrates the ideal configuration of its major components while ignoring the dynamic flow of subnuclear particles that either maintain or change the basic shape.

The international system is as dynamic as such a molecule, and any attempt to reduce it to fixed form necessarily diminishes its vitality. Nevertheless, because such descriptive models are typically referred to as indicators of major-power configurations, they are instructive despite their static character.

The Nineteenth-Century Balance-of-Power System

In illustrating different meanings of balance of power at the outset of this chapter, we used the sentence, "Britain was the crucial actor in the nineteenth-century balance-of-power system." What distinguished that system from the balance of power as we know it now?

Historians of the balance-of-power system (dated from the end of the Napoleonic Wars in 1815 until the outbreak of the First World War in 1914) identify the underlying conditions. They note that it could exist only among several nation-states in a fairly well-defined territorial area. Although it was an interstate system, it was not global. The system could not have worked except among participants relatively homogeneous in political culture, who had rational means of estimating one another's power (wealth, military potential, and so on).[2]

In retrospect, this international system seems to have resulted from several basic assumptions about states' previous behavior. First, each state would attempt to maximize its own power for its own purposes. Second, as a consequence, when states accumulated power and their interests (such as imperial interests) collided, there was potential for international conflict. Third, to enhance their respective power potentials, like-minded states entered into alliances, so alliance competition rather than state competition characterized the system.

In these first three assumptions, the balance-of-power model sounds no different from any other international system. But the subsequent premises were unique. It is assumed, for example, that each participant placed a high value on equilibrium and that in its alliance competition its objective was to achieve equilibrium rather than a disequilibrium, even one that would favor itself. To maintain equivalence, moreover, states were willing to switch alliances periodically to adjust the balance. Adjustment, therefore, can be said to have been automatic. Figure 8–4 diagrams the process of adjustment: (a) shows an existing equilibrium which is upset (b) by the addition of a new participant or by a major technical development that adds to the weight of one coalition. In (c), equilibrium is restored by the transfer of one state from one alliance to the other.

The concept of the adjustment function, and the notion of its automatic nature, have evoked criticism. As a result, supporters have offered several other means by which the classical balance was adjusted, apparently conceding that the process is, at best, semiautomatic. The means of adjustment are said to be vigilance, alliances, intervention, mobility of action, reciprocal compensation,

---

[2]Edward V. Gulick, *Europe's Classical Balance of Power* (Ithaca, N.Y.: Cornell University Press, 1955), chap. 1.

Figure 8–4 Adjusting the equilibrium.

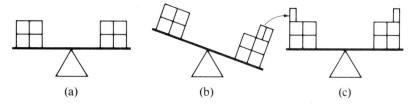

(a)　　　　　　　　　　(b)　　　　　　　　　　(c)

preservation of participants, coalitions, diversion into colonial expansion, and war. Beyond this, however, supporters have introduced the concept of holding the balance, which calls on a specific state to change its allegiances expressly to maintain the balance. This state is referred to as The Balancer.[3] The introduction of this concept means that the adjustment process is less than semiautomatic; rather, it is manual.

The concept of The Balancer is an effective modernization of this model only if The Balancer state has special characteristics. If a weak state were to take on this role, or a state that favors disequilibrium, then the function of manual balance would hardly be served. It follows that The Balancer must be an effectively powerful state, one whose strategic options enable it to have a major impact on the entire system. Moreover, it must be a state that favors equilibrium and, even more, one that demands for its own purposes that equilibrium be safeguarded. Of The Balancer one writer concludes:

> His task is difficult. A balancer is expected to be partial to no single national subject of the balance-of-power system but to direct his own mobile weight in such a way as to ensure the international object of an equipoise of power. He must be both at the focus of the system and outside it; otherwise he would not be free to withdraw and engage his weight in function of the system's requirements and thus manipulate the balance. An effective balancer must be both self-restrained and quick in imposing vigorous restraints on others. Only then can he frustrate and thus reduce the incentive to any one nation's quest for preponderance. A sufficiently powerful balancer of this kind might check the irrational drives and the miscalculations jeopardizing the balance of power and promote the realization of its objective norm.[4]

Among historians of this model, Britain is universally looked upon as having been The Balancer, although some also identify equilibrating functions in the policies of other states. Britain's virtues as The Balancer include its geographic location (which spared it from common boundaries with other powerful European states), its apparent interest in equilibrium as the most favorable climate for its imperial policies, and its great mobility of action.[5]

---

[3]The means of balance are derived from Gulick, *Europe's Classical Balance of Power*, chap. 3.

[4]George Liska, *International Equilibrium* (Cambridge, Mass.: Harvard University Press, 1957), pp. 36–37.

[5]This presentation follows the tradition of treating the entire balance-of-power century as having had a relatively unchanging political system. Recently, however, it has been shown that the period 1815 to 1914 actually consisted of three distinctly different balancing mechanisms, all governed by

Despite the modern refinements of this theory, skepticism continues to abound. One critic postulates that power is only one of the objectives of states, thus depreciating the assumption that power is the foremost national value. He also denies that nations are static and unchanging from within, insisting that through industrialization, marshaling of population resources, and improvements in governmental efficiency, states increase their potential power. These changes are not adjustable through the presumed mechanics of the balance of power. Third, because states are often tied to one another through economic, political, or psychological bonds, the freedom to switch alliances for no other purpose than balance is uncharacteristic of history. He interprets British policy as motivated by self-interest, not as fulfilling the self-appointed role of Balancer. In fact, he denies that any state in the nineteenth century preferred equilibrium to favorable disequilibrium. Finally, he concludes that imbalance of power is the characteristic pattern, particularly since the Industrial Revolution, with major states and their respective coalitions actually trying to maintain disequilibrium.[6]

Whether the classical mechanics of the balance-of-power model ever really operated is, therefore, in doubt. We may accept, nevertheless, the premise that in multiparty international systems favoring equilibrium, there must be some implicit rules of behavior. Based on his studies of the nineteenth-century system, one theorist sets out the operational rules of a system of international balance as follows:

1. Participants will increase their capabilities, but they will accept the responsibility to negotiate their differences rather than to fight.
2. Because increase in capabilities is the prime motive of foreign policy, states must be willing to fight, if necessary, rather than to forgo further development.
3. When at war, states will be prepared to terminate fighting rather than to upset the foundations of equilibrium by eliminating a participant. This is important because the model is built on the assumption of at least five major participants.
4. Every participant intent on equilibrium will contest any tendency to dominance by any state or coalition.

---

many of the same assumptions but necessitated by different relationships and dominated by different parties and different balancers. They were: 1815–1878 (Britain The Balancer, the most effective of the three experiments); 1878–1890 (Germany The Balancer, ingenius but not inherently stable); and 1890–1914 (Britain The Balancer; a desperate effort at maintaining order). See Gordon A. Craig and Alexander L. George, *Force and Statecraft: Diplomatic Problems of Our Time* (New York: Oxford University Press, 1983), chap. 3, "Balance of Power, 1815–1914: Three Experiments."

[6]A. F. K. Organski, *World Politics*, 2nd ed. (New York: Knopf, 1968), pp. 282–299. A contrasting view aggregates two principal assumptions of the balance-of-power system (alliance bonding and capability distribution across individual nations) into one ("bloc concentration") and then examines changes in the power distribution of the system to reestablish equilibrium when one or more states tend to move it into disequilibrium. The study concludes in favor of the balance-of-power hypothesis for the years 1824 to 1914. See Richard J. Stoll, "Bloc Concentration and the Balance of Power: The European Major Powers, 1824–1914," *Journal of Conflict Resolution*, March 1984, pp. 25–50.

5. Because the system is built on the power of states, participants must constrain tendencies toward supranational organization or organizations that would alter the sovereign status of the system's participants.

6. Each participant must be willing to permit defeated major actors to restore their positions, and they must encourage lesser actors to achieve the status of full participants. All major parties must be treated equally as acceptable role partners.[7]

These rules have a pragmatic basis: If the system is to be viable, the participating states must be viable. We shall return subsequently to the question of whether multipartite systems such as this or limited-bloc systems (such as bipolarity) tend toward greater stability.

The Tight Bipolar Balance of Power

The nineteenth-century balance-of-power system involved political relationships that ended with the First World War. Thereafter, international stability was not governed by the factors we have discussed. Other systems of power balance emerged, particularly after the Second World War. It is necessary, therefore, to explore the military relations of other balance-of-power systems in order to understand the contemporary distribution of power.

The Second World War probably changed international politics more than did any other single modern occurrence. Diplomats in the postwar years were confronted with the unprecedented problems presented by atomic weaponry and with the reduction of the number of effective major powers to two. Although the First World War had begun the process of restricting the number of major powers, the prostration of Western and Central Europe after the Second World War ensured that for the foreseeable future, world politics would center on Washington and Moscow rather than on London and Paris. But there was also a third critical development: the intense ideological hostility between the two principal powers, which opened an era of conflict, distrust, competition, and misperception.

These three factors together—the two-part division of power, the advent of atomic warfare, and unprecedented ideological rivalry—resulted in an international system of tight bipolarity, one in which virtually all the world's effective power was encompassed in two competing blocs. The institutional structure was that of two formal alliance systems, dominated by the Soviet Union and the United States, respectively. For diplomatic or geopolitical reasons, a few states did not participate (for example, Finland and Switzerland), but the fact remains that virtually all the measurable power in international relations was commanded through one or the other of these two structures.[8]

---

[7]Morton A. Kaplan, *Systems and Process in International Relations* (New York: Wiley, 1957), p. 23; and also Kaplan, "Balance of Power, Bipolarity and Other Methods of International Systems" *American Political Science Review,* vol. 51, 1957, pp. 684–695.

[8]This definition is only a slight adaptation of Kaplan's, which defines tight bipolarity as a system in which "non-bloc member actors and universal actors either disappear entirely or cease to be significant." ("Balance of Power, Bipolarity and Other Models of International Systems," p. 693.) Kaplan denies, however, that a tight bipolar system has ever existed.

The height of the Cold War, 1953. In the United Nations General Assembly, Ambassador Andrei Vishinsky of the USSR accuses the US of acting like a "master race" in trying to push through a proposal on the makeup of the Korean Peace Conference. American ambassador Henry Cabot Lodge and British ambassador Sir Gladwyn Jebb listen resignedly to the familiar invective.
Source: AP/Wide World

A tight bipolar international system may be said to have existed from 1946 to 1955, a decade that saw such momentous events as the breakdown of the wartime coalition, the emergence of the Soviet Union as a second nuclear power, the establishment of NATO and the Warsaw Pact, the Berlin Blockade, the accession to power in China by Mao Tse-tung, and the Korean War. In this era, the intense Soviet-American rivalry, particularly over Europe, resulted in the Cold War exchanges of threats and competing alliances. Technically, the Warsaw Pact did not come into existence until 1954 after the Western allies agreed to include West Germany in NATO membership; but long prior to this formal event the Soviet Union and Eastern Europe comprised a tacit alliance. Formal Sino-Soviet ties also existed. The American alliance structure was global [and remains so despite the collapse of the South East Asian Treaty Organization (SEATO) after the Vietnam War], and developed as follows:

1947   Organization of American States (the Rio Pact, or the Inter-American Treaty of Reciprocal Assistance) (22 members)

1949   North Atlantic Treaty (15 members)

1951   Security Treaty with Japan (bilateral)

1951   Security Treaty with Australia and New Zealand (trilateral)

1951   Mutual Defense Treaty with the Republic of the Philippines (bilateral)
1953   Mutual Defense Treaty with the Republic of (South) Korea (bilateral)
1954   Southeast Asia Collective Defense Treaty (eight members)
1954   Mutual Defense Treaty with the Republic of China (Taiwan) (bilateral)

Altogether, these treaties and the institutionalized alliances that they created encompassed some 44 nations including the United States, with several states belonging to more than one alliance. In addition, the United States had bases agreements and status-of-forces agreements with Spain and Libya (the latter agreement no longer exists), so that the United States was involved in some level of military activity with no fewer than 46 different governments on every continent in the world. Solidarity was furthered by the alliances sponsored by London, including the Central Treaty Organization and its military prerogatives in its colonial areas, particularly in Asia and the Mediterranean (for instance, Malta). Combined, the Anglo-American alliances and the Soviet alliances involved in excess of 60 states and almost half again as many non-self-governing areas. Compare this with the 1955 membership of the United Nations, which was only 76 nations, 16 of which were not admitted until 1955. Furthermore, of the original 51 signatories to the UN Charter, two—Byelorussia and the Ukraine—were not and are not sovereign states. Thus, at the start of 1955, while the United Nations had a membership of only 59 distinctly different sovereign states, the United States and Britain, on the one hand, and the Soviet Union, on the other, were formally allied with over 60 states. The universality of the alliance systems should be self-evident.

Based on this survey of alliances, we can now diagram the tight bipolar system, noting also the existence of several scattered but relatively powerless nonparticipants. Figure 8–5 demonstrates that although a tight bipolar balance of power existed from 1946 to 1955, the US-oriented bloc commanded more influence when all power sources are considered.[9] These included a superior number of allies, a larger supply of resources, and the global character of American alliances contrasted with the regional reach of the Soviet. The point is that tight bipolarity need not imply equality of capability.[10]

Because power is always relative, it does not necessarily follow from the lack of absolute equality that the political prerogatives of one bloc were less

---

[9]The exclusion of 1945 follows Robert Jervis, "From Balance to Concert: A Study of International Security Cooperation," *World Politics*, October 1985, pp. 58–79. Jervis argues that on three occasions—1815–1854, 1919–1920, and 1945–1946—after major hegemonic wars there appeared concerts prior to the reestablishment of balances of power. This resulted in each case from the fact that war had temporarily upset two of the fundamental assumptions of balance of power: the availability of war as an instrument of statecraft and the ability to change alliances on the basis of short-term objectives. The result is transitory cooperation rather than either defection or war. Thus, anarchy and the security dilemma do not dominate the international security system, rendering agreement.

[10]For a study suggesting that the power distribution be described in terms of symmetry and asymmetry, regardless of the number of major blocs, though especially in two-bloc systems, see Wolfram F. Hanreider, "The International System: Bipolar or Multibloc?" *Journal of Conflict Resolution*, vol. 9, September 1965, pp. 299–308. Hanreider provides alternative diagrams for depicting perfect and actual tight bipolarity.

Figure 8–5 (a) Perfect tight bipolarity. (b) Actual tight bipolarity, 1946–1955.

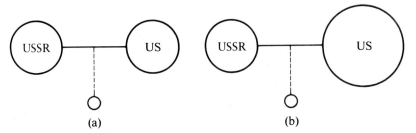

(a)   (b)

than those of the other in critical areas. In fact, in the tight bipolarity of 1946–
1955, the disparities operated outside Europe, beyond the sphere in which the
Kremlin generally wished to compete with Washington. Hence in the tight
bipolar era there existed European regional symmetry but global asymmetry.

The operating characteristics of the tight bipolar balance of power differ
markedly from those of the nineteenth-century system. The basic assumption
here is that international equilibrium is a second-best objective; the principal
aim of governments is to belong to the dominant coalition. Furthermore, the
system is built on the premise that all effective power is included in the major
blocs, or poles, with the result that there is no powerful state dangling free to
play the role of Balancer. Indeed, the objective of this pattern of power is to
anticipate the defeat of the other coalition should it breach the frontiers of
one's own members. It is for this reason, rather than mere coincidence, that
the ruling American political-military strategy of this era was massive nuclear
retaliation, although it is doubtful that the threat was ever taken seriously. It is
far more likely that the balanced conventional strengths of the European alliances ensured stability through this era. Nevertheless, the philosophy of tight
bipolarity renders massive retaliation quite logical as a strategic foundation.

Given the conditions that begat bipolarity and the strategic notions it fostered, this model of international order is maximally hostile.

The Loose Bipolar Balance of Power

In the mid-1950s, a number of fundamental changes occurred in the international system. The two superpower alliance systems began to loosen, with internal conflicts and losses of confidence appearing in each bloc, and
dependencies began to dissipate. In the Soviet sphere, events took several
paths. Eastern European dissatisfaction with Soviet control, foreshadowed a
few years earlier in East Germany, climaxed with the brief Hungarian revolt of
1956. Coupled with Nikita Khrushchev's campaign to de-Stalinize the Soviet
Union and Eastern Europe, this event resulted in increasing demands for
quasi-independence among the Soviet satellites, despite forceful suppression
by Soviet troops. The politics of the Soviet sphere came increasingly to be
identified as polycentric, suggesting reduced Soviet control over the states
within its orbit.

If polycentrism characterized Eastern Europe, only the term "schism" describes Sino-Soviet relations in the same era. Although not yet a major power,

after less than a decade of controlling the Chinese mainland, the Mao government found itself disaffected from Moscow and in search of independent power status. Formal relations were broken in 1956, and Soviet technicians and aid were withdrawn, leaving China to develop alone. Gone was the prevailing American notion that all communist power and authority emanated from the Kremlin; the international communist movement could no longer be regarded as monolithic. The Soviet Union's influence in Asia was sharply curtailed, leaving Soviet-American relations more asymmetrical. More important, the Sino-Soviet split represented a major break in the solidarity of the Soviet world.

The American bloc began to crack also. Latin America, increasingly disenchanted with Washington's sporadic paternalism, began to consider itself a member of the Third World despite its formal military and economic ties with the United States. Fidel Castro's seizure of power in Cuba under the banner of Marxism brought the first serious challenge to the ideological solidarity of the Western Hemisphere.

Europe presented other problems. The enormous success of the Western European economies in reconstruction led to gradual resentment of American economic domination. Charles de Gaulle's demand that Europe be de-Americanized threatened to dilute the potential effectiveness of the United States in facing the Soviet Union across Europe. Strategic policy in NATO led to other resentments and suspicions, with some Europeans doubting the credibility of the American nuclear umbrella, while still others feared that impetuous behavior in Washington in response to Soviet threats might unnecessarily embroil Europe in war.

Worldwide interests and associations tend to present worldwide problems, and the United States found that Latin America and Western Europe were not the end of its problems. The cornerstone of American policy in Asia, the alliance with Japan, also began to show signs of decay. In the years following the Korean War (1950–1953), Japanese resentment at American security policy grew steadily, focused on American nuclear strategy. Disharmony rose to the point of widespread rioting on the occasion of the renegotiation of the Security Agreement in 1960. The political climate in Japan grew so menacing that the Tokyo government successfully discouraged the planned state visit of President Dwight D. Eisenhower. The breakdown over security matters was compounded in Japanese minds by American efforts to prevent Japan from trading with China.

By 1960, then, it was clear that major shifts were occurring in the previous tight global bipolarity because of internal changes in the principal alliances. Another critical change was taking place too. Beginning in 1957, although more markedly after 1960, the number of nation-states burgeoned. In 1960, seventeen states were admitted to United Nations membership, every one of them newly independent. A world that had been revolutionary in several respects now added a new dimension—a sudden and unprecedented increase in the number of national actors. These new states, bound only by poverty, underdevelopment, and racial difference from the dominant white nations, were courted by both the United States and the Soviet Union, each one seeking

Figure 8–6 Loose bipolarity, 1955–1965.

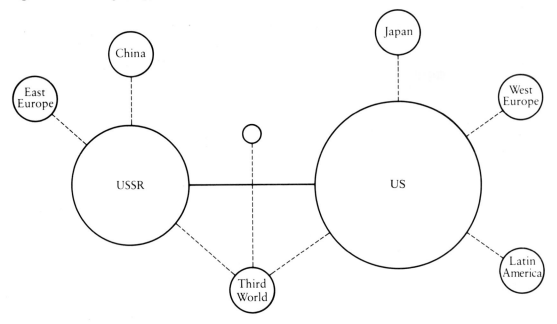

new adherents to its ideology. Most of the new states, however, did not tie themselves to either giant but accepted assistance from them with as little political cost as possible. Although they were not a solid bloc of states with coordinated behavior (except perhaps in voting patterns on economic matters at the UN), these states began to form a multistate group with potential collective impact.

In addition to the polycentrism of the Soviet sphere and the beginning of decentralization among American allies, the emergence of the Third World further loosened global polarity because it presented many nonbloc actors. Figure 8–6 shows the resulting loose bipolarity. Diagrammatically, the differences between this and the tight bipolar model are the presence of nonbloc actors and the splintering in the two main blocs. Yet the structure is still basically bipolar with respect to effective power relations. Only two bloc actors are portrayed as relating directly to the fulcrum. Each of the others either arises from a major bloc or is tied to one for power purposes, yet it may not be thoroughly allied.

For bloc members, the behavioral norms in tight and loose bipolar systems are essentially the same. Members are pledged to prepare to eliminate the opposing bloc but prefer to fight small wars rather than large. Members agree to strengthen their own bloc internally and to resolve differences by negotiation rather than open conflict. The threat of total destruction leads to a tacit agreement not to provoke war between the dominant members of opposing blocs.

But for the dominant members, the Soviet Union and the United States, there is an added objective in loose bipolarity—namely, to maintain optimum tightness under conditions that nurture fragmentation. The mechanisms for this function are like the normal rewards and punishments by which powerful states influence the less powerful: economic rewards and deprivations, offers and withdrawals of military supply beyond that needed for the state's contribution to bloc security, and so on. In extreme cases, strong states may use force, as the Soviet Union did in Hungary in 1956 and the United States did in Cuba in 1961 and in the Dominican Republic in 1965. In addition, especially when alliances are institutionalized, the polar states may use the alliance structure to prolong the perception of threat by playing to the self-aggrandizing behavior of pertinent elites, such as national military commands. In this sense, threat perception becomes an important aspect of dominant-member political strategy in loose bipolar systems.

The norms of nonbloc actors are considerably different. Their basic role is as a ground for peaceful competition of the major powers and blocs, each intent primarily on gaining the adherence of the nonbloc state but secondarily on preventing it from going over to the other side. Their conflicts must be internalized (Nigeria and Biafra), carefully circumscribed (Rhodesia and Zambia), or submitted to global settlement (Congo). They must resist great-power intervention if it is likely to bring in the other major power or result in subordination.

In the normal course of events, it might be expected that loose bipolarity would give way to multipolarity, with the quasi-independent blocs becoming independent power poles. Some observers argue that such a situation has existed for 20 years.[11] But although the loosening trend has shattered bipolarity, it does not appear yet to have arrived at multipolarity. Hence, an interim model is necessary.

The Incipient Multipolar Balance of Power

During the early 1970s, the years in which American foreign policy was established by President Richard Nixon and Secretary of State Henry Kissinger, the basic assumption was that the world power distribution was evolving into a "pentapolar" model, one in which five major powers would dominate international politics. In addition to the United States and the Soviet Union, this view included China, Japan, and Western Europe as critical participants in the power distribution. Events since 1973 have demonstrated that in addition, the ability of the resource-rich Third World to force a transformation of the international economic system requires that that group be regarded as a serious and independent part of the global power structure, although its military influence is small. It should be kept in mind, however, that power consists of several important nonmilitary characteristics (see Chapter 7). Indeed, although Japan is a mighty nation economically, its ability to influence international events through military action is negligible.

The notion of incipient multipolarity suggests that the global power distribution is in a transitional stage between bipolarity, clearly a thing of the past, and true multipolarity, in which six states (or groups of states) are more or

---

[11]See, for example, Cecil V. Crabb, Jr., *Nations in a Multipolar World* (New York: Harper & Row, 1968).

less equally capable of influencing the outcomes of major international events. But the reader is cautioned against the conclusion that such a stage will automatically lead to multipolarity. In fact, although it was widely speculated a decade ago that full multipolarity was safely predictable, recent developments in both the physical and diplomatic characteristics of the world suggest that the transition stage may be prolonged. Among these developments have been the growing awareness that the Western industrial powers are not energy self-sufficient and are thus vulnerable in their capabilities, the modest pace of political integration in Western Europe, and the temporary resurgence of interest in the trans-Atlantic defense structure as a response to the rapid Soviet military buildup in Central Europe (1981–1988), reversed in 1989 and 1990.

Nevertheless, if incipient multipolarity is a stage in which a fundamental realignment of world power is occurring, then we need to identify the principal political characteristics of a multipolar system in order to have a standard by which to measure the progress of the main participants toward it. The characteristic suggested here is that a major participant in a multipolar system would have the capability to determine the outcome of a direct (although not necessarily cataclysmic) confrontation between two other major participants. Another standard, both more modest and more practical, is the ability to determine the outcome of a distant event despite Soviet or American intention to achieve some other outcome(s). To what extent have the emerging major poles developed their international capabilities in these respects?

China The government of Mao Tse-tung used the Korean War to announce that it would not permit the two great powers to divide the world, and especially Asia. For the quarter-century that followed, American respect for China grew as a result of China's cautious diplomacy, its decision to limit strategic activities to its immediate Asian and Soviet border areas, and its general restraint during the Vietnam War. There is little doubt that American behavior throughout that war was guided by a careful assessment of Chinese tolerance of American control close to its borders.

Soviet respect for China was growing during the same time because of the latter's willingness to challenge Soviet territorial control of certain border regions and because of the growth of China's nuclear capability. Although both Washington and Moscow had considered China a bitter enemy and a clumsy diplomatic contestant through the 1960s, neither was concerned for China's strategic capability beyond the proximity of interests in Asia. Its nuclear capability was regional at most; its capacity to control external events by either military or economic means was meager; and its preference for self-imposed isolation from global politics was a tempting reassurance to both Washington and Moscow in the daily maneuvering of their worldwide interests.

But if little communication took place between China and either of the two giants between the end of the Korean War (1953) and the withdrawal of the United States from Southeast Asia (1973), in the years following the latter event there has been a startling change. The gradual normalization of relations with Washington resulted in formal diplomatic recognition in 1979, a rapid growth in Sino-American trade, and the conclusion of a Second World War peace agreement with Japan. With the deaths of both Mao and Foreign Secretary Chou En-lai, there was evidence of a new Chinese world perspective by the end of the 1980s. No longer interested in isolation and no longer fixed to the ideological notion of modernization that had resulted in the suffocation of education and a preindustrial rate of progress, China undertook to overhaul its educational system, to reawaken its scientific potential by welcoming foreign scientists as visitors and advisers, to stimulate diverse productivity, and to enliven its cultural life. (All of this was set back temporarily by the wave of political repression that followed the Tiananmen Square events of 1989.)

More strikingly, however, in 1979 China signaled to the world its intention of controlling the regional power distribution of Asia by invading Vietnam under a doctrine of punitive aggression. This was held to be payment for Vietnam's conquest of Cambodia. It may have been precisely this kind of expanded presence that the Soviet Union feared of post-Mao China and the reason the Kremlin resisted multipolarity. The Soviet leaders may have considered multipolarity an abstract Western notion of world politics, pitting state against state and ignoring the fundamental power question of international politics: the contest between world capitalism and world socialism.

For nearly a decade, while the United States viewed China's role as increasingly constructive in balancing regional power (save for Washington's displeasure at the Vietnam invasion), the Kremlin continued to view China as a deviant state capable of upsetting both Asian politics and world socialism. It viewed China as having seduced the United States into peaceful relations, military agreements, and industrial trade with the attractiveness of China's large and impoverished markets and with the richness of its natural resources, particularly petroleum. The Soviet Union deplored China's Westward leanings and collusion with capitalism and considered China's ideological deviations to have encouraged anti-Soviet influences in Poland. By 1982, however, Sino-Soviet relations began to thaw, a process symbolized by a visit of high-ranking Chinese officials to Moscow, the first such visit in a quarter-century. Western writers began to predict a Sino-Soviet détente. The most serious sign of change occurred in 1989 when Mikhail Gorbachev visited Beijing; debate raged in the United States as to whether a real Sino-Soviet détente would be desirable for American foreign relations and for the American role in Asia. Implicitly, this debate explored the question of whether or not a lasting thaw in Sino-Soviet relations would alter the power distribution regionally or globally. It was during Gorbachev's visit, however, that student demonstrations began, leading after the General Secretary's departure to military encampment, firing into the unarmed crowd, martial law, and a nationwide roundup of "anti-revolutionary hooligans." These events and the subsequent economic sanctions imposed by the United States and other governments turned China inward, and occasioned an abrupt (although presumably temporary) halt in the forward movement of Chinese diplomacy. The changes that might otherwise have resulted from the Gorbachev visit have yet to affect the power equation in Asia.

It is nonetheless true, despite the potential changes in China's role that these events signal, that Beijing's part in the power equation remains principally regional. Regardless of its nearly unlimited potential power and rapid advancement as a nuclear state, its capacity to determine the outcome of a direct confrontation between the Soviet Union and the United States is limited almost entirely to Asia. Furthermore, it is probable that with China's own power growing, the only area in Asia over which the two giants are likely to differ significantly—save possibly Korea—is China. Except as a matter of self-defense, therefore, it is difficult to imagine a situation in which China might be called to play a role in a Soviet-American confrontation in Asia. China's role in the brief war between India and Pakistan (1965) showed its willingness to take part in Asian politics outside its direct sphere, but in that case any Soviet-American confrontation was merely diplomatic. At present, then, within its Asian regional sphere, the likelihood of a confrontation between two major powers calling for China to play a third power role is very small. One quantitative assessment of comparative power status suggests that China's strategic reach is two-thirds that of the Soviet Union and only 20 percent that of the United States. The study concludes that by this index, China is roughly comparable as a world power with West Germany and Israel.[12] Although this study is more than two decades old, it is likely that its conclusion remains valid.

By the same token, because China's influence at its present stage of development has but a regional reach, it is improbable that it will effectively control distant events in a manner undesirable to Washington and/or Moscow. On the whole, therefore, China may be said to play a major role in its Asian tripartite relations with the United States and the Soviet Union; but given the current limitations of its capabilities and those of its preference for regional politics, China has not yet achieved the status of a third global power. The twenty-year rapprochement with the United States and the prospects for a serious effort at détente with the Soviet Union are less signals of a new global thrust for China than an indication of an evolving policy of expanding political and economic relations in order to accelerate domestic economic development. Although China shows increasing evidence of wishing to play on the global economic stage, its strategic reach remains regional.

Europe   Until recently, any discussion of the European role in incipient multipolarity was limited to Western Europe. The peoples of Western Europe, progressing toward economic integration, chaffing under American strategic control and feeling relieved of the Soviet military threat, have for two decades seen themselves as an increasingly important force in world politics. During the same period, as Eastern Europeans have longed for economic independence and freedom from Soviet control, progress toward any significant split from Moscow has generally been met by threats of force, as in the Warsaw Pact occupation of Czechoslovakia in 1968. In 1989, however, with the suspension of the Brezhnev Doctrine (the Soviet political rule that because the will of the Socialist Commonwealth supersedes that of any of its members, any threat of dissolution will be met by force from the community), Hungary became the first Eastern European country since the Second World War to open

---

[12]Ray S. Cline, *World Power Assessment,* as reproduced in George T. Kurian, *The Book of World Rankings* (New York: Facts on File Publications, 1979), table 49.

The reburial of Imra Nagy, 1989. Nagy, former Prime Minister of Hungary, was forced from power by the Kremlin in 1956 in the wake of anti-Communist uprisings, and was buried in exile and disgrace. Mikhael Gorbachev's policies in Eastern Europe permitted the reestablishment of his place in history.
Source: AP/Wide World

its boundaries by tearing down the barbed wire at its Austrian border; and only four months after it was removed from seven years of illegal existence, the Polish Solidarity labor movement managed to establish the first noncommunist government in Eastern Europe in almost 45 years. By the middle of 1990, communist governments had either collapsed or been replaced in East Germany, Poland, Hungary, Czechoslovakia, Bulgaria and Romania (where civil war accompanied political events). Furthermore, the Berlin Wall, for more than four decades the most vivid symbol of a divided Europe, had been opened both politically and physically, followed by the opening of the Brandenburg Gate and the removal of the famous Checkpoint Charlie. The two Germanys and the four occupying powers (United States, Soviet Union, Britain and France) had agreed to the reunification of Germany and its membership in the North Atlantic Treaty Organization. By the middle of 1990, then, the Cold War in Europe had ended and the process of reuniting Europe had begun, only 30 months before the anticipated economic union of the European Community members. These constitute momentous events for the evolution of the global power distribution. Hence, this section is entitled ''Europe'' rather than ''Western Europe,'' as in all previous editions of this book. Yet because the post-war histories of the two sectors differ considerably, they are necessarily treated separately.

Years have passed since the states of Western Europe were wholly dependent on the United States. Through their economic consolidation they have struggled against American economic domination, and they have labored to compete successfully with foreign goods in Europe and throughout the world. Declining apprehension of war has encouraged an awareness not only of Europeanness but also of Pan-Europeanness, a desire for the economic and political reconciliation of all Europe as inaugurated in the *Ostpolitik* of West Germany.

Far from continuing the decline (brought on by the destruction of the Second World War and the postwar gap) between their own productivity and that of the United States, Western Europeans perceive themselves, in the era of economic integration, to be a competitive economic force during the technological revolution. Advantaged by the steady fall in the value of the American dollar from the mid-1960s to 1982 and then again in 1985–1986 and by the always present American balance-of-trade deficit, the only external influences that the Western Europeans have not been able to control have been the instability in world fuel supplies and the uncertainty introduced in the world economy by huge annual American budget deficits. These problems notwithstanding, Western Europeans see themselves in the forefront of a world movement in which the status of the nation-state is changing. Political loyalty is gradually moving from the national government to an integrated Europe and to the transnational corporation with its worldwide connections. The growth of Eurocommunism until 1984, signaling the apparent death of anticommunist hysteria in Western Europe, further divided Europe from Washington and Wall Street. In fact, as these trends accelerate as Western Europe approaches full economic integration in 1992 and as free markets replace communism throughout Eastern Europe and the Soviet Union in the 1990s, the Atlantic alliance might easily disintegrate in either its economic or its military form, and quite possibly both.

Where strategic relations are concerned, there has been considerable evolution in the European position. In the early years of the 1980s, during which Soviet-American relations were characterized by rhetorical warfare, the European governments agreed to proceed with the stationing of new intermediate-range missiles despite opposition from a number of political parties, particularly in West Germany. By the end of the decade, though, a whole class of intermediate-range weapons had been eliminated by treaty and destroyed. Despite a brief flurry of debate over replacement of some short-range missiles, Western Europeans generally lost enthusiasm for the more bullish American strategic attitude in Europe. Much of this was due to a shift of focus to economic matters, and to Soviet diplomacy: the end of martial law in Poland; the withdrawal of troops from Afghanistan; the unilateral declaration of withdrawal of some troops from the Warsaw Pact territories; and official Soviet tolerance of liberalization in Hungary, Poland, and even the ''captive states,'' long symbolic of Soviet barbarism among Europeans, of Lithuania, Estonia, and Latvia. With the fear of a NATO–Warsaw Pact war eliminated by the end of 1990, Europeans East and West moved quickly to shed the vestiges of the Cold War and to establish a broad economic growth pattern unfettered by historical fears of capitalist encirclement or the menacing spread of communism.

Consistent with this Euroconsciousness as with the elimination of their global empires two decades earlier, the Western European governments generally spurned far-flung strategic obligations. British participation in the Falklands War against Argentina resulted from a long-standing commitment to retain the islands; and the brief French intervention in defense of Chad against Libyan invasion in 1983 was a reluctant postimperial attempt at preserving a special economic relationship. These were the only two departures from a strictly European defense focus in the decade. Western Europe's strategic interests, to the extent that they are distinct from NATO policy, are limited to that of a regional deterrent capable not of waging nuclear war but of inflicting unacceptable harm on any attacker. Although Western Europe will continue to be a major economic power, its strategic interests are almost exclusively regional.

Events in the Persian Gulf not only disrupted the dream of an era of global peace, but forced a reconsideration of extraregional obligations among Western Europeans. The end of the eight-year Iran-Iraq War in 1988 coincided with the early radical changes in Soviet policy and preceded by only months the democratization of Eastern Europe and the pacification of Central America. It appeared that the world's hot spots might be limited to regional or civil wars in remote places like Mozambique, Chad, Western Sahara and Cambodia, and to the guerilla wars in places like Peru and Colombia. The world was ever mindful of the potential for war between India and Pakistan; and while rhetoric ran high and tempers thin in the Israeli-occupied territories in the Middle East, the threat of war seemed slim.

But in mid-1990, powerful Iraq turned on tiny and defenseless Kuwait, conquering it in 48 hours. Over 100,000 Iraqi troops then assembled on the borders of Saudi Arabia, the conquest of which would have placed almost half of all Middle Eastern petroleum exports under Iraqi control. Within days the United Nations Security Council, for only the third time since 1945, voted a world-wide economic and arms embargo against Iraq. In an attempt both to deter Iraqi invasion and enforce the embargo, the United States assembled ground and air power in Saudi Arabia and a naval blockade of all Persian Gulf and Red Sea ports through which Iraqi trade, both import and export, might have been conducted. In an effort to secure the assistance of other states whose economic prosperity was threatened by Iraq's policies, Washington encouraged Arab and NATO states as well as the Soviet Union to provide both ground and naval forces. Britain and Italy responded with naval vessels and Egypt and Morocco with ground troops. France and the Soviet Union announced that they would participate in multinational deterrence and blockade only if specifically endorsed by the United Nations Security Council. These events together underscored several important elements of world politics and economics: (1) the fragility of world peace even in an era of unprecedented superpower harmony; (2) the willingness of Western European states to undertake tactical initiatives on behalf of their oil-dependent economies; and (3) their reluctance to do so except in concert with other governments.

The collapse of Soviet power and of communism in Eastern Europe and the reunification of the two Germanys contribute to an extraordinary acceleration in the evolution of the global power distribution. Gone is the protective ring around Soviet territory; gone for all practical purposes are both the Warsaw

Pack and the WTO-NATO confrontation across central Europe; and gone from the contemporary language of global politics are such expressions as "containment," "capitalist encirclement" and "cold war." The states of Eastern Europe are gradually withdrawing from the centrally-planned regional economy with its Soviet-centered distribution system, and are looking to the West for trade and for development capital. They suffer shortages of both industrial and agricultural goods, high unemployment, and environmental devastation. Although political oppression is greatly diminished, economic deprivation runs high. And Eastern Europeans are keenly aware that the former is due to the moderation and tolerance of Mikhail Gorbachev's *perestroika,* while the latter can be addressed only through economic contacts with the West. Their inclination to look first to Western Europe and only second to the United States is driven by a combination of history, proximity, and the lure of the anticipated riches of economic integration in 1992. Their break from the Soviet circle and their coveted integration into a united Europe influences the global power distribution in three ways: (1) it diminishes the strategic and economic reach of the Soviet Union; (2) it increases the aggregate economic potential of Europe; and (3) it both enhances the potential economic power of Western Europe and, in doing so, weakens the residual links of dependence to the United States, particularly as the political lever of NATO is reduced in importance precisely when the economic power of Europe is expanded.

These events and conditions serve to illustrate two important points. First, the global power balance does evolve, underscoring once again that the balance of power is driven by the dynamics of the system rather than by seemingly neat and cogent models. And second, they reveal that although China, Japan, and the Third World have traditionally been looked upon as the prospective sites of greatest change in the power distribution, the focus is once again on Europe. This time, however, the focus is not on Western Europe alone, but on the emerging probability of a Pan-European movement driven by economic growth and reform rather than by the Soviet ideological, economic, and military strategies of an extinct Cold War.

But there is a third lesson here too: that political change does not necessarily, or even commonly, occur in a linear fashion—events do not necessarily lead to their logical conclusions simply because they have been set in motion. To be sure, the changes in Eastern Europe are historic, but they are also very young and correspondingly unsteady. Scarcely two months before Solidarity's electoral victory in Poland, Chinese students had organized a demand for more democracy, particularly press freedom, greater nonsocialist economic incentives, and the elimination of corruption in government. As their protest turned to a hard-line demand for a change in the government, the government itself made the unequivocal decision that there would be no Chinese-style *perestroika.* This decision was reportedly made in the interest of preserving communism and of saving leading communists from mob justice. Powerful elements within the Soviet Union and throughout Eastern Europe find little value in *perestroika* and none in an Eastern European government in which the Communist party is the opposition rather than the dominant—if not the only legitimate—political party. Hence, it must be emphasized with respect to both the evolution of the global power distribution and a more general understanding of international politics, that the signal events in Eastern Europe in 1989–1990 are steps into the future, not necessarily incontrovertible predictors of the outcome.

Japan A third country that is regarded as a potentially effective third power is Japan, whose economic stature follows only those of the United States and the Soviet Union. Not only has Japan risen above American commercial domination; it has also proved its ability to compete in world markets and is preparing to be the dominant supplier of industrial goods throughout Asia, including China.

The growth pattern that Japan's economic power has followed alarms the West. During the 1960s, Japan achieved world domination in a number of small electronics manufacturers; in the 1970s, it dominated the international automobile trade; and in the 1980s and early 1990s, it is in a race with the United States, France, and West Germany to introduce the first megacomputers equipped with artificial intelligence. During each of these phases there have been charges that Japanese manufacturers have stolen Western designs rather than invent their own products; that Japan's export subsidy policies violate international free-trade laws and principles; that Japan violated international norms by closing its domestic markets to foreign goods and financial services; and that Japanese manufacturers have wantonly jeopardized Western security by selling to the Soviet Union, at substantial profit, manufacturing secrets that will make it more difficult to detect Soviet nuclear submarines in the future. Japan's economic prominence has been accompanied, then, by considerable diplomatic difficulties.

Despite its strong position, Japan is extraordinarily vulnerable to external pressures, so much so that even its economic productivity suffers significant external controls. Chapter 3 describes the susceptibility of Japan's economy to American economic policy, and its extreme exposure to the demands of the fuel-producing states. Consequently, the economic foundation of Japan's claim to third-power status is a peculiar one: More for Japan than for any other candidate for this global role, the greatness that Japan commands rests on its extreme dependency on both external markets and foreign energy sources. Although its productivity continues to increase, new threats loom. The formalization of peace with both the Soviet Union and the People's Republic of China seems to offer new economic hope for Japan with respect to markets for industrial goods and acquisition of desperately needed petroleum. Nevertheless, much of this promise seems to depend on the continuation of good diplomatic relations between Beijing and Washington and is threatened by the general strain in relations between the Soviet Union and Western-oriented nations that might result from economic imbalance within Europe.

The security sector reveals similar weaknesses. Prohibited at present by the Atomic Energy Law from developing nuclear weapons or deploying troops outside its home territory, and uncertain of the American security commitment at a time when the Asian power distribution is in disarray, Japan must rely on economic and political means to establish its regional and global role. Japan's role in Asia is constrained by the peculiarity of its being the indigenous economic giant without nuclear capability in a region that has two underindustrialized but nuclear states (China and India). And one of the most vexing problems of Japanese politics and of the Japanese role in the Western security network is the issue of Japan's increasing its financial commitment to its own defense.

In spite of its apparent strength, then, Japan is a state struggling to adapt to regional and global power relativities. Like Western Europe, it has escaped from the perpetual subordination of a bipolar system, but because of its dependence on others, particularly the United States and OPEC members, it is unable to establish a self-determined third-power role.

The Third World   For more than a decade, many observers have claimed that the Third World is, or is about to become, an effective third power in global relations. Because of its total population, its territorial vastness, and its richness in natural resources, the potential development here is extreme. But until recently this potential has not been mobilized. The population, growing at alarming rates, has caused a decline in per capita wealth even while the GNPs of most of the Third World states have been climbing. New forms of dependency implanted by Western-based multinational corporations have been added to the economic burden of population. Furthermore, the recessionary markets of the early 1980s devastated export potentials in the Third World and increased the burden in international debt to the point that Western bankers feared the collapse of international capital markets.

The establishment of OPEC and the events of 1973–1974 (both of which enriched the fuel-producing countries and forced changes in the foreign policies of more powerful states, including Japan and the United States) caused a reassessment of the long-range capabilities of the Third World. As described in Chapter 5, that reappraisal begins with a division of the Third World into the resource rich and the resource poor and then turns to the role of the former. Because much of the West is dependent on OPEC (and particularly on the Arab OPEC states) for industrial fuel, the oil-rich nations have discovered an effective lever for dealing with large dependent states. Simultaneously, they have greatly improved their regional bargaining position.

The 1973–1974 oil embargo was not an isolated incident. In the years that followed, the world's oil markets were shocked by the collapse of the Iranian economy after the revolution and then by the destruction of both Iranian and Iraqi oil production in a protracted war between the two. Moreover, the magic of OPEC dwindled even among its members, many of whom lost enthusiasm for a system of controlling international petroleum prices by limiting production. Those who preferred to take advantage of the increased demand by increasing production wanted also to maintain high prices. By 1979, internal conflict began to tear at OPEC, and by 1985 it appeared that OPEC's influence over the global economy was no more. Because of the severe market glut, oil prices dropped dramatically in less than a year from over $30 per barrel to approximately $9. In 1986, a renewed effort was made to reinstate production limits in order to drive up price again; but by the end of 1989, although the price per barrel of crude oil had reached $16 again, the political leverage of OPEC had not been restored. Meanwhile, as the technological revolution proceeds apace and governments invest heavily in alternative energy sources, predictions arise that the world's oil demand will drop sharply by about 2025,[13] leaving OPEC with only about 30 years to exploit its precious reserve to the fullest.

OPEC alone does not, of course, constitute the Third World. Nor have all of its consequences escaped the Third World, whose members suffered as much from exorbitant oil prices as did the industrialized economies. Furthermore, oil is the only commodity that has had a major effect on international economic determination. Other groups of Third World states have been unable to find the equivalents of oil to finance their development through economic pressure. Simultaneously, however, some of them have moved toward agricultural self-sufficiency (such as Bangladesh) and others toward industrial modernity (such as Taiwan, South Korea, the Philippines, and Singapore). By 1990, however, there were few visible bonds among Third World states that had not been present 30 years earlier, and those were more bonds of aspiration than of collective progress. Consequently, although the Third World has gained uneven and only occasionally significant influence on the global balance of power, it has not yet consolidated the ingredients that would make it an effective, independent pole in the international power equation.

These observations about China, Western Europe, Japan, and the Third World demonstrate that even though the world has outgrown the forms of subordination typical of loose bipolarity, it has not produced effective independent power centers that would usher in true multipolarity. Consequently, we conclude that the global balance of power is in a transitional phase of incipient multipolarity, in which the secondary power centers are still more attached to the primary than the independent poles. Figure 8–7 shows this configuration.

The Multipolar Balance of Power

If significant power increases should occur in the Third World, China, Western Europe, or Japan to the extent that two or more of these entities were able to challenge Soviet-American global interests, the international system could be defined as multipolar. Because the relative power capabilities need not be entirely equal, multipolarity might have either symmetrical or asymmetrical characteristics. The important issue is that several major power blocs would interact at virtually any place, without two-party domination. Such a system would appear as shown in Figure 8–8. As in the previous models, the important factor here is that each of these systems is depicted as affecting the fulcrum, rather than being derived from or dependent on some other power unit.

A New Balance-of-Power Model?

It has occasionally been suggested that multipolarity might restore the conditions of the nineteenth-century balance of power. This argument has two bases.

---

[13]Bruce Nussbaum, *The World After Oil: The Shifting Axis of Power and Wealth* (New York: Simon & Schuster, 1983).

Figure 8–7 Incipient global multipolarity, 1965 to the present.

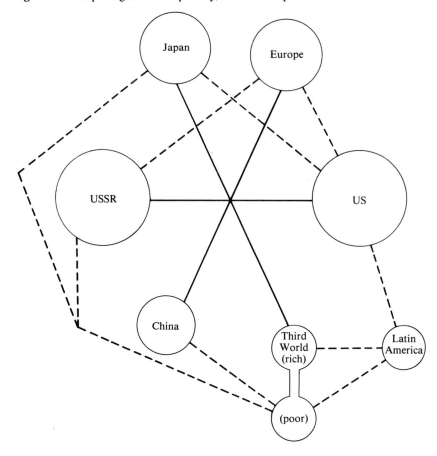

First, several independent power centers facilitate the switching of alliances and the realignment of interests and power. Second, the same feature—multiple power centers—is necessary for the appearance of a Balancer, at the service of the international system to balance the system consciously (manually). Presuming that multipolarity were approximately symmetrical, any of several power centers might serve in this capacity, and perhaps several would alternate in the role.

Because of its huge power potential, China is most likely the next effective independent power in global politics. If it is, then big-power confrontations calling for third-power intervention as a Balancer might take any of the following forms:

Contestants	*Balancer*
China–Soviet Union	United States
United States–China	Soviet Union
United States–Soviet Union	China

Figure 8–8 True global multipolarity, possible future.

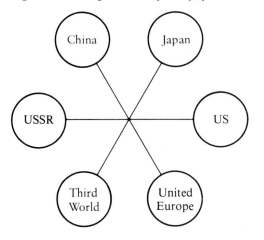

But there are several impediments to these relations. First, the power of each participant is so great that coalitions will necessarily overbalance. Hence, the proper designation for these relations is not balance of power but mutual superiority in noncoalition situations and disequilibrium in coalitions. Second, ideological barriers minimize the likelihood of each configuration. Third, balance-of-power theory assumes the dedication of each participant to the preservation of the others. Such devotion, whether out of strategy or sentiment, will be lacking for the foreseeable future. It follows that even the most probable form of global tripolarity is incompatible with a renewed balance of power on the nineteenth-century model.

The Contemporary Global Balance: Some Caveats

At the outset of this discussion of the balance of power, the student was cautioned to understand that the models presented (and argued) here are no more than structural depictions of the world power distribution at different stages of history. Such structural models are fraught with oversimplification and fall particularly to the criticism that structuralism is characteristically static, whereas the global political system is highly dynamic and even explosive. Before closing this discussion, therefore, it is necessary to impose on these models some comments about the dynamism of the system. But before we turn to that, there are other caveats that must be called to the student's attention.

Because this presentation is chronological, there may be in it a kind of momentum that suggests a necessary trend in power developments. This is not intended. First, we know that the development of the global system is discontinuous. The process is upset frequently, if not by wars, by changes, often radical, in the distribution of political forces, or by significant economic events such as the rise of OPEC or global economic recession. We have seen that for decades some observers have been proclaiming the existence of a multipolar system, but it is evident that such a day has yet to dawn. Even progress

in that direction was retarded by such things as the realization of Japan's industrial dependence on the deeply troubled Middle East, the debt crisis of the
Third World, and the temporary resurgence of support for NATO in Western
Europe as a consequence of the Soviet occupation of Afghanistan and many
other events. Hence, although there have been many trends toward multipolarity, there have been at least as many setbacks.

Second, even though our presentation is necessarily chronological, it represents nothing more than historical trend. For the events that mark these various stages of global history are, for the most part, random; any pattern is
more a consequence than a cause of the global power structure. This disclaimer is important because it is not claimed that a logical presentation of the
evolution of structural systems is driven by any laws of history. Unlike the
Marxist faith in the immutable laws of history that will result in global socialism and the disappearance of the state, the structures examined here claim to
have no predictive value. Rather, they are merely analytical instruments for
understanding the respective power distributions at frozen moments in history.
True multipolarity, even within the limited structural constraints suggested
here, may never occur.

Furthermore, although an effort has been made to include both economic
and military features of the balance of power, this is nonetheless exclusively a
state-oriented analysis. Nation-states may still be the principal actors on the
world stage, but they surely are not alone. They share the stage with nongovernmental organizations, intergovernmental organizations, the world's private
economy typified internationally by the transnational corporation, subnational
political forces, and even the powerful influences of international crime. Thus,
interstate power models are flawed, although still instructive. They lack the
realities of systemic dynamics and the submacropolitical forces that bring
about change in the global system and in interstate relations.

One observer examined the power theory of international relations in light
of the fundamental changes in the world in the last quarter-century. He found
six changes that have altered the traditional interstate power relations: rapidly
advancing resource scarcity; a growth in the demand for redistribution of the
world's wealth; a tendency among peoples to readjust their loyalties away
from the nation-state (''subgroupism''); a decline in governmental authority to
maintain order and cope with internal and external transformation; fragmentation of intergovernmental relations even within alliances; and the transnation-
alization of an increasing number of issues previously the preserve of
governments, or ''cascading interdependence.'' Together with the improved
ability of individuals to understand public policy and to initiate change in it,
these factors have lead to the simultaneous disintegration of the old world
order and integration into a new one, through a ''patterned chaos'' of sociopolitical relations within and among nations.[14] It is these dynamics that form
the framework of structural models of the balance of power, that determine the

---

[14]James N. Rosenau, ''A Pre-Theory Revisited: World Politics in an Era of Cascading Interdependence,'' *International Studies Quarterly,* September 1984, pp. 245–305.

pace, quality, and progress of interstate relations, and that determine whether or not structural change will occur in the balance of power.

Regional Balance of Power

Throughout this discussion of balance-of-power models, reference has been made to regional as well as global conditions. Although the concept has generally been applied to worldwide relations, the notion of a balance of power has critical interpretive meanings for regional conflict as well. This is true whether or not the major powers contribute significantly to the regional power equation.

Asia presents a highly complex power distribution. At the highest level, the two superpowers contribute directly because of their conflicting interests there. The Pacific Ocean, Taiwan, and South Korea are at the American nuclear frontier. At the second level, China transforms Soviet-American relations in Asia into nuclear tripolarity. Beneath that, India pursues a nuclear policy to enjoy mutual deterrence with China, but in so doing tilts the scale in its own favor against Pakistan. It is precisely because as an economic power Japan must venture into all of these relations that its military inferiority confuses its role in the overall Asian balance of power.

The situation is made less clear by the military events of 1978–1979, particularly the Vietnamese invasion of Cambodia and the subsequent Chinese occupation of Vietnamese territory. When a partial Chinese withdrawal was followed by the stationing of Soviet naval vessels in Vietnamese bases (built and previously used by the US Navy), the continental politics and power balance of Asia seemed once again to be thrown into disarray.

The balance-of-power question in the Middle East becomes more complicated annually. In a series of wars between 1948 and 1973, that balance was almost entirely one between Israel and its Arab enemies. But more recently, new political and military forces have come into play, with deeply disruptive consequences for the region. Among them we may simply list the following as the most important:

1. Egypt's peace agreement with Israel settled the Arab-Israeli conflict but broke the solidarity of the Arab nations.
2. The Iranian revolution, Iran's split with the West, and more than a half-decade of war between Iran and Iraq devastated the politics and economics of the southeastern portion of that region.
3. The civil war in Lebanon was complicated by Israeli-Syrian efforts to control both the internal factions and the use of Lebanese territory for purposes of preventing (Israel), or using it (Syria) for, continued guerrilla attacks on Israeli targets.
4. The factionalization of the Palestine Liberation Front is the focal point of revolutionary activity.
5. Libya has become increasingly radicalized; the Soviet and American navies have become more active in the Mediterranean; and the United States launched an air strike against Libya in retaliation for Libyan-sponsored terrorism, as did Israel on the Sudan.

6. The effects of the rise and fall of OPEC were felt by both the global and regional economies.

7. Iraq's annexation of Kuwait and threat against Saudia Arabia, and the resulting 26-member military coalition in Saudia Arabia.

All these circumstances exist simultaneously in the Middle East. As a result, when one addresses the Middle Eastern balance of power, one needs to specify which balance. Chapter 9 examines some of the world's most precarious regional balances.

Polarity and Stability: A Debate

The foregoing elucidation of past, present, and possible future power distributions produces a critical question: Is international stability better ensured by fundamentally bipolar political patterns or by multipolar balance? Each has advantages, but each also suffers from disadvantages.

One advocate of bipolarity finds four specific benefits in that system. First, with two overbearing world powers there are no peripheries from which significant conflict beyond the control of the great powers can occur. Second, the tighter the bipolarity and the more intense the interbloc competition are, the broader will be the range of the subject matter over which the great powers gain leverage and can control conflict. Third, pressure is constant, and crises recur at low levels rather than in major conflict. Finally, the combination of constant pressure within blocs and the superior power of the dominant members enables the blocs to tolerate potentially disruptive change, including revolution, which might otherwise lead to widespread conflict.[15]

The disadvantages and intrinsic dangers of bipolarity have also been elucidated. One is that bipolar systems accentuate antagonism because of the reactions of the blocs to each other, leading to a degenerative aspect. There is also skepticism over the maxim that peace is best ensured by a crisis atmosphere and mutual fear. As we have previously seen, the tighter a bipolar configuration is, the more tense will be the relations of the blocs and of their respective dominant members.[16]

Others have investigated the stabilizing potential of multipolar systems and have concluded that the increased interaction of a multipolar model promotes stability.[17] In addition, increased interaction reduces obsession with any single one, thus enhancing the trend toward moderation. Although multipolarity cannot maintain stability interminably, it may be preferable in the shorter term.

In an empirical attempt to resolve the dispute over the stability of bipolar and multipolar systems, yet another scholar has studied the stratification and

---

[15]Kenneth N. Waltz, "The Stability of a Bipolar World," *Daedelus,* vol. 93, Summer 1964, pp. 881–909.

[16]R. N. Rosecrance, "Bipolarity, Multipolarity, and the Future," *Journal of Conflict Resolution,* vol. 10, 1966, pp. 315–317.

[17]Karl W. Deutsch and J. David Singer, "Multipolar Power Systems and International Stability," *World Politics,* vol. 16, 1964, pp. 390–406.

stability characteristics of 21 separate situations. He concludes that unipolar systems (single-nation domination), although historically rare, are the most stable. Bipolar systems, he finds, tend to produce less frequent but more prolonged wars than do multipolar. Multipolarity, in contrast, produces war among major actors more frequently and with more casualties. This argument thus leads to a choice, because none of these configurations seems statistically to offer any guarantee against warfare.

> The choice between bipolar versus multipolar arrangements now seems clear. If a state or group of states is willing to accept long wars that are won by aggressor states, bipolarity provides an escape from the more war-prone character of historical multipolar subsystems. Multipolarity entails more violence, more countries at war and more casualties; bipolarity, fewer but longer wars.[18]

Conclusion

Equivalence or Nonequivalence of Power

What is the balance of power between the United States and the Soviet Union? Describe the balance of power in the Far East. Who held the balance of power in the Cold War? Expressions and questions of this sort are common in political discussion, and they suggest some of the ways in which the balance-of-power concept is applied to the direct relations of pairs or small groups of states. It is useful to think of balance for the moment not as a natural phenomenon but as the familiar inanimate object. This permits us to recast the opening questions in this way: In what position does the balance (scale) come to rest when the power of the United States is symbolically piled at one end and that of the Soviet Union on the other? For a tripartite situation (Sino-Soviet-American relations in Asia, for example), think of a perfectly balanced three-bulb chandelier hanging from a flexible chain. Now: How does it hang when the power of the United States is symbolically plugged into one socket, that of the Soviet Union into a second, and that of China into the third? Does it continue to hang on a perfect level, or does it tilt in the direction of one? It should now be evident that the expression "balance of power" in small-group interstate relations refers to a rough measure of power equivalence or nonequivalence.

Equilibrating Objectives

In the early part of this discussion of balance of power, we noted that many analysts include among its many meanings that of a policy or a set of objectives. If we assume that states are power conscious, then in their external relations they may have any one of three power objectives: (1) to maintain

---

[18]Michael Haas, "International Subsystems: Stability and Polarity," *American Political Science Review,* vol. 64, 1970, pp. 98–123.

equality with some object-state, (2) to achieve superiority over some other state(s), or (3) to decline to keep pace with some other state(s). Again, remember that power must always be determined and measured relative to the power of someone else: Italy is more powerful than Switzerland but less powerful than France. The power choices that a government makes with respect to its neighbors or competitors reveal its equilibrating objectives.[19]

Surprisingly perhaps, some states opt not to match the power of their neighbors. Finland cannot compete with the Soviet Union and does not care to compete with Sweden. Costa Rica has virtually no military forces. And Japan, despite its image as a powerful state, maintains but a small national defense force. The Republic of China (Taiwan), however, invests a disproportionate share of its public revenue in national defense, yet it could not conceivably defend itself against aggression from China should it occur. In all these cases, therefore, the potential adversaries of these countries hold the balance against them.

In other situations, particularly where the expectation of conflict is moderate to high, the contesting states will seek superiority and may even abandon the traditional power balance in favor of the balance-of-terror variant. In contrast, where the probability of violence is perceived as low, states will seek no more than equivalence or will arm themselves only up to the level of their alliance commitments (for instance, Canada). From the logic of these contrasting cases we may infer that in most bilateral situations, military allocations are governed by the quest for the safety of equivalence.

"Balance of power," then, is an expression with many political meanings. In the global context it is useful as an analytical concept for assessing the overall power capabilities of states and coalitions, and it serves as a generic title for a host of specific power distributions. On the interstate level, in contrast, balance of power is a device for bilateral and small-group power relativities. It also expresses the equilibrating or disequilibrating objectives of national arms policies.

The bilateral and interbloc relations of the superpowers since the Second World War have been so intense as to have outgrown conventional balance-of-power logic. Instead, the dominant contemporary variant is the balance of terror. After studying some specific regional military balances in Chapter 9, we will discuss the balance of terror in Chapter 10.

---

[19]Some authors have attempted to modernize balance-of-power theory in a variety of ways. One is to distinguish between "balance of power" and "balance of threat." This theory posits that states do not align their power relations solely by power equations, but according to their perceptions of threat to their interests. Says one author, "Threat is a broader concept than power, since it includes aggregate power, proximity to target, offensive capability, and perceived intentions." See Stephen M. Walt, *The Origins of Alliances* (Ithaca: Cornell University Press, 1987), and Robert O. Keohane, "Alliances, Threats, and the Uses of Neorealism," *International Security,* Summer 1988, pp. 169–176.

CHAPTER 9

Regional Military Balances

Maintaining international stability in a world of conflicting national values and perceptions depends on resolving or reconciling conflict, an objective that is in many cases unattainable, or on managing a world full of ideological, territorial, national, ethnic, and other antagonisms so as to prevent wars. Conflict management depends, in turn, either on the predominance of a single power center able to impose its will in contentious regions to maintain order, or on a network of regional balances of power that, taken as a whole, add up to a delicate global balance. In the contemporary world, in which there is neither a world government nor a single dominant power able to maintain systemwide peace, stability depends largely on such regional balances. The great powers are often important, sometimes vital actors in the regional balances, but in most cases only insofar as they affect the capabilities of the local actors who dominant their own regions.

Throughout this book, the concept of power is considered to encompass more than military capability. Economic abilities as well as geographic, psychological, and other factors of national strength constitute power. In this chapter, however, our concern is exclusively with military capability. Hence the chapter bears the title ''Regional Military Balances'' rather than ''Regional Power Balances.''

It is a sad fact that, for many regimes, maintaining an adequate military capability against external and internal enemies is a paramount objective to which many other needs must be subordinated. The net product of all these preparations is a global complex of antagonistic subsystems in the form of regional military balances. Until recently the preeminent fact of European life has been the opposition of NATO and Warsaw Pact forces across the vast central European front; South Asian politics is conditioned by the hostility of India and Pakistan and their opposed military deployments; planning in the two Koreas is dominated by their preparations for war with each other; and Somalia and Ethiopia spend immense amounts on their opposed armed forces in spite of the crushing burden of underdevelopment that afflicts both. Table 9–1 lists additional examples and illustrates the great variety of regional balances that comprises the contemporary international system.

In many of these regional balances, the great powers play important roles by providing arms and military advisers, financial support, and surrogate forces such as the Cubans and East Germans to support or actually lead military operations and, in some cases, direct military intervention. Although the great powers seldom control completely the elements of the local balance, what they do or do not do is often critical, as few of the local balances are fully autonomous. Local hostilities in Third World regions generally have local causes and are not merely reflections of the overarching competition of the superpowers, but their outcomes are viewed by the great powers as important developments in the evolution of the larger international system. A pattern in which one side is supported by the Soviet Union and the other by the United States or another Western country is typical. The local wars are therefore, in part, proxy wars between the two major power blocs.

The comparative involvements of the United States and the Soviet Union in the arms policies affecting regional balances vary greatly over time. From the onset of the Korean War in 1950 to the American withdrawal from Vietnam in 1973, Washington was directly involved in the establishment of arms programs in Europe, Asia, Latin America and parts of Africa. Following Vietnam, however, the American commitment to regional balances abated in many places, with only the European balance, the defense of South Korea and Japan, and the arming of Israel against the threat of Arab aggression as major exceptions. During those years (1973–1980), Soviet involvement in regional balances exceeded that of the United States. In 1979, for example, 25,600 Soviet tanks were in the inventories of Third World countries, compared with 11,000 American and European tanks (of which the United States accounted for 6700). This disparity shows up in a more pronounced way in local compari-

Table 9–1 The world as a collection of local military balances.

North Korea vs. South Korea	Iraq vs. Iran
Soviet Union vs. China	Ethiopia vs. Somalia and Djibouti
India vs. Pakistan	Ethiopia vs. Eritrea
China vs. Taiwan	Kenya vs. Somalia
Afghanistan vs. Pakistan	Christian Lebanese vs. Moslem Lebanese
Arabs vs. Israel	and Palestinians
Polisario/Algeria vs. Morocco	South Africa vs. Angola, Mozambique,
Libya vs. Egypt and Tunisia	Zambia, Zimbabwe, and Seychelles
Yemen vs. Oman and Saudi Arabia	Iraq vs. Kuwait and Saudia Arabia

sons of the high-intensity conflicts: Soviet-supported Ethiopia had 600 tanks compared with about 100 in Somalia (many of which also came from the Soviets when that country was on better terms with the USSR); North Korea had 2600 compared with 1360 in South Korea; Vietnam had 1000 main battle tanks from the USSR compared with Thailand's 170 supplied by the United States; and Algeria had 500 Soviet-supplied tanks compared with the 100 provided to Morocco by the West. Even Israel had 550 "supplied" (that is, captured) Soviet tanks in its active inventory, compared with 1460 provided by the United States as of 1979; and Syria, Iraq, Libya, and Egypt had 8000 provided by the Soviet Union.

In the 1980s, however, the relative contributions of Washington and Moscow to regional balances were approximately equal. This situation results in part from a general reduction of Soviet arms exports and a great increase in American exports under the Reagan administration. Until recently, the Soviet Union continued to provide arms for Libya and Syria in the Middle East, Cuba and Nicaragua in Central America, and Ethiopia and Angola in Africa, as well as to the Warsaw Pact countries and Afghanistan. But Washington had vastly increased its exports to Central America (particularly to Mexico, Honduras, and El Salvador, aid to the *contra* insurgents in Nicaragua having been discontinued even before the election of anti-*Sandanista* President Violetta Chamorro); to the NATO countries; to Israel, Egypt, and Saudi Arabia; and to South Korea, Japan, India, and Pakistan. Much of the increase in American arms sales to the Third World in Latin America and elsewhere is related to the Reagan Doctrine: Countries that have fallen to communist rule can be won back as liberal democracies by supporting disenchanted elements with military matériel, training, and logistical assistance.

As the 1990s opened, several events occurred that may eventually change these patterns materially. Because they were new at the time of writing, they are presented here without interpretative comment.

1. The permanent cease-fire in the Persian Gulf War between Iran and Iraq sharply curtailed the international shipment in arms among all the principal suppliers.
2. Iraq's conquest of Kuwait and threat of invasion of Saudi Arabia resulted in a United Nations-sponsored global embargo on arms shipments to Iraq. But it also led to the assembling of a huge multinational blockading navy in the Persian Gulf and Red Sea as well as a multinational ground and air force (mostly American) of over 475,000 with full battle materiel in 1990.
3. The United States and the USSR reached an agreement on the mutual reduction of ground troops in Central Europe and actually began troop withdrawals.
4. The United States announced its willingness to abandon its two largest military installations in the Pacific Ocean if asked to do so by a Philippines referendum.
5. The Pentagon announced its intention to reduce its troop commitment in South Korea by 5000.
6. Cuba announced that it would discontinue its pass-through of Soviet arms to the Nicaraguan *Sandanistas* after the free election of anti-*Sandanista* President Violetta Chamorro despite Daniel Ortega's early refusal to surrender direction of the police and the army to the new government.

Table 9–2 Recipients of Soviet and American arms, 1984–1988.

Soviet Exports		American Exports	
Importer	*% Total*	*Importer*	*% Total*
Iraq	25	Saudi Arabia	18
India	22	Japan	16
Syria	11	Egypt	16
Czechoslovakia	9	Pakistan	7
Angola	7	Canada	7
Poland	6	Netherlands	6
Libya	5	Israel	6
E. Germany	5	So. Korea	5
Total	90	Total	81

Source: SIPRI Yearbook, 1989, chap. 6.

7. The Pentagon continued to press the Japanese government to assume a larger share of its defense cost as a preface to reducing the American military commitment in the area.

Despite these promising events, arms continued to be shipped to the world's most troubled areas. These included the Middle East and Central America (other than Nicaragua and Afghanistan where, despite Soviet withdrawal, the communist government and American-armed insurgents continued to be locked in brutal civil war).

Lest it be thought that the United States and the Soviet Union alone are responsible for militarizing regional conflicts, it needs to be pointed out that their combined share of total international arms shipments is declining. Whereas in 1980 their combined share of the total was 80 percent, in 1984 it dropped to 62 percent but rose again to 65 percent in 1988. Part of the decline was a reflection of absolute reduction in Soviet and American arms shipments, but more of it was attributable to the increase in ability of other nations to manufacture weapons beyond their own needs. France ranks third among the world's arms exporters and Britain fourth, and the 1980s saw steep increases in the arms trade of both West Germany and China. Furthermore, Third World nations, particularly China, Israel, Egypt, and North Korea, now account for 8 percent of the world's total arms exports, having between 1984 and 1988 exported almost $3 billion in arms, all of it to other Third World countries.[1]

The impact is felt, of course, at the importers' end. As Table 9–2 indicates, from 1984 to 1988, the largest purchasers of Soviet arms were not the Warsaw Pact nations, but Iraq, India, and Syria; and except for Czechoslovakia and Poland, Angola and Libya also ranked ahead of the Warsaw Pact members. In fact, in that period both India and Iraq bought more Soviet arms than all the

---

[1]*SIPRI Yearbook, 1989,* chap. 6, "Trade in Major Conventional Weapons," especially pp. 195–199.

Warsaw Pact nations combined. And on the American side, Japan is the only industrialized nation among the top six for the same time period with Saudi Arabia, Egypt, Pakistan, Israel, and South Korea purchasing the most American arms. Japan ranks second among the six. In the Soviet case, 90 percent of arms exports in this period went to eight buyers, and only 25 percent of the Soviet total export of $63.8 billion went to the Warsaw Pact. In the American case, eight recipients accounted for 81 percent of all arms exports, valued at $50.3 billion, in this five-year period, with but two NATO members accounting for just 13 percent of the total American arms shipments.

Much of recent international history has been dominated by these regional tensions and military balances, and detailed examination of the many regional cases is an essential part of the study of international relations. It is not possible to consider all the tension areas here, but it may be worthwhile to review briefly three cases of particular contemporary importance: the European military balance, the Arab-Israeli case, and the conflict between the two Koreas. Although every region has its own "personality," these three cases may exemplify some of the major trends that are seen also in other areas, and they are of course worthy of study in themselves.

The European Military Balance

As these pages are written in 1990, the European military balance was undergoing its first substantial de-escalation in 45 years. In the summer and autumn of 1989, Mikhail Gorbachev's domestic reforms, centered about *glasnost* and *perestroika,* spread rapidly and dramatically to Eastern Europe. The "Iron Curtain that [had] descended across the continent" (in Winston Churchill's famous phrase from 1946) was virtually gone. Governments fell in Poland, Czechoslovakia, East Germany, Romania, Hungary, and Bulgaria; some Eastern European communist parties were disbanded; the Berlin Wall was partially dismantled and the Brandenburg Gate between East and West Berlin was opened; border crossing points were disarmed; formal negotiations completed the reunification of the two Germanys; and the Kremlin and Pentagon agreed to reduce their respective ground armies in Central Europe to 195,000. Europeans and Americans of all political varieties declared the Cold War to be over. Claimants on the US federal budget began arguing for shares of the "peace dividend"; Mikhail Gorbachev spoke frequently of "a single European home," adding that as a product of European civilization, the United States should be included in the concept; and George Bush countered with a campaign of "one Europe whole and free." Free, multiparty elections were held in several Eastern European countries.

The pace of these events was breathtaking, so great a departure were they from the established premise of the European military balance that 45 years after the Second World War, and after many failed efforts to reduce tensions and arms in the area, large NATO and Warsaw Pact armies, at relatively high stages of readiness, were the focal point of an uneasy European peace. Despite both Soviet and American weariness over the cost of Europe's defense, and despite growing feeling in Western Europe that the perpetuation of the Cold War addressed less European security than the global Soviet-American confrontation, the NATO–Warsaw Pact standoff was, prior to 1990, the central issue of East-West diplomacy.

What, then, is the balance of forces in Europe? Before exploring the facts, some background information is necessary. First, a study of the European military balance is not merely a comparison of Soviet and American strengths in the region, but of the combined strength of the Soviet Union and its Warsaw Pact allies, on the one hand, and the United States and its NATO allies, on the other. Second, although most statistical information about American and Western European military efforts is public, similar information for the Soviet Union and its allies is not. Hence, the best information available of Warsaw Pact military strength is a product of American (or other Western) intelligence. Third, when estimating military capability for the purpose of planning national or regional defense, analysts tend to underestimate their own strength and overestimate those of the potential adversary. Consequently, intelligence estimates are rarely accurate and equally unreliable for scholarly purposes. And finally, it is useful to divide the study of military comparison in Europe into (1) strategic (nuclear) capabilities, (2) conventional (nonnuclear) strengths, and (3) the small but critically important component of a regional arsenal known as tactical nuclear strength, a body of weapons that fire nuclear-tipped devices either from small, mobile vehicles such as jeeps or small trucks or from shoulder-mounted launchers.

The Strategic Balance

In Chapter 10, ''The Balance of Terror,'' we will discuss the capabilities of the United States and the Soviet Union to wage intercontinental nuclear warfare with the use of ICBMs. Our concern here, though, is slightly different: It is not with the vehicle capable of delivering weapons of huge megatonnage over distances of several thousand miles but with that capable of delivering moderate yields over the dimensions of the European theater only. This class of vehicle is technically referred to as the Long-Range Intermediate-Range Nuclear Force, meaning that it is on the long end of the intermediate-range class. For purposes of simplicity, it is usually referred to as the Intermediate-Range Nuclear Force, or INF.

Since 1979, most of the controversy over the defense of Western Europe has centered on the INF component of the arsenal. This debate resulted in part from a large and rapid increase in Soviet INF weapons from 1979 forward and in part from the 1979 NATO decision to deploy two new INF weapons (the ground-launched Cruise missile and the Pershing II) beginning in late 1983. Among other consequences, the arrival of the first new missiles touched off huge antinuclear popular sentiment, forced a reconsideration of policy in the West German government, drove Soviet diplomats from all arms negotiations then in progress, and prompted Moscow to increase its own INF deployment along the European dividing line.

Prior to the beginning deployment of the Pershing II and Cruise missiles in the European theater in 1983, the Soviet Union had, for five years, been deploying three classes of INF missiles. In early 1983 these consisted of 248 older SS-4 and SS-5 missiles, each with a single warhead, and 330 of the new SS-20 rockets, each capable of mounting three independently targeted re-entry vehicles. American intelligence estimates the range of the SS-4 to be 2000 miles, that of the SS-5 to be 4100 miles, and that of the SS-20 to be 5000 miles. With the deployment of the SS-20, many of the older weapons were being dismantled or moved to Asia; so even though the actual number of rockets declined in 1982 and 1983, the total nuclear striking capability of the Warsaw Pact forces increased considerably. In addition, the accuracy of the SS-20 is far superior to that of its predecessors, thus raising the threat of successful strike.[2]

During this period, the United States had no INF weapons in Western Europe. When the NATO decision was made in 1979 to install 542 of the new weapons beginning 1983, the Soviet Union responded by agreeing not to deploy the SS-20 in replacement of older missiles if the United States would cancel the decision to deploy Pershing IIs and Cruise missiles. The Soviet Union claimed that it was the 1979 NATO decision and the subsequent determination to execute the decision that led to rapid installation of SS-20s. The Reagan administration, which had come to power partly on its repudiation of the SALT II draft treaty, withdrew the SALT II draft from the Senate, terminated all negotiations relating to it, and called for the beginning of Soviet-American talks (the START negotiations) to reduce rather than simply to limit nuclear weapons. But when the controversy over theater nuclear weapons threatened the START conversations, President Reagan elected to separate theater from global negotiations, and the Soviet Union agreed to conduct START negotiations on worldwide strategic issues and INF talks on theater issues simultaneously.[3]

The controversy surrounding the INF competition went far beyond a mere counting of missiles or warheads. The main problems were the speed of delivery (about six minutes in either direction, thus considerably increasing the threat of unnecessary war from a decision to strike on warning of incoming missiles) and accuracy. The new generation of missiles on each side was capable of reducing to within 200 yards the probability of a direct hit on target by 50 percent of missiles fired. To both sides, this raised the threat of instantaneous destruction of command, control, and communications (C^3) systems, thus rendering defenses useless. That all these new missile systems were mobile (truck launched) resulted in increased intelligence problems. Despite these considerations, the Soviet Union continued to add about 50 additional

---

[2]Force estimates are taken from US Department of Defense, *Soviet Military Power, 1983*, pp. 34–35. *SIPRI Yearbook, 1983*, p. 6, reports the ranges of SS-4 and SS-5 as 1800 and 3500 miles, respectively.

[3]For a brief but excellent review of the diplomatic and strategic considerations behind START, see David Holloway, *The Soviet Union and the Arms Race* (New Haven, Conn.: Yale University Press, 1983), particularly chap. 4.

per year to its 330 SS-20s, as the United States began in late 1983 the plan to deploy 108 Pershing II (range: 1800 miles) and 464 Cruise missiles (range: 2500 miles). More striking than the numbers was the fact that these missiles were said to have controllable accuracy to within 40 and 50 meters of target, respectively.

Negotiations over this competition were complicated by differing perceptions of actual strengths. The Soviet Union, for instance, insisted that all NATO weapons be included in negotiations and in strength counts, whereas the United States, which has no direct control over French and British arms policies, argued that only American weapons should be included. Furthermore, the Kremlin was interested in discussing only missiles that were then deployed in Eastern Europe, but the United States, fearful of the degree to which the balance can be disrupted by new mobile missiles, wanted to consider all new generations of Soviet missiles east of the Urals. Moreover, the sides could not agree on a means of considering theater nuclear forces deliverable from aircraft or from submarines. The United States was particularly concerned about the capabilities of the new Soviet *Backfire* bomber. (The Pentagon had not deployed either its B-1 or its *Stealth* bomber.) Not surprisingly, with all these threshold issues at dispute, the two parties had very different assessment of their relative strengths.

Despite the rapid modernization of weapons in Europe from 1983 to 1986, a major thaw in Soviet-American relations in 1987 and 1988 presented important new possibilities. In 1988, the Intermediate-Range Nuclear Forces Treaty was ratified, and Soviet and American military observers began witnessing the removal and dismantling of one another's intermediate-range missiles in Europe. By the end of 1988, approximately 20 percent of the total previously deployed had been removed, with the remainder scheduled to be removed by 1992.

In the American arsenal, the principal INF weapons are the Pershing II and the Ground-Launched Cruise Missiles (GLCM), both deployed in 1983 and after, and the older Pershing I-A. The American side of the balance is shown in Table 9–3, using 1989 deployment figures that reflect the first phase of INF removal. For the Soviet side, 1988 saw the destruction of 525 missiles as required by the INF Treaty, approximately 28 percent of the total target, with the remainder to be removed by 1992. Those destroyed thus far are from among the SS-4, SS-12, and SS-20 classes. Table 9–4 demonstrates the Soviet side of the European balance for 1989, using only those weapons designed for land-based targets. (Antisubmarine, antiship and ship-to-air missiles are excluded, as they are for the United States in Table 9–3.) To complete the picture, see Tables 9–5 and 9–6 for the British and French contributions to the European balance, respectively.

The Conventional Balance

Not surprisingly, the NATO and Warsaw Pact nations together, including the United States and the Soviet Union, account for approximately 77 percent of the entire world's military expenditure. To be sure, the Soviet Union and United States have global military commitments, so not all of this expenditure

Table 9–3 US theater nuclear forces, 1989.

Type	Weapons Systems		Warheads	
	Number Deployed	Miles Range	Number Carried	Number Available
Land-based				
Aircraft	2250	1060–2400	1–3	1800
Missiles				
Pershing II	111	1790	1	125
GLCM	250	2500	1	325
Pershing I-A	72	740	1	100
Lance	100	125	1	1282
Nike Hercules	27	160	1	75
Artillery	3850	30	1	1540
Naval				
Carrier aircraft	1100	550–1800	1–2	1450
Land-attack missiles	200	2500	1	200

Source: Adapted from *SIPRI Yearbook, 1989,* table 1–2, p. 13. Adaptation includes only those weapons designed for use against land-based targets.

Table 9–4 Soviet theater nuclear weapons, 1989.

Type	Weapons Systems		Warheads	
	Number Deployed	Miles Range	Number Carried	Number Available
Land-based				
Aircraft	4600	700–4000	1–3	3960
Missiles				
SS-20	405	5000	3	1215
SS-4	65	2000	1	65
SS-12	135	900	1	405
SS-23	239	500	1	90
Other	1220	120–500	1	2770
Artillery	6760	10–30	1	2000
Naval				
Land-attack missiles	40	1400–3000	1	52
Carrier aircraft	340	3100–6500	1–3	480

Source: Adapted from *SIPRI Yearbook, 1989,* table 1–5, p. 16. Includes only weapons systems with land-based targets.

is directed at Europe. Moreover, much of the expense is for nuclear defenses, so not all of it pertains to the conventional balance in Europe or elsewhere. It is true, nonetheless, that up until 1990 there were more armed forces facing one another across the East-West border of Europe than across any other

Table 9–5 British nuclear forces, 1989.

Type	Weapons Systems		Warheads	
	Number Deployed	Miles Range	Number Carried	Number Available
Land-based				
Aircraft	245	1300–1700	1–2	175
Naval				
Carrier aircraft	42	450	1	?
Submarine missiles	64	4700	2	128

Source: Adapted from *SIPRI Yearbook, 1989*, table 1–6, p. 18.

Table 9–6 French nuclear forces, 1989.

Type	Weapons System		Warheads	
	Number Deployed	Miles Range	Number Carried	Number Available
Land-based				
Aircraft	113	600–1570	1	120
Missiles	62	120–3500	1	88
Naval				
Carrier aircraft	36	650	1	40
Submarine missiles	96	3000–6000	1–6	256

Source: Adapted from *SIPRI Yearbook, 1989*, table 1–7, p. 19.

border in the world, with the exception of that between the Soviet Union and China in Asia.

Throughout the Cold War, Western Europeans were concerned that American strategy within NATO tended to concentrate on nuclear deterence whereas the Warsaw Pact amassed a substantial conventional advantage. This led to fears that (1) the only effective response to a Soviet ground war against Western Europe would be nuclear and (2) the United States might be willing to sacrifice its European allies to a nuclear response rather than undertake the cost of an effective conventional deterrent. Americans, on the other hand, grew increasingly impatient with the unwillingness of the Western European governments to shoulder an appropriate share of defense costs.

Despite the huge commitment of both the Soviet Union and the United States to military expansion in the early 1980s, the conventional balance in Europe changed little. Although the balance of theater nuclear forces rocked back and forth with deployment of INF weapons, and the Kremlin undertook a massive conventional buildup of air and naval forces in the northern Pacific, the air, sea, and land balance of Europe was essentially stable. The INF Treaty and the subsequent dismantling of intermediate-range nuclear forces installed from 1979 to 1987 not only maintained stability, but did so at a lower level of ten-

The destruction of Pershing missiles, the backbone of the American intermediate-range nuclear force in Europe, after the US-Soviet agreement to eliminate the weapons.
Source: AP/Wide World

sion. New technologies replaced old, and the United States improved its ability to airlift troops and weapons to Europe in the event of armed hostilities.

On balance, by the end of the 1980s, the Warsaw Pact had achieved and maintained an edge of about two to one in conventional forces. Its greatest advantages were in the categories of troops (4.0 million as against 2.6 million for NATO) and divisions (173 as compared with 84). It maintained a three-to-one advantage in most categories of land warfare, including tanks, antitank launchers, artillery, and mortars, and a two-to-one advantage in transport vehicles and attack helicopters. The only ground combat category in which NATO held a discernible edge was transport and support helicopters.

With respect to air combat and support, the two parties are about equal in deployable fighter-bombers, but the Warsaw Pact has an advantage of nearly six to one in interceptor forces, and a two-to-one advantage in reconnaissance aircraft. And although the United States made a major investment in many categories of naval combat and support, it maintains a lead only in attack carriers, destroyers, and frigates; ocean-going amphibious ships; coastal non-ballistic missile submarines; sea-based aircraft; and antisubmarine aircraft. The Warsaw Pact continues to hold the lead in such categories as heavy cruisers, patrol boats, mine warfare ships, ballistic missiles, and long-range attack submarines.

NATO, in the past, has attempted to offset the Soviet advantage in quantity through Western advantages in quality, but these efforts, never fully satisfactory in the past, became more difficult over time. The Soviet Union outspends the West in military research and development by a considerable margin. There are inefficiencies in Soviet science and engineering and in the management of the Soviet military production effort; excessive bureaucratization seems particularly to plague the pace of development. But these are offset—at least partly—by Western inefficiencies, such as the frequent cancellation of programs after expenditure of large sums of research and development money. In addition, the continuity of Soviet leadership has an advantage in military development that the United States does not have. During the Carter administration, for example, it was decided to cancel a new bomber program even while the Soviets proceeded with theirs. After this long delay in modernizing the air force, the Reagan administration gave high priority to a new bomber. Despite the continuing debate about strategic air power, however, it is probable that the accuracy of surface-to-surface missiles for attack purposes and of surface-to-air missiles for defensive purposes makes obsolete the concept of nuclear bombing in a war between NATO and the Warsaw Pact.

Western observers are especially concerned that the Soviets are compounding their advantage in quantity of arms by reducing the quality gap. In some areas, such as surface-to-air missiles and armored personnel carriers, the Kremlin is achieving qualitative superiority on some performance criteria. Furthermore, there are signs of accelerated independent development in modern electronics, computer science, and computer applications for, among other purposes, military development. Until recently it was believed that Soviet computer science was five to ten years behind that of the United States, but Soviet-designed materials now at the disposal of Western scientists testify that the gap is more like three years.

By and large, then, until 1989, the Soviet advantages seemed to be expanding. In most scenarios, the Soviet bloc would enjoy the advantages of first strike, possibly including large elements of strategic and tactical surprise. Soviet divisions in the central theater are organized well for an offensive against weakly held positions of the NATO defense structure and are trained and configured for a rapid blitzkrieg offensive. Critical elements of the NATO defense plan depend on adequate warning to permit time for mobilization, whereas a considerable portion of the pact's armies are ready to fight from a standing start. NATO also depends on forward operating airbases, which could be vulnerable to a well-planned attack by new Soviet systems. Pact forces also use standardized Soviet equipment; NATO armies employ a wide variety of systems from different countries. This advantage in standardization and interoperability greatly simplifies problems of deployment, command and control, and logistics and is part of the greater technical integration enjoyed by the pact forces.

NATO did, however, enjoy significant advantages of its own. Foremost among these was that to penetrate fortified and prepared defenses, the attacker, presumed to be the Warsaw Pact, must have had a considerable numerical advantage, believed by many observers to be at least three to one. The

Soviet-bloc numerical advantage, although substantial, fell short of this criterion theaterwide. Wider margins of advantage might have been achieved in local sectors of the front, but it would have been difficult for a pact commander to initiate an attack with a high degree of confidence.

Moreover, aggression in Europe, although undertaken by conventional means, would, in the opinion of most observers, have led inexorably to nuclear escalation. The Soviet bloc was numerically superior at the nuclear level as well, but the devastating costs of an atomic war, even for the "winner," would have dissuaded adventurism at the subnuclear level in Europe. It should be noted, however, that not all specialists are convinced that nuclear deterrence would succeed if a conventional war-fighting capability is lacking. Some argue that if the Soviets were superior at all levels, they may have believed themselves capable of initiating a conventional attack without risking a NATO nuclear response or may even, through a devastating nuclear first-strike, so reduce NATO's retaliatory capability as to reduce the costs of a nuclear exchange to a level that they might find tolerable. The majority of analysts did not share these views, there was general agreement that conventional defense in Europe must be adequate in itself and not necessarily depend on a link to the nuclear deterrent.

This assessment led to a search for technological and organizational solutions that would cancel the Soviet numerical advantages and secure the Western defense without a massive increase in expenditures and forces. Foremost among these technical fixes was the search for antitank weapons that exploit precision-guidance technologies, such as smart missiles, bombs, and shells, to knock out expensive Soviet tanks with cheap Western countersystems. If, ideally, the West had a $10,000 missile that could reliably destroy a $500,000 Soviet tank on a one-shot/one-kill basis, for example, it could, at a given expenditure on both sides, deploy many more of these defensive systems than there are tanks and thereby cancel the value of the massive Soviet investment in armor. In actuality, the countersystems are sometimes as expensive as the tanks themselves; their reliability is not nearly one to one; and a wide variety of countermeasures can be employed to foil them and restore the offensive capability of the tank. Still, the current state of the art in military technology gives certain advantages to the defense, and the communist commanders would have to consider this as well as the compounded uncertainties of initiating an offensive engaging opposed systems whose battlefield capabilities in the European environment cannot be known in advance. Some believe that this uncertainty factor is the greatest deterrent of all, because communist planning is based on the scientific approach and not on the roll of the dice.

A final NATO advantage was the political weakness of the Warsaw Pact, and especially what must have been doubts in the minds of Soviet leaders as to the reliability of Polish, Czech, and other East European divisions assigned to the pact. Would these armies fight alongside the Russians, or would they seize the occasion to break the Soviet hold on their countries? In a real crisis, the Soviet Union might have been compelled to divert significant portions of its own forces to secure the rear of the empire. Even in a well-run colonial system, there must come a point when overexpansion stretches the resources of the imperial center so thin that control over the entire system is lost, and a robust offensive in Western Europe would under the best of circumstances demand a great deal.

Mutual (and Balanced) Force Reductions in Europe

Since 1973, the Warsaw Treaty Organization (WTO) and NATO have been discussing principles for troop reductions in Europe. From the name of the discussion on, progress has been painstakingly slow. From the American perspective, the goal has been to achieve mutual and balanced troop reductions, calling on the Soviets to reduce their troop commitment disproportionally so that the result will be balanced forces. The Soviets, on the other hand, have until recently rejected any proposal that went beyond mutual reductions, accepting the goal of bilateral reductions without agreeing to reduce in greater numbers in the West in order to achieve balance. The Kremlin regarded the existing balance as at least effective in maintaining peace, and thought that mutual reductions resulting in the same imbalance would both reduce tensions and maintain peace. The debate thus revolved around the conflicting concepts of percentage reductions, on the one hand, and common ceilings, on the other.

Modest progress was achieved in 1982, when both WTO and NATO presented draft treaties. Although far from achieving a settlement, these two attempts did establish some common ground, including the eventual total number of troops on each side (900,000), autonomous authority to determine the national proportions within the total number, establishment of verification stations on each side, and agreement on noninterference in satellite verification measures. Prospects for further progress were dimmed by an exchange of charges between Moscow and Washington regarding each other's propaganda objectives as the United States attempted to solidify Western European public opinion in preparation for the deployment of new theater weapons. By the end of 1983, as that deployment began, the Soviet Union reacted to the insincerity of American arms negotiations by postponing further MBFR talks. Although they resumed on an irregular schedule the following year, the prestigious Stockholm International Peace Research Institute concluded in 1985 that "it is becoming increasingly difficult to take these negotiations seriously."[4]

All this changed after 1988. Both the United States and the Soviet Union were overextended militarily. Gorbachev, committed to *glasnost* and *perestroika*, could not afford the costs of the Warsaw Pact indefinitely; and the budgetary and trade deficits of the United States called for a slow-down in military spending. Eastern Europeans, infected with the desire for Soviet liberalization to reach them, found little comfort in a rich military establishment when consumer goods were unavailable and food supplies were dwindling. And Western Europeans, sufficiently persuaded that the importance of NATO had waned, were more deeply committed to completion of their economic union than to perpetuation of the Cold War.

---

[4]*SIPRI Yearbook, 1985,* p. 21.

"You've got to admire the way George Bush congratulated Kohl and Gorbachev for working things out."

Source: Drawing by Lorenz; © 1990 The New Yorker Magazine, Inc.

In this new context, Mikhail Gorbachev gave two ground-breaking speeches in late 1988 and early 1989. In them he announced that the Kremlin would unilaterally reduce troops by 500,000, and would eliminate the conventional equipment that supported them. Of these, 50,000 troops would be recalled from Warsaw Pact territories, along with 10,000 tanks. He called for a 14 percent reduction in the Soviet military budget and nearly a 20 percent cut in arms production and procurement alone.[5] Together with INF reductions under the Soviet-American treaty, these announcements signaled Gorbachev's bid for an end to the Cold War.

The full rush of events followed almost immediately: the fall of communist governments virtually throughout the Warsaw Pact; the ethnic uprisings in the Soviet Union itself and the demand of some of the constituent republics for sovereign independence; Gorbachev's renunciation of the Brezhnev Doctrine,

---

[5]For a summary of these proposals, see *SIPRI Yearbook, 1989*, pp. 150–155.

thus offering self-determination to the nations of Eastern Europe; the flight of East Germans to the West and the fall of the Berlin Wall; the discussion of German reunification with no remnant of German membership in the Warsaw Pact; and the Soviet-American agreement to reduce to 195,000 their respective troop levels in Central Europe. By early 1990, Soviet troops and tanks were being removed from Czechoslovakia at the request of the Czech government. A scant two months later, the USSR and Hungary signed an agreement under which the Soviets began immediately to remove all troops and supporting equipment from Hungary, with the final phase to take place by the end of 1991. Together with Gorbachev's repudiation of the Brezhnev Doctrine, these two agreements essentially symbolized the changing geopolitics of the Warsaw Pact and perhaps, if not its actual demise, a fundamental reduction of the capacity of the East to threaten the West. The old debate over European security now shifted to a new agenda: the role of NATO after the Cold War; the future of NATO and the Warsaw Pact as political alliances with little military capacity and no role in intervening in the internal affairs of the member states; arms control and disarmament in Europe after the INF Treaty and the Cold War.

The Korean Military Balance

The Korean conflict is essentially a struggle between the two halves of a divided nation, one of which came under communist rule in the aftermath of the Second World War, while the other has been influenced by the West. As is often the case when people have been separated into two states pursuing different courses in their domestic and foreign policies (other examples include the two Germanys, China and Taiwan, North and South Yemen, and the former two Vietnams), reintegration of the nation is impeded by deep and often bitter differences between the rival regimes and social systems, yet each side is greatly affected by actions taken by the other. This combination makes conflicts of divided nations particularly bitter and difficult to resolve.

The Korean problem is a matter of global interest because of the strategic location of the divided nation: The Korean peninsula is a kind of bridge or strategic corridor between the Chinese mainland and Japan and is adjacent to the critical industrial region of Manchuria (now part of China), which has long been a theater of strategic competition among China, Japan, and Russia. At least three times during modern history (in 1592, 1894, and 1931), Japanese forces have used Korea as the principal corridor and axis to provide lines of communication for influence in China and Manchuria.

Indeed, the modern period of conflict over Korea began not after the Second World War but in 1895, when the forces of newly resurgent Japan defeated Chinese armies to gain control of Korea. Subsequently, and for the next seven years, Japan was opposed in Korea by Russia as Tokyo struggled to consolidate its hold over the peninsula. In 1905, in one of the climactic events of the Russo-Japanese war that figured importantly in modern Russian history, Japan defeated the tsarist forces and subsequently annexed Korea in August 1910.

Japanese influence in Korea continued until the end of the Second World War in 1945; indeed, the progressive waves of Japanese invasions of Manchuria and China from 1931 to 1945 moved primarily through Korea, enhancing the peninsula's importance. Japan's collapse in August 1945 brought an end to its control of Korea. When the Soviet Union joined in the fighting in Asia in the final days of the Second World War, its troops swept down into the northern portion of the Korean peninsula; and in the crucial General Order Number One setting the initial conditions of peace, President Truman established a demarcation line at 38 degrees of latitude as the line above which the Soviet Union would be responsible for the Japanese surrender and below which the United States would be responsible. As in Europe, the establishment of a line of liberation and occupation was to prove portentous.

Washington and the Kremlin had declared the independence and freedom of Korea to be an objective in their struggle against the Axis powers, but after the victory they were unable to agree on political measures to bring this about. Instead, postwar political developments were guided differently by the superpowers in their respective occupation zones. Soviet forces constructed a communist regime in the North, whereas the Americans attempted to organize a constitutional political order for the South. While these separate movements proceeded, the two sides engaged in rancorous negotiations, both in Korea itself and at the United Nations. Finally, when the Soviet Union announced its intention of preventing UN officials from entering the North to supervise elections designed to reunite the two halves of the country under a single constitutional rule, the United States encouraged the United Nations to proceed with elections in the South. Some looked upon the event as the first step toward reunification; others saw it as the final step of separation. In 1949, having established the independent and militarily secure state of South Korea, the United States withdrew its occupation forces. Meanwhile, the civil war in China was progressing toward a communist victory, and with the threat of war persisting in Europe, NATO was about to be established. In Japan, where the occupation had progressed toward its objectives with unanticipated speed, preparations for self-government were in motion, and the early removal of the American occupation forces was anticipated.

The withdrawal of American troops from South Korea seemed to signal, therefore, that this newly independent state would be outside the American strategic sphere. But within a year the pace of events quickened. Chinese communist forces had driven the Nationalist government from the mainland to the island of Taiwan and on June 25, 1950, North Korea mounted a massive invasion of the South by well-trained and experienced forces employing Soviet armor and artillery and supported by tactical aircraft. Overwhelmed by the vastly superior forces, the small and unprepared South Korean army was forced to retreat southward, surrendering the capital city of Seoul and facing the possibility of total collapse.

Within a day of the surprise attack the Security Council of the United Nations met in emergency session. In the absence of the Soviet Union, which had been boycotting the council over the refusal of the Western members to seat a Chinese communist delegation in place of the Nationalist, the council condemned North Korea for a breach of the peace and called for a cease-fire and withdrawal of North Korean troops to points above the thirty-eighth parallel. Two days later, in an effort to enforce their position, the Western powers were able to persuade the council to call upon member states to assist South Korea in repelling the aggressor. Under this act of legitimization, the United States transferred troop contingents from Japan, and these, together with troops and materials from some 40 countries, comprised the eventual United Nations Command. The communist victory in China had forced a revision of American policy in Asia. Now, contrary to its former policy, it intended to defend South Korea and, indeed, attempt to reunify the two Koreas by force. At the same time, it would now support the French in their struggle against communism in Southeast Asia (a decision that ultimately led to American involvement in Vietnam); and it would transform Japan not into the pastoral state envisioned by the occupation but into a powerful ally in the crusade against Asian communism. Other than the Berlin Blockade, then, the invasion of South Korea in 1950 was the most dramatic event in shaping America's Cold War strategy.

By October 1, the international force, composed largely of Americans but including major contingents from Australia, Great Britain and elsewhere, succeeded in reversing the tide, recapturing Seoul, and pressing the drive north to clear South Korea of communist forces. Under cover of an October 7 resolution of the General Assembly (the Soviet Union had returned to the Security Council, so this organ was no longer an effective instrument of Western policy with respect to Korea), the Western forces crossed the thirty-eighth parallel in an effort not only to repel, but also to defeat totally, the communist forces and to establish a single Korea. Within six weeks, the North Korean army faced extinction.

Now, however, as Western forces neared the Korean border of Manchuria and as the American Commander, General Douglas MacArthur, began to speak openly about attacking Chinese territory (even with atomic bombs), Chinese "volunteers" swept down out of Manchuria on behalf of the tiring North Koreans. Through the bitter cold of the winter of 1950–1951 there were small-scale territorial struggles, but the failure of either side to advance further led to the beginning of negotiations which were to last more than two years. The armistice of 1953, which has never been concluded in a formal peace agreement, preserved two Koreas along a border near, but no longer precisely at, the thirty-eighth parallel.

Because the armistice was a military rather than a political settlement, the military balance between the two Koreas is one of the world's most crucial, even four decades later. From 1953 to the present, each side has mounted a force-building campaign against the possibility of another round of fighting. Although there is neither peace nor war in Korea, there is a continuing arms race stabilized only by a precarious military balance. The balance has proved reliable to date, despite the occasional uncertainty of the US commitment to the South. The Nixon Doctrine, which declared America's intention of helping allies in Asia forestall communist aggression without direct intervention, shook the confidence of the Seoul government, and the general American distaste for intervention after the Vietnam War was another test of South Korea's resolve. The massive military buildup undertaken by the Reagan administration, and the firmly anticommunist stance accompanying it, resulted in closer ties between the two allies, in a presidential visit to Korea, and in Operation Team Spirit 84, joint Korean-American naval and military maneuvers held in 1984. (During those exercises, an American carrier was struck from below by a Soviet submarine, with no severe damage to either and without nuclear spill.) In any event, the absence of political peace and of steady economic relations between the two Koreas suggests that the military balance will continue to be the principal, if not the only, foundation of stability between these two bitter adversaries. Despite occasional reunification talks, enmity prevails; in 1983, when a terrorist attack on South Korean officials visiting Burma resulted in nearly a dozen deaths, including those of four cabinet members, the government of South Korea condemned the government of North Korea for the assassinations. Amid these events, however, the military balance promoted stability, as the South Korean government refrained from aggressive response.

What, then, is the status of the military balance in Korea? SIPRI reports that North Korea dedicates between 10 and 20 percent of its gross domestic product to military expenditures with the figure rising and that South Korea commits about 5 percent.[6] Although under a burden-sharing plan with the United States the actual cost of the South's commitment to defense is rising, the gross domestic product has risen so rapidly—more rapidly than any other country's throughout the 1980s—that defense as a fraction of gross domestic production is actually declining.

Because of the geographic location of Korea (see Figure 9–1), force comparisons are difficult to make. The US government maintains such figures, but they do not include men and matériel available in the heavily armed Northern Pacific, although not specifically assigned to Korea. Thus, the figures do not include naval and air forces available for easy deployment from Japan or elsewhere in the region. Recall that the first American troops deployed to South Korea in 1950 were transported from Japan in only a couple of days, and air cover was supplied within a few hours of a decision in Washington.

With these cautions, Table 9–7 outlines the current force comparisons between North Korea and South Korea, including American forces in the South. Note that nuclear forces in the Pacific are available on short notice in Korea. In addition, there may be as many as 1000 tactical nuclear warheads stationed permanently in South Korea.

Table 9–7 Force comparisons in Korea, 1987.

	So. Korea	*US*	*US/So. Korea*	*No. Korea*
Ground personnel	542,000	29,100	571,100	750,000
Air personnel	33,000	12,000	45,000	53,000
Naval personnel	23,000	400	23,400	35,000
	598,000	41,500	639,500	838,000

Source: United States Government, as reported in David E. Pitt, "Seoul, U.S. Forces and the North: The Balance Is as Delicate as Ever," *The New York Times,* April 8, 1987, pp. 1, 10.

[6]*SIPRI Yearbook, 1989,* pp. 164 and 190.

Figure 9–1 Geographic location of Korea.

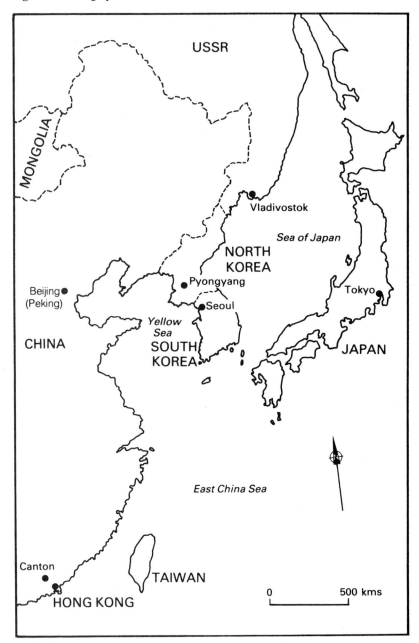

Source: Reprinted with permission of The Free Press, A Division of Macmillan, Inc., from *Korea: The War Before Vietnam* by Callum A. MacDonald. Copyright © 1986 by Callum A. MacDonald.

But personnel counts convey only part of the story. In equipment, including tanks and jet-fighter aircraft (excluding those of the United States that are deployable to South Korea on short notice), the North enjoys an advantage of nearly two to one. Only in armored personnel carriers does the combined strength of the South and the United States exceed that of the North. In many instances, however, South Korea has qualitative superiority, particularly in aircraft. Until 1984, North Korea operated with between 25 and 50 F-7 fighter-aircraft, old Chinese copies of the Soviet MIG-21. In 1984, it ordered 20 new MIG-23 fighters directly from the Soviet Union. And in 1988 alone, the Soviets supplied the North Koreans with 30 MIG-29 fighters, 18 Su-25 ground-attack fighters, 24 mobile surface-to-air missile systems, and more than a thousand air-to-air missiles, to cite only part of the list. At the same time, South Korea received arms from the United States, Britain, France, and West Germany, consisting of fighter craft, ground-attack planes, air-to-air missiles, ship-to-ship missiles, helicopters, transport vehicles, and a submarine.[7] This continues the expansion of the South's submarine fleet, which added two in 1985.

Even though the Korean military balance is currently stable, a number of specific concerns bother the West. The greatest is that the fastest-growing aspect of North Korean forces is the coastal craft capable of delivering shipborne surface-to-surface missiles. Given the long, slender geography of Korea and the dependence of South Korea on its ports for military and other imports, this capability is a major threat. The second concern is that although much of the recent development in North Korean military equipment is designed as defensive, the vehicles that comprise the largest increase make it apparent that North Korea is equipping for rapid, mobile, attack capability. For this reason, South Korean forces are on constant alert for attack without warning.

Beyond the disparity of numbers, the communist forces enjoy another cardinal advantage: Seoul, the South Korean capital, which is also the hub of the South's communications, industry, and culture as well as the heartland of the nation, lies only 25 miles south of the northern border. The defense of Seoul is the *sine qua non* of the South's security, and its capture or destruction is presumed to be the principal advance. These deployment strategies were accentuated during 1986 and 1987. During that time, North Korea raised the percentage of its ground troops within easy distance of the demilitarized zone from 50 percent to 65 percent. The South responded by moving more of its troops to the regions north of Seoul and accelerating a major road-building campaign to raise the speed of counterattack.

American analysts disagree deeply as to the stability of the military balance and the viability of the South's defenses. The US Second Division is maintained in Korea at the request of the South, and the need for it to remain there has been a matter of controversy in the United States. Those who favor its removal argue that the South, outnumbered but favored by technological advantages, can defend itself without the US presence. Those who believe the Second Division to be essential to stability on the peninsula argue that the North's wide advantage in numbers might comprise a temptation to aggression without the US presence. Some believe that the North could win even with the

---

[7]*SIPRI Yearbook, 1989,* pp. 255–256.

President Reagan views the demilitarized zone between North Korea and South Korea two months after the Soviet downing of a civilian Korean airliner, 1983.
Source: AP/Wide World

US presence, if it could consolidate control of the peninsula before American reinforcements arrived.

As tensions around the world subside, the issue of Washington's commitment to the Korean balance arises from time to time. In the last decade, the South Korean economy has grown about four times as fast as that of North Korea, and the current South Korean government has announced its intention to stop isolating the North from regional and global trading organizations. In the view of some, the demand in the North to enjoy the economic advantages of the South may eventually drive the two together. Moreover, Americans have grown uneasy with anti-American sentiments in South Korea and have begun to wonder why the South, so very prosperous, should not assume the cost of its own defense. This view is heated by increasing awareness that South Korea is one of the major contributors to the chronic American balance-of-trade deficit. As these attitudes develop, the Pentagon has announced its intention of reducing the American troop commitment in South Korea by 5000. Should China's strained relations with North Korea induce closer relations with the South, a major reason for maintaining a high-level American presence would be eliminated. A brisk debate has thus begun between those who anticipate the removal of American troops from the Korean balance in the near term, and those who regard the commitment as an ''inescapable entanglement.''[8]

---

[8]Contrast Doug Bandow, ''Leaving Korea,'' *Foreign Policy,* Winter 1989–1990, pp. 77–93, with

"Your father's a baby-boom liberal, dear—he's never had a war he could support before!"
Source: By permission of Doug Mariette and Creators Syndicate.

The Middle Eastern Military Balance

The most complex, and quite probably the most unstable, of the world's critical regions is the Middle East. It is complex because (1) it contains a number of subordinate balances, (2) the relationships among the regional parties change over time, and (3) the roles of the major powers change with international conditions and domestic politics. It is unstable because (1) the historic roots of conflict are so invasive as to defy political resolution, (2) much of the potential international conflict results from the regionally destabilizing consequences of domestic violence, (3) the worldwide economic changes ushered in by OPEC's power led to uncontrolled arms sales to the area, and (4) the degree to which local governments serve as proxy forces of the major powers is substantial. Each of these characteristics of the regional balance merits a brief comment.

Although the Middle East military balance usually brings to mind the Arab-Israeli conflict, there are several other influential forces in the region. For most of the last decade, the most visible was the Iran-Iraq War, or Persian Gulf War, fought with modern weapons provided by virtually all the international arms suppliers, but with primitive tactics. Because of the complete rupture in Iranian-American relations after the rise to power of the Ayatollah

James Chace, "Inescapable Entanglements," *Foreign Affairs*, Winter 1988–1989, pp. 26–44.

Khomeini, marked most importantly by the taking and holding of American hostages for more than a year, Washington quietly urged an Iraqi victory; and the Soviet Union, determined to seal one of its flanks by controlling both Afghanistan and its southern borders, favored an Iraqi victory to prevent Iran from intruding on Afghanistan's seeking religious unification with a major faction. As early as 1984, on the other hand, China provided Iran with 100 Chinese-made copies of the Soviet MIG-21 aircraft, and in 1987 sold Iran surface-to-surface antiship missiles for installation at the vital Strait of Hormuz, through which most westbound Middle East oil leaves the Persian Gulf. In order to protect the delivery of Kuwaiti petroleum to the west, Washington agreed to rename and reflag a number of supertankers in order to place them under the protection of the US Navy. While carrying out this policy, one American vessel was badly damaged (and American lives lost) by hostile fire, and an American destroyer mistakenly downed a loaded Iranian civilian craft, setting off a round of terrorism that reached to the United States. The war came to a permanent cease-fire, without a peace treaty, in 1988.

The new balance struck by the end of the Persian Gulf War was upset entirely in mid-1990 when Iraq conquered Kuwait in a brief but bloody invasion and threatened an invasion of Saudi Arabia by amassing over 100,000 troops at its borders. Surprised by the speed of the world's military, economic, and diplomatic reactions (United Nations-sponsored trade and arms embargo, the assembling of the troops and air forces of several nations in Saudi Arabia, and a multinational naval blockade of the Persian Gulf and Red Sea), Iraq reversed itself completely. It suddenly released Iranian prisoners of war in exchange for Iraqis similarly held, and unilaterally abandoned 1000 square miles of territory seized from Iran two years earlier in order to redeploy troops to the Saudi Arabian front. Saddam Hussein called for a holy war against the rich Arabs isolated in their oil-rich nations from the poor masses of the Arab Nation, and against all Western intervening powers. He held nondiplomatic Western citizens as "guests" in a number of military and industrial centers as hostages against bombing or attack, and threatened to respond to armed aggression by the massive use of chemical weapons, which he was known to have used previously against dissidents within Iraq and Iranian forces. His opportunistic reconciliation with Iran shifted the balance sharply in his favor, leaving Egypt (and the multinational forces in Saudi Arabia and nearby waters) as the only counterbalance in the region. And his threat to invade Jordan in order to keep Iraqi commerce flowing through the port of Aqaba revealed his willingness to abandon his neighbor and close friend King Hussein (not directly related) in order to pursue his intentions.

Another subordinate balance within the region exists between Libya, on the one hand, and Egypt on behalf of the Sudan, on the other. In late 1983 and early 1984, threat of a Libyan invasion of the Sudan mounted, and Egypt announced its willingness to assist the Sudanese cause. The United States entered the picture by offering to assist Egypt with military equipment and made available an AWACS early-warning aircraft, a sophisticated communications craft previously provided only to Saudi Arabia in the region. Indeed, Saudi Arabia and Egypt are regarded by the United States as the Middle Eastern powers most moderate in both economic and military policy and most capable of providing stability to the region as a whole.

Changing relations among the regional parties is a second characteristic of the balance. After more than 30 years of alternating between declared and undeclared war, the most dramatic change was the Israeli-Egyptian peace treaty (1979), a peace that stabilized a major determinant of regional conditions and divorced Egypt from more radical Arab politics. Similarly, the fall of the Shah of Iran and the rise of the Ayatollah introduced a reactionary theocracy determined to change the entire basis of both regional relations and the region's interplay with the major military and industrial powers.

Volatile relations among the region's nations precipitated the third characteristic of the region's complexity: the changing roles of the major powers in the Middle East. In the years between the two world wars, British and French influences dominated the Middle East. Later, because of the decline of Anglo-French interests, American oil aspirations, and the American commitment to defend Israel as the long-sought (since 1917) Zionist homeland, America's presence rose to preeminence. Yet the role of the United States has been less than consistent. In 1956, for example, when Britain and France attempted to assist Israel in a war against Egypt, the United States condemned the intervention of two of its closest allies. The successive policies of the Nixon, Ford, Carter, Reagan, and Bush administrations have varied so much that the foundations of the Israeli-American partnership are generally considered an unpredictable element in the Middle Eastern military equation. The big issues that best characterize the shift of Washington away from unerring support of Israeli policy are the opening of direct talks with Palestine Liberation Organization (PLO) leader Yassir Arafat in 1989 with the strong support of the American public, public criticism of Israeli policies in the occupied territories, and open encouragement to include the PLO in multinational talks aimed at peace in the region.

All these complexities are accompanied by a number of factors that render the region persistently unstable. The most important among these is the depth of emotion, engendered by centuries of animosity, which is a constant strain on stability. Because the Middle East is the historic center for several of the world's principal religions, contemporary events are colored by the legacies of religious conflict dating back over more than 20 centuries. To these roots must be added the consequences of modern imperialistic events, which intertwined traditional loyalties with growing ties to the nineteenth century's competing empires in the region, principally the French and British.

In the last 15 years, it has been necessary to add the regional consequences of the maturation of OPEC with its political and economic implications of worldwide power. Some of the region's members, particularly those that export petroleum, have modernized more rapidly than others. Iran, ten years ago the richest and most powerful militarily as the region's major non-Israeli recipient of American arms, has set aside its economic revolution in favor of fulfilling ancient spiritual aspirations. So while some Middle Eastern nations are busily modernizing, others are more concerned with perpetuating historic enmities. As Egypt and Saudi Arabia forge ahead, Libya and Syria long to settle old scores. Meanwhile, Israel plans and fights for survival, sometimes by territorial activity regarded by its adversaries (as well as by neutral Egypt) as imperialistic and aggressive. And the Palestinians, still homeless, continue acts of terrorism and war.

Domestic violence is an additional threat to the region's stability. The most outstanding example of this occurs in Lebanon, a republic of fewer than 4000 square miles (twice the size of Delaware, smaller than Connecticut) with a population under 3 million, coastally located at the eastern-most edge of the Mediterranean Sea. Its civic life is torn by hostility among Christians and Shi-ite and Sunni Moslem factions. Its strategic location in the unresolved conflict between Israel to its south and Syria to its east and north makes Lebanon's internal control of vital interest to both countries. Throughout 1983, to cite a year of particularly complex relations in Lebanon, all the following occurred: civil war among Christian and Moslem groups; civil war among factions of Palestinians; war between Syria and Israel, each with the assistance of one or more of the preceding factions; and Palestinian and Lebanese Moslem attacks on positions of American, French, and Italian "peacekeeping" forces. A full-scale American intervention was probably averted only by the fact that the Soviet role is limited to its support of Syria. Had similarly complex events occurred in another place, such as in Iran, Soviet and American interventions would have been a more serious threat, and the possibility of a major power war in the region greatly expanded.

All these complex factors notwithstanding, the most explosive aspect of the Middle East balance is the so-called Arab-Israeli balance. The Arab-Israeli conflict is, basically, a case of two national movements emerging from long years of suppression at the same time but making conflicting claims to the same piece of land. It is one of the perceptual analysts' favorite cases, because both sides have moving and persuasive stories, and the answer to the question "Who is right?" depends more on the particular question that the observer happens to ask than on any inherent superiority of the claims of one side or the other. No settlement could be devised that would fully satisfy the legitimate aspirations of both peoples at the same time, and although compromise solutions may someday be arranged, there is no way to slice the pie fairly for everyone.

The Arab-Israeli conflict is probably more familiar to many students than other regional tensions, yet it is worthwhile to review briefly the roots of the problem from the two perspectives. From the Arab point of view, the problem began when centuries of foreign rule—first by the Ottomans (Turks) and then by the European colonial powers—finally ended after World War II. Most of the Arab peoples gained independence and sovereignty, but in the case of the territory formerly known as Palestine, a new form of alien infringement on Arab sovereignty emerged—the creation of a Jewish state in the Arab heart-land by people whom the Arabs regard as European settlers. Israel is, in this perspective, a vestige of the colonial era—a colonial settler state, in a phrase borrowed from Marxist parlance—and its presence in the Middle East is a symbol of the indignities inflicted on the Arabs during their age of weakness. Now that the Arab nation is resurgent, the continued existence of this foreign body unnaturally grafted onto the Arabs' land is, at best, an insult to be tolerated. Moreover, the burden of the Israeli presence has fallen most heavily on the Arab people most directly affected—the Palestinians—and no solution will be possible without the agreement of the organization regarded as their spokesperson, the PLO.

The Israeli point of view begins with roots still further back in history—the expulsion of the Jews from their homes in the Holy Land by the Romans and other conquerors, and their forced migration to many distant lands where they lived at the mercy of often hostile peoples and suffered unspeakable degradations. Throughout this long history of *diaspora* (the Greek term meaning scattering or dispersion), the dream of returning to the homeland and gathering in the exiles was never forgotten.

The rebirth of Jewish nationalism in the modern period coincides with the Arab awakening, both stimulated by European nationalist thought in the late nineteenth and early twentieth centuries. But the main impetus to Zionism, the name of the national liberation movement of the Jewish people, came later when, in a genocidal campaign unprecedented in scope and scientific brutality, Adolf Hitler murdered 6 million Jews in ovens and gas chambers as part of the so-called final solution to the "Jewish question."

Germany had been considered by many before the war as the most civilized of nations and as the European state in which Jews had been permitted to live with the least harassment. The fact that evil on so massive and organized a scale could occur there convinced other Jews all over the world that the Jews who had escaped the slaughter, including the handful of shocked survivors of the European Holocaust, would never be safe and free without a Jewish state. In the many upheavals following the war, the plight of the Jewish survivors continued, as many other nations refused to take the desperate refugees.

At the same time, Britain was preparing to relinquish its control over Palestine but was willing, for the moment, to tolerate stepped-up Jewish immigration to Palestine. From the Arab point of view, this may have been a case of dumping Europe's unwanted people on the Middle East, but from the West's point of view it was the least that could be done for the pathetic survivors of this terrible experience.

Thus, the stage was set for the Arab-Israeli conflict: a vacuum of power created by the British withdrawal; the Arabs' expectation that now, at last, they would have independence and sovereignty in Palestine as throughout the Middle East; and a Jewish flight to safety led by men and women who, understandably, would fight to death for a haven.

Intercommunal fighting broke out between Arab and Jewish mobs and armies, and the surrounding Arab states sent expeditionary forces to support the Palestinians. In the war that ensued in 1948–1949, the Jews prevailed in the coastal areas, but the Arabs were able to retain the hills, including the Old City of Jerusalem. This was a bitter outcome for both sides. The Jews had a foothold, but not their goal of goals—Jerusalem—and the Arabs controlled commanding hills overlooking the Jewish flatlands below. The Arabs held major parts of the land, including Jerusalem, but had lost territory in which many of their brothers fell under Jewish rule. Also, several hundred thousand Palestinian Arabs felt compelled to flee the zones of Jewish control, creating a Palestinian refugee problem that has not been solved to this day. The outcome was satisfactory to neither side and was particularly unstable because of the lack of geographical separation and terrain obstacles between the two sides. The 1949 armistice line was easily penetrable by both conventional military forces and terrorist infiltrators and did not lend itself to a stable military balance.

A second round of fighting occurred in 1956, but this left the basic situation essentially unchanged. However, the third round, the 1967 Six-Day War, significantly altered the subsequent military and political terms of the conflict. It resulted in the Israeli capture of the Sinai desert on the Egyptian front, the commanding hills of the Golan Heights on the Syrian front and, most important, Jerusalem and the hills of the West Bank on the Jordanian front. This had several basic effects: (1) The borders were moved from some of the least defensible lines in the world (for Israel) to the strongest positions in the region. This would make future Israeli defense much easier. (2) Jerusalem, the holiest place of the Jews but also the third holiest of the Moslems, and Hebron, the second holiest place of the Jews but a city inhabited today almost entirely by Arabs, fell under Jewish control. (3) One million additional Palestinian Arabs fell under Israeli rule, creating a situation in which there are now half as many Arabs as Jews under the administration of the Jewish state. (4) Israel, which had previously been in an entirely defensive position, was now a military occupying power ruling over a large number of Arab civilians. Whereas the Jewish state had enjoyed considerable foreign sympathy before, this military occupation created a morally ambiguous situation for many in the West who sympathized with the Jewish state's right to exist and were alarmed by Arab efforts to destroy it but who could not condone Israel's extension of its authority over additional territory containing so many Palestinian Arabs.

The most important military result of the Six-Day War was the creation of more secure borders. The most important political result was the transformation of the conflict from one over the very existence of Israel to one over the future disposition of the territories captured in 1967. Although some of the Arabs continue to press for the final elimination of Israel, others are moving to the view that a compromise solution is possible: recognition and acceptance of Israel in exchange for the return of the 1967 territories.

However, turning this principle of "territory for peace" into a reality is impeded by several obstacles on both sides. On the Arab side, it is not clear whether all the parties in the coalition, particularly the so-called Steadfastness front and the more militant elements of the PLO, are prepared fully to recognize and accept the existence of Israel on a permanent basis. Some appear ready to accept back the territories, but only as a launching point for continued struggled against Israel.

On the Israeli side, there are several problems. First, Israel is being asked to retreat from lines that are relatively secure in a military sense, but unrecognized politically, to lines that might be recognized but will never be secure and defensible. This would make Israeli security dependent on the faithfulness of the Arabs to the agreement, and many Israelis are not willing to take this chance. Compromise regarding the Sinai was possible in order to achieve peace with Egypt, but the Sinai desert is different from the other fronts in that because of the wide separation it puts between the former adversaries, the element of risk was relatively small. By contrast, the West Bank hills and the Golan Heights are immediately adjacent to Israeli population centers, and the opposing parties are locked in a bear hug. The element of risk is inherently greater, and the adversaries on these fronts have so far been less compromising than the Egyptians. Indeed, Egypt's reward for peace, while other Arab states continue to call for a Holy War to eradicate Israel, has been diplomatic and partial economic isolation from the other Arab countries.

Second, the Sinai had no essential historic or religious importance to Israel. Jerusalem and the West Bank, which Israelis call by the biblical names Judea and Samaria, contain many places of great symbolic importance. The overwhelming majority of Israelis are opposed to returning the Old City to Arab rule, and many favor keeping the national capital there. An influential minority is opposed to the surrender of any other part of the historic lands of Judea and Samaria.

It appears that although solutions can be conceived abstractly and may, over an extended period of time, come to be accepted, the conflict will not be resolved soon. This means that a positive peace of political compromise and reconciliation is unlikely. However, it is conceivable that a "negative" peace can be achieved, in which there is no complete solution but there is a military balance to dissuade aggression and thereby prevent war. From the point of view of the United States, there are four possible conditions. In descending order of preference, they are (1) a comprehensive political settlement and an end to the state of tension, (2) no settlement but a stable military balance that prevents war, (3) a military balance that does not prevent war but does permit Israel to defend itself and bring about an acceptable military result in as short a round of fighting as possible, and (4) a military imbalance that leads to the destruction of Israel which presumably would not go down before taking very drastic actions against the Arab states as well.

All four, including the political solution, relate to the state of the military balance—the political solution because it is generally believed that the Arabs will settle with Israel only if they see that it is impossible to win completely on the battlefield. For this reason, in the Arab-Israeli conflict, as in Korea, the military balance has special importance for political and strategic stability.

If past wars are any guide, Arab coalition will greatly outnumber Israel in tanks, aircraft, artillery, and other categories of equipment as well as manpower. Moreover, the Arabs will be able to depend on a standing army ready to fight almost at once from their peacetime condition. By contrast, Israel will have to depend on the mobilization of civilian reserves—a process that takes 24 to 72 hours. This time gap will give the Arabs great advantages in the opening hours—particularly if they can successfully organize a surprise attack and catch Israel unprepared. The Arabs, who draw on a much larger population base, can also tolerate higher casualty rates.

It is difficult to quantify the Arab-Israeli balance because, over time, Israeli qualitative superiority has been more important than Arab quantitative superiority. This fact also makes it difficult to predict the future with certainty, because the balance will depend on the ability of the Arabs to close the gap in terms of quality of men and equipment.

In general, experts believe that the Israeli margin of superiority continues to be wide. According to some, it has a greater margin today than in the past. But Israelis believe that qualitative factors alone are not enough: a certain quantitative ratio must also be maintained, lest the Arab superiority in numbers grow to the point that it swamps the Israeli qualitative advantage. This creates a demanding and stressful situation for Israel, because it must compete with a coalition vastly larger and incomparably better financed.

Overall, Israel's strategy is progressively to convince its Arab adversaries, if necessary one at a time, that military action will not yield positive results and that the costs of resorting to force will greatly exceed the benefits. The most powerful member of the Arab coalition—Egypt—has already shifted from a military to a diplomatic strategy, resulting in the peace treaty between Israel and Egypt. The most significant remaining military challenge is Syria. Many Israelis are convinced that the Syrians have not given up the military option exactly because in past wars, they suffered less than Egypt did. This perception could lead Israel to adopt a punitive strategy in the event of another round of fighting, inflicting heavy damage on the Syrian armed forces to convince Damascus of the futility of continued confrontation. If Syria and Jordan gave up the military option, the war threat would, for practical purposes, be ended, because no combination of outer-ring regional states, however militant, could pose a credible threat without the front-line states adjacent to Israel. The purpose of a strong military balance, then, is both defensive and political—to create the preconditions for an eventual settlement that will require a greater spirit of willingness to compromise and make concessions than has been evident in the past.

Conclusion

This brief overview of three regional balances suggests several conclusions. (1) In high-tension areas, positive peace based on political solutions is difficult to obtain, and stability often depends on carefully calibrated military balances to prevent cold wars from becoming hot ones. (2) Allies of the Soviet bloc, such as the Warsaw Pact, North Korea, and many of the Arab confrontation states, tend to enjoy a numerical superiority deriving from the much higher levels of arms production sustained in the Soviet Union. Western and Western-associated states, such as South Korea and Israel, depend on qualitative advantages of technically superior equipment to offset their disadvantage in number. If, in fact, the current massive Soviet investment in military research and development closes the quality gap, the communist states may compound their advantage in quantity with equal or superior quality. This will upset the delicate regional balances. (3) Many of the regional balances are less stable, and more subject to decay, than is widely understood. Significant changes in both the relative number and the comparative quality of equipment held by rivals continually occur. And the management of regional tensions through military balances requires eternal vigilance.

CHAPTER 10

The Balance of Terror

Think, for a moment, about the unthinkable. Imagine a nuclear attack. Somehow, by accident or design, nuclear war has erupted. What would it be like?

The US Atomic Energy Commission's Nuclear Bomb Effects Computer gives us some horrifying estimates.[1] Let's say, first, that you are about 4 miles from the center of an important military installation, an industrial area, or a densely populated metropolis. Second, let's assume a nuclear surface blast, the bomb having detonated at ground level rather than in the atmosphere (an air blast). Third, to have a measure of the explosive potential of the weapon, we set the computer "yield" adjustment at one megaton, or the explosive equivalent of one million tons of TNT. That much TNT would comprise a stack reaching almost the height of the Empire State Building! One megaton is 50 times as great as the bombs used in 1945 at Hiroshima and Nagasaki (20 kilotons each, or 20,000 tons of TNT equivalent, each kiloton having the punch of 1000 tons of TNT).

---

[1]US Atomic Energy Commission, *The Effects of Nuclear Weapons* (Washington, D.C.: US Government Printing Office, 1962). For a more technical study, see Samuel Gladstone and Philip J. Dolan, eds., *The Effects of Nuclear Weapons*, 3rd ed. (Washington, D.C.: US Department of Defense and Department of Energy, 1977). *The Effects of Nuclear War* (US Congress Office of Technology Assessment, 1979) conducts several well-designed test simulations varying in assumptions and attempts to assess the physical, economic, and social consequences in each case. For more recent studies, see International Council of Scientific Unions, *Environmental Consequences of Nuclear War* (2 vols.) (New York: Wiley, 1985); and *The Effects on the Atmosphere of a Major Nuclear Exchange* (Washington, D.C.: National Academy Press, 1985). For a dissenting view, see Stanley L. Thompson and Stephen H. Schneider, "Nuclear Winter Reappraised," *Foreign Affairs*, Summer 1986, pp. 981–1005.

The effects of such an attack will be catastrophic. It will gouge out a crater half a mile across and 300 feet deep. Virtually everything in this area, pulverized by the blast and altered by its heat, will be engulfed in a fireball with a 1.5-mile diameter. The surface temperature of this fireball will be greater than that of the sun. A huge mushroom-shaped cloud will form, carrying up and away the particles that remain of former life and structure.

Although the effects on you, 4 miles away, will not be quite as bad, they will be severe. Everything combustible in your area will be ignited, and things normally resistant to heat will be melted and misshapen. If you survive, you will be burned badly. (More than half of the people who died in the 20-kiloton attacks on Hiroshima and Nagasaki died of fire and heat.) If you survive the skin burns, the heat of the air may destroy your lungs. Moreover, the supply of oxygen in your area will have been reduced by the nearby fireblast.

Percussion effects will also be devastating. Buildings around you will crumble from the shock waves of the blast. Glass and other torn materials will catapult through the air at a speed of 200 feet per second. The misery of your burns will be compounded by injuries sustained in collisions; and your eardrums will have been shattered by violent soundwaves and by the 80-miles-per-hour windstorm set off by the blast. If you survive the initial dangers at 4 miles distance, you will be among fewer than half who do.

Radiation effects are your next hazard. If you have not been severely injured by immediate irradiation, if your vital organs have not been damaged by its unique penetrating power, you will have a lengthy bout with radioactive fallout. All the particles vaporized and sucked up into the atmosphere in the mushroom cloud will carry radioactivity. As they precipitate back to earth, they will contaminate everything in their path. Once again the air you breathe will be hazardous; your skin will be exposed once again to potentially lethal radiation; and exposed water and food supplies will carry certain death. Even if you are alive and mobile, you will be confined to your location. Neither is the danger over when the fires have subsided and the rubble has been removed. Radiation sickness may strike at any subsequent point in life or may torment its victims for decades. In 1982, fully 37 years after the atomic bombings of Hiroshima and Nagasaki, 10,000 people died of radiation-related diseases attributed directly to exposure in August 1945. And the genetic effects on subsequent generations are unknown.[2]

All this destruction has been brought on by a single one-megaton bomb. Yet in actual nuclear attack it is unlikely that a single bomb would be used or that the yield would be limited to one megaton. Warheads of three and five megatons are now common in the stockpiles of the Soviet Union and the United States, and the Soviet Union is known to have tested a device of 50-megaton

---

[2]Studies conducted 15 years after the bombings suggested extensive genetic consequences for subsequent generations. More recent evidence, collected over a period of 35 years, suggests that there are trends toward genetic damage to the fetuses and children of those exposed but does not lead to statistically significant results. See William J. Schull, Masanori Otake, and James V. Neel, "Genetic Effects of the Atomic Bombs: A Reappraisal," *Science*, September 11, 1981, pp. 1220–1227.

yield. All together, the strategic operational nuclear forces of the United States are equipped with approximately 14,000 warheads capable of delivering about 8.4 trillion tons of TNT equivalent. The strategic delivery systems of the Soviet Union are equipped to carry as many as 19,000 warheads. Together, the Soviet and American arsenals are capable of delivering over 17 trillion tons of TNT equivalent, roughly equal to one billion times the firepower delivered to Hiroshima in 1945.[3] Thus, a yield of one megaton in our imaginary attack is conservative. But when compared with conventional weapons, this blast exceeds all the explosives used against Germany and Japan in the Second World War and equals the total of all bombing in the Vietnam War.

To return to our nuclear attack scenario, the attack on your area need not have been an isolated one. Suppose it were part of general nuclear war with an enemy seeking to destroy 50 percent of your nation's industry and 25 percent of its population. This would mean hitting several major cities in a matter of minutes, perhaps some of them with several warheads, in order to gain the advantage. In the United States, for example, almost one-third of the total national industrial might and one-fourth of the total national population are concentrated in the 12 largest metropolitan areas. These are, therefore, the areas with the highest concentration of defense industry and trained personnel; they also house some of the major military and governmental installations. Table 10–1 lists these concentrations. If the enemy prefers countervalue targeting, all these areas are vulnerable. If it chooses instead to knock out retaliatory forces (counterforce strategy), these areas might be spared.

The effect of total warfare on national survival and the human future is unmeasurable. Yet there are still subjects for speculation. Optimistic observers speculate that with intelligent planning, the consequences of a nuclear attack could be limited to losses of not more than 25 percent of the national population, with recovery of the gross national product (GNP) within as few as ten years. Others take quite a different view, arguing that the damage would be considerably greater and consequences for human survival incalculable. The Department of Defense estimated in 1974 that a massive Soviet strike would result in 95 to 100 million American fatalities; a strike limited to missile sites and strategic submarine and bomber bases would take 5 to 6 million lives; and a strike limited to SAC (Strategic Air Command) bases or ICBM (intercontinental ballistic missile) sites would result in 0.5 to 1 million deaths.[4] Such estimates are sensitive to assumptions about enemy intentions and targeting, the number of independently targeted warheads, delivery vehicle accuracy, and other variables.

This speculation accounts only for immediate devastation. Recently, a number of scientific simulations have been conducted to estimate the long-range

---

[3]*SIPRI Yearbook, 1985*, p. 44 for the United States and p. 52 for the USSR.
[4]Herman Kahn, *On Thermonuclear War* (Princeton, N.J.: Princeton University Press, 1960); Kahn, *Thinking About the Unthinkable* (New York: Horizon, 1962), the title of which inspired the opening sentence of this chapter; Linus Pauling, *No More War!* (New York: Dodd, Mead, 1958); and James R. Schlesinger, "Briefing on Counterforce Attacks," Senate Committee on Foreign Relations Committee Hearing, September 11, 1974.

Table 10–1 Principal American industrial and population centers: likely targets of Soviet countervalue attack. Populations are for metropolitan areas (primary metropolitan statistical areas) rather than for individual cities. Note that in 1980 the total American population was approximately 230,000,000, with the result that the 16 largest metropolitan areas accounted for over 28 percent of the national population.

Rank	Metropolitan Area (PSMA)	Population (1980)
1	New York City	8,275,000
2	Los Angeles–Long Beach	7,478,000
3	Chicago	6,060,000
4	Philadelphia	4,717,000
5	Detroit	4,488,000
6	San Francisco–Oakland	4,073,000
7	District of Columbia	3,251,000
8	Dallas–Fort Worth	2,931,000
9	Cleveland	2,834,000
10	Boston	2,806,000
11	Houston	2,736,000
12	Nassau–Suffolk counties (N.Y.)	2,606,000
13	Pittsburgh	2,219,000
14	Baltimore	2,200,000
15	Atlanta	2,138,000
16	Minneapolis–St. Paul	2,137,000

Source: 1980 census data reported in *Statistical Abstract of the United States,* 1984, pp. 20–25.

consequences of nuclear war. They deal with human and genetic consequences as well as with environmental, agricultural, biotic, and behavioral results. One simulation, conducted by a group of scientists and endorsed by a broader group of American and Soviet scientists and strategists, predicts a "climatic catastrophe and cascading biological devastation" complicated by smoke and dust obscuring the troposphere and the stratosphere, radioactive fallout, and partial destruction of the protective ozone layer, all producing a prolonged nuclear midnight and severe low temperatures.[5] Figure 10–1 outlines the long-term predictions of the various effects over time and the resulting dangers for populations in the United States and the Soviet Union and for the Northern and Southern Hemispheres.

The Doctrine of Strategic Deterrence

Despite this horrifying potential, a substantial fraction of the $6 trillion spent by the United States and the Soviet Union on defense since the Second World

[5]Carl Sagan, "Nuclear War and Climatic Catastrophe: Some Policy Implications," *Foreign Affairs,* Winter 1983–1984, pp. 257–292. See also Jeannie Peterson, editor for AMBIO, *The Aftermath: The Human and Ecological Consequences of Nuclear War* (New York: Pantheon, 1983).

Figure 10–1 Ten-year natural consequence of nuclear war and the accompanying hazards for populations in the United States and the Soviet Union and in the Northern and Southern Hemispheres. H = high risk; M = medium risk; L = low risk.

Effect	Time After Nuclear War	US/SU Population at Risk	NH Population at Risk	SH Population at Risk	Casualty Rate of Those at Risk	Potential Global Deaths
Blast		H	M	L	H	M–H
Thermal radiation		H	M	L	M	M–H
Prompt ionizing radiation		L	L	L	H	L–M
Fires		M	M	L	M	M
Toxic gases		M	M	L	L	L
Dark		H	H	M	L	L
Cold		H	H	H	H	M–H
Frozen water supplies		H	H	M	M	M
Fallout ionizing radiation		H	H	L–M	M	M–H
Food shortages		H	H	H	H	H
Medical system collapse		H	H	M	M	M
Contagious diseases		M	M	L	H	M
Epidemics and pandemics		H	H	M	M	M
Psychiatric disorders		H	H	L	L	L–M
Increased surface ultraviolet light		H	H	M	L	L
Synergisms	?	?	?	?	?	?

(Time After Nuclear War scale: 1 hr, 1 day, 1 wk, 1 mo, 3 mo, 6 mo, 1 yr, 2 yr, 5 yr, 10 yr)

War has gone to research, development, and deployment of nuclear weapons and related delivery systems. New generations of bombers, submarines, missiles, launching systems, nuclear defenses, and explosive devices have absorbed hundreds of billions of dollars, and the cost continues to rise even though the total military expenses of the United States, the Soviet Union, and NATO all started to decline in 1988. As the post–Cold War circumstances of Europe have led to conventional force reductions on both sides, the nuclear share of the Soviet and American military budgets has risen in percentage. On what grounds are such expenditures and such an astonishing potential for ''overkill'' justified? The unanimous response of nuclear strategists who are satisfied that a strong nuclear deterrent is the key to national security is that the nuclear arms race is not lunacy at all—that it is a carefully balanced system designed not to threaten peace but to guarantee it. This outlook assumes that the greater the capability of two or more parties to destroy one another, the less likely they are to engage in combat. This mutual deterrence, which some strategists regard as the sole guarantor of peace, is based on an uncomplicated message to any potential adversary: "Before you strike me, you had better consider that I will strike you back, and I will do more damage to you than will justify your attack on me." Hence, mutual deterrence is built on the twin abilities of conducting a first attack and of surviving that first attack so to be able to launch a retaliatory attack of insufferable proportions. This system of keeping the peace by mutual threat of destruction was labeled by Winston Churchill "the balance of terror." With time, it has been renamed mutual superiority or, with greater irony, mutually assured destruction (MAD)! One critic of the concept has labeled it "the dogma of consensual, mutual vulnerability."[6]

Despite the simple logic of this prescription for avoiding nuclear war, the theory of mutual deterrence has been reexamined in recent years and found wanting. Critics argue, first, that deterrence strategy is derived too much from anticipated behavior and too little based on the actual study of decision making during conflict, whether nuclear or nonnuclear. They also find a contradiction in the basic logic: On the one hand, the theory of deterrence emphasizes the strategic value of showing a willingness to increase the risks of military policy, whereas on the other hand, the objective of the policy is to make situations safer. Third, critics attack the theory for its stress on punishment and of directing too little attention to the potential value of compromise. Fourth, they charge the policy with being excessively rigid in the sense that nuclear weapons might be used in anticipation of an attack from the other party when, in actuality, policymakers have misunderstood or misinterpreted the intentions of the adversary. Finally, the policy has been attacked because of its absoluteness, in the sense that a commitment to nuclear deterrence implies an all-or-nothing response to international crisis above an uncertain, but nonetheless intolerable, threshold. In the view of the critics, this absoluteness is another potential cause for misunderstanding intentions, for ignoring the context of a crisis, for incorrectly evaluating deterrent capability because of domestic or bureaucratic politics, or for failing to recognize opportunities for compromise or alternative policies.

First- and Second-Strike Capabilities

Despite these criticisms, however, the conventional wisdom of nuclear strategy continues to dominate the policy establishments of both Washington and Moscow. According to that wisdom, mutual deterrence requires not only the possession of nuclear arms by two opposed parties but also the ability of each to absorb a first strike by the other without losing the capacity to retaliate. Atomic stability depends on a belief in the mind of the potential aggressor that

---

[6]Fred Charles Iklé, "Nuclear Strategy," *Foreign Affairs,* Spring 1985, pp. 810–826.

The scene is the attempted assassination of President Reagan in Washington in March 1981. Police, secret servicemen, and bystanders are jumping on the suspect; the president has been thrust into his car. Sprawled at the feet of the agent on the left, still gripping an attaché case, is the president's air force aide. In the case is the device which, by unleashing the nuclear arsenal of the United States, can signal the destruction of half of the world. This aide travels everywhere with the president and was even in the operating theater during the emergency four-hour operation that followed the shooting.
Source: Michael Evans/Contact Stock Images

it will suffer retaliation at an unacceptable cost (the essence of deterrence). This means above all that a considerable portion of the defending state's strike force must survive the initial assault. If either or both parties can achieve a first-strike capability—a capacity to destroy the adversary's strategic arsenal by surprise attack—mutual deterrence does not exist. Stable deterrence requires that both parties possess secure second-strike forces capable of surviving a surprise attack.

Those who advocate mutual assured destruction argue that it is in the interests of both parties that their adversaries have secure second-strike potential. Without it the retaliatory response, to be effective, would need to be launched before the arrival of the opponent's incoming attack forces. Intercontinental ballistic missiles travel at speeds that reduce warning times to 15 to 30 minutes. Thus, without second-strike security, a retaliatory force would need to be on hair-trigger alert during periods of political tension and ready for instant launch. Such a time-urgent system would be prone to catastrophe in the event of misinformation or miscalculation. Stable deterrence depends on a less sensitized system, one that permits time to verify the existence of an attack, and even to receive it, before taking irreversible counteractions.

On the American side, however, there is a contradiction between this goal of second-strike stability and the imperatives of defense in the European theater. It is the declared policy of the United States that if NATO forces could not turn back a Soviet attack at the conventional weapons level, tactical and strategic nuclear forces would be used. This nuclear umbrella is the heart of the Atlantic alliance. But it implies that the United States might be placed in the position of making first use of strategic nuclear weapons. To reduce retaliatory damage to the American homeland and to make the threat of an American nuclear attack credible, the United States has an incentive to develop the capability to destroy the largest number of Soviet strategic forces on the ground before they can be used against American targets. Thus, the logic of the NATO alliance presses Washington toward the development of a first-strike force—one declared to be defensive in intent but one sure to be perceived in Moscow as threatening an offensive potential. Indeed, President Carter announced in 1979 that American strategic targeting henceforth would be based on first-strike logic; American weapons would be aimed at the nuclear delivery vehicles of the Soviet Union. The Kremlin greeted this with a charge that the United States was planning a nuclear war by designing a strategy for destroying the Soviet Union's second-strike capability, thus eliminating the careful balance of retaliatory forces that ensures peace in a nuclear world.

The American commitment to Western Europe poses a dilemma between the objective of second-strike stability and the requirements of a first-strike force. The reality of this dilemma is the precise reason that the conventional wisdom of nuclear strategy (the assumption of mutual deterrence and mutual assured destruction) fails to stand up to the necessities of strategic policy. As a result, a new school of thought has developed, composed of nuclear utilization theorists (NUTs, as contrasted with MADvocates!), who hold that a doctrine built on second-strike capability is inferior to one constructed on the concept of first-strike advantage. This view derives only in small degree from the fear that a sufficiently destructive first strike will destroy weapons intended for a second strike. It is founded more on the notion that the satisfaction of having scored a second-strike victory over the aggressor hardly compensates for the carnage inflicted by the original attack. In brief, fearing that the nuclear future is subject to unforeseen imbalances, deterrence is an unreliable policy; and if deterrence fails and second-strike weapons are destroyed (or if a society is destroyed), then a doctrine that relies on second-strike technology or second-strike psychology may fail. As a result, in recent years, both in Washington and in Moscow, a quiet transformation of strategic doctrine has occurred, one that continues to stress deterrence but that is equipped increasingly to invoke nuclear weapons as a first-strike strategy. In a sense, then, the contemporary doctrine of both parties is a compromise between MADvocates and NUTs.

The ongoing debate between advocates of first-strike capability and those of second-strike retaliatory strategy blossomed into a major contest within NATO on the eve of deploying 572 new intermediate-range theater nuclear weapons in 1983 (subsequently removed as a result of the Soviet-American INF Treaty of 1988), as a purported response to the Soviet deployment of SS-20 theater weapons over the preceding three years. Second-strike traditionalists argued that a mutual Soviet-American guarantee not to resort to the first use of nuclear weapons is crucial to stable deterrence. Others, including the European advocates of first-strike thinking, argued that first-strike is an option that cannot be removed from the doctrine of flexible response to potential aggression, particularly in the European theater where Soviet and Warsaw Pact conventional weapons greatly outnumber NATO's.[7]

Nuclear utilization theory results from a rethinking of both the psychological and technological aspects of nuclear arms competition. Its advocates are aware that second-strike strategy depends not only on the will to deploy strategic forces in a certain way but also on the technical capacity to protect a retaliatory force from destruction. Up to now, this has been achieved by the so-called triad of delivery vehicles: land-based ICBMs protected in underground silos; submarine missile launchers protected from detection (and therefore destruction) by thousands of miles of ocean in which they prowl; and long-range heavy bombers kept in the air on routine alert to prevent their destruction on the ground. This triad has provided a considerable degree of security to second-strike forces.

Strategic Triads

Both the United States and the Soviet Union maintain strategic triads, but their respective compositions differ. The global distribution of military bases, abundant access to year-round, warm-water ports, and continued reliance on airpower result in an American triad proportionally stable. The Soviet Union, on the other hand, lacks such ports (except in Vietnam and Cuba), deploys the vast bulk of its strategic missiles within the Soviet territory, and places far less emphasis on the vulnerable aircraft. The result, as is indicated in the second column of Table 10–2, is greater dependence on land-based strategic forces. Between 1985 and 1989, the Kremlin undertook a planned effort to modernize its nuclear triad, and the result was a substantial reduction in nuclear-bomb-bearing aircraft and an increase in submarine-launched missiles. When the Soviet and American nuclear forces are compared by deployment of warheads rather than by delivery vehicles, several conclusions emerge. First, while from 1985 to 1989 the United States reduced its number of land-based missiles, its program of MIRVing (that is, replacing single warheads with multiple independently targeted reentry vehicles) significantly increased both the number of warheads on land-based missiles and the percentage of land-based warheads in the total triad. Second, although the Soviet Union reduced its number of sea-based delivery systems, it greatly expanded their delivery power as measured by average number of weapons carried.

---

[7]For a spirited written debate of these two positions, see McGeorge Bundy, George F. Kennan, Robert S. McNamara, and Gerard Smith, ''Nuclear Weapons and the Atlantic Alliance,'' *Foreign Affairs,* Spring 1982, pp. 753–768, advocating the no-first-use principle; and a German response arguing for the inclusion of first-use in a flexible response doctrine by Karl Kaiser, Georg Leber, Alois Mertes, and Franz-Josef Schulze, ''Nuclear Weapons and the Preservation of Peace: A German Response to No First Use,'' *Foreign Affairs,* Summer 1982, pp. 1157–1170.

Table 10–2 Force comparisons of American and Soviet strategic nuclear triad defense systems, 1989.

	Number of Delivery Vehicles		Number of Warheads Each	Total Warheads		Average Number of Warheads per Vehicle	
	Number	Percent		Number	Percent	1985	1989
Land-based							
US	1000	51	1–10	2450	19	2.1	2.5
USSR	1378	56	1–10	6860	59	4.8	5.0
Sea-based							
US	608	31	8–10	5312	41	9.0	8.7
USSR	926	37	1–10	3602	31	2.9	3.9
Air-based							
US	349	18	8–24	5238	40	14.2	15.0
USSR	170	7	2–8	1100	10	2.0	6.5
Total							
US	1957			13,000		6.2	6.6
USSR	2474			11,562		3.8	4.7

Source: SIPRI Yearbook, 1989, adapted from tables on pp. 12 and 15.

Which government holds the nuclear advantage? The answer depends on which category you select. It is apparent that although the United States has a slight edge in deployed nuclear warheads, the Soviet stockpile (deployed plus reserve) is slightly larger, but this is probably not a significant difference. The United States has the clear advantage in airborne nuclear strategy, with a slight advantage in number of strategic bombers, but a much larger advantage in payload. This is partially offset by sophisticated Soviet air defenses. The offense may regain the edge after the Pentagon deploys the Stealth bomber, capable of repelling radar and other detective rays, and the B–1 bomber, capable of flying at altitudes beneath radar detection. Both deployments are scheduled for the early 1990s. In regard to submarines, currently the most mobile and nearly undetectable leg of the triad, the Soviets have substantial superiority in number of vessels carrying weapons with multiple warheads, yet the United States has nearly twice the delivery capability, owing to a more efficient deployment of warheads. The greatest Soviet margin is in land-based ICBMs, which comprise 56 percent (as against 51 percent for the United States) of the total delivery vehicles, but 59 percent of deliverable warheads (as contrasted with only 19 percent for the United States). This is due largely to SS-17, SS-18, and SS-19 ICBMs, which carry four, ten, and six warheads respectively, and the SS-24, which carries ten; the American Titan and Minuteman II and III missiles carry a maximum of three warheads. The American MX Cruise missile carries ten MIRVs.

Loaded Trident submarine.

To the extent that the nuclear triad of either the United States or the Soviet Union is a deterrent and, therefore, a defensive complex, these new military technologies raise the possibility that the margin of safety will be reduced substantially in the future and even that one or the other contestant may have the option to develop a first-strike force able to overcome all existing defenses. A hardened silo, for example, the underground well where ICBMs hide, effectively defends its missile against all but very near hits by enemy warheads and is designed to withstand the fairly wide circular error probabilities (CEPs) of available long-range missiles. (The CEP is a measure of the probability that at least one-half the warheads targeted at an object will fall within a predicted radius of that object.) But recent advances in microelectronics have made possible offensive weapons with highly accurate terminal guidance, reducing the CEPs (or increasing the probability of one-half the warheads' falling within the predicted radius) and possibly opening a new era of silo-busting techniques. For the newest generation of American intermediate-range missiles (Pershing II and ground-launched Cruise missiles), for example, the CEP is 300 feet, meaning that one-half the warheads fired at a single target will fall within a radius of 300 feet of the target from a distance of over a thousand miles.[8]

---

[8]The value of the CEP in predicting the attack's effectiveness is not without detractors. Some argue that although the theory is mathematically sound, it fails to take into account a number of

Figure 10–2 Probability of a missile's surviving nuclear attack as a function of the explosion's megatonnage and the hit's accuracy (CEP).

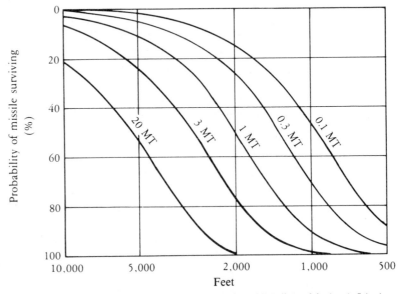

Source: Sidney D. Drell, "L + RV: A Formula for Arms Control," *Bulletin of the Atomic Scientists,* April 1982, pp. 28–34. Reprinted with permission of the *Bulletin of the Atomic Scientists,* a magazine of science and public affairs. Copyright © 1982 by the Educational Foundation for Nuclear Science, Chicago, IL 60637.

Figure 10–2 reveals a sliding scale of CEPs for warheads of differing megatonnage and the probability of a missile's surviving.

Similarly, the margin of security for submarines and strategic bombers is eroding. The submarine is protected by the physical properties of seawater, which impede the passage of detection impulses. But advances in antisubmarine warfare technology are extending the ranges over which detection is possible. Strategic bombers are vulnerable to precision-guided surface-to-air and air-to-air missiles, if radars are developed to respond to their characteristic low-level flight patterns. In general, and without overstating the point, it is fair to conclude that the new technologies will render obsolete many of the familiar means of protecting second-strike forces.[9] The probability that offen-

---

uncontrollable "bias" factors. Even if the CEP is demonstrated by firing repeated shots at a single target over a known test course, with the advantage of being able to correct the targeting on the basis of experience, it does not necessarily follow that the CEP will hold up when firing over an untested course. The detractors hold that the CEP may be a meaningless figure when missiles are fired between the United States and the Soviet Union over the North Pole because the "bias" factors peculiar to this untested course are unknown. See, for example, "A Question of Accuracy," *Science,* September 11, 1981, pp. 1230–1231.

[9]Authors differ on the effectiveness of nuclear defenses. One view holds that a "deterrent is deterred" because of the vulnerability of cities to retaliatory attack, whereas the other holds that the foremost weakness of American strategic policy has been to concentrate on offensive capability, leaving defenses weak, while the Soviets improve their defenses considerably. See, respectively, Robert Jervis, "Why Nuclear Superiority Doesn't Matter," *Political Science Quarterly,* Winter 1979–1980, pp. 617–633; and Daniel Gouré and Gordon H. McCormick, "Soviet Strategic De-

sive weapons will modernize more quickly than defensive ones will gives an edge to nuclear utilization theory, thus providing an added impetus to develop first-strike capability.

In the race between offense and defense, it can be safely predicted that new methods will be developed to protect nuclear strike forces. Suggestions include superhardening so as to give missile silos extremely high levels of blast resistance; camouflage and dummies, so that the enemy wastes its force on fake targets and misses the real ones; land mobile systems rather than fixed sites; electronic countermeasures to jam the sensitive guidance systems of the attacking force; high-energy laser beams to destroy missiles or their warheads in flight; and in the case of submarines, increased ranges and improved electronic warfare equipment to provide more cover against detection.

Behind all this competition, not only between governments but between proponents of offensive and defensive strategies as well, lies the logic of the nuclear arms race. No doubt the uncertainties of strategy and intent will force the competition to greater effort, higher cost, heightened technology, and greater probable loss. It seems that the arms race has gained so much momentum that it is unstoppable. Nevertheless, there are nuclear strategists who continue to insist that the race has reached the point of diminishing returns for both parties; that is, the current strategic balance, with respect to both deterrent capability and destructive potential, is durable and safe, so increasing the cost of weapons development provides ever smaller measures of security.

Counterforce and Countervalue Strategies

Some strategists have argued that deterrence may operate even during a nuclear exchange. Both sides have assets of greater and lesser value, and there may be a mutual interest or a tacit understanding to limit targeting in order to minimize the loss of human life. Former Secretary of Defense Robert S. McNamara suggested in 1962 that American planners seek not only the avoidance of nuclear war but also its limitation through a counterforce strategy. (He later abandoned this position.) This calls for the targeting of delivery vehicles on the forces of the adversary, rather than on its population, and for destruction of weapons rather than people. Although we ought to maintain a strike force targeted to cities and population centers to deter attack on our own civilian population, we should positively avoid striking cities. In this way, a level of deterrence could still operate even within a nuclear war.

Proponents of the counterforce strategy argue that any nuclear attacker realizes that its advantage comes not in killing people but in debilitating the enemy's forces. This is an especially acute consideration in warfare that will have a duration of only hours, in which no government would be able to utilize its population for manufacturing or any other purpose.[10]

But a counterforce strategy implies the ability to destroy missiles in silos, submarines in their hidden sanctuaries, and long-range bombers on the

---

fense: The Neglected Dimension of the U.S.-Soviet Balance,'' *ORBIS*, Spring 1980, pp. 103–127.
[10]See, for example, Kahn, *Thinking About the Unthinkable*, p. 66, and *On Thermonuclear War*, p. 115.

ground, at sea, or in the air. If this can be achieved against most or all of the enemy force, then the nation with such a capability will also have achieved a preemptive first-strike potential, whether or not this capability is intended. The opponents of counterforce argue, therefore, that the McNamara strategy which was reaffirmed in 1980 by President Carter and later by President Reagan as official American nuclear strategy, is a threat to the concept of stable mutual deterrence based on secure second-strike capabilities.

Although modern nuclear strategy is based on second-strike thinking, the original nuclear strategy was based on the countervalue concept, the notion of striking population and industrial centers. This notion was a natural extension of the saturation bombing strategy of the United States during World War II. But as the Soviet Union achieved nuclear strategic capability, newer considerations for deterrence entered the picture, and American strategy turned to counterforce coupled with notions of mutual deterrence and mutual retaliation.[11] Current strategy involves actual targeting at a combination of military and civilian targets, with the combined objectives of knocking out Soviet retaliatory forces, reducing the capability of the Soviet Union to recover from retaliatory attack, and eliminating the Soviet military and political leadership.[12] This may be interpreted as a strategy in which the basic planning is counterforce, but the targeting is a combination of counterforce and countervalue.

In an age of nuclear weapons, do the relative strengths of the United States and the Soviet Union in the number of missiles, bombers, and warheads make any difference? Each of the superpowers has an arsenal equivalent to several tons of TNT for every person. In 1974, Henry Kissinger offered the hypothesis

---

[11]For the evolution of the counterforce strategy, see Fred Kaplan, *The Wizards of Armageddon* (New York: Simon & Schuster, 1983), particularly chap. 13, "Counterforce." Also see Gregg Herken, *Counsels of War* (New York: Knopf, 1985), particularly chap. 15, "Eyeball to Eyeball."

[12]Although counterforce dominates current American strategy, countervalue planning (or "economic targeting") continues. See Benjamin S. Lambeth and Kevin N. Lewis, "Economic Targeting in Nuclear War: U.S. and Soviet Approaches," *ORBIS*, Spring 1983, pp. 127–149.

One account claims that the United States has 40,000 targets in the Soviet Union: 20,000 military targets (among the nuclear: ballistic missile launch facilities, nuclear-weapons storage sites, airfields with nuclear-capable aircraft, and bases with nuclear missile-carrying submarines; among the conventional: supply depots, marshaling points, conventional air fields, ammunition storage facilities, and tank and vehicle storage yards); 2000 urban targets to kill leadership of state and military forces; and 15,000 economic-industrial targets (divided between sites of war-supporting industry and industry capable of contributing to economic recovery). See AMBIO Advisory Group, "Reference Scenario: How a Nuclear War Might be Fought," in Jeannie Peterson, editor for AMBIO, *The Aftermath* (New York: Pantheon, 1983), pp. 38–48, at p. 40. The paper cites as its authority an unspecified report of the US Department of Defense in 1980 and a subsequent analysis by Desmond J. Ball, also unspecified.

Contrary to these reports, Defense Secretary Caspar Weinberger denied the use of countervalue planning as "neither moral nor prudent, neither necessary nor sufficient for deterrence," and as a strategy that would "invite the destruction of our own population." See *Annual Report to the Congress, Fiscal Year 1984*, p. 55.

For the first series of papers in the unclassified literature that contains much previously secret information about nuclear targeting, see Desmond Ball and Jeffrey Richelson, eds., *Strategic Nuclear Targeting* (Ithaca, N.Y.: Cornell University Press, 1984).

that ''when two nations are already capable of destroying each other, an upper limit exists beyond which additional weapons lose their political significance.'' Speaking in Moscow, he professed not to know what strategic superiority is, nor to understand its significance, nor to be able to imagine what to do with it. Winston Churchill put it succinctly: after a certain point, more bombs will only make the rubble bounce.

But in practice, diplomats and strategists take a different view and regard any change in the quantitative or qualitative balance of nuclear forces as a matter for the closest scrutiny. Does a new deployment signal a change of intentions by the other side? Is there a technological breakthrough that will confer an advantage to the adversary and upset the basis of the existing balance? Is the enemy achieving a first-strike option or gaining a local superiority in a particular region or theater? What political and strategic opportunities does it have under the new balance of forces, and how will our own policy alternatives be constrained? The major governments operate under the assumption that to ignore the strategic nuclear balance that underlies the panoply of relationships in the modern world system would entail great peril.

These questions give rise to two important distinctions. First, one must learn to distinguish between the implications of compiling more nuclear weapons, on the one hand, and the implications of improving the ability to deliver those weapons, on the other. Clearly, the emphasis in strategic decision making is on the latter; for it is the ability of the adversary to penetrate defenses, together with one's own ability to overcome the defenses of the adversary, that really drives the strategic debate and the pace of advancement in weapons technology. Second, and in contrast with conventional weapons, literal parity

Matter of Muscle?

When Richard N. Perle, Assistant Secretary of Defense for International Security Policy, and other arms control hardliners in the Pentagon talk about ''throw weights,'' they are not commenting on recent Olympic feats. A major issue in United States arms control policy is how persistently to press the Russians to agree to steps that would lead to equivalent ballistic missile ''throw weights,'' that is, the amount of weight, exclusive of the missile rocket, that the boosters can lift into ballistic space trajectory.

It would be difficult for the Russians to comply, even if they wanted to do so, because they took a different design path than the United States and built very large missiles with lots of throw weight. But the issue has become an obsession of Mr. Perle and some of his arms control colleagues in the Pentagon.

However, arms control specialists in the State Department generally seek other avenues to reduce any disparity in nuclear strength. One State Department office has on prominent display a handmade poster that reads: ''Real Men Don't Need Throw Weight.''

From *The New York Times*, August 13, 1984. Copyright © 1984 by the New York Times Company. Reprinted by permission.

in nuclear forces is meaningless. It is unimportant that one side's nuclear arsenal is as big as that of the other side. The critical issue is whether one's own side possesses sufficiency or practical equivalence. It is only that one have enough capability to meet the maximum strategic (both first-strike and second-strike) need, not that one side be able to match the other in a count of weapons. It is for this reason that comparisons of weapons arsenals, such as that shown in Table 10–2, are of limited value; it is also important to have a measure of the quality of defenses, the respective rates of developments in weapons technology, the efficiency of weapons as measured in distance and accuracy and so on.

Credibility of Intent

Deterrence, as has been noted, is more than simply the possession of weapons of mass destruction. There is a reciprocal psychological factor through which the parties signal one another as to their intentions and the depth of their commitments. The possession of power is not an effective deterrent unless accompanied by the will to use it in defined situations. Thus, the threat of nuclear retaliation must not only be horrifying; it must also be credible. The probability of nuclear attack is the product of capability and intent: if intent equals zero, then the probability will be zero.[13]

Credibility is also determined in part by the object of conflict. There is an obvious difference in expectation when (1) one's home territory is threatened or (2) one's vital allies are intimidated or (3) conflict brews over some remote areas or some remote interest. In the first case, there is little cause to doubt the credibility of deterrence. Doubt begins to spring up, however, in the second case. Although the United States would surely launch a counterattack if New York City were subjected to nuclear attack, would it do likewise if the object of the first strike were a Western European city? If the United States does respond with nuclear weapons, does it invite an attack on its own cities and its own defenses from the other side, after having already expended some of its deployed weapons? The European fear that for these reasons the American nuclear umbrella lacks credibility has greatly motivated the development of British and French nuclear forces. In the third case of remote areas and interests, of course, nuclear deterrence has little credibility whatever.[14]

Object of conflict is closely tied to commitment. There is no doubt of self-defense credibility, but commitment may become obscured as the issue in question wanders farther from home. This is the case with the American

---

[13]J. David Singer, "Threat Perception and National Decision-Makers," *Journal of Conflict Resolution*, 1958, pp. 90–105, also J. David Singer, *Deterrence, Arms Control and Disarmament* (Columbus: Ohio State University Press, 1962); and Dean G. Pruitt, "Definition of the Situation as a Determinant of International Action," in Herbert C. Kelman, ed., *International Behavior* (New York: Holt, Rinehart and Winston, 1966), pp. 393–432.

[14]Kahn, *Thinking About the Unthinkable*, pp. 110–125, suggests three types of deterrence pertinent to three distinctly different levels of interest.

pledge to defend West Berlin, a small island of the Western world surrounded entirely by East Germany in the Soviet world. Its size and location make it indefensible. The pledge to defend it seems impossible in the face of overbearing power from the Warsaw Pact nations. But the American pledge was boldly underscored by President Kennedy in 1961 when he declared in German to a cheering throng in West Berlin, ''I am a Berliner!'' A few years later President Nixon told a similar audience, ''All the world's free peoples are Berliners.'' Some politicians have gone so far as to say that even God may be a Berliner! The point is to dramatize to the Soviet Union the American commitment to defend what appears to be tactically indefensible.

But how is this commitment made credible? Among the NATO forces in West Berlin there are many thousands of Americans who, in the event of invasion, would be killed or captured. Their deaths or detention would commit the United States to retaliatory action (not necessarily nuclear), and the Soviets know this. Hence the commitment of the United States to the defense of a most unlikely piece of territory is made credible by the trip-wire character of the American forces there. It is based on mutual knowledge that a Soviet attack might force the United States to do something that it does not want to do. This process of voluntarily tying one's own hands is generally called the process of commitment and posits this rule: Credibility is ensured when you deprive yourself of the option of not honoring your own threat. Among other things, this process signals to the other side that the burden is on it to prevent a clash.

Thomas Schelling proposed the game of Chicken as a model of communicating to an enemy that a situation is out of control and that you are powerless to restore control because of the depth of your commitment. He likens international conflict to two hot-rodders on a deliberate collision course, each expecting the other to chicken out. If neither does, each is the loser in a bloody conclusion. Schelling suggests a strategy in which one participant becomes conspicuously drunk before the start. As the vehicles approach each other, the inebriated driver throws his steering wheel out of the car so as to signal to the other his inability to restore control. The burden is now on the other, because one is irrevocably committed. The major liability, of course, is that two may play at the same strategy, and instead of having one participant out of control, there may be two.

In the jargon of the nuclear era, this danger of uncontrolled escalation of commitments is called brinkmanship, or the process of proceeding stepwise to the brink of thermonuclear war. In this process, called by the late Herman Kahn "the rationality of irrationality," each side attempts to convince the other that its commitment is irrevocable and that it is the other's responsibility to defuse the situation. Irrevocability is communicated by tying it to larger values or to constituents who will not be satisfied with any other course. Language involving ideological necessity has been common in Soviet brinkmanship, especially in the Cuban missile crisis of 1962. By the same token, the specter of abandonment of allies and references to a determined Congress or electorate have accompanied American nuclear diplomacy. The danger is that if both sides play at the same tactics, issues and threats become magnified. The sole full threat of bilateral nuclear confrontation—the Cuban crisis—was defused only when the Soviet Union agreed to remove its offensive missiles as a *quid pro quo* condition for an American pledge not to sponsor further invasions like that at the Bay of Pigs in 1961.

Fortunately, that crisis and all others between nuclear powers up till now have been resolved short of the type of runaway commitment envisaged by Kahn. His image of a Doomsday Machine portrays a device running on computers that could not be drawn off the course of total destruction if an adversary were to undertake any of certain selected policies; it would be capable of universal destruction. Presumably it would be a totally credible deterrent, because it would be irreversible and able to compute events without human interference.

Risks of Nuclear War

The doctrine of deterrence presumes that all risks related to deployed nuclear weapons are calculated and controlled. But nowhere does uncertainty have potentially catastrophic consequences.

Proliferation of Nuclear Weapons

Up to this point, all references to nuclear politics have assumed the simplest of political configurations: a "binuclear world," or one in which only two states possess combat nuclear capability. In fact, this is a false situation, for at present, in addition to the United States and the Soviet Union, nuclear capability can be deployed by Britain, France, and China, and India has successfully detonated one nuclear device. Several other governments are within easy reach of nuclear capability should their policies call for it (although to develop it, many would have to renounce their ratification of the 1970 Nuclear Non-Proliferation Treaty). Among these are Iraq, Taiwan, South Korea, Australia, virtually all the Western European and Eastern European states, Israel, Egypt, Pakistan, Canada, Brazil, and Mexico. In all, there are perhaps 25 states that might in the foreseeable future opt for nuclear weapons, and there is evidence that South Africa tested one in 1983 (but it is not listed by SIPRI).

One needs to look briefly at the reasons that the present nuclear powers opted for such weapons. The United States did so in order to bring the Second World War to a fast and sudden conclusion and, in pre–Cold War spirit, to demonstrate its incomparable weapons strength to the Kremlin.[15] The Soviet Union was moved to nuclear capability by the rapid breakdown and polarization of world politics after the war. Britain and France undertook nuclear development both for reasons of prestige and in order to prepare European defenses that would not be dependent on the United States. China undertook the nuclear course for reasons of global prestige, regional political-military supremacy, and the dissolution of peaceful security relations with the Soviet Union. India, the newest (1974) of the nuclear partners, undoubtedly chose to enter the club principally for reasons of prestige (especially in relation to nuclear China and nonnuclear Pakistan), the Asian balance, and appearances of modernity.

On balance, then, there appear to be four reasons for nuclear weapons development: security, prestige, regional dominance or equilibrium, and reification of modern scientific development. Even though most citizens regard nuclear development as unreasonably costly, potentially aggressive, and generally useless, the competition among governments for security and recognition makes the nuclear option enticing. Quite possibly, were it not for the twin facts (1) that many states are protected by nuclear umbrellas through alliances (Western Europe and Canada by the United States through NATO and Eastern Europe by the Soviet Union through the Warsaw Pact) and (2) that despite public denunciation, nuclear equilibrium has contributed to East-West peace for four decades, there would be many more nuclear powers at present than there are. Basic nuclear weapons technology is known virtually throughout the world, and the cost of production is relatively low. In the hands of terrorists, a small, concealed weapon could have immense political effect; but for most governments attempting to base national strategic defense policies on nuclear deterrence, the cost of delivery technology will remain a barrier to entry for the foreseeable future.

It should not be assumed, however, that the other countries have progressed as far as the Soviet Union and the United States in weapons development. The

---

[15]Gar Alperovitz, *Atomic Diplomacy: Hiroshima and Potsdam* (New York: Vintage, 1965).

distribution by country of 1791 nuclear test explosions conducted between 1945 and the end of 1988 is shown in Table 10–3. During the 1970s, the average number of tests conducted annually was 42; from 1980 to 1985, it was more than 54, after which it fell to 36. The decline was due in part to a Soviet unilateral moratorium on testing, and in part to a 1988 Soviet-American agreement to conduct a joint verification experiment. Under the agreement, each hosted seismologists and other scientists at the site of a test explosion in the range of 100 to 150 kilotons TNT equivalent in order to obtain accurate yield measurements by which to monitor subsequent test detonations.

The relative ease by which nuclear weapons are acquired, either from allied governments or through independent scientific development, has raised a number of crucial questions about their spread or proliferation. In early nuclear jargon the problem was expressed as the "*n*th power problem," referring to the possibility that an indeterminable number of states might undertake nuclear weapons development. Was the world better off with only two (or a few) nuclear powers which fully understood the rules of the nuclear game in such a way as to establish a peace by threat? Or would the world benefit by being multinuclear, that is, by having several nuclear states, each capable of adjusting its own security without reliance on fragile alliances? Was a binuclear status anything more than a device of the two greatest powers to manipulate everyone else's security and to manipulate world politics in general to their conflicting outlooks? The modern problem, needless to say, places renewed emphasis on these questions, given that scientific knowledge enables the nuclear membership to multiply by five in a matter of a few years. Urgency is heightened by the fact that there are several critically important regional balances in the world where the Soviet Union and the United States play external roles, such as in the Middle East and continental Asia. Are the imperatives of regional balances and the demands for prestige sufficient to justify the rapid growth in number of nuclear states?

Table 10–3 Atomic and nuclear test explosions, 1945–1988.

	Before *Sept. 1, 1963*[a]	*After* *Sept. 1, 1963*[a]	*Country* *Total*
US	331	579	910
USSR	185	451	636
France	8	164	172
UK	23	18	41
China	0	31	31
India	0	1	1
	547	1244	1791

[a]The Partial Nuclear Test Ban Treaty was concluded in August 1963, yet the number of tests conducted since that time is double that of the pretreaty era. France and China have not joined the treaty, with the result that while all others restrict testing to underground sites, 44 French tests and 22 Chinese tests have been above ground.

Source: SIPRI Yearbook, 1989, pp. 59–60.

Most scholars and diplomats prefer to think of a world in which the management of nuclear power is kept in as few hands as possible. Controlling the spread of nuclear weapons has been an agreed goal of most of the leading powers. Efforts to stem proliferation of these weapons achieved a major success with the Non-Proliferation Treaty (NPT), which took effect in 1970. In this treaty, the nuclear members pledged not to transfer to nonnuclear states any form of nuclear explosive and not to assist in its development. Likewise, the nonnuclear members agreed not to accept such weapons or assistance. But, like most treaties, signature is wholly voluntary, and compliance with the terms is left to self-restraint. Furthermore, Article 10 of the treaty provides that any state may withdraw from the treaty's obligations upon a three-month notification by merely informing the other parties and the United Nations Security Council. The notification must be accompanied by a statement of the "extraordinary events it regards as having jeopardized its supreme interests."

Although 122 governments have ratified the NPT, it does not enjoy universal popularity. Nonnuclear states have often objected that the treaty is a luxury of the nuclear states, designed to freeze the international distribution for maintenance of special superpower privileges. Others have been reluctant to enter into the treaty without guarantees of deterrence assistance from one or another of the nuclear powers. We have already seen that such guarantees are without practical benefit, because the level of commitment embodied in them leaves much slack in credibility.

The nonnuclear states have not been alone in their objections. Among those who enjoy nuclear status, both China and France have vigorously opposed membership in the NPT. Each argues that it is a Soviet-American device to subordinate others and to profit from their unique ability to offer and then withdraw the nuclear umbrella. France, especially, insists that the possession of even minimal nuclear capability is a political and strategic equalizer. China adds the view that nuclear status promotes the decay of imperialism and is therefore a progressive international trend. The opponents of the NPT are not necessarily reckless, because their arguments are intended not to destabilize the international system but to challenge the political superiority of a few nuclear states. Although the United States pledges its aid against nuclear blackmail, France, China, and India refuse in turn to be blackmailed by the United States and the Soviet Union.

The fragility of the NPT as a safeguard against the spread of nuclear weapons is, however, becoming more a matter for concern, owing less to traditional reasons of security and prestige than to the global crisis of natural resources. Commencing with the petroleum embargo of 1973–1974, governments have been increasingly aware of the need to develop nonpetroleum energy reserves. A method particularly favored has been nuclear fuel. The ease of acquiring nuclear fuels in international trade has raised the issue of "innocent progress toward the Bomb," or the acquisition of nuclear capability for peaceful industrial reasons, only to succumb to the temptation to transform fuel for energy into fuel for combat potential. Not only does this possibility greatly increase the number of states that might in the foreseeable future have the nuclear military option; it also raises grave questions about the wisdom of nuclear fuel transfers, the management of nuclear policy internationally, and anticipatory controls over regional nuclear arms races. Indeed, India's single nuclear explosion resulted from nuclear fuel provided by the United States for peaceful purposes. The American charge that India violated the terms of the transfer agreement in using the material to develop a prototype nuclear weapon caused a serious rift in relations between the two governments. Israel's 1981 preventive attack on a French-built reactor in Iraq was undertaken because of evidence that the reactor would be used to produce weapons-grade nuclear fuel. (The world's fear of Iraqi nuclear development was reawakened in 1990 when British and American intelligence authorities captured California-made nuclear triggering devices bound for Baghdad at London's international airport.) And in 1987, threats were made in Washington against aid to Pakistan on the basis of reports that Pakistan had already achieved the most difficult steps in the production of a nuclear bomb by diverting nuclear fuels provided by the United States for peaceful purposes.

The problem is especially acute with respect to fast breeder reactors which produce plutonium, an artificial element, as nuclear fuel. In the view of the United States and other governments, the recycling of nuclear fuels threatens to close too rapidly the gap between nuclear energy technology and nuclear weapons technology, a threat both to the stability of international politics and to the control of terrorism. The threat is so severe that it has been estimated that by the turn of the century there will be enough breeder reactors in use to produce sufficient plutonium to build as many as 30,000 bombs as powerful as the one dropped on Nagasaki.[16]

In an effort to bring this under control, Washington sought to preserve time with the Nuclear Non-Proliferation Act of 1978, which purports to give the United States the authority to prevent the international transfer of plutonium in conjunction with its membership in the Nuclear Suppliers' Group, founded in 1975. In addition, the United States has succeeded in establishing the International Nuclear Fuel Cycle Evaluation, a project of some 40 governments, charged with exploring the international need, control, and storage of spent nuclear fuels. It is hoped in Washington and other capitals that these efforts will delay the excessive recycling of nuclear fuels long enough to develop reprocessing technologies that do not simplify the creation of weapons-usable material.[17] The Nuclear Non-Proliferation Act provides strict controls on the uses of fuel provided by the United States, but states that are not members of the Non-Proliferation Treaty and that have wanted to embark upon nuclear generation of electricity have been able to turn to other suppliers, most notably France, for nuclear fuels.

---

[16]Frank Barnaby, "World Arsenals in 1980," *Bulletin of the Atomic Scientists*, September 1980, reporting on the findings of the *SIPRI Yearbook, 1980.*

[17]Joseph S. Nye, "Non-Proliferation: A Long-term Strategy," *Foreign Affairs*, April 1978, pp. 601–623. See also Victor Gilinsky, "Plutonium, Proliferation and the Process of Reprocessing," *Foreign Affairs*, Winter 1978–1979, pp. 374–386. For a study of alternative policies together with pertinent technical information, see Ted Greenwood, George W. Rathjens and Jack Ruina, *Adelphi Paper No. 130*, Winter 1976 (London: International Institute for Strategic Studies).

Accidental Nuclear War

Popular literature throughout the nuclear era has given much attention to the possibility of unintended nuclear war ignited by accident, human error, nervous impulse, or unauthorized behavior. Occasionally, these horrors have been brought to life by close scrapes with nuclear disaster. On some occasions errant radar signals have indicated the possibility of incoming missiles over the North Pole. Soviet behavior in Germany, especially in the Berlin air corridors, has sometimes raised fears of nuclear war out of sheer nervousness. The projected "surgical strikes" on Soviet missile encampments in Cuba in 1962 might have brought a Soviet nuclear response. And the use of tactical nuclear weapons and even low-yield strategic nuclear weapons had been advocated by the political right in both Korean and Vietnam wars.

A vivid example of the possibility of accidental nuclear warfare occurred when a bomb-laden American Stratofortress crashed off the Spanish coast in the mid-1960s. Although its cargo did not detonate, two nuclear devices were temporarily lost, one on land and one in shallow waters. Do such incidents suggest that misunderstanding and coincidental happenings in international crises could touch off holocaust?

American strategists are convinced that the risk of Soviet-American nuclear war through technical accident is negligible. The risk may be increased, however, by the proliferation of cheap thermonuclear systems in the hands of states with inferior scientific development whose economies force dangerous shortcuts in safeguard systems. Although the giants invest heavily in careful electronic and mechanical shielding devices that make unintended detonation quite unlikely, similar protective devices may be either technically or economically beyond the reach of smaller states. It is believed that the bombs of the big powers are less accident prone than might be those of small future atomic powers.

American strategists are also confident that an accidental detonation would be unlikely to ignite a world conflagration. The superpowers depend on careful systems of bureaucratic checks and controls designed in part for exactly such a contingency. The maintenance of secure second-strike capabilities permits methodical inquiry rather than impulsive reaction. Here again, smaller powers, lacking protected capabilities and intricate verification devices, might be forced to react more hastily. The Moscow-Washington hotline was instituted after the Cuban missile crisis for the respective heads of government to communicate their intentions during times of tension. The hope was that an accident might not be taken as open hostility and that a single firing might not burgeon into global destruction.

Despite faith in fail-safe systems, strategists continue to acknowledge the remote possibility of accidental nuclear launchings. For that reason, Moscow and Washington have joined in an Agreement on Measures to Reduce the Risk of Outbreak of Nuclear War. Effective in 1971, this bilateral treaty calls upon the parties "to notify each other immediately in the event of an accidental, unauthorized or any other unexplained incident involving a possible detonation of a nuclear weapon which could create a risk of outbreak of nuclear war."

They agree in such cases to take measures to render the weapons harmless. They also pledge to communicate with one another upon sighting unidentified incoming vehicles and to notify one another in advance of missile tests that will extend beyond the home territory in the direction of the other. To ease such communications, they entered into executive agreement to update the hotline by adding communications links through two or more telecommunications satellites.

These arrangements have not succeeded, however, in resolving the question of whether or not each new generation of delivery vehicles raises the prospects of unintended nuclear war. Some observers retain the faith that fail-safe measures are adequate, but others are concerned that the speed with which missiles can round the globe leaves inadequate time for rational decisions about a response. Futhermore, according to the skeptics, command and communications systems are imperfect and not wholly defensible. According to the Senate Armed Services Committee, for example, in an 18-month period from early 1979 to June 1980, American nuclear forces received no fewer than 3703 alarms of in-coming nuclear attack, of which 147 were serious enough to require immediate evaluation. In addition, on the American side alone, there have been 32 accidents involving nuclear weapons, none of which resulted in a detonation. Some analysts argue, therefore, that the fail-safe measures are adequate, but others expect that the hair-trigger alert required by new missile technologies and the probability of subsequent accidents steadily increase the probability of accidental or unintended nuclear war.[18]

Another popular fear is the Dr. Strangelove syndrome, or the fear of a perverse individual who, for reasons known only to himself, uses military rank to launch an unauthorized nuclear attack on an enemy. Even the most careful psychological testing and training cannot, of course, guarantee that an anti-communist paranoiac on the American side, or an overzealous Soviet anti-imperalist, could not somehow gain access to the buttons. As a safeguard, the superpowers have installed elaborate multiple control systems, which require the coordinated acts of two or more persons at separate centers of decision to unshield nuclear weapons. Only a small group of people knows who operates the other button to the same weapon. In this way, an unauthorized use of weapons of mass destruction would require a conspiracy of people who do not know one another's identities. Short of an all-out conspiracy, achievable probably only through a coup of the entire armed forces, the two-key system prevents unauthorized firings.

Still another danger is that of catalytic war, or unwanted war between superpowers, provoked by a calculating third party. This concept arose in popular literature in the early days of the atomic race, especially from the book (and later movie) *On the Beach*, in which a nervous third party prompted a

---

[18]For a recapitulation of these events and for a skeptical view of fail-safe systems, see particularly Arthur Macy Cox, *Russian Roulette: The Superpower Game* (New York: Time Books, 1982), chap. 1, "Accidental Nuclear War." Jonathan Schell, *The Fate of the Earth* (New York: Knopf, 1982), pp. 26–27, raises the possibility that one human, mechanical, or electronic error could lead by chain of errors to unintended war.

Nuclear clock.
Source: Reprinted with permission—Toronto Star Syndicate

nuclear war between the two superpowers. In the days of America's policy of massive retaliation, many Americans feared that a nervous European decision maker might deliberately provoke war with the Soviet Union and force the United States to demonstrate the credibility of its defense doctrine. All in all, however, the increase in destructive potential makes it unlikely that any third party would provoke a war from which no nation could entirely escape.

But there is one type of nuclear threat over which governments have virtually no control: nuclear attack launched by terrorists or other nongovernmental actors. In recent years there has been growing concern that the basic science of nuclear weaponry is so well known that terrorist organizations might fall upon someone with the right background to provide them with crude nuclear devices. In addition, fears regarding the possible weapons-related consequences of reprocessing spent nuclear fuels are multiplied by the prospect of their falling into the hands of terrorists or revolutionaries. When the first known act of sabotage against a nuclear reactor occurred in France in early 1979, fears of clandestine access to nuclear fuel raised grave security questions about nuclear development.

Nonnuclear Terror

Although the expression "balance of terror" was created to describe the global nuclear balance, modern military tactics include other forms of weapons terror as well.

Chemical and Biological Warfare

Chemical warfare consists of several methods of using chemical agents to poison, burn, blind, expose, and otherwise incapacitate enemy troops. It has a long, and often colorful, history. The first known use was by Solon of Athens, who defeated the army of Kirrha in 600 B.C. by throwing bundles of hellebore roots into the enemy's water supply. While the enemy attempted to contend with the resulting diarrhea, Athenian troops marched in for the conquest. Other ancient uses were leaving poisoned wine in evacuated camps, tossing venemous snakes into enemy ships, and using poison for arrows and wells. Fire was used by Sparta as early as 429 B.C. in a mixture of pitch and sulphur used to ignite enemy cities. "Greek fire," first used in 350 A.D., acted as a primitive flame thrower by spurting burning liquid from a siphon. Smoke has been used since early times to seclude troop movements and naval maneuvers.

Chemicals have played a role in twentieth-century wars too. Tear-gas grenades were introduced by France during the First World War, and Germany responded by the full-scale use of lethal chlorine gas (contemplated, but not used, by the Union Army during the American Civil War). The United States fielded a Gas Regiment in the First World War, which launched as many as 2000 cannisters in a single battle. In 1936, mustard gas was dropped from Italian planes onto Abyssinian troops in the conquest of Ethiopia, causing incapacitating burns to bare feet. Only a year later, Japan used toxic gases against Chinese troops. During the Second World War, in the battle against Japan, the United States advanced modern incendiary warfare with napalm—a soap-thickened petroleum that cannot be extinguished, capable of igniting human torches. In the Vietnam War, American troops experimented with induced forest firestorms using the same principle.

Although toxic gases were not used during the Second World War, German researchers happened upon the discovery of the deadly nerve gases, which paralyze the motor nervous system. Through captured documents, the United States acquired the secret of sarin, while the Soviets seized a tabun plant. Either of these gases is lethal to a person if only a drop penetrates the skin. Contact causes instant nausea, vomiting, diarrhea, convulsions, respiratory paralysis, and death in a few moments. These agents would be most effective in local warfare for population attrition. Like other gases, their battlefield use is limited by the liabilities of windshift and the possibilities of self-infliction.

A new category of nonlethal chemical methods is called the incapacitating agent, designed to cause temporary paralysis, blindness, dizziness, and narcosis. The psychochemicals are a special category that have incapacitating mental effects such as paranoia, confusion, delirium, hallucinations, disorientation, giddiness, or maniacal behavior. These can seriously alter any army's fighting capacity, its will, its speed of movement, its reaction time, and other variables of ground warfare. General William M. Creasy, former chief chemical officer of the US Army, suggests that the future of warfare may lie in the psychochemicals.

The future of chemical agents for combat purposes is still under debate. There is strong sentiment for their uncategorical elimination, but others con-

American forces in Saudi Arabia prepare for Iraq's chemical weapons by conducting military preparations in protective equipment.

Source: AP/Wide World

sider incapacitation preferable to slaughter. Proponents of their prohibition insist that the greatest danger is from the thought-controlling potentiality of the psychochemicals, opening new and incalculable opportunities for tyranny. But fire, incapacitating agents, and defoliants have become so important to modern land armies that they are unlikely to be given up, especially when, with nuclear arms limitations, conventional arms are being restored to first priority. The flexibility, mobility, and visibility of flame, defoliants and "incaps" are likely to give them the stature of conventional machine guns, especially in guerrilla and counterguerrilla warfare. They are not apt to vanish from the conventional arsenals of major powers.[19]

---

[19]US Senate Subcommittee on Disarmament, *CBR Warfare* (Washington, D.C.: US Government Printing Office, 1960); *Chemical Warfare of Special Significance to Civil Defense,* Civil Defense Technical Bulletin, TB-11-28; J. Leiberman, "Psychochemicals as Weapons," *Bulletin of the Atomic Scientists,* January 1962; "Biological and Chemical Warfare: An International Symposium," *Bulletin of the Atomic Scientists,* January 1960; Marcel Fetizon and Michel Magat, "The Toxic Arsenal" in Nigel Howard, ed., *Unless Peace Comes* (New York: Viking, 1968).

This theoretical debate notwithstanding, both the Soviet Union and the United States began to reduce their chemical warfare stockpiles in 1989 under strong humanitarian and environmental pressures, and in an atmosphere of sharply reduced superpower tension. Yet the popularity of chemical weapons among the non-nuclear powers of the Third World remained as cause for alarm. For Americans, the potential horror of chemical warfare was more vivid than at any time since the First World War when Saddam Hussein of Iraq threatened the massive use of chemicals should the United States or any other government retaliate against Iraq for either its rapid conquest of Kuwait or the presence of more than 100,000 of its troops along the Saudi Arabian border. During these events in 1990, Americans were concerned about the ability of Western troops to conduct a desert war under the bulky protective cover and poorly ventilated masks required to withstand showers of chemical weapons.

Biological warfare has horrors of its own. Often called germ warfare, it utilizes infectious agents. It is the deliberate inducement of disease, either by spreading bacteria or viral microbes or by using their organic toxins. Although efforts have been undertaken sporadically since 1925 to outlaw these methods, not until 1972 was a multilateral treaty signed by states to that effect. Again, however, compliance is left to self-restraint and the possibility of investigation by the UN Security Council of alleged violations. Moreover, the Convention on the Prohibition of the Development, Production and Stockpiling of Bacteriological (Bacterial) and Toxin Weapons and Their Destruction permits any state to withdraw from its obligations by three-month notification accompanied by a statement of the jeopardy to national interests that motivates the withdrawal. The same treaty defers chemical elimination to the future and stipulates only that outlawing biological weapons may also be a step toward the prohibition of chemical weapons.

For much of the post–World War II period, the use of chemical agents in warfare has been rare, and of biological, nonexistent. A major exception was the American use of defoliants in Vietnam, a process of spraying thick vegetation from above in order to kill the leaves and thus deprive the North Vietnamese of the ability to move people and matériel behind their camouflage. More recently, the United States reported "unequivocal evidence" of the Soviet use of chemical and toxic weapons in Afghanistan and Southeast Asia.[20] In 1986, despite presidential objections, the US Congress denied funding for the replacement of old chemical weapons stockpiles.

World concern about the spread of both nuclear weapons and modern conventional weapons to the Third World has been accompanied by fear that other weapons might fall into the hands of Third World governments or terrorists. Two issues have been of particular concern. First, after several years of speculation that Eastern European governments were supplying undetectable plastic explosives to terrorists through certain Third World governments, the first postcommunist government of Hungary acknowledged in 1990 having found

---

[20]*Science*, April 9, 1982, pp. 154–155.

official records that such shipments had been made. Second, American intelligence sources accused Libya of mass producing chemical weapons, and subsequently speculated that it had done so with the assistance of a West German firm. In early 1990, the suspect plant was damaged by fire. Opinions on the cause varied from industrial carelessness and human error to sabotage (with the Libyan government accusing the United States and Israel). Within a few days of the fire, West German authorities arrested a chemical industrialist and charged him with complicity to synthesize chemical weapons abroad in violation of West German law and treaty obligations. The accused was convicted and sentenced. Only months later, at the time at which Saddam Hussein was threatening to use chemical weapons against American troops, or any other troops that might attempt to retaliate against Iraq for its conquest of Kuwait and the presence of over 100,000 Iraqi troops along the Saudi Arabian border, other West Germans were charged with having assisted Iraq in developing its notorious chemical stockpile. Those weapons had been known to have been used against Iranian troops in the 1980–1988 Persian Gulf War and against dissident political elements within Iraq.

Nonconventional Weapons

The focus on developments in the nuclear field ought not to obscure other parallel advances in the conventional arsenals. The Vietnam War, like all others, refined the human ability to destroy. The United States, for example, applied electronic science to conventional war, especially for automated air warfare. Other innovations included weather modification to disrupt movement of enemy troops and goods, and "smart bombs," which are able to seek out specific targets and aim themselves by reciprocating signals. Fragmentation bombs were used to inject painful fishhooks into the skin so as to demoralize troops and strain the enemy's medical facilities. Bomb targeting devices were developed that detected humans in the dark of night, thus depriving the North Vietnamese of the cover of darkness.

The major powers have exchanged charges that they have encouraged small wars as a means of combat-testing new military devices. For several months prior to the 1982 Israeli-Syrian war in Lebanon, it was charged by Western sources that the Soviet Union was encouraging Syria to provoke a war in order to observe the combat effectiveness of new Soviet equipment. Similarly, Soviet sources claimed that the military suppliers of Argentina, particularly France, encouraged the invasion of the Falkland Islands in 1982 in order to test certain antiship weapons against the British Royal Navy. Whether or not there were such conscious motives in these two cases is debatable; that new warring devices were unveiled is not.

The prospects for future arms seem limitless. Nuclear weapons may be miniaturized for movement by saboteurs, as plastic bombs are now used. Robot tanks will have multiple tactical uses, as will "kamikaze" bombers on suicide missions. Some writers envisage the use of anthropomorphic robots on the ground, within this century, to replace shock troops; and possibly even two-sided robot warfare. The robot may be the soldier of the future.

In addition, greater efforts at weather modification may have a role in future tactical warfare, both to slow the enemy through natural disaster and bad visibility and to facilitate one's own tactics by clearing techniques. Growing seismological understanding suggests that eventually it will also be possible to induce earthquakes in some regions.

Underwater and outer space zones will become more important. Undersea operations are ideal because the physical properties of salt water impede the passage of detection impulses. If downward-pointing antiaircraft devices are circulated in space, the role of supra-atmospheric space may increase. Control of interplanetary space may determine control of airspace, even national airspace. Despite the fact that the United States and the Soviet Union have entered into treaties prohibiting the orbiting of nuclear devices in space (1967) and the placement of such weapons in or on the ocean floor beyond a 12-mile national limit (1972), the military importance of both sea and space is steadily increasing and is likely to continue to do so.

Nuclear Defenses

Early in 1983, President Ronald Reagan instructed the Pentagon to begin immediately an investigation into the electronic weapons potential of the American armed forces for the turn of the century. His public announcement of this initiative became known as the Star Wars speech, and the policy, formally labeled the Strategic Defense Initiative (SDI), acquired the popular name of the Star Wars policy. The goal of the policy, first funded by Congress in 1985, is to establish an elaborate network of electronic instruments on the ground and in the air and space that will use laser technology to detect, locate, and destroy ballistic missiles that have already been launched by an enemy. The rationale for this policy is that this will provide the technology for the postnuclear era of strategic defenses in which the United States will base its security not on second-strike capability and the constant expansion of nuclear stockpiles and delivery vehicles, but on antimissile electronic technology.

The Strategic Defense Initiative sparked perhaps the most vigorous debate over defense policy since the Second World War. Hundreds of American scientists signed pledges not to accept research funding for Star Wars electronics; the president's estimate of $27 billion as the research cost was generally rejected as woefully understated; advocates of the demilitarization of space condemned it as the transgression of a barrier beyond which the control of events could not be ensured by governments; and until early 1987, the Soviet Union refused to enter into serious disarmament discussions unless and until the United States agreed to discontinue its Star Wars research. (President Reagan offered the compromise of postponing for ten years the projected date of deployment but would not agree to a discontinuation of development.) Proponents, on the other hand, lauded the policy as probably feasible, a reasonable basis for transcending dependence on nuclear defenses, and a strong bargaining item in nuclear arms reduction talks with the Soviet Union. President George Bush was less committed to SDI than had been his predecessor. Motivated by extraordinary budgetary pressures, by the rapidly evolving thaw in Soviet-American relations, and probably by doubts regarding SDIs scientific feasibility, he agreed to reductions in SDI funding. And for the 1991 fiscal year it was virtually eliminated from the Pentagon's appropriation.

The first solid evidence of America's preparedness to enter the space-war generation occurred in mid-1983 with the public disclosure of Pentagon plans to destroy a satellite in space. According to the published reports, the plan was to arm an F-15 fighter craft with an explosive cylinder called a miniature homing vehicle (MHV) and to fire the device at the upper reaches of the atmosphere. By electronic command, the MHV would seek out the target satellite and destroy it.[21] With knowledge that the Soviets were also working on advanced antisatellite weapons (ASAT), the US Air Force had already declared its intention of achieving superiority in space.[22]

Arms Control and Disarmament

Should arms races be controlled? If so, how? The answers to these questions may be critical to the human future. With respect to the nuclear race, have we reached the point of diminishing returns? At this point, each new increment of power is not only vastly more expensive than its predecessor but buys relatively less security than previous developments did. If so, what is the sense of undergoing the expense and the potential destabilization generated by further enlargement of nuclear stockpiles and development of more sophisticated vehicles? Does the respectability of membership in the nuclear club portend proliferation, despite treaties to the contrary? Does the temptation among nonnuclear powers to enter into the club because of lingering regional disputes raise the prospect of future nuclear blackmail and, with it, increased regional instability? In short, does the continuation of arms races, and the strategic nuclear arms race in particular, absorb more human and material resources than is now justified? Do arms contests prevent or delay peaceful transformation of the international system?

There is scarcely a student of public affairs who does not fault the logic of arms races on one or more of these bases. For those who find such competition important enough to exceed even treatment of social problems, the fear of nuclear proliferation is a major concern. Others lament the massive expenditures for small gains in security that thus serve to postpone correction of social inequities. Still others fear that the price of nonproliferation may be increased nuclear protection of many states by a few, and to ensure credibility of these defenses, there may be a greater impetus to brinkmanship. To reduce arms, a particular party must first build more in order to have negotiating advantages,

---

[21]Fred Kaplan, "We're About to Launch a Costly and Crazy Arms Race in Space," *The Washington Post*, October 16, 1983, p. B1.

[22]The first successful test of a Soviet ASAT occurred in June 1982, a test in which a killer missile was placed in a corrected orbit to seek and destroy a target satellite. See *SIPRI Yearbook, 1983*, pp. 437–439.

although this increase may itself delay political agreement until the other part catches up, thus prompting yet another turn of the upward spiral. However, regardless of what position one may take on the value of arms and their costs relative to other needs, arms control and disarmament are on everyone's mind—save, perhaps, for a few unthinking profiteers.

From the earliest attempts at disarmament in the beginning of this century, three principal motives for limiting arms races have been recognized: (1) the desire to reduce the likelihood of war, (2) the desire to decrease the amount of destruction that would occur if war were to break out, and (3) the desire to reduce the economic cost of defense. Secondary objectives include attempts to adjust the international power distribution by establishing permanent military relativities and by adjusting the number of effective military powers and the number of alliance systems. Each of these objectives is directly related to the structural characteristics of the international system. Finally, behind all other reasons for arms control is the desire of governments to maintain nothing less than military equality with adversaries and, when possible, a slight advantage.

If disarmament is thought of in grand terms—as the dismantling of all weapons, the stilling of munitions industries, and the total forswearing of the sovereign right to arm for national defense—then it is, indeed, a radical concept designed to alter the basic nature of the international system. In practical fact, however, twentieth-century attempts at arms control have never been this ambitious. Their objective has been the more conservative goal of managing arms races in such a way as to provide stability at the lowest possible price. Some have emphasized qualitative aspects of armaments (attempting to limit progress in the technological level and total destructive capability); others have concentrated on quantitative measures (the number of weapons deployed). Among the latter, some agreements have anticipated future arms deployment and have set limits for the future, whereas others have tried to reduce the number already in place. For the most part, strategic arms limitation has emphasized quantitative controls of future deployments.

The first Strategic Arms Limitation Treaty (SALT I) is illustrative. Through this instrument, the United States and the Soviet Union agreed in 1972 to absolute ceiling numbers of ICBMs, deployed nuclear warheads, and multiple independently targeted reentry vehicles, or MIRVs. They also agreed to limit antiballistic missile (ABM) sites to two each, a frank recognition of their faith in second-strike strategy at that time.[23] Quite obviously, the effort here is to prevent the strategic arms race from becoming still more threatening, still more horrifying, and still more expensive. Rather than reduce their respective arsenals, the two parties agreed only to limit the upward spiral.

The proportional reduction of nuclear weapons is far more complex. The variety of weaponry, the distances over which warheads can be delivered, the inaccessibility of some weapons to detection and surveillance—these problems

---

[23]This faith has been reiterated several times. For example, former Secretary of Defense Harold Brown: ". . . the absence of a widely deployed ABM system makes for stability." *The New York Times*, January 18, 1981.

and others greatly complicate mutual reduction. To make matters worse, neither side is eager to enter into negotiations while substantially ahead. Thus, parity seems to be the ideal negotiating posture, but it probably has never existed. The result has been to approach nuclear arms limitation item by item, or on the basis of direct trade-offs. It was formerly believed, for example, that the United States might decline to deploy ABMs if the Soviets would not proceed with MIRV. As timing and strategies dashed hopes for such an agreement, each party proceeded to deploy both ABMs and MIRVs. The SALT I agreements are the result.

Together, changes in strategic thinking (such as renewed interest in first-strike strategy) and development of weapons technology since SALT I made SALT II an even more difficult undertaking. The technological gap between the United States and the Soviet Union had narrowed considerably, and both sides were emphasizing offensive strategy in planning new developments. The increased MIRV potential of each side, commitment to new weapons such as the American Trident submarine and Cruise missiles, and confusion over whether or not a new Soviet-American strategic agreement would negatively affect the security of Western Europe (theater balances are not addressed in SALT I) contributed to a new negotiating and political environment. Furthermore, American relations with Turkey and Iran had fluctuated to the point at which access to tracking facilities to monitor Soviet missile development was in constant jeopardy. Despite all these obstacles, SALT II was conceived, although never born.

The détente atmosphere that enabled the Nixon administration to negotiate SALT I and the Carter administration to negotiate SALT II had vanished by the time Ronald Reagan assumed the US presidency. Furthermore, Soviet adventures in Afghanistan, the imposition of martial law in Poland, and American conservative dislike of SALT II (Reagan and others thought it advantageous to the Soviet Union and disadvantageous to the West) all combined to terminate the SALT II process. Because the SALT II treaty was never ratified by the Senate, Reagan withdrew it from consideration and announced a new arms limitation policy. When arms limitation talks resumed in 1981, they did so under the name START, or Strategic Arms Reduction Talks. This was more than a mere change in name, for the aim of the talks from the American viewpoint was not only to limit the upward spiral but also to begin the process of reducing the number of deployed strategic arms. Later, by Senate inspiration, a new gambit was offered: the so-called build-down, a system of arms reduction in which two missiles would be dismantled for each new one put in place. The eventual goal of American negotiations was the zero-zero option, the phased and eventual mutual reduction to no nuclear weapons. The Soviet Union viewed the American position as one designed to undo the balance created by SALT I, and a disguise for an American superiority.

Central to the Reagan strategy, however, was the prior Soviet-American agreement to separate the START negotiations from those regarding intermediate-range nuclear forces (INF) in the European theater. The INF discussions, in turn, were based on the supposition that the United States would be prepared to deploy in Europe more than 500 new-generation Cruise and

Pershing II missiles, either to counter the Soviet deployment of SS-20 rockets or to achieve their removal in return for a promise not to deploy Pershing II and Cruise missiles. The Soviets, in turn, refused to proceed with the START negotiations until the theater weapons question had been resolved. Thus, by the end of 1983, three sets of talks had commenced—START on global strategic issues, INF on European theater weapons, and MBFR on the mutual and balanced reduction of conventional forces in Europe—and progress in START and MBFR awaited events at INF, although officially they were to be conducted simultaneously.

The announcement of the SDI and the determination of the United States and its NATO partners to proceed with the Cruise and Pershing II deployments in Western Europe were seized by the Soviet Union as causes to discontinue all arms limitation talks. Hence, in early 1984, the INF, START, and MBFR talks all were recessed and did not resume until late 1985. During the interval, the Soviet Union continued its deployment of SS-20 and SS-4 missiles in Europe and Asia; NATO made considerable progress with its Cruise and Pershing II deployments; and funded research on Star Wars began in earnest.

Early 1987 was marked by a succession of contradictory, if loosely related, events, a sample of which follows:

1. The Kremlin, frustrated with Washington's refusal to enter into a nuclear test moratorium, broke its unilateral ban and resumed underground nuclear tests. Although this decision was vaguely attributed to the national economy, it was undoubtedly driven by strategic considerations, because the United States was both testing nuclear weapons and beginning systematic research on SDI.

2. Washington reversed its position on interpreting the Anti-Ballistic Missile Treaty. Having throughout the life of the agreement used a narrow interpretation in order to limit the development of Soviet defense systems, the Reagan administration, eager to remove all legal obstacles to Star Wars as a defensive system, announced that it would abandon its former position and apply a more expansive interpretation.

3. In another significant reversal of policy, the White House announced that it would disregard the informally recognized limits of the SALT II draft treaty by deploying a new nuclear submarine carrying strategic weapons without decommissioning an older one. To the charge of critics that this act would destabilize the strategic arms race and reduce prospects for progress on arms limitation, Washington responded that the SALT II agreement, had it been ratified, would have expired at the end of 1985, as a consequence of which voluntary compliance with its terms was no longer necessary.

4. Moscow unexpectedly decoupled its objections to Star Wars from its nuclear diplomacy. After having declared repeatedly that no significant progress could be made at the Geneva arms talks until the United States discontinued its SDI objectives, Gorbachev agreed to proceed with arms talks irrespective of American progress on Star Wars.

5. The Kremlin offered back to the Pentagon the zero-zero option previously made and abandoned by the United States. Gorbachev offered to negotiate the elimination of intermediate-range missiles from Europe on condition that the Soviet Union be permitted to maintain them in Asia and be permitted to maintain its short-range Euro-

pean missiles. The United States countered with a demand that it be permitted to build a short-range missile defense system in Europe before dismantling the INF weapons. The NATO partners, always fearful of the huge Warsaw Pact superiority in conventional (nonnuclear) weapons, were divided on the Soviet offer and fearful of a hasty agreement resulting from President Reagan's eagerness to avoid being recorded as the first president in nearly 30 years to make no progress with the Soviet Union on matters pertaining to the arms race.

Once the Intermediate-Range Nuclear Forces Agreement was reached in 1987 (although it did not go into effect until the following year), both Gorbachev and Reagan were eager to get on with the Strategic Arms Reduction Talks. The INF treaty covered only about 5 percent of combined Soviet and American nuclear fire power and was focused largely on Central Europe. President Reagan set as his "radical goal" a 50 percent reduction in strategic arms. The talks resumed in 1987 on the basis of some preliminary agreements achieved at the Reykjavik summit of 1986: a limit of 1600 strategic launchers each (including intercontinental ballistic missiles, intercontinental bombers, and submarine-launched ballistic missiles) and a limit of 6000 warheads apiece atop all these launchers. By late 1987, the ceiling on launchers had been reduced to 4900. But 1988, the last Reagan year, failed to produce a final START treaty, in large measure because of military opposition in the United States. At the time of writing in early 1990, the START treaty remained incomplete because of the Bush administration's preference for pursuing conventional forces reduction talks in Europe.[24]

Verification of Compliance

Even though governments might enter into arms control agreements in good faith, the need to verify compliance with such agreements is a paramount problem. If obligations are carried out by only one state, the other state's opportunity for blackmail is unlimited. This is regarded as a problem unique to the nuclear era, but it is not. Unilateral failure in convention reduction might produce such instability as to tempt the stronger. There is considerable likelihood that the threat here is greater than in noncompliance with nuclear control or reduction agreements, because both the United States and the Soviet Union have sufficient deterrent capability to tolerate even sizable imbalances in strategic potential. But if the two should arrange an agreement on mutual and balanced (conventional) force reductions for Europe and only one party were to comply, the danger of war through temptation might be increased.

On the nuclear side, the problem of verification is even more difficult. Ships, tanks, troops, air bases, and so on are more accessible to counting than are strategic submarines and hardened missile sites. In addition, even though exposed delivery vehicles may be counted with some accuracy, the problem of counting warheads and estimating their megatonnage remains. How many

---

[24]Strobe Talbott, "Why START Stopped," *Foreign Affairs,* Fall 1988, pp. 49–69; and James P. Rubin, "START Finish," *Foreign Policy,* Fall 1989, pp. 96–118.

missiles does a submarine carry? How many warheads does each bear? What is their total explosive potential? Similar problems arise with respect to hardened missiles.

Diplomats and scientists have shared the problem of perfecting verification systems. Early in the atomic age, the United States and the Soviet Union exchanged ideas for detecting atomic tests. These included on-site inspection plans involving neutral personnel and the use of "black boxes," or seismographic stations, which could be monitored for explosions and estimates of yield. Other plans included "open skies," in which the nuclear states would permit one another to enter national airspace for photoreconnaissance flights. None of these proposals ever materialized.

Modern technology has resolved much of the verification problem. The participants in the nuclear arms race have tracked one another's missiles firings and have been able to estimate rocket thrust. From this information, each has been able to estimate the amount of nuclear power capable of being delivered by specific missile systems. The United States knows, for example, that the successful testing and deployment of the giant SS-9 rocket by the Soviet Union represented MIRV potential. By the same token, the Soviet Union knows the lift potential of the Minuteman III and the Poseidon II. Furthermore, by orbiting reconnaissance satellites, each party is able to monitor the construction of missile sites and to determine satisfactorily the number of missiles poised for firing. ABMs are easily detectable from above because of the huge radar complexes that they require. About the only important thing that technology is unable to determine is the momentary location of nuclear submarines.

What is it, technically, that verification seeks? There are four general objectives. First, each party wishes to be satisfied with the other's compliance with immediate obligations of the treaty, such as dismantling, terminating site construction, or closing bases. Second, each party needs to know that the other is not undertaking to replace what has been removed. Third, each wants satisfaction that the other has not merely moved certain instruments to other places and concealed them from surveillance. Finally, each wants demonstrated assurance that remaining forces are what they are said to be. Therefore, verification of four objectives must be achieved: initial obligation, nonreplacement, nonconcealment, and remainders.[25]

The problem of enforcement of arms control and arms limitation agreements is even more difficult politically than is verification. If two states agree to limit their arms and only one complies, then it is difficult for the weaker to enforce the agreement against the stronger. Ideally, therefore, enforcement ought to be left to some neutral agent that has both the political capability to enforce agreements and the military wherewithal. Yet imagine states giving over to some other party or institution authority greater than their own and military power superior to their own, even though they are capable of creating

---

[25]Hedley Bull, *The Control of the Arms Race*, 2nd ed. (New York: Praeger, 1965), p. xix. For verification problems under SALT, see Stuart A. Cohen, "SALT Verification: The Evolution of Soviet Views and Their Meaning for the Future," *ORBIS*, Fall 1980, pp. 657–683.

more and better! To expect the United States and the Soviet Union to vest the United Nations, for example, with both the political power to order sanctions against a great power and independent nuclear capability is politically naïve. Hence, international arms agreements have traditionally left to states the privilege of "national means of enforcement." Often implicit in the reluctance to negotiate the reduction of arms is the argument that such a reduction would minimize the ability to enforce compliance against a treaty partner that violates its obligations.

Because every arms race is tied to a political context, arms reduction and political thaw are interdependent. Where favorable political opportunity is lacking, most progress toward arms reduction is dictated by cost factors. In 1899, Tsar Nicholas of Russia convened the First Hague Conference, not to negotiate a new political order for Europe, but because he felt economically incapable of competing in arms development with Germany. Likewise, the American "return to normalcy" after the First World War was motivated largely by budgetary fatigue, coupled with the desire to retreat from power politics. The SALT I agreements arose from the mutual Soviet-American desire to control the costs of yet another spiral in the race between offensive and defensive missiles. The abortive SALT II was likewise inspired in part by economic considerations but was complicated by the question of whether or not it would provide sufficient safeguards for Western security. The European anxiety over this issue was political: given the Soviet buildup, were the circumstances of the political context such as to justify marginal changes, through a treaty of self-denial, in the strategic balance of the theater? Western European endorsement of the START and INF negotiations faced the same question and rested on the assumption that if the talks failed, Pershing II and Cruise missiles would have provided deterrence against the Soviet Union for the remainder of the century.

The United States and the Soviet Union seem caught in a policy dilemma. Although they negotiate arms limitation agreements, they forge ahead with ever-advancing weapons technology and, at the same time, transfer modern arms to other governments in an effort to use the threat of force as a rationale for regional military stability. So far as the strategic arms race is concerned, weapons development becomes both the cause and the consequence of agreement. For although each new weapons system on one side may promote further development on the other, it also signals the need to bring the upward spiral under control. But this is to look at arms limitation as nothing more than a technical problem. Indeed, the technical problems probably lend themselves to resolution more readily than do the political and diplomatic problems. Just as Albert Einstein once remarked that scientific problems are easier to solve than are social scientific problems, so too effective control of arms development depends on the evolution of an East-West political context congenial to arms reduction. This serves to accentuate the dilemma of arms races and arms limitation: As strategic arms limitation depends in part on cordial political contexts, so too is it hoped that temporary management of the technical aspects of arms control will contribute to the evolution of such an environment.

War, Peace, and the Arms Race

Thermonuclear war, deterrence, brinkmanship, ABM, MIRV, tactical nuclear weapons, committal strategy, counterforce, nuclear proliferation, finite deterrence, accidental war, catalytic war, incendiary weapons, nerve gas, incapacitating agents, psychochemicals, robot warfare—to many people, all this sounds like Dr. Strangelove's inventory of madness. To the ordinary person, these preparations add up to less security rather than more. What chance of peace is there when every nation is armed to the teeth, when a dozen different arms races of differing proportions are conducted simultaneously, when the best of science is turned to killing? Many people share Kant's view in *Perpetual Peace* that standing armies and arms races are inextricably linked to war and that high levels of armament guarantee war rather than ensure against it.

But to diplomats, nuclear strategists, and students of war, the belief that nations fight because they have arms reverses history. Nations arm because they have conflicts with other states: conflicts over mutually exclusive goals cause war, not the maintenance of arms. The Cold War caused the arms race, because the incompatibility of potential objectives of the United States and the Soviet Union requires military preparedness. Only stable competition in arms prevents existing conflicts from erupting into war.

This conclusion does not, however, deny the wastefulness of arms races as measured both in economic cost and in nonproductive absorption of resources. "National strength," a nearly universal slogan, is easily sold to frightened populations. In addition, professional military elites want the most modern equipment available, in some cases if only for personal or service aggrandizement. As a result, a generous share of national resources is given by most countries to security. Although some governments have tiny to moderate military budgets, others have very substantial commitments. The United States and the Soviet Union rank highest in dollar expenditure. Israel, Saudi Arabia, Syria, and the People's Republic of Korea head the list measured by share of gross domestic product devoted to military commitments, which are in the range of 14 to 18 percent. Much larger amounts were recorded in the past. In the mid-1970s, for example, the Israeli military budget typically ran at about 26 percent of gross domestic product, and that of Egypt rose to as much as 33 percent.[26] In total, the world devotes over 7 percent of its total annual production to military expenditure, and the fraction would be much larger if veterans' benefits and military pensions were included.

Contrasted with critical social indicators, these amounts loom even larger. While most of the Southern Hemisphere seeks to modernize and while most of

---

[26]For a detailed study of national arms expenditures by dollar, by national currency, and by percentage of gross domestic product, see *SIPRI Yearbook, 1989*, pp. 178–193.

The figures offered by the Swedish International Peace Research Institute and by the US government often diverge considerably. As examples, the US government estimated that in 1983, Iraq devoted 47.2 percent of its GNP to the military, while the figures for other countries given much lower assessments by SIPRI were Israel, 29 percent; North Korea, 16.7 percent; Saudi Arabia, 24.3 percent; and Oman, 27.9 percent. See *Statistical Abstract of the United States, 1987*, p. 843.

the industrialized world searches for remedies to the social problems created by technology, the world's governments go on spending billions of dollars per year more on military expenditures than on such things as public health, foreign economic assistance, and international peacekeeping. In 1974, world expenditures on education exceeded the cost of the arms race by a slight margin, and for only the first time. They do no longer.

The human cost of this proliferation of arms is staggering. A single modern jet fighter, such as the McDonnell Douglas F-15, costs as much as a community hospital. A single second-generation nuclear submarine of the Trident class costs the equivalent of 500 schools. One modern nuclear-powered aircraft carrier equals four years' budget of the United Nations! American ABMs, if deployed in the numbers originally planned, would have equaled the cost of 2.5 million small homes. These costs are increasingly unacceptable in industrialized economies with constant growth in public revenue; but they are wholly unbearable in the poor countries that, ironically, are now increasing their military budgets the most rapidly.

National Perceptions of the Balance of Terror

The American Perception

Popular opinion about the balance of terror in the United States is sharply divided. Those who object to American participation insist that the arms race is unjustifiably costly, both absolutely and in relation to other needs. Each new generation of arms is more expensive than is justified by the minimal gains in security, and each new upward spiral may accentuate insecurity. Furthermore, the critics ask, are official assessments of need built on misperceptions? Are the nation's legitimate interests so vitally challenged as to require such exorbitant extremes to preserve them? Critics farther to the left wonder if such levels of arms are not maintained simply to safeguard less legitimate interests.

The official view is markedly different. It holds that in addition to the need for strategic balance, military threats to US interests are ever-present. American foreign interests have been targets of China and the Soviet Union, which sought to divide the Western allies, to undermine confidence in American leadership and the American economy, and to seize territories and governments not vigorously defended by the United States. Only the defense of Berlin and the resolute interventions in the Korean and Vietnam wars taught these foes that Washington will not tolerate encroachments on its interests. Establishment of the North Atlantic Treaty Organization, the Truman Doctrine (determination to prevent the spread of Soviet influence), and the incorporation of Japan and West Germany in defense alliances were the types of actions that signaled to the Kremlin an intent to resist challenge to American interests.

But there was another lesson as well. Soviet threats dramatized the need not only for intense political relations and institution building among allies but also for impressive arming. Only the ability to signal the Soviet Union, with credible threat, that the use of their arms would bring about massive retaliation, could ensure the allies against impediments to the founding or restoration of democratic political institutions. Arms policy was coupled with the "export of democracy" and provided the umbrella under which the United States could "help others to help themselves." If the Soviet Union proceeded to greater threats with improved weapons, the United States would improve its weapons. Each new Soviet development demanded American response: the Soviet Union was responsible for fueling the strategic arms race, through its combined political threats and strategic capability.

The interpretation of Soviet intentions as villainous abated only slightly with the death of Josef Stalin and Nikita Khrushchev's new policy of peaceful coexistence and de-Stalinization. But the tone did change. With the exception of rare direct confrontations (such as the Cuban missile crisis), the Soviet-American arms race began to yield to the need for rational policies of stable deterrence. The lessening of political tension did not result, however, in bilateral willingness to reduce stockpiles. Before such events could take place, a new factor arose: the prospect of China, with its immense potential power, as a nuclear state in enmity with both Washington and Moscow. The United States was finally obliged to acknowledge that there did not exist a communist monolith, that the threats of Moscow and of Beijing were politically and strategically distinct.

By the end of the 1970s, some of the uncertainties that dominated American strategic thinking had been better illuminated, but others seemed even more vexing. The sudden accord with China and the friendly Chinese attitude toward NATO substantially reduced American strategic concern with the nuclear capability of the Asian partner. In contrast with the preceding three decades, China now encouraged a strong American presence in Asia, in part for reasons of regional stability, in part as a deterrent to Soviet political offensives, and in part to reduce the probability of Japan's developing nuclear weapons.

But if the China puzzle in American nuclear strategy seemed to have abated, the Soviet buildup in Europe and its greatly improved weapons technology renewed the challenge to American strategic thinkers. European opposition to SALT II (which never became a ratified treaty), owing to the potential effect of a global strategic arms agreement on the balance of the European theater, led to division regarding new weapons systems. To be sure, since SALT I the United States had improved its MIRV potential and its accumulated nuclear warheads, and it had constructed Cruise missiles and begun the Trident program. In all this, the cost of defense was skyrocketing, and those political forces that regarded the strategic balance as stable and durable were calling for reduced defense spending. On the other hand, competing voices argued that Soviet military modernization presented a grave challenge to American security as well as European, and that new weapons were called for urgently. Only on the issue of proliferation of nuclear weapons to additional nations was there solidarity, and the president and Congress together attempted to take global leadership in preventing such proliferation. Meanwhile, America's arms transfers to Third World countries continued, both in order to maintain regional balances and to force restraint upon the Soviet Union's client states throughout the world.

With the resumption of the Cold War in the 1980s, Washington abandoned all détente-related notions of coexistence with the Soviet Union without still more modernization of its armed forces and, more specifically, its strategic forces. Furthermore, in face of an uncertain Sino-Soviet détente, fears grew that Soviet missiles pointed at Asia might be retargeted at Japan. This fear resulted in a Western declaration of intent to defend Japan against Soviet aggression. The declaration was the most important outcome of the 1983 Williamsburg, Virginia, economic summit meeting of the Western trading partners. Soviet deployment to Syria of SS-21 missiles, potentially nuclear tipped, also raised the threat of nuclear war in the Middle East in 1983.

The global circumstances under which the START negotiations commenced were, accordingly, severely strained. And the situation was further complicated by the imminence of antisatellite techniques that threatened intelligence systems and potential devices for mutual verification of arms reduction agreements. Finally, both the United States and the Soviet Union were aware of the vulnerability of their communications, control, and command systems, known in the United States as C^3. Washington was aware that the speed and probable accuracy of new Soviet weapons exceeded the capabilities of C^3 to ensure safe and secure responses; the Pentagon was aware that even a single nuclear explosion could destroy the delicate electronic and computer-programmed basis of American defenses and retaliatory capability.[27]

Given these immense problems, the White House chose to pursue two lines of arms negotiations. The first was START, designed to replace the scrapped SALT II, dealing with global strategic issues. The second, called the INF talks, addressed the immediate security questions related to the balance of intermediate-range nuclear forces within Europe. With the demise of détente, the Soviet Union had commenced the deployment of SS-20 intermediate-range, nuclear-tipped missiles targeted at Western Europe. The United States intended either to counter this deployment with 572 of its own Cruise and Pershing II missiles or to secure the dismantling of the SS-20s in return for an agreement not to deploy Cruise and Pershing IIs. From the viewpoint of the Reagan administration, this strategy was necessitated by the Soviet refusal to discontinue the deployment of SS-20s. Washington would negotiate only when its military technology put it in a position of either parity with or superiority over the Soviet Union.

Still, contrary to its professed interest in a peaceful balance resulting in mutual deterrence, the Soviet Union showed no sustained evidence that its strategic policy was based on anything but Khrushchev's 1960 declaration that the world would eventually know that "capitalism is the source that breeds wars and would no longer tolerate that system, which brings sufferings and disasters to mankind." The goal of the Kremlin, in the official American view, was not peace or mutual deterrence; it was a strategic military superiority for the purpose of world enslavement. Military buildup from 1975 to 1984 not

---

[27]See, for example, Jonathan B. Tucker, "Strategic Command and Control Vulnerabilities: Dangers and Remedies," *ORBIS*, Winter 1983, pp. 941–963.

only expanded Soviet influence in areas contiguous to the USSR's borders; it gave Soviet forces virtual worldwide basing capability in many areas previously allied to the West: Cuba, Central America, Ethiopia, Yemen, Vietnam, and so forth.[28] Hence, right up to the end of the first Reagan administration (January 1985), the official Washington view was that the Soviet Union was not the country of Lenin and Marxist-Leninist ideologists; it was a nation of imperialists ruthlessly directing economic potential to a war machine with global reach.[29] The American role in the balance of terror was a necessary corollary to this threat.

This view changed rapidly as the beginning of the second Reagan administration and the Soviet policies of *glasnost* and *perestroika* commenced almost simultaneously. There followed with unpredicted speed the INF treaty eliminating all intermediate-range nuclear forces from Central and Western Europe and the establishment of both warhead and nuclear delivery systems ceilings preparatory to a START agreement. The collapse of one Eastern European communist government after another in 1989 and 1990 brought rapid conventional arms removals as well. At the request of the noncommunist successors in Eastern Europe, the Soviet Union began withdrawing troops and matériel, as one columnist quipped, almost more quickly than the United States could ask that they be removed. In a world of rapidly shifting power and mutual recognition that economic strategies would become more important in Europe than military strategies, Americans began in large numbers to question the continued need to squander funds on a continued balance of terror.

By early 1990, the official view in Washington had shifted, but not dramatically. The Secretary of Defense announced his intention to reduce the defense budget by $80 billion over a 5-year period, arguing that any deeper cuts would deprive the United States of great power status. Moreover, conjecture and early planning regarding what items would be removed from the budget focused almost exclusively on conventional weaponry, troops, and bases (including both domestic bases and those in the Philippines, should the government decline to extend the lease and status-of-forces agreements). On the grounds that the Soviet Union had not thus far reduced its own strategic forces despite major shifts of policy in Eastern Europe, the Pentagon took the view that changes in American global strategy would be premature, and announced that it would continue to maintain and strengthen the nuclear triad, particularly its submarine-launched leg. Yet despite tacit understanding that nuclear bombs would never be delivered by aircraft because of the effectiveness of modern defense systems, the Defense Department insisted that it could not give up the B-1 or the B-2 bombers.

At present, then, the Bush administration has adopted a defense policy consisting principally of reduced conventional deployment alongside global strategic readiness resting primarily on nuclear deterrence emphasizing the

---

[28]See two publications of the US Department of Defense: *Annual Report to the Congress, Fiscal Year 1984*, pp. 27–28, and *Soviet Military Power, 1983*, chap. 6, "Soviet Power Projection."

[29]Edward N. Luttwak, *The Grand Strategy of the Soviet Union* (New York: St. Martin's Press, 1983).

submarine-launched portion first, the land-based missile second, and strategic aircraft third. In this context, the balance of terror is alive and well.

The Soviet Perception

Until recently, far from accepting the role of antagonist in world politics and in the strategic arms race, the Kremlin sought to defend its island of socialism from capitalist encirclement. Bolstering their traditional fears of exposed borders, the Soviets have experienced overt attempts by Japan and the West to bring down their power. Japanese and American landings in Siberia at the close of the First World War, shortly after the Bolshevik Revolution of 1917, were historic signals of the need to maintain rigorous defense against the capitalist industrialized states. More recently, American efforts after the Second World War to influence Soviet policy in Eastern Europe through atomic monopoly accentuated the need for vigilance. NATO in particular, and the string of anti-Soviet alliances in general, added further to the need. Incorporation of West Germany into NATO in apparent violation of the Potsdam Agreement of 1945 was the ultimate sign of American intentions of maintaining anti-Soviet tension throughout Europe; the Kremlin responded by forming the Warsaw Pact. Soviet arms policy, far from being the cause of the balance of terror, was a response to the capitalist (specifically American) political and strategic threats.

The Soviet view was confounded by questions about the basic assumptions underlying both SALT I and SALT II. During these talks, each party assumed that the other would continue to build its strategy based on the second-strike philosophy; that is, that neither would build systems principally for a surprise first nuclear strike but would base its strategy, instead, on a plan of retaliation against a first strike. But late in the Carter administration and during the Reagan administration, it appeared that the nuclear utilization theorists (NUTs) had gained ascendency over the second-strike philosophers, the advocates of mutually assured destruction (MADs). Evidence is obvious in several ways: (1) the Carter and Reagan administrations' belief that nuclear war is survivable; hence the risk of second-strike retaliation against an effective first strike may be worth taking; (2) American plans to test and deploy antisatellite weapons might indicate an American intent to prevent the Soviet Union from verifying American claims of retaining the second-strike philosophy; (3) the new generation of medium-range American weapons is sufficiently swift and accurate over intermediate distances to provide an effective first strike, at least within the European theater; and (4) open discussion in the United States about deploying antimissile lasers in space constituted a break with the SALT notion of a bilateral restriction on antimissile instruments as a means of stabilizing the nuclear arms race on second-strike premises.

In the mid-1980s' Soviet perception, these evidences belied American protestations about the desire for peace through a stable arms race. In practice, these protestations were a cloak for bringing fundamental change to the arms race by using new weapons technologies to shift from the trusted second-strike basis to the suspect first-strike strategy. This, in Moscow's view, was a deliberate destabilization of the nuclear arms race for purposes of superiority and domination.

From the Soviet perspective, the START negotiations and the INF talks were complicated by fear of the destabilizing prospects of the American Star Wars strategy. Yet, in an effort to lighten the burden of military costs, Mikhail Gorbachev agreed to proceed with both despite the refusal of Presidents Reagan and Bush to discontinue space-based defense research. This calculated gamble produced a successful INF Treaty under which all intermediate-range nuclear missiles in Europe were dismantled, and the preliminary agreements on delivery system ceilings and warhead ceilings for a strategic arms reduction treaty which has yet to be concluded. Events of seismic proportions then intervened: the collapse of communist governments throughout Eastern Europe; ethnic civil wars within some of the constituent republics of the Soviet Union itself; Lithuanian and Estonian declarations of independence from Soviet control; the restructuring of Soviet government in an effort to accelerate economic reforms; complete elimination of Cold War rhetoric and reduction of speed toward Star Wars by the Bush administration; the realignment of the Warsaw Treaty Organization in the context of reunifying the two Germanys; and a new Soviet-American agreement on troop reductions in Europe. Although none of these touched directly on the nuclear forces issue, they all pointed toward a new world order in which the global nuclear balance was less the focal point of reform than at any time in more than 40 years. Peace, stability, and reform would eventually demonstrate its diminished relevance.

The Perceptions of America's Major Allies

Caught between the need for security and the desire to liberate themselves from American domination, Washington's principal allies have an ambivalent outlook on the balance of terror. Yet there are considerable differences in their attitudes, owing particularly to their geographic locations, the external imperatives that guide their foreign policies, and the coincidence of their interests with those of the United States.

Japan   Throughout the history of the nuclear arms race, Japan has played the paradoxical role of being one of the most intensely interested states but one of the least involved. Its interest results in part from having been the only country to have been victimized by atomic bombs and in part because it is located in close proximity to Korea, China, the Soviet Pacific possessions including Sakhalin Island, and Southeast Asia. The superpower dispute, the Korean War, and the Vietnam War, together with the long containment of China by the United States, all threatened the possibility of nuclear action. Japan's vulnerability resulted both from geographic location and from the use of Japanese territory as staging bases for American military activity and matériel. Yet because of its close ties to the American security system, Japan has not been a principal participant in international military politics; and because of constitutional prohibitions, it does not participate at all in the nuclear balance of terror. Despite its anxieties regarding superpower strategies in Asia, Japan has, for the most part, profited from the Soviet-American arms race and from global bipolarity.

More recently, however, the Japanese outlook has shifted. American withdrawal from the mainland of Asia after the Vietnam War, together with the uncertainties introduced to national security by the Nixon Doctrine, necessitates a larger measure of self-dependence. Furthermore, because Japan has enjoyed a commanding role in international industrial trade, the United States has insisted that it cannot continue indefinitely to provide Japan's protection. On the other hand, the Sino-American détente has enabled Japan to enter into a belated World War II peace agreement with China that was followed by a treaty of friendship and commerce, both diminishing the security concern for China and opening new economic opportunities for both imports (raw materials and fuels) and exports (industrial goods). Despite closer economic ties with the Soviet Union, the growing Soviet military presence in the Pacific imposes new security imperatives. Given all these circumstances, including the uncertain reliability of the nuclear umbrella, Japan has concluded the first serious reconsideration of the level of its defense commitment since the establishment of its postwar constitution and a security alliance with the United States. (Refer to Chapter 3 for details.)

Nonetheless, Japan is not a participant in the strategic nuclear race and is unlikely to become one. Because it is limited to conventional armed forces, it sees the strategic race as wasteful; and because it must rely on a potentially unreliable American nuclear deterrent, it regards the race as threatening in the extreme.

Western Europe   Proximity to the Warsaw Pact nations, the degree of American security and economic domination, and the progressive reestablishment of Western Europe as a vital world center all contribute to the maturation of the attitude toward the global balance of terror. Through the years following the Second World War, American responses to what Europe perceived as a Soviet military threat were a welcome instrument of stabilization, one that permitted the gradual resurgence of economic activity and the integration of Western Europe.

During the détente period of the 1970s, however, Western Europeans found themselves Cold War weary and resistant to additional increases in military spending. They were happy to have more American security support and less American economic interference. But with the resurgence of the Soviet-American Cold War in the 1980s, attitudes changed markedly, although they are still divided. In face of the Soviet deployment of SS-20 theater (intermediate-range) missiles, the Western European governments all endorsed a decision made by NATO in 1979 to deploy 572 new-generation American missiles, starting at the end of 1983. This endorsement resulted in part from the election of conservative governments in Britain and Germany, the two countries where the initial deployments were to occur; but it was also endorsed by socialist governments in France and Italy, for which subsequent missiles were destined. Throughout Europe, this decision encountered resistance from antinuclear organizations, but the governments remained resolute.

As was demonstrated in the preceding chapter, however, Western Europe has its own balance of nuclear forces. NATO, the Warsaw Pact, SS-20s, Pershing II and Cruise missiles, the Anglo-French deterrent—these are the nuclear and conventional security issues that drive the European strategic debate. ICBMs, MIRVs, nuclear triads, Star Wars, hardened silos—these comprise the global nuclear balance. In an era in which the Western European countries have turned inward, abandoned their far flung colonial holdings, and determined to unify themselves economically, their interest in the global balance has waned and the stability of the regional balance has gained singular importance. But their dilemma is this: Because NATO is a major component of American global strategy, and because alliance management is a key element in Washington's political policy, the regional balance is dominated by an external ally. Until 1989, as American attention shifts back and forth from the global to the regional, a distinction less clear in Washington than in Paris or Bonn, the consequences of unwanted Soviet-American antipathy and of the global balance of terror seeped vexingly into trans-Atlantic affairs.

Canada   In contrast with Japan and Western Europe, Canada has been relatively removed from the balance of terror. Although it participated in the Korean War and is a member of NATO, it has avoided major military commitments and has chosen instead to be a significant participant in UN peacekeeping efforts. While maintaining a small but relatively modern defense force, Canada has avoided the nuclear option and has chosen to divert funds that might normally have gone to defense into economic development.

In part, the Canadian position is a fortuitous result of proximity to the United States. Even disregarding for the moment Ottawa's efforts to maintain friendly relations with Moscow and its relatively early recognition of China, it remains true that the closeness of Canada to the United States, and particularly to its industrial heartland, has lent a strategic immunity to Canadian policy. But this proximity is a double-edged sword. For like Western Europe, Canada has felt the penetrating effects of American industries and of the technological and industrial superiority that the balance of terror has enabled American manufacturers to develop. Thus, although Canada has remained aloof from the balance of terror as an active participant, it has quietly deplored its wastefulness and with increasing vigor has resisted its domestic economic consequences. In particular, the wastefulness that the balance of terror imposes on North America's natural resources now threatens to force upon Canada a continental allocation policy, one that will further erode national sovereignty. To Canada, then, the balance of terror may have produced coincidental security, but it has also resulted in economic relations with its continental neighbor that have been injurious to national self-esteem and integrity. Thus, although intact territorially, Canada perceives itself to have been a casualty of the balance of terror through indirect and continental economic exploitation.

The Joint Chiefs of Staff taking advantage of a lull in world affairs.
Source: Drawing by Ross; © 1990, The New Yorker Magazine, Inc.

On the purely military front, however, Canadians are aware of the extent to which the balance of terror has global implications. Canadians object, for example, to the American policy of selecting a course over their territory for any missiles that might be fired at Soviet targets from the United States. Any accidental firing or faulty missile could endanger Canadian lives and property. Neither of these has occurred, but Cruise missile tests have twice taken place in Canadian airspace, offering vivid evidence that in a Soviet-American nuclear exchange, Canada could be an inadvertent victim.

Another issue arose in 1987. With the global expansion of the Soviet navy both on and beneath the sea, the Canadian government has become concerned with its ability to assert sovereignty over its Arctic waters. As an expression of this concern, Ottawa announced in early 1987 that it was contemplating the deployment of as many as 15 nuclear submarines for service in these waters. It is to be assumed that the reference is to nuclear-powered vessels carrying conventional torpedoes rather than to nuclear-powered submarines equipped with either strategic weapons or nuclear-tipped torpedoes.

The Chinese Perception

Until recently, the Century of Humiliation and the growth of power under Mao Tse-tung shaped the Chinese view of the balance of terror. Hemmed in by the

Soviet Union to the north and America and its allies to the west and south, China experienced a modern history of containment. The achievement of nuclear combat potential was the sole means by which Beijing was able to demand recognition from both Washington and Moscow. If political advantage is a product of equality in arms, China must compete to gain full political potential in the international system. In this age of military technology, the ability to field millions of combat troops is no match in global security issues for strategic capabilities.

Both domestic and international events began to erode this viewpoint. At home, the death of Mao, the conclusion of the Cultural Revolution and the implementation of a careful diplomatic and economic plan for the modernization of the state resulted in a new view of relations with both the Soviet Union and the West. The international scene, too, changed. The conclusion of the Vietnam War and the withdrawal of the United States from the Asian mainland as a military power, the Sino-American normalization, China's participation in NATO military affairs, the growing prospects of a Sino-Soviet détente—all these international events have combined with new internal perspectives to alter virtually all vital Chinese interests. The emphasis now is on economic development, industrialization, improved education, international trade and cooperation, and diplomatic leadership of the Third World. While Beijing and Moscow warily test the feasibility of their new cooperation, China's closeness to NATO makes it an informal party to a global strategy of nuclear defense against the Soviet Union.

Despite its status as a nuclear state, China feels strongly that responsibility for global arms control lies principally with the United States and the Soviet Union. At the special session of the United Nations General Assembly on disarmament in 1978, China held firmly to the view that the lesser nuclear powers are forced by the Soviet-American arms race to make an effort to keep up, hopeless though that effort might be, in order to prevent a division of the world by threat and nuclear blackmail. Yet China's own nuclear development has proceeded very slowly. Since 1980, it has conducted only five nuclear tests, all of them below ground despite the fact that China does not subscribe to the Partial Nuclear Test Ban Treaty (1963) that outlaws atmospheric testing.

It is unlikely that China's self-conscious preoccupation with domestic events after the spring uprising of 1989 will have a long-term affect on its view of the global nuclear balance. Chinese modernization benefits from diminished antagonism with both the United States and the Soviet Union, although in their effort to reestablish the moral and legal order of Marxism-Leninism-Maoism they have branded Mikhail Gorbachev a fallen socialist and in 1990 they seemed less inclined to deal with him than in 1989. Nonetheless, as tension eases along the Sino-Soviet border and as the United States drifts away from Ronald Reagan's policy of arming Taiwan over Beijing's loud objection, there are perhaps only two contingencies that might alter China's nuclear strategy and its view of the global balance of terror: (1) an explicit sense of threat from Soviet military developments in Southeast Asia or the North Pacific and (2) a serious episode of mutual nuclear threat between India and Pakistan on the Asian subcontinent.

The Third World Perception

Faced with the costly and difficult problems of modernization in a world in which the rich get richer and the poor get poorer, the Third World nations deplore the unproductive squandering of natural, human, and economic resources. The balance of terror fits especially into this vision, inasmuch as it has absorbed a trillion dollars during the past quarter century.

But it is not merely the cost of the strategic arms race that is objectionable. Added to it is the unjustifiable vigor with which the United States and the Soviet Union deny their economic capability to assist fledgling governments or even to aid old and trusted, though impoverished, friends. The Third World has been a casualty of the nuclear era in still another way. At the height of the Cold War, when both the United States and the Soviet Union sought the allegiance of newly independent nations, their aid programs were considerably larger than they are at the present time. Since then, the strategic race has stabilized, and the expensive quest for friends among the ideologically uncommitted nations has become less competitive. As a result, development assistance from the superpowers has diminished, and the two wealthiest and most powerful governments have only reluctantly participated in enlarged multinational aid programs through international institutions.

But if this be the outspoken attitude of the Third World toward the balance of terror, then contradiction abounds. In the past decade, while decrying the nuclear arms race and the reluctance of the superpowers to sponsor more rapid economic and social development in the Third World, the governments of the developing states have been importing arms at record expense. In fact, most of the regional fighting in recent years has been in the Third World, principally in Africa, the Middle East, Southeast Asia, and Central America.

Conclusion

With or without arms races, the world will continue, for as long as the nation-state remains the dominant actor, to face problems of power, competition, and potential conflict. Disparities of wealth, ideological distrust, conflicts of interests, confrontation of objectives, perceptions, and misperceptions—these and other aspects of international relations will continue to ensure that states will apply their power in pursuit of their interests and their needs. And regrettably, they will also continue to ensure that humans will expend their scientific skill and their technological achievement as much to destructive purposes as to the betterment of the human condition.

CHAPTER 11

Principal Causes of War

One of the most pressing matters in the field of international relations is the causes of war. Why are international political controversies so often violent? The pages of international history are saturated with blood, and the moralist may fairly ask why people condone in war behavior that they would not tolerate in peace. Is war an international disease of the human social system, a collective insanity, a malfunction like falling down the stairs? Is it the product of conspiratorial behavior by certain interests and groups? Or is war a rational and functional, if horrible, component of the international system? In this chapter, we shall review 15 theories of the cause of war that have emerged from the growing field of conflict and peace research.

War is one of the most carefully studied human activities, and literally tens of thousands of books and tracts have been written about it. Many universities have established research centers and teaching programs that focus on conflict and violence, and several major journals are devoted exclusively to the subject (*Journal of Conflict Resolution*, United States; *Journal of Peace Research*, Norway; *Peace Research Reviews*, Canada). Findings by conflict researchers in various disciplines are exchanged at dozens of national and international conferences annually. Peace research has by now generated many scientific findings and spawned several distinct schools of thought. The theories of the causes of war reviewed in this chapter represent some of the most important propositions and findings that have emerged.

In studying these 15 theories of the origin of war, the reader will discover that although war is typically regarded as a political phenomenon, it springs not only from political events but also from economic motives, from ethnic and racial conflict, from cultural and anthropological differences, from individual personalities, and sometimes from psychopathology. A comprehensive study of the causes of war necessarily carries one into the literatures of

Table 11–1 Fifteen theories of the cause of war.

 1. Power asymmetries
 2. Power transitions
 3. Nationalism, separatism, and irredentism
 4. International social Darwinism
 5. Communications failure owing to misperception
 6. Communications failure owing to technical irony or error
 7. Arms races and the security dilemma
 8. Internal cohesion through external conflict
 9. International conflict through internal strife
10. Relative deprivation
11. Instinctual aggression and sociobiology
12. Economic and scientific stimulation
13. The military-industrial complex
14. Population limitation
15. Conflict resolution by force

politics, economics, history, philosophy, psychiatry, social psychology, anthropology, psychology, and other pertinent fields of study. In keeping with the central concept of this book, then, this chapter seeks to present not a single comprehensive theory of the cause of war, but a comparative and comprehensive review of the several principal theories.

Scientific research on war is based on a critical assumption: There are patterns and regularities in conflict behavior that can be identified systematically. If this assumption is not true—that is, if war behavior is idiosyncratic or unique from case to case—then research of this kind is unproductive. But historians and diplomats tend to agree with conflict researchers that orderly principles *do* underlie the complexities of warlike behavior. It follows that war is a serious question for social inquiry.

This chapter discusses 15 principal causes of war, as summarized in Table 11–1. Scholars of different orientations and tastes will argue that this is far from a comprehensive list, for there is scarcely a limit to the ways in which international (or intrasocietal) violence can be categorized. Nonetheless, the list that follows is based on this definition of ''war'': an organized conflict of major armed hostilities between social groups and nations. This definition enables us to consider internationally significant civil wars as well as international wars, the distinction between which has been eroded in the last quarter-century.

1. Power Asymmetries

The condition most feared among governments as a cause of war is the power asymmetry—that is, an unfavorable tilt in the distribution of power. There is widespread conviction that whatever other impetuses to war may be present, a careful equilibration of power between antagonists will tend to prevent war, whereas a disequilibrium will invite aggression. The maintenance of international peace requires that technological and other gains on each of two sides be matched and kept relatively even. A vacuum of power, such as that created by unilateral disarmament, destabilizes international relations and encourages military ventures. Proponents of this *Realpolitik* believe that occasions and issues for conflict always exist and that the immediate cause of warfare is usually a failure to balance power symmetrically. The operating principle of this doctrine is "If peace is your goal, prepare for war." Hence, the US Air Force boasts that "peace is our profession," and the MX missile is sold to the American people with its $30 billion price tag as the Peacekeeper missile.

In conflicts in which one side seeks a major redistribution of values while the other wishes to preserve the status quo—that is, when there is a clear distinction between the offense and the defense—peace may be preserved by a certain kind of asymmetry. An advantage to the defensive party will more reliably deter aggression than will a close balance. Conversely, an overbalance in favor of the offensive party will make war more likely. Thus, in the clear offense/defense case, peace is more nearly ensured by superiority of the non-revolutionary antagonist. For example, Winston Churchill argued in his iron curtain speech at Fulton, Missouri, in March 1946, that Soviet aggression would be stopped only by Western military superiority: "The old doctrine of a balance of power is unsound. We cannot afford, if we can help it, to work on narrow margins, offering temptations to a trial of strength." However, power asymmetries are inherently dangerous and tend to produce aggressive policies even when the favored state was previously peace loving and defensive.

Asymmetries pertain not only to different levels of industrial capacity, population, and other physical elements of war potential (see the preceding four chapters), but also to the more variable and volatile political elements. Of special importance is the ability to attract and retain allies willing to pool resources for mutual security. Only two states in the modern world, the United States and the USSR, are able to act alone in most contingencies, and even for them there are many political and strategic advantages in allied action. For lesser powers, it is vitally important to cement alliances to prevent asymmetries. For example, Israel depends on the United States while Syria relies on the Soviet Union.

Another important factor is will. Even very good capabilities and solid alliances can result in asymmetries if a party declines to fight. Conversely, a state with limited resources and support may be able to prevent asymmetry by showing a resolute determination to utilize its capacities fully. To prevent power asymmetries, it is not necessary that all possible pairs of states be balanced perfectly, but only that potential aggressors know in advance that the costs of overcoming resistance will outweigh the benefits. Thus, the asymmetry of power is one cause of war that can be controlled.

2. Power Transitions

One special adaptation of the theory that power asymmetries produce international conflict is the power-transition theory of war. Its unique feature is that it concentrates not on existing asymmetries but on evolving asymmetries, upsets in the international balance produced by rapid advantageous development among states inclined to challenge the international status quo established and protected by dominant states.

This theory postulates that states are differentiated by their relative power capabilities and by their satisfaction or dissatisfaction with the prevailing international system. Thus, in addition to the dominant states (United States, Soviet Union), some are powerful and satisfied (Britain, Germany, France, Japan, Canada); others are powerful and dissatisfied (China); still others are powerless and satisfied; and others are both powerless and dissatisfied. Similar relationships exist within regional settings. In the Middle East, for example, Israel and Egypt are powerful and satisfied; Syria and Libya are powerful and dissatisfied; Jordan is relatively powerless but satisfied; and Lebanon is powerless and dissatisfied.

The power transition is characterized by sudden and significant challenges to the status quo that result from rapid internal development in power capabilities. Whether they are a result of rapid social mobilization or of sharp advances in national economic capability, the roots of the challenge are in internal national development. Should the events occur in a state satisfied with the prevailing international or regional system, they are unlikely to be disruptive. But should they occur in a state that was not a party to the establishment of the prevailing norms and prefers to replace them, the development will be viewed by the dominant states as a challenge. Conflict will result, and war may follow. By the same token, if the development occurs gradually, the prospect of accommodating it to the existing system will be brighter than if it occurs at revolutionary speed.[1]

Although the United States and the Soviet Union have not fought war directly, the Cold War is an ideal example of the power-transition theory. At the close of World War II, many of the satisfied nations (for example, Britain and France) were in ruins, and the dissatisfied nations that had attempted through global war to replace the prewar system (Germany and Japan) were occupied by the conquering powers. The United States was the sole surviving dominant nation, determined to restore the political and economic systems of the prewar international system. The Soviet Union, socialist rather than capitalist, used its postwar geographic advantage and rapid economic and thermonuclear development to challenge Washington's exclusive right to restore the system. It

---

[1]The most influential work on the power-transition theory is by A. F. K. Organski and his collaborators. See particularly A. F. K. Organski, *World Politics*, 2nd ed. (New York: Knopf, 1968), chaps. 7 and 8, and *Stages of Political Growth* (New York: Knopf, 1965); also A. F. K. Organski and Jacek Kugler, *The War Ledger* (Chicago: University of Chicago Press, 1980). See also Michael D. Wallace, *War and Rank Among Nations* (Lexington, Mass.: D.C. Heath, 1973). Wallace deals with quantitative studies of international status and status redistribution as causes of war. For an analysis that attaches the power-transition theory directly to economic cycles, see Raimo Vayrynen, "Economic Cycles, Power Transitions, Political Management and Wars Between Major Nations," *International Studies Quarterly*, December 1983, pp. 389–418. Jack S. Levy, "Declining Power and the Preventive Motivation for War," *World Politics*, October 1987, pp. 82–107, argues that a power in decline will fear the consequences of that decline and provoke war in an effort to forestall them.

was this rapid development, filled with economic, military, and geographic credibility, that led to the measures and countermeasures later labeled the Cold War.

One variant of the power-transition notion is that of the power cycle. This postulates that as a state's capability, power status, and international political role change, there are specific points at which misperceptions, miscalculations, or overreactions to international events may trigger war. The most likely point is that when the state is at its peak as a power entity, principally because of rapid economic development. The second, in an urgent need to adjust international conditions as the state begins to slip in status, is at the point when the state's decline is detectable and its prospects for resurgence are recognized internally as minimal. The third most likely point is just before reaching the peak. And the least likely point is before the state begins its assent.[2]

3. Nationalism, Separatism, and Irredentism

Nationalism is a collective group identity that passionately binds diverse individuals into a people. The nation becomes the highest affiliation and obligation of the individual, and it is in terms of the national we-group that personal identity is formed: "I am a Canadian." From Hitler's celebration of the *Volk* to de Gaulle's near-mystical belief in the French, the most powerful elements of the political spectrum seem to agree that the ethnic nation is the highest form of identity.

This curious and compelling identification with one group tends to produce conflicts with others. A 1969 research team enumerated 160 disputes having a significant likelihood of resulting in large-scale violence within 15 years. This large inventory fell broadly into the following classifications:

1. Nationalist conflicts, including disputes between ethnic, racial, religious, and linguistic identity groups perceiving themselves as peoples.
2. Class conflicts, including issues of economic exploitation.
3. Other conflicts not characterized primarily by clashes between identity groups or classes.

Significantly, nationalist and ethnic conflict accounted for about 70 percent of the cases, whereas class and other conflicts divided the balance. Indeed, nationalism appears to be a potent factor in the causal chain to war, accounting for more bloodshed than any other cause.[3]

The disputes identified in 1969 were reviewed 15 years later in 1984, revealing that serious civil strife occurred in more than 30 cases at least once, and international conflict with significant damage and death occurred in 23.[4]

---

[2]Charles F. Doran, "War and Power Dynamics," *International Studies Quarterly*, December 1983, pp. 419–441.

[3]Steven Rosen, ed., *A Survey of World Conflicts* (Pittsburgh: University of Pittsburgh Center of International Studies Preliminary Paper, March 1969).

[4]The reader is cautioned that a study of this kind is fraught with pitfalls, principally concerning

In recent years, the main link between nationalism and war has been the survival of separate identities among populations whose geographical distribution differs from the international boundary lines. Peoples who do not feel that they belong to a country tend to feel an infringement of basic human rights in a world of nation-states. Populations submerged in other peoples' countries (Lithuanians), populations divided among two or more countries (Kurds), and populations denied the control of the governments of their own countries (black South Africans) tend to rebel against these denials. But territorial and political rearrangements often cannot be achieved without armed conflict between the deprived or oppressed groups and other interests. Thus, the link between nationalism and war today operates most importantly through militant territorial and political demands organized around certain principles of ethnic, linguistic, religious, and racial we-group identities.

Although this chapter attempts to draw fine lines between the several theories of wars' cause, several of these theories actually overlap. In this section, for example, discussion focuses on nationalistic causes of war, and section 11 addresses sociobiological explanations. One theory relates these two by arguing that over long stretches of time and in view of specific environmental circumstances including threat to security, social evolution may result in ethnic cohesion oriented to conflict.[5] If true, this would explain defensive nationalism in ethnically homogeneous peoples.

Two key forms of nationalist militancy predominate in modern war. These are the separatist form and the irredentist form. In the separatist form, a nationalist group attempts to secede from an existing state to form a new one. In the irredentist form, an existing state lays claim to a territory and population group presently subsumed within another state. These forms are illustrated in Figure 11–1.

Separatism and War

Most of the world's approximately 170 nation-states incorporate substantial minority populations. Even after prolonged periods of apparent assimilation among other groups, many minorities continue to think of themselves as separate and distinct (see Table 11–2). This feeling of distinctness becomes a separatist movement when a formal demand is made for territorial secession to form a state or, short of this extreme, for a considerable measure of internal autonomy from control by the existing political order. These separatist de-

---

definition and threshold conditions. How much destruction does it take to make an insurrection or terrorism a war? Are isolated instances of severe violence individual or continuous events? Is foreign occupation tantamount to war even if death and destruction do not occur? For these and other reasons, a count of the actual "wars" that occurred in a 15-year period is necessarily general. In the review of the original predictions, civil or international war has occurred only when conflict and violence have been sustained, when death has been substantial, and when violent events have been continuous or repeated with considerable frequency.

[5] R. Paul Shaw and Yuma Wong, "Ethnic Mobilization and the Seeds of Warfare: An Evolutionary Perspective," *International Studies Quarterly*, March 1987, pp. 5–32.

Figure 11–1 (a) The separatist mode. Territory *X* secedes from State *A* to form new State *X*. (b) The irredentist model. State *B* claims Territory *X* from State *A*.

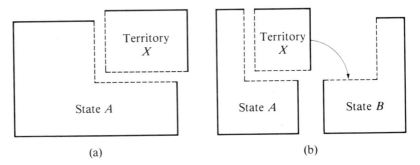

(a)   (b)

mands usually are resisted by the incumbent authorities because of the threat perceived to the state's political and territorial integrity. In this way, conflicts over separatist demands become common causes of war.

Minority movements take on added significance for the study of international relations when outside powers intervene. Often, one comes to the aid of the threatened government, while another lends its support to the restive minority. The various factions in the internal dispute become clients of outside sponsors motivated by their own interests. Foreign intervention is particularly important when a neighboring state allows its territory to be used as a sanctuary and staging area for guerrilla forays and political organization by the dissident population. This is seen by the threatened government as subversion and tends to lead to intergovernmental conflict.

Irredentism and War

Nationalist and ethnic disputes have still greater significance for international relations in their irredentist form. Virtually all the world's populated land surfaces are by now identified with the delineated territory of particular nation-states. But in many cases, the historic demarcation of boundaries (mainly through war and conquest) ignored natural lines of division between different peoples. Thus, political lines often are not congruent with ethnogeographic regions, and in many places one people straddles a border between two states. Irredentism is the struggle of such a people for reunification,[6] and the irredenta is a territory where a portion of the ethnic nation resides that is regarded as lost or stolen.

The irredentist territorial claim normally evokes resistance from the state, because its territory would be reduced in the event of a successful claim. The

---

[6]The term referred originally to the late nineteenth-century struggle of Italian patriots to redeem or reincorporate into Italy certain neighboring territories having a predominantly Italian population. As the term is used here, the impetus for reunification can come from the separated population (*irredenta*), the main body, or both.

Table 11–2 Some separatist and autonomist movements.

Recent wars of secession
1. Nigeria: struggle by Ibos for a separate Biafra; unsuccessful
2. Pakistan: secession of East Pakistan to form Bangladesh; successful
3. Sudan: black secessionists versus Arab state; unsuccessful
4. Chad: Arab secessionists versus black state; unsuccessful
5. Iraq: Kurds; unsuccessful
6. Ethiopia: Arabs of Eritrea, supported by Arab states; unsuccessful
7. Oman: Dhofar region; unsuccessful
8. Congo: Katanga; unsuccessful

Other separatist movements
1. Spain: Basques; Catalans
2. Yugoslavia: Croatians; Albanians
3. Uganda: Bugandans
4. Puerto Rico: Independista movement
5. France: Brittany; potentially Basques
6. United Kingdom: Ulster Catholics; Welsh; Scots
7. Indonesia: minorities in Moluccas, Sumatra, Celebes
8. Russia: Latvians; Estonians; Lithuanians; Ukrainians
9. Sri Lanka: Tamils
10. Switzerland: Jura
11. Canada: French of Quebec
12. China: Sinkiang; Tibet
13. Burma: Karens; Kachins; Shans; Chins; Mons; Arkanese
14. Pakistan: Baluchis
15. South Africa: Namibia (Southwest Africa)

Multiple secession movements
1. Kurds from Iraq, Iran, Turkey, and USSR
2. Bakongos from Zaïre, Congo, Cabinda, and Angola

Strained federations
1. Lebanon: Moslems versus Christians
2. Yugoslavia: Serbs, Croatians, and others
3. Guyana: Blacks, East Indians, and others
4. Ghana: northern versus coastal tribes
5. Czechoslovakia: Slav minority
6. Mauritius: Hindu, Creole, Moslem
7. Surinam: Creole, East Indian, Japanese
8. Rwanda and Burundi: Wa-Tutsi versus Bahutu
9. Belgium: Flemings and Walloons
10. India: many minorities
11. USSR: Moslem Azerbaijanis
12. India: Sikhs

challenged state often can base its own claim on historic ties and treaties regarded as legally binding. There is a fog of claims and counterclaims, and the stirring patriotic call of one side is a threat to the other. Even the most barren piece of territory is regarded as a sacred part of the national patrimony, and seldom does a border move a hundred yards in any direction without the spilling of human blood.

Resistance to irredentist claims occurs when

1. An existing state would cease to exist as an independent entity
2. One or more states would lose territory (both India and Pakistan lost territory in the establishment of Bangladesh)
3. Irredentism would reunify two halves with different political ideologies (the postwar reunification of the two Vietnams; the possible reunification of the two Koreas, and the reunification in 1990 of the two Germanies)
4. One population occupying the irredenta fears that it would be a disadvantaged minority in the case of reunification (Protestants in Northern Ireland; the Turkish population in Cyprus)

In all of these cases, some group stands to lose in the event of successful irredentism.

Issues in Separatist and Irredentist Conflicts

Economic Consequences   Although territorial issues of separatism and irredentism begin as ethnic questions, they also entail profound economic and natural resource issues. When Hitler seized the Sudetenland from Czechoslovakia in the name of 3 million Sudeten Germans, he also seized 70 percent of Czechoslovakia's iron and steel, 86 percent of its chemical, and 70 percent of its electrical generating capacity. Similarly, British support for the self-determination movement in Kuwait and Brunei is related to their oil wealth, and Belgian support for the Katanga secession attempt in the Congo was keyed to the copper deposits of that region. The secession of Biafra would have taken from Nigeria not just the Ibo people but also much of its national resource base and industrial capacity. Thus, nationalist disputes are also international economic issues.

The Moral Dilemma   Aside from economic issues, separatist and irredentist movements pose a moral dilemma for the international system. National self-determination is a cardinal value, and many concerned observers support struggling peoples seeking their own places in the sun. But the immense complexity of ethnogeography means that the world cannot possibly accommodate each splinter group with its own territory. All African states, for example, include members of tribes that straddle international borders. If each national group were given its own country, thousands of economically nonviable units would result. The 50 states of Africa, with a total population less than half that of India, are already too fragmented. When the Ibos sought secession from Nigeria, they were supported by only a few outside states (notably Tanzania, Zambia, Gabon, and Ivory Coast), despite the moral appeal of their position. Pan-Africanists hold that the real future of the continent is in regional amalgamation and federation, not further "Balkanization." In addition, wholesale border revisions probably could not be achieved without an unacceptable amount of conflict and warfare among interested states.

Colonial Boundaries   Many frustrated minorities blame their problems on past imperialism. Borders violate ethnic lines primarily because they reflect the points at which advancing armies stopped or deals between big powers were reached. They rarely reflect natural lines of human settlement. In many less developed regions, precolonial societies simply did not have officially drawn boundaries. When the Europeans came, they drew lines that seemed administratively, economically, and politically convenient in Paris, London, Lisbon, and Brussels but that often ignored tribal and ethnic lines. Unified peoples were splintered, and incompatible tribes and groups were often lumped together. This was not just chance but a calculated policy of divide and conquer. Many peoples have permanent problems as a consequence of past colonialism.

Unresolved and unresolvable irredentist and separatist issues are threats to the territorial interest of many nations (see Table 11–3). Nationalist conflicts may be latent and seemingly forgotten for prolonged periods, suddenly to emerge with renewed vigor as group identity reawakens. Recollections of lost territory tend to simmer beneath the political surface, and it is a simple matter for a jingoist leader or a demagogue to stir them up and ride to power on a nationalist tide. A latent irredentist or separatist feeling is a potent chemical reaction waiting for the right catalyst and is always, therefore, a potential cause of war.

Soviet General Secretary Mikhail Gorbachev's *perestroika*, or restructuring, has awakened nationalistic identities among non-Russian peoples incorporated in the Soviet Union after the Bolshevik Revolution of 1917. Sporadic episodes of Armenian nationalism have been relatively frequent since the death of Josef Stalin over 30 years ago, but more recently expressions of nationalism have arisen among Azerbaijanis and Usbekistanis, and from the Maldavian people annexed from Romania. All have demanded varied forms of political and linguistic independence. Moreover, the Baltic states annexed to the Soviet Union in 1939—Estonia, Lithuania, and Latvia—have used the occasion of *perestroika* and Gorbachev-supported liberalization in Poland, Hungary, and East Germany to express continuing discontent with Soviet control. Latvia has gone so far as to enact legislation requiring ethnic Russians to fulfill a residency requirement of several years before being eligible to vote. Unlike the official toleration of the growth of noncommunist power in Eastern Europe, the Kremlin has reacted to the Baltic peoples with implicit threats against what is termed "the virus of nationalism." Nonetheless, the growing volume of discontent among peoples in the many internal ethnic republics of the Soviet Union has led scholars and journalists around the world to focus on the Soviet Union's "nationalities problem."

Table 11–3 Some irredentist movements.

Claims to whole states
1. Tibet was reincorporated by China.
2. Togo has been claimed by Ghana on grounds of Ewe reunification.
3. Mauritania is regarded by some as part of Morocco.
4. French Somaliland (now Afar-Issa or Djibouti) has been claimed by Somalia.
5. Israel is regarded by Arab nationalists as a land stolen from the Arab nation.
6. Kuwait has been claimed by Iraq.
7. Gambia was carved artificially out of Senegal by the colonial power.
8. Cyprus is regarded as part of Greece by Greek Cypriots.
9. Taiwan is claimed as part of China.
10. Goa is claimed as part of China.
11. Armenia was incorporated into the Soviet Union.
12. Estonia, Lithuania and Latvia were annexed by the Soviet Union.

Divided states with different political orientations
1. North and South Korea
2. East and West Germany (now resolved)
3. The two Yemens
4. The two Vietnams (now resolved)

Claims to parts of states
1. United Kingdom is threatened by IRA demands that Northern Ireland (Ulster) be reunited with Ireland.
2. Algeria is threatened by Moroccan claims in Spanish Sahara, rich in phosphates, and Tindouf, rich in oil.
3. India is threatened by Pakistan's claim to Kashmir.
4. Kenya is threatened by Somali nationalist claims to the Northern Frontier District.
5. Guyana faces territorial claims by Venezuela and Surinam.
6. Italy has negotiated territorial claims by Austria and Yugoslavia.
7. China has extensive claims against the Soviet Union, Mongolia, and other states.
8. Malaysia has resisted Indonesian and Philippine claims to Sabah.
9. Germany, under Hitler, laid claim to regions of Czechoslovakia, Poland, and Austria on grounds of Aryan reunification.

4. International Social Darwinism

International social Darwinism is the belief that societies, like biological species, evolve and advance through competition, resulting in the survival of the fittest and the elimination of the weak. The social Darwinist sees the war of each against all as a cruel necessity for the progressive advancement of civilization. International relations is, in this perspective, the arena of combat between whole peoples where the global destiny of humanity is determined. The role of war is to pass the reins of power from the weak and decaying to the strong and dynamic.

Quebec's campaign for independence from Canada is one close-to-home example of the many nationalist and separatist movements that exist around the globe.

Source: Jean-Pierre Laffont / Sygma

In recent years, this philosophy has most often been associated with fascism. In advancing war as a positive aspect of fascism, Benito Mussolini declared: "Fascism sees in the imperialistic spirit—that is, in the tendency of nations to expand—a manifestation of their vitality. In the opposite tendency, which would limit their interests to the home country, it sees a symptom of decadence."[7] Moreover, "fascism above all does not believe either in the possibility or the utility of universal peace. It therefore rejects the pacifism which masks surrender and cowardice." And "war alone brings all human energies to their highest tension and sets a seal of nobility upon the peoples who have the virtue to face it."[8]

Carried to its logical conclusion in Nazism, the fascist philosophy views societies as biological entities united by blood ties. Two principles link Nazism with war: the principle of race and the principle of territory. Nazism, according to Adolf Hitler, "by no means believes in equality of the races, but along with their difference it recognizes their higher or lesser value. . . . Thus, in principle, it serves the basic aristocratic ideas of Nature." Moreover, because population expands but living space (*Lebensraum*) is limited, races must

---

[7]Quoted in S. William Halperin, *Mussolini and Italian Fascism* (Princeton, N.J.: Van Nostrand, 1964), p. 152.

[8]Benito Mussolini, quoted in Reo M. Christensen et al., *Ideologies and Modern Politics* (New York: Dodd, Mead, 1971), p. 70.

compete for territory. "Nature knows no political boundaries. First she puts living creatures on this globe and watches the free play of forces. She then confers the master's right on her favorite child, the strongest." The higher races must not agree "in their pacifistic blindness to renounce new acquisitions of soil," or they will leave mastery of the world to "the culturally inferior but more brutal and more natural peoples." Hitler was deeply suspicious of international law and diplomacy—"a cozy mutual swindling match"—and frankly set out "to promote the victory of the better and stronger, and demand the subordination of the inferior and weaker in accordance with the eternal will that dominates this universe."[9]

As these passages suggest, international social Darwinism glorifies conflict and focuses on incompatibilities among groups. It offers an appealing and simplistic account of history, providing a perfect rationalization for aggression. And, of course, it raises many questions for social theory.

Is race the basic human unit or only a biological accident that is promoted and distorted by corrupt politics? Is competition the basic law of nature, or are the most important human achievements attained mainly by cooperation and mutual effort? Do nations in fact face a shortage of living space, or are the most densely populated nations (for example, Japan) often the most prosperous? (It is interesting to note here that of the estimated 25 million square miles of arable land in the world, only about one-sixth is under cultivation.) Are people pressing outward from overcrowded population centers, or is the trend toward urbanization and concentration increasing while rural population is declining? Is the creative height of civilization reached in war or in peace?

Whatever the answers to these questions may be, and despite the fact that Nazism is now nearly dead, the philosophy of international social Darwinism is alive and well. Its sharpest critics are the Marxist-Leninist theorists who build their theory on dialectical materialism and believe that all war is a social phenomenon rooted in class differentiation across national boundaries. So to them, international social Darwinism is one of many attempts on the part of bourgeois theoreticians to substitute biological, psychological, and other factors for the social-class basis of war.[10]

5. Communications Failure Owing to Misperception

Another cause of war treated extensively in the conflict literature is the theory of communications failure. As we have found, national leaders and national peoples perceive one another through ideological lenses and with stereotypical images, with the result that their communication, whether formal or informal, may be distorted.[11] Several attempts have been made to identify and even to

---

[9]Adolf Hitler, *Mein Kampf* (Boston: Houghton Mifflin, 1943), pp. 134–157.

[10]For a collection of papers by Soviet authors, see *Problems of War and Peace: A Critical Analysis of Bourgeois Theories* (Moscow: Progress Publishers, 1972), trans. Bryan Bean, particularly part II, "The Origins and Essence of War."

[11]See, for example, H. C. J. Duijker and N. H. Frijda, *National Character and National Stereo-*

quantify the specific forms of misperception that interfere with communication. Among those that have attracted the most interest are a diabolical image of the adversary, a virile self-image, a moral self-image, a selective inattention to critical events and signals, an absence of empathy for the opposing party's problem(s), military overconfidence, a leader's self-perception, a leader's perception of his or her counterpart's character, perception of the adversary's intentions, perception of the adversary's power and capabilities, military overestimation, and military underestimation.[12]

The perceptual distortions that result from these phenomena result in the selective reception of messages and signals and in the mutual misperception of intentions.[13] For example, potentially threatening messages from another government may be more salient or perceptually prominent than are cooperative or concilatory statements. Listeners hear what they expect to hear, as in the theory of cognitive dissonance. The images that nations have of one another not only fail to match the realities they are supposed to represent, but these images are also highly resistant to change—even when evidence and experience contradict fixed expectations. (See Chapter 6 for a more detailed treatment of this process.) Communications failure and exaggerated fear contribute to escalatory processes by multiplying the consequences of international tensions.

As the speed and precision of modern weapons have increased the need for improved communications, so too should the communications revolution have assisted government leaders throughout the world in communicating their intentions better. There is no shortage of technical devices for these purposes: hotline telephone connections between the White House and the Kremlin, communications satellites that transmit information around the world in seconds, computers that communicate with one another over great distances, and so on. The difficulty, of course, is that as technical aids have become more sophisticated, leaders have become more, rather than less, wary of the spoken intentions of one another. Furthermore, international communications tend to be public statements secluded in political messages. It is not uncommon, for example, for the president of the United States to deliver a message to the Soviet communist party chief in a State of the Union speech, but in a politically popular way that risks distorting the message to the Kremlin.

Although the technical aspects of international communication have become modernized, the strategic aspects have become more complicated. This is particularly true in regard to the language of escalation. Only in its final stages

---

types (Amsterdam: North Holland, 1960); and O. Klineberg, *Tensions Affecting International Understanding* (New York: Social Science Research Council, 1950), Bulletin 62.

[12]For a review of the literature and extensive reference to original sources, see Jack S. Levy, "Misperception and the Causes of War," *World Politics*, October 1983, p. 76.

[13]See Anatol Rapoport, "Perceiving the Cold War," in Robert Fisher, ed., *International Conflict and Behavioral Science* (New York: Basic Books, 1964); also Kenneth Boulding, *The Image* (Ann Arbor: University of Michigan Press, 1956); and Karl W. Deutsch and Richard L. Merritt, "Effects of Events on National and International Images," in Herbert Kelman, ed., *International Political Behavior* (New York: Holt, Rinehart and Winston, 1965).

does the escalation of international events involve such things as deploying troops, making decisions regarding tactical nuclear weapons, or mobilizing alliances. The earlier, equally critical phases are largely verbal and symbolic. Often their form, designed as much for domestic political consumption as for international communication, may make de-escalation all but impossible. Threats, deliberate distortion of images, propaganda, public rejection of settlement proposals, legislative condemnation, domestic mobilization, economic restructuring, and political positioning among the loyal opposition—these and hundreds of other events, all of which carry messages of intractability to the adversary, precede actual preparation for combat. As patriotism begins to run high in public opinion polls, the difficulty increases of conducting more informative and accurate communications through diplomatic channels. Governments may simply lose the ability to communicate effectively to the adversary or to place strategic trust in the messages that are being received from abroad.[14] Instead they head straight at each other as if they were two drivers playing Chicken, each determined to force the other off the road by sheer resolve of purpose. But unlike the two drivers, neither can remove its steering wheel and throw it onto the highway to signal its inability to change courses. Lacking a last-minute communications display, the two collide in combat.

6. Communications Failure Owing to Technical Irony or Error

Not all communications failures in international politics result from the psychological aspects of human interaction. Many result from the contradictory purposes to which communications technologies are put, and still others are caused by human error or misjudgment or technical failure at a crucial time.

There is a great irony in the contemporary communications revolution with respect to international relations: Rather than improving communications between adversary governments, the revolution has been used to introduce precision warfare, to transform global powers into planetary powers by giving them military strength without occupation in distant lands, and to introduce new methods of concealing one's own strengths while improving the ability to detect another's. Together with sensing devices and computers, communications advances have produced a "transparency revolution" in which the competition for arms superiority is between the visible and the hidden. Thus, rather than enhance international communication for peace, the revolution has brought strategic competition to an unstable and dangerous condition. Whether or not the next generation of advances will emphasize mutual detection and verification rather than further competition in invisibility remains to be seen.[15]

---

[14]For a general treatment of escalation and its role in political communications, see Herman Kahn, *On Escalation* (New York: Praeger, 1965).

[15]For a systematic review of communications in world politics, see Andrew M. Scott, *The Functioning of the International Political System* (New York: Macmillan, 1967), pp. 68–70. For a pioneering discussion of the transparency revolution and its impact on international communications, see Daniel Deudney, *Whole Earth Security: A Geopolitics of Peace*, Worldwatch Paper 55 (Washington, D.C.: Worldwatch Institute, 1983), particularly pp. 20–32.

Unquestionably the most tragic example of failed communications in recent international relations was the Soviet destruction of a civilian Korean airliner over the Sea of Japan in September 1983. Apart from unanswered questions of why the plane was off course and over Soviet territory, the inability of the United States, the Soviet Union, and Japan (all of whom were monitoring conversations between the Soviet pilot and his command base) to avoid tragedy astonished the world. The Soviet Union claimed that because the plane had previously intersected paths with an American intelligence craft, they were unable to determine whether the intruding plane was the American spy craft or the civilian liner. (Later they claimed that they knew it was the Korean plane but that they had evidence it was conducting a spy mission over Sakhalin Island under the cover of civilian aviation.)

Whatever may have been the real Soviet motive in firing an air-to-air missile, however, we know that several communications opportunities were missed.

1. The plane was nearly out of Soviet air space when fired upon and had thus been followed for sufficient time to have enabled either Japanese or American officials to intervene by communication with the Soviet Union or for Soviet officials to have made international inquiries about the known locations of civilian craft in the vicinity of Sakhalin.
2. Translation difficulties between Japanese intelligence and the National Security Agency of the United States delayed a real understanding of the pending crisis longer than tolerable under the speed-of-sound flight of the Soviet intercepters.
3. There is no evidence that the Korean pilot was contacted by accepted international signals with the message that he was off course and in forbidden air space.
4. There is speculation, although no hard evidence, that the plane was off course precisely because of an error in operating a navigational computer or because of an electronic failure within the computer.
5. The communications hotline between the White House and the Kremlin was never activated.

All these failures of communication, and failures to use to best advantage the most sophisticated communications electronics ever known, demonstrate the precarious condition of international relations when military or intelligence events occur at speeds greater than the speed of the human link in a communications chain. In this case, inefficient use of intelligence data resulted from (1) the onset of the new Cold War, (2) the unexplained location of the Korean flight, (3) the earlier intersection of the civilian craft with an intelligence plane, (4) the Soviet eagerness to make a fire or no-fire decision before the plane left Soviet air space and entered international air space, and (5) delays caused by slowness in translating Soviet air-to-ground communications first into Japanese and then into English. Despite the speed-of-light communications capability among the three parties, it was actually the speed-of-sound chase 7 miles above ground that determined that 269 persons would die as targets of a Soviet missile. In August 1986 it was announced that a telephone hotline connecting Tokyo, Moscow, and Washington had been established in the hope of averting another such disaster in this strategically sensitive part of the world where private and military interests so often intersect.

7. Arms Races and the Security Dilemma

Another theory of the outbreak of war links it to runaway arms races that become strategically unstable and politically uncontrolled. Here, hostile nations lock into a cycle of mutual fear (a process called hostility reaction formation), in which each side believes itself to be threatened by the other. The defensive preparations of one are taken as evidence of offensive intentions by the other, who then arms in response. Each seeks a margin of superiority, leading to qualitative and quantitative competition in armaments and organized forces. This contest results in the security dilemma: Although one or both sides in a bilateral conflict may wish to have peace, the means by which they seek to secure it tend to destabilize the environment and reduce the prospects for peace. Another version of this argument says that arms competition up to some indefinite point may contribute to stability but that an incremental buildup beyond that point both diminishes the stability and contributes to the international environment in such a way that security is inversely related to incremental cost. In either instance, the basic concept of the security dilemma has generated several new mathematical approaches to the study of military power and war that conclude that arms actually contribute to insecurity.[16]

Many people on the liberal end of the American political spectrum argue that excessive military preparations and armaments accumulation are a cause of war. On the other side, conservatives tend to favor the adage *Si vis pacem, para bellum* ("If you want peace, prepare for war"). Do armaments cause wars or prevent them? Norman Cousins once invented a completely imaginary computer study of all the arms races in history to determine whether arms races were a cause of war or a guarantee of peace. He found that since 650 B.C., there had been 1956 arms races, of which only 16 did not end in war, and that most of the exceptional cases ended in economic collapse.[17]

More authentic studies have been much more equivocal and ambiguous in their findings. One well-known study found that arms races may be either a prelude to war or a substitute for it, depending on other conditions.[18] Even if a significant correlation were discovered between arms races and the outbreak of war, it could not be inferred that the former caused the latter. It is plausible that profound political disputes cause both arms races and wars, and so correlation in this case would not prove causation. *A* might correlate with *B* because both are caused by *C*.

The role of arms races in international conflict is closely linked to the issue of power symmetries or asymmetries. If an arms race has a stabilizing effect

---

[16]One of the earliest was Lewis Richardson, *Arms and Insecurity* (Pittsburgh: Boxwood, 1960). For more recent expressions, see Bruce Bueno de Mesquita, *The War Trap* (New Haven, Conn.: Yale University Press, 1981); and Stephen J. Majeski, "Expectations and Arms Races," *American Journal of Political Science*, May 1985, pp. 217–245.

[17]See Norman Cousins, *In Place of Folly* (New York: Harper & Row, 1961); also, Brownlee Hayden, *The Great Statistics of War Hoax* (Santa Monica, Calif.: Rand Corporation, 1962).

[18]Samuel P. Huntington, "Arms Races: Prerequisites and Results," in Robert J. Art and Kenneth N. Waltz, eds., *The Use of Force* (Boston: Little, Brown, 1971), pp. 365–401.

"There goes the 'peace dividend.'"
Source: Drawing by Ed Fisher; © 1990, The New Yorker Magazine, Inc.

because it results more in symmetry than in asymmetry, then it is not likely to be an immediate cause of war. If, on the other hand, the race tends toward asymmetry because of superior acceleration on one side, then war-related temptations may be irresistible. Hence, it is not mere existence of the race that influences the outcome, but its comparative characteristics.

For nearly four decades, the Soviet-American strategic arms race has tended toward stability, with neither side tempted to use a first strike of nuclear weapons. But a simple faith in the fact that thus far the race has been stable cannot form a logical basis for believing that further escalation of the competition will add to its security and stability. The difficult problem for analysts and diplomats alike is that the actual strategic and political conditions under which stability deteriorates dangerously are unknown. It is probable that the numbers of weapons on the respective sides are a less important indicator of stability than they once were, despite the sometimes simple arithmetic of arms reduction talks. Accuracy, penetrability and preservation of second-strike capability all seem to be more crucial to determining stability. As a result, it is the weapons systems that introduce new capabilities, rather than those that add to familiar capabilities, that seem the most threatening to stability. It is for this reason that the American goal of deploying electronically controlled defensive weapons in space so markedly raised the stakes in the Soviet-American discussions for a brief time in the 1980s.

It is not exclusively in Soviet-American relations, however, that these destabilizations may have consequences. In the many regional arms races to which Washington and the Kremlin contribute—from the Arab-Israeli arena to the two Koreas and the upheaved nations of Central America—the unbalanced introduction of new weapons systems could have revolutionary consequences. This underscores the conclusion that arms races alone do not determine outcomes; it is the stabilizing or destabilizing characteristics of those races that are the critical factors.

Arms races, like communication failures, are seldom the root cause of conflict. The decision to maintain extremely high military expenditures most often reflects a prior condition of discord and conflict with an opponent. Arms races and exaggerated fears may inflame an existing conflict but seldom create one that does not otherwise exist. The distinction should be underscored, however, between arms races as causes of conflict and arms races as causes of armed conflict (war). Arms, after all, expand the alternatives for dealing with conflict as a result of either rational or irrational decision making. In particular, perceptions of armed strength between adversaries may result in preventive war (armed conflict to prevent another party from expanding its decisional alternatives or its armed might) or preemptive war (armed aggression undertaken in anticipation of aggression from the other party and launched in order to beat that party to it).

8. Internal Cohesion Through External Conflict

Another theory sees war as the product of policies designed to promote internal group cohesion through the unifying effects of outside conflict—the process of drawing together to face a common enemy. Bismarck's calculated provocation of three external wars from 1866 to 1871 to integrate the German states is the classic example of wars fought purposely. Secretary of State William Henry Seward's fruitless proposal to President Abraham Lincoln that the United States precipitate international warfare to reunite the nation and to avoid civil war exemplifies the same tactic. There exists an extensive literature that demonstrates the relationship of external conflict to internal cohesion at all levels of social interaction.[19] In international relations, the implication of

[19]Anthony de Reuck and Julie Knight, *Conflict in Society* (Boston: Little, Brown, 1966), p. 32; D. Kahn-Freund, "Intergroup Conflicts and Their Settlement," *British Journal of Sociology*, vol. 5, 1954, p. 201; Georg Simmel, *Conflict and the Web of Group Affiliations* (Glencoe, Ill.: Free Press, 1955); Lewis Coser, *The Functions of Social Conflict* (Glencoe, Ill.: Free Press, 1957), pp.

this theory is that resort to international warfare may be preferable to internal dissolution.

Despite the apparent weight of this theory, however, most scientific studies conclude quite differently. If internal conflict tended to be externalized in foreign wars, it is hypothesized that there should be a statistical relationship between the frequency of internal and external conflict. But in the most careful quantitative research, no clear and consistent relationship has been found,[20] although one study demonstrated a slight relationship.[21]

9. International Conflict Through Internal Strife

In contrast with the preceding theory of the cause of war, one may observe that in the twentieth century many international military encounters have resulted from domestic dissolution. To a very large extent, in fact, the distinction between civil and international war has been blurred, particularly as a result of frequent external intervention. Although the superpowers manage by a symmetrical arms race to avoid direct military conflict, civil wars around the world result in international conflict.

Illustrations abound. At the close of World War I, when Russia was destabilized by the Bolshevik Revolution and the civil war that followed, American troops landed in Russia to assist the White Russian army in defeating the Bolsheviks and returning the government to non-Marxist-Leninist elements more sympathetic to the West and to capitalism. The Vietnam War, fought almost continuously from 1950 to 1973, involved first French (supplied in large measure by the United States as part of the Asian anticommunist strategy that led to American intervention in Korea) and, later, American intervention. In 1984, the United States intervened indirectly in Nicaragua to bring down the Cuban-oriented leftist Sandinista government there and in El Salvador to protect the pro-American government from falling to leftist insurrectionists. In each of these civil wars, direct American or Cuban intervention was possible at any time.

Governments often claim that they are forced to intervene militarily in their client states because of destabilization caused by adversaries. The Soviet

---

104–106, 92–93. For a thorough review and synthesis of the literature up to about 1959, see Robert North, Howard Koch, Jr., and Dina Zinnes, "The Integrative Functions of Conflict," *Journal of Conflict Resolution*, vol. 3, September 1960, pp. 355–374.

[20]Rudolph Rummel, "Testing Some Possible Predictors of Conflict Behavior Within and Between Nations," *Peace Research Society (International) Papers*, vol. 3, 1963, p. 17; Rudolph Rummel, "The Relationship Between National Attributes and Foreign Conflict Behavior," in J. David Singer, ed., *Quantitative International Politics* (New York: Free Press, 1968); Michael Haas, "Social Change and National Aggressiveness: 1900–1960," in Singer, p. 213; Raymond Tanter, "Dimensions of Conflict Behavior Within and Between Nations, 1958–1960," *Journal of Conflict Resolution*, vol. 10, no. 1, March 1966, p. 46; and Samuel P. Huntington, "Patterns of Violence in World Politics," in Huntington, ed., *Changing Patterns of Military Politics* (New York: Free Press, 1962), pp. 40–41.

[21]Jonathan Wilkenfeld, "Domestic and Foreign Conflict Behavior of Nations," *Journal of Peace Research*, vol. 1, 1968, pp. 55–59.

Union, for example, justified its interventions in Czechoslovakia (1968) and Poland (1981, with martial law rather than invasion), in part on the allegation that the United States and its NATO allies had, through propaganda and economic relations, created domestic instability that threatened the solidarity of the socialist commonwealth. In the case of Czechoslovakia, intervention resulted in the Brezhnev Doctrine, which proclaimed that the Warsaw Pact would not permit any political or economic change in an individual Eastern European state that would threaten the cohesion of the alliance. This does not differ greatly from the Theodore Roosevelt Corollary to the Monroe Doctrine that dominated inter-American relations from 1907 to 1932. Roosevelt's corollary attempted to stabilize South America, Central America, and the Caribbean under American influence by simply declaring Washington's willingness to use force if necessary to prevent the further establishment of European influence in the hemisphere. This led to American interventions in Venezuela, Colombia, and Mexico, to name only a few major examples.

Many twentieth-century interventions have resulted from revolt against imperialism and colonialism. Not only is this a major theme of Marxist international relations theory, but it also is observable in a number of concrete instances. The Boer War, for example (1898–1900), was a British imperial action designed to consolidate its rule in South Africa, which was mineral rich and strategically important to British shipping lanes from the south Atlantic to the Indian Ocean. At the same time, as China was being divided into sectors for Western and Japanese economic dominance, military occupations and forceful defeat of local opposition became common.

It has been argued that foreign intervention occurs when domestic strife threatens to establish governments hostile to the economic aspirations of specific external countries. For example, it has been claimed that the motive for American intervention in Vietnam was not simply ideological or geopolitical but economic and neoimperialist as well. This thesis claims that by 1960 the United States had determined to protect from Soviet-oriented or Chinese-oriented influence all Third World territories that have significant deposits of minerals and other raw materials critical to America's economic dominance in an era when history moved from the industrial age to the technological age.

The preceding examples vary in kind, but they all illustrate that external intervention in the domestic strife of nations, particularly economically less developed ones, has become so common and frequent, for a variety of reasons, as to have eliminated the distinction between civil and international war in current history. Although the thesis that external war results in part from an effort to preserve domestic cohesion is precarious, the idea that civil strife often results in international war has been abundantly demonstrated.

10. Relative Deprivation

The concept of relative deprivation is especially useful in describing the origins of internal wars. It maintains that political rebellion and insurrection are most likely when people believe that they are receiving less than their due. To

Figure 11–2 Level of economic development: The aspiration gap and rebellion potential (shaded).

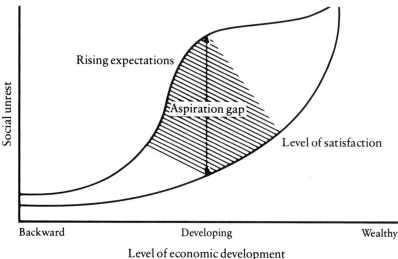

achieve greater benefits or to relieve the frustration of denial, groups may turn to aggression and political violence.[22]

This differs from simple common sense in one important respect: The objective or absolute conditions of poverty and oppression do not lead directly to rebellion, but rather, the subjective or psychological response to these conditions is determinant. To illustrate, studies of rebellion and revolution find that violence most often occurs when conditions are beginning to improve rather than when they are at their worst point. The beginnings of improvement after a long period of deprivation trigger a revolution of rising expectations. Hopes rise more rapidly than realities do, and an aspiration gap results, as shown in Figure 11–2. Careful statistical studies have found that violence has tended to increase during the transitional period from traditional to modern society, as predicted by the theory of relative deprivation. The shaded portion in the figure shows the general relationship between violence and level of economic development.

Since 1945, civil wars have been more frequent in the developing world than in already developed states. Although there were more than 85 wars of varying magnitude in the Third World between 1945 and 1984, some quite substantial, the developed countries experienced only sporadic incidents of

---

[22]See especially Ted Gurr, *Why Men Rebel* (Princeton, N.J.: Princeton University Press, 1970). Also Crane Brinton, *The Anatomy of Revolution* (New York: Vintage, 1965); James Davies, "Toward a Theory of Revolution," *American Sociological Review*, vol. 27, no. 1, February 1962; Peter A. Lupsha, "Explanation of Political Violence: Some Psychological Theories Versus Indignation," *Politics and Society*, vol. 2, no. 1, Fall 1971; John Dollard, Leonard Doob, and Neal E. Miller, *Frustration and Aggression* (New Haven, Conn.: Yale University Press, 1939); and Ivo Frierabend and Rosalind Frierabend, "Aggressive Behavior Within Politics, 1948–62," *Journal of Conflict Resolution*, vol. 10, no. 3, September 1966, pp. 249–271.

riot-scale violence on their own territories. In Korea, Vietnam, Nigeria, Bangladesh, Indonesia, Colombia, Algeria, Kampuchea, Laos, Zaïre, Angola, Mozambique, Guinea-Bissau, Chad, Sri Lanka, Lebanon, Nicaragua, El Salvador, Uganda, China, Sudan, Yemen, Iran, Iraq, and India, the dead numbered in the tens and hundreds of thousands and even in the millions. But in the highly publicized violent events in the developed countries, the dead have numbered only in the tens of hundreds: in the United States (the black revolution), Northern Ireland, French Canada, Belgium, Portugal, and Czechoslovakia. To explain this disparity between rates of violence in developed and less-developed countries, the theory of relative deprivation and the aspiration gap is attractive.[23]

However, several objections arise. Rich countries have engaged in many hostile confrontations outside their own borders, usually in the territory of dependent Third World client states. This displacement of violence to the developing countries may be a privilege conferred by the unequal distribution of influence in the international system. Also, Marxist critics have argued that there is an essential unity in the global revolutionary movement and that even revolutions in remote parts of the world are challenges to the worldwide system of imperialism. Today's struggles occur in the periphery rather than in the center because of the imperialists' relatively weaker hold in outlying regions. The overbalance of violence in the developing nations is, in the Marxist view, a transient historical phenomenon from which causal inferences cannot be drawn too hastily.

Another objection to this theory of political violence concerns the separation of physical bloodshed from other forms of abuse. The isolation of violence as the dependent variable in many studies ignores the fact that physical conflict exists on a continuum with other forms of harm, such as systematic oppression, imprisonment, and political denial. Such institutional violence can be quite as painful as physical abuse is, and it can continue over much longer periods of time. Singling out rebellious violence alone as a social disease ignores the everyday suffering of millions of people and may result in false theories and vacuous remedies.

---

[23]One of the overlooked facts of contemporary life is that many governments have increased expenditures for the use of force against internal upheaval much more dramatically than they have for international stability or war. From 1966 to 1975, for example, police expenditures in Africa rose by 144 percent, while appropriations for armies arose 40 percent. See Morris Janowitz, *Military Institutions and Coercion in the Developing Nations* (Chicago: University of Chicago Press, 1977). For a study of "macroparasitism" since 1000 A.D., see William H. McNeill, *The Pursuit of Power* (Chicago: University of Chicago Press, 1977). This is a study of the interaction of technology, armed force, and society, in which macroparasites are defined as "other men who, by specializing in violence, are able to secure a living without themselves producing the food and other commodities they consume. Hence a study of macroparasitism among human populations turns into a study of the organization of armed force with special attention to changes in kinds of equipment warriors used" (p. vii). For an empirical debate on whether lack of freedom—as contrasted to lack of material goods, food, or welfare—causes wars, see R. J. Rummel, "Libertarianism and International Violence," *Journal of Conflict Resolution*, March 1983, pp. 27–71, which draws an affirmative conclusion; and Jack Vincent, "Freedom and International Conflict: Another Look," *International Studies Quarterly*, March 1987, pp. 103–127, for negative findings.

11. Instinctual Aggression and Sociobiology

One of the most popular theories of war among laypersons is the idea of an instinct of aggression—the blood lust that is depicted in so many lurid movies and magazines. In the aggression theory, the root of war is seen as a vestigial instinct of pugnacity or bellicosity that has survived from our animal roots. Many observers have concluded that people like to fight and that at least in part, international conflict has its basis in male competitiveness *(machismo)* and even direct sadism. The outbreak of war is thus traced to biological proclivities and to individual and collective psychopathology.[24]

It is quite evident that people enjoy violence; otherwise television and the movies would not be so full of it. But there is much controversy concerning the relationship between aggressive impulses and the decision to go to war. One major study of 25 wars found that the decision to go to war was "in no case . . . precipitated by emotional tensions, sentimentality, crowd behavior, or other irrational motivations."[25] As organizations become more bureaucratic, controls are put on personal impulsiveness and deviance; studies have found that decisions made by groups are more likely to approximate rational choice than are decisions made in similar situations by individuals.[26]

On the other side, several theorists view aggression as a dominant impulse triggered by political disputes that provide the necessary rationalization for violence. As Albert Einstein said, "Man has within him a lust for hatred and destruction. . . . It is a comparatively easy task to call this into play and raise it to the level of a collective psychosis."[27] Bertrand Russell claimed: "War is accepted by men . . . with a readiness, an acquiescence in untrue and inadequate reasons."[28] Naturally, this opinion is more convincing to those who reject the official rationale but must account for the persistence of their opponents in adhering to it.

---

[24]William McDougall, "The Instinct of Pugnacity," in Leon Bramson and George Goethals, eds., *War: Studies from Psychology, Sociology and Anthropology* (New York: Basic Books, 1964), pp. 33–44; Edward Glover, *War, Sadism, and Pacifism* (London: Allen and Unwin, 1933); Elton McNeil: "Psychology and Aggression," *Journal of Conflict Resolution*, vol. 3, no. 3, September 1959, pp. 195–293; "Personal Hostility and International Aggression," *Journal of Conflict Resolution*, vol. 5, no. 3, September 1961, pp. 279–290; "The Nature of Aggression," in Elton McNeil, ed., *The Nature of Human Conflict* (Englewood Cliffs, N.J.: Prentice-Hall, 1965), pp. 14–44.

[25]Theodore Abel, "The Element of Decision in the Pattern of War," *American Sociological Review*, vol. 6, 1941, p. 855.

[26]See O. G. Brim, ed., *Personality and Decision Processes* (Stanford, Calif.: Stanford University Press, 1962). For an important view on the other side, see Harold Lasswell, *Psychopathology and Politics*, 2nd ed. (New York: Viking, 1960). Lasswell found a tendency for psychopathological individuals to go into public life out of proportion to their numbers in a group, displacing and rationalizing private disturbances in terms of the "public interest." For a review of literature on this question, see Brent Rutherford, "Psychopathology, Decision-Making, and Political Involvement," *Journal of Conflict Resolution*, vol. 10, no. 4, December 1966, pp. 387–407.

[27]From a letter to Sigmund Freud in James Strachey, ed., *The Standard Edition of the Complete Psychological Works of Sigmund Freud*, vol. 22 (London: Hogarth, 1964), pp. 199–202.

[28]Bertrand Russell, *Why Men Fight* (New York: Bonibooks, 1930), pp. 5–6.

Systematic studies distinguish between realistic and nonrealistic conflicts.[29] In a realistic conflict, the cause of struggle is rational disagreement over goals. In a nonrealistic conflict, the immediate issues are merely a pretext for fighting, and the real purpose of the combatants is violence itself. When we have both an instinct of combativeness and a disagreement over political issues, we have a chicken-and-egg problem, of deciding which is the real cause. Are the political issues only rationalizations to justify violence and to permit the relaxation of normal inhibitions against bloodshed that are applied unless reasons of state are involved? Or is it the reverse—leaders facing realistic disagreements with opponents take advantage of the aggressiveness of their followers to arouse a spirit of national struggle? Is aggressiveness a cause of war or only a consequence of it?

No final answer to this question has emerged from conflict research, but it is a reliable maxim that the aggressive urge is important only insofar as it is translated into ideology. Sheer blood lust plays a relatively minor role, but aggressive and demanding definitions of the political situation are commonly behind warlike disputes. If the aggressive urge distorts perceptions and magnifies perceived threats (the Cold War, for instance), it is a causal contributor to war. Thus, serious researchers tend to reject the crudest forms of the aggression theory and to accept the more complex and subtle formulation.

There is, however, a substantial research literature on the nature and function of the aggressive urge and its relation to political violence. Much of it focuses on animal behavior for clues to human aggression. In the best known of these reports, Konrad Lorenz examines the logic and functions of aggression in a variety of animal species. He finds that aggression is useful in many ways: for self-defense and protection of the young for forcing territorial spacing over the available food area, preventing depletion in one location; or for mate selection through male rivalry, leading to the upward evolution of species. He then asks, What keeps aggressive behavior within tolerable and useful limits and prevents it from destroying the species altogether?

This question leads Lorenz to his key finding: that a second, previously unknown factor exists alongside the aggressive urge. This is a built-in inhibition against the use of violence, which is present in every species whenever aggression occurs. The inhibition is biologically triggered when the victim of an attack gives an appropriate signal of submission; the signal is different for each species. Most important, the strength of the inhibition in each species is proportional to the innate lethality of the species—the stronger are the natural weapons of the species, the firmer will be the inhibition. The supposedly vicious wolf, for example, is quite incapable of continuing an attack on another wolf once the victim signals submission by exposing a vulnerable section of its neck. The dove, on the other hand, supposedly as peaceful as the wolf is warlike, is actually quite vicious. Having poor equipment for aggression, it has little inhibition against aggression and has been known to pluck apart another dove ruthlessly over a 48-hour period of torment, disregarding signals of submission.

---

[29]Lewis Coser, *The Functions of Social Conflict* (New York: Free Press, 1957).

Lorenz extends this theory to an explanation of human aggression. He reasons that people lack teeth, claws, poison, and other natural weapons of great power. Hence, the corresponding level of their inhibition is relatively moderate, but they have used their brains to develop artificial weapons that greatly enhance their lethality. Their programmed inhibitions are exceeded by their unprogrammed potential for destruction, and they are able to release their aggression with relatively little restraint. Aerial bombardment, long-range artillery, and other remote-control weapons interfere with the passing of signals that would restrain the attacker. Thus, humans, according to Lorenz, have upset nature's balanced design, and their aggressive urge threatens to destroy them.[30]

Among humans' inhibitions, of course, is the power of rationality, and that is accompanied by the ability to institutionalize critical decision making such that the instinct of aggression of one or a few people need not result in society-wide violence. Thus, as in all social relations, one must distinguish between individual aggressiveness and the social organization of violence. Lorenz's work attempts to build a bridge between the two. On the individual level, modern science has made some small contributions to understanding. For about 20 years there has been a sporadic attempt to link criminal aggression with specific genetic defects, but with inconclusive results. More recently, studies of lower primates that demonstrated a biochemical basis to power seeking have been confirmed in humans.[31] Researchers have found a high statistical correlation between levels of whole-blood serotonin and three characteristics of the Type A personality (aggressiveness, competitiveness, and drive) and distrust and self-confidence. Whether or not these studies will subsequently explain an individual's fighting instinct, as contrasted with social aggressiveness, is a question of interest to theorists of war.

But even if science does hold the key to understanding the aggressive behavior of individuals, social scientists interested in war will still need to understand the translation of individual instinct into aggressive political movements. We may trust that except in the presence of such genuine psychopathology as a national leader who takes it upon himself or herself to launch nuclear war, the instinct of aggression will not develop into war until transformed into principle, national imperative, or a sense of mission, whether offensive or defensive. It is the predisposition of an ideology or a national people to transform aggressive instincts into formal policy that is crucial to the understanding of war. And in the absence of scientific explanations or antidotes, only political controls will suffice to maintain stability.

Cultural Differences and Aggression

Are some countries and cultures more aggressive than others? Many historians and social scientists have attempted to match degrees of aggressiveness with

---

[30]Konrad Lorenz, *On Aggression* (New York: Harcourt Brace Jovanovich, 1966); see also Robert Ardrey, *The Territorial Imperative* (New York: Atheneum, 1966).

[31]Douglas Masden, "A Biochemical Property Relative to Human Power Seeking," *American Political Science Review*, June 1985, pp. 448–457.

different national characters. Germany, for example, has been identified as a country with a cultural background particularly conducive to authoritarianism and the use of force, as reflected in prevailing child-rearing practices, the martial quality of German music, and other cultural attributes.

Nineteen hundred years ago, Tacitus gave this classic account of the German propensity to war:

> Many noble youths, if the land of their birth is stagnating in a protracted peace, deliberately seek out other tribes, where some war is afoot. The Germans have no taste for peace; renown is easier won among perils, and you cannot maintain a large body of companions except by violence and war. . . . You will find it harder to persuade a German to plough the land and to await its annual produce with patience than to challenge a foe and earn the prize of wounds. . . . When not engaged in warfare, they spend some little time in hunting, but more in idling, abandoned to sleep and gluttony. All the heroes and grim warriors dawdle their time away, while the care of the house, hearth, and fields is left to the women, old men and weaklings of the family. The warriors themselves lose their edge. They are so strangely inconsistent. They love indolence but they hate peace.[32]

This opinion accords with the views of many observers of German behavior during the present century.

But is there a scientific basis for the opinion that different cultures have varying propensities to political violence? Careful studies disagree on the answer. Some relate various cultural attributes to the occurrence of aggressive behavior, taking the frequency of violence as an indicator of the cultural propensity for war.[33] But others doubt that the frequency of violence and war is attributable to culture. A more important factor may be the number of common borders that a country shares with other nations. This is the theory of "geographical opportunity"—the more borders, the more war.[34] Another factor unrelated to aggression is the territorial distribution of ethnic groups. As we have seen, multiethnic countries have more opportunities for conflict than do homogeneous populations. Against these and other factors, purely cultural variations in aggressiveness may be a weak explanation for warlike behavior. At least one study concludes that there is no good evidence for a cultural propensity to aggressiveness:

> Although culture patterns may be fruitfully compared in terms of their ways of handling and expressing hostility/aggression, it is essentially meaningless to describe one culture as more or less hostile/aggressive than another in any absolute terms, since no external criterion exists that is not in some sense arbitrary.[35]

---

[32]Tacitus, *On Britain and Germany* (Baltimore: Penguin, 1948), pp. 112–113.

[33]For example, Tom Broch and Johan Galtung, "Belligerence Among the Primitives," *Journal of Peace Research*, 1966, pp. 33–45; and Wright, *The Study of War*, apps. 9, 10, 20.

[34]James Paul Wesley, "Frequency of Wars and Geographical Opportunity," *Journal of Conflict Resolution*, vol. 4, December 1962, pp. 387–389.

[35]R. T. Green and G. Santori, "A Cross Cultural Study of Hostility and Aggression," *Journal of Peace Research*, vol. 1, 1969, p. 22.

In general, one may say that the present evidence for cultural propensities to aggressiveness (in the sense of warlike violence) is inconclusive.

War-Peace Cycles

Another strand of aggression research is the search for cycles of violent behavior. Does the amount of violence in human society ebb and flow in patterns? Is there a "war curve"? Such research is generally based on the aggression view of war, but sometimes the aggression theory is left implicit.

Early quantitative research into this matter varied in its conclusions, with some researchers rejecting the cycle theory, some demurring from it by finding certain trends, and others accepting it.[36] Most recent studies point more conclusively toward validating the war-cycle theory. One finds a trend of an upswing in the level of violence about every 25 years, with a 20-year cycle prior to 1680 and 30 years the apparent cycle after that. Another hypothesizes that the observed cycle of war is caused by patterns in social psychology. After a war, memories of suffering are vivid, and so further fighting is avoided. As time passes, unpleasant memories fade or are repressed, and "the themes employed in the descriptions of the last great war shift from 'horror'-dominant to 'glory'-dominant." War is then romanticized again until a new opportunity arises to satisfy violent needs. There is a parallel rotation of decision makers every 20 to 25 years, and the new leaders, it would appear, need to have their own war. This seems to assume that "the opportunities for employing violence are always present."[37]

Although there is in this conventional wisdom an appeal to human sensibilities regarding mass killing, most quantitative studies of war reject the notion of periodicity. Some go the additional step of disproving the war-weariness hypothesis that armed conflict engenders images that forestall the next war. One study concludes, for example, that there is no statistical support for the contention that great-power wars are followed by periods of predictable length during which none of the participants will engage in another war. It also concludes that there is no relationship between the intensity and the ruinousness of war, on the one hand, and the length of time before the outbreak of another war, on the other hand.[38] These conclusions and others like them would seem to indicate that the frequency of war is not primarily a function of culture or of time but of political conflict. War cannot be understood apart from politics.

---

[36]See, respectively, Pitirim Sorokin, *Social and Cultural Dynamics* (New York: Bedminster, 1962), vol. 3, p. 357; Lewis Richardson, *Statistics of Deadly Quarrels* (Pittsburgh: Boxwood, 1960), pp. 137–141; and J. E. Moval, "The Distribution of Wars in Time," *Journal of the Royal Statistical Society,* vol. 112, 1949, pp. 446–458.

[37]Frank Denton and Warren Phillips, "Some Patterns in the History of Violence," *Journal of Conflict Resolution*, vol. 1, no. 2, June 1968, p. 193. A similar conclusion positing 50-year cycles is found in Oswald Spengler, *Decline of the West* (New York: Knopf, 1926), vol. 1, pp. 109–110.

[38]Jack S. Levy and T. Clifton Morgan, "The War-Weariness Hypothesis: An Empirical Test," *American Journal of Political Science*, February 1986, pp. 26–49.

12. Economic and Scientific Stimulation

Another theory of war concerns its economic functions. Both war and the threat of war have promoted the acceleration of scientific discovery, technical innovation, and industrial development. It might be said that a major external economy of war is this great industrial spinoff. Sluggish economies may be stimulated by the creation of artificial demand: "The attacks that have since the time of Samuel's criticism of King Saul been leveled against military expenditures as waste may well have concealed or misunderstood the point that some kinds of waste may have a larger social utility."[39] There is little doubt, for example, that the Great Depression of the 1930s ended for America only with the onset of the Second World War. Military demands put Americans back to work and primed the pump of economic recovery. Today, with economic pump priming managed principally through manipulation of the public sector, military spending is a crucial factor in most industrialized nation-states.

Again, empirical studies challenge intuitive logic. Some argue that on the whole, the economy would prosper with substantial cuts in defense spending. However, some industries would feel harsh effects, while the gainers would profit only slightly.[40] The supporters of military spending are therefore better organized than are the opponents.

Nevertheless, even if high levels of military spending can be shown to be good for the corporate economy, it does not follow that war is good for business. Major wars tend to produce side effects such as inflation, the tightening of credit, and the interruption of international trade and financial flows—all of which harm the largest corporations. The New York Stock Exchange averages declined in response to escalation in Vietnam and Kampuchea (Cambodia) and recovered their losses only with the de-escalation of the war.[41] Even firms specializing in the production of military hardware did not flourish during the Vietnam years. US defense profits ran at substantially higher rates from 1961 to 1964 than from 1965 to 1972. Thus, we are led to the paradoxical conclusion that defense spending might be good for the capitalist economy, but war definitely is not. Perhaps the perfect combination from a profit

[39]Arthur Waskow, *Toward the Unarmed Forces of the United States* (Washington, D.C.: Institute for Policy Studies, 1966), p. 9. Also David Bazelon, "The Politics of the Paper Economy," *Commentary*, November 1962, p. 409; and Michael Reich, "Military Spending and the US Economy," in Steven Rosen, ed., *Testing the Theory of the Military-Industrial Complex* (Lexington, Mass.: D. C. Heath, 1973), pp. 85–86. See also John Nef, *War and Human Progress* (Cambridge, Mass.: Harvard University Press, 1950).

[40]Stanley Lieberson, "An Empirical Study of Military-Industrial Linkages," in Rosen, ed., *Testing the Theory of the Military-Industrial Complex*. For more general issues, see especially Robert G. Kokat, "Some Implications of the Economic Impact of Disarmament on the Structure of American Industry," in US Congress, Joint Economic Committee, *Economic Effects of Vietnam Spending* (Washington, D.C.: US Government Printing Office, 1967); Wassily Leontief, et al., "The Economic Impact of an Arms Cut," in Wassily Leontief, ed., *Input-Output Economics* (New York: Oxford University Press, 1966). See also Emile Benoit and Kenneth Boulding, eds., *Disarmament and the Economy* (New York: Harper & Row, 1963).

[41]See Betty Hanson and Bruce Russett, "Testing Some Economic Interpretations of American Intervention," in Rosen, ed., *Testing the Theory of the Military-Industrial Complex*.

viewpoint is a prolonged state of controlled international tensions (such as the Cold War) with high military spending but without the actual outbreak of war.

Even if warlike policies were clearly and unambiguously favorable to business, it would not automatically follow that governments would act in these interests. It was shown in 1935 that financial and industrial elites had played a relatively secondary role in the expansionist policies of the imperialist states. Investors supported governments interested in expansion for other reasons, but the political elite used the business groups, rather than the reverse.[42] Another study found that economic causes figured directly in less than a third of the wars from 1820 to 1949 and that they have been more important in small wars than in large wars.[43] The results in studies like these often depend on the way that the question is posed and the measures that are used for key variables.

Apart from the well-known relationship between conflict and arms innovation, the role of scientific stimulation in causing war is less well understood. Clearly, a government with an economic advantage over its adversary in terms of matériel, ability to sustain long logistical lines, and the like may be tempted to provoke a war of conquest. And a technological advantage may diminish prospects for strategic security, as might have been the case with the American Strategic Defense Initiative, because it might have given a new dimension to the Soviet-American nuclear arms race. But probably the most important consequences of scientific stimulation for peace are regional. First, as the technological transfer in arms and other goods destabilizes regional power balances, the threat of war through asymmetries arises. Second, as aspiration gaps are widened because of the disparity between the promise of technology transfer and the actual performance, internal forces may grow violent through visions of relative deprivation.

But these details of and speculations about the roles of economy and science in promoting war should not obscure the basic theoretical issue at hand. Economic factors play a part in virtually every theory of war except those that are based wholly on psychological factors. Furthermore, the purpose of war is to bring about by force a redistribution of resources (for example, territory, population, industry, raw materials, wealth). Economic development stimulates not only competition but lust and covetousness as well. One of the potential means of avoiding war, therefore, is the peaceful redistribution of wealth to reflect the distribution of power so that war will not be invoked for forceful redistribution. One quantitative study shows that when both sides in a conflict have adjusted their economies to a war footing, the probability of war can be measured by each party's understanding of the other's balance of consumption utility and war disutility, and the clarity with which these are revealed in the diplomacy of the prewar conflict phase.[44]

---

[42]Eugene Staley, *War and the Private Investor* (Garden City, N.Y.: Doubleday, 1935). See also Kenneth Boulding and Tapan Mukerjee, eds., *Economic Imperialism* (Ann Arbor: University of Michigan Press, 1962); and Steven Rosen and James Kurth, eds., *Testing the Theory of Economic Imperialism* (Lexington, Mass.: D. C. Heath, Lexington Books, 1974).

[43]Richardson, *Statistics of Deadly Quarrels*. Contrast John Bakeless, *The Economic Causes of Modern War* (London: Yard, 1921).

[44]Degobert L. Brito and Michael D. Intriligator, "Conflict, War and Redistribution," *American*

13. The Military-Industrial Complex

One issue of special interest in the debate over the causes of war is that of the military-industrial complex. Powerful domestic groups within the major states that have vested interests in military spending and international tension use their influence to promote antagonistic relations among nations, according to this theory. These domestic groups that comprise the military-industrial complex include (1) professional soldiers, (2) managers and, in the capitalist states, owners of industries deeply engaged in military supply, (3) high government officials whose careers and interests are tied to military expenditure, and (4) legislators whose districts benefit from defense projects.

These core members of the military-industrial complex are supported by associated and lesser groups such as the veterans and military service associations who do defense-related research. These groups occupy powerful positions in the political structures of the major states, and they exercise their influence in a coordinated and mutually supportive way to maintain optimal levels of war preparation and to direct national security policy. According to proponents of this theory, the influence of the military-industrial complex exceeds that of any opposing coalitions or interests.

This complex rationalizes high levels of military spending with an ideology of conflict, such as the mythology of the Cold War. This ideology may be a deliberately manufactured deception to mislead the public, or it may be a militaristic false consciousness that arises spontaneously with high military spending. Whether or not the complex is a conscious conspiracy, it requires an ideology of international conflict to guarantee its position within the society's political and economic structure. To the conventional theorist, arms races are caused by realistic conflicts and a cycle of mutual fear between opposing states. To the military-industrial-complex theorist, the external threat is merely a necessary projection for the self-aggrandizing activities of domestic military-industrial complexes.

In its classic formulation, this theory applies to both capitalist and socialist states.[45] In the latter, the professional military combines with the managers of state defense industries and with the related functionaries within the communist party apparatus and the ministries and bureaucracies. There is a natural and effective alliance of interests among Soviet heavy industry, the armed forces, and the conservative wing of the communist party, forged on ''their understanding of the interdependency that exists between security, heavy industry, and ideological orthodoxy.'' Without it, harm would befall the career interests and social positions of both the professional military elite and some of the most highly paid civilian personnel in the country. Thus, despite state ownership of productive facilities, the USSR also has a military-industrial complex interested in the continuation of international conflict.[46]

Political Science Review, December 1985, pp. 943–952.
[45]C. Wright Mills, *The Causes of World War III* (New York: Ballantine, 1958), and *The Power Elite* (New York: Oxford University Press, 1956).
[46]Vernon Aspaturian, ''The Soviet Military-Industrial Complex: Does It Exist?'' in Rosen, ed.,

The theory of the military-industrial complex is far from flawless. It fails to account for the decline in percentage of national production devoted to defense in both the United States and the Soviet Union in the early 1970s. The US defense budget in constant dollars (that is, discounting inflation) declined in 1973 to a level comparable to that of the 1950s, and the decline in both constant dollars and percentage of the gross national product (GNP) continued throughout the decade. This occurred even as the cost of designing and building military technology increased, although some of the cost was offset by the decrease in the military population after the Vietnam War. Several congressional battles over military procurement have resulted in the elimination of entire weapons systems. For a brief period, several aerospace industries faced bankruptcy, one of which (Lockheed) had to be rescued by the government. In many ways, then, the defense sector shows signs of decline and weakness rather than the omnipotence attributed to it by military-industrial-complex theorists, at least in the United States (which alone accounts for about 40 percent of the entire world's military expenditures).

But even when the defense sector expands rather than shrinks, other doubts still apply. The theory of the military-industrial complex assumes that political behavior is motivated essentially by private interest rather than public good or national interest. At the core of the theory, critics charge, is a crude and simplistic economic determinism. Careful studies of international events generally find a much more complex pattern of motivation behind national policies. Particularly in warlike conflicts, where the highest values of life and death and national survival are at issue, behavior tends to be guided by principled conviction rather than by crude self-interest.

The theory of the military-industrial complex gains plausibility if ideology is considered alongside self-interest and conflict behavior. Behavior may be determined by convictions, but where do these come from? Perhaps self-interest sets the frame for broader values and perceptions. If so, military-industrial dependency might produce a conflict-filled world view.

This analysis is similar to the view taken earlier of the relationship between the aggressive instinct and warlike behavior. War decisions are guided by rational calculations, but the conscious values and perceptions themselves may conceal an underlying aggressiveness. Similarly, values and perceptions may sublimate private interests into the supposed national interest. Social scientists are only now beginning to inquire where political ideologies, convictions, and beliefs come from. More research on this question will be needed before we can arrive at a definitive analysis of the role of the military-industrial complex and the aggressive instinct.

14. Population Limitation

One of the precursors of Hitler's theory of *Lebensraum* is the theory of population expansion and war suggested by Sir Thomas Malthus. In his *Essay on*

Testing the Theory of the Military-Industrial Complex.

the Principle of Population (1798), Malthus argued that there is an innate tendency for population to expand geometrically while food resources expand only arithmetically. Thus, "the power of population is infinitely greater than the power in the earth to produce subsistence for man." Because population must be proportioned to food supply, there must be controls on population growth. One of these is war.

This theory of war as a control on surplus population growth still remains attractive to laypersons, although not to conflict researchers. The rate of global population expansion is much greater now than in Malthus's time. Indeed, more people have lived on the earth since 1900 than in the sum of human history before that date! And this number is expected to double and redouble in the next one hundred years. Some observers, echoing Malthus, predict cataclysmic wars and famines in the future to dispose of surplus population.

This theory, however, does not accord with the facts. Wars have in general taken very few lives when measured as a percentage of populations, even when the deaths have been in the millions. Only the most exceptional wars have taken more than 5 percent of the populations of the warring parties; more than half of all wars end with battle losses under one-half of 1 percent (see Figure 11–3). Even during the Second World War, the loss rate did not significantly depress populations. The losses of the North and South Vietnamese, staggering as they were, were lower than the birthrate, so the population con-

Figure 11–3 Percentage of population lost in battle deaths in major international wars.

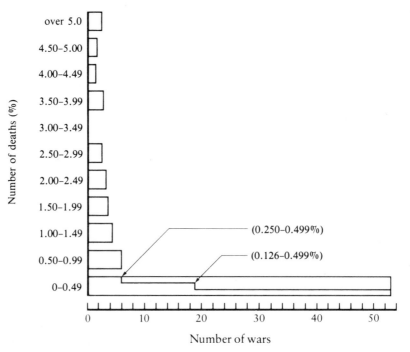

tinued to grow.[47] These figures do not agree with the Malthusian view of war as a significant population-limiting device. In addition, the technology of the Green Revolution now promises to multiply the capacity of the earth to produce food geometrically—finally putting to rest the theory of Malthus unless, of course, we include nuclear war in the analysis. But an atomic cataclysm would destroy arable land as well as population.

15. Conflict Resolution by Force

We have saved for last the most general and comprehensive theory: war as a device for conflict resolution. In the general theory, conflict exists when two or more groups make mutually exclusive claims to the same resources or positions, and war is a means of allocating scarce values to resolve the conflict. War, in this view, is a rational instrument of decision, and war policies are decided by a logical computation of costs and benefits.

The claim of rationality is controversial. Conflicts can be decided by arbitration, elections, courts and tribunals, administrative decisions, direct negotiation, and compromise—even the flip of a coin. How is it rational to spill blood when nonviolent means are available?[48]

The answer lies in the importance of the issues typically involved in warlike disputes. Every nation or movement has a few core values that cannot be compromised and many shell values that it would also like to satisfy but are not vital. Secondary interests can be compromised with an opponent, but leadership is obligated to defend core values by all available means—including, if necessary, violent defense. War is the *ultima ratio*—the last resort. In the words of Walter Lippmann, war is "the way in which the great human decisions are made."[49]

In recent years, the image of the armed forces and military policy has been depreciated in the United States and other countries, partly as a consequence of the unpopular Vietnam War. At the same time, most people reject absolute pacifism and retain a belief in the "just war." For example, on May 24, 1969, the World Council of Churches resolved: "All else failing, the church and churches would support resistance movements, including revolutions, aimed at

---

[47]See Steven Rosen, "War Power and the Willingness to Suffer," in Bruce Russett, ed., *Peace, War, and Numbers* (Beverly Hills, Calif.: Sage, 1972).

[48]Just as war may be used to resolve differences among nations, so too may the escalation of war be used to bring about fast results. The theory of applying maximum force, even to levels that have previously been regarded as disproportionate to the conflict and to the objectives of the parties, was labeled the "madman theory" during the Vietnam War. President Nixon is reported to have suggested massive bombings of North Vietnam and the mining of Haiphong Harbor (at risk of destroying Soviet and other Eastern-bloc ships) as a means of forcing a conclusion to the war prior to the elections of 1972. Henry Kissinger is reported to have endorsed the "madman theory." See Seymour M. Hersh, *The Price of Power: Kissinger in the Nixon White House* (New York: Summit Books, 1983); refer to index for several references.

[49]Walter Lippmann, "The Political Equivalent of War," *Atlantic Monthly*, August 1928, pp. 181–187.

elimination of political or economic tyranny which makes racism possible.''
Although most people value nonviolence, they evidently value other things
even more and are willing to pay the exorbitant price of human lives in their
pursuit of core value objects.

Conclusion

Many of the theories that we have reviewed imply that the cause of war can be
found in conspiracies, irrationality, hidden motives, and the influence of certain elites. One is attracted to the conclusion that calm and thoughtful people
who are not involved in the munitions industry or the military high command,
who are not particularly aggressive or greedy or sinister, who neither hate the
enemy unreasonably nor willfully misunderstand it, and who detest the idea of
war as a waste of life and treasure do not make wars but are led or duped into
them.

But most wars involve very real incompatibities between the basic moral
objectives of the two sides, and it is historical fact that ordinarily the population of each side deliberately and without any element of crowd irrationality
supports the carefully formulated policy of the leadership. In their zeal to
eradicate war, political scientists cannot ignore the nonconspiratorial and quite
rational processes in social life that turn the peace loving into warriors. It is
the behavior of these people that is at the core of the theory of war as a
rational instrument of conflict resolution.

PART III

The Logic of the International Political Economy

CHAPTER 12

The International Political Economy

ny discussion of power in international relations is likely to leave the impression that most of the content of world affairs relates to conflict and military preparedness. In fact, however, the principal interactions of governments and peoples are economic, although to be sure, in areas like international arms sales, power politics and global economics are identical. Even in intergovernmental relations, however, the frequency of economic transactions and events greatly exceeds the number of military events. And in the broader universe of international relations involving public organizations, corporations, individuals, and other nongovernmental actors, economic transactions comprise the great majority of activities. It is for this reason that this book has not distinguished between the political and the economic content of international relations. Not many years ago it was thought that international politics was for the political scientist, and international economics for the economist. But today, just as it is faulty to present global politics from a single national perspective, so too is the study of international relations insufficient if it is restricted to politics unenlightened by economic content. This part of the book, then, deals not with technical economics and econometrics but with the economic motives, activities, and policies that cross the boundaries of national politics.

What, then, is the international political economy? Simply stated, it is the global interaction between politics and economics. This simple premise recognizes the essential reciprocity of politics and economics.

On the one hand, politics largely determines the framework of economic activity and channels it in directions intended to serve the interests of dominant groups; the exercise of power in all its forms is a major determinant of the nature of an economic system. On the other hand, the economic process itself tends to redistribute power and wealth; it transforms the power relationships among groups. This in turn leads to a transformation of the political system, thereby giving rise to a new structure of economic relationships. Thus, the dynamics of international relations in the modern world is largely a function of the reciprocal interaction between economics and politics.[1]

The international political economy, then, is "the reciprocal and dynamic interaction in international relations of the pursuit of wealth and the pursuit of power."[2]

Economic aspects of the international system have been a dominant force since the Industrial Revolution. As distances have become shorter and competition keener, the need for markets and for inexpensive skilled labor, not to mention such other driving forces as raw materials and sources of energy, has stimulated volumes of international political implications. The quest for development in the post–World War II era has added another impetus, as has the central political-economic antipathy between the capitalist West and the socialist East. Although all these problems stem from economic issues, they nevertheless fuel the international political system. In order to regulate these relations, the world has created an elaborate international economic system, much of which has become institutionalized (that is, it is organized around formal intergovernmental institutions) since the United Nations was formed. Such agencies as the International Monetary Fund, the International Bank for Reconstruction and Development, the General Agreement on Tariffs and Trade, the Organization of Petroleum Exporting Countries, the Organization for Economic Cooperation and Development, and dozens of others contribute to the orderly regulation of the international political economy. Yet other aspects remain conspicuously unorganized: East-West economic relations, economic intervention in the developing world, and political-economic subversion, to mention only a few.

Goods pass daily between nations, and payments are adjusted through systems of international credit. But international trade is a source of more than profit; for as nations compete with one another for natural resources, labor, capital, and world markets, they collide with one another's interests. We have seen, for example, that despite the closeness of Japanese-American relations since the Second World War, the great success of Japan's technological growth has threatened American sales throughout the world, has eroded profits within the United States because Japanese imports are less expensive than are similar American products, and has made Japan so nearly self-sufficient industrially as to need fewer and fewer American goods. The result is that two friends are engaged in a constant effort to adjust their economic relations so that there will not be severe conflict over economic competition. Their respective abilities in international trade, generally looked upon as two independent capabilities for enrichment, in fact become a source of tension.

---

[1]Robert Gilpin, *U.S. Power and the Multinational Corporation* (New York: Basic Books, 1975), pp. 21–22.
[2]Gilpin, *U.S. Power and the Multinational Corporation*, p. 43.

Economic relations between states are strained by more than trade. East-West trade, for example, is hampered by ideological differences and the great difficulties of establishing meaningful price comparisons between capitalist and socialist economies. Even within the capitalist world, however, price comparisons and currency values impose severe strains on international activity. Domestic inflation, international trade volume, and the numerical ratio of a state's exports and imports all affect the value of that state's currency. For 20 years after the Second World War, the American dollar and gold were regarded as the most precious media of exchange. Now, however, the decontrolled value of gold (which went from $35 per ounce to as high as $900 per ounce in a 5-year period, only thereafter to drop again to $300) provides little stability to international business; and the value of the American dollar has slipped, despite two official devaluations, to the point that central banks outside the United States have preferred to hold German marks or Japanese yen. For all these reasons and more, a comprehensive understanding of international relations requires that not only economics but also international trade and the international organization of money be considered as sources of international conflict.

As the great power conflicts of the postwar world have receded from the brink of war, the normal peacetime issues of commerce and trade have played a larger role in foreign policy and international interaction. The spread of industrial capability, the onset of the technological era, the huge increase in international trade volume, the fluctuation of national currency values, foreign aid, the desire to protect national economies from foreign-made goods, the domination of international economic activity by transnational corporations—these and other characteristics of contemporary international political economy ensure that economic topics often dominate front-page political news. Theoretical refinements, counterarguments, and mathematical treatments important to the economist are left aside in our discussion in favor of concentration on a few essential principles particularly important to the student of politics, many of which have been touched upon elsewhere without having been flagged as uniquely economic topics. Before we turn to the business of this chapter, it may be useful to list some of these.

1. Conflicting economic philosophies as a basis for the Cold War (Chapters 1 and 2).
2. Discussion of capitalist imperialism (Chapters 1 and 2).
3. Interallied economic competition as a source of tension (Chapter 3).
4. Economic aspects of China's power growth (Chapter 4).
5. Economic development in the Third World (Chapter 5).
6. Economic components of national power (Chapter 7).
7. Technological bases of modern arms competition (Chapter 10).
8. Economic causes of war (Chapter 11).
9. Economic causes and effects of international integration (Chapter 17).
10. The transnational corporation as a global actor (Chapter 17).

In addition, this part explores two of the dominant issues in the international economy: trade and the international monetary system. These 12 topics together suggest the breadth and variety of the global political economy as well as the variety of players in it. This chapter attempts to mold this diffuse subject matter in the form of an annotated outline.

National Politics and Global Interdependence

Before turning to that outline, it is necessary to establish the conditions of the international political economy. As "the pursuit of wealth and the pursuit of power" indicates, the most fundamental characteristic is competition. Whether through their governments or by direct action, individuals and groups of individuals (through organizations or corporations) use the international economy to increase their power and wealth. When this is done through government, it is seen as a national goal achieved through foreign policy. When it is done apart from government, it is known as transnational activity, even though it may occur under the legitimacy or even the protection of some governmental policy. Indeed, most such activities are governed by public policy. Trade, for instance, occurs within the context of governmental policies and even intergovernmental policies; but these, too, take their shape from normal political give-and-take. Materials deemed sensitive to national security are traded only under special license. And although trade is for the most part a bilateral matter, third-party interests may occasionally intervene. In the early 1980s, for example, President Ronald Reagan attempted to prevent Western Europe from becoming dependent on the Soviet Union for natural gas by refusing to grant trade permits to American corporations or their European subsidiaries to sell gas-line and pumping equipment to the Soviet Union. And in 1987, after it was revealed that a subsidiary of Japan's Toshiba company had sold submarine propeller-boring equipment to the Soviet Union, the United States Senate adopted a resolution calling for a two-year ban on import of all Toshiba products. This was because of fears that this technology would make Soviet submarines more difficult to detect because of quieter propulsion and that the development cost of improved detection equipment for the United States would exceed $30 billion. From the American perspective, a Japanese company's pursuit of wealth had a high price for the American pursuit of power and security.

The literature of American history regarding the public-private nexus and the simultaneous pursuit of wealth and power grows steadily. Three examples stand out. First, one of the most compelling explanations of the American decision to abandon neutrality and intervene in World War I is that American economic interests in England and France—both war related and nonwar related—had to be preserved from German victory. Second, it is widely believed that behind the apparent altruism of the Marshall Plan—under which $14 billion was invested in rebuilding Western Europe after World War II— lay such motives as reconstructing capitalist economies for short-term profit among American businesses and reconstructing constitutional democracies for the preservation of American power in Europe against the growing threat of Soviet communist expansion. And third, a popular antiestablishment explanation of the American intervention in the Vietnam War (and for American interventionism in general in the Third World from 1948 into the 1970s) was to safeguard American access to natural resources that might be needed by American manufacturers.

Such interpretations are not unique to American historical revisionism. Indeed, from ancient times, conquest has more often than not been motivated by such economic imperatives as securing arable land, gaining warm-water ports for year-round use, and controlling natural resources ranging from timbers to oil and metals. France's intervention in the American Revolution was designed to deprive Britain of using North America's natural riches to pursue its European policies, and France's subsequent sale of the Louisiana territory to the United States was to provide badly needed capital for the Napoleonic wars. The Monroe Doctrine was an American statement of hemispheric hegemony intended to prevent the spread of European imperialism from Africa and the Middle East to Latin America and the Caribbean. Soviet expansion into Eastern Europe and its unsuccessful efforts to control southwestern Europe after World War II were designed in part as a defense against capitalist encirclement and the perceived threat of economic strangulation that Marxism-Leninism posited as the likely consequence. All these are examples of national politics in the global political economy. So too are corporate acquisitions in foreign lands; direct private investment abroad; manufacture of goods abroad in order to avoid higher labor costs at home; the creation of international debt by the private acquisition of foreign governmental securities; changes in OPEC price and volume policies with all their consequences for Western industries and trade balances; legislation designed to restrict imports of foreign goods; secret arms sales to Iran during its war with Iraq and, perhaps, the subsequent diversion of the profits of those sales to assist the antigovernment *contra* forces in Nicaragua—even if in violation of American domestic law; and scores of thousands of other events that take place hourly. As examples of either governmental or private political-economic activity, they also are illustrations of the simultaneous pursuit of wealth and power and of the conflicts that may result.

Cooperative (Reciprocal or Symmetrical) Interdependence

The magnitude of the global political economy indicates the extent to which peoples and nations are interdependent. For example, Indonesians welcome the construction of factories by American corporations because they create jobs, attract technology, provide export products for earning foreign exchange, and generate public revenue. All these contribute to Indonesia's economic and social development and domestic tranquility. If any party loses in this arrangement, it is the unemployed American worker whose job may have gone to Indonesia in the decision to build there rather than in Atlanta or Chicago. The US government, for its part, enjoys some gains and sustains some losses. On the positive side, corporate income rises and, with it, its federal tax bill. On the negative side, the import of the company's Indonesian-produced goods contributes to the balance-of-payments deficit, and individual income taxes are lost. Perhaps the most important consequence, however, is that Indonesia's development removes it from the list of capital-starved Third World nations dependent on American (and other) support and reduces the prospect that Indonesia will gravitate into the Soviet political orbit. On balance, then, although the United States is not entirely benefited by this arrangement, in the simultaneous pursuit of wealth and power the advantages are roughly reciprocal.

Provocative (Nonreciprocal or Asymmetrical) Interdependence

Not all such international political-economic activities are so well balanced. Indeed in recent years, the concept of global reciprocity has come erroneously to have almost exclusively a positive value in describing the political economy. It has virtually come to imply approximate reciprocity in political-economic relations, regardless of the participating parties' relative strengths, wealths, sizes, or international standings. It would be more nearly accurate to say that although the example of the American factory in Indonesia is one of cooperative or reciprocal interdependence, there are many contemporary instances of exploitative or nonreciprocal interdependence. In our earlier discussion of economic development (Chapter 5), for instance, we contrasted the conservative and radical viewpoints. Although the traditional argument focuses on direct private investment and stimulated trade as helping develop an unindustrialized economy, the radical view sees them as extensions of exploitation. Trade may well be stimulated, but at terms dominated by the industrial states, resulting in cumulative debt that surpasses annual export increases. Thus, although some benefits accrue to the developing economy (jobs, public revenue, improved social stability), the economic benefits to the industrialized participants are far greater, more stable, and more subject to control. This conclusion applies to all forms of imperialism (political and economic domination) and neoimperialism (economic imbalance and exploitation in the presence of apparent political independence), even though each may contain some interdependent characteristics.

In modern history, no people have seen exploitative interdependence developed to a greater extreme than have the native people of South Africa. Conquered by Europeans at the turn of the century, they have transformed their nation's economy under white domination. Today, although still a major supplier of gold and diamonds to the world, the South African economy is the most vigorous in sub-Saharan Africa, as a result of direct American and Western European private investment in both mining and manufacturing. And it is a nation virtually free of international debt. For the last 20 years, as South Africa through its white minority has enjoyed an interdependent relationship with virtually all the Western industrialized nations and their multinational corporations, pressure has mounted for recognition that behind the country's economic growth resides a racial majority that is enslaved in its homeland, restricted by the national *apartheid* (absolute racial separation) to housing in impoverished townships, to entrance to commercial areas only by permit, to only partial use of public transportation, and to inadequate health and educational facilities. This majority is prohibited altogether from holding public office. Under cover of the Sullivan principles—a code of morally permissible business activity in South Africa that uses benefit to the black majority as one of its legitimacy criteria—American and Western European corporations have continued to operate in and earn great wealth from South Africa. But as the unwillingness of the white minority to loosen its stranglehold became more apparent, the legitimacy of those principles diminished. One company after another has abandoned its South African holdings, under a number of pressures, including the divestment by hundreds of American colleges and universities of all their stock holdings in companies conducting business in South Africa. To date, however, despite the efforts of the deKlerk government to break the absolute chains of apartheid, there has been little real impact upon the majority black population. Significant but not definitive political change, including the release of many political prisoners, has done little to reduce the virtual enslavement of the majority. Despite a reduction in American investment, South Africa continues to prosper for its minority population through interdependence with the Western world, while an only slightly modified *apartheid* continues to rule the lives of black people. From the white South African perspective, therefore, global interdependence is cooperative; whereas from the black perspective, it is exploitative in the extreme, fostered as it is by both foreign and domestic forces.

With the exception of the domestic complexities of the South African situation, these examples of both cooperative and exploitative interdependence are based wholly on bilateral situations. To be sure, even though most of the world's daily transactions are principally bilateral, many of them have important consequences for third parties. Even cooperative interdependence may, as a result, have adverse effects that have to be weighed outside the bilateral advantages. The Middle East provides an instructive case in point. The formal establishment of peace between Israel and Egypt occurred at the time at which OPEC enjoyed its greatest power. Egyptian-Israeli peace gave the United States an opportunity to adjust its relations with Egypt, Saudi Arabia, and other moderate Middle Eastern countries at a time when oil imports were the most important factor in both the burgeoning American balance-of-trade deficit and a sharp rise in domestic inflation. One of Washington's responses to this combination of opportunity and crisis was an extensive arms agreement with Saudi Arabia by which the latter received large shipments of the most current military technology, including AWACS aircraft, the world's most sophisticated airborne early-warning defense system. For its part, Saudi Arabia kept up the flow of oil to the United States and its allies and continued to exercise a moderate influence over OPEC. Despite this interdependence, the arrangement led to a severe, although reparable, disruption in American relations with Israel, specifically, in the Israeli view, because the arrangement threatened the always-delicate regional balance of power. Again we see the interplay of power and wealth, with the United States adding to Saudi Arabia's power in order to continue the pursuit of its own wealth, seen by Israel as a potentially adverse regional adjustment in the power column.

Because the pursuit of wealth may influence power distributions, the concept of provocative interdependence may have a domestic variant. Recent events in the Philippines and in South Korea illustrate this point. Because each is vitally important to the American defense perimeter in the Pacific, the US government and American corporations have for decades sponsored economic development through aid and direct private investment. And in each case one of the results has been the expansion of the middle class and the improvement of the distribution of wealth. In the Philippines, the middle class developed a growing dissatisfaction with the government of Ferdinand Marcos, regarding it as corrupt and despotic, rejecting court findings that close associates of Marcos were innocent of assassination charges resulting from the death of his most prominent political rival, and charging the government with political fraud and the private use of inestimable amounts of public funds. Thus, it was the redistribution of political forces nourished principally by the American sponsorship of economic development that brought down the Marcos government in 1986. Well-established interdependence, formerly cooperative, had led to a realignment of political forces to the extent that the interdependence helped bring down a government.

The situation in South Korea holds some similarities to that in the Philippines, though there are also considerable differences. The twin avenues of American-sponsored industrialization and democratic access to higher education contributed to a redistribution of political forces and a growing disenchantment with an antidemocratic military government in the mid-1980s. A rapid growth in the middle class, rising per capita income patterns, growing sentiment among the student generation for reunification with the North (accompanied by a substantial measure of anti-Americanism because of the continued presence of American armed forces at the border between the two Koreas) all contributed to growing demands for political liberalization. A South Korean population restive for democracy came to regard the traditional cooperative interdependence as an instrument for sustaining a non-democratic government (and to some, an unnecessary division of the two Koreas) and was thus provoked to violence in demand of national political transformation.

These multiple forms of interdependence suggest yet another condition of the global political economy: the influences of political stability, orderly change, and revolutionary change on political-economic activity. As the definition of the international political economy indicates, the interaction of politics with economics influences the international and domestic distribution of both material wealth and political power. Thus, the conditions of stability and change are important to determining the frequency, quality, and political and economic effects of political-economic transactions.

A few contrasting illustrations will illuminate this point. First, because of political stability in Indonesia, American and Japanese firms are eager to construct plants there and to take advantage of high productivity and relatively low labor costs. Their presence assists in reaching the next stage in modernizing the nation, as we have seen. Political change is orderly and controlled; the government enjoys a high degree of legitimacy; there is a sense of advancement toward the national goals and personal aspirations; and the security and profitability of foreign investment are ensured by domestic conditions.

A second and contrasting example is that of Pakistan. A young nation with a history of political violence and little success in coalescing disparate ethnic and political elements around vitally important national goals, Pakistan has been unable to attract the kind of foreign interests that might assist in its development. It has been relatively unsuccessful in using international aid, either from other countries or from international organizations, to develop the kind of economic infrastructure (transportation, trained labor, financial networks and so forth) that leads to economic modernization.

Yet a third class of example is found principally in Latin America, although also in Africa, and is seen in industrializing states (such as Argentina) as well as in those that are still dependent on a small number of primary products (coffee, copper, fruit) to fuel their economies. Nicaragua is an example of the latter. These environments differ from those of South Korea and the Philippines. In the latter, the demand for change has been abrupt, but it has resulted from forces for democratization and has been infrequent; the tendency toward political instability, although profound, is generational rather than repeated in short cycles. In contrast, many of the lands of the Third World have gone through rapid and broad swings of political control. Since World War II, Argentina has gone from fascism to democracy and then to military rule before a return to democracy. Nicaragua has passed in a short time from a despotic right-wing dictatorship to Soviet-backed military state, but without a socialist economy. Chile passed by constitutional means from a moderate government to an elected socialist government that was destroyed by a combination of domestic and international elements, possibly including the Central Intelligence Agency of the United States, and then fell to right-wing military control. Many peoples of the Third World are accustomed to one *coup d'état* after another in which a group, often military, seizes the reins of government simply by taking over its offices and its official radio, killing or imprisoning its officials, and securing the loyalty of the armed forces. In all these instances, the prospects for the continued profitability of industrial development are slim, and nations choosing these political paths find themselves consigned to a role in the international political economy characterized by poverty, debt, adverse terms of trade, and perpetual exploitation.

At this point we may summarize the basic characteristics of the global political economy. It consists principally of (1) the dynamic interaction of politics and economics; (2) the simultaneous pursuit of wealth and power; (3) the intermingling of public activities, focused first on power and second on wealth, with private activities, centered first on wealth and second on power; (4) global interdependence, whether it be cooperative (described as balanced, reciprocal, or symmetrical), exploitative (described as imbalanced, nonreciprocal, or asymmetrical), or provocative (as measured by primary international consequences or by primary domestic consequences and secondary international results); and (5) domestic conditions of political-economic stability and change that influence the manner in which a nation will play its part in the global political economy. Underlying all these is the constant exchange of domestic politics and its spillover onto the global scene.

The International Political Economy: An Annotated Outline

We turn now to the subject matter of that spillover. As was indicated earlier, the following material is organized as an annotated outline, or an organized outline of the principal components of the global political economy, accompanied by a series of descriptive notations or explanations. It begins with a fundamental distinction, namely, that between the policy domain of the political economy and the material domain. Each of these is then subdivided into its major components, and these, in turn, are segregated into specific political-economic activities, with notations about the relation of the public sector to the private, and vice versa. In instances in which these are discussed at length elsewhere, there is but a brief annotation here. Other activities are introduced in greater detail. For the student's convenience, the organization of the reminder of this chapter is summarized in the outline found in Table 12–1.

Certain cautionary notes are important before exploring this outline. First, although any outline imparts a sense of descending logic, all the elements here are interactive. The policy and material domains depend on each other all the time and are not as distinct in content or logic as they may appear. That is, if the outline were constructed in a circle, the ends would meet, and there would be no real beginning or end; and if the entire outline were arranged as a sphere, both the vertical and horizontal boundaries would disappear.

Second, the outline is intended to be illustrative rather than exhaustive. Moreover, more than half the items identified are discussed elsewhere in this book, most of those in considerable detail. Their repetition here is to provide an idea of the ways in which they affect the political economy when removed from their individual contexts as elements of national power or problems of contemporary diplomacy. The addition of new items not only shows their places in the global political economy, but also provides a place to introduce them as subjects in international relations that have not been touched upon elsewhere.

Third, in capitalist economies such as that of the United States, there is a tendency for power to be pursued at a more macroscopic level than is wealth. Many interests converge to form the national interest that determines foreign policy. Some of these are wealth-seeking interests, but they are highly different in kind and source. Hence, the pursuit of power is primarily a public-sector matter even when one of the components of the power sought is the wealth of the government's constituents. Foreign policy seeks wealth only to the extent that disparate wealth-seeking interests are able to gain the protection of foreign policy. Thus, in capitalist economies, governmental participation in the global political economy is primarily for the pursuit of power and secondarily for the pursuit of wealth. For the private sector, wealth is the primary objective and enhancement of governmental power the secondary;

Table 12–1 An outline of the international political economy.

I. The Policy Domain: Public-Sector Primacy

  A. The pursuit of power
    1. Expansive activities
      a. military aid and arms sales
      b. hegemonic policies
      c. intervention and aggression
      d. covert activities
      e. space policies
    2. Protective activities
      a. military modernization
      b. alliance policies
      c. maintenance of political stability
      d. securing of boundaries
      e. espionage
      f. export controls
    3. Regulated activities
      a. law of the sea
      b. laws of war
      c. regulation of aggression: United Nations Charter

  B. The pursuit of wealth
    1. Expansive activities
      a. economic aid
      b. international trade and technical assistance
      c. imperialism and neoimperialism
      d. intervention and aggression
      e. international integration
      f. primary-products diplomacy
    2. Protective activities
      a. national restraints on trade
      b. preservation of natural resources
      c. labor controls
      d. fiscal and monetary policies
    3. Regulated activities
      a. international trade
      b. international debt
      c. customs unions
      d. codes of conduct

II. The Material Domain: Private-Sector Primacy

  A. The pursuit of wealth
    1. Cooperative activities
      a. exchange of goods and services
      b. educational and cultural exchange; tourism
    2. Competitive activities
      a. utilization of Third World resources

continued

Table 12–1 *continued*

b. technological development
c. competition for talent
d. exploitation of global money markets
  B. The pursuit of power
    1. Cooperative activities
      a. maintenance of profit-oriented ideology
      b. responsiveness to economic needs of national government
      c. responsiveness to economic needs of allied governments
      d. expansion of employment for government power
    2. Competitive activities
      a. international trade in arms
      b. protection of world markets and natural resources
      c. maintenance of advantageous terms of trade

and domestically, the private sector contributes to the power of the state largely because it needs the protection of state power to sustain its continued pursuit of wealth beyond the nation's boundaries. Because of these distinctly different roles, the outline used here emphasizes the power seeking of the public sector and the wealth seeking of the private sector. It is, therefore, an outline distinctly influenced by capitalist political-economic philosophy. Major modifications would be necessary to describe the world political economy from a socialist perspective.

Fourth, the policymaking bodies of the international global economy are national governments and intergovernmental organizations. It is they that promulgate international law and other regulations of interstate activity. And it is governments alone that, through domestic politics, determine the manner in which their individual and corporate constituents will interact with the global system. Those constituents, on the other hand, are the subjects rather than the creators of policy, and they use those policies and regulations to guide their participation in the global political economy. Consequently, it is the public sector that plays the primary role in the policy domain, and the private sector that is the primary actor in the material domain. Again, however, these roles are not mutually exclusive. To protect its goals in the material domain, a wealth-seeking interest participates with governments in the policy domain; and in order to sustain the growth of the economic sources of national power, governments assist their corporate constituents in their material-domain activities.

The Policy Domain

Except on matters wholly anarchical, the international political economy operates under a vast complex of rules, policies, and regulations produced by governments and intergovernmental organizations. Some of these have virtual global application, and others are more narrowly multilateral, bilateral, or individual. All these together comprise the policy domain of the political economy, as they form the policy structure for the simultaneous pursuit of wealth and power. National policies form the framework for expansive and protective activities utilized in the pursuit of power and wealth, whereas governments are bound to restrict themselves to regulated behavior in other sectors.

As we have seen earlier in this book, governments both seek and use power in expansive ways. The use of military aid and the sale of arms are devices by which governments extend their influence abroad, acquire military and economic uses of foreign territories, and attempt to influence orderly political change for maximizing the profitability of investment by their domestic constituents. When geopolitical, economic, or military interests are threatened, they may engage in military intervention in order to determine the outcome of events in a manner compatible with their broader interests. On occasion they may move aggressively to conquer territories that are vital to their interests but unavailable to them by means other than military aggression. On other occasions they may limit their activities to assisting domestic revolutionary forces or domestic resistance forces, or they may engage in covert military or paramilitary activities under a cloak of secrecy protecting the activity from either domestic or international critics.

Sometimes, however, the scope of conflict or potential conflict expands beyond a single nation or region. From ancient times, imperial forces have sought to control whole sectors of the globe. The great empires of antiquity were built on the notion of complete domination of vast regions, as were the empires of the nineteenth and twentieth centuries. Now in the age of bipolarity and even incipient multipolarity, two great powers—the United States and the Soviet Union—regard the entire globe as within the scope of their respective protectorates. These twin perceptions have led to hegemonic policies in which American air and ground forces are found virtually throughout the nonsocialist world, and Soviet or Soviet-sponsored forces are broadening their geographic reach considerably. Soviet and American naval forces span the oceans and the great seas and gulfs almost as though they were territorial waters. By means of these deployment policies, Washington and Moscow extend their respective influences, protect their economic interests, restrain each other's territorial expansion, and encompass whole quarters of the globe in their respective national interests. On the one hand, this is a modern application of traditional hegemonic military policy; on the other hand, it is related to wealth as well. The perceived military imperative begets technologies that find their way into global commerce; protections granted to distant peoples affect the global flow of goods and services; neoimperialism may proceed even in the presence of rising expectations; and military presence controls the pace of political change and, with it, the redistribution of political and economic power.

Today the forum of this hegemonic struggle transcends land, oceans, and air and reaches into space. The age of technology, and of military technology in particular, has enabled the Soviet Union and the United States to embark upon the most expansive policies in the pursuit of power thus far imagined. Each is prepared to use space to deliver strategic nuclear weapons over courses measuring more than 5000 miles. Each is now able to use space for stationing and destroying satellites. And each is now pursuing electronic means to use an enormous ground, air, and space network of devices to introduce antimissile strategies to the next century.

Together with expansive activities, governments employ protective activities in the pursuit of power. Most of these are extensions of traditional means. Among them are continuous military modernization by either indigenous production or foreign military assistance, securing national borders from threats of aggression, engaging in military alliances to enlarge power and to gain access to territories of geopolitical advantage, and maintaining political stability domestically and in areas of economic or strategic importance. They also engage in espionage by a variety of electronic and personal means, varying from satellite and microwave interception of communications to sex and money for secrets. And to secure their power advantages, they forbid their constituents, the foreign subsidiaries of their constituents, and friendly governments from selling or otherwise transmitting or revealing the existence of specified technologies that are of potential military interest to adversaries.

As we will indicate in Chapter 15 (''International Law''), most international transactions are regulated by international law. This is because governments agree that on matters of minimal or moderate political interest on which they ask only moderate modifications of one another's policies, predictable behavior based on formal regulation is beneficial to all. But on the keenly political matters, particularly where interests are highly incompatible, such agreement is rare; in those areas that touch upon the world's political and military context, there is little mutually recognized regulation. Hence in the pursuit of power in the context of the global political economy, regulation is rudimentary. Governments operate by a fairly mature maritime law and a body of regulations pertaining to commercial air carriage, for both people and cargo. Only in the last decade has there been a law of the sea regulating economic rights to the sea and the seabed beyond territorial limits and continental shelves. In most other areas, governments have resisted regulation and have, instead, maintained almost complete discretion in the manner in which they use the political economy to pursue national power and the wealth of their domestic constituents.

Expansive, protective, and regulated activities also occur in the pursuit of wealth within the policy domain. Among the expansive activities that we have previously encountered are economic aid to international friends, potential friends, peoples in vital places, and potential friends of the adversary. Trade and technical assistance are often used for the same purposes. Intervention may occasionally be used when either political or military events portend a threat of losing control of these areas; and less frequently, aggression may be employed to secure vital areas when economic or political events appear to advantage the adversary.

On a larger policy front, governments may attempt to protect their ability to compete economically by taking rather dramatic political measures such as international integration. As is the case with the European Community, the ability of individual members to compete with the United States and Japan may be extremely small (although it is not with West Germany or France at present), whereas the ability of 12 politically and economically sympathetic neighbors to compete together may be multiplied many times. The integration of policy through political agreement involving such sensitive matters as common tariffs, common labor policies, agreed-upon industrial and agricultural subsidies, and even cooperative long-term economic planning is a singularly promising means, under the right circumstances, for simultaneously enhancing both national power and aggregate wealth.

Great variations in the distribution of the world's natural riches and potential for agricultural production place primary products, including food, among the top national priorities with respect to the simultaneous quest for power and wealth within the policy domain. For the better part of a decade, the OPEC nations were able to demonstrate the enormous power of oil diplomacy in forcing major changes in the world's distribution of both political and economic power. But beyond this dramatic example of the extraordinary interplay of politics and economics are scores of examples of the role of natural resources in international relations. Much of European imperialism in Africa and the Middle East was motivated not by territorial conquest but by the need to secure politically stable areas for exploiting the mineral resources necessary for the Industrial Revolution a century ago. Similarly, much of the United States'

A symbol of the failed East European economies falls into history with the Cold War.
Source: © DPA, Photo reporters

exploitation of Central and South America has resulted from a need for a steady supply of such things as bauxite, aluminum, copper, and tin. Despite huge riches in coal, oil, natural gas, and ferrous metals, the American territory is devoid of some of the less abundant metals needed for newer industrial and technological generations. Although the United States leads the Soviet Union in virtually every category of technological development needed for military modernization, it is far more dependent than the Soviet Union on foreign sources of crucial natural resources. This is a major determinant of both governmental and corporate behavior in the American use of the global political economy for the simultaneous pursuit of power and wealth.

Protective activities accompany these protective devices. Here, for example, we see the opposite of acquisition of natural resources: their protection. In some instances, natural resources flow in international commerce as a normal part of cooperative interdependence. This is true, for example, in Canadian-American trade and in coal and iron trade among the European Community members (through the European Coal and Steel Community). Elsewhere, however, they flow by rationing policy (the Soviet Union to Eastern Europe), by trade policies that permit resource exportation in return for military or technological transfer (OPEC to Japan and the West), or by exploitative interdependence (Bolivia to the United States). Under most other circumstances, governments guard their natural resources because they are exhaustible and irreplaceable. Hence, to export them now is to create a need to import them in the future under unpredictable political and economic conditions. In many countries, therefore, prohibitions on the export of select minerals are deemed a matter of national security.

Another common protective policy in the pursuit of wealth is restraint on trade. This is one of the major subjects of the next chapter. For the moment let it suffice to say that although most governments profess to prefer free, unrestricted international trade, most engage in some form of multilateral or unilateral restraint. Most often this is done to protect a domestic industry from competition within the home market; and although this usually applies to the so-called infant industries that cannot succeed except under temporary monopoly conditions, it is frequently used as a general measure of protection.

Labor control is another protective measure. Many nations, faced with high rates of unemployment, attempt to reserve jobs for the domestic population by preventing others from entering to work. For example, several African nations forbid cross-boundary labor flows. Even American integration policy limits work by aliens to certain industries and professions in which there is an undersupply of labor. The European Community, which has adopted a policy of free flow of labor beginning in 1992, is a major exception to the attempt by governments to use national policy for protecting domestic jobs for the domestic population.

Fiscal policy, designed primarily for its effects on the domestic economy, is another protective device within the policy domain. Under its fiscal authority, a government determines the economic relationship between the government and the private economy. A few examples from the American political economy will clarify this. Congress and the president determine the national budget and, by tax policy, predict the public revenue, thus establishing the annual national debt. The Federal Reserve, with an eye to such things as economic activity and the national debt, establishes interest rates for borrowing by national banks, with the rates designed to influence the general health of the economy. If the rates encourage business activity, unemployment will decline; if they climb so high as to discourage borrowing and investment, unemployment will rise. Rates of borrowing also influence rates of earning, thus affecting savings and investment patterns and the flow of foreign capital into or out of the domestic financial market. As a consequence of the magnitude of the American economy, the direction of international capital flow will influence other economies together with such things as currency values, exchange rates, the costs of imports, and the value of exports. These, in turn, will be felt in international trade and subsequently in national trade balances. All these factors combined, together with scores of others, will affect the global economy and help determine whether there will be global recession, recovery, or stability. And although much of the global economy operates spontaneously, still more of it is subject either deliberately or inadvertently to adjustment decisions made by governments, unilaterally or multilaterally. Each impact will have some effect on the distribution of economic wealth and power and hence on the international political economy.

Although fiscal policy begins at home and may be felt internationally, one of the adjustment measures that has direct international effects is monetary policy. And this is one of the devices most often used by governments to protect their countries in the pursuit of wealth in the global political economy. This is one of the principal subjects of Chapter 14, ''International Monetary Exchange.'' For the moment it is necessary only to observe that differences in currency values brought about by currency shortages, currency gluts, or complex economic factors—including confidence, productivity, and stability—can have profound effects on governments' relative abilities to use economic manipulation to pursue power and wealth in the global political economy.

As is the case with the pursuit of power, these expansive and protective activities undertaken within the policy domain are accompanied by some forms of international regulation. Some of these are international regimes, including the regulation of international trade under the General Agreement on Tariffs and Trade (GATT) and the control of international debt and accounts through the International Monetary Fund (IMF). These are discussed in detail in Chapters 13 and 14, respectively. Other regulatory activities occur on a regional basis. A customs union is a prime example. Here, as is the case with the European Economic Community, regulation centers on the elimination of barriers to trade among the members, and common or unified principles for dealing economically with external parties.

In the last 25 years, the main instrument of international commerce has been the transnational corporation (TNC), discussed under the section entitled ''Transnational Participation'' in Chapter 17. The TNC is viewed by some in a predominantly positive light, as the principal vehicle to transfer technology and to spread the world's industrial produce. Others see the TNC as a uniquely effective means of perpetuating and even deepening the dependence of the Third World on the Western industrialized nations. Because by its nature the TNC is almost beyond the legal control of governments, and because its role in the international political economy is so powerful and controversial, many attempts have been made to subject it to a code of conduct that would enable it to maximize its beneficial characteristic and force it to minimize its capacity for exploitation. The United Nations, in particular, has made major efforts of this kind, but with only modest results. Still today, therefore, the TNC is a relatively unregulated and extremely powerful actor in the global political economy.

The Material Domain

We turn now to the material domain, in which the private actor is the main player in the simultaneous pursuit of wealth and power. As was indicated earlier, the private sector uses the international political economy to enhance its wealth and contributes to the pursuit of power through the international political economy by assisting the national government in enhancing its influence on the political economy. It is from this protective power that the private sector gains economic advantage.

Because private commerce is naturally competitive, there is little formal cooperative activity in the pursuit of wealth in the material domain. What little cooperative activity there is results from cooperative interdependence and consists of peaceful international trade, sponsorship of educational and cultural exchanges, tourism, and such informal arrangements as may exist among chambers of commerce, labor unions, or conspiracies to violate patent laws, antitrust laws, and the like.

In the main, the activities of the material domain are competitive and are more typically out of balance than in balance. It is in the pursuit of wealth in the material domain that the private sector of the industrialized nations conducts exploitative interdependence with the Third World with respect to primary products, food, and even semimanufactures. It is here that corporations take advantage of relatively cheap labor in foreign lands, often to the benefit of the host people, but always to the enormous profit of the corporation. Direct private investment in the Third World is almost invariably more profitable for American corporations, for example, than is similar investment either at home or in other developed economies. And outside the Third World, financiers play the money markets to earn huge sums by buying and selling currencies at small marginal rates—buying by computer in one city at a low rate and selling by computer in another where the currency has a slightly and momentarily higher value.

Among the industrialized countries, one of the main manifestations of competition is the search for talent. After World War II, the American economy was so far ahead of the European economies that much of the best European scientific and business talent left Europe for North America. Thus began the "brain drain" phenomenon. Although the reawakening of Pan-European pride has reduced the frequency of this flow, there continue to be episodes of it. The most recent was in the early 1980s, when the American economy recovered from the global recession faster than did others. Investment in American manufacturing greatly outpaced investment in Europe, creating a sudden spurt of opportunity in the United States that did not exist until a few years later in

Europe. During that time there was a minor brain drain. The same phenomenon has not occurred among the Japanese, whose national pride has been invested steadily in domestic economic development. The consistent trend of that development has not created vacuums of opportunity, as have occasionally occurred in Western Europe. Those Japanese who do reside in the United States for long periods typically do so in order to work in Japanese corporate offices in the United States or in subsidiaries of Japanese corporations. Unlike their European counterparts, they are not expatriates.

The relocation of exceptional talent has been an intermittent problem for Third World governments. After World War II, a first generation of Third World young people went abroad to study engineering, science, medicine, education, and other specialized professional fields and returned to become the national intelligensia. The return rate was very high. More recently, as the frustrations of development have surpassed the cravings, more young people sent to Western Europe, the United States, Eastern Europe, the Soviet Union, and China for higher education have attempted to remain in their host countries. Their success in achieving their wishes has been determined by the country of location, economic circumstances, and visa provisions imposed by the host government.

Without question, the area of keenest competition in the material domain is that of technological development. The electronics revolution, the computer age, the worldwide quest for improved military technology, and the economic

Source: CORAX, © 1990, Cartoonists & Writers Syndicate

spinoffs of space exploration all have combined to create fierce competition in the discovery, development, and commercial exploitation of technological products. And what the electronics revolution has done in engineering competition, the genetics revolution has repeated in the biochemical and pharmaceuticals industries.

Because of the astonishing applications of engineering technology to the contemporary Soviet-American arms race, there is a tendency to think of technological competition as a Soviet-American phenomenon. From a different perspective, because of the growing bitterness in Japanese-American economic competition in areas such as computers and electronics, it is sometimes seen as a race between Japan and the United States. In fact, although each of these is an accurate assessment, there is at the same time a third competition: the effort of Western Europe to remain in the technology race with the United States and Japan on commercial applications and with the United States and the Soviet Union on military applications. There is considerable evidence of Europe's success: French military aircraft and air-to-surface antiship missiles are among the finest in the world; France and West Germany lead the world in the export of nuclear technology for the generation of electricity; and although Japan is reputed to produce the world's best small cars, French and German vehicles are in great demand in the luxury class. This evidence notwithstanding, there continues to be a brisk debate over the status of Western European technological competition.[3]

The subject of Europe's competitiveness in technology sheds light on one of the region's great advantages in the global political economy: the European Economic Community's ability to undertake collaborative research and to conduct cooperative long-term economic planning. Already there are several significant results. The region's Integrated Services Digital Network (ISDN), which first operated in 1988, restores Western Europe's competitive position in the field of telecommunications, a technological area important to competition in other areas, particularly those that require high-speed, around-the-world data transmission. A second program, called the European Strategic Program for Research/Development in Information Technology (ESPRIT), is aimed at making Europe competitive with the United States and Japan in computer technology and at establishing international norms for the industry in the next century. A program entitled Basic Research in Industrial Technologies for Europe (BRITE) has been launched with the objective of improving production and synthesizing new manufacturing materials for the future. Project Stimulation rounds out this set of programs by providing incentives for collaborative scientific investigation within the community.[4]

Although it is widely denied that President Ronald Reagan's Star Wars speech of 1983 was an extraordinary stimulus to European planning, it is nonetheless true that when, in 1985, the United States invited Europe to par-

---

[3]Andrew J. Pierre, ed., *A High Technology Gap? Europe, America and Japan* (New York: Council on Foreign Relations, 1987).

[4]Hubert Curien, "The Survival of Europe," in Pierre, ed., *A High Technology Gap?* pp. 44–66, particularly pp. 55–58.

ticipate in the American Strategic Defense Initiative (SDI) by joining in technological research, Europe responded by adopting the EUREKA proposal of French President François Mitterrand. This European Research Coordinating program proposal is not a replication of the American SDI, but a collaborative effort in both engineering and biotechnology to mount a regionwide development effort specifically designed for commercial applications. Hence, although the SDI is an antimissile research program that may have coincidental commercial benefits, EUREKA is more modest in its ambition but broader in its intent. Furthermore, whereas the SDI is addressed to international strategic issues, EUREKA relates directly to the global political economy and is a conscious regional effort at pursuing wealth and power simultaneously through public-private cooperation.[5]

In the pursuit of wealth within the material domain, the private sector plays a direct and independent role. In the pursuit of power, in contrast, its role is less direct, working through governments and intergovernmental organizations. This is a symbiotic, or mutually beneficial, relationship in which the private sector provides the economic wherewithal by which the government develops its power and, in return, the private sector is given governmental power and protection for the further pursuit of wealth in the world political economy.

With respect to cooperative activities, the private sector provides jobs and, with them, public revenue and political stability for the growth of state power. It also responds to the government's economic needs by readjusting production and conducting product-oriented research for both the military and civilian economies. Through its relations with the government, the private sector also seeks to respond to the needs of allied governments, particularly with respect to armaments. Underlying all this is the goal of perpetuating the symbiosis with government and, thereby, preserving the profit-oriented ideology for application in the global political economy.

This relationship of mutual benefit between the public and private sectors is enhanced by the competitive activities of private corporations. They provide the arms that are used by the government to extend influence, and the quality and price competitiveness of those arms will determine which government will succeed in its plan to use arms for influence. The private corporations contribute to the integrity of the domestic economy by competing internationally for favorable position, even monopoly position, in the acquisition of natural resources and by competing for a dominant position in the world markets for manufactures. With respect to the Third World, these corporations improve the advantage of the home economy by driving terms of trade that favor industrial exports as a means of attracting primary products, including minerals.

The list of illustrations of international political-economic activity could be extended for volumes. The preceding presentation should suffice, however, to

---

[5]Curien, "The Survival of Europe," in Pierre, ed., *A High Technology Gap?* pp. 44–66, particularly pp. 58–64. See also Thierry deMontbrial, "The European Dimension," *Foreign Affairs, America and the World 1985 edition,* pp. 499–515, particularly pp. 512–515.

demonstrate the manner in which various concepts of interdependence, national politics, domestic conditions, the public-private nexus, and the interplay of politics and economics all operate within the global political economy as public and private actors simultaneously pursue power and wealth.

Conclusion

The contemporary study of international relations recognizes the crucial interplay of politics and economics. Moreover, it acknowledges the extent to which international behavior is guided by domestic politics, domestic economic imperatives, and the international objectives of dominant economic elites within nations. For these reasons, scholars have in the last decade or so begun to explore the concept of the global political economy as one of the fundamental elements of international relations. Here we have attempted to define the global political economy and then to outline its essential elements and to illustrate them with specific activities that characterize the political economy. Two of the dominant issues within this subject are international trade and the international monetary system, each built upon economic theory but important to the conduct of global political relations. The next two chapters deal with these subjects in greater detail.

CHAPTER 13

International Trade

No activity occurs among the world's peoples more frequently or with greater regularity than does international trade. A quick study of the hailing ports of trade vessels in the world's great harbors conveys a sense of the distance over which trade occurs and the variety of places from which goods come and to which they go. A visit to the cargo terminals of the major international airports will impart a similar sense, although perhaps with somewhat less appreciation for variety. Or one need spend only a few hours watching commercial barges crossing the Detroit River between downtown Detroit and Windsor, Ontario, to see the billions of dollars in trade value that crosses the international boundary annually. More than any other activity, international trade underscores the interdependence of nations despite their political disagreements.

Interdependence in the trading environment is far from just a one-for-one exchange of goods and services. In the simplest setting, a number of units of one commodity is traded for a number—perhaps not the same—of items of another after the parties agree on the relative values of the two commodities. But global life is rarely so simple. Thus, before exploring the complexities of international trade, it is useful to set out the specific reasons for which it occurs.

Historically, trade was closely related to territorial conquest. Ancient empires expanded in part to secure goods that were not available within the realm; and if the owners of such goods resisted unequal exchange, that is, if the stronger party exploited foreign goods at a discernible disadvantage to the lesser party, territorial conquest was a likely consequence. Hence, although we tend to think of a trading relationship as one of equality over relatively brief periods of time, the concept was actually born of inequality.

In modern times, this notion is illustrated in a number of ways. The great European explorations that resulted in the discoveries of sea routes to the Far

East and the settling of the Americans were financed not as scientific adventures but as searches for trade routes. Later those routes were used to exploit the lands and peoples thus encountered. By the same token, the efforts of a small number of economic powers to carve China into spheres of economic influence in the early years of the twentieth century were an extension of the concept of unequal trade, providing cheap and exotic goods for the West with little regard to the economic betterment of the exploited peoples. And a broader application of the principle is found in the massive colonization of Africa, Latin America and the Caribbean, the Middle East, the Pacific, and Asia by a handful of economic powers, even in places in which political independence was presumed to have developed.

Even before the Industrial Revolution, the major powers recognized their dependence on foreign supply. North American timbers, for example, were essential to the growth of Britain as the world's leading naval power. But industrialization multiplied the need for foreign goods, at first mainly natural resources. Ores and fuels led the list and, in fact, continue to. Then urbanization and the decline of agricultural workers gave rise to the need for foods, particularly grains, dairy products, and meats. The growth of the textile industry led to demands for greater supplies of cotton and wool. By now, however, the number of industrially productive countries had begun to grow, and the concept of reciprocity evolved as a critical element of international trade.

But the Industrial Revolution and its aftermath had other consequences as well. The first was excess production. As industrialization progressed, more units of industrial goods were produced than could be consumed by the domestic economy. Rather than reduce production and with it both efficiency and profit, manufacturers turned to other countries as potential markets. In some they were the only source of the goods in question; in others they competed with domestic manufacturers or with other exporters, sometimes with both. And whereas in some instances they extracted large cash profits, in others they used their industrial exports as the means for purchasing primary products or other manufactured goods. Whether such exchanges constituted equal trade or exploitation of foreign markets depended on value equity. As we saw earlier in our discussion of international economic development, the conventional theorists tend to see such exchanges as bilaterally beneficial when they result in capital for investment; but the radical theorists of development look upon this early system of trade as the foundation of a global economic structure that perpetuates the exploitation by the rich and the dependence of the poor.

The second major consequence of industrialization and trade was competition. The drive to elevate profits took a variety of paths, among them the constant effort to control the costs of production. This meant, among other things, attempting always to widen the gap between the price of industrial goods and the prices of the primary goods from which they were produced. With this, trade between the industrial exporters and the primary goods exporters became imbalanced. But in many industries, the cost of production is controlled more by the price of labor than of primary goods, and so the manufacturers attempted to minimize the number of employees and their wages and to maximize their productivity, often through brutal labor practices. Gradually governments intervened, imposing on industry laws designed to humanize working conditions: child labor laws, laws governing female employees, fair labor practices, minimum wages, workers' compensation and unemployment benefits, standards for health and safety in the workplace, and so on. And at other times labor itself intervened by organizing to influence the terms and conditions of employment. All these drove up the cost of production, often even as the gap between the price of manufactures and primary goods became increasingly advantageous. Now industries began to relocate; for example, the American textile industry abandoned the northern states and moved to the South, leaving many of the boomtowns of the Industrial Revolution (such as Lawrence, Lowell, Fall River, and New Bedford in Massachusetts and Providence and Pawtucket in Rhode Island) virtually prostrate economically. Others sought cheaper supplies of labor outside their own countries, constructed plants abroad, exploited local labor conditions, and began to import their own products.

With this practice was born the multinational or transnational corporation (TNC), the entity that has its headquarters in one country but manufactures its product in at least one additional country. Today the web of the TNC encompasses the world. Consider General Motors as an example. Motors Trading Company, one of its subsidiaries, uses foreign currency reserves and both primary and manufactured goods to buy other primary goods in areas whose local currencies are of little value in the international market. These goods are then shipped to other GM subsidiaries around the world. For instance, motor casings made in one country may meet in another country transmissions made in yet another country, and these and other parts may be shipped to Canada for assembly, after which the finished automobile is imported into the United States and sold as a domestic product. Meanwhile, an auto from the same assembly line may be shipped to another foreign market and booked as an American import. In other industries, few if any units are manufactured in the United States, yet their American labels identify their country of origin because of the location of the maker's headquarters.

These are just a few of the complexities of global trading. They arise not from economic theory but are the natural consequences of the history from which they evolved. In subsequent pages we shall explore international trade at greater theoretical depth. Before doing so, however, it is useful to look briefly at the magnitude of world trade. In 1963, nearly two decades after the end of World War II, total world exports stood at $154 billion (in 1963 dollars). It was not until 1977 that this amount crossed the $1 trillion mark, and by 1980 it was nearly at the $2 trillion level. After a substantial decline in the recession of 1981–1983, this amount again approached $2 trillion in 1984. In 1987, the total exceeded $2.5 trillion. Figure 13–1 illustrates this dramatic growth in world exports.

Why Nations Trade

At the simplest level, a nation will import a commodity that it does not produce and export one that it produces beyond the needs of the domestic market. For example, a nation that lacks fuel will import oil and gas, whereas another

Figure 13–1 Total annual world exports, 1963–1987.

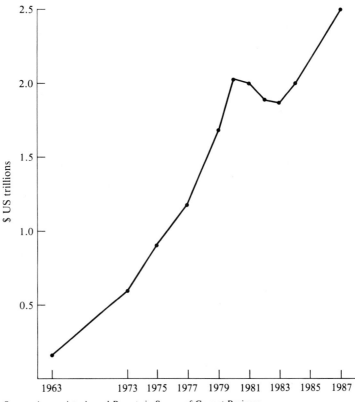

Source: Appropriate Annual Reports in Survey of Current Business.

nation, which produces more automobiles than it needs (because they are cheaper individually when produced in large numbers), will export the excess. If all nations imported and exported different items, if there were a perfect international division of labor in the production of goods such that competition were absent, and if all participants kept constant both their need (demand) for imported goods and their production (supply) for export, then a perfect natural regulation of international trade would result. But with modern innovation and demands for improved standards of living worldwide, such circumstances are as unlikely as a single, rigidly regulated and centrally directed world economy. In fact, most nations engage in international trade in a vast array of goods even while their domestic corporations attempt both to control domestic markets and to produce goods at prices that will compete in international export markets.

Furthermore, many nations import goods that they themselves also produce in large numbers; some goods might be both imported and exported! A standard example is the United States, which was until 1980 the world's largest producer of cars, trucks, and buses but which is also the largest export market for Japanese cars and the German Volkswagen. In the latter case, the German producer was in danger of falling behind the American demand and of losing its share of American market to Japan, so it purchased an abandoned automobile production facility in Pennsylvania, modernized it, and commenced to produce VW cars actually in the United States. Meanwhile, American manufacturers were finding production costs in the United States so high that they were producing automobiles abroad and selling them in the home market as American goods: Fords made in Canada and England, Buicks made in Italy, Mercurys made in Germany, and Dodges made in Japan. (The 1975 Mercury Capri, which was sold to Americans as an American product, called attention to the need for unleaded gasoline by the command "Achtung!" on a sticker over the tank cap.) Now Nissan and Honda produce automobiles in Tennessee; and Ford and Toyota have joined forces to produce the Nova in California.

If all this seems comical, it is nonetheless vitally important to international relations. For when VW produces in the United States, German workers lose jobs while Americans gain them; and the establishment and management of the production facility represent huge financial transactions for Germany, which must export funds (probably from the surplus of American dollars within its currency reserves) to the United States. On the other hand, the external production of autos by American manufacturers represents a loss of jobs for Americans as well as a large capital export. In addition, when producing overseas, American manufacturers spend capital and production costs abroad (thus producing no tax revenues at home) and bring home (repatriate) only their profits.

Obviously, the real circumstances of international trade are unlike the simple example with which we started. In the modern context, then, the theory of international trade begins with a question: Why, if a nation can produce a given product at home, should it import from abroad? Imports, after all, cut into domestic jobs and the demand for domestic produce. Beyond a certain point, the growth of imports might even lead to the collapse of domestic firms and the loss of employment for an entire labor sector. It is well known, for example, that the production of color television sets in the United States has halted almost entirely, with the loss of thousands of jobs. Similarly, imported shoes, steel, and other products have flooded the American market, devastating whole industries and geographic regions. It is now common in the United States and elsewhere to encounter demands that the government protect domestic industries by stopping or controlling imports of selected items or that it apply such high tariffs (import charges) as to make imported goods significantly more expensive than similar domestic goods. Why, it is often asked, should a nation expose its products and workers to competition from abroad and to the perils of international competition? Everyone would agree that we should buy from abroad what cannot be produced at home, but why allow imports of those same commodities to threaten domestic production and employment? Even for nations that espouse the philosophy of free trade (trade without political restraint), what justification can there be for the potentially calamitous effects of imports, even if free trade does enhance international cooperation?

The answer to these vexing questions is found actually at the heart of this familiar argument. What should strike us immediately about it is the exclusive focus on imports and the lack of reference to exports. If indeed imported goods do substitute for domestic products and do replace domestic jobs, it is equally the case that exports represent jobs performed and goods produced at home. A thorough comparison of the gains and losses in employment from international trade would be complicated and would entail the actual volume and composition of import and export flows, the labor intensity (the degree to which the cost of production represents the contributions of labor rather than capital) of production in pertinent industries, economic multiplier effects, economic and scientific spinoffs, and several other critical details. Nonetheless, it is quite possible that a large volume of imports and exports will lead to a net gain in total employment, even if the dollar value or volume of imports is greater than the value and volume of exports.

It would seem that imports are inherently dangerous and that exports are of extreme value. In fact, there is a popular myth that a few overproducers are madly flooding foreign markets with goods, while the recipients import with equal vigor and produce little or nothing. The myth relies on the assumption that the world's major producers will accept worthless currency in return for imported goods—that importers need only print more and more of their respective currencies to meet the import demand. In fact, however, money has value only insofar as it is able to pay for a subsequent claim, and that ability is determined in part by the vitality of the economy that produces it. In order to maintain the promise of the currency, a nation must maintain a steady flow of imports and exports. Such a policy ensures (1) that the value of exports will to some degree offset (and may even exceed) the cost of imports and (2) that the vigor of the economy will enable the national currency to maintain its position relative to others.

Before looking at the notion of an international trade balance, it is instructive to return with this new perspective to a question posed earlier: Why do nations trade at all? Part of the answer is found in the comparative prices of goods in two countries. If the price of autos produced in Country *A* is significantly lower than for those produced in Country *B*, and if the cost of transporting them from *A* to *B* is less than the production cost difference, it will be sensible for *B* to import automobiles from *A* because of the lower price. But given the impact on employment in *B*, it will be of far greater advantage to *B* to import *A*'s autos if in return *B* is able to produce and transport some other commodity, such as computers, at a lower price than *A* can build them. This is the beginning of a rational exchange between the two: *A*'s autos for *B*'s computers.

Although this situation is considerably more complex than the primal circumstances used earlier, it is still atypical of international trade. Such reciprocal advantage is quite rare, especially given the broad array of goods that nations produce and demand. Moreover, it is common that one country in a trading partnership may be more productive and more cost-efficient in several, or even all, of the goods that might be exchanged. Even under these circumstances it may be rational for them to maintain a bilateral trading relation. To explain this paradox and to lay the foundation for a deeper understanding of international trade, it is necessary to go beyond isolated examples and to introduce the basic theory of comparative advantage that underlies the global exchange of goods and services.

The Theory of Comparative Advantage

The Ricardian theory of comparative advantage, named for the eighteenth-century classical economist David Ricardo, holds that the general welfare of two or more countries will be higher for all if free trade among them is permitted than if each attempts a policy of restricting trade and producing only for itself. Moreover, the theory holds that this will be true even if some countries are absolutely more efficient in the production of all goods than the others are and even if, in theory, each country could produce everything for itself.

To explain this essential principle, let us imagine a two-country, two-commodity world in which we have only the United States and Taiwan and only two products, automobiles and wheat. Let us further assume that American labor is absolutely more efficient in the production of both items: it takes an average of one person-year to produce a car in the United States compared with two person-years in Taiwan, and one person-year to produce 1000 tons of wheat in the United States compared to four person-years in Taiwan. We will make the simplifying assumption that these direct labor costs represent all the factors of production in each country and, for the moment, assume a world without money in which there is a direct barter exchange of goods.

At first glance, it might—incorrectly—appear that the United States will be in a better market position as a producer. But this impression is immediately corrected when we consider the *comparative* production advantages in the two countries, as reflected in their internal barter rates of exchange.

In the United States, if we assume that labor is the only cost of production and that all workers are paid equally within the country, an automobile, which represents one person-year of labor, will be worth exactly 1000 tons of wheat, because each thousand tons also contains one person-year. However, in Taiwan the internal barter rate of exchange will be different. There, it will take two automobiles to buy 1 ton of wheat, because the two person-years contained in a Taiwanese automobile is only half of the four person-years it takes to produce 1 ton of Taiwanese wheat.

The comparative advantage of each country is inherent in this difference of the barter rates of exchange—one car equals 1000 tons in the United States, compared with 500 tons in Taiwan. Both sides will gain if there is a trade of American wheat for Taiwanese cars. For example, if the American wheat producer offers the Taiwanese car producer 750 tons for an automobile, the American will be spending less wheat than would be needed to buy an American car—750 compared to 1000 tons—and the Taiwanese will be receiving more wheat for a car than he would in a home trade—750 compared with 500 tons. Clearly there is a mutual advantage in the trade.

Note, however, that the opposite exchange does not work. The American car producer wants at least 1000 tons of wheat per automobile, because this is the price at home. But the Taiwanese producer of wheat will not be willing to accept such an exorbitant price, because 1000 tons at home will net only two cars. Therefore, the exchange of American cars for Taiwanese wheat does not work. Only the exchange of American wheat for Taiwanese cars is sensible.

In this example, there is likely to be a thriving trade in American wheat for Taiwanese autos at 750 tons of wheat per car because this barter rate of exchange is advantageous for both sides. Is there a loser? As trade grows, the short-term loser will be the American producers of cars and the Taiwanese wheat farmers. Neither will be able to export, and it is to be expected that both will also lose shares in their domestic markets as their products are undersold by foreign competition. The American producer was able, for example, to buy 1000 tons of wheat for each automobile before international trade, but in the changed market a car brings no more than the Taiwanese price in wheat: 750 tons. The industrialist might profit, in fact, from leaving the car business to produce wheat instead, because one person/year of labor will produce 1000 tons, with which to buy a Taiwanese car and still have 250 tons of wheat. By remaining in the automobile business our industrialist produces one car per year and has no wheat at all.

The advantage of free trade will be clearer after considering two economies as a whole. Imagine that there are 100 workers in each country and that workers are freely transferable between industry and agriculture. Assume further that in each country workers are in the pretrade situation, evenly distributed between the two production sectors. We have, then, the picture as presented in Table 13–1.

Now, to compare the situation that might result after the introduction of trade, assume that a certain volume of American wheat is exchanged for Taiwanese autos at the barter rate of 750 tons of wheat per auto—an exchange rate that we have already indicated is advantageous to both sides. Assume also that as a result of the trade, there is a growth in US wheat production, which now produces for both the home and foreign markets, and a reduction in the size of the US auto industry, which loses part of the home market and is unable to export competitively to Taiwan. Similarly, there is a decline of the Taiwan wheat sector and a growth in the Taiwan auto sector. These changes will be reflected in a reallocation of the work force in the two countries away from the declining industries and into the growing ones. Table 13–2 represents the result.

Table 13–1 Total output without trade.

	Number of Workers (A)	Output per Worker/Year (B)	Total Production (A × B)
US wheat	50	1000 tons	50,000 tons
US autos	50	1 auto	50 autos
Taiwan wheat	50	250 tons	12,500 tons
Taiwan autos	50	0.5 auto	25 autos

Table 13–2 The gains of free trade.

	Col. A	Col. B	Col. C	Col. D[a]	Col. E[a]	Col. F	Col. G	Col. H
	No. of Wkrs.	Output per Wkr./Yr.	Total Prod. (A×B)	Minus Exports	Plus Imports	Net Supply (C−D+E)	Supply Before Trade from Table 13–1	Gains of Trade (G−F)
US wheat	65	1000	65,000	12,750		52,250	50,000	+4.5%
US autos	35	1	35		17	52	50	+4%
Taiwan wheat	10	250	2500		12,750	15,250	12,500	+22%
Taiwan autos	90	0.5	45	17		28	25	+12%

[a]Assumes trade at the barter rate of 750 tons wheat = 1 auto.

We see that with the same number of workers and the same output per worker/year (labor productivity rate), the total world production of both products increases significantly when each country specializes in the line of production in which it is *comparatively* more efficient (even though the United States is in our example *absolutely* more efficient in both production sectors). Before trade (Table 13–1), the combined production of wheat was 62,500 tons, and the combined production of autos was 75 units. With trade and its accompanying reallocation of the work forces, the combined production is 67,500 tons of wheat and 80 autos. By having each country concentrate in the area of its comparative advantage, and permitting free trade between the two at the mutually advantageous rate of 750 tons = 1 car, the final supply of goods in both countries is significantly higher in every area than it was before trade. That is, the result of free trade increases the aggregate standard of living for both partners, and conversely, a refusal to trade would result in a lower standard of living for both.

This is the powerful economic principle behind the call for free trade. With all its problems and dislocations, a free flow of goods, under normal conditions, has the potential to enhance the welfare of all countries. The results illustrated by Tables 13–1 and 13–2 could be extrapolated to apply to any number of countries and any number of products, although such a demonstration would require complex examples and calculations beyond the requirements of our analysis.

The Problems of Free Trade

But despite the attractiveness of the free-trade argument as set forth in Ricardian theory, free trade is not without its practical problems. It is generally acknowledged that international trade raises a variety of conflicting interests that must be reconciled in order for the international political economy to function smoothly and profitably. Some of these difficulties can be managed within the framework of a free-trade regime, such as that established by the United Nations—consisting principally of the International Monetary Fund,

the World Bank Group and the General Agreement on Tariffs and Trade—
whereas others are considered sufficiently important to merit restrictions on
trade. It is important to differentiate, therefore, between world trade problems
that are sensibly resolved or regulated by a free-trade program and those for
which such a program might be counterproductive. Keep in mind also that the
extension or withdrawal of free trade can be used as an instrument of power in
world politics. Governments may use free trade as a means of strengthening
friendly governments and may discontinue trade individually or through collective sanctions in order to weaken hostile governments. Clearly, the philosophy of free trade is not entirely divorced from higher political principles and
objectives in international relations.

The most frequent objection to free trade arises from workers, managers,
and owners in industries adversely affected by imports, who quite naturally
wish to protect their jobs and investments by reducing the price advantages of
imports or banishing them altogether. In recent American experience, loud
calls to Congress and the White House for such protection have come from the
shoe industry, fishing interests, steel, automobile manufacturing, textiles, pet-
rochemicals, and electronics, to mention just a few representative sectors in
which domestic productivity and market dominance are severely threatened by
import competition. Typically, advocates of protection call for some or all of
the following instruments.

1. **Tariffs, import surcharges, or other import taxes.** All these are designed to increase the selling price of imported goods relative to the prices of domestically
   produced goods. If a compact Japanese car normally sells in the American market
   for $200 less than does a comparatively equipped American-made car, then an im-
   port tax of $300 on the Japanese car should result in increased sales of the Ameri-
   can product and decreased sales of the import. But discriminated governments do
   not take lightly to changes in tariff policy and are likely to threaten or even to
   undertake tariff retaliation. Such action and reaction can result in trade warfare or
   tariff warfare, which is antithetical to the concept of free trade. In order to prevent
   this, the major capitalist nations have engaged in intermittent multilateral trade negotiations in order to regulate as much as possible the character of tariffs and import taxes among them, both as a stimulus to world trade and as a means of
   preventing disruption in trade relations. In addition, the establishment after the Second World War of the General Agreement of Tariffs and Trade (GATT) as an integral part of the United Nations system provided the international machinery for
   dealing with the same problems.
2. **Preferential tax treatment for domestic producers.** One of the major reasons that
   imports become a threat to domestic producers is differences in the rate of investment for modernization in different countries. If an industry in Country *A* continues
   to produce a commodity by out-of-date means, it is possible that it will keep its
   price unnecessarily high. If at the same time the same industry in Country *B* has
   adopted innovative means of production, it may be able to bring down the world
   price of the item and therefore invade the domestic market of Country *A* at a lower
   price than that of domestic production. One rational response in Country *A* would
   be to invest heavily in modern production techniques and attempt once again to

surpass the efficiency of Country *B*'s producer. But if this investment erodes the stockholders' profits while sales fall to imports, investment may require an incentive. Often the incentive that industries call for is preferential tax treatment for producers in selected sectors, specifically in order to permit them to divert dollars to production that would otherwise go to taxes. The threat of import underselling is a common cause for preferential tax treatment in capitalist economies. In economies in which the government controls all means of production, such preferences are always present, but more as a matter of public policy and economic philosophy than as an exception under duress.

3. **Import restrictions including prohibition.** Whatever combination of remedies might be sought, import restrictions almost invariably are included. This mechanism, a device that simply prevents or limits subsequent importation of the threatening commodity, can scarcely be undertaken without severe disruption in the other relations of trading partners. It is a unilateral act without compromise, and reasonable as it might seem in light of urgent domestic circumstances, it is highly destructive of international relations. Its impact on employment, investment, and fiscal policies in the target countries is immediate and profound, and it runs the risk of provoking economic retaliation and subsequent escalation.

4. **Licensing and advertising restrictions.** These more subtle means of alleviating perceived threats from import competition work against the foreign competitor within the domestic setting. Domestic importers may be prohibited from importing certain goods from some or all countries, and domestic exporters may be denied licenses to export their goods to certain places as a retaliation for trade practices in the target country. Similarly, although foreign goods may be permitted to enter the country, advertising restrictions may prevent their effective sale.

5. **Product regulation.** This is a deterrent to sales competition that involves the strict stipulation of standards of production and product that may and may not be sold in the import market. This is commonly applied to food imports, generally using public-health safety standards as the ostensible rationale. In the automobile industry, protection was given temporarily to American manufacturers in the United States by suddenly raising the environmental control standards, an act that rendered thousands of imports unsalable and required redesigning and retooling abroad. Among other things, this policy required that Japanese and European automobile manufacturers increase their investment in their plants, a cost that was reflected in the price of cars imported to the United States.

The student is cautioned that these instruments of protection apply only in the bilateral economic relations of countries and that they have little application to relations among groups of states. Two caveats are appropriate, however. First, although protection is usually an act of a single country, the multilateral trade negotiations and the GATT both are collective means of regulating trade-restraint decisions by individual governments. Second, when states enter into agreements to combine their economies in order to compete more effectively in world markets, they adopt group trading policies that may run counter to the prevailing principles of the international political economy. This ''customs union'' arrangement is typical of international economic integration and results in the elimination of trade restraints among the participants and common trade policies by all the participants in their trade relations with nonmembers. These arrangements are central to the concept of the European Economic Community and other economic integration agreements.

To assess the merit of a protectionist case, it is necessary to consider whether the advantage of the foreign producers grows out of their real comparative efficiency or is an artifact of unfair and unnatural advantages conferred by their own governments. If there is a real comparative advantage enjoyed by the foreign producer, it is not generally considered wise to restrict imports solely because they are of lower cost. Indeed, it is the very fact that the imported good is cheaper that provides the rationale and advantage of free trade, and denying cheaper goods to one's own people solely because they are produced abroad is a hidden form of taxing the majority to protect an inefficient minority. In such a case, the more rational response is to allow the foreign goods in and to devise compensatory measures to divert some of the gains of trade to the expansion of export industries. For example, advocates of free trade often propose governmental assistance to workers in adversely affected industries, to train them in new skills better suited to areas of production in which the home country has a comparative advantage. In our example, this might take the form of a tax on the savings from the importation of foreign autos to retrain American auto workers for the booming electronics industry.

As this example implies, the real-world problems of transferring workers from one industry to another, particularly if the two production sectors are widely separated by geography and work patterns, can be substantial. The dislocation may be unacceptable to the affected workers, particularly if large-scale changes in the market take place in a compressed period of time. In a democracy, the adversely affected workers will use their political influence, through the legislative process and the electoral system, to soften the impact of changes on them.

Realistically, it is unlikely that the perfectly logical model of free trade, unfettered by restrictions and protectionism, can be consummated. Instead, the potential gains of unrestricted trade act as an inducement to liberal exchange, while the adverse effects of free trade act as a counterbalance. Thus, there is a tug-of-war, both nationally and internationally, between those who stand to gain and those who stand to lose from free trade, and the overall trade regime that exists at any moment represents the balance of power between these two forces. This controversy is well known to students of American economic history, who have observed wide fluctuations between periods of liberal trade and periods of protectionism.

The arguments for protection are stronger when the foreign products enjoy their advantages not because of inherent efficiencies and inefficiencies but because of unfair advantages enjoyed by the foreign producers. For example, it is sometimes the case that American tax treatment of home products is prejudicial, compared with the tax systems of foreign countries. If the total effect of American taxes is to double the price of an American automobile, whereas the Taiwanese automobiles produced for export are effectively exempt from taxation, the final price difference between the two goods may have less to do with production efficiencies than with government policy. In such a case, it is reasonable to expect that the workers in the US auto industry will call upon the US government either to reduce taxes or to make representations to the foreign government to equalize the difference. If neither of these approaches proves effective, the demand for tariff protection will grow. Such issues are often lively subjects of international trade negotiation.

Beyond these considerations, there are several special classes of protectionist argument that are worthy of note. One is the problem of an infant industry, one that has just started in a country and must face competition with the imports of a mature firm in the same industry of another country. For example, in the first years of automobile manufacture, a new firm in a developing country cannot be expected to match the efficiency, quality, and cost-effectiveness of a huge foreign producer that has been in the business for years and has established firm markets abroad, even perhaps in the country in which the new firm is being established. The new firm will not have achieved the scale of production at which large savings can be realized (economies of scale); it will not have developed a competitive network of sales and service facilities; and it will not have solved all the problems of engineering, design, manufacture, finance, and marketing necessary to achieve its eventual level of efficiency. During this period of infancy it may be rational and consistent with the national interest to restrict imports to assist the fledgling producer. If it does not have to compete with cheaper foreign products in the early years, it may eventually realize its own comparative advantage as a domestic producer and even as an exporter competing in world markets with the older foreign producer.

This is a rational approach, but two dangers should be recognized. First, the new industry may never become fully competitive and may demand to be treated preferentially long beyond its infancy. In such a case, indefinite restrictions on imports can no longer be justified strictly on economic terms, with respect either to the domestic economy or any sensible regime of free international trade. Second, once an industry is created it becomes a political fact and possesses a reality of its own. In effect, an inefficient industry may bear the seeds of its own perpetuation even if it never realizes a comparative advantage. For these reasons the infant-industry argument, properly applied, should pertain only to those lines of production in which there is a reasonable expectation that a comparative advantage will eventually accrue. It is not rational to apply this argument for protection to any and every industrial endeavor. Too often, particularly in developing countries and those in the second industrial rank, new projects are undertaken for reason of national pride or in the absence of adequate business judgment, rather than because of reasonable anticipation of long-term comparative advantage.

Another special class of protectionist argument applies to strategic industries. These are industries in which the domestic suppliers recognize that they have a permanent comparative *disadvantage* relative to that of the foreign producers but in which this disadvantage is offset by the decision that the higher national interest precludes dependence on the foreign supply. For example, if it is judged that the supply of a vital product could be interrupted by international conflict, that the long-range commitment of the external supplier is uncertain, or that the political relations between the government of the country in need and that of the supplier are either untrustworthy or adversely affected by overdependence, then the country in need may wish to be self-sufficient even at a higher economic cost.

Strategic self-sufficiency is often a compelling argument in this world of conflict, but it is an argument that lends itself to gross overextension in practice. For example, radio manufacturers have been known to demand protection on the grounds that the military applications of their products must be protected; watchmakers produce chronographic instruments for the army; and agricultural interests point out that an army marches on its belly. It behooves the policymaker to raise a skeptical eyebrow when every interest group wraps its self-interest in the sacrament of the national flag. Even in the area of arms production, it is by no means self-evident that dependence on foreign producers is *ipso facto* against the national interest. The strategic value of self-sufficiency must be weighed against the larger interests of the economy, which are also strategic concerns. If a country sacrifices all other interests to pursue absolute strategic autarky, it may weaken rather than strengthen its international position. Conversely, a nation like Japan, which accepts its dependence on foreign producers of many strategic goods, may enjoy a favorable international position. Moreover, defense is not the only criterion; at some point, an obsession with strategic needs may unduly sacrifice other needs of the people, including their aspiration to an improved standard of living that often comes with freer trade. Whether or not protection of a particular strategic industry is a rational choice will depend on the sober consideration of all these factors.

A third class of special protectionist argument applies particularly to the Third World countries struggling to escape the shackles of underdevelopment. It concerns the effort to diversify production so that the country's development pattern need not rely on only one or two primary products that may comprise the whole economic system as inherited from colonial days. Diversification is aimed at a more healthy balance of production and of export potential, which both diminishes reliance on too few commodities and enables the developing economy to adapt to fluctuations of international demand. The older, prediversification pattern of single- or dual-commodity dependence in exports while importing an array of goods from industrialized nations, often termed foreign-oriented development, is now recognized as pernicious in most cases and adverse to the long-range interests of most developing countries, however powerful the short-run economic logic might have seemed. For this reason, many developing countries seek to nurture a limited number of domestic industries through protection against import competition, irrespective of the normal calculations of comparative advantage.

Although diversification contains a number of obvious symbolic attractions, it may not always correspond to the real enlightened self-interest of a country. It is unlikely that many of the world's poorest countries can achieve competitive production efficiencies in the thousands of product lines that they consume and in which they rely on imports at present. Some infant industries may be deserving of protection, but attempts to replicate in small populations the industrial miniatures of a world economy are not rational. (Most of the world's poorest 100 countries have populations of less than 5 million, and fully 55 have populations of less than 1 million each.) Most either will fail miserably or will be forced by economic inefficiencies to charge their domestic customers far higher prices than would be required by imports. The result of such uncontrolled diversification will be to lower rather than to raise the aggregate economic level. Selective diversification, on the other hand, will carefully apply the infant-industry argument to the protection of a few especially promising sectors.

The final class of protectionist argument applies to countries that suffer chronic trade imbalances. This is a situation in which, year after year, a country's imports have a higher monetary value than its exports do, resulting in a form of chronic debt from trade. Typically this type of debt leads to unemployment, as jobs lost to imports are not made up by employment created by exporting industries. Moreover, such a situation weakens a nation's currency relative to those of countries with stronger trade positions. Here protection against imports may be seized as a partial corrective, but it is not the principal solution. The principles of international monetary exchange, discussed in the next chapter, take over where simple barter fails.

Trade Balances and Contemporary Strain in Western Trade

Because export trade is so vital to a nation's economy, competition among trading partners frequently becomes acrimonious. Moreover, because the trading activities of the principle Western industrialized nations are so intricately interwoven, multilateral trade negotiations have virtually replaced bilateral economic diplomacy. Five times since World War II those partners have engaged in long, elaborate efforts to reduce barriers to trade. Conducted under the auspices of the General Agreement on Tariffs and Trade (GATT), these several rounds of negotiations have gradually, but not entirely, reduced the tension that results from unilateral efforts to secure advantage.

By 1980, Western trade was troubled by significant events. The first was that the economic law of the European Economic Community (also called the European Common Market) permitted financing subsidies for export industries at interest rates of 4 percent to 6 percent below the prevailing rates in the Western world. In the view of the United States and others, these rates gave an artificial advantage to Western European producers, enabling them to sell products on world markets at prices that reflected lower capital and production costs. The European resistance to change on this issue led to predictions of a trade war against them.[1]

The more severe cause of disruption, however, was the enormous success of the Japanese automobile industry in world trade. In 1980, Japan became the world's largest producer of motor vehicles (cars, trucks, and buses, although the United States continues to lead in trucks and buses). At the same time, the

---

[1]For a summary of the problem, see "Is Trade War with Europe Inevitable?" *World Business Weekly,* December 15, 1980, p. 6.

American auto industry was suffering its worst single-year loss in history (approximately $5 billion). European producers, particularly in Italy, France, and Germany, were also failing to keep pace with Japan's exports. To make matters worse, while Japan was courting foreign investment in the Japanese economy because so much of its capital was flowing out to places of less expensive production in Asia and Australia, the automobile industry remained under the sole control of Japanese investors. And because it was clear that the majority of the autos produced were for export (about 6 million of the 11 million produced in 1980), it was also clear that the Japanese denial of stockholder influence on production and marketing policy indicated an aggressive attitude toward world markets.

The Japanese view was, of course, very different. In response to the United States the Japanese claim that their domination of the American market results not from marginal international practices but from wiser production policies, superior technological applications, and better marketing strategies. Most especially, Tokyo argued, US auto manufacturers failed to recognize in time the impact of the 1973–1974 petroleum embargo on consumer tastes. Rather than adjusting production to small, fuel-efficient models, American manufacturers treated the slump in big-car sales as an anomaly and returned to their old production habits.

Whatever might be the accurate argument regarding the imbalance of Japanese-American trade, the fact remains that such imbalances invariably result in cries for the protection of domestic industries. In this case, the demands were heightened by growing American awareness of the Japanese intention of dominating the electronics market worldwide, and of the tangible and less tangible means being used by the Japanese to restrict imports. These included metallurgical coal and natural gas, pharmaceuticals, cigarettes, telecommunications equipment, and certain agricultural goods, principal among them beef and citrus fruits. As Congress began officially to consider protectionist measures, the president headed off an embarrassment to the United States—the embarrassment of the principal champion of free trade engaging in official protectionism—by negotiating agreements with Japan. These resulted in 1981 through 1987 in both increased American exports to Japan (the United States' largest customer in agricultural goods) and a voluntary annual freeze on the number of Japanese automobiles exported to the United States. One result was that the US auto industry rebounded from the recession, and the number of foreign autos sold in the United States as a percentage of total consumption returned in 1983 to approximately the 1980 level. American production declined steeply from that in 1980 to 1982 and began to climb again in 1983. In these same years, both Japanese production and exports to the United States were virtually constant.

But the Japanese auto dominance is only a single symptom of the trade imbalance problem. As the American economy is transformed from heavy industry styles of production to modern electronic applications (including robotics manufacturing), it has faced demands for protectionism in other areas. Steel is a major example. The steel trade between the United States and the European Economic Community was regulated in 1983 after exchanges of trade-war

Figure 13–2 Japanese-American trade imbalance, 1974–1989.

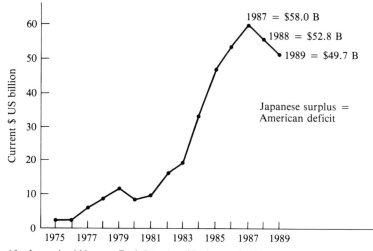

After International Monetary Fund, *Direction of Trade Annual*; US Department of Commerce, *Business Statistics*, 1982 (Supplement to the Survey of Current Business), November 1983, pp. 75–79. For 1987, International Monetary Fund, *Direction of Trade Statistics Yearbook*, 1988.

threats. In areas of lighter manufacturing, too, the demand for protectionism has risen: shoes, textiles, rubber goods, electronic appliances, and the like. In 1987, charging Japan with willful violation of an international agreement on computer chip sales, President Reagan declared retaliatory increases in tariffs on $300 million in Japanese electronic goods exported to the United States each year. Although this is a tiny fraction of Japan's total exports to the United States annually, it was symbolic of the frustration of American manufacturers and public officials over unequal trading relations with Japan and the chronic deficit position of the United States at a time at which the American taxpayer was taking on an increased burden for the cost of Japan's national security.

From the American perspective, world trading patterns have undergone a major upheaval since 1974. It may be helpful to list some of the reasons.

1. **The enormous success of the Japanese export industries, particularly automobiles, but other industries as well, including electronics and computers.** This success is coupled with the relative hostility of Japan's public policy to the import of foreign manufactures, thus making it difficult for the United States to balance its trade with Japan. Figure 13–2 depicts the recent trend in that imbalance.
2. **The growth of the combined economic might of the European Community nations and their common import policies.** This strength results in part, in the American view, from unfair subsidy practices in which governments underwrite the costs of capital modernization in order to reduce the cost of industrial production. Whereas between 1972 and 1982 American industrial subsidies ran at a nearly constant rate of 0.5 percent of gross domestic product (GDP), in the European Community the average annual subsidy was approximately 2.5 percent of GDP. To be

sure, West Germany and France were generally the lowest in the group, with Belgium (at 3 to 5 percent) and Ireland (running as high as 10 percent) leading the list.[2]

3. **OPEC's temporary strength combined with the dependence of the capitalist industrial states on Middle Eastern oil.** From 1974 to 1980, and to a declining extent thereafter, the cost of oil had an immense inflationary effect on the Western economies and a severely detrimental consequence for their trade balances.

4. **The mounting success of the industrial exporting sectors of the industrialized Third World.** Imports from such places as Singapore, Taiwan, and South Korea invaded American domestic markets in this period and provided additional competition in distant markets. Taiwanese steel and Korean steel and automobiles are among the outstanding examples.

5. **Declining worldwide dependence on American agricultural production.** Although the growing world population continues to demand more food production, agricultural improvements elsewhere in the world have reduced the demand for American products. For example, American fruits and vegetables have been replaced on the world market by the produce of Latin America, Southern Europe, and Israel; meats have been replaced by Brazil and Argentina; the Northern European countries and the Soviet bloc have gained dominance in providing sea products; and the world demand for American grains has become sporadic.

As a result of these and other factors, the United States has gone in a short time from being the dominant Western trading nation to having a chronic trade deficit.

From the point of view of a single nation, the ideal goal of international trade is to secure wealth. From a global perspective, however, it is better for each state to achieve a balance between the value of its exports and that of its imports, so that through trade, no nation becomes a significant debtor unless it is able to make up its trade debt by international exchange of services or capital. Chapter 14 will deal with monetary exchange; here we are concerned only with the global consequences of international commodity trade.

Among the major market economies of the world, only West Germany, Japan, and the OPEC countries have been able, over the last decade, to retain consistent balance-of-trade surpluses. The United States and the remainder of the EEC members have become chronic debtors. There are several reasons for this. First, structural changes in the world economy have had a marked impact on international industrial trade, and the long period of adjustment has not yet ended. Second, particularly since 1982, some countries have emerged from recession faster than others have, with faster growth in earnings and greater import demand as results. Third, exchange rates have not yet adjusted to world economic conditions, resulting in artificial pricing structures. Fourth, the debt-laden nations, particularly of the Third World, are using so much of their earnings from productivity development to service their debts that they are unable to afford imports, thus reducing the worldwide demand for the industrial products of the developed market economies. Fifth, the terms of trade for the

---

[2]International Monetary Fund, *Trade Policy Issues and Developments*, July 1985, p. 31.

Table 13–3 World trade balances, 1970–1987, expressed in billions of US dollars.

	OPEC Rise 1970–1981			OPEC Decline 1982–1985		OPEC Stabilization 1986–Present
	1970	*1975*	*1981*	*1983*	*1985*	*1987*
Developed economies	(11.4)	(33.6)	(102.0)	(76.6)	(129.3)	(84.5)
US	0.5	2.2	(39.6)	(69.4)	(143.8)	(173.7)
Japan	0.4	(2.1)	8.6	20.6	39.6	80.4
EEC	(5.3)	(7.0)	(32.9)	(16.3)	(12.7)	3.5
Developing economies	—	—	—	—	—	(14.9)
OPEC	7.0	59.6	117.4	30.3	24.6	32.5
Other	(7.5)	(36.8)	(71.0)	(27.0)	(6.4)	—

Source: For 1970 through 1985, *Economic Report of the President, 1986*, p. 375. For 1987, figures are derived from individual country reports in International Monetary Fund, *Direction of Trade Statistics Yearbook, 1988.*

products of the Third World are both unfavorable and deteriorating at a rapid rate, reducing the international trade earnings used to purchase industrial goods.

Together, these five factors result in the trade balances shown in Table 13–3. All the figures in parentheses represent trade deficits; that is, the country's import value exceeds its export value (or it buys more than it sells), resulting in a negative balance. Several observations are possible from this table. Among them, the United States, with its chronic trade imbalance, had a 1985 deficit that exceeded that of the entire industrialized world, and a deficit in 1987 that was double that of all industrialized countries. Only Japan and the combined OPEC countries (owing largely to Saudi Arabia, Kuwait, and the United Arab Republics) have had consistent trade surpluses. The European Community countries achieved a combined surplus only in 1987, while the non-OPEC developing countries remain in annual deficit. Finally, however, as both the politics of OPEC and world petroleum prices stabilized, oil trade ceased to be the disruptive influence in world trade that it was for a decade and contributes more modestly to trade imbalances among the industrialized nations than it did. Ironically, despite the steady growth in its annual trade balance, Japan's reliance on oil results in a deficit trade position with respect to the OPEC states. The effect of Iraqi policies in 1990 is considered subsequently.

The Resurrection of Protectionism

As the victorious nations set out after World War II to organize world politics around international institutions of varying authority, they addressed the question of the world political economy. Although the capitalist members among them declined to establish the World Trade Organization (WTO) on the ground that it might regulate trade to the point of eliminating free trade (the huge American advantage led the United States to oppose the WTO), they did establish the GATT. The GATT has some of the characteristics of an organization, but it is more a code of international economic conduct. Most modern trading relations, particularly among the market economies, are conducted under its terms; and when in the judgment of the participating governments the terms are inadequate, lengthy trade negotiations are established under the aegis of the GATT. In the 1960s, when the United States was particularly concerned about the mounting strength of the EEC, the so-called Kennedy Round of GATT negotiations was initiated. Over a period of seven years, the Kennedy Round resulted in an across-the-board reduction in tariffs of 35 per-cent in manufactured goods. In the 1970s, with the United States still con-cerned about the EC and now about the rise of Japan as a trading partner, another round, termed the Tokyo Round, was undertaken, with the result of additional tariff cuts of 31 percent.

Despite these substantial achievements toward free trade, in the 1980s there have been calls for protectionism unprecedented in the postwar political economy. This results from a number of factors. First, the chronic deficit position of the United States is seen domestically as a result of either illegal or unfair trading practices instituted by Japan, South Korea, Western Europe, Taiwan, and others. Even when the practices are marginally legal, the White House has adopted the view that free trade is free trade only when it is fair trade to all.

Second, the structure of global trade is changing rapidly. Agricultural trade, for example, is growing rapidly, but it is moving away from traditional patterns. For the United States, agricultural trade is in a sharp decline, because of both new international competition and carefully protected markets in Japan and the EC. And although the GATT negotiations have a proud history in opening trade in manufactures, they have not effectively addressed agricultural trade. Furthermore, in the last decade, the global trade in services—financial services, data services, and the like—has risen to as much as 20 percent of the annual global exchange. Such trade is wholly unregulated by the terms of the GATT or the negotiations undertaken in its name.

Third, because the actors within the GATT are competing national governments, the GATT's dispute-settlement machinery moves very slowly. For instance, accusations of illegal practices may not be resolved for years, leaving the charged party to continue its practices and the aggrieved to suffer its frustration.

Fourth, the GATT permits protectionist practices under certain specific circumstances, one of which is a chronic balance-of-trade deficit. When a participant as large as the United States fell into chronic deficit, domestic forces began to demand that the government avail itself of these passages. One protectionist measure after another was introduced in Congress, but as of early 1991 none of any particular force had found its way into law.

Given the contemporary circumstances, governments have used a combination of GATT-justified and national means to protect their markets from unfavorable international trade. In the current decade alone, they have taken hundreds of protectionist actions. Among the industrialized members, who together have taken considerably fewer such actions than have the developing nations, the rationale has usually been defense related or protection of resources. Many others have been by consent of other parties (such as the agreement to limit the number of Japanese automobiles shipped to the United States). Many of these restrictions fall under specific articles of the GATT; many more are unilateral actions taken outside the GATT. The major consequence, however, is that protectionist acts have become relatively frequent. In 1985, the EC members had subjected fully 41.9 percent of their trading partners' trade to some form of protection. Japan had achieved the same with 8.7 percent of its contracting parties' exports, and the United States with 15.1 percent.[3] Not surprisingly, the three leading proponents of free trade, all allies but also fierce competitors, lead the world in contemporary protectionism.

In addition to such international agreements as the GATT, American foreign trade is regulated by the Trade Act of 1974, Section 301 of which empowers the president to act upon petitions submitted by American corporations that charge foreign interests with unfair practices against the United States. Between 1975 and 1986, 57 such petitions were submitted, resulting in 12 American trade retaliations. Fifteen additional cases were pending at the end of 1986.[4] This device was used most frequently in the mid-1980s, when several acts of retaliation were taken against the EC, Japan, and South Korea. In 1986 and 1987, retaliations were threatened against the Canadian lumber industry but were not implemented.

The Special Case of Petroleum Trade

While the world's fossil fuel reserves are dwindling, industrialized nations find themselves in need of greater and greater amounts of energy resources to run factories, to power transportation systems, to generate electricity, and so on. At the same time, with the advent of OPEC and its escalating pricing policy, they find themselves more and more dependent on expensive oil from the Middle East. From 1974 through 1982, OPEC increased the price of crude petroleum an average of twice a year, eventually raising the price of a barrel from slightly over $3 to about $34. Not until early 1983 did OPEC unity begin to crumble, with the ensuing dispute between moderate demands for stable prices and controlled productivity, on the one hand, and radical demands for continued price increases and uncontrolled production, on the other, resulting in the first moderate price decreases in a decade. Note in Table 13–3 the performance of the OPEC trade balance beginning in 1975, the year after OPECs maturation, and then the drop in 1983 and stabilization thereafter.

This stabilization was set askew in mid-1990 by Iraq's conquest of Kuwait, its threatened invasion of Saudi Arabia, and subsequent events. United Nations-sponsored sanctions, including a global embargo of trade into and out of Iraq, removed both Kuwaiti and Iraqi oil from the world market. Contradictory messages went out from both Iran and Saudi Arabia about their

---

[3]For extensive details, see International Monetary Fund, *Trade Policy Issues and Developments*, July 1985, table 7, pp. 104–105.
[4]*Economic Report of the President*, 1987, p. 132.

Source: Reprinted with special permission of King Features Syndicate.

willingness to increase production to meet the import gaps in Japan and the United States particularly. Iraq vetoed the calling of an emergency meeting of OPEC to review production and price schedules. Iraq's sudden reconciliation with Iran in order to redeploy troops from the Iran border (and occupied territory) to the Saudi Arabian and Jordanian borders raised fresh questions about Iran's willingness to assist the West on the eve of a new holy war. Prices rose immediately. Throughout the West, national energy policies were reviewed hastily, nuclear debates once apparently closed were reopened, and the public cry for conservation of fuels echoed the winter of 1973–1974. Oil was once again at the center of the global economic stage as President Bush announced that the Iraqi menace in the Persian Gulf posed an economic threat to a way of life in the West.

For most industrialized countries, oil represents the largest single portion of a trade deficit. Table 13–4 shows the extent to which petroleum and petroleum products have dominated American imports for nearly two decades. The center column, "Value of Petroleum Imports," is also shown graphically in Figure 13–3. To avoid misunderstanding these observations, remember two important things: (1) not all oil is imported from OPEC nations (Canada is a major supplier to the United States); and (2) the cost of oil has been subject to wide variations in OPEC prices, at which virtually all the world's oil is sold, so the figures are influenced simultaneously by price and volume.

In addition to appreciating the cost of oil and oil products as a function of total import value, it is useful to show it in relation to overall annual trade performance. Figure 13–4 plots oil imports against the annual trade deficit as

Table 13–4 Oil as a percentage of total American imports, 1970–1987, expressed in billions of US dollars.

	Total Value of Imports	Value of Petroleum Imports	% Petroleum of the Whole
1970	39.9	2.9	7.3
1973	70.5	8.4	11.9
1974	103.7	26.6	25.6
1976	124.0	34.6	27.9
1978	176.0	42.3	24.0
1980	249.8	79.3	31.7
1982	247.6	61.2	24.7
1983	261.2	53.8	20.6
1984	334.0	57.5	17.2
1985	338.9	50.5	14.9
1986	365.2	34.4	9.4
1987	409.9	42.9	10.5

Source: Economic Report of the President, 1989, pp. 426–428.

measured in percentages. The graph shows clearly that in every year since OPEC first flexed its muscles, the value of annual American oil imports have exceeded the total trade deficit. The record high year was 1980, in which the cost of petroleum imports was 253 percent of the entire trade deficit, or more than two and one-half times higher in value. The low year was 1986, in which the trade deficit grew so high that the portion attributable to oil was only 22 percent. (There was actually a small trade surplus in 1975, for which reason

Figure 13–3 US import costs for petroleum and petroleum products, 1973–1987.

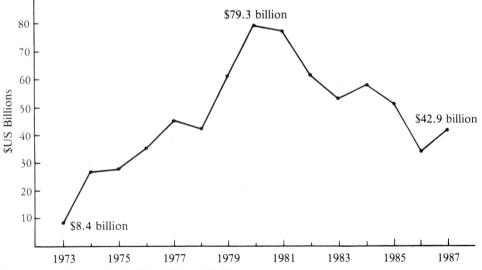

From *Economic Report of the President*, 1989, pp. 425–426.

Figure 13–4 US oil imports as a function of the annual trade deficit, 1973–1989.

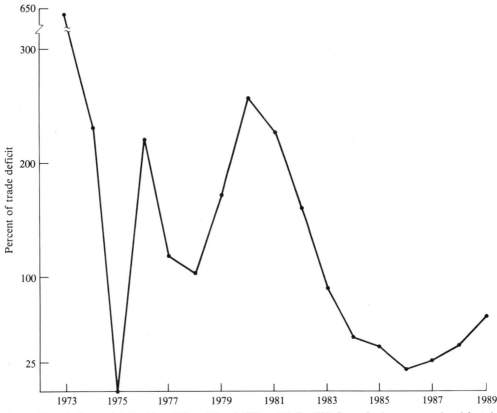

Source: Economic Report of the President, 1989, p. 426 and *1990*, p. 418. For 1989, figures for the year are projected from the actual performance through the first two fiscal quarters.

Note: Read this graph as follows: In 1989, the value of American petroleum imports was equivalent to 50 percent of the nation's balance-of-trade deficit. In 1980, in contrast, the value of petroleum imports was equivalent to two and one-half times the balance-of-trade deficit. For 1990 and 1991, it is expected that the curve will climb sharply as a result of higher prices following the Iraqi invasion and annexation of Kuwait.

the graph falls to the base line.) Look now at Figures 13–3 and 13–4 together. They show that from 1973 to 1978 the annual cost of imported oil rose steadily, although those exports as a fraction of the annual trade deficit declined. Then in 1980, both the price and oil's part of the trade deficit spiked to their high records, after which both declined almost at the same rate until 1987, when both rose once again. But the entire period of decline was marked by huge increases in the annual deficit, with the result that while oil imports declined by less than half ($79.4 billion in 1980 to just over $30 billion in 1986), oil's portion of the total deficit dropped dramatically, from 253 percent in 1980 to only 22 percent in 1986. So although the importance of oil remained a very substantial American economic problem, other serious problems, such as the chronic trade deficit with Japan, began to overshadow it.

These are important observations because of the crucial role of oil in firing American industry. Moreover, in 1989, the United States met its lowest point since 1973 in the production of domestic oil: less than 25 percent of all the oil consumed in the United States in that year came from American wells. This was caused by several things including stability in the international supply, stability in the global price, refusal of the government to release drilling permits because of environmental factors, and repeal of tax incentives for drilling new wells. Hence, although the domestic politics and the global politics of oil were relatively quiescent at the beginning of the decade, it is certain that America's 1974–1985 preoccupation with oil will return.

Oil importation does not occur in a vacuum but in the context of trade in other commodities. Indeed, as we have seen elsewhere, the price of OPEC oil and the volume available might have been much more unfavorable to the developed economies had it not been for three things: (1) the enormous increases in agricultural exports to the oil-producing states, from which the United States profited most in controlling its petroleum-caused deficit; (2) huge increases in arms sales to the entire Third World, but particularly to the oil-producing members, from which the United States, France, and West Germany took the greatest advantage; and (3) the so-called oil-for-technology agreements, by which oil was kept flowing at a partially controlled price in return for technology transfer in arms and other goods. All the developed Western countries took advantage of these oil-for-technology arrangements, but Japan profited the most.

Because Japan is nearly totally reliant on other nations for fuel to support the manufacturing productivity on which its world stature depends, the OPEC maturation was particularly threatening to Tokyo. Contrary to common opinion and to its government's own prediction, the Japanese consumption of imported energy did not skyrocket from 1974 to 1981. In fact, the total consumption in 1974 and in 1981 was almost identical, although in 1979 the demand grew to a level of approximately 111 percent of the base year. But given the huge price increases during those years, the cost of maintaining even a steady supply of fuel was staggering and had a severely detrimental influence on Japan's trade balance with OPEC as Table 13–5 suggests.

Clearly, the cost of petroleum, not an increase in volume, resulted in the burden of Japan's trade balance with OPEC. Even a tenfold increase in the value of exports to OPEC could not offset the ravages of OPEC's price increases. Although it is of no lasting significance to the global economy, because adjustments are made annually from Japan's overall trade surplus, it is

Table 13–5 Japan's trade deficit with OPEC, 1973–1987, in billions of US dollars.

1973	(3.4)	1980	(31.9)
1974	(11.9)	1981	(26.8)
1975	(10.8)	1982	(28.1)
1976	(12.5)	1983	(24.8)
1977	(12.9)	1984	(27.5)
1978	(11.3)	1985	(26.0)
1979	(20.5)	1987	(16.7)

Source: International Monetary Fund, *International Financial Statistics*, as reproduced in and compiled from *Europa Yearbook*, 1979 and 1981. For 1982–1987, International Monetary Fund, *Direction of Trade Statistics Yearbook*, 1988, p. 245.

nonetheless shocking to find that for the period 1974–1987, Japan incurred a cumulative deficit of $280 billion in its trade with the OPEC states. In fact, during OPEC's strongest years, this deficit ensured an annual worldwide balance-of-trade deficit. But as OPEC's prices began to drop, Japan's global trade balance began a sharp rise, going from a deficit of $10.9 billion in 1980 to a modest surplus of $8.6 billion in 1981. By 1985, despite a continuing deficit of $26 billion with the oil-exporting Third World, Japan's global trade surplus rose to $46.7 billion. And in 1987, while the deficit regarding OPEC dropped almost $10 billion (to $16.7 billion), Japan's global trading surplus rose to a record high of over $80 billion. Through its trade surplus alone, in that year Japan amassed wealth greater than the gross domestic product of either Argentina, South Africa, or Saudi Arabia; twice that of Greece; and roughly equal to that of Denmark, a member of the wealthy European Community.

Recall, however, that our interest here is not simply in the troubling facts of global petroleum trade but in the consequences of those facts for the global political economy. From the American perspective, the strength of OPEC was nearly crippling. Almost by itself, it sent the domestic inflation rate soaring to record heights, with interest rates following. At the same time, industrial productivity declined, creating both a loss of confidence in the economy among investors and consumers and a demand for durable goods that could be met only by foreign production and imports. The Japanese took a reciprocal view: They adjusted their pattern of oil consumption, established a national policy giving industrial consumption first priority, and multiplied their industrial production. In this way they were able greatly to increase their exports of manufactures and thus to offset their trade deficit with OPEC even during the years of its greatest ascendancy. As the United States emerged from recession, the dollar gained strength in world markets, with the result that American goods became increasingly costly. Hence, as Japan's trade surplus widened, that of the United States continued to slide even after OPEC lost its control of the world oil trade. This, in turn, led to demands of protectionism in the United States, particularly with respect to Japan.

East-West Trade

If trade among friendly nations committed to the same economic philosophy is prone to such hostilities, it is easy to imagine the difficulties of establishing reliable and well-regulated trade between the capitalist economies and the socialist world. Strained in the first place by political differences severe enough to appear irreconcilable, the economic relations of these countries are complicated by differences in methods of assigning value to goods and by the deeply troubling question of whether one should trade with one's potential adversary and, in so doing, strengthen and improve the enemy's potential advantage.

During the age of containment, a basic Cold War political maxim was that Western industrialized states should not trade with the Soviet Union or China and their respective friends. Certain exceptions (mostly of food and consumer goods) were made for Eastern European countries, particularly by the Western Europeans. But it was not until the era of détente that the idea of using trade deprivation as a political instrument was replaced by the one that mutual trade is a potential route for intercultural understanding and improved international tolerance. In essence, this view interpreted trade as a functional instrument, one with which to build trust and confidence. This general revision of thinking was accentuated by the growing Western European tolerance of socialism and communism and by the growth of Eurocommunism. Moreover, the trans-European policies of Germany, commencing with Konrad Adenauer, and of French Gaullism became a suitable rationale for trade between East and West Europe, although more with the smaller satellite states than with the Soviet Union itself. Finally, in addition to détente and Pan-Europeanism, the Sino-American political thaw of the 1970s was accompanied by vigorous Western and Japanese overtures to China in order to trade industrial products for natural resources.

By the mid-1970s, then, East-West trade was growing quickly, but it was not to grow at a steady pace. The Carter administration reacted to the impo-

Source: AISLIN, © 1990, Cartoonists & Writers Syndicate

Table 13–6 Direction of Soviet trade with the West, 1979–1987, in billions of US dollars.

	World			US			EC		
	Exp.	*Imp.*	*Bal.*	*Exp.*	*Imp.*	*Bal.*	*Exp.*	*Imp.*	*Bal.*
1979	26.6	30.9	(4.3)	0.8	4.0	(3.2)	10.5	9.9	0.6
1980	32.4	38.8	(6.4)	0.4	1.7	(1.3)	13.9	11.9	2.2
1981	33.2	42.6	(9.4)	0.3	2.7	(2.4)	14.0	10.2	3.8
1982	34.1	40.7	(6.6)	0.2	2.9	(2.7)	15.8	10.0	5.8
1983	33.3	39.9	(6.6)	0.3	2.2	(1.9)	15.4	12.2	3.2
1984	33.8	38.6	(4.8)	0.6	3.6	(3.0)	16.5	10.9	5.6
1985	31.1	38.7	(7.6)	0.4	2.7	(2.3)	14.5	10.4	4.1
1987	37.2	44.9	(7.7)	0.4	1.6	(1.2)	13.6	11.7	1.9

Source: International Monetary Fund, *Direction of Trade Statistics*, 1986, pp. 394–395, and 1988, pp. 399–400.

sition of anti-Solidarity martial law in Poland and to the Soviet invasion of Afghanistan with retaliatory trade policies; and throughout most of two Reagan administrations, the notion of the Soviet Union as the "evil empire" was used to prevent technological trade with the East. Moreover, until the launching of *perestroika* in the late 1980s, there was little export potential in Eastern Europe beyond what was required by the common production and distribution system among the participating states.

Table 13–6 details the Western trade of the Soviet Union. In the year immediately preceding *perestroika* (1987), the Soviet Union exported to the entire world $37.2 billion in goods and services, and imported $44.9 billion, yielding a worldwide trade deficit of $7.7 billion. Barely a third of Soviet exports went to the West; almost all of it ($13.6 billion) went to the EC countries. The amount of trade with the United States (as well as with Japan, which is not included in the table) was tiny by major power standards. Most of Soviet trade, then, is within the Council for Mutual Economic Assistance (COMECON) or with the Third World, including importantly in this period Cuba, Nicaragua, Syria, and India.

From 1979 to 1987, Soviet trade with the EC remained stable, involving about $14 billion of Soviet exports and $11 billion of Soviet imports annually. In the same period, trade with the United States was stagnant. This resulted from a 1980 recommendation of the President's Export Council, an excerpt from which follows.

> As to the Soviet Union, the Council recommends that the process of normalizing trade relations, which was broken off by the Soviet invasion of Afghanistan, be resumed only if and when there is significant improvement in U.S.–U.S.S.R. relations. Meanwhile, the U.S. should continue non-sensitive trade as circumstances make appropriate, while indicating a willingness to increase trade and resume normalization steps if and when the Soviet Union changes its policies to a peaceful cooperative course.[5]

---

[5]President's Export Council, *The Export Imperative*, December 1980, vol. 1, p. 104.

Soviet-American relations for most of this period of Presidents Carter and Reagan and Soviet General Secretaries Brezhnev, Andropov, Chernenko, and Gorbachev resulted in little to warrant the repeal of this recommendation. With *glasnost* and *perestroika,* however, followed by a distinct thaw in Soviet-American relations late in the Reagan years, economic prospects began to unfold rapidly. The Gorbachev summit visit to the United States in late 1988, interrupted by a devastating earthquake in Soviet Armenia, opened the way to a Soviet proposal of most-favored-nation trading status with the United States, a doctrine under which the United States would give terms of trade to the Soviets equal to the most advantageous granted any other trading partner. The Bush-Gorbachev summit at Malta a year later further improved the climate for economic change, and in the joint news conference that followed, President Bush agreed to explore the proposal fully prior to the opening of formal economic diplomacy. At the time of writing, this matter had not been carried to a conclusion.

The trading pattern of Eastern Europe follows closely that of the Soviet Union, although the volumes are much smaller. Most of the trade of these nations occurs within the COMECON, that is, among these countries and the Soviet Union itself, in a commonly planned production and distribution system. Table 13–7 reveals what little trade these nations have with the United States and the EC members. Trade with the United States is minimal, and that

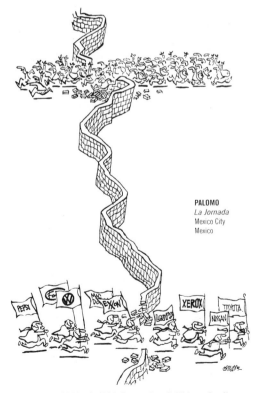

PALOMO
La Jornada
Mexico City
Mexico

Source: PALOMO. © 1990 Cartoonists & Writers Syndicate.

Table 13–7 Direction of Eastern European trade, 1987, in billions of US dollars.

	World			US			EC		
	Imp.	*Exp.*	*Bal.*	*Imp.*	*Exp.*	*Bal.*	*Imp.*	*Exp.*	*Bal.*
E. Germany	6.2	5.7	(0.5)	0.1	0.1	—	1.4	1.4	—
Poland	10.8	12.2	1.4	0.2	0.3	0.1	0.2	0.0	(0.2)
Czechoslovakia	7.0	6.5	(0.5)	0.1	0.1	—	2.7	2.2	(0.5)
Hungary	10.8	10.5	(0.3)	0.4	0.3	(0.1)	2.1	2.6	0.5
Romania	10.6	12.5	1.9	0.3	0.8	0.5	1.0	2.2	1.2
Bulgaria	4.0	2.1	(1.9)	0.0	0.1	0.1	1.9	0.5	(1.4)
Yugoslavia	11.8[a]	10.4[a]	(1.4)	0.7	0.6	(0.1)	6.3	4.9	(1.4)

[a]Figures from 1986 rather than 1987.
Source: International Monetary Fund, *Direction of Trade Statistics Yearbook*, 1988; individual country charts.

with the EC amounts to no more than one-third of exports or imports for any member of the group (Czechoslovakia, with Hungary trailing close behind) except Yugoslavia. And Yugoslavia is a special case in Eastern Europe, having from 1948 maintained an uncommon degree of both political and economic independence from the Soviet Union. Although it is not in Table 13–7, Eastern European trade with Japan is no greater than that with the United States.

China's recent global trading pattern indicates the extent to which China had, at least prior to the events in Tiananmen Square in 1989, abandoned isolation on its path to economic modernization. From 1979 to 1987, China's global exports and imports each approximately tripled, as did its trade with the United States, the European Community, and Japan, respectively. (See Table 13–8.) The pattern is one of steady growth although, ironically, not the growth anticipated in 1979 following formal diplomatic relations between Washington and Beijing. During the same period, ideological differences with the Soviet Union prevented Sino-Soviet trade from developing. Again ironi-

Table 13–8 Direction of China's trade with the West, 1979–1987, in billions of US dollars.

	World			US			EC			Japan		
	Exp.	*Imp.*	*Bal.*	*Exp.*	*Imp.*	*Bal.*	*Exp.*	*Imp.*	*Bal.*	*Exp.*	*Imp.*	*Bal.*
1979	13.7	15.7	(2.0)	0.6	1.9	(1.3)	1.7	3.4	(1.7)	2.8	3.9	(1.1)
1980	18.1	19.5	(1.4)	1.0	3.8	(2.8)	2.4	2.8	(0.4)	4.0	5.2	(1.2)
1981	21.5	21.6	(0.1)	1.5	4.7	(3.2)	2.5	2.7	(0.2)	4.7	6.2	(1.5)
1982	21.9	18.9	3.0	1.8	4.3	(2.5)	2.2	2.2	0	4.8	3.9	0.9
1983	22.1	21.3	0.8	1.7	2.8	(1.1)	2.5	3.4	(0.9)	4.5	5.5	(1.0)
1984	24.8	26.0	(1.2)	2.3	3.8	(1.5)	2.2	3.3	(1.1)	5.2	8.1	(2.9)
1985	27.3	42.5	(15.2)	2.3	5.2	(2.9)	2.3	6.2	(3.9)	6.1	15.2	(9.1)
1987	39.5	43.4	(3.9)	3.0	4.8	(1.8)	3.9	7.3	(3.4)	6.4	10.1	(3.7)

Source: International Monetary Fund, *Direction of Trade Statistics Yearbook*, 1986, p. 137–139, and 1988, p. 136.

Table 13–9 Direction of China's trade, 1987, in billions of US dollars.

Destination	Exports	Imports	Balance	Total Value
World Total	39.5	43.4	(3.9)	82.9
Indust. World	14.6	26.5	(11.9)	41.1
Developing World	22.7	13.9	8.8	36.6
Non-oil Developing	21.7	13.1	8.6	34.8

Source: International Monetary Fund, *Direction of Trade Statistics Yearbook*, 1988, p. 138.

cally, Mikhail Gorbachev was visiting Beijing in May 1989 to begin the process of normalizing relations between the two capitals when, presumably taking advantage of the worldwide press coverage of the Gorbachev visit, demonstrations began in Tiananmen Square that resulted two weeks later in massive bloodshed. Although the Gorbachev government made only mild statements of protest, like the Western governments, the Soviet Union downplayed its economic policies with respect to China for an extended time thereafter.

If the growth in China's global trade is not with the West, Japan, or the Soviet Union, where is it? Table 13–9 indicates that more than half of China's exports go to the Third World, almost all of them to the non-oil-producing developing countries. At the same time, more than half of its imports come from the industrialized world, all but $4 billion of those from Japan, the EC, and the United States, with exports to the developing world nearly offsetting the trade deficit caused by growing imports from the industrialized countries. The reason for this mixed pattern is no mystery: China exports large volumes of nonindustrial goods (other than arms) to the Third World in order to be able to import a growing volume of industrial goods from the West. How this pattern will continue to develop as China puts Tiananmen Square behind it politically and diplomatically will be one of the interesting things to observe in the 1990s.

Conclusion

International trade is one of the principal measures of global interdependence. At the same time, the harmony or acrimony with which it is conducted says much about not only the international economy, but the political economy as well, simply because the presence or absence of conflict in international trade governs to a large extent such important features of international politics as barriers to trade, economic retaliation, and the distribution of wealth within the global power equation. But it also cuts directly to the heart of many politically sensitive domestic subjects such as employment and unemployment, public tax revenues and the services provided by them, capital accumulation, and industrial investment. Each of these in its turn affects domestic politics and eventually foreign policy. The relation of the political to the economic and of the international to the domestic is thus apparent.

World trade continues to grow steadily, and it is likely that the return of China to active participation in the global economy and the economic reconstruction of Eastern Europe and the Soviet Union under *perestroika* will stimulate new investment, new wealth, new demand for goods, and new avenues of expanded trade. But future growth is not without political obstacles. The approach of Western European economic union in 1992 may greatly increase the aggregate wealth of the EC countries, but it may accentuate the growing fears of Americans that their place in international commerce is being eroded not by better products, but by unfree and, therefore, unfair trade. Japan's growing annual trade surplus, the envy of the world, continues to irritate in part because it results partly from import restrictions that ensure an excess of exports over imports, and in part because Japan is seen as having been slow to use its wealth to stimulate economic growth in the Third World. And the Third World itself, always struggling against adverse terms of trade, finds the wealth gap widening as their debt obligations erode the value of their exports, so that no matter by how much trade balances improve, their standard of living continues to slip relative to the industrialized world. This interplay of trade, money, debt, and investment in the global political economy is the subject of the next chapter.

CHAPTER 14

International Monetary Exchange

While it is handy to discuss international trade in terms of a steady flow of imports and exports that offset one another in value, such perfect reciprocity rarely exists. Even in the uncommon case in which one nation's trade with a single partner is in perfect balance, it would not follow that the country's world trade for the same period would be in perfect balance. More typically, a nation may have an export surplus with respect to some trading partners and an import surplus with respect to others, putting its total trade in surplus (higher total export value than import value), deficit (higher import value than export value), or balance (equal import and export values). A nation's annual trade performance and its performance trend over a period of a few years are important indicators of its economic condition, irrespective of its standard of living.

But note that the discussion of international trade in Chapter 13 emphasized the importance of trade value rather than trade volume. (Although volume units were used in the hypothetical example of wheat and autos in Taiwanese-American trade, certain assumptions were made in advance with regard to the value of labor and produce.) Needless to say, given the complexities of international trade, simple barter is rarely if ever used. Value is measured in monetary units, and because of social and economic differences among countries, national currency units have different absolute values. As a result, their values have to be compared with one another. To an American, for example, a dollar is worth a dollar (although with inflation it purchases less even in the domestic market than it did at any earlier time). To an Italian, a hundred lira are worth a hundred lira, and to a Briton, a pound is worth a pound. But when an American dollar is offered in Canada, it may bring anywhere from 90 Canadian cents to 1 dollar and 30 cents Canadian. In London, it will draw about 2.2 pounds sterling, and in Rome, a cascade of lira. Hence, while a dollar is worth a dollar, it is also worth a specified amount in foreign currencies. The same is true of all national currencies: A national unit has a price in international exchange, and the price may vary frequently, perhaps even daily, and sometimes violently. Goods are traded internationally according to the prevailing relative values of the currencies of the importing country and exporting country. Table 14–1 provides sample exchange rates for eight capitalist countries on a given date.

Note that in this table only capitalist currencies are considered. Comparing values of currencies in the capitalist world with those of the socialist is extremely difficult, because of the different way in which these two fundamentally different economic philosophies attach value to goods. This is one factor that hinders the growth of East-West trade and one reason that trade between, say, the United States and the Soviet Union usually takes place in massive, celebrated, long-range contracts rather than through a consistent flow of traded goods that are constantly repriced according to market value. Virtually any licensed American corporation can trade with a British counterpart in a legal commodity, but the exchange of grain between the United States and the Soviet Union calls for a long-range contract at permanent terms that are worked out in advance.

Also note that the figures in Table 14–1 are for a specified date. This suggests, correctly, that currency values change constantly. In a stable and unchanging relationship, currency values fluctuate in only small amounts. But in a dynamic complex of trading relations among nations, fluctuations can be extreme, and divergences of value can be dramatic. These changes will be influenced by such factors as volume activity, different rates of capital investment, different degrees of productivity, variations in incentives, domestic inflation or deflation, and the like. From 1979 to 1983, for example, the American dollar became steadily less valuable in international finance, while the German mark and the Japanese yen gained in value. It gradually took more American dollars to purchase German and Japanese goods because it took more dollars of lower value to purchase marks or yen of higher value. Then in 1984 the value of the dollar began to rise, more nearly equating the values of

Table 14–1 Sample currency exchange rates in the capitalist world.

January 8, 1981 Middle Rate For	US Dollar	Belgian Franc	British Pound	Canadian Dollar	French Franc	German Mark	Italian Lira	Japanese Yen
1 US dollar	1	31.57	0.416	1.188	4.537	1.963	932.4	201.5
100 Belgian francs	3.168	100	1.318	3.763	14.37	6.219	2954	638.3
1 British pound	2.405	75.90	1	2.856	10.91	4.720	2242	484.5
1 Canadian dollar	0.842	26.58	0.350	1	3.820	1.653	785.0	169.6
110 French francs	2.204	69.57	0.917	2.618	110	4.326	2055	444.1
1 German mark	0.509	16.08	0.212	0.605	2.311	1	475.0	102.6
1000 Italian lira	1.072	33.85	0.446	1.274	4.866	2.105	1000	216.1
1000 Japanese yen	4.963	156.7	2.064	5.895	22.52	9.742	4627	1000

Source: World Business Weekly, January 19, 1981, p. 56. Adapted and published with permission.

the three currencies. At that point, German and Japanese goods became relatively less expensive for Americans, and American goods became relatively more expensive for people spending marks or yen. In 1986, the fall of the dollar resumed and hit record low values against the yen. This resulted once again in a relative rise in the price of Japanese goods for American consumers and a reduction in the cost of American goods on international markets. The rule that emerges is a simple one: As a currency rises in value relative to others, the price of goods originating in the country of that currency will rise; and as it loses relative value, those prices will fall.

This simple rule has profound political economic consequences. International economic activity is, after all, designed to strengthen the domestic economy and to contribute to domestic political stability. If changes in currency values have far-reaching effects on relative import and export values, both the economic and the political goals of global activity may be undermined. If, for example, the rise of the dollar's value makes American-built machinery so expensive internationally that consumers turn to German or French imports (assuming roughly equivalent quality), then the machine tool industry in the United States will be adversely affected. Fewer units will be exported, and because the overall production level was set with the assumption that exports represented productivity in excess of domestic demand, buyers at home will not be able to consume those units that are no longer exported. Results: Production goes down; investment is curtailed; income is reduced; employees are released; and plants may be closed. But the ramifications run still deeper: The loss of income results in reduced bank deposits, a decline in capital accumulation, and a reduction of investment in other industries. Meanwhile, both the industry and the unemployed workers pay less to tax revenues—the source of public investment—commensurate with their lost income. In fact, the workers may now draw subsistence from public welfare, thus not only eliminating them as taxpayers but also transforming them into financial liabilities for public revenue. Hence, as public revenue declines, public expense rises, and changes are forced upon the distribution of the public treasury. The variation in currency value has now resulted in social and economic changes at home. The domestic political consequences will depend on the intensity of the change and on public reaction to it, but could range from mild changes in political alignment to revolution. Almost invariably, one of the consequences is hostility to foreign goods and a demand for protectionism.

Return now to the simpler level of international trade and consider this question: Does it pay for an American to buy an Italian car priced at 1 million lira rather than an American car priced at $5000, assuming the quality of the two products to be identical? Or does it pay for the Italian consumer to buy the American car at these prices? The questions cannot be answered without knowing the exchange rates between the two currencies. Americans do not ordinarily carry lira to the market, and Italians do not ordinarily carry dollars. The exchange rate is, therefore, the instrument through which the price system of one country is related to the price system of the other. Pegged at one level, the exchange rate might stimulate American interest in Italian products and discourage Italian interest in American products. Pegged at a different level, the exchange rate might reduce American interest in Italian goods and increase Italian receptivity to American products. At some intermediate point, the exchange rate might result in mutual trade: Some Italian goods would be less expensive for buyers in both countries, while other American products would be advantaged in both markets. The exchange rate determines the price of each country's goods in the other's markets.

Now take another example. Suppose that on some hypothetical Day One the German mark and the American dollar are exchangeable one for one. Suppose also that identical automobiles are made in the two countries such that the American model will sell in Germany for $10,000 and the German model will sell in the United States for $10,000. Now suppose that at some subsequent Day Two, because of a variety of national and international factors, the mark has become twice as valuable as the dollar; it would now take two dollars to buy one mark. It follows that it will now take two of the American models to purchase (or trade for) one German model. If one is exchanged for one, Germany will be owed the cash value of a second in order to get its full value from the trade, since trade is measured in value. Without such a payment, Germany will have suffered a trade deficit in the transaction; but in order to compensate Germany's trade balance by making a payment of $10,000, the United States must incur a payment deficit of $10,000.

The constant change in relative currency values adds further complication. Whether by official governmental policy, international agreement, or the informalities of the international currency markets, changes occur daily. United States citizens who live along the Canadian border watch the value of the Canadian dollar to determine when, even after calculation for import duties, it is more advantageous to shop across the border than at home. When the variation in the US and Canadian dollars is small, the border crossings will drop. But between 1984 and 1989, when the Canadian dollar was valued at about 66 US cents, crossings went up sharply as shoppers, diners, and vacationers looked forward to the lucrative advantage. By the same token, in 1984 the value of the US dollar was at a record high relative to virtually all the Western European currencies. Americans traveling in Europe raved about the purchasing power of the dollar, and European companies ran special excursions to lure American shoppers. Meanwhile, however, the value of the dollar was making American goods prohibitive to foreign buyers; so while American shoppers enjoyed their binge in Europe, the US balance of trade began to become an emergency for public policy. Three years later, through a combination of international agreements and natural fluctuations in the currency markets, the dollar had reached record low values against the Japanese yen and other national currencies. Only by making American goods less expensive in foreign markets than those of competitors would the decline in the trade balance be reversed. And as the dollar dropped in value, using it for international travel became far less advantageous, and Americans began to complain that international vacations were beyond their means.

These everyday phenomena of the global political economy comprise little more than the crust of an enormously complex system of trade and payments. In the preceding chapter we dealt with trade and balances of trade. Here we launch into the far more complex—and, to some, the more mysterious—aspects of international economic life, seen not from the perspective of the foreign traveler but from the macroeconomic viewpoint of governments. As material interdependence has increased the importance and volume of international trade, so too has the global exchange of goods and services strained the machinery by which nations balance their accounts with one another.

The International Monetary System

Among the most important characteristics of the global political economy is the international monetary system. It is a web of international organizations, national policies, bilateral and multilateral agreements, currency markets, and business behaviors of governments, corporations, and individuals. Here we will be concerned principally with the intergovernmental portion, which is designed to aid national governments in regulating international economic behavior, encouraging international economic activity, and facilitating the balances of national trade and payments. In the preceding chapter, the discussion of the General Agreement on Tariffs and Trade (GATT) was our first encounter with the international monetary system.

Before World War I, the world operated almost exclusively on a gold standard of exchange. National currencies were fixed in value at some percentage (or multiple) of gold's value. When a nation's trade fell into deficit, the balance was made up by payment in gold, either by the physical transfer of gold blocks or by accounting between central banks. In the interwar period, as international trade reached new heights and as the dollar rose above all others in desirability, gold and the dollar together ruled the international monetary system and gradually became almost interchangeable. But as dollars were shipped

International monetary system out of control.
Source: Oswaldo/Excelsior/Mexico City

to Europe for recovery and reindustrialization, the debt burden of the European governments mounted. With this history in mind, much of the non-military diplomacy of the last two years of World War II addressed the postwar configuration of the monetary system, with all parties seeking official safeguards against a repetition of the debt crisis of the interwar years.

Out of this diplomacy came the Bretton Woods system, named for the 1944 conference in the United States at which the outline of the new monetary system was introduced by the American delegate. Complex and intricate by the standards of the 1940s, today it seems remarkably simple in its original design. Indeed, because of its simplicity, this system was unable to endure all the problems of the postwar global economy and succumbed to major changes in the 1970s. Its main components are the International Monetary Fund (IMF) and the International Bank for Reconstruction and Development (IBRD or the World Bank). In 1956, in an effort to stimulate private investment in the developing countries, the newly created International Finance Corporation was affiliated with the IBRD, as was the International Development Association (IDA). The role of the IDA is to provide loans at subsidized rates to the developing nations. Because only the IMF is directly involved in settling national accounts, our attention here will be limited to that.

The International Monetary Fund

The Bretton Woods system was a response to the dual needs of a standardized code of behavior for international trade, finance, and payments, and a source of borrowing for nations with temporary balance-of-payments deficits. Consistent with the informal practice of the later interwar years, the IMF was based on the principle of a gold-exchange standard in which the dollar was equated with gold at $35 per ounce, and the US government guaranteed to exchange dollars for gold at a ratio of one to one. All other currencies were given fixed rates relative to gold and the dollar and were allowed to rise or decline in market price by a maximum of 1 percent. If market forces changed a currency's value more than this, the country of that currency's origin was pledged to draw on its reserves (originally gold and dollars but later other valuable or "convertible" currencies) to purchase the excess of its own currency on the international exchange at a price within the plus or minus 1 percent band. Changes in par value could be made only with permission of the IMF upon the satisfactory demonstration of a fundamental disequilibrium between the current par value and the international economic forces affecting the currency.

This concept of equilibrium was central to the theory of the IMF, for it appeared not only in the standards for revaluation but also in the quota system for borrowing, in the voting system, and in the borrowing machinery. Upon entering the fund, each government was given a quota based on the global ranking of its trade and other factors related to its economic stability and currency value. This quota then dictated three important factors: the distribution of voting rights, the obligation to store financial reserves with the fund, and the magnitude of the borrowing rights. Voting rights were weighted by quota (proportional voting), thereby giving the greatest power over the international monetary system to the economically strongest nations. And because voting was used to determine currency values, borrowing rights, and subsequent changes in the fund's reserve holdings, this was one of the most important political decisions that gave rise to the postwar international monetary system.

The assignment of a quota determined how much of its reserves a government would store with the IMF. Once this was established, 25 percent of the total was submitted to the fund's accounts in gold and the remainder in the national currency. Thereafter, upon sustaining a (presumably short-term) balance-of-payments deficit, the government could go to the fund to borrow back some of its reserves. It was limited to borrowing 25 percent of its quota per year for a maximum of five years, and its first 25 percent increment had to be its own gold deposit. In subsequent years, its borrowing would be not in its own currency but in convertible currencies (originally US dollars) that were more desirable to international creditors than was the debtor's currency. Repayment was to be within five years of each annual borrowing and was made by buying back from the fund the debtor's own currency, by depositing convertible currencies presumably gained by the strengthened trade position enabled by the borrowing. At the end of the repayment cycle, the fund would again hold no more than 75 percent of the country's quota in its own currency.

With a number of policy changes, the IMF dominated the international monetary system from 1947 to 1970. Among the most important changes were the establishment of the two-tier gold system in 1968 and the introduction of the Special Drawing Rights (SDRs) in 1970. Both were responses to declining international financial reserves in the face of an enormous increase in international trade and the resulting disequilibria. The two-tier gold system, invented primarily as a means of protecting the American gold supply—recall that under Bretton Woods the United States was obliged to exchange dollars for gold, and the glut of dollars in Europe was beginning to find its way into the demand for gold exchange—maintained the value of gold at $35 per ounce among the central banks but permitted it to fluctuate by market forces outside official circles. The SDR, sometimes called "paper gold," was a wholly new invention and will be discussed later. Despite the importance of these modifications, by 1971 the Bretton Woods system was strained beyond repair. As a consequence, the first fundamental changes in the postwar international monetary system were introduced.

After the Bretton Woods System

By 1971, the global economy was already undergoing major structural changes. Although OPEC had not yet embarked upon its meteoric rise, trade and exchange between the Third World and both the Soviet Union and the West had already begun to alter some of the assumptions on which the Bretton Woods system had been constructed. At the same time, both Europe and Japan had recovered fully from the economic ravages of World War II and were rapidly invading America's reserve domains in international trade. The European Economic Community (EEC) was beginning to challenge the United

States and, furthermore, used its customs-union characteristics to diminish the access of American goods to Western European markets. Japan's export industries were beginning to threaten American exclusivity elsewhere. In an effort to overcome the Western European import barriers, American companies began constructing manufacturing plants in Europe, thus unleashing a vast flow of private capital out of the United States. And in contrast with the Bretton Woods assumption that balance-of-payments deficits would be temporary, some nations, including the United States, fell into chronic debtor status. SDRs and the two-tiered gold system notwithstanding, world reserves relative to trade continued to dwindle. The dollar shortage of the early Bretton Woods years evolved into a dollar glut, with such an abundance of dollars in foreign markets, especially those of Western Europe, that their real value declined despite the artificiality of the fixed-rate system of currency values. As European central banks sought to retrieve the full value of their dollars, they demanded American gold, the supply of which was falling into dangerously short supply (because of the gold backing requirement ensuring that for every dollar of circulating currency there would be a gold reserve of at least 20 cents). The international monetary system was in crisis.

This crisis was addressed by the dominant members of the IMF in Washington in 1971, and the result of their deliberation was the Smithsonian Agreement. The fixed-rate system of currency values was abandoned in favor of freely fluctuating rates, and the United States was released from its obligation to exchange dollars for gold at a one-to-one ratio. The official value of gold was raised to US $38, a device for effectively devaluing the dollar by about 9 percent. Other currency values were also officially changed before going to market fluctuation, the most important among them being the German mark, at the time the most desirable of the convertible currencies. Subsequent changes have introduced the so-called managed float system, a combination of valuing currencies by both market forces and government policy (by purchasing excess currency). The separation of gold from the dollar was a formal departure from the gold-exchange standard established by the Bretton Woods system and effectively placed the Western world on a dollar system, with all currencies valued in relation to the American currency. Because the dollar now fluctuates, sometimes wildly, a practice has emerged of periodically adjusting the dollar value of an SDR and then presenting currency values and certain international economic statistics in SDR-equivalent values.

The Smithsonian Agreement is broadly regarded as the triumph of monetarism in the international global economy, that is, the recognition of the superior role of adjusting monetary policy to resolve the disequilibria of international payments. The system continues to evolve. Throughout the 1980s, for example, there was a series of intergovernmental meetings (variously called G–5, G–7, and G–10 meetings, depending on the number of participants), some of them hastily, and even secretly, called to deal with urgent matters of adjustment. In 1986 and 1987, when, after a period of high valuation, the American dollar once again fell precipitously, the finance ministers met several times to determine methods either to stabilize the dollar or to stem its fall at a level at which it would contribute positively rather than negatively to the US balance-of-trade deficit. Once again we come to the interrelation between trade and payments and between the international political economy and the forces of domestic politics.

The importance of currency valuations cannot be overstated. The value of a national currency relative to others will not only have direct consequences for international activity but may have major impacts on the domestic economy as well. In the era of fixed rates, those governments whose currencies were artificially undervalued did not wish to revalue upward, because such actions tend to diminish the profitability of international activity. Meanwhile, those countries whose currencies were artificially overvalued did not wish to revalue downward for fear that such action would be interpreted either domestically or globally as a sign of economic decline. Fluctuating rates, whether by free float or managed float, overcome these difficulties; but in return, they increase the burden on those responsible for national monetary policy to invoke both monetary policy and diplomacy to direct currency values to levels that will maximize the value of international trade and minimize the effects of international disadvantage on the domestic economy.

National Accounts

Having studied both international trade and the international monetary system, we now turn to the concept of national accounts, of which both trade and payments are important parts. In the simpler days of the past, national accounts consisted almost entirely of the import and export of goods and services and the import and export of funds. Today, however, fluctuating currency rates have introduced international currency speculation; transnational corporations move capital around the world creating simultaneously capital deficits for the home accounts and improved overseas assets; governments use their reserves for both anticipating future payments needs and purchasing their own currencies from foreign central banks in order to control their value and may also buy other currencies to affect their values.

These complexities notwithstanding, we begin with the assumption that the comprehensive balance of a nation's accounts is a product of the import and export of goods and services and the import and export of funds, both public and private. The export of a load of tractors means a financial earning, so that the transaction contributes positively to a trade balance. An import of a similar load contributes negatively. The use of domestic funds to support an undertaking overseas, on the other hand, means that the domestic economy is deprived of those funds, and so the export of funds contributes negatively to a payments balance. When those funds are returned to the domestic economy, however, they contribute positively to the domestic payments balance. A simple rule of thumb will help sort out some of the first-order confusions of these differences: Goods going out contribute positively, but funds going out contribute negatively; and goods coming in contribute negatively, whereas funds coming in contribute positively. The reason for this apparent contradiction is that exchanges are viewed in terms of value. The sale of tractors means receipt of payment. If that payment comes from another country, it represents a net addition to the domestic account. Conversely, when investment capital is sent abroad, the action represents a net reduction in the domestic account. Only when that investment begins to profit and only when the earnings from the investment or the proceeds of its subsequent sale are returned to the domestic economy, does it enter the books as a net increase in the domestic account.

As recently as a decade ago, this simple rule and its direct consequences told most of the story of national payments balances. Today, however, as global economic activity continues to become more extensive and complex, statements of payments balances include many other factors, and the older notion, that the so-called current account (composed of the balance of goods and services together with the balance of direct investment and other long-term capital movements) accurately states a country's payments condition, no longer holds. Today the annual payments statement adds to these such things as net reserve position (in gold, foreign exchange, SDRs, and IMF credit), short-term capital movements, and liabilities constituting the foreign reserves of other countries. Table 14–2 is a simple organization of the contributing factors, identifying the activities that are typical of the public sector and the private sector. The right-hand column aggregates these activities into the specific categories of payments accounting. We will review each of those here and then explore how the IMF actually follows and states national balances.

The Public Sector

The simplest influences in the public sector on the national balance are the payment or collection of fees, debt, and the interest on debt. For the collector, the influx of the payment means a net positive increase on the national account; for the payor, the outflow of funds represents a withdrawal from the national account. Foreign aid has much the same reciprocal influences: The lender withdraws funds and ships them away, and the recipient has a net positive increase in its cumulative capital resources. Also relatively simple is the payment of direct expenses abroad, or the payment by foreigners of direct expenses in a host economy. The stationing of American troops in Europe, for example, is extremely costly for the United States and represents a continuous outflow of funds. From the Western European perspective, on the other hand, the funds used for the payment and support of American military personnel and their dependents are spent in the local economies for food, housing, education, entertainment, and the like. This is a constant stimulus to the Western European economies, providing not only individual livelihoods but savings and capital accumulation as well. And in periods in which the value of the US dollar is high relative to the local currency, every dollar expended in this way represents increased wealth.

The international sale of public securities has become one of the major devices of international exchange in the last decade. The annual expenditures of many governments exceed their revenues. Although many borrow abroad, others choose to enlarge their revenues by selling public securities. Until the last decade, most of these were consumed at home. Millions of Americans, for

Table 14–2 Factors influencing national balances.

	Positive Influences	*Negative Influences*	*Balancing Factor*
Balance of Trade	1. Export of goods 2. Export of services	Import of goods Import of services	1.⎫ 2.⎭ Net trade position
Balance of Payments			
1. Public sector	1. Collection of debt 2. Collection of fees 3. Collection of interest on debt 4. Direct expenses paid by foreigners	Payment of debt Payment of fees Payment of interest Direct expenses abroad	1.⎫ 2.⎪ 3.⎬ Net cash position 4.⎭
	5. Receipt of foreign aid 6. Sale of public securites abroad	Payment of foreign aid	5.⎫ 6.⎭ Net capital position
	7. Preservation of IMF credit 8. Preservation of SDRs 9. Acquisition of gold 10. Currency-strengthening policy	Use of IMF credit Use of SDRs Loss of gold Currency-weakening policy	7.⎫ 8.⎪ 9.⎬ Net reserve position 10.⎭
2. Private sector	1. Import of capital 2. Repatriation of capital 3. Repatriation of foreign earnings 4.	Export of capital Purchase of foreign public securities	1.⎫ 2.⎪ 3.⎬ Net capital position 4.⎭
	5. Corporate expenses of foreigners 6. Personal expenses of foreigners 7. Collection of interest 8. Collection of foreign debt	Corporate expenses abroad Personal expenses abroad Payment of interest Payment of foreign debt	5.⎫ 6.⎪ 7.⎬ Net cash position 8.⎭
	9. Successful currency speculation 10. Reinvestment of foreign earnings abroad	Unsuccessful currency speculation	9. Net reserve position 10. Postponement of effect

example, own savings bonds, one of the simplest forms of government security. More recently, however, as the discrepancy between the national budget and the government's annual revenue from taxation has increased (the national debt doubled between 1981 and 1986), government securities have been sold more frequently and in unprecedented amounts. Today a declining percentage of this paper is bought by domestic consumers, and more by foreign governments and corporations. Increasingly the United States depends on Japanese investors to purchase US government securities and releases them at long-term interest rates designed specifically to attract Japanese buyers. These sales represent capital inflow for the United States and capital outflow for Japan, although ironically, they also represent a tremendous long-term debt for the United States and a long-term profit for Japan. Once they come to maturity and are paid off, the cumulative and final payments to Japanese investors will represent a substantial capital gain for the Japanese and a significant long-term outflow of capital for the United States.

The final device available to the national government is the enhancement of its reserves. It is true, of course, that all the foregoing are instruments for increasing government reserves. But it is more accurate to say that they all are means of improving a government's net capital position. The distinction is that net capital is for current investment, whereas reserves are intended as savings in specific forms to be used subsequently to meet payments problems. The means by which governments do this are, specifically, acquiring gold at advantageous prices; acquiring and/or saving diverse currency reserves, emphasizing those that are most likely to be convertible in the future; minimizing credit obligations to the IMF; and maintaining a balance between net increases in capital outflow and anticipated revenue from capital investment and foreign aid.

Given the fluctuations of the global economy, a government's reserve position is crucial to both its liquidity and its solvency. Before the establishment of the postwar international monetary system, reserves consisted entirely of gold and foreign currencies held in reserve. The advent of the IMF changed that, first with the invention of fund credit as previously described, and later (1970) with the addition of the SDRs. Unlike ordinary fund credit, the SDR represents a recognition that balance-of-payments problems can be chronic. The SDR is an artificial unit of credit that the IMF allocates to a government. The fund may, upon the satisfactory demonstration of a chronic problem in the payments balance, authorize a government to use the SDR to borrow convertible currencies from the central banks of the participating governments. The SDR's own value is based on the values of a "basket" of dominant currencies—the American dollar, the German mark, the British pound, the French franc, and the Japanese yen. Thus, as in the case with individual currencies, the SDR's value is subject to fluctuation; but because it is based on several currencies simultaneously, whose values frequently change with respect to one another, these fluctuations are small compared with those experienced by the individual currencies.

Once authorization is granted to a government to use its SDRs, each participating country is required to accept the SDRs in exchange for convertible currencies up to a level of twice its own SDR allocation. Although SDRs are not literally currency and cannot be spent for commodities, they have the effect of expanding governmental payment capabilities by making convertible currency reserves available. This right is subject at all times to the IMF's

Table 14–3 SDR distribution, 1970–1988, expressed in SDR value units.

	1970	1975	1980	1985	1988
Industrialized nations	2.6	7.2	8.9	14.9	17.6
Developing nations	0.5	1.5	2.9	3.3	2.6
Total	3.1	8.7	11.8	18.2	20.2

Source: International Monetary Fund, *International Financial Statistics,* 1986, pp. 48–49; for 1988, *International Financial Statistics Yearbook,* 1989, pp. 53–55.

Table 14–4 Fund credit distribution, 1970–1988, expressed in SDR billions.

	1970	1975	1980	1985	1988
Industrialized nations	6.6	7.7	10.7	25.2	19.5
Developing nations	1.0	4.9	6.1	13.5	8.8
Total	7.7	12.6	16.8	38.7	28.3

Source: International Monetary Fund, *International Financial Statistics, 1986,* pp. 52–53; and 1989, pp. 53–54.

voting procedures, which are complex and weighted in favor of the most important currencies, including the American dollar. Nevertheless, their creation has been regarded as "a genuine breakthrough in monetary thinking,"[1] and has contributed considerably to easing the currency reserve problem of countries with chronic trade deficits.

The importance of SDRs as reserve units is underscored by the degree to which their total value grew in only 15 years. When the units were first distributed in 1970, they totaled only $3.124 billion. But by the end of 1985, the total amount had risen to $18.2 billion, $14.9 billion of which were held by the industrialized countries and only $3.3 billion by the combined developing countries.[2] These figures indicate both the extent of the industrialized world's reliance on expanded reserve assets and the degree to which the chronic debtors in the international payments scheme are industrialized rather than developing nations. Table 14–3 indicates the SDRs' evolution and distribution, and Table 14–4 shows the traditional fund credit for the same period of time. Note the much greater difference between the developed and the developing nations with respect to SDRs, compared with traditional fund credit.

For most of the postwar years, international financial statistics were kept and expressed in US$ billions. Today, however, with fluctuating exchange rates and the dollar's unreliability, the IMF expresses such statistics in value equivalents of the SDR. Hence, its value with respect to the dollar or any other currency has become a matter of importance. When the SDR was established, it was equated with gold. Their relative values were expressed as one

---

[1] Fritz Machlup, *Remaking the International Monetary System* (Baltimore: Johns Hopkins University Press, 1968), p. 34.
[2] See William J. Byrne, "Evolution of the SDR, 1974–81," in John Adams, ed., *The Contemporary International Economy,* 2nd ed. (New York: St. Martin's Press, 1985), pp. 340–350.

to one or as SDR/US\$ = 1.0 and, conversely, US\$/SDR = 1.0. As both the dollar and the basket of currencies have fluctuated, however, the equivalence has changed, the SDR being sometimes more valuable than the dollar and sometimes less valuable. In 1979, the SDR reached its high point with respect to the dollar, rising to a value of \$1.32 per SDR. That is, an SDR was no longer worth \$1.00 but, rather, \$1.32. Its low point was in 1984 when the dollar was at an extremely high point in the international exchange, with the SDR falling to US \$0.98. Thereafter, it rose to a new high of \$1.42 in 1987 and settled back to \$1.35 in 1988.

Another reserve unit available to governments, although outside the IMF structure, is the European Currency Unit (ECU), often called an E–note and abbreviated as *Æ*. Originally established for the sole use of EC members in balancing their payments, the E–note is now used between the EC and its major trading partners, such as the United States, Canada, and Japan. The E–note's value is determined in much the same way as is the SDR. In 1979, it was worth US \$1.442, and fell in 1985 to \$0.888. By 1987, it had risen again to \$1.303, and in 1988 tailed off again to \$1.173. Like virtually everything else financial in nature—national currencies, stocks and bonds, SDRs, and even gold—the ECU is subject to significant shifts in value according to the other pressures of the international markets.

In sum, then, national financial reserves in the current global economy consist of fund credit, SDRs, foreign currencies held in reserve, and gold at the official rate. Table 14–5 depicts the evolution of the US reserve position for the years 1970 to 1988. Note particularly the following features of Table 14–5: (1) the American gold stock has remained almost perfectly stable for 15 years, after a substantial fall in the 1960s; (2) only after OPEC began its slide from power did the United States once again begin to amass foreign currency reserves; and (3) the greatest increase in the net US reserve position has been through the devices of the IMF, in both traditional credit and SDRs. In the case of Japan, the great advance has not been through the IMF, in which its SDR credit is \$2.9 billion and its traditional credit is \$3.3 billion, but in vast holdings of foreign currencies, \$90.5 billion in 1988 as contrasted to a mere \$3.2 billion in 1970 and only \$22.3 billion in 1985. Table 14–6 shows the trends in foreign currency holdings from 1970 to 1987 for Western and OPEC nations. No other reserves figure in this table. The extreme right-hand column is not read in dollars, but in the maximum extent to which a country's cur-

Table 14–5 US net reserve position, 1970–1988, in billions of US dollars.

	1970	*1975*	*1980*	*1985*	*1988*
SDRs	\$ 0.85	\$ 2.33	\$ 2.61	\$ 7.29	\$ 7.16
IMF credit	1.94	2.21	2.85	11.95	9.75
Foreign exchange	0.63	0.08	10.13	12.86	17.36
Gold	11.07	11.60	11.16	11.09	11.06
Total	\$14.49	\$16.22	\$26.75	\$43.19	\$45.33

Source: International Monetary Fund, *International Financial Statistics Yearbook*, 1989, pp. 720–721.

Table 14–6 Comparative trends in national currency reserves, 1970–1987, in billions of US dollars.

	1970	1976	1980	1985	1987	Maximum Multiple
Industrialized nations						
US	$0.6	$ 0.3	$10.1	$12.1	$13.1	21.8
Canada	3.0	3.5	2.1	2.5	6.2	2.1
France	1.3	4.4	25.3	24.3	29.6	22.8
W. Germany	8.5	25.5	43.9	39.0	72.9	8.6
Japan	3.2	13.9	21.6	22.3	75.7	23.7
OPEC nations						
Kuwait	$0.0	$ 0.9	$ 3.4	$ 4.7	$ 3.4	470.0
Saudi Arabia	0.5	24.3	20.7	13.8	10.8	21.6
Venezuela	0.5	6.9	5.6	8.9	4.5	17.8
Iran	0.1	7.5	14.6	NA	NA	146.0
United Arab Emirates	0.0	1.8	1.9	NA	NA	19.0

Source: Statistical Abstract of the United States, 1981 (Washington, D.C.: US Government Printing Office, 1982), p. 889; *1982/83*, p. 888; *1987*, p. 838; and *1989*, p. 838. For Iran, the final figure is for 1979; thereafter, figures are unavailable owing to the revolution and war with Iraq. The data source discontinued Kuwait in 1987.

rency reserves have multiplied in the 18-year period. Note that Japan, the United States, and West Germany have steadily amassed these reserves, each multiplying about 22 times from its lowest level during the period. Note also that with the decline and stabilization of OPEC in the mid-1980s, the currency reserves of its richest members declined sharply from their peaks.

The Private Sector

The private sector's contributions to the national payments account are considerably easier to understand, even though they include currency speculation and the purchase of foreign public securities. Corporate and personal expenses paid by foreigners, or the payment of such expenses received from foreigners, play the same role as do the payment and receipt of direct expenses by governments. And the payment or receipt of interest on a foreign debt is identical to the corresponding category in the public sector.

The other categories all relate to private investment, either directly into industry or into securities portfolios. Sending investment capital abroad represents an account deficit, even though it also creates a net investment advantage and a potential long-term capital gain. It is an immediate capital improvement in the recipient country. This relationship lasts only until the profits from the investment are repatriated or until the investment is sold and the original capital and profit are returned home, now representing a net capital advantage to the home economy and a net deficit to the host.

In recent years, the net American position on US investment abroad and foreign investment in the United States for all categories—direct private investment (construction of plant, and so on), indirect private investment (pur-

Inside Fort Knox
Source: Fred Conrad /Sygma

chase of stocks and bonds), and public securities (sale and purchase of government securities, a major means by which governments borrow money)—has reversed; and in the mid-1980s, the United States went from being the world's largest creditor to the world's largest debtor. In a subsequent section, ''The World Debt Crisis,'' this is demonstrated statistically.

Not all money invested abroad represents additional capital outflow. Foreign investments, like investments at home, appreciate regularly. The annual earnings may be reinvested (for example, an American-owned manufacturing plant in Spain is enlarged using funds from annual earnings) or repatriated (returned home) to be distributed to stock holders. How much will be reinvested and how much repatriated will be determined by such issues as tax policies in the home and host countries, corporate priorities, competition, long-range planning, and so forth. Or foreign earnings may be moved to another foreign site for investment or reinvestment. Table 14–7 demonstrates the pattern of earnings reinvestment by Americans abroad and for foreign investors in the United States for 1987 and 1988. It shows that for Americans abroad, earnings declined slightly in 1988, but the fraction that was repatriated doubled. For foreign investors in the United States, both earnings and the portion reinvested doubled. The table does not show that in 1987 American investments abroad returned earnings of 19.3 percent and dipped in 1988 to 15.2 percent, while earnings on foreign investments in the United States rose from a mere 3.9 percent to 5.6 percent.

Table 14–7 Distribution of earnings on foreign investment, 1987–1988, in billions of US dollars.

	Earned	*Reinvested*	*Repatriated*	*% Reinvested*
US investment abroad				
1987	$58.5	$34.3	$24.2	59
1988	52.3	15.2	37.1	29
Foreign investment in US				
1987	$ 6.0	$ 1.5	$ 4.5	25
1988	12.1	6.6	5.5	55

Source: Survey of Current Business, August 1989, pp. 48–51 and 64–65.

The advent of fluctuating currency values introduced a whole new profession to the realm of international finance, that of the currency speculator. As we have seen, a currency unit that has a value of $100 today may rise to $110 next year or fall to $70. The wise speculator will buy currencies that are low but climbing in value. The speculator is a student of gross economic trends: interest rates, economic stability, employment trends, political stability, and other factors influencing currency values. A thorough knowledge of these trends will tell him or her when to buy a currency, just as if buying the stock of IBM or Boeing, in the expectation of selling it later as its value increases.

But not all currency speculation is for such a long term. Unlike the stock markets where trading takes place in public, the global currency market is a network of computerized private selling floors, worldwide telephones, and satellite communications. The selling rooms are in New York, Hong Kong, Zurich, London, Tokyo, Rome, and a few other places. In one of these, a currency may be selling for $1.03 and in another only $.97. In the latter a trader may buy 10 million units and then alert his or her correspondent in the former to sell 10 million units. The transfer from one city to another around the world takes place by a computerized transaction, and if the sale works out, the two traders will have made for their client a half-million dollars in a few moments. And because these transactions frequently take place in magnitudes of hundreds of millions or even billions of dollars, the profits are often multiples of a million. In fact, it is no longer uncommon for the trader to make several million dollars in commissions on such activities. From an international perspective, while these funds are in foreign hands, they represent a net liability for the country of origin and a net increase in the reserves of the country in which they are deposited.

These, then, are the basic components of a nation's balance of payments. The many parts are regularly brought together by governmental agencies and by such international organizations as the World Bank and the IMF. Table 14–8 uses the recently redesigned IMF format. It serves both as an example of the manner in which this accounting is presented and as statistical information about changes in the global economy in the first half of the 1980s. (The lines are numbered so that the text can refer more easily to some of the table's important features.)

Table 14–8 Aggregated balances, 1980 and 1985, for the United States, West Germany, Japan, and Saudi Arabia, expressed in billions of SDRs.

	United States 1980	United States 1985	Germany 1980	Germany 1985	Japan 1980	Japan 1985	Saudi Arabia 1980	Saudi Arabia 1985	Line No.
A. Current account	1.45	−115.66	−12.19	13.29	−8.25	48.00	32.849	−12.769	1
Merchandise exp.	172.38	211.53	140.73	170.85	97.42	170.96	77.38	27.50	2
Merchandise imp.	−191.95	−333.44	−134.05	−142.89	−95.77	−116.24	−19.64	20.06	3
Services: credit	90.84	141.66	39.47	48.75	24.20	44.83	8.66	15.12	4
Service: debit	−63.99	−120.74	−48.75	−53.02	−32.92	−49.92	−25.87	−26.96	5
Other	−5.83	−14.67	−9.60	−10.40	−1.17	−1.63	−7.68	−8.64	6
B. Direct investments and other long-term capital	−6.53	69.28	2.12	−2.19	1.81	−61.98	−21.04	11.02	8
Direct investments	−1.81	−0.31	−2.99	−2.90	−1.62	−5.72	−2.45	2.47	11
Portfolio investments	2.20	66.22	7.12	3.05	7.23	−40.81	−18.13	8.54	12
Other	−6.92	−7.37	−0.74	3.26	−3.80	−15.45	−0.46	−0−	13
Total A & B (basic balance)	−5.08	−46.38	−10.07	11.11	−6.44	−13.98	11.81	−1.75	15
C. Short-term capital	−21.07	28.74	−1.80	−14.02	12.71	9.68	−8.78	1.06	18
D. Net errors/omissions	19.19	23.29	−0.24	3.55	−2.39	4.48	−0−	−0−	20
E. Counterpart items	0.80	1.23	−0.4	−1.26	0.62	−2.82	0.71	−1.79	22
Total A–E (official Settlements balance)	−6.16	6.88	−12.16	−.63	4.50	−2.64	0.74	−2.49	25
F. Exceptional financing	0.90	−0−	−0−	−0−	−0−	−0−	−0−	−0−	28
G. Liabilities constituting foreign reserves	11.45	−2.04	4.67	1.33	−0−	−0−	−0−	−0−	30
Total A–G (summary balance)	6.19	4.85	−7.49	0.70	4.50	−2.64	3.74	−2.49	34
H. Change in Reserves	−6.19	−4.85	7.49	−0.70	−4.50	2.64	−3.74	2.49	36
Monetary gold	0.13	0.05	5.60	−1.14	−0−	−0−	0.01	0.06	37
SDRs	0.02	−0.88	0.13	−0.2	−0.8	0.4	0.06	0.48	38
Fund reserve (IMF)	−1.29	0.90	0.58	0.36	0.8	0.19	0.61	1.95	39
Foreign exchange	−5.06	−4.91	1.08	0.21	−4.49	2.41	3.08	−0−	40
Use of fund credit	−0−		0.09	−0.11	−0−	−0−	−0−	−0−	41
Conversion to SDR	US$/ SDR= 1.3015	US$/ SDR= 1.0153	Mark/ SDR= 2.3657	Mark/ SDR= 2.9891	Yen/ SDR= 295.11	Yen/ SDR= 242.19	Riyals/ SDR= 4.3299	Riyals/ SDR= 3.6777	44 / 45

Source: International Monetary Fund, *International Payments Statistics,* 1986.
Note: "Direct investments" go directly into another economic activity, as in constructing a manufacturing plant, whereas "Portfolio investments" are purchases of stocks, bonds, and other securities.

We look first at the format. Note the following features:

1. Line 1 is a statement of the current account balance, consisting exclusively of the balance of trade in goods and services. This portion of the current statement is identical to the types of net trade figures used in the preceding chapter. The contributing parts are listed on lines 2 through 6, each of which provides useful detail on trade.

2. Line 8 states the current balance of investment and other long-term capital, with the net capital-flow detail following on lines 11 through 13.

3. Line 15 sums up sections A and B and presents the so-called basic balance, the sum of the current account balance, and the current net capital position.

4. On line 18, short-term capital flows are added to the equation, and then small adjustment items are added on lines 20 and 22.

5. Line 25 adds all of the preceding items and presents the so-called official settlements balance. Lines 28 and 30 factor in other small adjustments.

6. The summary balance, which adds all the preceding items, is presented on line 34. It is at that point that the actual intergovernmental settlements are made. Note that section H on line 36 is, in every case presented, the reciprocal of line 34. The reason for this is that whereas line 34 indicates a government's total surplus or liability for the period in question, line 36 is a statement of the manner in which the adjustment was made. The following detail indicates the various amounts taken from (or added to) the different reserve resources in order to bring the entire account into balance.

7. Finally, because it is now customary to present these accounts in SDR value rather than in billions of American dollars (owing to the relatively greater stability of the SDR than of the dollar), lines 44 and 45 state the SDR value of the national currency for the period in question. For example, in 1980 it took 1.3015 American dollars to purchase an SDR. To convert any figure in the 1980 column for the United States into billions of American dollars, then, because the table is expressed in billions of SDR, merely multiply that number by 1.3015

Turn now from the format itself to its practical meaning. There are countless conclusions that can be gleaned from a review of the actual figures. For instance, look at the 1980 and 1985 American figures. It is immediately apparent that between 1980 and 1985 the United States suffered a devastating trend in its current account balance (line 1), caused largely by a massive growth in merchandise imports relative to exports and to less pronounced growth in the gap between service credits and debits. When we move from section A to line 8 we find that there has also been a reversal in the long-term capital balance owing principally to a massive increase in the net portfolio investments being made in the American market from abroad. Short-term capital reveals a similar trend. The table also shows that the US government prefers using foreign exchange reserves to balance its summary account. Finally, whereas in 1980 it took $1.3015 to purchase an SDR, by 1985 the dollar had strengthened to the point at which it took only $1.0153.

The tabular format belies the diplomatic and political complexity of all these transactions but, at the same time, indicates to some extent the degree to which we are misled about some of these things. In the United States, for example, there is so much concern over the deteriorating international trade position of domestic manufacturers and farmers that little attention is given to the fact that the overall balance of payments has been remarkably stable during the decade. But behind even this contradiction lies an important political-economic conclusion: Despite the relative balance-of-payments stability, the international trade picture persistently presents an image of declining American competitiveness in both the basic industries and the more modern manufacturers, calling into question such profound things as future employment patterns in the United States, loss of domestic production and commensurate dependence on uncertain foreign supply, and major swings of capital into the United States for portfolio enrichment but out of the United States for direct investment in industries elsewhere that will accentuate the loss of jobs at home and American dependence on foreign manufactures. In this cycle of events, the modern transnational corporation is the paradoxical element: Even though it invests directly in other economies and thus provides employment abroad at the expense of employees at home, and even though its products are imported into the United States as part of the net balance-of-trade deficit, it nonetheless produces substantial portfolio wealth for both American and foreign investors.

The World Debt Crisis

Although our discussion of global payments mechanisms reveals certain trends in the world's flow of wealth, the period between 1980 and 1988 was one of marked disruption in the world economy. Several events or series of events contributed to the darkest years in the global economy in a half century. Although it is impossible to place them in order of importance, it is nonetheless useful to outline them briefly. Special attention is given to the Third World and American debt crises, for these carry the greatest likelihood of causing protracted difficulties.

Worldwide Recession of the Industrialized Market Economies

Throughout the Western world and Japan, the recession that began in 1978 deepened through 1982, and the major trading partners emerged from it at different growth rates from 1983 to 1985. At its depths, unemployment rose to ten-year high points; interest rates on borrowing soared to the extent that acquiring capital for business growth and modernization was prohibitive; and the total value of world trade diminished temporarily. The developing countries suffered substantial setbacks in their trade and interest rates, and the reduction in their exports relative to the cost of their imports prevented them from repaying their capital debts. The trade deficit of the United States became chronic, and even after recovering from the recession it continued to dive, until it hit its historic low of $173.7 billion in 1987.

The United States was the first of the major trading partners to rise out of the recession. Opinions differ as to why, with some crediting the fiscal policies of the Reagan administration (tax reductions to produce rapid capital accumulation, coupled with the deregulation of several industries and tighter control on official interest rates), whereas others credit the growth of worldwide demand. Whatever might have been the causes, the relatively early American recovery had a number of international consequences. First, the rise in the stock market, particularly in 1986 and 1987, presented an exceptional attraction to foreign capital, thus depleting Japan and Western Europe of the capital needed to fuel their own recoveries. In the first fiscal quarter of 1987, the Japanese gross national product (GNP) dropped for the first time since 1948, and unemployment remained at ten-year high levels in Britain, France, Italy, and even West Germany. Furthermore, the rapid growth of the American national debt, rising from a cumulative total of approximately $1 trillion in 1980 to about $3 trillion by the end of 1989, resulted from annual budgetary shortfalls (owing largely to tax reductions and huge military investments) that required the sale, often international, of public securities as a means of expanding the government's annual revenue. Thus, more foreign money was attracted to the United States at the expense of recovery elsewhere. And the dollar, exceedingly strong in 1984 and 1985, was deliberately driven down, particularly against the Japanese yen, as a device for reducing the cost of manufactured goods relative to those of the Japanese, all in an effort to reduce the annual balance-of-trade deficit. But the cheap dollar had a greater effect on the weaker currencies, such as the British pound and the French franc, than on the yen, leading to renewed economic friction between North America and Europe. And in an effort to improve the American trade position by means other than monetary policy, the Reagan administration took several trade actions against Canadian lumber products, European agricultural products and spirits, and South Korean and Taiwanese manufactures, charging all those governments with illegal or unfair international trading practices.

OPEC's Fluctuating Influence Over World Oil Price

From 1979 onward, OPEC's ability to control world oil prices diminished consistently, largely because of a dispute among its members. The more radical members called for rapid increases in price and freedom among members to determine output, and the more moderate members wished to control the total output on a quota basis while also controlling prices. War between Iran and Iraq, together with the continuing uncertainty of the international consequences of the Iranian revolution, led not only to disruption of supply but also to fears that the Strait of Hormuz would be closed as a military measure and that oil would no longer be able to leave the Persian Gulf by ship. In 1986, furthermore, OPEC had regained enough of its unity to raise the price of crude oil once again. In the 12-month period from mid-1986 to early 1990, the price of unleaded gasoline at the American pump rose by over 60 percent, from approximately $.70 to $1.10.

During the period of OPEC's greatest strength, from 1974 to 1982, American oil investments had soared in an effort to achieve national self-sufficiency and to reduce dependence on the Middle Eastern supply. When OPEC prices fell after 1982, Middle Eastern oil once again became cheaper than domestic, and both investment and petroleum development declined sharply in the United States. The sudden increase in OPEC prices in 1986, coupled with desperate Iranian military moves in 1987, significantly changed the global petroleum picture. One result was that in mid-1987, the Strait of Hormuz became the single most important geopolitical point in the world. To prevent Iraqi oil commerce from reaching its destinations, Iran began a policy of air-to-surface missile attacks on oil supertankers. Shortly thereafter it installed Chinese-built short-range missiles on the ground approaches to the strait. Iraq, apparently in retaliation for Iranian air attacks, mimicked the policy and in one attack accidentally struck the American cruiser *USS Stark* with at least two French-built Exocet missiles, killing 37 American servicemen. So as to ensure the safe passage of oil tankers from the Persian Gulf to destinations in North America, Western Europe, and Japan, the United States adopted a policy of reflagging Kuwaiti tankers, thereby placing them under American military protection; the presence of the US Navy in the gulf was enhanced by several vessels. With the permanent cease fire between Iran and Iraq (although no peace treaty yet), this special role of the US Navy was discontinued, and OPEC began once again to assert its role in the determination of global petroleum. By early 1990, prices were on the rise once more.

Political Instability and Loss of Confidence in Investment

The increase in political instability of many areas of the world disturbed the climate of international investment. Western investments, including American, were rocked by the increasing prospect of widespread civil war in South Africa, where an unyielding right-wing government repeatedly selected force over diplomacy to resolve the consequences of its apartheid policy. In Central America, Washington's commitment to the *contra* forces of Nicaragua, and the domestic political scandal resulting from the use of profits from illegal arms sales to Iran to provide funds illegally to the *contras,* contributed to the mounting instability in the area. Heated rhetoric between the two Koreas and continuing conflict among China, Vietnam, Cambodia, and Thailand, together with the unrelenting Soviet war in Afghanistan and persistent political unrest in India, Pakistan, and Sri Lanka, kept virtually all of Asia unsettled. The new constitution of the Philippines subjected to public referendum the question of whether or not the United States should be able to retain its military bases there, thus throwing further into question the Asian power distribution. New Zealand's refusal to permit visits of American nuclear-armed vessels prompted the United States to terminate the ANZUS Council, the device that linked New Zealand and Australia to the American worldwide alliance scheme. And the growing resentment in the United States over export competition from South Korea, Hong Kong, Taiwan, Singapore, Indonesia, and the Philippines raised serious questions about the wisdom of additional industrial investment in those places.

The Third World Debt Crisis

The Falkland Islands War and the imposition of martial law in Poland were the first two events that illuminated the pending inability of Poland and the Third World to keep abreast of their debt payments. It is an error, however, to consider that these events themselves caused financial prostration. They can be understood only in the context of a sluggish global economy, the economic consequences of political instability both regionally and between the superpowers, deteriorating terms of trade for Third World exports (including oil), the demand by overcommitted lending institutions for repayment, and the depletion of national credit reserves in the IMF to rescue them.

Many of the consequences of these problems have been considered elsewhere in this book, particularly in Chapter 5, which dealt with the global perspective of the Third World. In this chapter, therefore, we shall address the problem only as it relates to the global economy, having dealt already with its impact on the Third World.

The Third World debt crisis charged into the global scene in 1982. At that time, the aggregate Third World debt exceeded $680 billion, with 14 countries having the greatest difficulties. Brazil and Mexico led the list of debtors with outstanding amounts of $92 billion and $87 billion, respectively, after which the amounts dropped sharply: Argentina's foreign debt was $39 billion. The geographic distribution of the debt was also alarming, with approximately $283 billion of the total attributed to only six Latin American countries, out of a total of $330 billion owed by the entire region. The total Third World debt was rising by about $40 billion per year, and reached $875 billion by early 1988, of which $325 billion was owed to private-sector sources and the balance to governments and international organizations. It is expected to exceed $1 trillion by 1991. (See Table 14–9 for national systemization of Third World debt as of the end of 1987.) More alarming even than the aggregate figures is the relationship of debt to economic development. By the end of 1987, for example, combined Third World debt equaled 37.6 percent of the combined Third World GNP and among the most highly indebted, that fraction was 56 percent. Moreover, because exports are a major source of economic advancement, the ratio of debt to exports is also an important measure of urgency; and in 1987, the aggregate Third World debt equaled 21 percent of aggregate exports. For the most deeply indebted, the fraction was 33 percent. Annual payment must be made on debt and interest; therefore, a significant portion of annual exports cannot contribute to the development of the economy.

The Third World debt problem is, then, two crises in one. On the one hand, the debt severely erodes the capacity of developing states to improve their economic performance through exports. And on the other hand, throughout the industrialized world and the network of financial international organizations governments, corporations and agencies await payment of interest and principle needed to meet their own obligations, in a global environment in which the prospect for repayment seems to decline steadily.

From the Third World perspective, nonpayment, postponement of payment, or rescheduling of payment are options available at various levels of despera-

Table 14–9 Twenty principal Third World debtor nations ranked by total gross external liabilities in 1987, expressed in billions of US dollars.

| Rank | Country | Long-term | | Other Debt | Total Gross External Liabilities |
		Public/Publicly Guaranteed Debt	Private Nonguaranteed		
1	Brazil	$ 91.7	$14.4	$ 17.8	$123.9
2	Mexico	82.8	14.1	11.0	107.9
3	Argentina	47.5	2.9	6.4	56.8
4	Indonesia	41.3	4.1	7.2	52.6
5	India	37.3	3.4	5.7	46.4
6	Poland	35.6	—	6.5	42.1
7	Turkey	30.5	0.9	9.4	40.8
8	So. Korea	24.5	6.1	9.9	40.5
9	Egypt	34.5	1.1	4.7	40.3
10	Venezuela	25.2	7.5	3.8	36.5
11	China	23.7	—	6.3	30.2
12	Philippines	22.3	1.5	6.2	30.0
13	Nigeria	25.7	0.4	2.6	28.7
14	Israel	16.8	5.7	3.8	26.3
15	Yugoslavia	14.4	5.0	4.1	23.5
16	Greece	17.4	1.4	4.3	23.1
17	Algeria	19.2	—	3.7	22.9
18	Chile	15.5	2.5	3.2	21.2
19	Morocco	18.5	0.4	1.8	20.7
20	Thailand	14.0	3.1	3.6	20.7
	Total	$638.4 billion	$74.5 billion	$122.2 billion	$835.1 billion

Source: World Bank, *World Development Report, 1989,* Table 21, pp. 204–205.

tion. Nonpayment is politically risky, and postponement of payment has been invoked in a few instances. But the favorite means of handling debt among the Third World governments has been rescheduling, a device by which the creditor and the debtor agree to a new schedule by which payment of interest and principle are due. As Table 14–10 indicates, rescheduling was relatively common for four years prior to the deepened crisis of 1983, when the frequency of rescheduling multiplied. The numbers need no explanation, because their magnitude speaks volumes about the extent of the debt crisis for both debtor and creditor. Although the frequency of rescheduling declined after 1985, it is nonetheless true that in 1986 Venezuela and Brazil postponed payment of debts in amounts of $22 billion and $31 billion respectively; and in 1987, Nigeria, North Korea, Venezuela, and Ecuador rescheduled payment on a total of $49.4 billion while the Philippines postponed interest payment on another $13.2 billion.[3]

---

[3]"Chronology 1986," *Foreign Affairs,* America and the World 1986/87 issue, pp. 690–691; and 1987/88 issue, pp. 644–646.

Table 14–10 Third World debt reschedulings, 1979–1985, in billions of US dollars.

	Public Sources		Private Sources		Total	
	Number	Amount	Number	Amount	Number	Amount
1979	4	2.0	4	3.0	8	5.0
1980	3	2.5	3	1.5	6	4.0
1981	3	1.5	5	4.0	8	5.5
1982	6	1.5	4	2.0	10	3.5
1983	17	10.0	14	41.0	31	51.0
1984	13	3.5	10	9.0	23	12.5
1985	19	7.0	12	88.0	31	95.0
Total	65	28.0	52	148.5	117	176.5

Source: World Bank, *World Development Report, 1986,* p. 38.

From the creditors' perspective, three major methods have been used to come to grips with unpaid debt aside from rescheduling. The first is a series of attempts by the IMF to ease the crisis using their special capabilities. Political wrangling in the United States between conservatives who wished to expand the IMF's credit capacity and liberals who thought the extension of credit a bailout for American banks and a device for deepening the Third World's dependence on banks, prevented the IMF from making a major contribution. Furthermore, the IMF rejected a proposal for a joint operation with the World Bank to have been called the Debt Adjustment Facility. The Facility's role was to have been to serve as a body for purchasing Third World debt at discount prices and contributing the savings to the debtor. This is similar to a collections agency which pays an unpaid creditor a fraction of the debt's value, then attempts to collect whatever he can from the debtor. The difference is that while the collector in such a scheme keeps any profit, in the case of the Debt Reduction Facility the difference would have been subtracted from the debt owed. The World Bank did, however, create a Multilateral Investment Guarantee Agency, which guarantees private investors against certain types of losses. The purpose of this mechanism is to discourage private investors from exiting the Third World credit business.

The second approach is that of the private banks themselves. Convinced by 1987 that some Third World debt would never be paid, some began the process of preparing for large losses by establishing set-aside programs. These are programs in which profits are placed in reserve (rather than paid out to stockholders or used for other investments) to be used to balance defaults in the future. In the first such moves Citicorp, Bank of America, J. P. Morgan, and Manufacturers Hanover moved simultaneously to create this protection using $4.6 billion. Later in the year, Citicorp added $3 billion to its set-aside account, and the Bank of Boston began its own program with $200 million.

The third major approach, one that is American rather than multilateral, is the Brady Plan (named for its author, Treasury Secretary Nicholas Brady). Unlike its predecessor the Baker Plan (named for former Treasury Secretary and later Secretary of State James Baker), the Brady Plan assumes that most

Third World debt will never be repaid at full value. The other central features are these:

1. Although all 39 Third World debtors that have previously resorted to rescheduling are eligible to participate, its main target is the six or eight principal debtors to banks.
2. It addresses not the entire external indebtedness of these countries, but only that portion that is owed to banks.
3. In order to be eligible to participate, a debtor must show substantial progress toward economic reform, a standard often used by the World Bank as well. The plan calls on the IMF and the World Bank to supervise economic reform.
4. Because it is assumed that most Third World debt will never be repaid at full value, the plan is based on a discount, or secondary market, principle. Table 14–11 shows the US bank-related indebtedness of ten major target nations, listing their debt to American banks at full value and at discount market value. The final column identifies the discount value as a percentage of the full value.

Although the Brady Plan has limitations (for example, it addresses only part of the debt; it is concerned only with American banks), it is seen as an advance toward resolution of the Third World crisis. It provides incentives for banks to liquidate debt at discount prices without suffering stock market value,

Table 14–11 Mid-1989 market value reduction approach to Third World indebtedness to American banks.

Country	Debt (billion $)	Market Value (billion $)	Market Price (% of face value)
Argentina	33.6	6.3	19
Bolivia[a]	.9	.1	10
Brazil	62.2	21.0	34
Chile[a]	11.2	6.6	61
Costa Rica[a]	1.5	.2	14
Ecuador[a]	5.5	.8	14
Mexico[a]	63.8	24.1	38
Nigeria	11.5	2.4	21
Philippines[a]	10.5	4.8	46
Poland	12.3	4.9	40
Venezuela[a]	22.6	8.2	37
Total for 39 eligible countries	279.4	96.7	35
Total for 11 countries listed	235.6	79.4	34

[a]Indicates initial targets of the Brady Plan.
Source: World Bank Debt Tables as compiled in Jeffrey Sachs, "Making the Brady Plan Work," *Foreign Affairs,* Summer 1989, pp. 87–104 at p. 91, adapted and reprinted with permission. Poland has been included despite its radically changed status.

and it encourages the Third World governments to practice sound fiscal policies, noninflationary market adjustments, and incentive for capital to remain at home rather than to seek larger profits abroad. It "denationalizes" criteria for sound economic practices by having the IMF and the World Bank provide the criteria and supervision. It attempts to secure investment guarantees from the World Bank and the IMF. And it hopes to lure Japanese capital into the general problem of Third World debt relief. Because debt reduction was in occasional practice prior to announcement of the Brady Plan, it is not original to the plan. But as a comprehensive package, the Brady Plan is seen as a new and promising device for bringing Third World debt, at least to the private sector, into line.[4]

Third World debt has been a major feature of the international political economy for four decades, but the urgent call for solutions has been with us for only about one. Among the most important economic phenomena of the last decade has been realization in public policy—not merely in individual minds—that the magnitude of debt is such that repayment is almost certainly out of the question. The trick, of course, is to reduce debt burden in the Third World without transferring that burden to creditors, whether they be taxpayers who supported government loans, commercial institutions, or international organizations which, like governments, get their resources primarily, and in some cases exclusively, from member contributions and assessments. Whether or not current efforts result in easing of the burden, the Third World debt problem remains "a long-term economic and political barrier to development that is slowly strangling world economic growth."[5]

Additionally, the collapse of communism in Eastern Europe during 1989 and 1990 will introduce complicating factors to the global political economy and to international finance. The industrial economies of East Germany, Hungary, Czechoslovakia, Poland, Bulgaria, and Romania are very old and unintroduced to the technological age. The political revolution that resulted in the opening of the Berlin Wall and the ouster of communist governments throughout the region was inspired in very large measure by economic hardship, industrial backwardness, and a public realization that the standard of living of Western Europeans is far better than that of their Eastern European peers. Now, following the political revolution, must come the economic reconstruction of Eastern Europe. Although the problems there differ from those of the Third World of the Southern Hemisphere, the demand for investment capital will be at least as great. Thus, even before significant progress has been made in cleaning up one debt crisis, another potential such crisis descends on the global economy.

---

[4]For a partial text of the Brady speech that outlined the plan, see *The New York Times,* March 11, 1989, p. 37. The summary here leans heavily on Jeffrey Sachs, "Making the Brady Plan Work," *Foreign Affairs,* Summer 1989, pp. 87–104. For a view that sees the Brady plan as little more than an American refinement of practices already well established, see Benjamin J. Cohen, "A Global Chapter 11," *Foreign Policy,* Summer 1989, pp. 109–127. Cohen calls for a more radical approach to debt reduction along the lines of Chapter 11, the American bankruptcy code.

[5]Christine A. Bogdanowicz-Bindert, "World Debt: The United States Reconsiders," *Foreign Affairs,* Winter 1985–1986, pp. 259–273, at p. 259.

The United States as a Debtor Nation

When World War I broke out in Europe in 1914, American investors gradually provided the financial wherewithal for France and Britain to carry on the fight, even during the official period of American neutrality (1914 until the American intervention in 1917). Indeed, some have argued that the United States might not have abandoned its neutrality and been drawn into war had it not been necessary for the administration of President Woodrow Wilson to go to the rescue of those investments. Be that as it may, from that time forward the United States was continuously a creditor nation, providing capital, both public and private, for both the peacetime and the wartime sustenance of other countries. The Lend-Lease Program through which Washington armed the wartime allies, including the Soviet Union, throughout World War II and the Marshall Plan that financed Western Europe's postwar recovery are major examples of massive public efforts to provide capital for the maintenance and survival of strong market economies abroad. The history of private capital parallels that of the use of public revenue for these purposes.

In 1986, however, this historical continuity came to an end amid some most extraordinary circumstances. On the one hand, despite a conscious policy of lowering the dollar's value in order to improve the trade deficit, the stock market rose to one record level after another. While personal wealth was being amassed through portfolio investment, the nation was growing poorer. Moreover, the attraction of the stock market drew unprecedented amounts of foreign private capital out of other countries while, simultaneously, the US government sought to balance its books by selling public securities in huge amounts, thus doubling the national debt in six short years. By the end of 1986, the net capital position of the United States in the combined public and private sectors had been reversed; and for the first time in 72 years, the United States had become a debtor nation. Depending on one's political perspective, either because of or despite both domestic fiscal policy and international monetary policy, the United States had fallen to a position in which its debt was, for the first time, being financed by foreign interests.

Yet despite its debtor status, the United States continued to see the Dow Jones average rise (despite wild daily swings and a severe temporary "crash" of over 500 points in October 1988, the general trend continued upward) and enjoyed the lowest unemployment rate among its principal trading partners, even allowing for differences in the way that governments count the unemployed. Domestic interest rates were stable through 1986 and began to rise only modestly in 1987. The executive branch of government continued to hold the line against tax increases as a means of balancing the government's books without enlarging its dependence on foreign capital. Although the standard of living was not immediately disturbed, public opinion polls indicated that for the first time ever recorded, college graduates of 1987 predicted that their living standard would not be as high as that of their parents. For the first time, the interconnection between the global economy and the standard of living of Americans at home became a matter of outspoken public concern. Some political forces called for remedies rooted in nationalism, protectionism, retalia-

Table 14–12 Net investment position of the United States, 1981–1988, in billions of US dollars.

1981	$ 140.9 billion
1982	136.7
1983	89.0
1984	3.3
1985	(111.4)
1986	(267.8)
1987	(378.3)
1988	(532.5)

Source: Survey of Current Business, June 1989, table 2, p. 43.

tion, and military buildup; others, concerned that without American leadership the global political economy would fall utterly out of control, called for a reassessment of international policies in order that global conditions might lead the way to domestic improvement.

The trend toward American indebtedness is measured by its annual net investment position, that is, the annual balance of American-owned assets abroad and foreign-owned assets in the United States. Among these assets, the most familiar are direct investments and portfolio investments, and each of these will be studied in this chapter. But some of the assets are less well known, and call for explanation here. These include gold, currencies, SDRs, IMF drawing rights, and outstanding loans. The evolution of the American net investment position from 1981, when it reached its highest positive number in history, to 1988, when it reached its deepest negative position up to the time of writing, is displayed in Table 14–12. Note the steady decline of the American positive net balance from 1981 to 1984, and the steady decline into a negative balance of over $532 billion thereafter. In 1988, the net negative position with respect to Western Europe was $437 billion, and with Japan $128 billion. Although a little of this was offset by positive positions elsewhere in the world, both the overall negative balance and the degree of indebtedness to Europe and Japan are alarming. Unquestionably, the close of the 1980s brought with it a seriously eroded American international economic picture.[6]

With the dawning of the 1990s, the harsh truth was no longer avoidable: Despite such evidence of a strong economic condition as low interest rates, high employment, a booming stock market, and high industrial output relative to capacity, the United States was not only the world's largest debtor nation, but one in severe long-term danger of losing control of its own economic destiny. As evidence, the following:

- An annual trade deficit chronically in excess of $150 billion
- Net outflow of capital annually to cover approximately $50 billion in interest on debt

---

[6]For full detail with extensive charts and tables, see Russell B. Scholl, "The International Investment Position of the United States in 1988," *Survey of Current Business*, June 1989, pp. 41–49.

- A cumulative budget deficit of almost $3 trillion, equal to about 75 percent of the GNP
- Foreign direct investment in the United States exceeding American direct investment abroad, with a growing tendency for major sales of real estate, the entertainment business, and department stores to go to foreign interests from Canada to The Netherlands and Japan
- Annual federal budget deficits in excess of 3 percent of the budget despite legislative efforts to set an annual cap on expenses above revenues
- A practice of resolving very large financial problems "off budget," meaning making large expenditures without calculating them into the annual budget deficit
- A neglected and decaying economic infrastructure threatening to paralyze some aspects of life such as education, fresh water supplies, urban transportation, homelessness, and medical care while lavishing hundreds of billions annually on a bloated military capability that is increasingly out of step with the national need

Observations such as these have inspired one American writer to declare that US economic policies

> have contributed not only to our economy's interdependence with the rest of the world, which is perfectly healthy, but to its *dependence* on outsiders, which is not. The necessity to finance part of the U.S. budget deficit with foreign capital; the necessity, over the last two years, for foreign central banks to acquire more than $150 billion to support our currency; our trade deficit and growing foreign debt; the steep increase in domestic assets sold abroad to finance our deficits— all of these factors, and more, have created a dependence on the policies of other sovereign governments and private interests that affect every U.S. domestic issue.[7]

Having looked at trade and payments balances previously, we will concentrate here on the other factors that contribute to American dependence: net direct investment, net sale and purchase of government securities, and net sale and purchase of private securities.

Table 14–13 sets out the comparison between US direct investment abroad and foreign direct investment in the United States. Remember that direct investment is the purchase of land, property, industrial facilities, real estate, and so on, as contrasted to portfolio investment which consists of stocks, bonds, and other securities. As Table 14–13 indicates, right through the mid-1980s, the United States held a net capital surplus of foreign direct investment, although the parentheses in the final column indicate that in return for this net investment position we had also seen an outward capital flow. But by 1988, the net position had reversed, with foreign interests owning more direct investments in the United States than Americans did abroad. Although the figures for 1989 were not available at the time of writing, it is probable that the trend accelerated in 1989, during which there were several very large foreign purchases made in the United States, particularly in the real estate and entertain-

---

[7]Felix Rohatyn, "America's Economic Dependence," *Foreign Affairs,* America and the World 1988/89 issue, pp. 53–65 at pp. 54–55.

Table 14–13 Net US direct investment position, 1970–1988, in billions of US dollars.

	US Direct Investment Abroad	Two-Year Change	Foreign Direct Investment in US	Two-Year Change	Two-Year Net	Cumulative US Net Capital Position
1970	75.5		13.3			(62.2)
1972	89.9	14.4	14.9	1.6	(12.8)	(84.0)
1974	110.1	20.2	25.1	10.2	(10.0)	(85.0)
1976	136.8	26.7	30.8	5.7	(21.0)	(106.0)
1978	162.7	25.9	42.5	11.7	(14.2)	(120.2)
1980	213.5	50.8	65.5	23.0	(27.8)	(148.0)
1982	221.3	7.8	101.8	36.3	29.5	(119.5)
1983	207.2	(14.1)	137.1	35.3	49.4	(70.1)
1985	232.7	25.5	183.0	45.9	20.4	(49.7)
1988	326.9	94.2[a]	328.9	145.9[a]	51.7[a]	2.0

[a]Indicates a three-year interval.

Source: Economic Report of the President, 1982, p. 351; and *Survey of Current Businesss*, August 1983, p. 14; August 1986, pp. 70–74; and August 1989, pp. 48–51.

ment markets. These purchases bring with them capital from abroad, but they also represent the dwindling of American assets for capital which is then used to support the global deficit position of the United States. It is for this reason that one concludes that the sale of such assets to international interests is for financing deficits.

As to nation of ownership of American assets, it is reported that in 1987, of the $260 billion in foreign direct investment in the United States, approximate national percentages were as follows:[8]

United Kingdom	30%
Netherlands	20%
Other Europe	22%
Japan	13%
Canada	7%
All other	8%

And in 1988, when total foreign direct investment in the United States climbed to $329 billion, $216 billion was attributable to European interests ($194 of that within the European Community), and $53 billion to Japanese. Journalistic accounts suggest that in 1989, the Japanese portion of new foreign direct investment in the United States may have increased substantially.

Table 14–14 deals with the net portfolio position of the United States for three sample years in the 1980s. The figures are for new purchases annually; they do not represent cumulative amounts. They indicate that in any typical year, foreign purchase of new portfolio issues substantially exceed new over-

---

[8]*Economic Report of the President, 1989*, chart 3–6, p. 135.

Table 14–14 Net American portfolio investment position, 1980–1987, annual (not cumulative).

	US Purchase of Foreign Securities	Foreign Purchase of US Securities	Net
1980	$3.1 billion	$15.8 billion	($ 12.7 billion)
1985	7.9	78.2	(70.3)
1987	6.5	69.7	(63.2)

Source: Statistical Abstract of the United States, 1989, p. 505.

seas portfolio investments by Americans. And the trend is widening: In 1987, foreign purchases in the United States ran at a rate ten times those of Americans abroad, and the net negative position was growing in an equal amount. Although these differences mean a short-term inflow of capital to the United States, they are another measure of the extent to which American assets are now foreign owned, of the extent to which periodic dividends represent future capital outflow, and the extent to which this initial influx of capital is required to cover American trade, payments, and budget deficits.

But Table 14–14 tells less than the entire story; for as we have seen, portfolio investment may be either private-sector securities or issues offered by governments. For foreign interests to own considerable interests in, say, IBM stock is a problem of its own; but for the same interest or another government to own a substantial share of another country's government securities is quite another.

Turn, then, to Table 14–15, which distinguishes net portfolio positions for commercial and governmental securities. The table indicates that in the seven-year period, foreign portfolio purchases in the United States jumped by a multiple of 4.4, even after having slid from the high level of 1985. It also indicates that an average of about 44 percent of those investments are in government securities annually; and by adding the second and third columns one finds that in 1980 foreign interests owned only $7.5 billion in US government securities, but that the level rose to $33.3 billion in 1985 before falling off to $30.8 billion in 1987. Once again, journalistic reports suggest that the number may have reached a record high in 1989.

Now for the final pieces of the puzzle. Remember that Tables 14–14 and 14–15 represent new securities purchases annually, and do not contain cumu-

Table 14–15 Government securities as a fraction of foreign portfolio investment in the United States, 1980–1987, annual (not cumulative).

	Total Purchase	Treasury Notes	US Govt. Bonds	Commercial Securities	% Government
1980	$15.8 billion	$ 4.9 billion	$2.6 billion	$ 8.3 billion	47.5
1985	78.2	29.2	4.3	44.9	42.6
1987	69.7	25.8	5.0	38.9	44.2

Source: Statistical Abstract of the United States, 1989, p. 505.

Table 14–16 Cumulative American portfolio indebtedness, 1981–1988, in billions of US dollars.

	Total Invested	US Govt. Securities	Commercial Securities	% Government
1981	$ 93.6	$18.5	$ 75.1	20
1982	118.6	25.6	93.0	22
1983	147.6	33.8	113.8	23
1984	185.5	58.2	127.3	31
1985	289.8	83.6	206.2	29
1986	400.3	91.5	308.8	23
1987	422.6	78.3	344.3	19
1988	490.2	96.6	393.6	20

Source: Survey of Current Business, June 1989, table 2, p. 43.

lative numbers. Table 14–16 goes this extra step. It shows accumulated (new and old) foreign portfolio investment in the United States each year from 1981 to 1988, breaks the total into its parts (government securities and commercial securities), and then tabulates the percentage of the total represented by the government securities. It demonstrates that in the years in which the major turn in the net investment position of the United States (see Table 14–12), the percentage of government securities rose sharply, then returned to a stable norm. Hence, although the percentage column is not particularly alarming, the amount of purchase by foreign interests in American government securities is, for these represent loans made to the government by foreign interests, all of which earn interest and all of which someday will have to be repaid.

Now combine all these factors studied either here or previously: (1) the annual foreign deficit, (2) the annual foreign payments deficit, (3) the negative net position in direct investment, (4) the negative net position in portfolio investment, and (5) the extent to which the growing foreign portfolio of American securities consists of government issues. Not only is the United States an economically dependent nation, but one in which both commercial assets and government debt are increasingly held by overseas interests.

Conclusion

Even though we think of the international system principally in political terms, much that fuels global politics is economic in nature. Trade, exchange, currency values, international investment, payments balances, surpluses and deficits, competition, economic development, barriers to trade, protectionism—all these lie prominently beneath the surface of political rhetoric daily. One can even go so far as to argue that the Cold War might not have occurred had it not been for the determination of two very different economic systems, capitalism and socialism, to rid the world of one another. Although surely not every international event is economic, there is scarcely one that has neither economic content nor economic consequence.

It is for this reason that this section is entitled "The Logic of the International Political Economy" rather than simply the "International Economy." The purpose is less to convey volumes of economic data than to clarify the inseparability of the economic from the political in international relations.

Until recently, the only two isolated events that changed the course of the international political economy in this century were the Bolshevik Revolution and the coming of Marxism-Leninism to the Soviet Union in 1917, and the Keynesian adjustments to capitalistic economies in the West after the financial crash of 1929. Today, however, the rush of economic events is spellbinding. Among them, the most notable are (1) the inadequacies of economic development and the debt problem of the Third World; (2) the evolution of the United States into a precarious economic condition as the world's largest debtor after years of having been the mainstay of global economic stability; (3) the political collapse of communism in Eastern Europe with all the unknown consequences for international economics; (4) the gradual development of free enterprise alongside planned socialism in both China and the Soviet Union; and (5) the approach of complete economic union within the European Community by 1992. The decade of the 1990s promises to students of the international political economy a laboratory of unprecedented excitement.

PART IV

The Logic of World Order

CHAPTER 15

International Law

As the preceding section has stressed, certain economic mechanisms accompany day-to-day international transactions. These are intended to adjust the relations among states as they compete for natural resources, markets, development opportunity, and national enrichment. These adjustments contribute to the pacification of international practice and do their part to bring order to a global political system that, in their absence, would tend to be characterized by self-assertion and disruption for national purposes.

But other relations among nation-states are not subject to such mechanisms. Adjustments of payment balances has little bearing on the ability of the nuclear powers to destroy the planet; and currency revaluations, although a great help in the stabilization of relations among nations, are of little assistance in offsetting nuclear arms races, aggressive intervention, or border clashes. Specifically, because power is a relative concept (power with respect to what?), some international actors will always be able to threaten others with coercion, enslavement, or destruction. Whenever states are unwilling to exercise self-restraint (or autolimitation), there are but two alternatives for ensuring international stability: holding the future of other states in ransom by threat of superior force, or submitting to collective means for making international decisions and for enforcing compliance. This chapter deals with the second of these alternatives by exploring one specific method that, for over three centuries, has been practiced by governments with varying amounts of enthusiasm and varying degrees of performance: international law. The succeeding chapters continue that examination by looking at other practical methods: international organization and international integration and transnational participation. How do legal and organizational processes in the international system promote a more stable world order?

The Nature of International Law

In a well-ordered domestic society, there is a complex legal system with specific organs for making, adjudicating, and enforcing laws. The state has the authority to call individuals to account for their behavior relative to the law. Laws are made on their behalf; they can be called to court against their will; and legal regulations are enforced whether or not an individual likes them.

The international system is not so well ordered. Because only the nation-state is sovereign, it is not subject to the decisions of external institutions in the way citizens are to the institutions of their societies. No legislative body exists above the state; no international court has the capacity to compel its behavior; and there are few organs to execute international regulations. If a parallel between the domestic legal system and the legal attributes of the international system is lacking, just what is international law? If it is not by nature a formal system of regulations made by a supreme legislature, judged by supreme courts, and enforced by a supreme executive agency, what is it?

No student need feel alone in skepticism about the existence or the nature of international law. It is a matter that scholars and governments have been debating for centuries. The debate among scholars is in the realm of jurisprudence (science of law), within which countless interpretations have been offered. It will be useful to look into two theoretical interpretations that differ vastly: positivism and neorealism.

Positivism

Positivist theory is based on an analogy between domestic law, with its rules and institutions, and the international setting. It understands the law to be a system of rules (norms) that specify the rights and obligations governing the external behavior of states. Positivist theory holds law to have a consensual basis—that is, states become subject to rules only by voluntary consent. These two concepts are summarized in an opinion of the Permanent Court of International Justice, to which France and Turkey voluntarily submitted the *Lotus* case for decision in 1927.

> International law governs relations between independent States. *The rules of law binding upon States therefore emanate from their own free will* as expressed in conventions [treaties] or by usages generally accepted as expressing principles of law and established in order to regulate the relations between these co-existing independent communities or with a view to the achievement of common aims. *Restrictions upon the independence of States cannot therefore be presumed.*[1]

The progressive development of an international legal order depends, accordingly, on convincing governments that their relations are best protected by mutually arranged norms with which they will comply consistently and voluntarily.

---

[1] PCIJ Series A, no. 10. The emphasis has been added to illuminate the twin positivist principles of rule orientation and consent.

Neorealism

At the other end of the theoretical spectrum is the neorealist school. This interpretation denies that rules are at the center of a legal order and argues instead that policy and values are the foci. This theory is said, therefore, to be policy oriented and value oriented. Because international relations are in constant change, regulatory law must be a process of decision making in which all states and international agencies participate, with the content of the law changing at every moment. There are no fixed rules that can be relied on tomorrow as they are today. Thus, international law is not a system of rules but "a constitutive process of authoritative decision." The law is what the policies of the contributors make it, and it is imposed on the world by power of the actors in accordance with the values that they wish the law to promote and defend. When major actors dispute the outcomes of the constitutive process or when they disagree on the values to be promoted, then international law is identified with the foreign policy of that state whose value objectives most nearly approximate the pursuit of human dignity. The highly subjective standard is a product of the Cold War.[2]

The political uses to which these two theories can be put by governments are as different as are the doctrines themselves. If a government accepts the positivist definition, it will presumably regulate its behavior by existing treaties and other agreements, and it will expect other governments to regulate their actions by formal norms as well. In this way governments will be able to predict one another's actions and will have solid ground on which to question one another's motives. Compliance or noncompliance with formal agreements communicates the intentions of governments.

If, however, a government prefers the neorealist interpretation of international law, it will shun the reliability of formal agreements and justify its behavior on the claim that its value objectives are superior to those of its adversary, that its foreign policies more nearly approximate the goals of human dignity than do those of someone else. In this way, declarations of foreign policy become international law. One neorealist author, for example, argues that the Truman Doctrine "has gradually evolved . . . into a kind of common law of international order, a prudent rule of reciprocal safety."[3] The doctrine was announced in 1947 as a unilateral policy of the United States for restraining the growth of international communism. It was an instrument of contain-

---

[2]For statements of the neorealist theory, see Harold D. Lasswell and Myres S. McDougal, "Jurisprudence in Policy-Oriented Perspective," *Florida Law Journal,* vol. 19, 1967, pp. 486–513; Myres S. McDougal, "The Comparative Study of Law for Policy Purposes: Value Clarification as an Instrument of Democratic World Order," *Yale Law Journal,* vol. 61, 1952, pp. 915–946; Myres S. McDougal, "International Law, Power and Policy," *Recueil des Cours,* vol. 82 (The Hague: Academy of International Law, 1953), pp. 133–259; Harold D. Lasswell, Myres S. McDougal, and W. Michael Reisman, "The World Constitutive Process of Authoritative Decision," *Journal of Legal Education,* vol. 19, 1967, pp. 253–300, 403–437, in two parts.

[3]Eugene V. Rostow, *Law, Power, and the Pursuit of Peace* (Lincoln: University of Nebraska Press, 1968), p. 43. (Also published in paperback edition by Praeger.)

ment undertaken by the United States against the Soviet Union. The neorealist sees it otherwise.

No government accepts either view of the law exclusively. In fact, for most powerful states, the choice of legal interpretations depends on the facts at hand. A safe rule of thumb emerges: Governments will seek to maximize their rights (neorealist interpretation) and minimize their obligations (positivism), but they will attempt to minimize their adversaries' rights (positivism) and maximize their adversaries' obligations (neorealism). When governments have genuine concerns for legal interaction, they will speak as positivists; but when they have politicized concerns for the law, they will come forth as neorealists.

The Sources of International Law

Think again about the analogy of international law to domestic law. Rules arise from constitutions, formal legislation, custom, and the decisions of formally constituted courts. Such institutionalization exists in the international system to a far less authoritative degree. From where, then, do the norms of international law come? What are its sources?

The authoritative statement of the sources of international law is found in Article 38 of the Statute of the International Court of Justice, the permanent judicial organ of the United Nations. The statute lists the sources as (1) international conventions (treaties) in force between parties, (2) international customary rules, (3) general principles of international law, and (4) such subsidiary sources as prior judicial decisions and the writings of the highly qualified publicists.

Treaties, bilateral and multilateral, are the most logical primary source. Whether a convention be one of codification (merely formalizing in codes practices already accepted through custom) or of a legislative character (creating new rights and obligations), it represents the maximum explicit consent of the signatories. Much of the business of twentieth-century intergovernmental organizations has been the codification of existing principles and customs. Only in the last few years has the bulk of international law come to be treaty law.

Custom, until recently the largest component of positive law, is the practice of states. It is generally held that usage becomes an international legal norm when it has been repeated over a period of time by several states, when they have generally acquiesced in such behavior by one another, and when governments begin to act in certain ways out of a sense of legal obligation. In this manner, most of the international laws of the high seas originated, as did the laws of diplomatic and consular privileges and immunities, and the rules governing neutrality and international commerce, to mention only a few.

General principles of international law are less clearly defined, partly because it is difficult to demonstrate widespread acceptance and partly because the distinction between a firm principle and a customary rule is an obscure one. Nevertheless, there are general principles that can be readily identified. Many of the amenities of international relations are general principles that arise out of the theory of sovereignty. Other general principles emerge from the necessity for sovereign equality, including the principle of legal equality and the expectation of fair treatment of one another's nationals.

Subsidiary sources are still less specific and merit last place among the sources of international law. In judicial tests of legal rules, the rules themselves must undergo interpretation. The business of courts is to interpret the law and to apply it. In international adjudication, rules may be interpreted by national courts, standing international tribunals, panels established to deal with specific problems, or international courts, among them the International Court of Justice. In most national systems, courts are bound by the rule of *stare decisis,* meaning that what the court has previously decided is the law and is precedent binding on courts. International tribunals generally subscribe to the same principle, and the decisions of such courts contain references to former cases, just as the decisions of American courts do in domestic cases. The International Court of Justice (ICJ), however, while availing itself of its prior decisions and of those of other courts, does not feel itself so firmly bound by precedent. Unlike other tribunals, the ICJ may interpret the legal significance of declarations and resolutions of the political organs of the United Nations. This is especially the case in its advisory jurisdiction, which enables the ICJ, upon request from the UN organs, to render constitutional interpretations that may have political effects on member states.

Viewed from a big-power standpoint, the most significant example of this action was embodied in the advisory opinion *Certain Expenses of the United Nations* (1962).[4] Because the Soviet Union and other governments had refused to pay their apportioned shares of financing UN peacekeeping operations in the Middle East and the Congo, the General Assembly requested clarification of its authority under the charter to bill members for such expenses against their will. The court dealt with the legitimacy of the operations themselves, rendering a constitutional interpretation on the limits of UN authority. It favored an expansive view. Out of this controversial decision an argument has arisen that the charter contains implied powers of UN organs over and above the explicit ones.[5] The contrary view holds that the most effective contribution that the ICJ might make to the progressive development of international law is through the cautious use of advisory jurisdiction—that the court might thus earn the trust of states, which might then be more willing to submit to it their bilateral disputes.[6] Whichever of these positions may carry the greater hope of eventual judicial contributions to a more stable international order is for the

---

[4]International Court of Justice, advisory opinion of July 20, 1962, found in *ICJ Reports,* 1962, pp. 151–180.

[5]Rahmattullah Khan, *Implied Powers of the United Nations* (Bombay: Vikas Publications, 1970). For a demonstration of use of implied powers by the secretary-general, see Hugo Caminus and Roberto Lavelle, "New Departures in the Exercise of Inherent Powers by the UN and OAS Secretaries-General: The Central American Situation," *American Journal of International Law,* April 1989, pp. 395–402.

[6]Leo Gross, "The International Court of Justice and the United Nations," *Recueil des Cours,* vol. 120 (The Hague: Academy of International Law, 1967), pp. 313–330.

moment less important than that the *Expenses* case reveals the potential political impact of international judicial activity.

The Sanctions of International Law

How is international law enforced without international government or police? Merely to posit the existence of a body of international law is not to claim that the international system is capable of legal regulation. We must demonstrate the extent of states' willingness to comply with legal norms. What, then, is the compelling force of international law, and by what mechanisms is it presumably enforced? Is international law "law, properly so called," or is it merely "positive international morality" that lacks the enforceability necessary to make it law?[7]

Any form of law has as its incentives a variety of normative, utilitarian, and coercive sanctions. An individual may drive his or her automobile lawfully because of fears of the consequences of wrongdoing (fear of coercive sanction) or as a matter of personal safety (utilitarian sanction) or as a contribution to orderly social coexistence (normative sanction). Likewise among states, compliance with rules of law is rather consistent and is grounded in normative and utilitarian motives. Governments do generally regard reciprocal behavior as mutually beneficial and are often sensitive to international pressures. They wish to avoid reprisals and embarrassing declarations and resolutions brought on by improper behavior, except when perceived needs exceed the risk of external criticism. Furthermore, states rarely enter into formal international agreements unless they intend to benefit and unless they intend to comply with them. Nor do they acquiesce in custom over the long run without anticipating benefits. Accordingly, it is not at all extraordinary that states should normally comply with their voluntary obligations.

Coercive sanction takes over where all else fails. Indeed, the necessity for coercion occurs only when a state departs from its normal pattern of behavior under existing rules, when a behavior pattern is devoid of legal restraint, or when a state does not participate in what is considered by other nations to be law. All this is just another way of saying that when a state is not party to formal normative or utilitarian sanctions that are generally applicable, its behavior with respect to others may be controllable only through the threat of coercion.

Coercive theories of law abound, especially of international law. Some claim that norms are not legal norms unless they are capable of coercive enforcement by some political entity juridically superior to the actor. Hence, un-

[7]This is the classic distinction made by the English positivist John Austin. For American expressions and discussions of the argument, see particularly Westel W. Willoughby, *Fundamental Concepts of Public Law* (New York: Macmillan, 1924), pp. 224 ff, and "The Legal Nature of International Law," *American Journal of International Law,* vol. 2, 1908, pp. 357–365; and Hans Kelsen, "The Pure Theory of Law and Analytical Jurisprudence," *Harvard Law Review,* vol. 55, 1941, pp. 44–70.

less international law is enforceable by some power above the sovereign state, it is not really law. Others go so far as to define law in terms of its enforceability: Only if violation of a norm elicits a coercive response can that norm be interpreted as a legal rule.[8] It is the response that defines the character of a norm, rather than the mere content. Law is a statement of coercibility.[9]

Among the coercive measures that states utilize are a vast array of forceful and nonforceful acts. Nonforceful acts are referred to as retorsions, which are reciprocal punitive acts, and often referred to as nonforceful acts of retaliation. If one state should take steps to restrict the imports of another, the victimized state may respond by freezing the assets of the first state held in the banks of the second. In general, such acts are proportionate, so as to minimize the likelihood of escalation.

Retaliatory acts that are responses to forceful violations and that themselves involve actions that would otherwise be considered illegal are called reprisals. Because such acts involve use of military material, it is difficult to measure and to maintain proportion. Yet it is normally held that reprisals ought to be equivalent to the original violation. Familiar recent acts of reprisal are the American bombing raids of North Vietnam as a response to the alleged attacks on American destroyers in the Tonkin Gulf in the summer of 1964, Israeli air strikes on guerrilla sites in Lebanon after that country's government failed to prevent terrorist activities, and American air strikes on Libya in retaliation for state-sponsored terrorism.

The ultimate sanction in international relations is war. War is a political instrument, not always undertaken to destroy, but to deprive the target state of the ability and will further to violate normal behavior. The threat of war, then, may deter states from aberrant behavior, and the use of war as a response to prior actions is punitive. But in either case, the major intention of a state undertaking responsive warfare is to force political submission.

Collective Sanctions in International Law

Traditionally, responses to illegal behavior have been left to the aggrieved states. Indeed, international law includes a doctrine of self-help, which permits each state to launch punitive responses to illegal or other noxious acts. Although the doctrine of self-help (a by-product of absolute sovereignty) tries to provide international politics with formal and legal means for sanction, abuses or excesses actually contribute to international anarchy. Primarily for this reason, twentieth-century international organizations have striven to replace unilateral sanctions by collective sanctions. Because the next chapter

---

[8]See Kelsen, ''The Pure Theory of Law and Analytical Jurisprudence,'' p. 58; ''The Pure Theory of Law,'' *Law Quarterly Review,* vol. 50, 1934, pp. 474–498; and *General Theory of Law and State* (Cambridge, Mass.: Harvard University Press, 1949), pp. 51–58.

[9]The coercive theory of law is not, however, universally accepted. For major exceptions, see Gerhart Niemeyer, *Law Without Force: The Function of Politics in International Law* (Princeton, N.J.: Princeton University Press, 1941); and Michael Barkun, *Law Without Sanctions: Order in Primitive Societies and the World Community* (New Haven, Conn.: Yale University Press, 1968).

deals with some of these institutions, detailed discussion is deferred. Nonetheless, a comprehensive study of international legal sanctions requires some discussion of international organizations here, but not without a cautionary note.

International organizations are political creatures. They are made up of national governments; they derive their operating funds from their members; their powers and procedures are results of political compromises among the members; and every action that they take, they take on behalf of the members and as a result of the members' agreements and compromises. Governments form and join these organizations for the principal purpose of improving their own means of advancing their own international goals; they do not, in the main, join for the purpose of limiting their policy flexibility. From the point of view of international law, therefore, international organizations are the sum of their powerful parts, with little political will of their own. When international law is made, its content reflects struggle and compromise; when it is violated, the consequence of the violation is determined by the same kind of struggle and compromise; and when it is enforced by the organization, it is enforced to the extent that the members wish collectively.

From these common observations emerge several caveats regarding the capacity of an international organization to make and enforce law.

1. Like any other bilateral or multilateral agreement, law sponsored by any international body is the product of the member governments.
2. In both making and enforcing law, an international organization cannot exceed the political will of the member states.
3. Under the auspices of the organization, the member states at most will agree to enforce the law sponsored by that organization.
4. Law is not self-contained policy; every use of it is a result of a group political decision.

Each of these observations results not from an esoteric theory of international organization, but from the fact that all international law is based on the consent of the participating states.

When the League of Nations was established after the First World War, an effort was made to create machinery for collective sanctions in the sole instance of a government's decision to undertake war. Chapter XI of the League's Covenant inscribed the principle that "any war or threat of war . . . is hereby declared a matter of concern to the whole League." This concern was to be activated by the decision of the Council—meaning, of course, the member states of the Council—to act under Article 16:

> Should any Member of the League resort to war . . . it shall *ipso facto* be deemed to have committed an act of war against all other Members of the League, which hereby undertake immediately to subject it to the severance of all trade or financial relations, the prohibition of all intercourse between the nationals of the Covenant-breaking State and the State, and the prevention of all financial, commercial or personal intercourse between the nationals of the Covenant-breaking and the nationals of any other State, whether a Member of the League or not.

The covenant further authorized the council to recommend to states what military forces they should contribute for the implementation of Article 16.

These principles of the League of Nations were greatly expanded in the Charter of the United Nations. Chapter 7 of the charter, entitled "Action with Respect to Threats to the Peace, Breaches of the Peace, and Acts of Aggression," authorizes the Security Council to determine the existence of a threat to international stability and to recommend either peaceful measures for its resolution or coercive acts short of force. Ultimately, however, in Article 42, the Security Council is authorized to call on states to use armed force on behalf of the organization:

> Should the Security Council consider that measures provided for in Article 41 would be inadequate or have proved inadequate, it may take such action by air, sea, or land forces as may be necessary to maintain or restore international peace and security. Such action may include demonstrations, blockade, and other operations by air, sea, or land forces of Members of the United Nations.

This principle of all against one—the entire world against the aggressor—is termed collective security. This differs both from self-help, which is a doctrine of unilateral action, and from collective self-defense, which is an alliance arrangement by which a few states agree that an attack on one shall be considered an attack on all.

Because the United Nations is not a government and must depend on separate nation-states for military forces, much of Chapter 7 is devoted to the means by which such forces are to be placed at the disposal of the Security Council. The Military Staff Committee has been wholly unable to create a standby force, so the ability of the Security Council to act still rests on the states' willingness to be the council's agents. To this end, Article 48 provides that "the action required to carry out the decisions of the Security Council for the maintenance of international peace and security shall be taken by all the Members of the United Nations or by some of them, as the Security Council may determine."

Despite the apparent limitlessness of Security Council authority on enforcement action, the council has never undertaken an act of enforcement within the full meaning of the expression and of the charter's provisions. Demands for action have been highly politicized and have failed to achieve the concurrence of a majority of the Security Council members—including the permanent members, which are the United States, the Soviet Union, Britain, France, and China (until 1971 the last of these having been represented by an envoy of the government of the Republic of China in Taiwan). Among the great impediments to Security Council action is that when the United Nations was created, the great powers sought to prevent action against their own interests by including in the charter the principle of great-power unanimity. Article 27 requires that matters of substance be decided by a majority of 9 of the 15 members "including the concurring votes of the permanent members."

In only two instances has the Security Council been able to transcend its internal politics to vote enforcement measures. In the first, Western governments responded to the North Korean invasion of South Korea in 1950 under a

Security Council resolution authorizing them to do so. But in this instance the Soviet Union did not participate in the voting (because of its boycott after the UN refusal to seat the Beijing representative following the Communist victory in civil war). Hence it cannot be said that collective security as intended by the frames of the charter was involved in the Korean incident. The second instance was a remarkable post-Cold War moment in which the five permanent members of the Security Council and eight other governments joined in a series of resolutions that (1) condemned the Iraqi invasion and annexation of Kuwait, (2) created a sea and land embargo on Iraqi inward and outward trade, and (3) extended the embargo to the air. In creating the land and sea embargo, the resolution of the Security Council

> Calls upon those member states cooperating with the Government of Kuwait which are deploying maritime forces to the area to use such measures commensurate to the specific circumstances as may be necessary under the authority of the Security Council to halt all inward and outward maritime shipping in order to inspect and verify their cargoes and destinations and to insure strict implementation of the provisions related to such shipping [previously resolved].

The subsequent resolution confirmed that the embargo "applies to all means of transportation, including aircraft," and laid down specific provisions for states to prevent aircraft departures to or arrivals from Iraq and Iraq-occupied Kuwait. Later, for the first time ever, the full council authorized the 27 governments cooperating militarily with the exiled government of Kuwait "to use all necessary means" to enforce the prior resolutions should Iraq not withdraw from Kuwait by January 15, 1991, an authorization of force under Article 42:

> Should the Security Council consider that measures [short of force] would be inadequate or have proved to be inadequate, it may take such action by air, sea, or land forces as may be necessary to maintain or restore international peace and security. Such action may include demonstrations, blockade, and other operations by air, sea, or land forces of Members of the United Nations.

Only if such forces were used under this authorization could it be said that the full power of the Security Council to provide sanctions in international law had been invoked. More broadly, although one promising series of events scarcely constitutes a trend in world order, the post-Cold War occurrence of the Iraq-Kuwait crisis demonstrates that a convergence of political wills at the Security Council as foreseen by the framers of the charter may now be possible. If the major powers agree under new global circumstances to act in concert to preserve peace, the council may for the first time in United Nations history have a major role to play.

Enforcement measures are not the sole means of UN sanction. Indeed, skeptics of the coercive theory of international law note that forceful sanctions through the United Nations are limited to situations involving threats to the peace, breaches of the peace, and acts of aggression. In all other instances of noncompliance with international law, the charter's own general provisions outlawing the threat or use of force actually prevent forceful sanction. Those same skeptics regard this as an appropriate paradox in a decentralized state system of international politics.

Nonetheless, other means of collective sanction through the United Nations involve diplomatic intervention and economic sanctions. In its economic sanctions, the United Nations has followed in the path of the League of Nations, which undertook economic sanctions against Italy in 1935–1936 for its attack on Ethiopia. In the UN period, the most celebrated sanctions have been those voted against China by the General Assembly in 1951 as a result of Chinese intervention in the Korean War; and the 1967 decision of the Security Council to isolate Southern Rhodesia (now Zimbabwe) for its policy of racial separation following its unilateral declaration of independence from Britain.

As in other cases of economic sanctions, effectiveness in the Rhodesian situation was limited by the twin problems of (1) achieving universal participation and (2) the resistance of national elites to external coercion, especially when the issue was one of prominent internal concern. With respect to universal participation, even states usually sympathetic to Britain's policy demonstrated weak compliance.[10] For example, by executive order, the United States imposed restraints on imports originating in Rhodesia,

> *Provided,* however, that the prohibition against dealing in commodities or products exported from Southern Rhodesia shall not apply to any such commodities or products which, prior to the date of this Order, had been lawfully imported into the United States.[11]

As a matter of international interest, the United States sought formally to implement the Security Council sanctions. But as a matter of self-interest, the US government demurred from full implementation by interpreting the sanctions to affect only commodities in which trade had not customarily occurred between the two nations. The reason was that Southern Rhodesia was a prime supplier of chromium to the United States, and continued flow of this resource was necessary for production of steel alloys needed in, among other things, military hardware.

This decentralization of sanctions remains one of the major weaknesses of international law. Although international bodies sometimes make decisions in the implementation of sanctions, member states must implement them. The states are the importers and exporters in the international system. They command industrial economies and the passage of goods across national boundaries. Just as Stalin once remarked that the pope has no military divisions, so too does the United Nations have no troops of its own, no industries to produce the coveted commodities that, if withheld, might alter the external or

---

[10]Report of the Committee Established in Pursuance of Resolution 352 (1968) of May 29, 1968 (New York: UN Publications S/8954, dated December 30, 1968); also Johan Galtung, "On the Effects of Economic Sanctions, with Examples from the Case of Rhodesia," *World Politics,* vol. 19, no. 3, April 1967, pp. 378–416; Frederick Hoffmann, "The Functions of Economic Sanctions," *Journal of Peace Research,* no. 2, 1967, pp. 140–160; and Ronald Segal, ed., *Sanctions Against South Africa* (London: Penguin, 1964).

[11]US Department of State Release no. 176, July 29, 1968; in *US Department of State Bulletin,* vol. 59, 1968, p. 199, and as reprinted in *American Journal of International Law,* vol. 63, 1969, pp. 128–130, in the section entitled "Contemporary Practice of the United States Relating to International Law."

internal policies of states. The United Nations has no chromium deposits to withhold from the United States! Furthermore, the United Nations is wholly dependent on its members for operating funds, so no matter what decisional authority its members give it, its ability to take action depends not only on decision but also on means. Without the support, the wealth and the material assistance of national governments, the United Nations is incapable of effective sanctions. The resistance of governments to a financially independent UN arises principally from their insistence on maintaining control over sanctioning processes in international politics.

Despite sweeping language regarding "threats to the peace, breaches of the peace, and acts of aggresion," the role of the United Nations in the enforcement of international law is quite limited. Indeed the purpose of the United Nations is not to enforce international law, but to preserve, restore, and ensure international peace and security. Viewed slightly differently, the role of the Security Council is to enforce that part of international law that is either created or encompassed by the Charter of the United Nations. When aggresion occurs, the members of the council may decide politically—but are not obliged legally—to undertake collective action that will have sanctioning result. In instances of threats to or breaches of the peace short of war, they may decide politically to take anticipatory action short of force. Moreover, it is for the members of the Security Council to determine when a threat to the peace, a breach of the peace or an act of aggression has occurred. Even this determination is made by political rather than legal criteria. The Security Council may have a legal basis for acting, but self-interest determines how each of its members votes, irrespective of how close to aggression the incident at issue may be. Hence by virtue of both its constitutional limitations and the exercise of sovereign prerogatives by its members, the Security Council's role as a sanctioning device in international law is sharply restricted.[12]

Individual Sanctions in International Law

In the absence of a reliable system of collective sanctions, individual and group sanctions must be accepted as legitimate within current international law. Until states can achieve their demands through collective actions, govern-

---

[12] For a more restrictive interpretation of the Security Council's role in international sanctions, see Robert E. Riggs, "The United Nations and the Politics of Law," in Lawrence J. Finkelstein, ed., *Politics in the United Nations System* (Durham and London: Duke University Press, 1988), pp. 41-74. Riggs refers to the council's "paper enforcement powers" (p. 63) and concludes that "the Charter appears to confer upon the Security Council substantial power to issue commands in matters relating to international peace and security, but the power has seldom been used and in practice has not been very significant." (p. 53.) The author also acknowledges the assistance of Dr. Finkelstein (personal correspondence) in appreciating the constitutional limits of the council's powers, but nonetheless prefers a somewhat broader view because the charter itself is an integral part of international law. Note also that the Riggs paper and the Finkelstein-Jones correspondence preceded the council's actions regarding the Iraqi invasion and annexation of Kuwait in 1990, discussed earlier herein.

Text of U.N. Security Council Resolution on Using Force in the Gulf

Special to the New York Times

*UNITED NATIONS, Nov. 29—
Following is the text of Resolution 678,
which was approved today by the Security Council:*

THE SECURITY COUNCIL,

RECALLING AND REAFFIRMING its
Resolutions 660 (1990), 661 (1990),
662 (1990), 664 (1990), 665 (1990),666
(1990), 667 (1990), 669 (1990), 670
(1990), 674 (1990) and 677 (1990),

NOTING that, despite all efforts by
the United Nations, Iraq refuses to
comply with its obligation to implement Resolution 660 (1990) and subsequent resolutions, in flagrant contempt
of the Council,

MINDFUL of its duties and responsibilities under the Charter of the United
Nations for the maintenance and preservation of international peace and security,

DETERMINED to secure full compliance with its decisions,

ACTING under Chapter VII of the
Charter of the United Nations,

1. DEMANDS that Iraq comply fully
with Resolution 660 (1990) and all
subsequent relevant resolutions and
decides, while maintaining all its decisions, to allow Iraq one final opportunity, as a pause of good will, to do so;

2. AUTHORIZES member states cooperating with the Government of Kuwait, unless Iraq on or before Jan. 15,
1991, fully implements, as set forth in
paragraph 1 above, the foregoing resolutions, to use all necessary means to
uphold and implement the Security
Council Resolution 660 and all subsequent relevant resolutions and to restore international peace and security
in the area;

3. REQUESTS all states to provide
appropriate support for the actions undertaken in pursuance of paragraph 2
of this resolution; and

4. REQUESTS the states concerned
to keep the Council regularly informed
on the progress of actions undertaken
pursuant to paragraphs 2 and 3 of this
resolution;

5. DECIDES to remain seized of the
matter.

ments and their close allies will invoke collective self-help. As a result, the
imposition of individual and group sanctions is common.

Some cases in which sanctions are threatened see no actual implementation.
The United States, for example, did not impose measures on those Latin
American states that nationalized privately owned American property, despite
legislation that authorizes the president to discontinue aid in the absence of
adequate compensation.

A most interesting case of sanctions between major powers was raised by the Soviet Union's refusal to permit Jews to emigrate and, later, its consent to do so only after payment of an exorbitant "education tax." This became an issue of public debate when hopes for expanded Soviet-American trade brightened (1972–1974). Several interest groups demanded withholding agreement until after relaxation of Moscow's emigration policy. These pressures were expressed in the Jackson-Brock amendment, which imposed restraints on American trade with the Soviet Union until the latter recognized the open right of its citizens to emigrate. Because Moscow regarded these restraints as interventionary and politically exorbitant, it declined to enter into a commercial agreement offering it most-favored-nation status (tariffs no higher than those required of other major trading partners of the United States). Later, in 1980, when Soviet troops invaded and occupied Afghanistan, the United States responded with a number of sanctions, including the unilateral discontinuation of treaty-regulated grain trade with the Soviet Union.

Other acts of unilateral sanction may also be noted. In the fall of 1975, after the United States suffered several embarrassing defeats at the United Nations, including the majority declaration equating Zionism with racism, it became American policy to threaten with economic sanction those of its friends who contributed to the continuing embarrassment. In another instance, as a potential recipient of sanctions, the United States was informed by Britain and France early in 1976 that if it refused limited landing rights in American airports to the supersonic plane Concorde, they would initiate economic sanctions against the United States.

Between global sanctions urged by the United Nations and individual sanctions lies an area in which several states apply sanctions through informal cooperation. A classic example is the non-UN sanctions undertaken against South Africa by the states of the British Commonwealth (with only Britain dissenting), the United States, and a large sector of the Third World. These resulted from the failure of normal diplomacy to persuade the South African government to discontinue its policy of racial separation (apartheid) that forces the black majority population to live in isolated and squalid townships, to be licensed for work outside the townships, and to play no part in the civic life of the nation. Although many people who were opposed to sanctions, including President Ronald Reagan, insisted that the people most likely to be injured were the black people in whose behalf the sanctions were adopted, others felt that the world's conscience had been awakened to the repugnance of apartheid to the point that failure to make a political statement through formal sanctions would be tantamount to concurrence in it.

The frequent resort to individual sanctions leads some to conclude that international law is incapable of restraining states. Yet we know beyond doubt that much of the conduct of states is regulated and that it is regulated by legal means. We know, for example, that the law of the high seas is highly developed, although laden with modern complications; that under all but the most peculiar political circumstances, such as those in Iran in 1979 and 1980 in which dozens of American diplomatic personnel were held hostage for more than a year, diplomatic and consular personnel may rely on foreign governments for specified treatment; that there exist developed principles for the international exchange of fugitives through extradition; and that a host of relatively nonpolitical functions is regulated by international conventions.

We know equally well, however, that the power relations of governments are but sparsely regulated, and even then imperfectly. The General Pact for the Renunciation of War (the Kellogg-Briand Pact, 1928) was considered inapplicable in cases of self-defense, and each state retained the right to determine the conditions and needs of its defense. Article 51 of the United Nations Charter continues to permit "individual or collective self-defense" prior to Security Council assumption of responsibility. By the same token, neither France nor China has entered into the Nuclear Non-Proliferation Treaty, nor is either likely to do so until after having achieved its desired level of deterrent capability. And although the United States, the Soviet Union, and Britain have forsworn nuclear testing at sea and in the atmosphere, they have reserved the right to continue nuclear competition by underground testing.

The Effectiveness of International Law

If we are to conclude that international law provides effective restraints on states, then we must demonstrate not merely the existence of legal principles but also the willingness of states to comply with them. Compliance is a function of several factors, among them: (1) the subject matter that law seeks to regulate, (2) changes in the motives and needs of governments, (3) the ability of states to violate the law without serious threat of sanctions, and (4) the importance of the outcome of an event. So while we are concerned here with international law, each of these elements is subjected to the political judgment of the state. The decision as to whether one will be law-abiding is a decision for the state's political apparatus. A state's compliance with legal obligations is a function of (1) the degree to which issues are politicized and (2) the state's ability to behave in a lawless manner without serious threat of adverse consequences.

International law consists of norms of varying political levels.[13] On some subjects, states readily recognize the utility of collective regulation, especially where the subject matter is relatively mechanical and depoliticized. This level of law, referred to as the law of reciprocity, is a network of treaties and customs through which governments acknowledge reciprocal benefit. Compliance with these norms is predictable.

As the subject matter of the law becomes more politicized, however, states are less willing to enter into formal regulation or do so only with loopholes for escape from apparent constraints. In this area, called the law of community, governments are generally less willing to sacrifice their sovereign liberties. In a revolutionary international system where change is rapid and direction un-

---

[13]Although this concept has been expressed by several legal scholars, this analysis follows most closely that of Stanley Hoffmann, "International Systems and International Law," *World Politics,* vol. 14, 1961, pp. 205–237.

clear, the integrity of the law of community is weak, and compliance with its often flaccid norms is correspondingly uncertain.

The law of the political framework resides above these other two levels and consists of the legal norms governing the ultimate power relations of states. This is the most politicized level of international relations; hence, pertinent law is extremely primitive. Those legal norms that do exist suffer from all the political machinations that one might expect. States have taken care to see that their behavior is only minimally constrained; the few international legal norms they have created always provide avenues of escape such as the big-power veto in the UN Security Council.

The question of states' compliance with international law, and, therefore the effectiveness and credibility of international law, has been crucial throughout interstate system history. Some theorists base effectiveness exclusively on the built-in sanctions of the law, but more modern studies tend to emphasize the behavioral aspects of political decision making related to law, such as domestic political considerations or profit-maximization strategies of foreign policy.[14] A third school finds problems of compliance rooted particularly in global cultural and ideological diversity, a condition that makes it difficult to frame a cohesive world order without attempting simultaneously to bring about fundamental changes in political relations.[15] A fourth view concerns the diversity of ethical standards.[16] One scholar has examined these several literatures and found no fewer than 13 explanations of compliance and noncompliance with international law.[17]

Uncontrollably rapid changes in the current international political system have multiplied the need for a sound world order built on the rule of law. Some of those changes involve military technology, speed and stealth of military delivery, command and control communications, international intervention, and economic coercion. Others, however, involve the social and legislative foundations of the law itself. One scholar summarized the patterns of contemporary change related to international law in this way:

1. The emergence of the quasi-legislative functions (see Chapter 16) of the United Nations and other international institutions that purport to prescribe conduct without any formal legal codification.

---

[14]Oran Young, *Compliance and Public Authority* (Baltimore: Johns Hopkins University Press, 1979).

[15]George Schwarzenberger, "The Credibility of International Law," *The Year Book of World Affairs* (London), 1983, pp. 292–301.

[16]Schwarzenberger and Stanley Hoffmann, *Duties Beyond Borders: On the Limits and Possibilities of Ethical International Politics* (Syracuse, N.Y.: Syracuse University Press, 1981).

[17]Oscar Schachter, "Towards a Theory of International Obligation," in Stephen M. Schwebel, ed., *The Effectiveness of International Decisions* (Dobbs Ferry, N.Y.: Oceana Publications, 1971), pp. 9–31. Schachter identifies these explanations as consent, customary practice, juridical conscience, natural law or natural reason, social necessity, international consensus, direct intuition, common purposes of governments, effectiveness, fear of sanctions, systemic goals, shared expectations, and rules of recognition.

2. The evolution of informal international rules regarding apparent understandings or unilateral actions and acquiescence.

3. The frequency with which social revolutions have overturned traditional order and challenged assumptions on which authority was previously based.

4. Cooperation and reciprocal behavior resulting from global interdependence but not yet institutionalized in traditional forms of law.

5. The increased permeability of states by technology and economic interdependence, which blurs traditional distinctions between matters of domestic concern and those of international concern.

6. Scientific and technological expansions that have led to informal means of setting standards and exercising supervision without formal legal instruments.[18]

Considering these circumstances, the normative basis of international law is, in the opinion of some, deteriorating just as the probability of major international conflicts is rising; and the deterioration is not accompanied by a strong will to return to the difficult act of codifying a legal order acceptable to the majority of states. Those who hold this view have also concluded that there is a direct relation between the threat to world order and the deterioration of the normative basis of law.[19] Will the end of the Cold War reverse this?

If the law attempts to depoliticize international relations, then what exists today in one level of law may tomorrow reside in another. International conditions may change, or domestic politics may alter a government's willingness to depoliticize an external issue. Thus, the predictability of compliance may be determined not merely by the level of the subject matter, but also by a state's determination to affect certain outcomes of international events. Compliance, then, and the overall effectiveness of positive international law may be viewed as a horizontal problem as well as a vertical one and may be represented as in Figure 15–1. Behind these indicators of compliance are social and political motives. It is the intent of this book to demonstrate that the sociopolitical motivation is attributable primarily to the respective perceptions that the major actors hold of the international system. Therefore, after noting briefly some of the areas in which effective international law is most urgently needed at present, we will turn to an exploration of the views that the principal world actors hold in international law, in order further to reveal some of the sources of cooperation and resistance.

Areas of Urgency in International Law

Each observer of the international scene has his or her own priorities as to the areas most urgently requiring the attention of international law. By the same token, each views differently the probability of achieving effective legal control in these respective areas, and the matter of national or multinational

---

[18]Schachter, "Towards a Theory of International Obligation," pp. 9–31.

[19]See, for example, Richard A. Falk, *The Year Book of World Affairs* (London), 1982, pp. 3–16.

Figure 15–1 Levels of compliance and political salience.

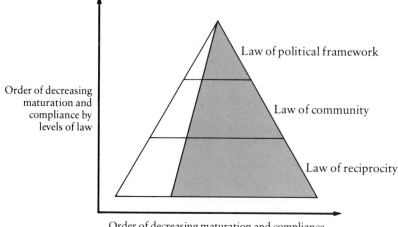

Order of decreasing maturation and compliance by levels of law

Law of political framework

Law of community

Law of reciprocity

Order of decreasing maturation and compliance by determination to affect outcome

primacy in undertaking to achieve legal control. All these differences notwithstanding, there are a few areas of political activity where the effective control of law is visibly insufficient. Some of these are outlined next as a primitive agenda of legal issues.

Prevention and Control of Aggression

No issue is more vital to the global political context than are prevention of aggression, serious disruption of important international transactions, and massive destruction and death. Once preventive measures have failed, control of the level and territorial scope of aggression is the next most crucial issue, as is the restriction on the number of participants, particularly in instances that may involve the crucial interests of the most powerful and nuclear-armed states.

Given the degree of contemporary international economic interdependence and the far-flung interests of governments, there is scarcely a corner of the earth where aggression would not be a major threat to the security and survival of most nations. Although the scope of the Vietnam War was ultimately contained, the degree to which it touched on the political and geopolitical interests of three nuclear powers carried civilization to the danger point and beyond. War between Iran and Iraq not only added to the instability of the Middle East, already fraught with threats of war between Arab and Israeli interests (and ultimately Soviet and American interests) but also threatened the entire Western industrialized world with fuel depletion should the area of the Persian Gulf become fully embroiled or should the straits through which petroleum is shipped to the high seas be closed. Similarly, the transformation of Lebanon into a battleground, first between Israel and Syria and then by a combination of local factions and, simultaneously, by factions of the Palestine Liberation Organization with Syrian participation, threatens major-power confrontation and territorial expansion of fighting.

The crisis that began in 1990 in the Persian Gulf and the Arabian Peninsula opened additional questions of conflict containment. Iraq's invasion and annexation of Kuwait, followed by its threat to overrun Saudi Arabia as well, resulted in a large and complex multinational force on the ground in Saudi Arabia and in the Persian Gulf. Within a month of the invasion of Kuwait, 27 nations were participating. Washington alone contributed a force of over 450,000. Historic moments occurred at the Security Council where the United States and the Soviet Union voted together first to embargo all Iraqi trade and then to authorize the enforcement of the embargo at sea. But neither wanted the other's ground forces in the area. At the UN, the Soviets made clear their fear that the crisis would result in a permanent American armed presence in the Middle East, and the Bush administration breathed a collective sigh of relief when the Soviets informed the Japanese that they would not send ground troops of their own. At a summit meeting in Helsinki, Finland, a mere five weeks after the start of the crisis, Presidents Bush and Gorbachev reiterated their demand that Iraq comply with the Security Council's order to withdraw from Kuwait, but President Bush insisted that he had not asked the Soviets to contribute ground forces. For his part, Mr. Gorbachev succeeded in getting public assurances from his American counterpart that the American presence would not exceed the duration of the crisis.

As we have seen, the United Nations Charter addresses matters that constitute "Threats to the Peace, Breaches of the Peace, and Acts of Aggression." But in UN law, as in all international law, effective action begins with agreement on definitions, and it was not until 1974 that the General Assembly adopted, without balloting, a consensus definition of aggression: "the use of armed force by a State against the sovereignty, territorial integrity or political independence of another State, or in any other manner inconsistent with the Charter of the United Nations."

But even in the presence of general agreement on a definition, collective security is not likely to serve as an effective deterrent or remedy. Individual or multinational responses are much more likely for the foreseeable future to be the act of choice. In rare instances when the political and geopolitical interests of the involved states have been uniquely suited, UN peacekeeping has been substituted for unilateral response. For the most part, however, only self-restraint and fears of escalation and nuclear consequences have deterred would-be aggressors or restricted the expansion of wars. As sophisticated weaponry overspreads the world through arms transfers, particularly as a form of trade to secure Middle East petroleum, the threat of regional wars may increase, and the impulse of third parties to intervene may grow. The simultaneous rapid change in the international economy, with its uncertain direction, adds to these threats.

Meanwhile, when aggression is not checked, it is rewarded. For whatever reasons the Soviet Union may have decided to invade and occupy Afghanistan in 1980, it is certain that its objectives were simplified by the unwillingness of the Western alliance to respond with force. Therein lies the dilemma of an international legal order that lacks effective collective sanctions: It is unable to deter aggression under some circumstances, and having allowed it to occur, it can respond only with silent acquiescence or with military force, which risks enlarging beyond control the intensity, geographic scope, and number of participants.

Arms Control and Disarmament

As with the case of legal controls of aggression, arms control and disarmament are matters that touch directly on the political context and are therefore so sensitive to national governments as to be submitted rarely and only partially to effective legal control. Furthermore, in eras of instability and of vastly changed economic relations, modern weaponry becomes not only a coveted prize of governments but also a major instrument of international trade. As a result, while the superpowers negotiate limitations on strategic nuclear arms, they are busily and enthusiastically supplying other governments, many of them unstable, with conventional arms at the same level of sophistication as those with which their own forces are equipped. Control of resort to arms is made more difficult in an international legal order where there is no control of access to arms.

The New International Economic Order

Until the past decade, international economic law was restricted largely to trade and currency agreements, international economic aid, and agreements between (or among) imperial states dealing with forms of competition in colonized territories. The formation of the European Economic Community and other regional customs unions expanded the scope of interest to investment controls within protected areas. But the commencement of the New International Economic Order called for a comprehensive legal order.

Views of what the prospective content of that law should be depend on national perspectives. The industrializing countries call for a legal order that limits the political activities of the transnational corporations, ensures the transfer of technology, protects agricultural and semifinished products from dangerous variations in international prices, protects natural resources from foreign exploitation, removes political strings from intergovernmental aid, and places restrictions on foreign direct investment. For their part, the industrialized states call for protections against nationalization of property by host governments, assurances of controlled increases in the price of natural resources, guarantees against repudiation of contracts to purchase industrial produce, and guarantees of a steady export flow of raw materials. The concern of the latter group is directed especially to the oil-exporting countries of the Third World which, from 1973 to 1983, demonstrated their ability to influence the industrial productivity of the West and Japan by controlling the export and price of oil and which, in the meanwhile, disrupted the international currency exchange system by amassing nearly $100 billion annually in reserve currencies.

The vast and sudden change in world economics, which occurred over a span of barely five years, calls for legal control not only because of its economic aspects but also because of its immense impact on political and social conditions both globally and within the industrialized world. Because modern arms are a major instrument of trade from the industrialized side of the equation, the uncertain directions of world commerce gain an additional destabilizing characteristic. Without an effective, comprehensive legal order, the new economics will continue to be regulated by hazardous self-help.

Law of the Sea

Although the law of the sea may have the sound of a maritime problem, it is an intensely economic one. Not only does the sea provide a large share of the world's nutrition (all of it, in some societies); it also contains a treasure of minerals and proteins. The floor of the sea at great depths beyond the continental shelf and beyond national territorial waters is strewn with metal deposits, and the suboceanic floor may contain fossil fuels that today's technology cannot reach.

It is for these economic reasons that the members of the United Nations struggled for more than a decade to arrange a comprehensive legal regime for the seas. National positions are often incompatible because the value of the sea's resources is determined roughly by the technology necessary to exploit them, thus giving the advantage clearly to a handful of states, an event that the rest of the world vows to avoid. Furthermore, not all the world's nation-states have coastal territories; nearly 20 percent are wholly landlocked. What rights to the oceans' resources do they have?

As the world's accessible and known resources are depleted at an accelerating pace and by more and more competitors, ownership of rights to the riches of the seas becomes one of the most vital issues in international economic law. Conclusion of a treaty on the law of the sea in 1983, which will not enter into force until ratified by the required number of governments, still leaves many important issues inadequately addressed.

Terrorism and Skyjacking

Aggression is not the exclusive province of national governments. In recent years, the frequency of terrorist violence by national and transnational extremist groups has become a common element in political activity. Although most of it occurs internally and is therefore solely within the domestic jurisdiction of the state, there are a number of international considerations. First, many acts of terrorism have occurred against foreign nationals, as in the many cases in which foreign businesspeople have been shot by Italian and Latin American terrorists. Prevention, apprehension, and conviction are the responsibilities of national governments, and international substitutes for ineffectual national actions do not yet exist. Furthermore, some terrorist acts have occurred on the territories of third parties, most notably the massacre of Israeli athletes by Arab terrorists at the 1972 Olympic Games in West Germany. Although this fell within the responsibility of the West German government, the international implications are evident. Terrorism has also spread to nonnational airspace, as illustrated most dramatically in 1988 by the bombing of an American

International terrorism: Officials inspect scene of bombing in which seven horses of the Queen's guard were killed in London, 1982.

Source: AP/Wide World

commercial airliner over Scotland, an act subsequently proved to be the work of Middle Eastern terrorists.

A recent episode of terrorism on the high seas illustrates the jurisdictional difficulties in controlling these events. Middle Eastern insurgents aboard a cruise ship in the Mediterranean killed one person and injured others before the ship reached an Egyptian port. Egyptian officials put the presumably guilty parties aboard an aircraft bound for Libya, but it was intercepted by American fighters and forced to land in Italy. There, many of the alleged criminals were released; others were tried and found guilty of relatively minor crimes on the basis of the court's finding that they had not been engaged in politically inspired terrorism.

A new phenomenon has crept into the world's concern about terrorism, namely, state-sponsored terrorism. This consists of terrorist acts—such as shootings, bombings, and hijackings—planned, supplied, and assisted by a government. Whereas in most instances an individual terrorist is anonymous (there are notable exceptions in the Middle East and in West Germany) and difficult to capture except when caught in the act of violence, governmental institutions are visible and easily subject to reprisal if blame can be placed confidently on them. Such an event occurred in 1986 when having determined that the Libyan government had participated in the terrorist bombing of a West German restaurant and the resulting death of an American soldier, President Reagan ordered air strikes against the Libyan central government compound. There were several deaths, allegedly including a child of Libyan chief of state, Colonel Muʿammar Qaddafi. The sort of self-help retaliation is invited by the absence of international alternatives. It also illustrates the dangers of military retaliation for terrorism, and of retaliatory terrorism for acts of military defense. The latter is exemplified by attempts of presumed Iranian terrorists to assassinate the wife of the American naval officer whose ship, stationed in the Persian Gulf during the Iran-Iraq war, downed an Iranian commercial airliner mistaken for a military craft on an attack path toward the ship. This incident illustrates the tendency toward intercontinental terrorism.

Yet another aspect eagerly awaits international legal supervision. Many terrorists have sought protective refuge in countries in which they are aliens but which fail to prosecute them under domestic jurisdiction or to return them to their national governments or to the governments of territories from which they have fled. In the absence of extradition treaties or of formal international obligations to do otherwise, these governments are free from all pressure, save moral suasion, to bring law to bear on terrorists. In one recent instance, the courts of West Germany chose to try a terrorist whose extradition had been sought by Washington so that he could be tried in the United States for terrorist crimes against Americans. In sharp contrast, the government of Colombia agreed in 1989 to extradite to the United States Colombian nationals under indictment in the United States for international drug smuggling. The cost was extremely high for Colombia: Terrorists representing the drug interests conducted retaliatory assassinations against public officials and set off almost daily explosions against both public and private buildings.

A special case in point is the form of terrorism called skyjacking, in which a commercial aircraft crew is commanded by armed terrorists to divert the craft to an unintended destination, usually a foreign one where the individuals will be free from prosecution. Many such acts are not directly linked to international terrorism, but many have been, as is evidenced by the common occurrence of a negotiated political demand in return for release of the craft and its crew and passengers. Once again, the absence of established international norms compelling national governments to act on behalf of the international community in the legal prosecution of such terrorists contributes to the frequency of the act. Despite the many differences between Cuba and the United States, they have entered into an agreement regarding strict Cuban treatment of skyjackers who land in Cuba. As a result of this agreement, incidents of skyjacking with Cuban destinations have virtually ended.

International Refugees

Throughout the twentieth century, one of the principal objectives of international law and organization has been to extend legal rights to the millions of people who have been displaced from their homes and homelands and who swarm across the world as refugees. Handling of the refugee problem was one of the main activities of the League of Nations after the First World War; and at the close of the Second World War, the United Nations, as one of its earliest efforts, organized machinery on behalf of refugees.

Not all homeless people crossing international boundaries are refugees by international legal definition. It is doubtful, for example, that thousands of East Germans who, in 1989, reached the West when Hungary, in defiance of a demand from its East German ally, opened its boundary to Austria in deliberate assistance to East Germans wishing to leave the Eastern bloc territories permanently, are protected refugees. Nor are Mexicans seeking better economic conditions in Texas or Southern California, and who cross the border into the United States in violation of American immigration law, considered refugees. They are, instead, regarded as illegal aliens and are subject to involuntary return to Mexico. In contrast, Cambodians seeking refuge in Thailand from the civil war at home are considered refugees by international legal standards, as are Ethiopians in Sudan and Nicaraguans in El Salvador. What, then, constitutes a refugee in international law?

Because international law is made by agreements among sovereign states, the legal definition of refugee status reflects in large part the willingness of governments to accept large numbers of refugees in their territories without the freedom to return them upon the elimination of the cause for their refugee status. Indeed, the 1951 United Nations Geneva Convention on Refugees stipulates that refugee status is dependent on "a well-founded fear of persecution for reasons of race, religion, nationality, membership in a particular social group or political opinion." The narrowest view, accordingly, is that an international migrant is a true refugee only if the cause for migration were political persecution, and only if the return home carries with it the inception or resumption of such persecution.

But a broader view holds that migrants may be classed as protected refugees when the cause behind migration is some other threat to life and security, such as naturally caused territorial desimation (for example, fire, flood, earthquake), or chronic drought and famine. As the number of refugees began to swell again in the 1980s, many governments preferred the tighter language of the Geneva Convention, which enabled them to return refugees to their homelands after the causes of migration had been eliminated, thus avoiding the tremendous costs of housing, nutrition, and so on.

Recently, however, a United Nations Group of Governmental Experts on International Cooperation to Avert New Flows of Refugees has presented to the General Assembly a two-part report that adopts the broader definition, including as internationally protected refugees people escaping natural disasters as well as political persecution.[20] By this definition, it was estimated that in 1988 there were approximately 14.5 million refugees in the world, contrasted with about 10 million just four years earlier. According to the United States Committee on Refugees, they were distributed geographically as shown in Table 15–1. Unless and until the United Nations adopts this definition, its numbers will continue to be somewhat smaller. In 1988, for example, the United Nations reported in excess of 12 million internationally protected refugees. To underscore the magnitude of these numbers, think of them as approximately equal to the total population of Venezuela, or equal to the

---

[20]Luke T. Lee, "United Nations Group of Governmental Experts on International Cooperation to Avert New Flows of Refugees: Part II," *American Journal of International Law,* April 1987, pp. 442–444. For a thorough history of the issue that adopts the narrower definition, see Guy S. Goodwin-Gill, *The Refugee in International Law* (New York: Clarendon, 1984).

Table 15–1 The world's refugees, 1988.

Origin	Approximate Number (in millions)
Afghanistan	5.9
Africa	4.1
Middle East	3.2
Asia and Pacific	0.9
Latin America and Caribbean	0.3
Europe	0.06

Source: The United States Committee on Refugees as reported in, and adapted from, *Time,* July 3, 1989, p. 26.

combined populations of Sweden and Switzerland. (Note that these figures do not include approximately a quarter of a million refugees in Jordan and Turkey in 1990, all fleeing from Iraqi-occupied Kuwait and Iraq itself. All of these were awaiting transportation to their homelands.)

But the refugee problem is far greater than mere definitions and numbers. All these people are without homes, food, protection from weather, sources of income, medical care, education, clothes, stable social and political organizations, and protection from violence. Most are unable to communicate in the languages of the host countries. And because all the basic necessities of life must be provided by the host countries when international relief efforts fall short, in the main they find themselves inhospitably received as added burdens on the public revenue systems of poor countries already unable to meet the needs of citizens. Moreover, their international legal protection means that they cannot be forced to return to their homelands, thus prolonging indefinitely their absolute dependence on international and host-country assistance. It is, therefore, the role of international law to protect them from the threat of involuntary return to the ravages of war, to political persecution, or to natural disaster, but it is the role of international organizations and national governments to provide the basic ingredients of survival.

International Illicit Drug Trafficking

As dependence on illegal drugs sweeps many countries, and as the documentation of drug-related violence begins to dominate the front pages of many urban daily newspapers, virtually every legal jurisdiction in the world has attempted to find solutions to the problem of illicit drugs. City, state, and national governments turn to law enforcement, border patrols, searches of suspicious vessels, and surveillance of airports to stop the flow of drugs, while they attempt to find programs of drug treatment and education that will reduce the demand for these substances. Many aspects of the global drug problem belong properly within national and local jurisdiction, but there can be little progress in reducing the international flow of supply without effective international law.

Although several bilateral and multilateral agreements on drug trafficking existed prior to 1984, the huge increase in social problems—addiction, drug-related violence, and drug-related spread of acquired immune deficiency syndrome (AIDS)—prompted the United Nations General Assembly in 1984 to call for the creation of new global measures for dealing with international drug trafficking. This call was reiterated by an International Conference on Drug Abuse and Illegal Trafficking in 1987. At the end of 1988, the United Nations convened a conference at the home of its drug-control agencies in Vienna, Austria, from which emerged a new United Nations Convention Against Illegal Traffic in Narcotic Drugs and Psychotropic Substances. One indication of the urgency with which governments viewed the situation was that the convention was adopted unanimously by the representatives of 108 participating governments. As national governments formally adopt this treaty by their normal constitutional processes, and as it gains enough national ratifications to go into effect, the participating states will acquire new rights and obligations. Among the rights will be the ability of courts to confiscate drug profits and to extradite drug offenders to the countries in which they conducted their illegal acts. And among the obligations will be passing laws to open banking practices so that drug money laundering will become more difficult, and to forbid the employment of children in any aspect of creating, processing, transporting, or disseminating illicit drugs.

Questions of Jurisdiction

One of the frequently debated topics among theorists of international law is the relationship of domestic law and jurisdiction to international law and jurisdiction. Although most theories and judicial findings subordinate domestic law to international law, there are several that endorse the superiority of national law and jurisdiction. In drafting the Statute of the Permanent Court of International Justice and later of the International Court of Justice, negotiators debated this relationship in connection with the obligation of states to submit international disputes to the jurisdiction of the court. Still today, international organs and international jurisdiction extend into the state only on the rarest of occasions.

Until states agree on the extent to which national jurisdiction is subordinated to or defined by international law, there will be little opportunity for international organs to pursue international criminals into protective jurisdictions. Furthermore, only under certain regional codes of law (such as the agreements attendant to the European Court of Human Rights) does international jurisdiction address itself to individuals rather than to governments. These twin problems of jurisdiction—the place of the individual in international law and the relationship of international jurisdiction to national jurisdiction—are major obstacles to a more effective international legal order.

The American View of International Law

The view of the United States of international law arises from America's European origins and from the fact that the United States is heir to the central political position previously held by Great Britain. The United States is a by-product of Western European culture and civilization and is the first offspring of the British Empire. Despite its revolutionary separation from Britain, in its legal traditions and international outlook the United States behaves as the progency of Europe.

International law evolved in a Eurocentric world, its norms originally serving the reciprocal convenience of European monarchs. But as the trade of the European states became global and as European empires swelled, the European view of international law became imprinted upon much of the inhabited world. Law came to protect and serve capitalist economic interests; the doctrine of noninterference in the policies of other states was used in part to foster imperialism; and the law of the seas facilitated the commercial and military shipping of the richest and most powerful. Many of these laws were oblivious—and occasionally hostile—to the interests of competing economic systems and to colonized populations. Yet they enjoyed a high degree of integrity, because they had the political protection of the states whose interests they served. Thus, the United States, reared in the cultural, economic, and legal traditions of Britain and Europe, inherited dominance of a Euro-American world prior to the Second World War, in which existing international law was much to its advantage. In the interwar period, the United States took a major role in expanding this legal system along the same lines, seeking, for example, to sponsor a vast network of treaties for the peaceful settlement of international disputes. It also participated in the functional activities of the League of Nations, and sought international economic regulation through bilateral and limited multilateral pacts.

The postwar world presented different conditions, as the Euro-American domination of international politics began to dissolve. The security of Western-oriented concepts of international law fell under stern challenge. The breakup of colonial empires strained legal norms, as did the rapid proliferation of new states. The bellicose unwillingness of the Soviet government to comply with formal norms threatened American interests throughout the world. Soviet refusal to permit self-determination in the countries of Eastern Europe; the brutal absorption of Latvia, Lithuania, and Estonia; the Soviet-inspired Czechoslovakian coup d'état in 1948; the launching of the Korean War; guerrilla fighting in Greece, Turkey, and Iran; and the invasion and occupation of Afghanistan—all these events and more underscored the lawbreaking character of Soviet foreign objectives.

Besides codifying customary law to formalize the international legal order, the United States turned to the United Nations as a focal point of international political and ideological struggles. It relied on the General Assembly to pass quasi-legislation designed to foster peaceful change. At the time of the Korean War (1950), it utilized the Security Council in calling for the defense of the aggrieved South Koreans. The refusal of the Soviet Union to participate in this collective deliberation gave further testimony to the Kremlin's refusal to cooperate in the legal order. The military intervention of Korea by China accentuated the lawbreaking character of international communism, but the General Assembly joined with the United States in labeling China as an aggressor and retaliating with economic sanctions.

But the revolutionary international system in the years following the Second World War was not always receptive to the positivist concept of international law. Soviet and Chinese behavior often threatened global norms and just as often made compliance with them quite dangerous for the United States. As new forms of politics appeared, they escaped from positivist regulation. Finally the United States was forced by Soviet policies to adopt neorealistic attitudes toward the law. Hence, the Truman Doctrine occurred outside the United Nations, the occupation of Japan was replaced by a close Japanese-American security arrangement for the Far East, and West Germany was re-armed. Whenever possible, then, Washington pursued a policy of enhancing the positivist approach to international law; but whenever Soviet foreign policy prevented this, the United States was forced to resort to the broader standards of neorealism.

But it was the Soviet-inspired revolutionary policies of the Third World that brought on Washington's greatest impatience with the changing foundations of international law. Fed up with the continued Soviet supply of the socialist Sandinista forces in Nicaragua and determined to reverse the revolution, the United States intervened by giving military aid to the Western-oriented rebel forces and assisted directly by mining Nicaraguan harbors. When the leftist government of Nicaragua submitted to the ICJ a legal claim against American actions, Washington announced the first modification in its 40-year-old declaration of acceptance of the court's compulsory jurisdiction, excepting from the declaration all matters pertaining to Central America, and declaring that it would neither participate in the proceedings nor comply with the outcome. Despite subsequent findings in favor of the Nicaraguan government, and in defiance of several attempts to embarrass the United States at the United Nations, Washington held fast to its refusal to be subjected to the court's jurisdiction in the Nicaraguan matter.

The View of America's Major Allies

Because of the Cold War, rapid rates of industrialization, and the Westerniza-tion of Japan after 1945, Washington's principal allies have had similar atti-tudes toward positive international law in all three categories: community, reciprocity, and the political context. Indeed, because of the social and eco-nomic origins, the United States and Canada derived much of their perception of international law from Europe. Japan, earlier a victim of such a legal order, after 1950 came to enjoy its fruits and thus adopted a Western-sympathetic attitude.

Recent events have forced changes in the attitudes of these industrialized states, however. The burgeoning resource scarcity in Europe and Japan, in par-ticular, has resulted in a call for new systems of allocation; but more specifi-cally, it has given rise to new attitudes toward economic coercion. Although industrial states have always appreciated the coercive capability of resource boycott, they have only recently felt the negative effects of such boycotts themselves. Now at last, although they hardly share with the resource-rich

Third World the same objectives concerning international economic law, they are prepared to clarify economic rights and duties on a reciprocal basis. Thus, necessity has forced on them a reassessment of the economic portion of the law of community. Canada, itself richly endowed in natural resources, is driven to the same sense of reciprocal adjustment, not out of fear of boycott, but out of sympathy for the Third World's sovereign compromises in asymmetrical economic relations, a sympathy engendered by Canada's own asymmetrical relation to the American economy.

The Soviet View of International Law

In contrast with the United States, the Soviet Union gained major-power status in a world fundamentally hostile to its political, ideological, and economic principles. Its view of international law arose from the writings of Karl Marx, who had seen the state as an instrument through which one class oppresses others. To Marxist jurists, law is the formal instrument of such oppression. They look upon the law of nations, therefore, as a body of rules and principles through which powerful classes in several societies undertake jointly to promote class exploitation in the international system. International law, like all other law, is of class origins.

Yet Soviet leaders have found reason to cooperate with prevailing international law. Their principal justification is the Stalinist premise that the withering away of states must await the universal socialist revolution; and meanwhile, Soviet politics is partly motivated by the fear of capitalist encirclement. It is thus necessary to participate at least minimally in capitalist international law to escape this encirclement. In later years, after Nikita Khrushchev introduced his notion of peaceful coexistence, it became the fashion of Soviet international legal science to promote cooperation with the institutions of interstate law as a means to achieve peaceful coexistence.

Although it is officially denied by Soviet spokespersons, the contemporary view, for practical purposes, is founded on the notion that three bodies of international law exist concurrently. The first is the body of law that regulates the class interests of the capitalist nations. The second pertains to the relations between capitalist and socialist worlds. Finally, they posit a totally separate body of law among socialist states.

The second body is the law of peaceful coexistence. The Soviets agree that a body of rules and principles exist that govern diplomatic and economic relations between East and West. Although they take a positivistic view of its content, they nevertheless insist on distinguishing between textbook law and political reality. While they opt for treaties, particularly bilateral treaties, as the source of choice, they nevertheless hold that politically outmoded rules have lost the quality of law. Probably because of their political minority status in international organizations, they are more sensitive than is the United States to political controls of international law.

Intrabloc law is another area in which Soviet outlooks appear more forthright than do those of the United States. Although the United States purports to respect the self-determination of its friends and allies, it has not always demurred from commanding domestic politics abroad. Recent examples are the American manipulation of the government of South Vietnam, especially from the mid-1950s to the mid-1960s, intervention in the Dominican Republic in 1965, invasion of Grenada in 1984, and intervention in the Nicaraguan civil war on behalf of the antigovernment *contras* throughout the 1980s. From the Soviet viewpoint, the Monroe Doctrine is more a doctrine of unilateral intervention than of hemispheric self-determination.

On the matter of intrabloc law, Soviet policy has undergone a rapid evolution. The first illustrative event occurred in the invasion and occupation of Czechoslovakia in 1968. The legal rationale for this act, the Brezhnev Doctrine, held that among socialist states, sovereign liberties are subordinate to the needs of all the states collectively. The Czech government, it held, is free to establish internal policy, but not to the detriment of the overall interests of socialist states collectively. To the Soviets, the Brezhnev Doctrine enjoyed as much legitimacy in international law as did the American Monroe Doctrine.

Although never formally declared to be the legal justification for the Kremlin's response to events in Poland in 1980, undoubtedly the Brezhnev Doctrine was in the minds of the Soviet leaders. In that year, a workers' strike led to an official acceptance of the independence of labor unions from the government and from the Communist Party. The Polish government's capitulation to the workers' demands resulted in a Soviet-directed change of governments. This is consistent with the dictum that member states of the socialist commonwealth are politically independent up to the point at which their actions or policies countervene the basic ideological foundations of intrabloc law.

Despite the prominence of this thinking prior to the Gorbachev era, events in Poland in 1989 gave some indication of the legal implications of *perestroika*. In that year, the growing strength of the Solidarity Union forced the government to grant it legal status for the first time in seven years (despite the 1980 recognition). At about the same time, Mikhail Gorbachev gave an address in which he made no explicit mention of the Brezhnev Doctrine, but hinted nevertheless that intervention would no longer be part of Soviet intrabloc policy. There followed general elections in which the Solidarity Union became the Solidarity party, and in every contest in which it fielded a candidate, it defeated the incumbent communist. In a rapid rush of events that captured the attention of the world, Gorbachev himself publicly implored the Communist Party to cooperate in establishing the first noncommunist government in Eastern Europe since immediately after the Second World War. In place of the tanks of the summer in 1968 in Czechoslovakia and the forced change of Polish governments in 1980, the Kremlin of the *perestroika* era openly encouraged political self-determination. This formed the first indication that in law, politics, and even ideology, *perestroika* would alter vastly not only the Brezhnev Doctrine, but intrabloc law, the law of peaceful coexistence, and even the notion of proletarian internationalism.

Only weeks later East Germany erupted in political crisis. The opening of the Austro-Hungarian border gave dissident East Germans an open route to the West through Hungary, and thousands chose to take it. Others fled by rail and air through Poland. The crisis of East German solidarity coincided with the planned celebration of the communist government's fortieth anniversary, at which General Secretary Gorbachev was a scheduled participant. During his brief visit and speech, Gorbachev asked the East German people to be patient in their demands, but gave public assurances that the Soviet Union would do nothing to intervene in the outcome of East Germany's domestic struggle. As the anticommunist wave spread across Eastern Europe in 1989 and 1990, it became clear that in the intrabloc law of the *perestroika* era, the Brezhnev Doctrine had been replaced by a doctrine of nonintervention to the point at which the "bloc" as previously known virtually ceased to exist. The final blow was struck to the Brezhnev Doctrine when the Kremlin gave its blessing to the reunification of the two Germanys and gave its consent for the new Germany to be a member of the North Atlantic Treaty Organization, the very alliance that had been the adversary of the Warsaw Treaty Organization throughout the cold war.

Outside of the Eastern European sphere, evidences of new official Soviet attitudes regarding the law of peaceful coexistence—*glasnost*-related legal applications—are lacking. Declaration of willingness to pay old UN assessments for peacekeeping operations, reduction in economic support for both Cuba and Nicaragua, and the removal of armed forces from Afghanistan are undoubtedly more closely related to the demands of the Soviet economy and to the thaw in Soviet-American relations than to international law. Soviet scholars, on the other hand, have adjusted their views of international law as *perestroika* and *glasnost* have evolved. One has written, for example, that the Soviet jurisprudence rejects the neorealistic notions on the basis that they cause "complete uncertainty in international law." Instead, the Soviet scholars prefer a theory of international law based on "the coordination of wills" among governments, a doctrine more nearly correlated to the consensual theory of international law held by the Western positivists. In this Soviet theory, international law is a body of principles and norms that form a subsystem of the larger global system designed to regulate the common interests of the market economies and the socialist economies, shaped by a variety of economic, political, sociological, ideological, and other factors.[21]

In broader terms, the new Soviet theory of international law begins with the declaration of the Soviet Communist party in 1986 that peaceful coexistence is no longer understood to be a specific form of class struggle. Modern communications, the Western technological race, and the growth of socialism as a worldwide system have all reduced the expectation of war among capitalist states as well as war between capitalist states and the Soviet Union. Peaceful coexistence, in face of these historical and doctrinal developments, is no longer an instrument of international class struggle, but of urgency to all humankind. The trend toward multipolarity has loosened American control of

---

[21]R. A. Mullerson, "Sources of International Law: New Tendencies in Soviet Thinking," *American Journal of International Law*, July 1989, pp. 494–512. The author is Head of the Department of International Law, Institute of State and Law of the Academy of Sciences of the USSR.

world capitalism, and the debt compiled through the arms race has forced Washington to diminish its capacity for military threat against the socialist world. As the Soviet government recognizes these advances and adjusts the Kremlin's ideological content, new forms of adherence to international law enter. The result is an appeal to a more positivist concept of international law; greater reliance on international institutions such as the United Nations to foster legal norms, security, and economic development; and a greater distribution of economic produce by increased trade between the market and the socialist economies regulated by treaties and other formal arrangements.[22]

The Chinese View of International Law

Although the Chinese share with the Soviet Union the notion of the class origins of international law, they face the additional problem of having been a major victim of Western treaty law. During the Century of Humiliation, China was subjected to treaty relations based on Western power superiority and the ability of other states to imperialize its territory and its commerce. More recent events, such as exclusion of the People's Republic of China from the Japanese Peace Treaty (1951), have accentuated the Chinese alienation from prevailing international legal norms. All Chinese governments of the present century have deplored the unequal treaties and have shared the determination to repossess territory granted to other states, yet none has coupled these determinations with other diplomatic grievances more vigorously than did the government that ruled China from 1950 to 1977. It looked upon Western-oriented international law as vacuous humanistic platitudes designed to attract China's support and participation on Western grounds. The concept of President Woodrow Wilson's Fourteen Points as the gospel of the First World War and the Atlantic Charter of the Second World War, with its stress on fundamental freedoms, seem to the Chinese to have been withdrawn in time of peace and the actual destiny of China to have been cynically given over to other "legal" agreements. Most vexatious among these is the Soviet-American Yalta Protocol (1945), which enlisted Soviet military assistance against Japan at the cost of Chinese political and territorial integrity.

As much as these perceptions persist justifiably, the Chinese view of Western-dominated international law is thawing considerably because of its newfound diplomatic, economic, and military relations with the United States, relations that not only accelerate China's economic development but also diminish the likelihood of Soviet aggression on Chinese territory. For the first time, then, save for a brief period of Western support to the Chinese Nationalist government between 1939 and 1949 (much of which was designed to assist the Nationalists in defeating the domestic communist forces), China has begun to profit from the Western content of international law.

---

[22]G. I. Tunkin, Address to the American Society of International Law, Washington, April 21, 1988. This paragraph is based on John Quigley, "Perestroika and International Law," *American Journal of International Law*, July 1988, pp. 787–797. Quigley based his comments on a translation of Tunkin's address prior to its publication in English.

The contemporary Chinese view of international law, then, is shaped by three factors: (1) the historical perception that Western-oriented law has aided Western growth at the expense of China and that the Soviet Union increasingly benefits from the same; (2) that international law has class origins that make it a peculiar instrument of transnational class struggle through economic oppression and intervention; and (3) that as an industrializing socialist state, China's sympathies on the restraints and licenses of law lie more with the Third World nations than with the Soviet Union.

Although the Chinese understanding of international law shares with the Soviet view the notion that law has class origins, the Chinese view rejects the idea that there are several types of international law in operation simultaneously. The Chinese accept the notion of a single general international law that represents the will of the ruling classes in any particular agreement. With respect to the theoretical basis of international law, however, the Chinese strike a difference between a bourgeois theory founded on assumptions derived to preserve the capitalist world order, and a proletarian theory founded on assumptions designed for a socialist world order uniting classes across national boundaries. The first emphasizes the state and the ruling class; the second stresses the liberation of the working class (proletariat). This view concludes that "only the proletarian science of international law established on the base of Marxism-Leninism is genuine science."[23]

Unlike the highly industrialized states whose interests are worldwide, China's growth phase dictates that its interests be regional and, for the most part, defensive. Except for attempts to repossess former territories lost under duress and except for its intervention in Korea when its borders seemed threatened, modern China has not behaved as an aggressive or expansionist state. Even its invasion of Vietnam in 1979 was explained in legal terms: China's was a punitive attack, designed to punish Vietnam for its earlier aggression against Cambodia. But in broader terms, because China's interest in international law and in the international power distribution is principally regional, the attack may be looked upon as a device for punishing Vietnam for altering by aggression the balance of forces among the Asian states.

China's interest is not so much in expanding its rights as in attempting to restrict the rights, and formalize the obligations, of other major powers that have interests in Asia. Thus, China argues for the sanctity of treaties, although it acknowledges membership in few. As its fundamental statement on international law, it has accepted the content of a Sino-Indian declaration of 1954, which encompasses the five Primary Principles of Peaceful Coexistence:

1. Mutual respect for sovereignty and territorial integrity
2. Mutual nonaggression
3. Mutual noninterference in internal affairs

---

[23]For a Chinese statement on the basis of international law, see Ho Wu-shaung and Ma Chun, as reprinted in Jerome Alan Cohen and Hungdah Chiu, *People's Republic of China and International Law: A Documentary Study,* 2 vols. (Princeton, N.J.: Princeton University Press, 1974), vol. 1, pp. 33–36.

4. Sovereign equality and mutual advantage (or benefit)

5. Peaceful coexistence

(Unlike the Soviet formulation enunciated by Khrushchev in 1961, peaceful coexistence in Chinese terms does not mean peaceful competition. By the same token, there has been no formal restatement subsequent to Gorbachev's reformation of the peaceful coexistence concept in the era of *glasnost*.)

Although most of these principles do not depart substantially from the classical notions of Western international law, the Chinese formulation stresses mutual advantage more than others do. Imbued with an historical sense of inequality in treaty relations, the Chinese argue that unless a treaty exists for mutual benefit, it is not binding, regardless of the apparent formalities of consent. Chinese jurists argue explicitly that treaties need not be renegotiated or formally terminated if their obligations were imperialistically imposed. It is held, rather, that in these cases the victim state may simply renounce its obligations. Despite ideological origins similar to those of the Soviet Union, the Chinese view of international law is tempered more by history and policy imperatives than by ideology.

The Third World View of International Law

The Third World nations share China's perception of having been victimized by the Western international order, and they view much of its legal content as designed to facilitate Euro-American growth at their expense. New states of revolutionary birth sympathize, furthermore, with the Chinese view that the law of nations still is pitted against their interests. But even old Third World states, and those that became independent through peaceful means and with formal preparation for self-government under UN surveillance, have found that much existing international law is inimical to their needs and politics.

The element of succession that distresses these states most is devolution. Upon achieving independence, many states have found themselves left with debts and commitments that they are expected to honor. Certain obligations have developed upon new governments, some informally and others through the formal device of the inheritance agreement. Some of these may be bilateral obligations easily renegotiated into modified arrangements called novations. In other cases, however, the other partner may be unwilling to change the agreement. Here the new state is likely to adopt the Chinese view that conditions having changed, the obligation no longer holds. Some new states have taken up the clean-slate doctrine, which insists on the nullity of all prearrangements.

Multilateral treaties present a more complex problem, because renegotiation with multiple partners is more difficult. The pressure to accept responsibility may be heightened by the former's controlling capital on behalf of third parties. Furthermore, upon entry into international organizations, the new state assumes obligations that it did not create. Certain unwanted restraints may have to be undertaken as the price of membership benefits.

Customary law creates larger problems too. The Third World countries are expected to partake virtually without consent, and it is here that they find themselves most disadvantaged by the legal rules and principles created by, and in the interests of, the more powerful states. This is especially true in the economic sphere, where the desperate need for investment capital and favorable terms of trade may be held in ransom by externally imposed trade principles, liquidity agreements, and tariff regulations.[24] In this regard, the Third World has combined efforts to develop a more advantageous structure of positive international law designed to overcome some of the collective economic strength of the industrialized states. Their principal mechanism has been the creation of the United Nations Conference on Trade and Development (UNCTAD) and its use to press their common needs upon the wealthier countries in the United Nations. More recently, the voting majority that the Third World has achieved at the United Nations has enabled it to pass the Declaration of the Establishment of a New International Economic Order and its companion Programme for Action, as well as the Charter of Economic Rights and Duties of States. It is now clear that the efforts of the underindustrialized world toward the establishment of an international legal order will turn principally upon effective law for economic self-determination. Accordingly, it will applaud the efforts of both the Organization for Economic Cooperation and Development and the United Nations Task Force on Multinational Corporations to conclude codes of conduct for international business, with the hope of reducing by law some of the neoimperialistic patterns justified under existing Western-oriented international law. So too will it welcome the recent efforts of the International Criminal Law Commission to define international economic crimes.

To the Third World, and especially to its newly independent members, the main objection to international law combines the notion of sovereignty with the philosophical understanding of self-determination. The achievement of independence illuminates a bold fact of international life—that in the face of disparate power, sovereignty is an abstraction; although formal self-determination may have been achieved, it does not confer all the latitudes of an economically powerful state. The destiny of the state is in large measure determined from without, both because it is expected to comply with certain established rules and because relations with more powerful states and corporations may limit economic and political prerogatives. In place of formal colonialism, the economically less developed states find that international law provides few, if any, defenses against the neoimperialistic trend by which the developed states encroach upon their economics.

Conclusion

The diverse outlooks toward contemporary international law exist because four fundamental bases of the Western legal order no longer enjoy universal valid-

---

[24]An exhaustive study of the problems of succession is found in D. P. O'Connell, *State Succession in Municipal Law and International Law,* 2 vols. (New York: Cambridge University Press, 1967).

ity. First, it is no longer accepted that there is a fundamental distinction between law, on the one hand, and ideology and politics, on the other. Second, there has been a breakdown in the practical distinction between war and peace, and the mere conviction of the desirability of peace. Third, the revolutionary international system does not accept the sanctity of the coexistence of independent, territorially discrete states. And finally, it is no longer universally held that governments are able to undertake mutually binding obligations through consent and voluntary compliance.[25] These premises have deteriorated primarily because we live in a multicultural world that the West no longer dominates.

The future of international law, however, is not bleak. Although multiculturism will continue to mark the international system, there is encouraging evidence that material interdependence, especially among states of equivalent power, fosters the growth of positive legal principles. In addition, as friendships and enmities change, some bilateral law may cease to be observed among new enemies, but new law may arise among new friends who have newfound mutual interests. In the meanwhile, some multilateral law may have been developed. Finally, research suggests that the social effects of industrialization are universal and that they result in intersocietal tolerances that did not exist during periods of disparate economic capability.[26] On social, political and economic grounds, therefore, international law is intrinsic to the transformation and modernization of the international system, even though the "law of the political context" has remained primitive so far. To what extent does modern international organization help here?

[25]Adda B. Bozeman, *The Future of Law in a Multicultural World* (Princeton, N.J.: Princeton University Press, 1971), pp. 35–48, 180–186.
[26]Edward L. Morse, "The Transformation of Foreign Policies: Modernization, Interdependence, and Externalization," *World Politics,* vol. 22, 1970, pp. 371–392.

CHAPTER 16

International Organization

In the discussion of international law in the preceding chapter, the point is made repeatedly that the development of an effective international legal order is impeded both by the sovereign equality of states and by the lack of authoritative international institutions competent to govern the international system. Since 1648, and more especially since 1815, creative statespersons have sought to remedy this institutional defect by founding a network of international agencies for international decision making. Although there is little expectation that these will replace nation-states as principal actors, there is considerable evidence that their presence contributes to the settlement of disputes, prevents the occurrence of disputes, and facilitates decision making on a broad spectrum of problems.

But the notion of collective decision making should not be interpreted to excess. Only in rare cases are international institutions authorized to impose their decisions on members. *Inter*national organizations conduct their business among states and do not exist separately from them. *Supra*national organizations, in contrast, have authority above the state and are capable of dictating to it, within carefully defined limits. International organizations, as presently constituted, do not pretend to supplant the nation-state or its authority over internal or external policies.

In a world of hostilities and power politics, students of international relations have traditionally focused their attention on public international organizations (also called intergovernmental organizations, or IGOs). Recently, on the heels of communications and travel revolutions, and recognizing that business and other interests often transcend international boundaries, attention has been directed to private international organizations (also called nongovernmental organizations, or NGOs). These facilitate transactions by means other than governments, and they are the vehicles of transnational participation.

Governments become involved in their business only indirectly or secondarily. Their principal subjects are individuals and organized social groups, corporations, and so on. Whereas the IGO is a government-to-government institution, the NGO deals people to people. They are, respectively, intergovernmental and intersocietal.[1]

Throughout the last century there has been a steady growth in the number of both IGOs and NGOs. At present there are more than 300 IGOs and in excess of 2000 NGOs. Moreover, even among the IGOs the variety of content and intent is so wide that further subdivision is needed. That the North Atlantic Treaty Organization (NATO) and the International Court of Justice (ICJ) both are IGOs ought not to imply that they have very much in common, except that each has several member governments! The following typology (breakdown of types) suggests some of the important classifications and provides familiar examples:

I. Global Organizations
   A. Multipurpose (United Nations)
   B. Single purpose or functional
      1. Economic (Economic and Social Council)
      2. Security (Security Council)
      3. Anti-imperial (Trusteeship Council)
      4. Nutrition (Food and Agricultural Organization)
      5. Transportation—sea (International Maritime Consultative Organization), air (International Civil Aviation Organization)
      6. Communications—mail (Universal Postal Union), telegraph (International Telegraphic Organization)
      7. Judicial (International Court of Justice)

II. Subglobal Organizations
   A. Intrabloc organizations
      1. Economic (International Monetary Fund)
      2. Security (North Atlantic Treaty Organization)
   B. Regional Organizations
      1. Economic (European Economic Community)
      2. Security (Organization of American States: Rio Pact aspects)
      3. Sociocultural and economic (Organization of American States: Bogotá Pact aspects)
   C. Integrating Organizations
      1. Economic (European Coal and Steel Community)
      2. Judicial (European Court of Human Rights)

---

[1]Historically, the study of international organizations has concentrated entirely on intergovernmental organizations as defined here. Recently, however, it has been recognized that not all organized intergovernmental activity occurs in formal institutions such as the United Nations. Many take place, rather, in less formal "regimes," defined as "sets of implicit or explicit principles, norms, rules, and decision-making procedures around which actors' expectations converge in a given area of international relations." See Stephen D. Krasner, ed., *International Regimes* (Ithaca: Cornell University Press, 1983). Although the treatment here makes occasional reference to regimes, its central focus is on the more formally constituted international institutions.

International Organization and World Politics

The expression "international organization" has two related but different meanings. First, the expression can be considered synonymous with international institution. The United Nations, for instance, may be labeled an international organization or an international institution (or group of institutions). In the other context "international organization" refers to a major international political process, one in which member states attempt through collective measures and diplomatic experimentation to facilitate their transactions, particularly when the subject matter is deemed to be handled more efficiently collectively than competitively.

Whatever form an IGO may take, states enter into it because of anticipated benefits. But in determining the effectiveness of such institutions from a collective viewpoint, it is not mere service to governments that matters. There are three critical measurements of organizational ability to draw states into collective policies and, therefore, to overcome the potentially anarchical characteristics of the nation-state system.

Association or Disassociation?

The first of these is the associating or disassociating character of the organization. Does the activity of membership tend to draw states closer together, or does it accentuate their differences and drive them farther from collective decision making? Does parliamentary diplomacy facilitate the discovery of workable common denominators, or does it magnify the differences among states? Does it help to remove the clouded images that states hold of one another, or does it further distort them?[2] From a global perspective, even associating organizations have a paradoxical component: The more associating they may be with respect to members, the more disassociating they may be in relation to outside states. NATO is a case in point. Although it intends to be associating among the members, its existence maintains the disassociation of Europe. But it exemplifies also a second phenomenon: As Europe has embarked upon other paths of association, NATO has come to have internal disassociating effects.

Contributions to Future Improvements

The second test of organizational capability is its contribution to change in the international system. Although institutions are often imprisoned by the will and power of their members (which, as sovereign states, safeguard their supreme decision-making capability), they may make independent contributions to world politics, often by helping members clarify obscured possibilities in their relations. But they may also contribute through a more complex mechanism. Dag Hammarskjöld, second Secretary-General of the United Nations,

---

[2]Bruce Russett, *International Regions and the International System* (Chicago: Rand McNally, 1967).

visualized two distinctly different models of UN effectiveness. The organization might be either a "static conference machinery" or a "dynamic instrument of governments" for introducing a new world order. Far from prescribing a supranational role, Hammarskjöld hoped only that a politically immune international civil service, together with quasi-legislative competence of the deliberative body, might help states overcome their immediate and narrow interests.[3] The extent to which an international organization is able to emulate the second model may be taken as one of the criteria of its effectiveness in stabilizing the international system.

Most studies of international organization suggest that regional organizations are understandably more effective than are global organizations. The usual explanation is that regional states share historical understandings, have had a long history of diplomatic and international relations, and have built an informal sense of understanding among themselves owing to the frequency of their transactions. Although the Western European experience with international integration partially vindicates this outlook (see Chapter 17), at least one quantitative study suggests that global organizations are actually more effective in improving the relations of members than are regional institutions. Based on comparative data, the study concludes that through international institutions, states may find solutions to problems that they are unable to resolve through bilateral diplomacy; that the degree of cooperation in international institutions is determined more by the expanse of the organization's mandate than by the characteristics of the member states (ideological, economic, and so on); and that, on balance, global institutions are more effective than are their regional counterparts.[4] One plausible interpretation of these findings is that in multipurpose global institutions, competing states are able to isolate their conflicts, so that while they undertake bilateral diplomacy on those issues, they are free in the multinational forum to cooperate on other issues.

Constraints on Member States

The third criterion of institutional effectiveness is closely related to both of the preceding. It is taken for granted (1) that states enter IGOs in anticipation of benefits to their individual interests and (2) that institutions become the instruments of their members' foreign policies. Under these circumstances, are such institutions ever capable of restraining the states' behavior? True, they serve definite purposes for specific governments; but in the long run, are they able to constrain governmental behavior?

If the principal objective of international organization is to overcome some of the anarchical characteristics of a decentralized, state-centered global system, then the capacities of any institution to be associative, to contribute to future improvement in the system's transactions, and to constrain the behavior

---

[3]Dag Hammarskjöld, "Two Differing Concepts of United Nations Assayed," *United Nations Review,* vol. 8, no. 9, September 1961, pp. 12–17.

[4]James M. McCormick, "Intergovernmental Organizations and Cooperation Among Nations," *International Studies Quarterly,* March 1980, pp. 75–98.

of member governments become important measures of effectiveness. Because we are concerned here with the global system, the discussion that follows addresses only global organizational efforts, and because of space limitations, the discussion centers entirely on the components of the UN organizational system.

The United Nations System

The United Nations consists of six permanent organs and a vast array of specialized agencies, conferences, funds, and commissions. Table 16–1 categorizes some of these. Each body has different objectives and capabilities. As a result, each relates differently to the sovereignty of the state, and each has a different potential impact on the international system and change therein.

The General Assembly

If modern IGOs attempt to emulate the American doctrine of separation of powers, then the General Assembly may be said to be the legislative branch of the UN system. Yet such a claim does not hold up much beyond form. The work of the assembly is done through parliamentary diplomacy, which combines the techniques of legislation and negotiation.[5] Yet while the General Assembly has broad competence to consider virtually any subject so long as it does not intrude on the domestic jurisdiction of states, it has little authority to make binding decisions. Except for final decision-making authority on certain matters internal to the organization (budget, membership, temporary members of the Security Council), its conclusions are expressed in three forms, none of which is decisive.

Declaration The first of these is the declaration, which is a pronouncement of principle. Such pronouncements do not have binding capacity, although they may result in subsequent treaties and may have customary or moral impact. One of the declarations of the General Assembly that has been most celebrated but least observed is the famous Universal Declaration of Human Rights (1948). Its principles have found their way into several constitutions, and it has become the substance of two international covenants on human rights. But the declaration itself lacks the force of law, despite adoption without a dissenting vote. Because lawmaking is a highly political process, states are not generally willing to subordinate their sovereign controls to the General Assembly.

Resolution The General Assembly's second decision-making instrument is the resolution, around which there swirls a controversy. Is it or is it not a

---

[5]Philip C. Jessup, ''Parliamentary Diplomacy,'' *Recueil des Cours,* vol. 89 (The Hague: Academy of International Law, 1956), pp. 181–320.

TABLE 16–1 The UN system.

All Permanent Organs	All Specialized Agencies	Some Commissions, Funds, and Institutionalized Programs
General Assembly	World Health Organization	Conference on Trade and Development
Security Council	Food and Agricultural Organization	Children's Fund
Trusteeship Council	Intergovernmental Maritime Consultative Organization	Special Fund
Economic and Social Council	Intergovernmental Maritime Consultative Organization	Peacekeeping and Observer Forces
Secretariat	International Civil Aviation Organization	Disarmament Commission
International Court of Justice	Universal Postal Union	High Commission for Refugees
	International Telecommunications Union	Institute for Training and Research
	World Meterological Organization	Development Program
	International Labor Organization	Environment Program and Earth Watch
	Educational, Scientific, and Cultural Organization	Disaster Relief Office
	International Atomic Energy Agency	Fund for Population Activities
	International Monetary Fund	World Food Programme
	World Bank Group[a]	World Food Council
	General Agreement on Tariffs and Trade	Center for Transnational Corporations
	World Intellectual Property Organization	
	United Nations Industrial Development Organization	

[a]The World Bank Group consists of the International Bank for Reconstruction and Development, the International Development Association, and the International Finance Corporation.

source of international law binding upon states? If a resolution encompasses a previously accepted law, then the resolution will do little more than illuminate existing law. But what is the effect of a resolution that imposes some new standard? Presumably, until many states acquiesce, law cannot be said to have been generated.[6]

---

[6]Leo Gross, "The United Nations and the Role of Law," *International Organization*, vol. 19, 1965, pp. 537–561.

But may it not be that policy has been implemented through the subsequent actions of states? If a resolution is of a recommendatory nature, calling upon states to act as agents of the General Assembly, then perhaps the General Assembly has transcended the will of some states in bringing about collectively determined policy. The recommendatory resolution, then, may not be legally binding, yet its execution by eager states may nevertheless place the imprimatur of the General Assembly upon their policy.[7] This distinction between legally binding norms and nonbinding norms engenders the notion of the quasi-legislative competence of the General Assembly.[8]

But all this assumes the willingness of states to act on behalf of the organ, usually indicating prior intention to act. As a result, the recommendatory resolution may have less of a policymaking function than a legitimizing function—one of the major activities of the United Nations.[9] In some instances, when states have flocked to the support of the General Assembly's legitimizing resolutions, the result has been profound, both in impact on international events and in the evolution of the United Nations. The most outstanding example of this was the Uniting for Peace Resolution (1950), passed by the General Assembly during the early months of the Korean War. With the Soviet Union's return to the Security Council after a lengthy boycott, the United States was unable to use the council for legitimizing its policy in Korea. In face of Soviet vetoes of American-sponsored resolutions, Washington moved its policy to the General Assembly. The Uniting for Peace Resolution expanded the assembly's legitimizing capability in the area of international peace and security, a province over which the Security Council claimed sole jurisdiction. More important, the resolution effectively and swiftly removed the Korean War from the veto-prone Security Council and enabled the Western majority of the time to make a political statement. Under the resolution, the United States and other Western powers continued their military actions in Korea and, at the same time, opened a debate not yet formally resolved regarding relative constitutional positions of the Security Council and the General Assembly on matters pertaining to international peace and security.

Convention　The third mechanism by which the General Assembly expresses its will is the convention, or multilateral treaty. Although we have previously noted the primacy of the treaty as a source of international law, the treaty-making power of the General Assembly is more qualified. In fact, the expression "United Nations treaty" has two meanings. The first refers to treaties signed by a state and by an organ of the United Nations, such as the General Assembly. These treaties, envisioned by the charter, concern relations not

---

[7]Jorge Castañeda, *Legal Effects of United Nations Resolutions* (New York: Columbia University Press, 1969).

[8]For example, Richard A. Falk, "On the Quasi-Legislative Competence of the General Assembly," *American Journal of International Law*, vol. 60, 1966, pp. 782–791.

[9]Inis L. Claude, "Collective Legitimization as a Political Function of the United Nations," *International Organization*, vol. 20, 1966, pp. 367–379. This article does not deal specifically with the General Assembly.

The founding of the United Nations, San Francisco, June 1945. US President Harry Truman stands on the speaker's right, in front of the assembled delegates.
Source: United Nations

between states but between a state and the IGO. As a rule, these do little to alter the behavior of the state with respect to other states, although there are exceptions. When, in 1956, the Egyptian government agreed with the United Nations to permit the dispatch of peacekeeping troops to Egyptian soil, that agreement resulted in a major temporary change in the area's political events.[10]

The more common meaning of "United Nations treaty" concerns conventions generally applicable among members. Such treaties are debated on the floor of the assembly and then put to votes. With passage, the treaty is carried back to member governments for domestic ratification. Ultimate decision making, therefore, lies not with the membership collectively but with individual governments. No government is bound until it has given formal constitutional assent or until the treaty is formally in effect, conditions of which are determined by the treaty itself. Thus, despite the favorable position that treaties hold as sources of international law, treaties arranged by the General As-

---

[10]Rosalyn Higgins, *The Development of International Law Through the Political Organs of the United Nations* (London: Oxford University Press, 1963), especially part 5, "The Laws of Treaties: United Nations Practice."

sembly represent minimal concession to collective decision making, and the process is not so centralized as the title indicates.[11]

The strictures placed on the General Assembly by the charter suggest that it is rare that the assembly makes authoritative decisions regarding the vital interests of states. Yet through its legitimizing role, the assembly has occasionally made significant contributions to the theory and practice of international stability. The Uniting for Peace Resolution, for all its political aftershocks, is one such example. Another, much more original in form and reusable in content, was an action of the General Assembly pursuant to an initiative of the secretary-general in 1956. Because of their participation in Middle East (Suez) combat, Britain and France had immobilized the Security Council. When the issue was shifted to the General Assembly, it was suggested that Britain and France remove their forces in favor of a UN presence. The result was an assembly mandate to Secretary-General Hammarskjöld to formulate the principles of a new system that came to be known as "peacekeeping"—a specific way of keeping peace. The idea was not to enforce a political objective of one party against that of another, but to interpose a lightly armed force between the belligerents to gain time for diplomacy. This was, then, preventive deployment of troops made available to the assembly by states. Not only was its concept a departure from UN standards, its implementation was as well. Most remarkably, the membership accepted Hammarskjöld's suggestion that the great powers be excluded from the action, on the ground that their presence would tend to expand, rather than contract, the scope of conflict.

The Soviet Union's reaction to this step was consistent: The General Assembly had exceeded its powers and once again eroded the exclusive authority of the Security Council to take action on security matters. Furthermore, although the same principles were invoked by the Security Council in the handling of the Congo crisis of 1960, the Soviet Union objected to the Western-oriented manner in which the secretary-general executed his mandate. Hence, by 1962, the Soviet Union, along with France and other governments, refused to pay its apportioned shares of the operations. A major financial crisis ensued. The crisis was legally, but not politically or financially, resolved by the ICJ in the *Certain Expenses* case, which elucidated constitutional principles, derived from the chapter, applicable to financial obligations.

The details of these situations are presented here only as illustrations of the informal manner in which General Assembly resolutions may change the course of multilateral relations, sometimes with the added authority of the ICJ. Although the assembly's ability to make final decisions is limited to nonpolitical issues (except in electing the temporary members of the Security Council and establishing financial assessments), the strength of its majority may, through either authorization or legitimization, give it a capacity to influence international events and behavior beyond what the great powers envisioned when they attempted to balance the roles of the General Assembly and the

[11]For a comprehensive treatment, see Henry H. Han, *International Legislation by the United Nations* (New York: Exposition Press, 1971).

Security Council through the charter. Not all issues fall within the scope of international peace and security. Examples include the expulsion of the delegation from the Republic of China and the seating of the delegation from the People's Republic of China, an event that had profound consequences for great-power relations and Asian politics; the labeling of Zionism as racist—raising the call to the Third World countries to support Palestinian and other Arab enemies of Israel; and the declaration of the New International Economic Order, an event that both formalized and fueled a major redistribution of wealth and influence during the 1970s.

Although government viewpoints on the effectiveness of the General Assembly may differ from one event to the next (with their differing evaluations resulting from the incompatibility of their objectives), scholars have concluded that the General Assembly's effectiveness is greater than public opinion and conventional wisdom will admit. One study, for example, that attempts to correlate effectiveness of action with the willingness of states to comply with assembly resolutions, concludes that in 29 resolutions concerning international political situations between 1946 and 1962, effectiveness of action reached 87 percent among those resolutions complied with by states. Where compliance was not forthcoming, the level of effectiveness was a scant 21 percent. The study also substantiates that in matters dealing with threats to the peace, breaches of the peace, and acts of aggression, the level of compliance and effectiveness was higher than in less dangerous and nonmilitary situations.[12] But these data pertain only to compliance with, and effectiveness of, General Assembly resolutions, which often deal only with parts of disputes. To this extent, and except for specified situations, the General Assembly shares other international agencies' failure to prevent war situations, as detailed in the empirical data of yet another study.[13]

This discussion of the General Assembly's role has been confined largely to matters of international peace and security. But given the broad competence of the body, it is unjustifiable to write off its successes on social and economic issues. These, however, are left to later discussion of functional activities.

The Security Council

In comparison with the General Assembly, the Security Council of the United Nations is both more complex and more simple. It is more complex because it is the forum not only of general world politics but also of great-power politics more intensively than is the General Assembly, with the result that clashes of opinion tend to wound the international system more deeply. Complexity is added by the type of subject matter dealt with by the council. Yet it is less complex because the veto power of the permanent members is able to prevent effective decision making. Even more than the General Assembly, the Security Council suffers from the inability to pass meaningful resolu-

---

[12]Gabriella Rosner Lande, "An Inquiry into the Success and Failures of the United Nations General Assembly," in Leon Gordenker, ed., *The United Nations in International Politics* (Princeton, N.J.: Princeton University Press, 1971), pp. 106–129.

[13]J. David Singer and Michael Wallace, "Preservation of Peace, 1816–1964: Some Bivariate Relationships," *International Organization*, vol. 24, 1970, pp. 520–547.

tions—a problem that logically precedes that of seeking compliance and effective implementation.

The Security Council grew out of the so-called grand design or grand alliance of the Second World War. During the war, despite the mutual suspicions and antipathies between the West and the Soviet Union, the necessity of alliance against the fascist menace resulted in cooperation that led some to believe that the victorious great powers, including the Soviet Union, could continue through the United Nations to ensure international peace and security by collective means. But the lingering suspicions, coupled with the historic American fear of being dragged unwillingly into foreign warfare, are expressed in the Security Council's complex voting formula. On matters of substance, decisions of the council are made by a majority of nine votes "including the concurring votes of the permanent members." The final phrase is the veto power of the permanent members. Abstentions are not counted as negative votes, and over time all the permanent members have chosen to abstain from voting with the understanding that their abstentions will not affect the outcomes of decisions. Earlier, however, a controversy raged over the meaning and political impact of abstentions, because it was during the Soviet absence in June and July of 1950 that Washington's Korean War policy was legitimized by the Security Council. At that time, many observers (including Soviet) held that in the absence of one of the five permanent members, the votes of the council had no binding effect on the organization.[14] More recently, the issue has ceased to have meaning, and often votes are recorded as "in favor," "opposed," "abstaining," and either "absent" or "not participating."

The main impediment to effective Security Council action is great-power dominance. Although the council is composed of 15 members, only five of them (the Soviet Union, the United States, the United Kingdom, France, and China) are permanent members and have the veto power. The result is that while decision making is relatively centralized for ten members, the ability of any single permanent member to prevent action means that ultimately the Security Council is highly decentralized. It is true that if all five permanent members abstain and nine of the others constitute a majority, then a decision can be reached. But what is the likely effectiveness of Security Council resolutions in which the great powers take no part? Will they respond, obligated or not? As in the General Assembly, the making of formal norms by majority voting can be deceptive; unless states are willing to put their power behind decisions, there will be no effective impact on the international system.[15]

Even the membership of the Security Council fails to reflect international political reality. True, the belated seating in 1971 of the delegation from the

[14]For starkly contrasted interpretations of this matter, see the works of a positivist and of a neo-realist, respectively: Leo Gross, "Voting in the Security Council: Abstention from Voting and Absence from Meetings," *Yale Law Journal*, vol. 60, 1951, pp. 210–257; and Myres S. McDougal and Richard N. Gardner, "The Veto and the Charter: An Interpretation for Survival," *Yale Law Journal*, vol. 60, 1951, pp. 258–292.

[15]Leo Gross, "Voting in the Security Council: Abstention in the Post-1965 Amendment Phase and Its Impact upon Article 25 of the Charter," *American Journal of International Law*, vol. 62, 1968, pp. 315–334.

Chinese People's Republic erased a long-standing misrepresentation. But the changing global power distribution complicates the situation in other ways. West Germany, one of the most powerful economic competitors in the world, was denied membership on the Security Council because of Germany's East-West division; and it is doubtful that German unification will alter the structure of the council. Likewise Japan, now restored to full power except for its non-nuclear status and working out its relations with the Soviet Union and China as it rejects American paternalism, may eventually seek a permanent seat on the Security Council, but not without prior charter amendment, the success or failure of which will, itself, be a reflection of the great-power politics of the time.

But the expansion of Security Council membership would not of itself generate greater effectiveness. In fact, the opposite is more probable. The more the council reflects conflicting policies and outlooks, the less likely it is to achieve its objectives. Indeed, granting the veto power to more states by charter amendment would decrease the likelihood of Security Council effectiveness. It is regrettable but nonetheless true that despite the grand design, the major powers consciously created such a situation by insisting on veto power.

Again, however, all is not hopeless, though Security Council performance has been less than fully encouraging. While it has occasionally achieved peaceful settlement of incipient crises, it has instituted enforcement measures in only two cases: (1) the 1950 case of the Korean War, when Soviet absence from the council enabled the Western governments to adopt a resolution legitimizing the use of responsive force; and (2) the 1990 instance of the air and naval enforcement of an embargo on Iraq in response to its invasion and annexation of Kuwait and its threat to overrun Saudi Arabia. With the sole exception of the Iraq situation, since 1956 the Security Council has favored peacekeeping over collective security as a less politically charged method by which to exercise its responsibility. Logically, the Security Council is the proper organ for the use of peacekeeping, although politically it is the most difficult forum from which to get action. The remarkable permanent-member unanimity on Iraq was solid testimony to the end of the Cold War, but only time will tell whether or not the Security Council will be able to find regularly such political consensus.

The logical argument stems from the historical anticipation that the great powers should make the critical decisions regarding international peace and security. Yet politically, the hope of their electing enforcement procedures against their own interests is unrealistic. Because peacekeeping is intended to be preventive rather than enforcing, neutral rather than carrying the stamp of a great power, and impartial rather than serving the will of one party against another, it is not so inimical to the interests of great powers as is collective security. War (and the implementation of collective security is war) is intended to erase political alternatives. Peacekeeping is intended only to prevent warfare while political wrangling proceeds.

The International Court of Justice

The International Court of Justice (ICJ), or World Court, enjoys a dual role in the international system. It is simultaneously the constitutional court of the

United Nations and the court of law among states. In its relation to the United Nations, the court has the authority to render advisory opinions on formal request from official bodies of the United Nations. As we have seen in the *Certain Expenses* case concerning the funding of UN peacekeeping actions in the Congo and the Middle East, these opinions may lend to the strength and operating scope of the organization. At the same time, however, the opinions are unenforceable, so their effectiveness is determined by the voluntary willingness of member states to comply with any organizational policy that results from an advisory opinion of the court.

In its role among states, the World Court is authorized to hear contentious cases, or cases involving disputes between or among states, and to render judgments. But unlike domestic courts, the ICJ is limited in this activity by the willingness of states to bring their disputes before it. Domestic courts possess compulsory jurisdiction, which means that they determine their own jurisdiction according to law and that subjects of the legal system are bound to appear when called. In the United States, for example, individuals can be summoned into court, corporations can be sued against their will, and governmental officials can be enjoined from certain acts. In the international system, such authority does not exist. All members of the United Nations are members of the ICJ, but their obligation to utilize the court is restricted by the court's own statute.

The statute was created by a Committee of Jurists in 1921 for the establishment of the Permanent Court of International Justice, a court affiliated with (but not a permanent organ of) the League of Nations. The committee recognized both the desirability and the political impracticability of imposing compulsory jurisdiction on the states, knowing from the outset that inclusion of compulsory jurisdiction in the statute would prevent many states from joining the court's membership. They sought, therefore, to establish an interim, although it is still in effect, arrangement by which states could specify in advance their acceptance of the court's limited compulsory jurisdiction with respect to certain matters, with or without reservation, and on condition of reciprocity. These conditions comprise the optional clause of the statute.[16]

When the ICJ was established as a permanent organ of the United Nations, the statute was adopted virtually unchanged. The critically important passages regarding the obligations of member states to use the United Nations' principal judicial organ are found in Article 36.

Article 36.–1. The jurisdiction of the court comprises all cases which the parties refer to it and all matters specially provided for in the Charter of the United Nations or in treaties and conventions in force.

2. The states party to the present Statute may at any time declare that they recognize as compulsory *ipso facto* and without special agreement, in relation to

---

[16]For a history of the optional clause's origins, told from a British perspective, see Lorna Lloyd, " 'A Springboard for the Future?': A Historical Examination of Britain's Role in Shaping the Optional Clause of the Permanent Court of International Justice," *American Journal of International Law,* January 1985, pp. 28–51.

any other state accepting the same obligation, the jurisdiction of the Court on all legal disputes concerning:

    a. the interpretation of a treaty;

    b. any question of international law;

    c. the existence of any fact which, if established, would constitute a breach of an international obligation;

    d. the nature or extent of the reparation to be made for the breach of an international obligation.

    3. The declarations referred to above may be made unconditionally or on condition of reciprocity on the part of several or certain states, or for a certain time.

. . . .

    6. In the event of a dispute as to whether the Court has jurisdiction, the matter shall be settled by the decision of the Court.

Because the court is a permanent organ of the United Nations, all UN members are automatically its members. Yet, as Article 36.2 indicates, recognition of the court's limited compulsory jurisdiction requires an act separate from joining the organization. By the end of 1987, only 46 of the United Nations' 159 members had such declarations in force, only six of these without some form of reservation. Reservations typically excuse the state from use of the court on matters that lie within the domestic jurisdiction of the state or that are classified as matters of vital national interest. Some national reservations effectively nullify Article 36.6 by declaring that the state alone shall determine whether or not an issue lies within its domestic jurisdiction.[17] Moreover, states are free to terminate their declarations of acceptance (as France has done), to allow them to lapse after a given period of time (Turkey) or to modify them to fit new and unforeseen circumstances. In a most celebrated instance, the United States notified the secretary-general of a change in order to avoid responding to a Nicaraguan suit in the ICJ regarding American intervention in the Nicaraguan civil war. Washington indicated that the declaration would no longer pertain to matters in Central America. Given all these protections against the court's compulsory jurisdiction, there now exists a brisk debate among scholars on the value of retaining Article 36 of the statute.[18]

Under the conditions of membership, then, there is little obligation to use the court; thus a decision to use the World Court is a political rather than a

---

[17]For example, one of the four reservations included in the recently canceled US acceptance read: "Provided that this declaration shall not apply to . . . [d]isputes with regard to matters which are essentially within the domestic jurisdiction of the United States of America *as determined by the United States of America*" (emphasis added). The emphasized final clause is referred to as the Connally amendment, after the senator who sponsored it.

[18]For the current debate, see Anthony Clark Arend, ed., *The United States and the Compulsory Jurisdiction of the International Court of Justice* (Charlottesville, Va.: Center for Law and National Security, 1986); Thomas J. Franck, *Judging the World Court* (New York: Priority Press Publications, 1986); Jonathan I. Charney, "Compromissory Clauses and the Jurisdiction of the International Court of Justice," *American Journal of International Law,* October 1987, pp. 855–887; and Gary L. Scott and Craig L. Carr, "The International Court of Justice and Compulsory Jurisdiction: The Case for Closing the Clause," *American Journal of International Law,* January 1987, pp. 57–76.

legal decision. Studies have considered why nations use the court. The most recent study compared the decision processes on each side of four suits brought to court: the *Nuclear Test* case in which Australia and New Zealand sued to prevent France from conducting nuclear tests in the South Pacific; the *Fisheries Jurisdiction* case in which Britain and Germany brought suit against Iceland to determine the territorial limits of exclusive fishing rights; the *North Sea Continental Shelf* case in which Germany sued both Denmark and the Netherlands on division of the North Sea continental shelf for purposes of fishing and mining rights; and the *Prisoners of War* case between Pakistan and India. The study determined that six motives lead plaintiffs to invoke the authority of the World Court. First, such a decision may be a tactical move to speed up negotiations. Second, it provides the suing party an opportunity to save face in domestic politics. Third, such a suit may focus worldwide critical attention on the opponent and its international policy. Fourth, although the parties may not be equally powerful and influential in world politics, the judicial environment tends to equalize them and to remove disparities. Fifth, the acting state may wish to use the court in order to establish or clarify a norm or rule of international law. And sixth, in cases of suits between states that have generally friendly relations, utilization of the court permits isolation of the dispute from the full body of their relations, thus preventing contamination of other issues between them.[19]

If the decision to bring suit in the World Court is political, then a decision to be sued will be doubly political. When threatened with action in the World Court, states generally react by claiming that they have exempted themselves from the court's jurisdiction. In the cases examined in the same study, the respondent states also felt that it is politically preferable to seek a partial solution by agreement or compromise than to await an absolute solution based on court procedure and a potentially embarrassing decision. In other words, states prefer to avoid suit than to face outcomes that they are politically unwilling to execute. Finally, states attempt to avoid the jurisdiction of the court because of the vagueness, uncertainty, or absence of the law to be applied—all circumstances that make it more difficult for respondents to assess the probable outcome.

In rare cases when both parties agree to a court decree and the court renders a final judgment, the international legal system is faced with its second problem: compliance. It is commonly thought that states ignore or violate the court's decisions. In fact, however, that is not so. A high degree of compliance exists, for two reasons. First, the ICJ is capable of rendering either declaratory or executory judgments. In declaratory judgments, it declares itself on a point of law and may in effect advise states as to their rights or may limit behavior by clarification of existing law. These judgments are not intended to favor one state over another in specific issues, and neither contestant need make restitution to another. Executory judgments are quite a different matter. These arise

[19]Dana D. Fischer, ''Decisions to Use the International Court of Justice: Four Recent Cases,'' *International Studies Quarterly,* June 1982, pp. 251–277.

when the court finds for one contestant rather than for another and orders one to undertake remedial or compensatory action. Much misinformation has circulated about these judgments, leading to the impression that states have rarely carried out judicial awards made against them. In fact, however, such cases are exceptional.

The second reason is closely akin to an argument used in earlier discussion of states' compliance with treaties. Because, in the absence of compulsory jurisdiction, use of the court is almost wholly voluntary, it stands to reason that a government will not make the political decision to seek a judicial settlement without having assessed possible outcomes and without having accepted the obligation to carry out an award in case of an adverse decision.

What remedies exist when states refuse compliance? As the traditional standards of sanctions suggest, a judicial award gives a state an actionable right. This may be exercised through general IGOs, functional organizations, or regional organizations. Conceivably, even the Security Council might be called upon to enforce compliance, as provided by Article 94 of the United Nations Charter. Such actions, however, may serve merely to repoliticize a dispute previously depoliticized by having been taken to the court in the first place. The other alternative is to rely on self-help, with all its potential anarchical and escalatory effects.

Remarkably illustrative of many of these principles and their limitations was the American behavior with respect to the *Case Concerning Military and Paramilitary Activities In and Against Nicaragua*, a suit entered in the ICJ by Nicaragua in 1984. The Nicaraguan government sought court orders terminating alleged American intervention in its country's civil war, in the form of arms supplies to the *contra* (antigovernment) forces and mining of the Nicaraguan port. It also sought $370 million in reparations for damages attributed to American intervention.

Just three days before the action was filed, the Reagan administration notified the Secretary-General of the United Nations of a change in the longstanding American acceptance of the court's limited compulsory jurisdiction. Effective immediately and for a two-year period, the notification stipulated, American acceptance "shall not apply to disputes with any Central American State or arising out of or related to events in Central America, any of which disputes shall be settled in such manner as the parties to them may agree." The purpose, according to Washington, was "to foster the continuing regional dispute settlement process."[20] The logic, however, was to deny the court's jurisdiction in anticipation of its refusal to evaluate American policy in the full context of regional events to which the United States was reacting.

In its response to Nicaragua's application for trial, the United States formally argued that the court was without jurisdiction for several reasons.[21]

---

[20]*Case Concerning Military and Paramilitary Activities In and Against Nicaragua (Nicaragua v. United States of America)*, 1984 *ICJ Reports*, pp. 169 ff, at pp. 174–175. For a summary, see a case note by Monroe Leigh, *American Journal of International Law*, October 1984, pp. 894–897.

[21]For a transcription of the American argument on jurisdiction, see *US Department of State Bulletin*, January 1985, pp. 24–29.

Principal among them was that Nicaragua's own acceptance of the court's compulsory jurisdiction, a carryover from the Permanent Court of International Justice in 1929, was procedurally incomplete and, therefore, invalid (even though Washington had never before presented this analysis in judicial dealings with Nicaragua). Assuming its invalidity, then, Washington claimed its reciprocal right under the statute not to be subjected to the court's compulsory jurisdiction, despite it historic acceptance and notwithstanding its recent modification. Over these objections, the court ruled unanimously that the case fell properly within its jurisdiction, and it agreed to proceed with an examination of the facts and merits. At the same time it decided that the United States should desist from restricting access to Nicaraguan ports and that Nicaragua's sovereignty should not be endangered by any military or paramilitary activities prohibited by international law. Now, having lost its argument regarding the court's jurisdiction, Washington declared that it would not participate further in the deliberations. Nicaragua's case was branded "a misuse of the Court for political purposes." Furthermore, the State Department rationalized, "The haste with which the Court proceeded to a judgment [on the matter of jurisdiction] . . . only adds to the impression that the Court is determined to find in favor of Nicaragua in the case." Under such circumstances, American participation is unjustified.[22] Washington had decided that it could ill afford the political consequences of an adverse judicial decision.

Nicaragua and the court proceeded without the United States, and in 1986, the court ruled in favor of Nicaragua's claims. In a series of 16 votes on individual matters, the court found the United States in violation of customary international law regarding the use of force, violations of Nicaraguan sovereignty, and intervention in the internal affairs of another state. It rejected only Nicaragua's claim that all damage done should be attributed to the United States. Although the court determined that Nicaragua was due reparations, it declined to establish an amount.[23] Having by these decisions acquired an actionable right, Nicaragua proceeded to the Security Council, where it invoked its right under Article 94 of the charter to seek council enforcement of the court's decisions. Taking full advantage of the permanent-member escape clause in Article 27.3, which requires the unanimity of the permanent members on matters of substance, Washington vetoed action against itself and nullified Nicaragua's only political recourse to the enforcement of a judicial award.

The case prompted within the Reagan administration a comprehensive review of the American acceptance of the court's compulsory jurisdiction. Even before the court's final award to Nicaragua, the United States had determined that for a number of reasons, acceptance of compulsory jurisdiction no longer benefited its foreign policy. It noted the imbalance between its obligations and

---

[22]For the text of the State Department's news statement on the discontinuance of participation, see *US Department of State Bulletin*, March 1985, pp. 64–65. The statement was released on January 18, 1985.

[23]For the summary of the court's findings and the Security Council's debate, see *United Nations Chronicle*, August 1986, p. 110; and *US Department of State Bulletin*, November 1986, p. 57.

those of the Soviet and Eastern European nations, none of which had accepted compulsory jurisdiction. But its principal argument was that as a founding member of the United Nations, it had never expected the principal judicial body to become involved in matters of high politics that were presumably reserved for the Security Council. Hence, in accepting jurisdiction in the *Nicaragua* case, the court had enlarged its scope in a manner potentially injurious to American security interests. In explaining the administration's decision to the Senate Foreign Relations Committee, the legal adviser to the State Department argued as follows:

> The fact that the ICJ indicated it would hear and decide claims about the ongoing use of force made acceptance of the Court's compulsory jurisdiction an issue of strategic significance. Despite our deep reluctance to do so and the many domestic constraints that apply, we must be able to use force in our self-interest and in the defense of our friends and allies. We are a law-abiding nation, and when we submit ourselves to adjudication of a subject we regard ourselves as obliged to abide by the result. For the United States to recognize that the ICJ has authority to define and adjudicate with respect to our right of self-defense, therefore, is effectively to surrender to that body the power to pass on our efforts to guarantee the safety and security of this nation and of its allies.

Having thus constructed its case, the United States notified the secretary-general in 1985 of the withdrawal, effective six months later, of its acceptance of the ICJ's limited compulsory jurisdiction, under Article 36.2 of the statute.[24]

Social, Economic, and Humanitarian Functions

Although media attention usually focuses on the contribution of the United Nations to global security, the organization engages in a vast array of social, economic, and humanitarian activities that receive far less attention or acclaim. These activities are consistent with the functional theory of international relations introduced in the early 1930s. The theory of functionalism posits that in the long run, peace is preserved by growing international trust and reciprocity constructed around specific common objectives of states. It assumes, not entirely accurately, that as trust builds around relatively nonpolitical interests, it will spill over to the crucial political interests of governments. Its first practical verification occurred in 1936 when, even while the African and Asian conflicts of the Second World War were already in progress, with little lingering hope of effective action on the part of the League of Nations, a major evaluation of the nonsecurity activities of the League found them to be still healthy and productive.

The postwar endorsement of functionalism was signaled by inclusion of the Economic and Social Council and of the Trusteeship Council among the per-

---

[24]For the full statement and the text of the letter to the secretary-general, see *US Department of State Bulletin*, January 1986, pp. 67–71.

manent organs of the United Nations. Thereafter, specialized agencies were created on the basis of perceived international needs with respect to health; refugees; economic development; children; educational, social, and cultural activities; labor; trade; and so forth. At the same time, two venerable functional organizations, the Universal Postal Union and the International Telecommunications Union, were incorporated into the UN system. Special programs, commissions, and funds continue even now to be added as world attention is focused on new humanitarian needs: the environment program, the development program, the population program, and so forth. Today, a survey of the activities of the United Nations in areas not directly related to international peace and security is a virtual tour of world political, social, economic, and humanitarian concerns. Although the world has stumbled into nearly 100 wars since the World War II armistice, functionalism through the United Nations (and elsewhere) has flourished and has been a major force of change.

Many of these functional activities are discussed elsewhere in this book, particularly those related to international economic development. One that merits specific mention here, however, is the progress made through the United Nations toward self-government of formerly colonized peoples. The United Nations shares with the League of Nations, however delicately, formal commitment to the self-determination of national peoples, largely on the ground that competitive imperialism is a cause of war. To deal with this problem, the League created a system of mandates by which established states undertook formally to prepare colonized peoples for self-government in the League's behalf. The United Nations has provided a dual system, consisting of a Trusteeship System and a Declaration Regarding Non-Self-Governing Territories.

The Trusteeship System was arranged (Chapters 12 and 13 of the charter) for international surveillance of progress toward self-government. To colonized peoples, the trusteeship was a progressive mechanism, for it included formal terminal dates and the promise of international pressure to enforce major power compliance with the terms of the agreement. But to the major states, trusteeship agreements involve too much obligation and exposure. As a result, trusteeship has not been the main route to independence.

But out of this gap between plan and performance emerged one of the great success stories of UN history. In Chapter 11 of the charter, the framers had arranged a Declaration Regarding Non-Self-Governing Territories. Although it was initially assumed merely to inscribe principles rather than legal obligations, this declaration became the United Nations' prime peaceful mechanism through which sovereign status has been achieved in the postwar era. The focal point of this development has been the evolution of Article 73(e). Here UN members who controlled non-self-governing territories accepted as a "sacred trust" the responsibility to achieve well-being for the inhabitants, and in pursuit of this goal they consented

to transmit regularly to the Secretary-General for information purposes, subject to such limitation as security and constitutional considerations may require, statistical and other information of a technical nature relating to economic, social and educational conditions in the territories for which they are respectively responsible.

By evolution, this hope has been transformed into an obligation. Article 73(e) became a source of international scrutiny. (It would be excessive to say surveillance.) It shares significant responsibility for the huge increase in the total number of states and in the membership of the United Nations. More than half of the UN member nations have become independent in the last 35 years. Even more remarkable as the result of this emancipation, between 1945 and 1985 the number of people living in dependent territories declined from 750 million to 2.8 million.[25] This reduction occurred while the world's total population increased by 50 percent, with a disproportionate amount of that increase in the newly independent, underindustrialized areas of the world.

Table 16–2 reveals the distribution of dependent peoples of the world as late as 1989, all of whom were in non-self-governing territories with the exception of the last entry, a trust territory. Note that fully half of the total lived in a single place, Namibia, formerly the South West African Territory originally governed by South Africa under a League of Nations mandate, and more recently by South Africa in defiance of a series of ICJ and UN decisions transferring governmental power to the United Nations itself. At the time at which this book went to press, free elections under UN auspices were planned, after which Namibia would become an independent state, the final stroke in eliminating colonialism from sub-Saharan Africa. Assuming the conclusion of these plans, by late 1990 less than one-twentieth of 1 percent of the global population lived in dependent or colonized territories. This remarkable reduction in the number of dependent peoples occurred over a span of barely 40 years, during which the last of nineteenth- and twentieth-century empires dissolved. Belgian and Portuguese power yielded to black self-government in Africa; the French abandoned virtually all their colonial holdings from Southeast Asia to Africa; and the once nearly global British Empire dwindled to the few remnants identified in Table 16–2. In an effort to underscore the rapidity of these events, one historian has written the following comment about the sun's setting on the British Empire:

> Until 1947—within the lifetime of half the world's population—the Government in London ruled more land and people than any other government in history. In the thirty-three years between India's independence in 1947 and Southern Rhodesia's in 1980, the British Empire ended. Territories that gained independence from Britain before then—for example the American colonies and Ireland—were part of the imperial ebb and flow. After 1980 the dozen territories that remained—were no longer an empire, merely the leftovers. Relative to its size, no great ship ever sank so quickly.[26]

---

[25]*United Nations Chronicle,* January 1986, pp. 76–80, at p. 79. The decline is the more dramatic in light of the continuing and alarming increase in population in the Third World. In 1982, for example, the number was estimated as 4 million, out of a Third World population several hundred million fewer than in 1985. See United Nations, *Report on the World Social Situation,* 1982.

[26]Brian Lapping, *End of Empire* (New York: St. Martin's Press, 1985), p. xiv.

TABLE 16–2 The world's dependent peoples, 1990.

	Territory	Administering Authority	Area (sq. km.)	Population (est.)
Africa	Namibia (until 1990)	United Nations	824,292	1,465,000
	Western Sahara	Spain	266,000	147,000
Asia	Hong Kong (until 1997)	United Kingdom	667	5,000,000
Atlantic	Anguilla	United Kingdom	96	78,000
and the	Bermuda	United Kingdom	53	55,000
Caribbean	British Virgin Islands	United Kingdom	153	13,000
	Cayman Islands	United Kingdom	250	19,000
	Falkland Islands			
	(Islas Malvinas)	United Kingdom	12,173	2,000
	Montserrat	United Kingdom	103	13,000
	St. Helena	United Kingdom	412	5,000
	Turks and Caicos Islands	United Kingdom	430	8,000
	United States Virgin Islands	United States	343	101,000
Europe	Gibraltar	United Kingdom	6	29,000
Pacific	American Samoa	United States	197	34,000
and	Guam	United States	540	111,000
Indian	Pitcairn	United Kingdom	5	55
Oceans	Tokelau	New Zealand	12	2,000
	Wallis and Futuna	France	159	14,000
	New Caledonia	France	11,930	155,000
	French Polynesia	France	2,510	185,000

Source: From *United Nations Chronicle*, January 1986, p. 79. © United Nations 1986. Adapted to 1989 in Asia and Pacific and Indian Oceans.

Encouraged by the great progress made toward the elimination of colonialism in sub-Saharan Africa, the states of the Non-Aligned Movement within the United Nations persuaded the General Assembly to adopt in late 1988 a resolution declaring the 1990s as the International Decade for the Eradication of Colonialism. The reader is cautioned, however, that political independence is not necessarily independence in its entirety. As Chapter 5 has indicated, political independence in the underindustrialized world has often been followed by economic subservience and neoimperialism.

To a large extent, these newly emancipated people make up the Third World, and for the United Nations as well as for the major powers, they have created huge new problems. Although sovereign equality enables them to control much of the decision making in the General Assembly and in the Economic and Social Council, more than 90 of them declared themselves underdeveloped economically. Thus, while they make a small dollar contribution to the UN system, they profit mightily from its grants and other programs. Yet it has been shown that relative to gross national product and in comparison with national expenditures on armaments, the two poorest categories of states have had better UN financial records than the two richest have.[27] In the political realm, these new states present other problems. Foremost among them is the "ministate problem"—the difficulty of equal voting when many of these states are very small, ranging even below 100,000 inhabitants.

Can the United Nations Keep Peace?

Few questions in international relations are so frequently asked. The ability of the United Nations to safeguard international stability rests on three issues: (1) the fostering of peace, (2) the making of peace, and (3) the keeping of peace. Can it improve international perceptions so that the impulse to war will be less frequent? When conflict does occur, can the United Nations rise above some of the political muddle and restore order? And once a conflict has been extinguished, can the United Nations provide a consistent influence to maintain the peaceful status quo?

In the long run the prevention of aggression is the objective of international organization in the security realm, but the more immediate issue for the United Nations is the control and termination of war once in progress. The framers of the charter chose as the primary method of controlling aggression a concept derived from the Covenant of the League of Nations: collective security. This doctrine claims that a war against one member is a war against all and that the world's governments should be prepared collectively to meet aggression anywhere in the world. In the United Nations Charter, the concept resides in Chapter 7, entitled "Action with Respect to Threats to the Peace, Breaches of the Peace and Acts of Aggression." This chapter authorizes the 15-member Security Council to determine the existence of a threat and, thereafter, to prescribe nonmilitary or military sanctions. Because the only source of military action is its member states, the United Nations calls upon states to make troops available to the Security Council and provides that the decisions of the Security Council will be carried out "by all the members of the United Nations or by some of them, as the Security Council may determine" (Article 48). All decisions are subject to the formal voting arrangements of the Security Council and, therefore, to the possibility of veto by any permanent member (United States, Soviet Union, United Kingdom, France, and China). Given the disparate interests and global objectives of these states throughout the Cold War, the probability of Security Council action under Chapter 7 remained hopelessly low.

Indeed, during the Cold War, as we have seen, Chapter 7 had only one partial test: the Western response to aggression in Korea in 1950. But this occurred only because the Soviet delegation, boycotting the council over the question of Chinese representation after the Red Army had chased the Kuomintang (Nationalist) government from the continent, was not present to exer-

---

[27]Edward T. Rowe, "Financial Support for the United Nations: The Evolution of Member Contributions 1946–1969," *International Organization,* vol. 26, 1972, pp. 619–657.

cise its veto power. In all subsequent instances, one or another of the great powers prevented Chapter 7 action by use of the veto. (The three post-Cold War resolutions of 1990—first creating then enforcing an embargo against Iraq for aggression in Kuwait followed by authorization to remove Iraq from Kuwait by force—are the other major exceptions to the political paralysis of the Security Council's authority under Chapter 7.)

An early test occurred in 1956 when Britain and France joined with Israel in war against Egypt, but because of British and French participation and veto power, the Security Council was unable to influence the situation. Secretary-General Dag Hammarskjöld, in one of the boldest initiatives in the United Nations' history, although not without partial precedent, proposed to the General Assembly that it establish, consistent with the Uniting for Peace Resolution, a lightly armed, multilateral force (deliberately excluding the superpowers, lest the scope of the conflict widen). This force would interpose itself between the combatants, not to enter into the fighting, but to create a neutral zone that would separate the parties while diplomatic efforts at ending the conflict were conducted. Over the objections of the Soviet Union, France, and a handful of other governments, the first UN peacekeeping operation was conducted under the principles enunciated by the secretary-general. The United Nations Emergency Force (UNEF, 1956) thus became the first attempt by the United Nations to formulate a substitute for the failed notion of collective security. Summaries of the principal uses of the new method follow.[28]

Egypt

Although Egypt expected the United States to finance construction of the Aswan High Dam, Secretary of State John Foster Dulles announced in 1956 that Washington would not do so. In disgust over this announcement Colonel Gamal Abdel Nasser, Egyptian head of state, seized the Suez Canal, despite a treaty ensuring its international ownership. This seizure affected Israeli imports, threatened the flow of Middle Eastern oil, upset the British, and infuriated the French, who were beset with problems in Algeria. Jointly, these three nations drove Egyptian troops away from the Suez region and reestablished control.

At the United Nations, Britain and France prevented the Security Council from assuming responsibility for order in the area, voting against everything from censure to action. During the voting, a most unusual event occurred: The United States and the Soviet Union voted together against two of Washington's

---

[28]For a synopsis of UN interventions and peace observer groups, see Larry L. Fabian, *Soldiers Without Enemies* (Washington, D.C.: Brookings Institution, 1971), pp. 261–268. An exhaustive treatment of military, logistical, and budgetary details is found in David Wainhouse, *International Peacekeeping at the Crossroads* (Baltimore: Johns Hopkins University Press, 1973). More recent historical comments and summary appraisals, some by authors from countries to which peacekeeping has been applied, may be found in Henry Wiseman, ed., *Peacekeeping: Appraisals and Proposals* (New York: Pergamon Press, 1983). For a thorough analysis of the law, politics, origins, practice and prospects for peacekeeping, see Indar Jit Rikhye, *The Theory and Practice of Peacekeeping* (London: C. Hurst, 1984).

most prestigious allies. This American reaction ought not to have surprised its friends, because President Dwight D. Eisenhower had warned that he would not support their operations. Yet not until faced with the American vote did the British will begin to subside. France was more deeply committed, but British second thoughts sent Paris scurrying for an alternative policy. Thus, when the issue arrived in the General Assembly, the point of contention was not a superpower confrontation but the embarrassment of two second-rank powers who by then were amenable to collective decision. The atmosphere was receptive to the new principles of peacekeeping, which resulted in the stationing in Egypt of a multinational interventionary force (the UNEF) from 1956 to 1967.

The Congo

The situation in the Congo in 1960 was wholly different, There, immediately after achieving independence from Belgium, Katanga province announced its secession, and civil war commenced. Within a few days, the Belgian government began returning troops to restore order, and the Congolese government responded by asking the United Nations to provide troops both to counter Belgian aggression and to suppress the secessionist movement. The matter was handled this time by the Security Council where, in the early weeks, Soviet and American goals were sufficiently similar to enable the council to establish ONUC, the initials of the French-language expression for United Nations Operation in the Congo. Very quickly, however, their objectives diverged. The United States vigorously supported with airlifts, military aid, economic aid, and evacuations what the Soviets considered an increasingly pro-Western policy on the part of the secretary-general. And for their part, the Soviets found themselves with what have been described as ''conflicting, even irreconcilable, goals . . . ,'' such as ''supporting the Congolese government without alienating more moderate Congolese factions which might win out'' and ''how to push for strong UN action against the Belgians and Katanga and weak UN action elsewhere.''[29] For a brief period, the Soviets attempted to resolve their policy dilemma by direct, unilateral support to the ruling Congolese, but in the longer run they focused their policy on a continual attack on the pro-Western leanings of Secretary-General Hammarskjöld and refused to pay their financial assessments for ONUC.

Without Soviet (and French) financial support, ONUC continued through 1964. It was on a visit to the area for inspection of UN operations that the secretary-general was lost in an air crash. Only later with the *Certain Expenses* decision of the ICJ was it determined that the United Nations has full constitutional powers to bill its members for political and military actions with which they disagree. But this juridical decree, although presumably clarifying the organization's constitutional powers and resolving a financial crisis, did nothing to move the recalcitrant powers to pay their arrears.

---

[29]David W. Wainhouse, *International Peacekeeping at the Crossroads* (Baltimore: The Johns Hopkins University Press, 1973), p. 325.

Cyprus

Cyprus was still a different problem. A small insular state in the eastern Mediterranean, its domestic politics suffered from a power struggle between the majority Greek population (about 80 percent) and the smaller Turkish population. As far back as 1931, there had been moves by the Greek population to merge Cyprus with Greece. In the years immediately prior to independence in 1960, there was sporadic violence. Fed up with responsibility and under pressure to divest itself of colonial holdings, Britain agreed to the formation of a Republic of Cyprus in 1960, with guarantees that the president would be elected by Greek Cypriots and the vice president by Turkish Cypriots. The former were also to hold 70 percent control of the national legislature.

But independence was only a palliative for the social and ethnic problems of the tiny republic. By 1963, Turkish Cypriots were charging the Greek majority with denial of rights. Open hostilities began. In March 1964, amidst crisis, the Security Council voted a peacekeeping operation, which it still maintains, despite Turkey's seizure of much of Cyprus in a brief war in 1974.

Again, the objectives of the great powers are a critical consideration in the successful utilization of peacekeeping principles. Because both Greece and Turkey are formal allies of the United States, Washington saw the crisis as a threat of intra-alliance warfare. Although Britain had retained two small military posts on the island, it wanted collective responsibility lest anyone accuse the British government of resort to imperial tactics. France, by then extricated from both Algeria and Indochina, was receptive to any plan for stability in the Mediterranean. And the Soviet Union, although always ready to profit from disruption among the Western security allies, wanted peace in the Mediterranean. Most particularly, Moscow wished to court the favor of Turkey, because Turkey controls the Bosporus and the Dardanelles through which Soviet ships must move from the Black Sea to the Mediterranean. With plans for a major naval buildup, the stability of Turkish foreign policy was critical to Moscow. The conditions were optimal for interventionary peacekeeping. The Security Council continues periodically to extend the mandate of the United Nations Force in Cyprus (UNFICYP), despite the Turkish sector's 1983 declaration of an independent republic.

The Middle East, 1973

The resumption of war in the Middle East in 1973 threatened once again to plunge that area into catastrophe. This time, the interests of the United States and the Soviet Union were more directly touched. The United States strongly supported Israel, and the USSR was determined to support its Arab friends and to maintain a naval balance in the Mediterranean. A written Soviet threat to intervene militarily in the fighting, reported to the American people without detail as "a brutal note," resulted in a temporary worldwide alert of American forces, including the mobilization of some reserve units. In withdrawing from this potential superpower crisis, the Soviet Union proposed a joint Soviet-American peacekeeping operation for the region—a proposal vigorously rejected by Washington on the traditional ground that such an operation would threaten larger crisis. As an alternative, the Security Council agreed to establish a multimember peacekeeping force consisting of the troops of smaller powers, to be commanded by a Finnish general. The initial troop contingents were ferried to the area from Cyprus. The command assumed the functions of interposition, administration of prisoner repatriation, exchange of checkpoints, and logistical facilitation of truce talks in the desert.

The council's decision to establish this force signaled the growth of a Soviet-American consensus on the utility and political acceptability of peace-keeping as a means of ensuring regional security. This promising characteristic was partly offset by Chinese refusal to take part. Although the force was established without a negative vote, the Chinese were recorded as "not participating." They repeated their view that such operations are instruments by which the two largest powers use the United Nations as a tool for perpetuating their control of world events and regional conflicts. That China did not veto the proposal, however, restored expectation that the major powers might now have come to accept peacekeeping as the most appropriate means of maintaining regional stability. The Security Council's willingness and political ability to reaffirm the mandate of UN functions both in the Sinai (where American diplomacy had arranged for Egypt-Israeli agreement) and for the Golan Heights (where no Syrian-Israeli agreement applies) adds encouragement to peacekeeping as a means of ensuring regional tranquility. Indeed, although we must await memoirs to confirm the possibility, the quiet success of the 1973 UNEF operation in the Sinai may well have contributed to the healthy environment leading to the long-awaited Egyptian-Israeli peace in 1979, after which the Security Council dissolved the UNEF in the Sinai. It continues, however, to extend the mandate of the United Nations Disengagement Observation Force (UNDOF) in the Golan Heights.

Lebanon

Throughout the hostilities between Israel and its Arab neighbors, the Israeli government has repeatedly reaffirmed its intention of striking against Palestine Liberation Organization (PLO) positions in southern Lebanon from which terrorist attacks have been launched frequently. The interests of Israel were closely touched by the Lebanese civil war, which resulted in the arrival of a Syrian interventionary force charged with establishing peace in an environment in which Lebanon would be oriented to Arab views of regional politics. To help neutralize Lebanon in the regional struggle, Israel threw its weight behind the Lebanese Christians.

In 1978, the frequency of terrorist attacks launched from southern Lebanon increased, and Israeli air and ground forces retaliated with attacks against suspected positions, even briefly occupying Lebanese territory. Both Lebanon and Israel called the issue to the attention of the secretary-general of the United Nations. Lebanon considered itself to have been occupied, and Israel wanted to bring world public pressure to bear on the Palestinian terrorists. Not only did immediate events cause discomfort, but they seemed also to jeopardize the delicate Egyptian-Israeli peace talks.

After studying the situation, the Security Council voted (without dissent) to establish a United Nations Interim Force in (southern) Lebanon (UNIFIL). The Soviet Union and Czechoslovakia both abstained, in part because of larger considerations of foreign policy in the area and because the Security Council had not declared Israel an aggressor. Interestingly, the Security Council resolution establishing UNIFIL also established a system of financing the operation by which the General Assembly would bill the organization's members. This was based on a formula of size, wealth, and dues to the United Nations, a method the Soviet delegation disliked but did not ultimately reject. China, in keeping with its suspicion of peacekeeping, was recorded as "not participating." Again, however, it was gratifying to peacekeeping advocates that China did not exercise the option to veto the establishment of UNIFIL, lending further evidence to the cooperative spirit of China in such multilateral efforts to maintain international peace and security.

UNIFIL was charged with the responsibility of supervising the withdrawal of Israeli forces, of restoring peace and security in the area, and of assisting the government of Lebanon in reestablishing effective control over southern Lebanon. This was a far more complicated mission than had originally been envisioned for peacekeeping forces. Far from merely interposing a lightly armed force between two combatants who had accepted the general principle that such a force would be beneficial to both, UNIFIL was introduced into a conflict involving multiple interests. These included Syria, Israel, Palestinians, and both the Christian and Arab forces within Lebanon. Boundaries and lines of demarcation were thus absent, and as a consequence of the complex situation, UNIFIL was as much a political force as a military operation. Success in its mission demanded that its leaders arbitrate virtually every move among the competing domestic and international interests.

In the spring of 1983, the situation in Lebanon changed dramatically when several wars erupted simultaneously. Rival Lebanese factions resumed the civil war, and Syrian and Israeli troops engaged each other. In the midst of conflict, UNIFIL positions in southern Lebanon were overrun by Israeli troops, but the Security Council continued its periodic extension of the UNIFIL mandate to try to moderate the situation in the south and to provide humanitarian aid to refugees and local victims of occasional shelling. By summer, the PLO agreed to vacate the Beirut area under the protective cover (from Israeli shelling) of a multinational force consisting of American, French, and Italian troops. The United Nations did not take a direct part in this exodus. Subsequently, the United States, France, Italy, and Britain agreed to station a few thousand troops in different areas of Beirut as a multinational peacekeeping force, separate in mission and command from UNIFIL in the south.

As factional fighting continued and as terrorist attacks on both American and French positions increased in number and intensity (with nearly 300 deaths and hundreds of injuries in a six-month period), the PLO slipped back into the Beirut area and conducted its own civil war. At the end of 1983, the PLO loyalist faction led by Yasir Arafat was evacuated from Lebanon once

*Troops of the United Nations Force in (Southern) Lebanon maintaining friendly
relations with the local population, 1989.*
Source: Pierce/Sygma

again, this time in rented Greek vessels flying the protective flag of the
United Nations. The Security Council had agreed to this extraordinary condition to help reduce the carnage in Beirut, a city near total destruction. During
the evacuation, the presence of the French navy prevented Israel's gunboats
from firing on the fleeing Palestinians, its mortal enemy.

Meanwhile, under political pressure at home, increasing criticism of the role
and indefensibility of marine positions in Beirut, President Ronald Reagan first
"redeployed" the marines to vessels off Lebanon's coast and then removed
them from the zone altogether. American efforts failed to secure the consent of
15 nonaligned governments to form a new multilateral force outside the
United Nations' command. During this entire period, there was no formal dis-

cussion of a UN peacekeeping role in the Beirut area, although the UNIFIL mandate in the south of Lebanon continues.

Altogether, among these operations and many lesser UN observer missions, over one-half million men and women from 58 countries had participated in 15 UN peacekeeping from 1956 to 1988. Among them, 733 had lost their lives in military duty. At the end of 1988, there were 10,000 peacekeeping troops still on station in eight operations. Perhaps the prime indication of the value placed on this type of international operation occurred in 1988, when the Swedish Academy awarded to UN peacekeeping forces past and present the Nobel Prize for Peace as it had previously to Dag Hammarskjöld, Lester Pearson, and Ralph Bunch—the three leading figures in the initial development of the concept.

Apparently reassured of the value of peacekeeping, the Security Council agreed in 1989 to dispatch four additional missions consisting of various mixtures of military, police, technical, and election officials. These were:

- The United Nations Namibia Force—to maintain peace during transition to independence and to supervise national elections.
- The United Nations Angola Verification Mission—to supervise and certify the withdrawal of 50,000 Cuban troops from Angola after a negotiated end to civil war.
- The United Nations Good Offices Mission in Afghanistan and Pakistan—to observe the full withdrawal of Soviet troops from Afghanistan and the repatriation of Afghanistan rebels from sanctuary in bordering Pakistan.
- The United Nations Iran-Iraq Military Observer Group—to monitor the cease-fire of the Persian Gulf War.

In addition, preliminary agreements were struck for stationing observer groups in both Cambodia and Nicaragua if permanent cease-fires could be arranged in those two long-standing civil wars. They were used in Nicaragua in 1990.

Evaluation of Peacekeeping

These brief histories are provided less in an attempt to detail international events than to demonstrate the evolution of peacekeeping as a substitute for collective security and to demonstrate the benefits and liabilities of this method as well as the way it fits into great-power politics.

It is widely agreed today that except in matters touching directly on the interests of the superpowers, peacekeeping is a promising method for restoring regional stability. Although it began as a General Assembly decision, thus calling into question the relative roles of the Assembly and the Security Council in matters pertaining to international peace and security, since the United Nations Emergency Force of 1956, it has been used exclusively by the Security Council. The UN operation in the Congo was a Security Council operation, and it was threatened not by matters of initiation but by the Soviet Union's objection to the West-leaning manner in which the secretary-general carried it out. Even though the United States and the Soviet Union have grave disagreements over the uses and execution of peacekeeping operations, they have co-operated on all recent decisions regarding the Middle East and Cyprus. Even China, which originally believed that peacekeeping was a form of organized aggression, abstained rather than vetoed peacekeeping decisions until 1981. In a 1981 vote on one of the several periodic extensions of the UNFICYP mandates, China voted affirmatively for the first time. Scholars and diplomats seem now to agree that in the hands of the Security Council, where peacekeeping can be subject to great-power unanimity and where issues affecting international peace rightfully belong under the original intentions of the charter's framers, peacekeeping is a major hope for stability. One distinguished scholar of international relations provided this assessment:

> Perhaps the most significant development in the thinking of scholars and statesmen about international organization in the postwar period has been their gradual emancipation from the collective security fixation, their breaking out of the intellectual rut in which it was taken for granted that the suppression of aggression was so crucial a function of general international organizations that if this function could not be exercised, the only issue worth thinking about was how to make its exercise possible. Dag Hammarskjöld gave dramatic and forceful expression to the new and less constricted approach to international organization when he put the question of how the United Nations could contribute directly to keeping the peace when it could not enforce the peace and answered the question by formulating the theory of preventive diplomacy, now generally known as peacekeeping.[30]

Even in the hands of the Security Council, however, peacekeeping's role in the international system is not assured. Foremost among the difficulties is that it can be used only in very special circumstances. First, there must be relative equivalence of power among the local forces, because the United Nations can usefully interpose a force only if neither party can gain a quick military advantage; second, unless the Security Council is willing to use its special privileges under Chapter 7 to bypass host-state rejection of forces, it is able to operate only with the consent of one or more of the local disputants; third, either the General Assembly or the Security Council must be able politically to agree on the mandate and organization of the emergency force. This is a lengthy catalogue of politically sensitive conditions, and it cannot be expected that many local disputes will fit it. Only under special and peculiar circumstances will political and military conditions permit a UN peacekeeping role.[31]

---

[30]Inis L. Claude, "The United Nations, the United States, and the Maintenance of Peace," *International Organization*, vol. 23, 1969, pp. 621–636.

[31]James Stegenga, "United Nations Peace-Keeping Patterns and Prospects," in Robert Wood, ed., *The Process of International Organization* (New York: Random House, 1971), pp. 299–316. For a study of proposed methods of overcoming both national and international barriers to peacekeeping, see Indar Jit Rikhye, Michael Harbottle, and Bjorn Egge, *The Thin Blue Line: International Peacekeeping and Its Future* (New Haven, Conn.: Yale University Press, 1974). See also Lincoln Bloomfield, "The United States, the Soviet Union, and the Prospects for Peacekeeping," *International Organization*, vol. 24, 1970, pp. 548–565; Larry L. Fabian, *Soldiers Without Enemies* (Washington, D.C.: Brookings Institution, 1971), especially chaps. 5–8. For another general dis-

Given the special positions and prerogatives of the major powers, however, agreement in principle on the conditions and scope of peacekeeping is a required precondition for reliable utilization. The manner in which peacekeeping originated, over the Soviet protest of a General Assembly action, means that even today peacekeeping is accompanied by substantial residual distrust. To help resolve this underlying difficulty, in 1965 the General Assembly established a United Nations Special Committee on Peacekeeping Operations, charged to enunciate general principles. This committee, also referred to as the Committee of Thirty-Three, worked amicably but unsuccessfully through its session of 1983, when it reported that it had been unable to resolve problems related to the financing of peacekeeping operations, the creation of a Ready Force (although Canada, Norway, Iceland, Sweden, and Denmark already have standby agreements with the United Nations), and on the extension of its own mandate. It is the General Assembly's decision whether or not it should continue its work, and at the time of this writing, the General Assembly had not taken up the question.

The financial matter has always been at the center of the problem. The Soviet Union and others originally objected to being billed for peacekeeping because they had opposed it. Proposals have been exchanged ranging from supporting the operations with voluntary contributions, billing only the participating nations, billing only the governments that voted affirmatively on the establishment of an operation, and billing the combatants whose activities resulted in peacekeeping operations. In the midst of it all, while reimbursing those governments that supply troops to the United Nations at a rate of only $950 per soldier per month, the United Nations has run up an unpaid bill of $300 million exclusive of the unmet costs of the operations in the Middle East and of the Congo in 1956 and 1964! Moreover, at least $195 million is currently regarded as a permanently uncollectible bad debt.[32]

But cost and politics are not the only sources of contention regarding peacekeeping. Although it is unquestionably true that for the United Nations the UNEF and ONUC operations were the most traumatic, both financially and politically—not to mention constitutionally—UNIFIL has, in many respects, been the most agonizing. Largely because of the perils of attempting to establish a fixed position in a situation in which the warring parties change frequently, UNIFIL has been deeply frustrated in its effort to serve the United Nations' mission. In addition, from its founding in 1978 through late 1986, 132 members of the force had been killed while on duty. These soldiers were from among the nine countries that had contributed troops to the 5829-member unit. Moreover, by 1986, the annual cost of UNIFIL had risen to $141 million, with little hope that the United Nations would be able to reimburse the contributing parties.[33]

---

cussion of the future, see Arthur M. Cox, *Prospects for Peacekeeping* (Washington, D.C.: Brookings Institution, 1967).

[32]For a thorough review of the history of financing UN peacekeeping operations, see James Jonah, "Funding United Nations Peacekeeping," *United Nations Chronicle*, May 1982, pp. 65–70.

[33]*United Nations Chronicle*, November 1986, p. 57.

With collective security virtually a historic vestige of international organization and with peacekeeping still hostage to the geographic and political interests of the permanent members of the Security Council, it is still an unanswered question whether or not the United Nations is able effectively and consistently to maintain international peace and security. One study has shown that even though the veto was used in the Security Council in 46 of the armed conflicts between 1945 and 1981, the United Nations had a great impact in 12 cases, some impact in 12 others, and virtually none in 22 cases.[34] The potential ability of the United Nations to maintain peace, therefore, is subject not only to the use of the veto by the great powers but also to the willingness of states to permit third-party interests to enter into diplomacy, a decision closely tied to domestic politics and regional histories.

Evaluation of United Nations Performance

The United Nations is not a political system acting in a vacuum, nor does it operate above the international system. Its effectiveness depends on the quality of world politics and the degree of community among members. In a revolutionary system, community is at best fictitious, with the United Nations representing victories for legal authorization but only modest advances in the political impact. Although it presents a picture of utmost institutionalization, its structure contributes only intermittently to change in the international order. In 1970, it was predicted that with the termination of the Vietnam War and the quickening pace toward multipolarity, the sense of global community might intensify, and collective decision making through international institutions might be more acceptable to states. But since that time the North-South confrontation has replaced the Vietnam War as the obstacle to progress, and the upsurge of political activity in the Third World has produced new uneasiness. The principal difference, of course, is that although the Vietnam War was not fought diplomatically at the United Nations, the North-South controversy is being acted out principally in the United Nations' organs.

Just as the international system undergoes change, so too does the United Nations, and change in the United Nations may alter national attitudes toward its effectiveness. In American public opinion, for example, the United Nations has declined in popularity in recent years, principally because it has not consistently endorsed or legitimized American foreign policy. Disapproval has occurred partly because of the character of American overseas operations and partly because the United Nations has seen a fundamental change in its membership that has resulted in strong voting coalition of the Third World members and with it a new policy orientation, one that seems threatening to American economic stature.

---

[34]Ernst B. Haas, ''Regime Decay: Conflict Management and International Organizations, 1945–1981,'' *International Organization*, Spring 1983, pp. 189–256.

When the United Nations was founded in 1945 it had 51 members, each represented in the General Assembly. Today the total membership is 159. Virtually all the states admitted after 1956 are newly independent states (see Table 16–3). Before 1957, the membership of the assembly was such that the United States could count on being in the majority on virtually every issue, although often only after difficult political bargaining. But the new membership deprived the United States of that certainty. Not willing to align themselves with American foreign policy and not willing to be taken into the vituperative politics of Soviet-American relations, these new states have taken a highly independent course. Sometimes neutral to American objectives and sometimes critical, the attitudes of the assembly have eroded American confidence in the United Nations, and the new voting patterns rarely support American policy. This has been especially true in regard to issues concerning the international economy and the Middle East. On each of these the United States has suffered major diplomatic setbacks at the hands of the automatic majority.[35]

Changing voting patterns in the United Nations have had even more profound effects. The Third World's voting majority had made advancement of industrialization the United Nations' first concern. But within that goal there has taken root a Third World ideology, sympathetic to neither the Soviet Union nor the United States. Instead, it is an ideology of independent leftism, scornful of industrial states but covetous of industrialization. To the West it is ill conceived and petulant; to the Soviet Union it is useful as a constraint on American control of UN decision making. But in any event, it has diverted the United Nations, and particularly the General Assembly, from its old obsessions with security as an East-West problem. The United Nations is now more typically a forum for the war of wits and dollars between the industrial North and the maturing South.

As Figure 16–1 indicates, one study links the declining effectiveness of the United Nations to the decreased American satisfaction with the organization and with the declining American hegemony in the world. The study, however, deals exclusively with matters directly related to international peace and security.

Whether or not the United Nations is an effective organization depends foremost on one's perspective, as the following section illustrates. It also depends on recognition of major changes in world politics that have had significant impacts on the UN system: the global redistribution of power and wealth that

---

[35]Robert E. Riggs, "The United States and Diffusion of Power in the Security Council," *International Studies Quarterly,* December 1979, pp. 513–544, discusses and analyzes American public opinion regarding the Security Council and the General Assembly, respectively. He concludes that since the "automatic majority" of the Third World was consolidated in 1972, American faith in that body has deteriorated steadily. In contrast, although the Assembly was once held in high esteem by Americans and the Security Council low because of Soviet-American confrontations there, since 1972 American opinion has swung back in favor of the Security Council because it gives the United States "an institutional foundation for maintaining a tolerable political position within the U.N."

Table 16–3 Growth of UN membership, 1945–1989.[a]

Year	Number	Original Member States
1945	51	Argentina, Australia, Belgium, Bolivia, Brazil, Byelorussian SSR, Canada, Chile, China, Colombia, Costa Rica, Cuba, Czechoslovakia, Denmark, Dominican Republic, Ecuador, Egypt, El Salvador, Ethiopia, France, Greece, Guatemala, Haiti, Honduras, India, Iran, Iraq, Lebanon, Liberia, Luxembourg, Mexico, Netherlands, New Zealand, Nicaragua, Norway, Panama, Paraguay, Peru, Philippines, Poland, Saudi Arabia, South Africa, Syria, Turkey, Ukrainian SSR, United Kingdom, USSR, United States, Uruguay, Venezuela, Yugoslavia

		New Member States
1946	55	Afghanistan, Iceland, Sweden, Thailand
1947	57	Pakistan, Yemen
1948	58	Burma
1949	59	Israel
1950	60	Indonesia
1955	76	Albania, Austria, Bulgaria, Democratic Kampuchea, Finland, Hungary, Ireland, Italy, Jordan, Lao People's Democratic Republic, Libyan Arab Jamahiriya, Nepal, Portugal, Romania, Spain, Sri Lanka
1956	80	Japan, Morocco, Sudan, Tunisia
1957	82	Ghana, Malaysia
1958	83	Guinea
1960	100	Benin, Burkina Faso, Central African Republic, Chad, Congo, Côte de'Ivore, Cyprus, Gabon, Madagascar, Mali, Niger, Nigeria, Senegal, Somalia, Togo, United Republic of Cameroon, Zaïre
1961	104	Mauritania, Mongolia, Sierra Leone, United Republic of Tanzania
1962	110	Algeria, Burundi, Jamaica, Rwanda, Trinidad and Tobago, Uganda
1963	112	Kenya, Kuwait
1964	115	Malawi, Malta, Zambia
1965	118	Gambia, Maldives, Singapore
1966	122	Barbados, Botswana, Guyana, Lesotho
1967	123	Democratic Yemen
1968	126	Equatorial Guinea, Mauritius, Swaziland
1970	127	Fiji
1971	132	Bahrain, Bhutan, Oman, Qatar, United Arab Emirates
1973	135	Bahamas, Federal Republic of Germany, German Democratic Republic
1974	138	Bangladesh, Grenada, Guinea-Bissau
1975	144	Cape Verde, Comoros, Mozambique, Papua New Guinea, Sao Tome and Principe, Suriname
1976	147	Angola, Samoa, Seychelles
1977	149	Djibouti, Vietnam

continued

Table 16–3 *(continued)*

Year	Number	Original Member States
1978	151	Dominica, Solomon Islands
1979	152	Saint Lucia
1980	154	Saint Vincent and the Grenadines, Zimbabwe
1981	157	Antigua and Barbuda, Belize, Vanuatu
1983	158	Saint Christopher and Nevis
1984	159	Brunei Darussalam

ª The countries' names are those in use in 1986.
Source: From *United Nations Chronicle*, February 1986, inside front cover. © United Nations 1986. Reprinted by permission.

has diminished American satisfaction with the United Nations; the rise of the Third World to where it controls the voting majority at the United Nations on all issues pertaining to global economics; the Chinese competition with the Soviet Union for the allegiance of the Third World; and so forth. It depends also on a careful study of different functions of the UN organs, because they function at different levels of effectiveness.

We have already looked at the United Nations' record of keeping and restoring peace. Elsewhere in this book, we look at the United Nations' success in specific functional areas. In general, however, it is important to point out that although public opinion condemns the United Nations for its relative inability to maintain regional peace in several areas of the world and to reduce arms trade between the developed world and the less developed world (not to mention its failure to slow down the strategic arms race between the Soviet Union and the United States), many of the United Nations' functions proceed with remarkable effectiveness.

One of the United Nations' restrictions is its total dependence on the member governments for financial support. For the two-year period 1988 and 1989, the formal UN budget was $1.77 billion, an amount apportioned to the member states according to an elaborate formula. In addition, however, whereas in 1950 the specialized agencies received only $40 million in additional voluntary contributions, the corresponding amount in 1983 was over $1 billion. Similarly, voluntary contributions for the United Nations Development Program exceed $2 billion (up from $8 million in 1950), and World Bank Group commitments increased from $0.5 billion in 1960 to over $12 billion in 1983. These increased contributions result from a broad recognition of the growing functional needs of the world, particularly in the economically less developed regions. Through improving coordination among the functional agencies and gradually reducing the vulnerability of the programs to political fighting, particularly between the industrialized North and the developing South, the functional activities of the United Nations will be increasingly productive.[36]

---

[36]Evan Luard, "Functionalism Revisited: The UN Family in the 1980s," *International Affairs* (London), Autumn 1983, pp. 677–692.

Figure 16–1 UN success in influencing action on disputes referred to it, compared with US opinion of those actions and with general US dissatisfaction with the UN as measured by the decline of frequency of US voting with the majority on all issues, 1945–1978.

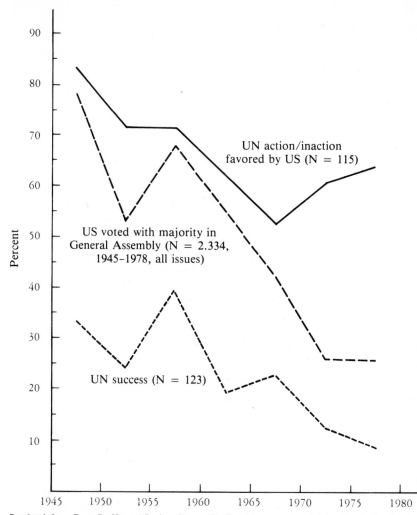

Reprinted from Ernst B. Haas, "Regime Decay: Conflict Management and International Organizations, 1945–1981," *International Organization*, Spring 1983, pp. 189–256, at p. 231, by permission of the MIT Press, Cambridge, Mass. Copyright © 1983 by the World Peace Foundation and the Massachusetts Institute of Technology.

Organic Growth and Humanitarian World Politics

In addition to changes in political patterns at the United Nations brought on by the maturation of the Third World, events of the age have also refocused the concerns of the world organization. In the past decade, the world has undergone the crisis of recognizing that humanity is imperiled by its own excesses, that the catastrophes that one may safely predict will result not from natural forces but from peoples' overzealous efforts to conquer those forces. In search for a better life we have contaminated our biosphere, polluted our environment, and offended all our senses. Through the battles against disease, old age, and premature death, we have created a global population boom that now threatens to exceed food supplies even as nonreplaceable resources are consumed at an increasing pace. These three crises—ecocide, excess population, and agricultural limitation—have forced a reassessment of the trend toward undifferentiated growth and have called forth an attempt at balanced, planned development the world over. This latter concept, often labeled organic growth, is at the center of the United Nations' new concern for humanistic world politics.[37] It is treated in the final chapter of this book as an issue of future world order.

The American View of the UN System

The American record of participation in international institutions has been erratic. To avoid involvement in European war after 1918, the Senate rejected American membership in the League of Nations in a fascinating and tragic struggle with President Woodrow Wilson. Despite only rare participation in the League's political activities, the United States was an active contributor to its functional activities. Most American policy between the world wars, however, was conducted with little regard for the League. Furthermore, despite the efforts of the European states to enlist the United States in the Permanent Court of International Justice (going as far as offering to alter the statute and to limit the advisory jurisdiction of the court if the United States should wish), Washington steadfastly declined membership.

Relations between Washington and the United Nations have been quite another story. Finally convinced during the Second World War that global international organization and collective security were indispensable to future

---

[37]Mihajlo Mesarovic and Eduard Pestel, *Mankind at the Turning Point* (New York: New American Library, 1974). This is the Second Report to the Club of Rome, in which the authors report computerized projections regarding the human condition and reflect on the consequences of delaying action toward resolving the principal human crises. The references to "undifferentiated" and "organic" growth are biological analogies, the former representing growth for the sake of growth (as cells dividing without changes of function) and the latter, coordinated growth (as cells dividing into organized units for interdependent activity).

For a less specialized but equally informative treatment of these issues, see Ronald Higgins, *The Seventh Enemy: The Human Factor in the Global Crisis* (New York: McGraw-Hill, 1978). Higgins lists the first six enemies as the population explosion, the food crisis, resource scarcity, environmental degradation, nuclear abuse, and science and technology unleashed. The seventh enemy is the "human factor," consisting of the political inactivity that prevents dealing with the global crisis and the blindness of individuals to the need to contribute through self-restraint to solving the global crisis.

Because "science and technology unleashed" is a unique problem of the technological (or postindustrial) age, attention is beginning to be given to it as a political problem of the future. See particularly Langdon Winner, *Autonomous Technology: Technics Out-of-Control As a Theme in Political Theory* (Cambridge, Mass.: MIT Press, 1977).

world stability, the United States played a leading role in the creation of the United Nations. Virtually throughout the war, planning groups—at first quite secret—worked on drafts of the charter. The major political parties declared their support for a renewed outlook on international organization. In September 1943, the House of Representatives resolved, with the Senate concurring,

> That the Congress hereby expresses itself as favoring the creation of appropriate international machinery with power adequate to establish and to maintain a just and lasting peace among the nations of the world, and as favoring participation by the United States therein through its constitutional processes.[38]

Not to be outdone in its influence upon the foreign-policy process, the Senate resolved two months later,

> That the United States, acting through its constitutional processes, join with free and sovereign nations in the establishment and maintenance of an international authority with power to prevent aggression and to preserve the peace of the world.
>
> That the Senate recognizes the necessity of there being established at the earliest practicable date a general international organization, based on the principle of sovereign equality of all peace-loving states, and open to membership by all such states, large and small, for the maintenance of international peace and security.[39]

American interest in establishing the United Nations was portrayed most vividly by its sponsorship of the Dumbarton Oaks Conference in May 1944, at which delegates of the United States, the Soviet Union, Britain, and France studied draft proposals for the United Nations Charter. Finally, after an additional year of diplomatic exchanges, including the great-power agreement at the Yalta Conference (February 1945) on the veto provision, the United States hosted the San Francisco Conference (April–June 1945) for the formal signing of the charter.[40]

American interest evolved from two directions. First, there were those believers in the grand design of continued Soviet-Anglo-American cooperation who anticipated great-power enforcement of the peace and who looked upon the veto in the Security Council as insurance against unwilling involvement in

---

[38]House Concurrent Resolution no. 25, 78th Cong., 1st sess., sponsored by Congressman J. William Fulbright of Arkansas, passed by the House on September 21, 1943. *Congressional Record*, vol. 89, p. 7729; as reprinted and footnoted in Ruhl J. Bartlett, ed., *The Record of American Diplomacy*, 4th ed. (New York: Knopf, 1964), p. 675.

[39]Senate Resolution no. 192, as amended, 78th Cong., 1st sess., vol. 89, p. 9222, November 5, 1943. This resolution was offered by Senator Tom Connally of Texas and is generally referred to as the Connally resolution.

[40]For a comprehensive study of the American role in the founding of the UN and of the various political and diplomatic forces that shaped that role, see Robert A. Divine, *Second Chance: The Triumph of Internationalism in the United States During World War II* (New York: Atheneum, 1967). See also Ruth B. Russell (with the assistance of Jeannette E. Muther), *A History of the United Nations Charter* (Washington, D.C.: Brookings Institution, 1958). Russell was a staff member of the Leo Pasvolsky Committee, which prepared the American draft proposal.

war. Second, there were others who more realistically assessed the postwar situation. Why, they asked, ought we to expect that the Soviet Union will not return to its prewar attacks on capitalism and on the West? The other side of this question, which plagues revisionist scholars of the Cold War, was this: Because the postwar bipolarity was likely to necessitate a *pax Americana,* why not create international machinery through which American foreign policy toward the Soviet world could be pursued with collective legitimacy? Depending on one's historical outlook, therefore, the American interest in the United Nations originated either from naïve expectations of Soviet-American cooperation in power politics or from the American intent to establish global institutions for facilitating American foreign relations.

It stands to reason that in an American-dominated world, Washington would consistently seek to enlarge the United Nations' authority insofar as such increases helped American policy. This explains the American approval of the ICJ's interpretation of UN legal status in the *Reparations* case, in which the United Nations was held to be a subject of international law with certain characteristics resembling those of states and having implied powers to fulfill specified functions and responsibilities. It also illuminates American sponsorship of the Uniting for Peace Resolution, which eased recourse in security matters to the General Assembly, free from Soviet veto. The American position was similar to the ICJ's advisory opinion in the *Certain Expenses* case, which rejected the Soviet argument that security measures that circumvent the special prerogatives of the Security Council are illegal.

In organizing the economic sector, the United States also played a leading role. It hosted the Bretton Woods Conference in 1944 which created the International Monetary Fund (IMF) and the International Bank for Reconstruction and Development (IBRD). Washington rejected the founding of the International Trade Organization in 1948, which would have limited the exercise of unilateral restraints to trade. The General Agreement on Tariffs and Trade (GATT), now with permanent institutional structure, has adopted much of this function.

This Western economic structure was created in an era when the United States was undisputed king among the trading partners. It was the most productive and largest exporter; it enjoyed the most favorable balance of trade (income from exports greatly exceeding cost of imports); and the American dollar was not only in great demand overseas but was virtually the standard medium of international exchange.

Recently the American position has deteriorated. Inflation has reduced export potential; Western Europe and Japan have regained productivity and favorable trade and payments balances; and the European Community has enough combined strength to spurn the American dollar and to compete with American manufacturers. All these contributed to a reversal of the American balance of trade in 1971, when imports exceeded exports for the first time in 60 years and have continued to do so ever since.

Looked at from abroad, American reactions to these problems have been retaliatory. Western Europeans in particular feel that after years of attempts to persuade Germany, Japan, France, and other countries to alter their currency values in relation to the dollar, the United States in 1971 undertook vigorous changes that either frankly or marginally violated international economic rules. The imposition of a 10 percent surcharge on all imports—a unilateral act designed to reduce the imports that were throwing the trade balance into deficit—was clearly a violation of the GATT. Furthermore, only months later Washington forced wholesale changes in the world's currency valuations by informing other governments of the changes that the United States would expect in return for an American devaluation. All this was done without formal adherence to the rules of the IMF.

Washington's interpretation of these events differs. The official view is that because of its postwar economic superiority and Europe's need for special trade conditions, the United States voluntarily endured trade discrimination. Now, however, having restored Europe's economic vitality through its foreign assistance programs and having encouraged the European community to establish still further trade restraints disadvantageous to the United States, the American competitive position has been eroded to the point that Washington must demand international trade equality. The official view holds that the United States started from a weak position and is bargaining back to equality.

On other economic fronts, the record of the United States is unsurpassed. No government contributes more to the economic programs of the United Nations than does the United States (although relative to its total wealth American contributions are not great). Overall, the United States bears about 40 percent of the total burden of financing UN programs. Thus, it has resisted the proliferation of UN programs, having worked assiduously to prevent the founding of the Special United Nations Fund for Economic Development (SUNFED) and having shown little if any early enthusiasm for the United Nations Conference on Trade and Development (UNCTAD). The motive for this resistance is that such changes in institutional structure do not contribute to American interests but turn the collective voting strength of the less developed nations into a bloc intent on availing itself of American wealth.

The General Assembly's decision of 1972 to reduce the American share of the apportioned budget (as contrasted with the total budget, which includes voluntary contributions) from 31.5 percent to 25 percent, at American request, was not acquiescence in a reprisal based on declining American confidence. Rather, the request was made as part of the Nixon administration's general distaste for UN activities and as a domestic budget-cutting measure. Although the organization needs American money, the proposal was acceptable to the General Assembly mainly because payment of one-third of the apportioned budget symbolizes American domination. Immediately after the assembly's decision, the Soviet delegation announced that it would reserve the right to request reduction in its apportioned share as well.

But just as the members of the United Nations do not want their organization dominated by the United States, so too does Washington look with disfavor upon the current trend in which the Third World uses the United Nations as a forum for global anti-Americanism. Throughout 1975 in particular, the string of American embarrassments over economic questions and over policy with respect to Israel and the PLO resulted in outspoken counterattacks by former Ambassador Daniel Patrick Moynihan. Washington made clear its dissatisfaction with the United Nations as an instrument of global diplomacy. Whereas Washington once used the United Nations in the battle against the Eastern (communist) world, it is now being used against the United States by the Southern (underindustrialized) world. American governmental and popular reactions to this reversal add up to public hostility to the United Nations and declining willingness to fund its programs.

The greatest American frustrations with the United Nations General Assembly have occurred over North-South issues and over efforts by the underindustrialized world to adjust the world economy such that the industrialized West pays not only the economic price of development but the social price as well. The degree to which the United Nations and its agencies are the forum for this policy explains the deterioration of American public opinion regarding the United Nations. The ultimate frustrations occurred in 1979 and 1980 when the United Nations was unsuccessful in securing the release of 53 Americans held hostage by Iranian militants, even after the formation of a presumably responsible government.

Among the presidential administrations in the post–Korean War years, that of Jimmy Carter attempted most often, and in the most difficult times, to improve relations between Washington and the United Nations. Perhaps because of his concern for human rights as a cornerstone of foreign policy and perhaps out of a broader faith that the United Nations might once again become consistently useful to American foreign policy, Carter was quicker than were his predecessors to refer to the United Nations or to utilize its capabilities. Needless to add, much of this occurred over issues on which the United States had little alternative: use of the General Assembly and the ICJ in attempts to secure the release of Americans held hostage in Iran, protest over the Soviet occupation of Afghanistan, attempts to limit the impact of the New International Economic Order of the American domestic economy, and so forth. But in other areas, such as in the general effort to improve relations with the Third World, Carter took unprecedented steps, such as the selection of two black Americans, Andrew Young and Donald McHenry, as Washington's ambassadors to the United Nations. In other areas, however, Carter was notably resistant to UN participation, particularly in respect to the Middle East, a matter on which he rested politically and diplomatically on the Camp David accords. These were a series of agreements forged by Carter with the leaders of Egypt and Israel on which he pinned long-range hopes for a peaceful Middle East.

The Reagan administration's view of the United Nations was very different. Apart from having named the first American woman ambassador to the United Nations since Eleanor Roosevelt, the administration treated the organization with disdain. It lost patience with Third World and Eastern bloc resolutions on the Middle East, particularly on Israel and the Palestinians; it was frustrated by failure of the United Nations to reverse Soviet policies; it withstood Third World efforts to use the United Nations to resolve civil wars in Nicaragua and El Salvador; and it resisted further American obligations to the New International Economic Order. The conservative frustrations of the administration were summed up by Charles Lichenstein, a member of the US delegation at the United Nations, when he said in the fall of 1983:

> If in the judicious determination of the members of the United Nations, they feel that they are not welcome and that they are not being treated with the hostly consideration that is their due, then the United States strongly encourages such member states seriously to consider removing themselves and this organization from the soil of the United States. We will put no impediment in your way. The members of the US mission to the United Nations will be down at dockside waving you a fond farewell as you sail into the sunset.[41]

Two other issues created political friction between the United States and the United Nations in 1983. The first was an administration request that Congress authorize additional contributions to the World Bank Group in order to provide added borrowing power for the Third World nations unable to pay their international debts. Liberal factions took the position that this was a request that taxpayers' money be used to drive foreign governments deeper in debt to American banks, the solvency of which was threatened by the mounting inability of the Third World to service its huge debts. Conservatives, on the other hand, wanted to supply the additional money as a form of assistance to American banks, but only on the condition that the new funds not be lent to communist or other anti-American governments. When an amendment to this effect was defeated in Congress, conservative Republicans released public letters to the constituents of the Democrats who had voted against it, claiming that they had communist tendencies.

The second issue was President Reagan's announcement late in 1983 that the United States would withdraw from the United Nations Educational, Social and Cultural Organization (UNESCO) on December 31, 1984, the mandatory one year after announcement.[42] This declaration capped a long-standing frustration with UNESCO and its secretary-general over ideological, financial, policy, and management issues. Specifically, the United States charged the organization with having politicized every issue and allowed itself repeatedly to be used as a Third World, anti-West forum. And it objected to the secretary-general's attempt to fashion a New International Information Order that would have restricted the rights of the Western press operating in Third World countries.

---

[41]Lichenstein's remark is reported in *The New York Times*, September 20, 1983, p. 1. It was made in reference to charges made by the Soviet Union that the United States had violated its responsibilities as the host state of the United Nations by refusing permission to Soviet Foreign Minister Andrei Gromyko to land at a civilian airport in the United States on his way to the fall session of the General Assembly. Both New York and New Jersey had announced that in retaliation for the Soviet downing of a Korean civilian aircraft, the Soviet jetliner would not be permitted to land at any of its accustomed destinations. The federal government had offered use of a US Air Force base as a substitute, but the Soviets declined the offer and announced that Gromyko would not attend the session.

[42]For the full text of notification from the State Department, see *American Journal of International Law*, April 1984, pp. 428–429.

The 1984–1986 period was one of continued American frustration with the United Nations. The traditional disparities between the developed and less developed world were accentuated during these years of emergence from worldwide recession, with the result of more strident demands among the Third World members for reform in the international economy. Soviet-American relations, although very promising throughout most of the period, deteriorated severely and rapidly toward the end, restoring some of the familiar rhetoric between the parties, particularly over such issues as Soviet military activities in Afghanistan and American intervention in the Nicaraguan civil war. The latter issue, one on which the Third World was especially critical of the United States, was fought not only in the political organs but in the ICJ as well. Those events culminated in the American withdrawal of its acceptance of the court's limited compulsory jurisdiction.

One other issue haunted the United States at the United Nations in this period: South Africa and the efforts of black South Africans and most other peoples to use the United Nations to bring an end to apartheid, the oppressive policy of racial separation and exploitation on which South African society and economy are constructed. Insisting on continuation of its diplomatic policy of "constructive engagements" as a means of persuading the South African government to change its policies, Washington opposed the Security Council's efforts to mandate sanctions against South Africa. For this, American (and British) policy was condemned by the UN Special Committee Against Apartheid. The United States was also roundly attacked for its air strike against Libya in retaliation for the Libyan government's participation in terrorist attacks on Americans in Europe and the Middle East; for vetoing Security Council action against Israel for its air strikes against Tunisian territory in which anti-Israeli terrorists were trained and protected; and for the American invasion of Grenada in a successful attempt to eliminate a left-leaning government. In light of these and other situations, the American public and their government were increasingly critical of the UN as an institution,[43] tending to think more and more that the institution and the nation were public adversaries. Despite this growing public view, however, one study showed that the American accusation of a double standard at the United Nations—that is, that the members readily condemn the United States for acts that they would condone or ignore had they been undertaken by Third World or socialist countries—is inaccurate.[44]

But the differences between the United States and the United Nations from 1981 to 1987 constituted more than a war of words. And withdrawal from UNESCO was not the sole action on the part of Washington to demonstrate its displeasure with the United Nations. We have seen, for example, that in this

---

[43]See, for example, Richard Bernstein, "The United States versus The United Nations," *The New York Times Magazine*, January 27, 1984, pp. 18–24, 26, 68. The principal theme is that the United Nations is ruled by a "Third World ethos" that is inimical to American foreign policy interests.

[44]Thomas M. Frank, "On Gnats and Camels: Is There a Double Standard at the United Nations?" *American Journal of International Law*, October 1984, pp. 811–833.

same period the United States first altered and then canceled its 40-year-old declaration of acceptance of the compulsory jurisdiction of the ICJ. And although most of the heated exchange originated in the executive branch, Congress played its own part. Apparently persuaded that many of the American woes in the United Nations were a result of the Third World majority in general and of the rich state/poor state/ministate problems, Congress adopted in 1985 the Kassenbaum-Solomon Amendment. Under this law, there was to be a 20 percent reduction in the annual American contribution to the regular budget of the United Nations beginning in 1987 and a continuation of selected reductions in contributions to special UN functions. These reductions were not to be canceled until the United Nations and its specialized agencies adopt a formula of proportional (weighted) voting giving the greatest influence over the organization to those who contribute most to it.[45]

The deterioration of the American attitude toward the United Nations reflects the general decline in America's satisfaction with the international system. One study of UN effectiveness correlates it with the general decline of American economic and political hegemony and with the rapid decrease in the frequency with which the United States has voted with the majority of the General Assembly on all subjects.[46]

Paradoxically, any resurgence of American interest in the United Nations is centered not on the General Assembly, but on the Security Council which for so long was paralyzed by the veto power of the five permanent members. President George Bush, himself a former United States Ambassador to the United Nations, turned to the Security Council in 1990 to organize global condemnation of Saddam Hussein after Iraq's invasion and annexation of Kuwait and its threat against Saudi Arabia. In a history-making series of events made possible by the end of the Cold War, the Soviet Union and China joined the United States, Britain, France, and eight nonpermanent members of the council in creating an embargo on all Iraqi imports and exports, and less than a month later in authorizing the use of naval forces to interdict any such trade in the Persian Gulf. Later the council authorized the forceful removal of Iraq from Kuwait.

But whatever course any American presidential administration may take with the United Nations, a dangerous paradox emerges in US-UN relations. If the UN system reflects an American-dominated world order, if the United States is its largest financial supporter, and if the United Nations is an important element in international progress, American dissatisfaction with the United Nations may either destroy the organization's role or drive the United States farther from support of the United Nations and from willing participation in collective decision making. If the United Nations lacks the authority to compel the United States and if the United States is unable to manipulate the

---

[45]For a review of the political and legal aspects of this event, see Elizabeth Zeller, "The 'Corporate Will' of the United Nations and the Rights of the Minority," *American Journal of International Law*, July 1987, pp. 610–634.

[46]Ernst B. Haas, "Regime Decay: Conflict Management and International Organizations, 1945–1981," pp. 189–256.

membership to its policy needs, the disaffection between Washington and the United Nations may destroy the organization's role in a changing world.

The Views of America's Major Allies

Because they have generally shared the Cold War preoccupations of the United States, the major American allies have held views of international organization similar to those of the United States. There have been, however, some outstanding exceptions.

The Japanese position has been anomalous. Having been one of the wartime enemies against which the United Nations was founded, Japan was excluded by the terms of the United Nations Charter. It was nearly a decade before East-West agreement permitted the seating of a Japanese delegation. Since then, Tokyo has served as a loyal American ally in the United Nations, although its role has been a quiet one. It has not wanted to serve American interests to the detriment of normal relations with the USSR, and it has not wanted its American ties to make more difficult the problem of working out effective relations with both China and Taiwan. Probably for these reasons, Japan has disavowed any intention of requesting a permanent place on the Security Council, even though its accession to great-power status in all but the military sense might otherwise justify such a claim.

The Western European attitude, too, is similar to that of the United States, although there are marked differences. During the peak of the Cold War, trans-Atlantic objectives were identical, so Western Europe clung to the anti-Soviet successes of the United States at the United Nations. European dissatisfaction with the extent of Washington's commitment to Asia during the Korean War, and American criticism of Britain and France over the Suez venture of 1956, were the only substantial exceptions.

But in the dynamics of world politics, the Western European partners have begun to move away from the United Nations and away from some of the positions that the United States holds there. Most important, the progress of European regionalism and dissolution of its empires have both altered the focus of Europe's organizational attention from the global to the regional and created the strength with which to pursue policies independent of Washington. On global issues such as petroleum, the Europeans prefer a policy of industrial states' consortia; and on the political issues of the Middle East that threaten the steady flow of oil they have abandoned such major American concessions to Israel as excluding from UN debate representatives of the PLO.

The Canadian attitude is genuinely unique among Washington's principal allies. Having for the first ten postwar years been caught in the flow of Soviet-American events at the United Nations, including participation in the Korean War, Ottawa's independence began to show in 1956. It was Ambassador (later Prime Minister) Lester Pearson who conceived the idea that Dag Hammarskjöld later developed into peacekeeping, and Canada has since been one of the prime contributors to interventionary peacekeeping. It also served a brief and unhappy term as part of an international (non-UN) truce observer team in Vietnam.

On economic matters, the Canadian position is also a unique one. Resource rich but industrially dominated, it is subject to all the fluctuations of American demand and American business. In a peculiar sense, then, Canada is an industrialized state that confronts many of the problems that are typically those of the Third World. On issues of the New International Economic Order, therefore, Canada is defensive when the United States is assertive, and often assertive when the United States is defensive. The role the United Nations plays in Canadian foreign policy, accordingly, is increasingly different from the one it plays in American policy. Consequently, the attitude that Canadians hold toward international organization is gradually diverging from that of its southern neighbor.

The Soviet View of the UN System

The Soviet view differs spectacularly from those of the United States and its principal allies. All the latter have traditionally taken a Western view of matters of organization, as of law, pertaining to the world confrontation between communist and socialist states, on the one hand, and noncommunist and capitalist states on the other. Because of its sharply divergent perspective on these matters, the Soviet political attitude differs vastly.

The Kremlin sees international organization as an instrument of Western, and particularly American, policy designed to weaken the Soviet Union and to enhance capitalistic imperialism. Traditionally, then, its approach to the UN system has been defensive. Because of the organs' composition, the Soviets have been able to pursue few if any major policies through the United Nations; they hope at best to prevent American intrusions in their interests. If they have outdone the American delegations in maximizing the propaganda potential of the United Nations, it is only because the makeup of the organization makes necessary a negative approach to collective diplomacy.

Several focal points have emerged in Soviet outlooks. The first was opposition to the Uniting for Peace Resolution on the ground that it subverts the prerogatives of the great powers in the very founding spirit. Second, the ICJ's advisory opinion in the *Certain Expenses* case further infuriated the Soviet Union on the ground that it illegally expanded the authority of the General Assembly at the expense of major-power domination in security matters. A third major issue has been the principles of peacekeeping, toward which the Soviets have taken the view that the Security Council must control the issue to preserve great-power authority. Connected to the issue of peacekeeping finance is the Soviet complaint that the secretary-general managed the Congo operation in a pro-Western manner.

It would be a grave error to suppose that as the membership has become less sympathetic to American foreign policy, it has become more oriented to the Soviet Union. Although voting patterns in the 1960s gave greater strength to Soviet positions, it was not because increasing numbers of states were adhering to the Soviet line. Yet the Kremlin took a more patient view of the United Nations during the latter half of the 1960s. Attacks on the organization were both less frequent and less vehement, and aside from refusal to pay for peacekeeping operations, Soviet willingness to fund the United Nations improved. Although it is a passive policy, the increasing failure of the organization to support American policy must have raised Moscow's spirits and its view of the United Nation's viability.

Because of the long-standing conflict between Moscow and Beijing, the seating of the Chinese delegation at the United Nations was not a victory for the Soviet Union—as it would have been in 1950 or 1955. Indeed, the presence of the Beijing delegation has changed the Soviet outlook on the United Nations. It is the avowed intent of the Beijing delegation to champion the cause of the Third World, and in the long run this means new losses in the Soviet voting column. The deliberate Chinese strategy of labeling the Soviet Union a ''social-imperialist,'' a concept alien to Marxism-Leninism because all imperialism is regarded as fascist and capitalist, is an ideological and rhetorical device by which China deliberately drives a wedge between the Soviet Union and the Third World countries at the United Nations.

Aside from the political organs and the economic programs, the Soviet Union is not an active participant in the UN system. It has never agreed to submit a dispute to the ICJ. Because of its different economic system, it has refused to participate in the institutions of Western imperialism. Neither it nor its allies takes part in the GATT. It was not until 1972 that Romania became the first Soviet ally to enter the IMF and the IBRD.

Historically, then, the Soviet attitude toward the United Nations was almost uniformly one of dissatisfaction. But there are evidences that this will undergo substantial revision in the era of *glasnost*. In the fall of 1987, Mikhail Gorbachev addressed the opening session of the General Assembly in a manner that was widely interpreted as a broad statement of Soviet internationalism rather than propaganda. He called for an expanded role for the United Nations in regional stability and international economics and declared the Kremlin's intention to pay much of its outstanding debt to the United Nations: $28 million in arrears to the regular budget, $172 million for the United Nations Force in (southern) Lebanon (UNIFIL), and $25 million for other peacekeeping missions since 1973. The statement excluded the possibility of payments for three operations that the Soviet Union still regards as illegal because they resulted from the unconstitutional evasion of the Security Council: the Korean War, the 1956 United Nations Emergency Force in the Middle East (UNEF, 1956), and the United Nations Operation in the Congo (ONUC, 1960). This was taken as a significant event for at least three reasons: (1) the Soviet Union seemed to be putting hard cash behind its call for greater UN influence; (2) it came at the same time as the congressionally mandated reduction of American funds to the organization; and (3) the payment of funds explicitly directed to post-1973 peacekeeping operations appeared to signal a Soviet proclamation of acceptance as legal and legitimate both those operations and the concept of peacekeeping itself.[47]

---

[47]For a review of the Gorbachev statement, see *The New York Times,* October 16, 1987, pp. 1 and A10.

With the close of the Cold War, Gorbachev's interest in the United Nations system grew rapidly. By 1989, as he began to seek comprehensive solutions to the failed socialist Soviet economy, he began to build a case for membership in the International Monetary Fund as a source of development capital. And in the Security Council, the Kremlin agreed to support a Washington-sponsored resolution authorizing the use of naval power to enforce the economic embargo against Iraq only if the resolution made explicit reference to the Military Staff Committee of the council, a body that had been created on paper prior to the onset of the Cold War, but which had never convened. Whether or not this was an early sign of renewal of Soviet interest in the Security Council, provided multilateral safeguards are applied (rather than concede to the view that the council should merely legitimize the forceful intentions of individual states), will be revealed by time and circumstances.

The Chinese View of the UN System

China is the youngest of the major powers. Its development toward full status has been retarded by the United States and the Soviet Union. American resistance was facilitated by the United Nations, through which Washington conducted a consistent anti-Beijing policy from 1949 until the General Assembly session in the fall of 1971. It follows that Beijing shares the Soviet view of the United Nations as the handmaiden of American foreign policy and of Western imperialism. More specifically, the United Nations is the forum through which the fraud was perpetuated until 1971 that the nationalist government on Taiwan was the real representative of the Chinese people, although over 800 million Chinese people on the Asian mainland were ignored.

The Korean War is also at the center of Beijing's memory. In the hands of pro-American majorities, the General Assembly labeled China an aggressor, despite obvious threats to its borders and despite the urgings of General Douglas MacArthur that the Western allies in Korea attack Chinese targets. The United Nations, moreover, submitted to American pressures to vote an economic boycott against China. The continued refusal to seat the Beijing delegation was the largest single source of China's sense of isolation from world politics and was interpreted in China as an extension of the Century of Humiliation. Its embarrassment was further heightened by the comparative diplomatic positions of the two Chinas prior to the seating of Beijing. By that time, 66 states had recognized the People's Republic, of which 60 still had active diplomatic relations. Of these, 55 were UN members. Meanwhile, 61 states had formally recognized the Taiwan government, and 59 had active diplomatic relations, of which 56 were UN members.[48]

When finally seated at the United Nations, the Beijing delegation was notably restrained. It insisted before arriving that it would take no part until remnants of the Nationalist Chinese representation had been expunged from all

---

[48]Summarized from Byron S. J. Weng, *Peking's UN Policy* (New York: Praeger, 1972), apps. B1–B3, pp. 232–235.

UN agencies (except the IMF and the IBRD). Beijing joined the IMF and the Asian Development Bank in 1986; it began applying for development loans and drawing on its IMF rights immediately. Its other uncompromising position was refusal to pay for maintenance of military cemeteries in South Korea. Otherwise it announced, quietly but resolutely, that it recognized its duty to pay a larger share of UN expenses than the weaker Nationalist government had and volunteered to increase its contribution from 4 percent of the budget to 7 percent, over a five-year period.

In other respects China's introduction to the United Nations was not quiescent. The first major event that followed the seating of the Beijing delegation was the Pakistan civil war and fighting between India and Pakistan, out of which Bangladesh was born. Because China sided with Pakistan and the Soviet Union with India, Bangladesh's subsequent request for admission to the United Nations was vetoed by China. Second, at the global United Nations Conference on the Human Environment at Stockholm in 1972, China used the opportunity to obstruct the meeting by condemning American use of defoliants in Vietnam.

In many respects, China's early days at the United Nations were characterized by outspoken criticism of the United States and the Soviet Union. It was apparent from the beginning that China intended to use its new status as a permanent member of the Security Council—a proud and prestigious position—as a new and unique opportunity to campaign against the perceived intentions of the two superpowers of dividing the world into two, giant armed camps, commanding the allegiance of all others. In those early years, then, China's diplomacy at the United Nations was of two kinds: a bitter invective against the political intentions of Washington and Moscow, and a passionate involvement with the demands and expectations of the developing world. The developing world had already come to command General Assembly majorities on virtually all economic and development issues and sympathized with China on matters of development and on its dislike of Soviet-American manipulation of the international system.[49] China's intention of taking a world lead among the developing countries was first enunciated at Bandung (Indonesia) in 1955, so the advancement of this policy at the United Nations is consistent with well-established Chinese foreign policy objectives. It is not sheer opportunism, as is often argued by anti-Chinese and anti-United Nations political elements in the West and in the Soviet world. China, after all, is the largest of the underindustrialized countries. It feels that it has been driven into a position of inferiority and that its achievement of national self-fulfillment is tied to nonwhite nations, regardless of politics or ideologies, more than to the industrialized world or to other Marxist societies.

Quantitative studies reveal that on matters dealing with security, social policy, human rights, and economics, the Chinese delegation at the United Na-

---

[49]For a thorough analysis of China's early role at the United Nations, based on documentary UN information, see Samuel S. Kim, *China, the United Nations, and World Order* (Princeton, N.J.: Princeton University Press, 1979), particularly chaps. 3–7.

tions has voted more frequently with the Third World than with the Soviet Union and Eastern Europe. The inclination to vote with the Third World is most pronounced on economic, human rights, and social issues and somewhat less on political and security issues. It has voted more frequently with the Eastern European bloc on colonial and race issues than it has with any particular region of the less developed world.[50] The great improvement in Sino-American relations, even in the Asian military sphere, has not altered the Chinese voting pattern at the United Nations.

Within a year or two of the arrival of the Chinese delegation at the United Nations, interest grew for a review of the United Nations Charter to determine whether or not it would be possible to strengthen both the Security Council and the General Assembly. These efforts were opposed by all other permanent members of the Security Council, but China took an ambivalent position. On the one hand, China wanted to signal its support for the interests of the Third World, which wanted foremost to reduce the abuses of the veto in the Security Council and to increase the authority of General Assembly decisions. In short, China and the Third World favored steps that would "democratize" international decision making at the United Nations.

On the other hand, as a permanent member of the Security Council after 20 years of exclusion from the United Nations, China was not eager to sacrifice the privileges of membership, including its new veto capability in the council. Prior to admission and in the early years thereafter, China took the position that the veto is one of the building blocks in the Security Council's authority in international peace and security and that the unanimity of the permanent members is critical to progress. As this position became unpopular with the Third World, which wanted to eliminate the veto, China took the position that the problem is not with the existence of the veto privilege but with its abuse by the other four permanent members.[51]

China's view of peacekeeping has changed substantially. Since the original peacekeeping initiatives were carried out by the General Assembly in part under authorization of the Uniting for Peace Resolution, a resolution under which China and the United Nations had conducted war against each other in Korea, it should not be surprising that China's early attitude toward peacekeeping was that it is a form of organized aggression. Not until the end of 1981 did China finally vote affirmatively on extending the mandate of a UN peacekeeping force, after nearly a decade of having abstained on all related questions. Nonetheless, China joins the Soviet Union in insisting that because peacekeeping is an instrument of maintaining international peace and security, it belongs exclusively to the Security Council where it is subject to the unanimity of the permanent members.

---

[50]Trong R. Chai, "Chinese Policy Toward the Third World and the Superpowers in the United Nations General Assembly 1971–77: A Voting Analysis," *International Organization*, Summer 1979, pp. 391–404.

[51]Suzanne Ogden, "China's Position on UN Charter Review," *Pacific Affairs*, Summer 1979, pp. 210–239.

The Third World View of the UN System

Although the Cold War has left the impression that all international conflict is arranged along East-West lines, it is the feeling of the less developed states that the focus of world politics is really North-South. The bulk of the world's industrial power is in the Northern Hemisphere, whereas most of the southern half of the globe languishes in poverty. As a result, the less developed states have a mixed view of the UN system. On the one hand, they see it as the special preserve of the major powers, through which the latter have promoted economic domination and resisted adequate development programs. But on the other hand, much of the Third World enjoys national independence principally because of the United Nations' activities in promoting self-government; and they see in the UN agencies hope for relatively depoliticized programs of aid, trade, and technical assistance. Thus, although the ideologically uncommitted states play an active and often vocal role in higher politics, their principal energies in the United Nations are reserved for the organs and agencies that serve their development needs.

The Third World's relations with these agencies are not entirely smooth. Because the funds for these programs come from the industrialized states, attempts to control the politics of assistance are never far off. The developed states, insisting on maximum efficiency in the expenditure of funds, impose difficult criteria. They insist on preinvestment development, designed to mature the nonvisible aspects of an economy so that larger and more productive projects can follow with maximum probable success. Less-developed countries (LDCs) view this sequence with impatience. Likewise the LDCs, in their long-range planning, seek commitment of funds from plan to completion, whereas the lending agencies generally prefer to fund in stages and to require the successful completion of each stage before releasing money for the next. More recently, the lending institutions have required consideration of ecological hazards in development projects. The LDCs view this requirement with disdain, because in their quest for rapid development, they view environmental protection as a luxury appropriate only to developed economies. All impediments to accelerated development are viewed by the Third World as attempts to retard the pace of economic sovereignty in the Southern Hemisphere and as methods of collective neoimperialism. Nevertheless, acquiring funds through the UN system is less costly, both economically and politically, than is attaining them directly from other governments.

The need second to capital is trade concessions. The Third World has a difficult time trading in a world dominated by enormous economies in which trade regulations serve industrial states. To counter this situation, the Third World pressed for the establishment of the United Nations Conference on Trade and Development (UNCTAD), which provides a collective voice in confronting the GATT for more advantageous terms of trade with industrial countries. Specifically, UNCTAD seeks to press upon the GATT a unified program of preferential trading conditions. As we have seen, in 1974 and 1975 the underindustrialized states succeeded in focusing the attention of two special sessions of the General Assembly on economic problems and achieved passage of the Charter of Economic Rights and Duties of States and the Declaration on the Establishment of a New International Economic Order, together with a Programme of Action.

Technical assistance is the third principal area of need. The United Nations' contribution began in 1949 with the founding of the Expanded Program of Technical Assistance (EPTA). Technical assistance continues to be provided through the Technical Assistance Board (TAB), the United Nations Industrial Development Organization (UNIDO), and appropriate offices of such functional agencies as the Food and Agricultural Organization (FAO) and the World Health Organization (WHO). Administrative personnel are offered to governments through the OPEX program (Operational and Executive Services), which locates administrative talent and places it on loan to Third World governments.

To meet the combined needs of the LDCs with respect to aid, trade, and technical assistance, the United Nations General Assembly designated the 1960s the "development decade" and combined the Special Fund, the TAB,

Figure 16–2 Defection rate among Third World countries on UN economic resolutions, 1971–1985.

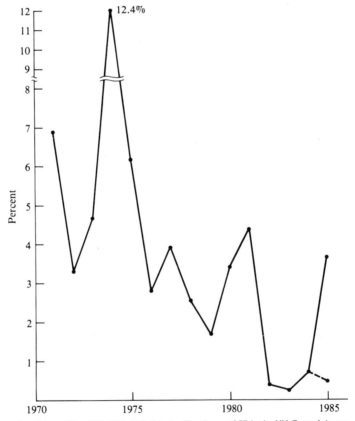

After Keisuke Iida, "Third World Solidarity: The Group of 77 in the UN General Assembly," *International Organization*, Spring 1988, pp. 375–396.

and the EPTA into the United Nations Development Program (UNDP). The aim was to achieve 5 percent per year economic growth among the LDCs and to raise foreign assistance to a level of 1 percent of the annual gross national products of the industrialized states. During this period, however, unilateral nonmilitary aid did not increase substantially, and the United Nations' own programs were only a little more successful than they had been. The modest successes of the UNDP did, however, restore hope for collective advancement, and the 1970s were designated the "second development decade." UNDP II was launched. UNDP III progressed throughout the 1980s.

In all these undertakings, the Third World nations are engaged in the difficult process of turning the United Nations to a goal that in practice has taken a decidedly secondary role to the great-power struggle. And as American opinion regarding the United Nations is irritated by the cohesion of the Third World, so does the Group of 77 profit diplomatically from its voting solidarity. One recent study has measured this cohesiveness by calculating the annual "defection rate" among the Group of 77 on all economic issues placed before the General Assembly. This is defined as "the likelihood that a country randomly chosen from the Group of 77 will deviate from the common position on any given resolution." The results for the years 1971 through 1985 are shown in Figure 16–2. On the graph, a low percentage indicates a high rate of cohesion; and the higher the percentage, the less cohesive for the Group of 77 throughout the year. Moreover, a different presentation of the data shows that Africa and the Middle East, particularly the OPEC countries, always scored the strongest cohesion, and throughout the 1970s Latin America, Asia, and the Pacific generally showed the least cohesion. Since then, however, their cohesion rate tightened also, thus recording the strongly cohesive findings after 1981. (The author of the study notes that the unexpected upturn in the defection rate in 1985 was the result of a single factor—a vote regarding an economic embargo against Nicaragua. If that issue were removed, the aggregate defection rate for the year would have been only 0.5.)[52]

No similar studies have been conducted thus far on matters other than economic. Nonetheless, in view of the reliance that the Third World governments place on the UN's economic agenda, this study alone is sufficient to demonstrate their cohesion in utilizing the organization for their major foreign policy objectives. Now, as *glasnost* holds the promise of a reduction in East-West bipolarity, the hope is kindled that the United Nations might turn to saving "succeeding generations from the scourge of war" by employing "international machinery for the promotion of the economic and social advancement of all peoples," as envisaged in the preamble to the charter. Patient and long-suffering, the LDCs look to the UN system to lift them above exploitation by the great powers and to carry them over the seemingly impassable barriers of neoimperialism.

---

[52]Keisuke Iida, "Third World Solidarity: The Group of 77 in the UN General Assembly," *International Organization*, Spring 1988, pp. 375–396.

CHAPTER 17

International Integration and
Transnational Participation

Centuries of study of the nation-state system have raised doubt regarding governments' ability to preserve international peace and stability. International law and organization have assisted, but neither has ensured lasting international harmony. What, then, are the alternatives to the nation-state system? What new political contexts might be framed through which familiar international transactions might continue and peace be possible?

At present, attention is focused on two possible alternatives: international integration and transnational participation, the subjects of this chapter. Will political history reach beyond the nation-state?

International Integration

International integration is the process by which a supranational condition is achieved, in which larger political units conduct the business now carried out by national governments. Defined succinctly, it is

> the process whereby political actors in several distinct national settings are persuaded to shift their loyalties, expectations, and political activities toward a new and larger center, whose institutions possess or demand jurisdiction over the pre-existing national states.[1]

Unlike international organization, which establishes institutional machinery *among* states, international integration provides decision-making machinery

---

[1]Ernst B. Haas, *The Uniting of Europe: Political, Social and Economic Forces 1950–57* (Stanford, Calif.: Stanford University Press, 1958), p. 16.

above them. It constructs procedures and institutions capable of making obligatory decisions on behalf of national governments. It consists of the merger of separate authorities and jurisdictions, usually in a well-defined geographic region, into a larger unit, a higher unity, and a single polity. This slow and gradual process, which may occur unevenly in different sectors of interaction, leaves different states intact; but it progressively blurs the distinctions of international policy among them.

Before commencing an analysis of the theory and progress of international integration, a note is appropriate regarding the frequency of integrating efforts. Most have begun with economic integration. Among the market (nonsocialist) economies of the world, progress toward economic integration is most easily observed in Western Europe, where two collaborations of different memberships, the European Community (EC)[2] and the European Free Trade Association (EFTA), are well on their respective paths to integrated economies. Because the progress of the EC has so far exceeded others, and because of the rich theoretical and analytical literatures it has inspired, the sections that follow rely heavily on theory and data pertaining to the EC. In fact, however, outside Western Europe there have been no fewer than 14 efforts of regionally related market economies at some level of integration, involving virtually every part of the nonsocialist world except North America. Among these the Andean Group, formed in 1969 and composed of Bolivia, Colombia, Ecuador, Peru, and Venezuela (Chile having withdrawn in 1976), is generally considered the most advanced and the one that has most effectively limited direct foreign investment in order to maintain regional control over the economic future.[3] In the analysis that follows, occasional references are made to economic integration efforts outside the EC, but only when they are more instructive than are similar observations about the EC.

Integration and the Functional Model

Integration by any means is a long and arduous process. Although some observers have predicted integration through federation, most hold that integration is a testing process tied to compiled successes. This functional model of integration rejects rapid constitutional consolidation and looks instead to

---

[2]The integrating states of Western Europe are commonly referred to in the aggregate as "the European Community." However, the larger community consists of a number of functionally organized activities, each of which is also labeled a "community." As a result, the European Community consists, in part, of the European Economic Community (EEC), which Americans call the Common Market, and the European Coal and Steel Community (ECSC), through which coal and steel resources are regulated. Hence, if one wishes to speak of the community as conceived totally, one refers to the European Community; but if one wishes to connote the specific functional activities, the reference is instead to the European Communities. In this book, the singular form is used except where technical accuracy calls for the plural.

[3]Lynn Mytelka, *Regional Development in a Global Economy: The Multinational Corporation, Technology and Andean Integration* (New Haven, Conn.: Yale University Press, 1979). Also see Elizabeth G. Ferris, "Foreign Investment as an Influence on Foreign Policy Behavior: The Andean Pact," *Inter-American Economic Affairs*, Autumn 1979, pp. 45–69.

progress in specific sectors. The functionalist view holds that even compatible societies cannot integrate all public functions simultaneously. Collectivization may be based on economics, on politics, or on security. Gradual and parallel progress in several sectors may converge into general, cross-sectoral integration. Without this convergence, integration is encapsulated or isolated, having no carryover effects in other sectors.[4]

1. The Sectors of Integration

What functions have been given over to the integrative process? What purposes, normally served by national governments, have been entrusted to higher political levels? The answers to these questions lie in the different sectors of integration.

Economics Historically, the sector most frequently integrated has been the economic sector. The most familiar integrative organizations are "common markets," in which the member states consolidate all or part of their economic activities. The European Economic Community (EEC), the Central American Common Market (CACM), the Latin American Free Trade Association (LAFTA), and the European Free Trade Association (EFTA) are among the most familiar.

The function of a common market is to raise economic potential through policy consolidation. Two particular instruments are used. First, the members eliminate barriers to trade among themselves, so that goods flow freely in trade. Second, they agree to treat outside states with a single economic policy; their economic policies concerning nonmembers are not only coordinated but are also identical and mutually enforced.

Because economic interaction is highly complex, it is instructive to consider economic subsectors. In the European experience, for example, progress toward a full free trade area has developed at different rates and with vastly different amounts of enthusiasm in the industrial and agricultural subsectors. Although it has not been easy, principles for industrial free trade areas were more readily achieved than were those for agriculture. In addition, Britain's entry into the Common Market was delayed not only by French politics (on Britain's first serious attempt to gain entry in 1963, President Charles de Gaulle vetoed its membership), but also by British fears of the impact on its agricultural subsector. Upon entry in 1973, Britain suffered inflation in food prices but anticipated that gains in industrial trade would favorably affect its

---

[4]For a study of the distinction between the federationist and the functionalist approaches, see particularly David Mitrany, "The Prospect of Integration: Federal or Functional?" *Journal of Common Market Studies*, vol. 4, December 1965. A useful study of the multivariate nature of integration is found in Leon N. Lindberg, "Political Integration as a Multidimensional Phenomenon Requiring Multivariate Measurement," *International Organization*, vol. 24, 1970, pp. 649–731. The neofunctionalists hold that federation can ultimately occur on a well-established and solid functionalist base. See, for example, Joseph S. Nye, "Comparing Common Markets: A Revised Neo-Functionalist Model," *International Organization*, vol. 24, 1970, pp. 796–835.

balance of payments (increase exports over imports) and would stabilize the British economy.

Another distinction involves production and producer. Although an economy consists of production of goods and services, these are produced by people; therefore, there are important labor aspects to a free trade area—standardization of wages in industries, community agreement on fair labor practices, free flow of labor across national boundaries, and agreement on pension and unemployment benefits.

In addition to labor and produce, another aspect of economic integration is the availability of capital, without which efficient, coordinated growth cannot occur. If this means borrowing from abroad, then one state (even perhaps an outside state) may dominate growth by controlling both capital and decisions about capital utilization. Creation of a common medium of exchange among participating central banks facilitates payments. Western European integration achieved this milestone in 1971 with the establishment of the Euronote or E-Note (E), which is exchangeable only among the member treasuries.

Social Considerations   The second major sector is the social sector. Although it may be technically feasible to integrate economies, ultimate integration requires mutual toleration and common social and political values. Social integration means transforming national preferences into loyalty to the larger political community. *Supranational* attitudes must evolve.

Evidence has developed over a number of years to suggest that such a process is occurring in Western Europe. Studies as old as 20 years have revealed that the degree of ''Europeanness'' evolving among nations of various European states—the degree to which people sense themselves part of a larger political community—grew steadily in the early days of the EC. These studies demonstrated variations among age groups toward the growth of community, with younger people generally more favorably disposed toward supranational attitudes.[5] Furthermore, data nearly 20 years old suggest that as early as 1971, the growth of a supranational consciousness was accompanied by outward-looking attitudes: A united Europe was seen not only as a political community for self-service, but as a stabilizing force in the international system.[6]

More recent events highlight attitudes about a common social policy. With the approach of 1992 and the goal of a single economic market within the community, the European Commission began in 1989 to think beyond economic union. One of the products of its thinking was a draft Community Charter of Social Rights with three principal goals: (1) to create standards for the freedom of movement within the community and the right to establish residency; (2) to provide social and economic cohesion within the community; and

---

[5]See, for example, Ronald Inglehart, ''Public Opinion and Regional Integration,'' *International Organization*, vol. 24, 1970, pp. 764–795, and ''The Silent Revolution in Europe: Intergenerational Change in Post-Industrial Societies,'' *American Political Review*, vol. 65, 1971, pp. 991–1017.

[6]Ronald Inglehart, ''The New Europeans: Inward or Outward Looking?'' *International Organization*, vol. 24, 1970, pp. 129–139.

(3) to promote employment and ensure solidarity among the members. This was publicized at a time at which several controversial debates were in progress, including debates over such vexing issues as a common agricultural policy, a common banking system with monetary union, and growth of the political authority of the European Parliament and the European Commission. These difficult background issues notwithstanding, fully 75 percent of people questioned responded that adoption of the Community Charter of Social Rights would be desirable.[7]

Politics   A third sector of concern to integration theory is the political sector, although it is not neatly distinguished from other sectors. Societies are replete with bonds of patriotism, loyalty, historical mythology; and a sense of national difference. Political integration refers, therefore, to the relatively narrow concept of integration of basic political institutions—with transfer of sovereignty over external policy to common international institutions. It aims not to eliminate national governments but to alter their control over specific functions. These changes may affect internal matters of the state, such as fiscal policy or production policy. In integration short of full federation, there is no pretense to transfer of full sovereignty over internal matters.

Despite this limited expectation, political integration is more difficult to achieve than is economic integration, chiefly because the latter is expected to strengthen the national economy, thus encouraging dual loyalty to nation and larger community. Political integration, in contrast, directly affects the state's sovereignty over decision making with respect to its nationals. Its institutional effects are more visible, and the assault on nationalism is more nearly frontal. The state is reduced in stature. Only where this is regarded as a desirable objective has the concept of political integration caught on.

A variety of interpretations exists about the relationships among political integration, social integration, and general governmental cooperation. Some hold that social predisposition is the critical measure of integration potential. Others insist that the creation of institutions among generally sympathetic states will create the social conditions necessary for political integration. Empirical studies indicate, however, that improvements in intergovernmental relations must precede both institution building and changes in societal attitudes.[8] Western Europe integration illustrates this point.

It was apparent by the mid-1960s that political unification of Europe required a revival of internationalism in France. Always conscious of French historical and cultural uniqueness, President de Gaulle's view of European organization was pragmatic: How much can France profit from integration without sacrificing national identity? Toward the end of his long public career, de Gaulle confided to Christopher Soames, British ambassador to France, that he anticipated as an ideal "a looser form of free trade area with arrangements by each country to exchange agricultural produce, and a small inner council of

[7]"Eurobarometer: Public Opinion in the European Community," *European Affairs*, Autumn 1989, pp. 26–32.
[8]See Barry B. Hughes and John E. Schwarz, "Dimensions of Political Integration and the Experience of the European Community," *International Studies Quarterly*, vol. 16, 1972, pp. 263–294.

a European political association consisting of France, Britain, Germany, and Italy.'' Broad political integration was not part of Gaullist politics, and both the entry of Britain into the EC and French acceptance of political unity awaited the passing of the Gaullist era.[9]

The forthcoming entry of Britain along with Denmark and Ireland in 1973 set the stage for a forward-looking summit conference in October 1972, at which ministers from the three incoming states participated. There a general agreement was signed calling for a phased schedule of political unity by 1980. Details of the unity were to be culminated in the first phase, scheduled to end in 1975. The departure of de Gaulle, the enlightened attitude of his successor, the willingness of the British Conservative government to withstand the attacks of the Labour opposition in entering the EC—these and other events converged to give new life to the spirit of political supranationalism among the Nine. By January 1976, major achievements had been scored: the Tindemans Report on progressive integration was published; a formal agreement had been made for direct election of the European Parliament in 1978 (as contrasted with assignment of members from the respective national parliaments); and the members had intentionally presented a common front at the United Nations on the economic matters considered at the special session on the new international economic order. In addition, within the community new political alliances had formed; and on matters of deliberation there had developed a tendency for cross-national parties and interest groups to discuss policy on the basis of shared interests rather than to resort to the more primitive device of national caucuses.[10]

As is not uncommon, however, progress toward political integration was minimal. The direct election of the European Parliament was postponed to 1979, but even in advance of the event some observers expressed the view that the very preparation for such elections had had a profound effect on the national politics of the member states. One such observer noted that in the preparations, European subjects had become more important in public debate, that European voters were aware that Europe itself would soon become a fourth level of politics for their consideration—local, state, national, and now continental. In addition, it was apparent that the forthcoming elections were promoting latent transnational links among European political parties.[11] All these trends seemed to revive earlier attitudes toward the probable political spillovers of economic integration and seemed to give new life to the notion of at least a partial transfer of loyalty from the nation as the source of services and economic vitality to the union of nations.

Another little-noticed trend gave added evidence of progress toward political union. By the end of 1978, based on a nine-year-old agreement on European

[9]The words are those of British Foreign and Commonwealth Secretary Michael Stewart, as he reported the de Gaulle–Soames conversation to Parliament in February 1969, as described by Hugh Corbet, ''Role of the Free Trade Area,'' in Hugh Corbet and David Robertson, eds., *Europe's Free Trade Area Experiment* (Oxford, England: Pergamon Press, 1970), pp. 1–42.

[10]*The New York Times*, February 9, 1976, pp. 1, 18.

[11]See, for example, Karl Kaiser, ''Europe's Parliament,'' *The New York Times*, February 18, 1979, p. E10.

political cooperation, a substantial EC diplomatic presence was discernible around the world, which might in time result in the development of a structure for a common foreign policy. Working principally through a presidential commission, the directors-general responsible for various aspects of the community's affairs (such as external relations, agricultural trade, international development, and the like) had begun consulting regularly on the behalf of the community in several capitals, including Washington, Tokyo, Beijing, and Ottawa. They had placed 50 representatives in the developing world and elsewhere, and they had stationed conferences with several international organizations. In the words of two commentators on the subject, "Without any clear or agreed plan for developing the Commission's role in bilateral diplomacy, incremental growth [had] nevertheless produced an extensive pattern of Community missions in [nonmember] countries."[12] In 1981, the EC's diplomatic activity resulted in an elaborate but unsuccessful proposal to the Kremlin for the withdrawal of Soviet forces from Afghanistan.

Even though the direct election of the European Parliament in 1984 had a disappointing voter turnout as contrasted with the election of 1979, the 1983–1985 period showed substantial declaratory progress toward political integration. During that time, the EC produced a draft treaty on a European Union and a Solemn Declaration on European Union, each in one way or another calling for improvement in the EC's institutions and policies concerning economic activity, social policy, international relations outside the community, and the union's finances. In a climactic event, the European Council of Ministers met at Luxembourg at the close of 1985 to review reports and strategies, most particularly the report of the ad hoc Committee for Institutional Affairs (the Dodge Committee), and from their deliberations produced the Single European Act and called for its ratification by member governments by the end of 1987.[13]

Adoption of the Single European Act, frequently referred to as simply the Single Act, greatly accelerated progress toward unification and made talk of a single Western European economic market by the end of 1992 quite reasonable. Two British writers assessed its importance in 1989 as follows:

> The Single Act has unexpectedly become the [European] Commission's vehicle for . . . ambitious aims. The Act is no longer a modest intergovernmental compromise, or even a framework treaty . . . , but is instead to be regarded as binding law. . . .[14]

The same authors characterize the goal of the commission as one in which a single economic market will create a single economy, and with it a single

[12]Christopher Hill and William Wallace, "Diplomatic Trends in the European Community," *International Affairs* (London), January 1979.

[13]Juliet Lodge, "The Single European Act: Towards a New Euro-Dynamism?" *Journal of Common Market Studies*, March 1986, pp. 203–223.

[14]Christopher Brewin and Richard McAllister, "Annual Review of the Activities of the European Communities in 1988," *Journal of Common Market Studies*, June 1989, pp. 323–357, at pp. 323–324. The remainder of this paragraph relies on the same source.

currency managed by a treaty-based institution with power to control credit within the EC. They cite the president of the commission as predicting that by 1995, some form of European government will be needed, perhaps a higher form of American-style federalism in which the member states and the communitywide organs of government share social and economic power on a prescribed basis. These predictions are based on the expectation that by the turn of the century, as much as 80 percent of all economic matters, and perhaps fiscal and social matters as well, will be regulated by community legislation rather than by the laws of the individual member states.

These events demonstrate the occasional interdependence of integrating sectors. In the judgment of at least one recognized expert on EC affairs, this progress resulted from a recognition that without another leap forward in integration, Europe would continue to suffer the effects of the absence of common planning during recession and to lag behind the United States and Japan in such vitally competitive fields as information technology.

One critic of the pace of Western European integration argues that without a renewed political impulse, the region will be unable to compete in the technological revolution with the United States and Japan. Although great progress has been made in the area of trade, integration in the economic sector has not made sufficient progress to permit the EC to compete effectively. Only with new awareness of the need for political integration can the EC achieve the kind of comprehensive economic policy and investment program to promote production and financial integration so that it will no longer be limited by the forces of the market and American financial agents.[15]

The interplay of the political and the economic is obviously crucial in these events. On the one hand, progress toward economic integration cannot be made without substantial political compromise and accommodation; yet, on the other hand, progress made at untoward speed may ring alarms among those political forces that see beyond economic integration to the loss of national sovereignty. Indeed, in 1988 and 1989, as the EC made strides toward the goal of full economic union in 1992, Britain, together with Luxembourg and Denmark, attempted repeatedly to apply the political brakes, with British Prime Minister Margaret Thatcher frequently reiterating the view that her nation would never subordinate its sovereignty to that of the community.[16] Despite this official view, 75 percent of British citizens questioned favored union in 1992. On a communitywide basis, a series of periodically scheduled opinion surveys from 1978 to 1989 indicated that 70 percent of the public has always favored union.[17]

Security   The fourth major area in integration is the security sector. Integration may follow from existing alliances, but it implies considerably more than

[15]John Pinder, "The Political Economy of Integration in Europe: Policies and Institutions in East and West," *Journal of Common Market Studies,* September 1986, pp. 1–14.

[16]See, for example, *The New York Times,* September 28, 1988, p. I 1.

[17]"Eurobarometer: Public Opinion in the European Communities," *European Affairs,* Autumn 1989, pp. 26–32.

mere alliance. Generally, an alliance is a political instrument through which the dominant member gains political access to the decision-making processes of the lesser members, in return for which the weaker states are guaranteed strategic assistance. Integration calls upon all members, whatever their relative power potentials, to contribute to decision making at all levels of planning, deployment, and command.

Integrated alliances are rare. Despite the frequency of alliances since the Concert of Europe (1815), governments have generally resisted giving total strategic control to common institutions. The Warsaw Pact—the military alliance of the Soviet Union and its Eastern European allies—was about as integrated as an alliance can be. The Soviet Union, through its political control and economic supremacy, regulated the power and the respective roles of the other allies, thus virtually dictating policy. The North Atlantic Treaty Organization (NATO) has more collective decision making, although in nuclear affairs Washington has consistently dominated despite the presence of British and French nuclear forces. Much of the recent history of NATO diplomacy has revolved around attempts by the Western European members to break down this American position. Although troops and conventional war materials have been integrated to a considerable extent, fully integrated decision making does not yet exist.

These observations lead to two preliminary conclusions. First, considering the importance of strategic policy to national survival and to powerful national elites, security integration must follow political integration. The mere creation of alliances does not ensure integrated policymaking, integrated commands, or integrated allocation of resources. Second, given the same political realities, moves toward security integration occur mainly in times of crisis. They are the result not of political and social preferences, but of immediate vital need.

2. The Momentum of Integration

What causes integrating energy to continue to gain? If the impetus exists for sector integration at all, what forces permit it to surpass mere organization and to enter into supranationalism? And what are the prospects that success in one sector will catch on in others?

Each of these questions is answered by a single word, although neither connotes a simple process. First, sector integration, once begun, gains steam by *feedback*. This is analogous to gravity: A falling object gains velocity. In like manner, if a snowball rolls down a sharp decline, it gains mass. Put simply, integration theory posits that if a formal process of sectoral interaction is allowed free forward propulsion, it will gain in intensity.

The analogy is oversimplified, of course. Social phenomena are obstructed from free forward propulsion, in the same way that wind alters the free downward fall of an object or that friction reduces the energy of a rolling snowball. Social scientists have as their laboratory only political systems, and the data invariably show the feedback process to be halting and sporadic. The ideal condition is continuous, growing, and mutually perceived success and equal sharing by all the participants in the continuing benefits. Generally, these inside conditions must be accompanied by external inducements. The impetus to advancement must, on the whole, exceed occasional setbacks.

What of the second question: What forces carry the energy of integration from one sector to another? The answer is found in the *spillover* phenomenon, in which integrative successes in one sector awaken integrating objectives in another: The integrative energy from one sector spills over to another. But once spillover has occurred, there is no assurance that feedbacks within the new sector will keep pace with the first, or that one spillover will energize the next.

The relatively rapid pace of economic integration in Western Europe, as contrasted with political and security integration, illustrates both the necessity for spillover in the aggregate integrative process and the practical limitations of its progress. One writer finds four basic causes for the slower speed of spillover than was originally predicted by the neofunctionalist theory: (1) the mixed quality of performance by the EC from national perspectives; (2) the failure of the EC to select and administer policies that would become self-evidently critical to the national publics; (3) the difficulty of securing either public or governmental identification with processes with constantly shifting definitions and emphases; and (4) the tendency of national governments to prefer intergovernmental cooperation through the EC organs rather than a direct shift of authority to the EC.[18]

Thus far we have considered four basic issues of the integrative process: (1) the distinction between organization and integration (or internationalism and supranationalism), (2) the notion of sector differentiation, (3) the concept of feedback, and (4) the concept of spillover. Behind these concepts is an array of social and political conditions that determine the start of the process, as well as its pace, progress, and end products.

3. Goals of Integration

Integration is a conscious process, so nations and governments must have explicit motives for seeking it. This is especially true because self-preservation is one of the major aims of statehood and of governmental activity. What expectations are sufficiently intense to motivate governments toward integration?

Economic Potential   Historically, the largest single motive has been the desire to maximize economic potential. In the presence of a few giant economies, smaller states have been unable to keep pace with competition. Whether they are less developed states or old industrial states, the hope of fully competing may be a call to integration.

After the Second World War, the Western European states rebuilt their industries only to discover that once-great national economies were lost in the

[18]William Wallace, "Less Than a Federation, More Than a Regime: The Community as a Political System," in H. Wallace, W. Wallace, and C. Webb, *Policy-Making in the European Community,* 2nd ed. (London: Wiley, 1983), pp. 1–41.

American shadow. The economy of the Western world had become asymmetrical, with the United States commanding the greatest produce for export, the largest and most technically developed labor force, and the most innovative entrepreneurial skill. For reconstructed Western Europe to compete, it was necessary to merge national economies. Although this meant hardships for agriculture, six governments agreed in 1957 to establish the European Economic Community (the Common Market), with an elaborate plan for integrating trade among themselves and for a common trade policy with respect to nonmembers. In the first 16 years of their integrating experience, during which the EC consisted only of the original six members, they were able to develop a combined economic potential second only to that of the United States.

Subsequently, however, the membership grew to the current 12. With the admission of Greece, Spain, and Portugal in particular, the geographic reach, the total population, and the aggregate gross national product (GNP) soared. By 1989, the Twelve had a combined population of over 320 million and a combined GNP of over 4 trillion. But because of the economic disparity between the original members and the new, the per capita GNP had begun to decline relative to those of both the United States and Japan. Nevertheless, the fear of being left behind economically by the United States and Japan in the 1990s spurred interest in advancing integration at a level unseen since the 1960s. In the face of trepidations from some regarding the potential long-range consequences for national sovereignty, economic imperative ruled the day. Long-standing obstacles regarding agricultural subsidies were resolved; agreements were made removing all legal obstacles to the free flow of capital among the members; preliminary agreements were reached on eliminating border crossing posts to facilitate the free flow of labor; and agreements were struck on common recognition of all university degrees, again to facilitate and encourage the interunion flow of talent. These details notwithstanding, the important thing here is that the maximization of combined economic benefit was the principal motive of progress.

Political Potential A second major motive for integration is the desire to maximize political potential. With rare exception, small and politically powerless states have had little impact on the international system, especially during the bipolar era that followed the Second World War. Small states have felt either left out of, or victimized by, a world of two massive power centers. Some view integration as the route to reestablishing a multipolar world in which their diplomacy might achieve more favorable results.

The experience of the EC demonstrates the dual-edged nature of political combination as a motive for integration. Although some Europeans view political integration as a route to a stronger role in a politically multipolar world, others see it as too great a price with respect to national sovereignty. The latter would generally prefer to settle for economic integration.

Conflict Resolution A third impetus to integration is the desire to resolve potential conflict among territorial neighbors. If there be nascent conflict among states forced by geography to be interdependent, integration of vital sectors of their interaction may outweigh the existing sources of strife.

The most notable instance of such motivation was the founding in 1951 of the European Coal and Steel Community by the same six states that founded the EEC a few years later. Although the ECSC was the first implementation of a long-range plan for European economic integration, it was addressed more immediately to a specific problem: the age-old Franco-German rivalry over coal and steel resources. At a press conference in 1950, French Foreign Minister Robert Schuman declared:

> The gathering of the nations of Europe requires the elimination of the age-old opposition of France and Germany. The first concern in any action undertaken must be these two countries.
>
> With this aim in view, the French Government proposes to take action immediately on one limited but decisive point. The French Government proposes to place Franco-German production of coal and steel under a common "high authority," within the framework of an organization open to the participation of the other countries of Europe.

The Schuman Declaration, previously approved by the French Council of Ministers, resulted in the ECSC. Most important, however, is the specific intent that Schuman emphasized—the interdependence of European economic integration with elimination of this historic cause of war.

How effectively does progress toward supranationalism actually diminish conflict among the participants? Although integration does not eliminate strife, it does reduce its frequency. Denying that this proves a casual link, one scholar, examining a non-European context, contends that "when combined with awareness and concern on the part of Central American elites about the relationship between economic integration and violent conflict, it does provide some useful evidence for the existence of the probable relationship."[19]

But not all students of integration are persuaded that organizations reduce the likelihood of war among members. Using five measurements of integration (common institutional membership, proximity, economic interdependence, sociocultural similarity, and UN voting behavior), for example, another scholar reviewed the history of conflict among 41 pairs of states. He found that "all five of these conditions may be necessary to prevent war between states . . . , but not even all five together are sufficient to do so." The greater the interdependence among nations, the more sensitive their interests will become, and the greater will be their prospects of conflict.[20] Unfortunately, the closest neighbors may have the largest number of chances to fight—and may do so despite their interdependence. Thus, the desire to resolve conflict is not invariably an adequate cause for integration. Even in such circumstances the duties and expectations placed on integrative processes may exceed the stabilizing capabilities of organization.

---

[19]Joseph S. Nye, *Peace in Parts: Integration and Conflict in Regional Organization* (Boston: Little, Brown, 1971), p. 120.

[20]Bruce M. Russett, *International Regions and the International System* (Chicago: Rand McNally, 1967), chap. 12, "Conflicts and Integration," especially pp. 198–201.

Even though Western Europe now exemplifies a high degree of integration, conflict has not disappeared. Raymond Aron, the late French political scientist, warned that Europe is a place and an idea, but that it is not a unity. Another European has written a Ten Commandments for the EC, the first of which is, "*Do not confuse Europe with Uniformity. Europe is not uniform and attempts to make it so will be rightly resented and resisted.*"[21]

Others have adopted the same tone. Noting that community is built upon a growing sense of cooperation, we are reminded:

> The members of the Community do not confront each other only or chiefly as diplomatic gladiators; they encounter each other at almost every level of organized society through constant interaction in the joint policymaking contexts of officials, parliamentarians, interest group leaders, businessmen, farmers, and trade unionists. Conflicts of interest and purpose are inevitable. *There is no paradox between the progress of economic integration in the Community and sharpening political disagreement;* indeed, the success of economic integration can be a cause of political disagreement. The member states are engaged in the enterprise for widely different reasons, and their actions have been supported or instigated by elites seeking their own particular goals. Therefore, conflicts would seem endemic as the results of joint activity come to be felt and as the prointegration consensus shifts.[22]

Progress aside, integration is a dynamic process. Goals change, roles shift, new leaders and elites emerge; old influences wane, and new ones burst onto the scene. Integration may thus proceed in a regional system of constant conflict. Indeed, because progress toward supranationalism creates stresses of its own, the process may have negative effects on the overall relations of members. Reason dictates that although the resolution of regional conflicts may be one of the expectations of integrating members, the very process itself may be the cause of strife.

4. Background Conditions for Integration

Alone, common expectations about regional future are not sufficient to promote integration. Certain preconditions must be satisfied, although subconsciously for the most part.

Social Assimilation   To some observers, the foremost precondition of regional integration is social causation, resulting in a so-called sociocausal paradigm of integration.[23] Focusing on transnational attitudes, this posits that

---

[21]John Pinder, "Ten Commandments for 'The Nine,' " *European Community,* vol. 161, December 1972, pp. 18–19.

[22]Leon N. Lindberg, "Decision Making and Integration in the European Community," *International Organization,* vol. 19, 1965, p. 80. The emphasis has been added.

[23]See particularly the classic study by Karl Deutsch, et al., *Political Community and the North Atlantic Area* (Princeton, N.J.: Princeton University Press, 1957). See also Deutsch's several contributions to Philip E. Jacob and James V. Tascano, eds., *The Integration of Political Communities*

social assimilation is a precondition of integration. Critics of this concept reject the assumed necessity of social assimilation. Nevertheless, most observers agree that minimal social prerequisites do exist and that among them are mutual tolerance of cultures, common identity of foreign-policy goals, and generally cordial contacts of governments and respective nationals.

Value Sharing A second precondition is value sharing, especially among elites. In the economic sector, for example, unless the elites of participating states share common values, such as capitalism or socialism, or free markets as contrasted with central controls and subsidies, they will expend little energy on integration, and little pressure will be exerted on governments. Again, this is a sociopolitical condition.

Mutual Benefit Expectation of mutual benefit is the third precondition. Because states will enter into a process that fundamentally alters national prerogatives only with sufficient incentives, states must be able to predict that benefits will accrue from the process. Some states may expect to profit in one sector, whereas others seek advancement in another. Remember, however, that the integrative process involves not only international politics but intense domestic bargaining as well. A government may be willing to sacrifice major industrial gains to achieve agricultural integration, but the industrial elites may resist. Thus, their expectation of benefit is just as important as are aggregate national expectations.

Congenial Past Relations A fourth precondition is experiential: a history of frequent pacific transactions. This acknowledges the functionalist precept that nothing succeeds like success itself; and it posits that elites, nations, and governments are unlikely to integrate without already operating cordiality.

Importance of Integration Itself Closely related to congenial past relations is the fifth criterion—the salience of transactions. If interests are only remotely related, integration is unlikely; but if participants recognize the importance of activities in other countries, impetus for integration may awaken. The prospects for integration in these cases are governed by "the law of inverse salience," which holds that the growth of integration is inversely related to the political importance of the subject matter. Another functionalist proposition, this argues that because integration proceeds only with prior progress, it is seen first in matters that are politically expendable. Only through feedbacks and spillovers does the process begin to invade politically sensitive areas.[24]

(Philadelphia: Lippincott, 1964), including "Communication Theory and Political Integration," "Transaction Flows as Indicators of Political Cohesion," and "Integration and the Social System: Implications of Functional Analysis." For an evaluation and critique of the sociocausal paradigm, see William E. Fisher, "An Analysis of the Deutsch Sociocausal Paradigm of Political Integration," *International Organization,* vol. 23, 1969, pp. 254–290.

[24]Nye, *Peace in Parts,* pp. 23–24.

Low Relative Costs   Because there are bound to be costs as well as benefits, another precondition must be the anticipation of low costs relative to benefits, measured economically, socially, or nationalistically.[25] Likewise, such costs will probably be assessed principally in domestic policy, yet a prospective participant may wish to predict the effects on other foreign policies or other regions. Britain's delayed entry into Europe resulted partly from the potential effect on the British agricultural sector, on its relations with members of the British Commonwealth, and on its special relationship with the United States.

External Influences   The last issue raises what generally has been an underestimated precondition of integration: external influences. Virtually every integration movement can be attributed in part to external stimuli. In Western Europe, for example, economic integration may have had external stimuli. The threat of American domination of European economies after the Marshall Plan was completed unquestionably increased the demand for economic consolidation. Also, the desire to coordinate trade policy with respect to the United States contributed to the establishment of the Central American Common Market and the Latin American Free Trade Association. External conditions may even have spillover effects. For example, although French military policies during the 1950s in Algeria and Indochina may have contributed to the French defeat of the European Defense Community (EDC), they also helped change the older notion of forceful maintenance of an overseas empire and inspired new demands that the de Gaulle government turn French national resources and energies inward to Europe.

5. Maintaining the Momentum of Integration

Starting along the integrative path and maintaining continued progress toward the goal of supranationalism are quite separate issues. In addition to certain preconditions that permit the process to begin, certain combinations of "process factors" must be present to govern steady progress.

Functional Satisfaction   First among these process factors is functional satisfaction, that is, recognition by pertinent elites and officials of the degree to which integrated policy is serving their interests. This recognition promotes feedback, thus fueling greater sectoral integration and encouraging spillover.

Public opinion polls taken at irregular intervals during the Western European integrating experience reveal a steady faith in the process. Even during the years following the first OPEC petroleum boycott, when the Western industrial states suffered declining productivity and inclining inflation and unemployment, functional satisfaction continued to be high in the participating countries. Although there were some irregularities in the late 1970s, satisfac-

---

[25]For a systematic study of costs and benefits in supranationalism, whether or not in regional settings, see Todd Sandler and Jon Cauley, ''The Design of Supranational Structures: An Economic Perspective,'' in *International Studies Quarterly,* June 1977, pp. 251–276.

tion with functional performance was directly correlated with national economic condition and with the duration of membership in the EC. Satisfaction was lower in Britain, Ireland, and Denmark, which joined in 1973, but these were also the member states that suffered the worst inflation during this troubled period. Later, when Greece, Spain, and Portugal were admitted to membership, satisfaction reached new heights, particularly because of satisfactory settlement of common agricultural policies in 1988 and 1989.

The issue of monetary union in Western Europe provides an example of functional satisfaction. The European Monetary System was originally established in 1979 as a means of stabilizing exchange rates and promoting economic integration in an era of high inflation. It made little progress toward greater integration, despite a competent performance, until the late 1980s, at which time the role of the monetary system within the context of the 1992 goal of economic union was raised. As part of the push toward 1992, the members agreed on the liberalization of capital movements within the community; and pursuant to the Single European Act, they agreed to remove all technical, administrative, and legal barriers to the free flow of labor, goods, services, and capital. By the beginning of 1990, talks were in progress regarding the future of the European Monetary System and its role relative to the central banks of the member states.

Control of capital is to national governments the economic equivalent of sovereignty in the political realm. Why, then, would the member governments risk going beyond a unified trade market toward a unified monetary system? Two British authors respond with reference to functional satisfaction. They demonstrated that in the first ten years of the EMS (European Monetary System), three major successes had occurred: (1) inflation had been reduced and maintained at controlled levels; (2) there had been a sharp reduction in exchange rate volatility among the member currencies; and (3) money-supply growth rates had been held down and their unpredictability reduced. All these had contributed to low inflation and general economic stability. The authors conclude that it was as a result of this successful EMS performance that the community members were willing by 1988 to risk its growth as a regulatory influence in the final phases of integrating the Western European economies.[26]

Increased Pacific Transactions   A second process factor is an increased frequency of pacific transactions. The rate and number of transactions are measures of mutual reliance, revealing governmental willingness to compromise sovereignty in specific sectors. Because increasing interdependence is indispensable, the rate of transactions is a critical measure of progress. One study, however, has cautioned against overvaluing transactions as a causal factor in the growth of integration; increased transactions are more a reflection of integration than a cause.[27] Yet it is probable that satisfaction in these contacts,

---

[26]Frank McDonald and George Zis, "The European Monetary System: Toward 1992 and Beyond," *Journal of Common Market Studies*, March 1989, pp. 183–202, at p. 184. This entire issue of the *Journal of Common Market Studies* is devoted to the European Monetary System.

[27]Donald J. Puchala, "International Transactions and Regional Integration," *International Orga-*

originally an effect of integration, now encourages additional contacts and is thus a major determinant of sectoral feedback.

Regulation   Gradually, the transactions of integrating sectors must become institutionalized. Informal regulation cannot continuously serve the objective of formal integration. Hence, a third major process condition is the proliferation of institutions with sufficient authority to regulate. Ultimately, these institutions must assume the national governments' normal legislative and executive prerogatives. Complete transfer of such authority from national governments to common institutions is the final stage of the integrating process, and with its completion a supranational community may be said to exist. At present, the maximum progress toward complete integration of a subsector is represented in the High Authority of the ECSC, which has been authorized by its members to exercise sovereign authority over the allocation of the pertinent resources.

The achievement of full multisectoral supranationalism requires establishment of sufficient institutional machinery to govern the community. This means development of legislative, executive, and judicial institutions, each vested with full authority in its realm. At present, one of the most interesting developments in Western Europe is the drive, inspired principally by Great Britain, to wrest legislative control from the Council of Ministers of the European Communities and to invest full legislative authority in the European Parliament. Advocates of the ultimate federation of Europe hope that eventually this body will be a true multinational legislature.

Bureaucracy   The institutionalization of a political process requires the creation of a bureaucracy, specially trained to manage sectoral activities. Because a high degree of technical competence is needed in addition to administrative skills, these bureaucracies are customarily referred to as "technocracies." Technocrats not only manage the day-to-day affairs; they must also coordinate the expectations of elites, soothe the sensitivities of governments, and make the unremitting case for further development. They are at once technical experts, intergovernmental managers, and the guardians of the integrative process.

Bureaucratic development in a community that is both multinational and multilingual is far from automatic. From the start, the integrating European states established national formulas and quotas for employment in several of the important organs of community. These were designed for equity and balance, but they have had some divisive consequences. The tensions of multinational staffing have accentuated the contrast of national loyalties with community loyalty. In addition, it has been shown that nation-based informal organizations of staff members develop spontaneously, and the tensions among these groups have significant impacts on community work.[28] Moreover, such

---

nization, vol. 24, 1970, pp. 732–763.

[28]Hans J. Michelmann, "Multinational Staffing and Organizational Functioning in the Commis-

organizations may serve as vehicles for special-interest groups in the decision making of the community.[29]

The recent experience of the EC demonstrates the importance of institution building on the path to integration. The organ most commonly credited with the acceleration of progress in 1988 and immediately thereafter is the European Commission, an organ with a commissioner and some 17 cabinet officers appointed by the member governments. It has become evident that without the work of the commission, political compromise would have been much more difficult than it has been. Furthermore, Commissioner Jacques Delors, a French socialist and former foreign minister, is so generally credited with having managed crucial compromises between the liberal views of West German Chancellor Helmut Kohl and Britain's conservative Prime Minister Margaret Thatcher, that he has been compared in his influence with Jean Monnet, one of the founders and visionaries of the EC.

Community Jurisprudence   Another though less visible process condition is the development of a community jurisprudence, a commonly recognized body of law that governs the legal relations of the respective states. If governments or corporations of different states become involved in legal problems, it is not productive in an integrating community to rely on the judicial practices of one state or another. Furthermore, if a community institution and a state have a legal disagreement, the development of a body of law and of community courts is eventually necessary in the development of supranational politics. The Court of Justice of the European Communities serves this need and has already developed a large body of case law governing the relations of the communities, the member states, and individual technocrats.

The evolution of a community legal system that supersedes the legal systems of the member countries is fraught with collisions of nationalism and the political primacy of the state. After all, the goal of integration is to subordinate many of the state's traditional functions and prerogatives to a higher political community, but the complex conditions of this evolution ensure that there will be setbacks, periods of little progress, and occasional conflicts between state interests and community goals.

In the area of jurisprudence the potential for strife between state and community is particularly acute, especially when basic constitutional premises are at stake. Although the primacy of community jurisprudence was firmly established as early as 1963, a decision of the Court of Justice of the European Communities in 1978 provoked a sharp constitutional debate in Britain, which at the time had belonged to the EC for only five years. In the *Simmentha* case, the court declared that "every national court must, in a case within its jurisdiction, apply Community law in its entirety and protect rights which the latter confers on individuals and must accordingly set aside any provision of national

---

sion of the European Communities," *International Organization*, Spring 1978, pp. 477–496.

[29]Juliet Lodge and Valentine Herman, "The Economic and Social Committee in EEC Decision Making," *International Organization*, Spring 1980, pp. 265–284, deals generally with the role of interest groups in functional integration.

law which may conflict with it, whether prior or subsequent to the Community rule.'' Such a prescription boldly subordinates all acts of Parliament, those that occurred before entry into the community as well as those that succeeded entry, to the law of the EC. Membership had indeed had a deep impact on Britain, whose tradition of common law is centuries old.[30]

All member states are affected by ascendency of community law. One study uses the case law of the Court of Justice of the European Communities to demonstrate the extent to which the Commission of the Communities and the Advocates General for the Communities have expanded the court's power on matters of direct application of community law, on supremacy of community law over national members' law, and even on treaty making.[31] Another study concludes that the European Court of Justice has evolved into one of ''the world's great constitution makers.'' Noting that few courts enjoy the power of judicial review (that is, the power to declare a legislative act unconstitutional), a reviewer of this study concludes that ''[o]nly the European Court of Justice . . . has taken what proclaims itself as something else, namely, a treaty, and turned it into a constitution so that it itself could engage in constitutional judicial review. And no other court . . . has ever played so prominent a role in the creation of the basic governmental and political process of which it is a part.''[32]

Increased Decisions Increased transactions, formation of institutions and technocracies, and the establishment of a common core of jurisprudence all point to the next process condition: increased decisional output. It cannot be said that integration is under way merely because of institutional appearances; rather, measurable and reliable decisions, on which governments and pertinent elites willingly depend and with which they comply consistently, are indispensable. Institutions can have no productive effect on national elites unless they are able to command the external transactions of those elites. Only through actual decisions does the institution become the authoritative vehicle of an international process.

Mass Attitudes All the foregoing process factors imply increased relations and communications among elites. But the process of integration requires that mass political and social attitudes also be nurtured. Thus, a seventh important process factor is the development of mutual mass attitudes. Although progress toward integration may build on elite pressures, governments are not likely to sacrifice national prerogatives or to respond to narrow demands for suprana-

---

[30]J. D. B. Mitchell, ''The Sovereignty of Parliament and Community Law: The Stumbling Block That Isn't There,'' *International Affairs* (London), January 1979.

[31]Eric Stein, ''Lawyers, Judges and the Making of a Transnational Constitution,'' *American Journal of International Law,* January 1983, pp. 1–27.

[32]Quoted from Martin Shapiro's review in *American Journal of International Law,* October 1987, pp. 1007–1011, at pp. 1008–1009, of Hjalte Rasmussen, *Law and Policy in the European Court of Justice: A Comparative Study in Judicial Policymaking* (Dordrecht, Boston, and Lancaster: Martinus Nijhoff Publishers, 1986).

tionality until appropriate attitudes have been established among their electorates. This development must take place in most of or all the participating nations. In this way, mutual expectations are regularly communicated across national boundaries; the benefits of continued progress become more familiar to individuals; and nationalistic attitudes begin to recede.[33] British entry into the community was paradoxical in this regard, because polls showed in 1973 that the population did not favor membership. It was thus expected that although Britain's membership might eventually accelerate integration, there would be a time lag during which British elite and popular attitudes would need to catch up with those on the continent.[34] In fact, it was not until 1975 that a British referendum demonstrated decisively the public desire for full membership in the EC.

Despite the continuing trend of opinion polls to indicate sustained public interest in European integration, at least one important event in 1984 seemed to indicate a setback. The direct election of the European Parliament in 1979 is generally regarded as a landmark in integrative progress, but the election in 1984 is broadly considered as having been disappointing. Pre-election enthusiasm was diminished, and public participation declined considerably. One analysis of the results demonstrated that interest was more along the lines of transnational party interest than of mass or nationally oriented interest. The author of this analysis concluded that the sense of distance from the EC as a political system is not diminishing at present.[35]

External Factors   External factors of either of two types may influence the integrative process. First, they may be external events that absorb the energies of one of the participants in the community. These events may prevent full and earnest participation or, in some cases, accentuate regional preferences. French foreign policy provides examples of both phenomena. Before the Gaullist era, French participation in European integration was impeded by preoccupation with problems in North Africa and Indochina. But for a decade commencing in the mid-1950s, President de Gaulle turned these problems around and directed energies inward. Those years witnessed the most vigorous steps toward European supranationalism. Hence, integration may depend on external events in which one of the community members is vitally engaged. These are *member-centered* external events.

Other external events are not member centered but may nevertheless have major impacts on the integrative process. The foreign policies (potentially even

---

[33]A pioneering effort to measure the impact on the individual reward structure of internationalization of business enterprise in Europe (specifically Germany) is found in Bernard Menns and Karl P. Sauvant, "Describing and Explaining Support for Regional Integrations: An Investigation of German Business Elite Attitudes Toward the European Community," *International Organization*, vol. 29, 1975, pp. 972–995.

[34]For a study of mass opinion as well as elite opinion with respect to European integrative progress, see Donald J. Puchala, "The Common Market and Political Federation in Western European Public Opinion," *International Studies Quarterly*, vol. 14, 1970, pp. 32–59.

[35]Geoffrey Pridham, "European Elections, Political Parties, and Trends of Internationalization in Community Affairs," *Journal of Common Market Studies*, June 1986, pp. 279–296.

domestic policies) of other nations may touch on one or more of the members of a growing community with either integrative or disintegrative effects. The unpopularity among Europeans of American policy in Southeast Asia during the 1960s heightened their sense of Europeanness and correspondingly diminished their psychological bonds with Washington. Except in the security sector (NATO), then, the Vietnam War (as a *nonmember-centered* external factor) had integrative effects on Europe. Warsaw Pact occupation of Czechoslovakia in 1968, a resort to long invisible Soviet politics, was an event of similar meaning to Western Europe. Conversely, the Soviet-inspired imposition of martial law on Poland in response to the liberal demands of the Solidarity Labor Union (which resulted in a 1983 Nobel Prize for Peace for the movement's leader, Lech Walesa), had little integrating impact on Western Europe. Indeed, these events unfolded even while a new peace movement resisted the deployment in Western Europe of new American nuclear-tipped missiles.

A most instructive nonmember-centered external event occurred in 1962, with telling effect on European economic integration. Already concerned about future competition from Europe, American merchants sought long-term relief from tariff barriers. As a result, the Kennedy administration sought and secured from Congress discretionary authority to negotiate substantial reciprocal tariff reductions. The Trade Expansion Act of 1962 authorized executive discretion for a period of five years, during which major changes in American trade policy might be negotiated.

The EEC members entered into the subsequent negotiations, called the Kennedy Round, with full awareness of the American intent to safeguard industrial exports against future competition. This awareness sparked renewed activity in the EEC toward eliminating internal restraints to trade and resulted particularly in the resolution of many of the thorny agricultural problems that had previously retarded progress toward a full free trade arrangement.

These negotiations, together with American direct investment in Europe designed to "get behind" the tariff barriers, comprised a clear signal to EEC members that major industrial competitors feared the successful culmination of the free trade area and provided added incentives for conscious development. Resentment over this form of exploitation also sparked European attacks on the American balance-of-payments deficit, accentuated European criticism of American policy in Vietnam, gave credence to President de Gaulle's efforts to de-Americanize Europe, and generally raised the level of Europe-consciousness. These were significant social and political spillovers.

Transfer of Loyalty The final process condition is really the measure of all the others: the transfer of loyalty gradually from national to community values, objectives, and institutions. It means the adoption by national majorities of far-reaching supranationalist attitudes. As this itself is a functional requisite, such a development does not occur except through individual recognition of the profitability of integration. Nor will it occur in several nations unless there is sufficient communication by which societies can measure attitudinal progress in neighboring lands. Social communication is thus vital to the transfer of loyalties.

The loyalty-transfer process is one of continuing socialization in which positive value communication substantiates the need for community-oriented attitudes. Several studies have concluded that Europeans look less and less to national governments for critical decisions and increasingly to community institutions. Socialization data point almost incontrovertibly to further integration in economic, social, and political sectors in Western Europe.[36] Public opinion polls in 1962, for example, showed overwhelming preference for unification and widespread expectation that it would occur within 10 or 15 years. Furthermore, responses to questions pertaining to internal matters of the European Communities showed huge favorability of integrated policy.[37] A survey of French attitudes was conducted (within three weeks of British entry in 1973). On questions of direct election of the European Parliament, the evolution of a formal community government, and community supremacy in such critical areas as defense, diplomacy, economics, and nuclear and space development, the number of respondents who preferred community-oriented solutions consistently exceeded those who favored state-oriented policy, although approximately one-third of respondents gave no opinion.[38] Repeatedly, therefore, socialization data have underscored the public preference for, and acceptance of, regional integration to the extent of spillover from the economic to the political sector.[39]

As important as these indicators may be, they deal with the business of state rather than the nature of the state. Loyalty transfer at the economic level—even at the extreme level of the proposed full economic union by 1992—falls short of the most elemental issue in loyalty transfer: recognition of a political authority higher than the state and its assumption of duties previously exercised by the state and, indeed, demonstrating its sovereignty. The direct election of the European Parliament over a decade ago was the first substantial step taken by the EC toward transformation of sovereignty. The growth in the influence of the European Commission is another, particularly in view of the political advantage it has taken of the Single European Act. By late 1989, opinion surveys were beginning to reveal the attitude of the public toward this change in the balance of political forces between the community, on the one

---

[36]Leon N. Lindberg and Stuart A. Scheingold, *Europe's Would-Be Polity: Patterns of Change in the European Community* (Englewood Cliffs, N.J.: Prentice-Hall, 1970), especially chap. 8 and 9; Carl J. Friedrich, *Europe: An Emergent Nation?* (New York: Harper & Row, 1969); Karl W. Deutsch et al., "Integration and Arms Control in the European Political Environment," *American Political Science Review,* vol. 60, 1966, p. 355.

[37]*Communauté Européenne,* December 1962. For well-organized reproduced data, see W. Hartley Clark, *The Politics of the Common Market* (Englewood Cliffs, N.J.: Prentice-Hall, 1967), pp. 111–113.

[38]*Le Figaro,* February 27, 1973, as reproduced in Ernest H. Preeg, *Economic Blocs and U.S. Foreign Policy* (Washington, D.C.: National Planning Association, 1974), p. 109.

[39]For summary socialization data pertaining to transfer of loyalties, see particularly Ronald Inglehart, "An End to European Integration?" *American Political Science Review,* vol. 61, 1967, pp. 91–105. The paper is framed as a response to the article by Deutsch et al.; also Puchala, "The Common Market and Political Federation in Western European Public Opinion"; and Inglehart and Rabier, "Economic Uncertainty and European Solidarity."

Table 17–1 Summary of integration factors.

Integration Sectors	Momentum	Objectives	Preconditions	Process Conditions
Economic	Feedback	Maximize	Social assimilation	Functional
Social	(intrasector)	economic	Elite value sharing	satisfaction
Political	Spillover	potential	Expectation of	Increased
Security	(intersector)	Maximize	mutual benefits	frequency of
		political	History of pacific	transactions
		potential	transactions	Institution building
		Resolve	Favorable ratio of	Technocracy
		regional	costs to benefits	building
		conflict	External	Community
			influences	jurisprudence
			a. Member-	Growing decisional
			centered	output
			b. Nonmember-	Mass attitude
			centered	assimilation
				External factors
				a. Member-
				centered
				b. Nonmember-
				centered
				Transfer of loyalty

hand, and its member states, on the other. Fully 82 percent of those questioned recognized the importance of community affairs even though only 45 percent of respondents considered themselves interested in political affairs and only 42 percent expressed interest in specific community policies.[40]

Summary of Critical Elements

With the conclusion of this discussion of sectors, objectives, preconditions, and process conditions of integration, we are now ready to summarize the critical issues of the supranational quest (see Table 17–1).

Before turning to an evaluation of integration, a few theoretical notes are necessary. Earlier in this chapter it was noted that the integration of Western Europe has generated the greatest interest and the richest literature among the 15 supranational movements in the nonsocialist world, with the result that virtually all the foregoing presentation concentrated on the EC. The apparent implication is that the Western European model is reproducible elsewhere and that to understand the integrative trends of Western Europe is to understand similar phenomena in other parts of the world.

---

[40]"Eurobarometer: Public Opinion in the European Communities," *European Affairs,* Autumn 1989, pp. 26–32.

Studies of integration in the Third World suggest, on the contrary, that the Western European model does not have universal application owing to the fundamentally different political economies of Western Europe and of the developing world. Although Europe has its own technological and industrial bases, integrating economies in the Third World are dependent economies, dependent for growth and development on the spread of technology from elsewhere, as well as on foreign capital and aid. As has been demonstrated earlier in this book, these circumstances produce political strains between integrating developing economies, on the one hand, and the industrialized economies that control the flow of capital and technology, on the other, and limit the capacity for political and economic independence of the former. Thus, integration without dependence calls for extraordinary political cooperation among the participating states. The process must begin with political cooperation among transnational coalitions that, together, are able both to promote the integrative objectives and to overcome the sources of dependence. The patterns of underlying political cooperation in the Third World thus differ from those in Western Europe, where spillover from the economic sector to the political sector has been the norm. Hence, it may be that the nature of integration in the developing world undermines the assumption of political spillover in the neofunctional model, as demonstrated in the experience of Western Europe.[41]

Nevertheless, although the tensions of economic development in the Third World may not duplicate precisely those of Western Europe, there is even more reason to think that functionalism and integration may have useful roles there. We know, for example, that the one great experiment in integrating economic policy—OPEC—was an enormous temporary success in spurring economic development. This was not a true example of integration, but it did represent a form of international organization around a single asset aimed at a common goal. Furthermore, as the issue of planetary degradation owing to pollution and deforestation spreads increasingly to the Third World, where conservation has traditionally been regarded as a luxury of the industrial nations, the demand for cooperative economic policies within specific geographic regions is likely to grow. These two examples suggest that where there is relative regional peace and ethnic harmony within the Third World, where the law of comparative economic advantage suggests a value in common resource and trade policies, and where integration would promote development without deepening dependence on foreign capital, the functional integration model might serve the Third World well.

An Evaluation of Integration

This examination of integration assumes that supranationalism is healthy and that it is to be encouraged and lauded. But if integration occurs, its impact on people and international order is worth exploring.

---

[41]W. Andrew Axline, "Underdevelopment, Dependence, and Integration: The Politics of Regionalism in the Third World," *International Organization*, Winter 1977, pp. 83–105.

First consider the effects of integration on the population of an integrated community. Although it is conventionally assumed that these persons will, for the most part, profit from integration, some observers raise negative aspects. Integration may very well raise standards of living, indices of production, and so on, but what will life be like? Does supranationalism necessarily make the individual's life more pleasant?

Although these questions remain unanswerable, perhaps skepticism is appropriate. The consolidation of economies and politics does, to be sure, have the effect of eliminating competition and some differences among participants, but it creates a new form of political community. Is this new form merely an enlarged nation-state? Is there anything fundamentally different between an integrated community and a large nation-state that is multilingual and culturally and socially heterogeneous?

These are not merely abstract questions. In their concerns with mass anxiety, crises of identity, breakup of the nuclear family, lack of pride in work, and the generation gap, social observers today have begun to explore the social and psychological consequences of mass industrialization. They have turned their attention to whether there are ill effects from the philosophy of the modern industrial state: "There's more of it where that came from!" Does integration for purposes of successful international economic competition rush a society blindly toward these effects? Does it hasten the alienation of men and women from the politics, institutions, and lip-service ideals of mass society?

Another concern is with the antidemocratic effects of centralization and bureaucratization. As policy becomes less the result of public participation and more a consequence of administrative pragmatism, does a society relinquish to functional technocracies its grip on its own destiny? What is the likelihood that increased reliance on technocracy will degenerate into new forms of oligarchy? Are there major divergences between the values, needs, and expectations of technocrats, on the one hand, and those of society, on the other? What is the future of the political role of nonelite social sectors?

These and other quality-of-life questions have led to a call for a normative critique of integration theory and for research into the social consequences of regional supranationalism. To be socially tolerable in the long run, life in supranational communities must be preferable and superior to life in contemporary nation-states. Otherwise, the achievement of higher political community may be merely a new organizational stage in the destruction of societies.[42]

The view from outside raises equally troubling questions. Even if one accepts the intragroup benefits of integration, what are the effects on intergroup relations? Do the consolidated policies of like-minded states necessarily contribute to international order, or do they merely accentuate the effects of the nation-state? What are the prospects that European economic integration will lead to trade warfare even with the United States if European production and

---

[42]These questions have been broached in a most incisive manner in John W. Sloan and Harry R. Targ, "Beyond the European Nation-State: A Normative Critique," *Polity,* vol. 3, Summer 1971, pp. 501–520.

trade volumes should have long-term detrimental effects on the American economy, its exports, and its balance of payments? The answer may already exist in American foreign policy: the unilateral increase in tariffs on imports from all industrialized countries in 1971 and 1972, and the frequency of threats of trade war between the United States and the EC throughout the 1980s. How will the United States, Japan, and the EC's other external industrial trading partners react if complete economic union is achieved by the end of 1992? Will Western Europe's success stimulate trans-Atlantic trade or further unbalance the American account? The possibility exists that even if regional integration tends to have associating characteristics among its members, it may have disassociating consequences in overall international stability.

The potential for global disassociation is especially apparent in security communities, which exist as the result of previously identified enemies. Because the enmities exist before the security arrangements do, disassociation is a product of earlier political relations. Yet, like all other institutions in society, security institutions tend to become self-sustaining. The elites that manage them continue to have interests, and their operations may depend on perpetuating the initial causes. In security communities, the original cause is a threat; and the perpetuation of security institutions may thus depend on the ability to convince public and appropriating agencies of the persistence of potential crisis. Should this occur—if persons propagandize and even romanticize crisis potential for institutional or personal aggrandizement—then institutions may prolong crises, contributing to the disassociating effects of the original antipathy. Institutionalized alliances always carry this danger; and because integrated institutions magnify the political potential of elites, supranational security communities may impede global stability.

There may also be a dangerous aspect to the connection between supranational institutions and domestic institutions. Successful integrative trends require close cooperation between regional technocrats and domestic leaders, yet they may learn to use one another for personal purposes. Thus, the command officers of an integrated military community may gain inordinate access to legislative politics, to the great detriment of domestic policy. Strong and semisecretive national-regional competition among interacting elites may hasten the erosion of beneficial aspects of national life.

Despite the dangers implicit in integration from both domestic and international perspectives, at present the prevailing attitude is that regional integrative trends are healthy, productive, and promising of a brighter future for national peoples and for global stability. Indeed, one French student of EC affairs has gone so far as to write that "Europe as a whole could well become the first example in history of a major centre of the balance of power becoming in the era of its decline not a colonised victim but the exemplar of a new stage in political civilisation."[43] But two others have entered an incisive condition:

---

[43]François Duchêne, "The European Community and the Uncertainties of Interdependence," in Max Kohnstamm and Wolfgang Hager, eds., *A Nation Writ Large? Foreign Policy Problems Before the European Community* (New York: Wiley, 1973), pp. 1–21.

''[T]he Community's capacity to act constructively in the world depends in the last resort on its success in establishing within its boundaries a more united and more just society.''[44] It is safe to conclude that integration over any geographical region will encounter a similar variety of pressures.

The American Perception of Integration

Having maximized its own political, social, and economic potentialities through federative integration and having undergone a bloody civil war to preserve union, it is natural for the United States to favor integration. Indeed, at the close of the Second World War the United States not only encouraged but also paid about $15 billion to reconstruct Europe through the Marshall Plan (European Recovery Program). From the start, the United States assumed that the Western European participants would plan together a forerunner to the economic integration that the United States intended to encourage. Taking cues from Winston Churchill, Jean Monnet, and others, Americans such as Secretary of State George C. Marshall, William L. Clayton, and Christian Herter joined from this side of the Atlantic in constructing the foundations for a United States of Europe.

The dramatic recovery of Western Europe depended in large measure on America's assistance and willingness to undergo a decade or more of disadvantageous trade principles so that Europe might speed its reconstruction. Although the principles of the international monetary system and of free world trade were dictated principally by the United States, they benefited Western Europe even more. They opened wide American markets to European produce, and they protected the infant European industries from American competition. Now that the EC has matured, time has come to restructure the system, for the United States ought no longer be asked to bear the burdens of trade and monetary disadvantages. For economic purposes, a USE (United States of Europe) now exists, and its competitive ability has surpassed the American concessions to its maturation. So that the EC might not produce disassociating effects in the Western Hemisphere, the rules of the road must be changed. In Washington, the debate is now limited to the question of how to change the rules. Should the United States take the patient route of international agreements while the nation's trade deficit continues to soar to new records, or should it take the forceful and expedient route of unilateral trade restrictions, despite the probability of global trade war as a consequence? By 1986, Congress was so impatient with these questions that the nation's traditional commitment to the principles of free trade were nearly abandoned. And in a historic reversal of roles, the Democratic party—for which principles of free trade had long been a building block of foreign policy—was leading the demand for unilateral restrictions in defense of failing basic industries in the United States, industries whose work forces are overwhelmingly Democratic. Partisan politics aside, the fact remains that trade protectionism was a major theme in American do-

---

[44]Kohnstamm and Hager, ''Conclusion'' to *A Nation Writ Large?* pp. 256–264.

mestic politics in the 1980s, stimulated primarily by a huge chronic trade deficit with respect to Japan and secondarily by the industrial success of the EC. It remains to be seen how the United States will react to completion of the EC's economic union in 1992. By 1989, many American transnational corporations were expanding their production capacities within the EC member territories in order to gain full advantage of the union, but their individual corporate policies will have little influence over the ultimate policies of the US government. The urge of American corporations to establish bases of operation within the EC territories resulted in large measure from the fear of a "fortress Europe," from which the EC might in the future coordinate its industrial subsidy policies as well as its import policies in order to perpetuate an American trade disadvantage behind the economic walls of the EC.

The approach of 1992 and the completion of Western European economic union was complicated in 1989 and 1990 by the collapse of Soviet control of Eastern Europe and the fall of communist governments in Hungary, East Germany, Czechoslovakia, Poland, Romania, and Bulgaria. Some Americans lept quickly to the conclusion that the drive for political liberty was one with a demand for capitalism. Others viewed the situation more moderately as a demand for liberty and improved economic conditions through a combination of socialist planning and a free market in goods and services. But together they recognized two things: (1) that the restoration of political self-determination opened countless new export opportunities as well as new investment possibilities, and (2) that the dawn of possible unification of East and West Europe, with or without the reunification of the two Germanys, could multiply Europe's advantages in trade should the EC eventually expand eastward. Some American corporations began contemplating major direct industrial investment in East Germany, Poland, Hungary, and Czechoslovakia as a way of offsetting this eventual situation.

Other than in Europe, the United States continues to encourage economic integration, although successful industrial competition that might alter American attitudes has not arisen from any other integrated region.

On the matter of political integration, the United States takes a somewhat dimmer view. Washington is ambivalent about political supranationalism, even in Europe, that would deprive Washington of the ability to negotiate with European capitals individually on certain matters and would remove the traditional rite of playing one power against another. Preservation of the American role in the larger trans-Atlantic community thus dictates a cautious approach to European political integration.

The Perceptions of America's Major Allies

As the world's prime promoters of integration, the attitude of America's Western European allies is in the record of their experience. But what of Japan and Canada?

The Japanese view is not entirely clear, although logic would seem to predict a negative attitude. In the first place, just as the United States had retaliated against Japanese economic success, so too has it retaliated against the resurgence of Europe. Because the target of such actions is rarely specified, any Western-oriented industrial producer is likely to feel the brunt of American protection. Second, Japan's exports are industrial, and Europe is a large industrial market. The efficiency of European industry, together with the common barriers to trade raised against external competitors, reduces the probable sales of Japanese goods in Western Europe. Although it cannot be said that Japan is hostile to European integration, it appears that integrative success is detrimental to the distribution of Japan's industrial exports.

In its own region of the world, Japan is actively promoting development through both public assistance (largely through the Asian Development Bank) and private capital flows, but its interest is not now in integration. Instead, Japan is attempting to construct industrial markets, particularly in places rich in natural resources.

Canada's view of integration is typically restrained. Itself a federal state, integrative experience is understood by custom. Yet the British entry into EC placed economic strains on Canada which, as a member of the British Commonwealth, had previously enjoyed a free-trade relationship with Britain and had particularly profited as an agricultural supplier. British entry not only removed those advantages but also presented the added strain of making industrial trade more difficult at precisely the point when Canada was undergoing a major industrial development. Even in 1973 (the year of British entry), Canada's balance-of-trade surplus with respect to Britain continued to rise. Because Canada suffers a substantial deficit with respect to the world at large, it is probable that the EC will eventually present costly barriers to Canada's industrial trade.

The Soviet Perception of Integration

The forced integration of the Soviet regions in the civil war that followed the Bolshevik Revolution, succeeded by years of intense "Russification" of the non-Russian peoples of the Soviet Union, speaks vividly for the Soviet tendency to favor integration, at least among its friends and allies. Post–Second World War incorporation of Eastern Europe in a related economic supranationalism directed from Moscow, as center of the socialist commonwealth and of proletarian internationalism, accentuates this view. But as for integration in the West, the Kremlin's view is mixed and has changed with progression from the Cold War to the era of peaceful coexistence, back to Cold War, and now to *glasnost*.

Initially, the Soviet Union saw American interest in the integration of Europe not as a move toward economic stabilization, but as part of the effort to subject the Soviet Union and Eastern Europe to capitalist encirclement. In the wake of the Second World War and the division of Europe, the United States sought to isolate the East politically and economically by strengthening Western Europe as a huge economic colony and political puppet of American interests. Prior to the Gorbachev era, and in a view increasingly shared by Western Europeans, the Soviets saw American economic restoration of Europe less as a mechanism for promoting international trade than for extending the American economic empire overseas. And in a view increasingly shared by American revisionist historians, the Kremlin saw economic restoration principally as a step toward preventing the kinds of economic and social conditions that might have made Marxism attractive to Western Europeans. American motives were, therefore, either imperialistic or ideological, or perhaps both.

More recently, with the advent of *glasnost, perestroika,* and improved East-West relations as Mikhail Gorbachev attempts economic modernization in the Soviet Union, this view has transformed markedly and rapidly. The economic progress of a uniting Western Europe that has no aggressive intentions related to Eastern Europe is not only a source of potential supply to the USSR, but an example of how to modernize a large, unwieldy economy as well. Moreover, the combined economic strength of the EC is so great that it is capable of self-sufficiency within the global economy, thus removing it from the influences of the United States which, to the conservative hard-liners in the Kremlin, remains imperialistic and subject to lapses into containment and encirclement. (Nor has it been lost on the Soviet Union that trade with integrating Western Europe has greatly exceeded that with the United States for several reasons, among them the greater willingness of Europeans to deal with the Soviets than their American counterparts. In 1988, for example, Soviet trade with the EC reached $22.7 billion, whereas with the United States, it was a mere $3.4 billion.) As Gorbachev has openly supported political liberalization throughout Eastern Europe, so too has he encouraged close economic ties with the EC, even as the Warsaw Pact defense system has followed Eastern European communist governments into history in face of a strong NATO now including a reunified Germany

The Soviet attitude about economic integration of Eastern Europe has undergone a rapid and vast change. Prior to the Gorbachev era, the objectives of all Soviet policy, including economic policy, in Eastern Europe were the advancement of the socialist commonwealth and the achievement of a distribution system that strengthened the ability of the Soviet Union itself to maintain the solidity of its military and economic alliance. It was not fully interdependent and was not operated by equal participation of all the Eastern European governments. In essence (although not in every detail), the Eastern European states were part of the central planning of the Soviet economy through the Council for Mutual Economic Assistance (COMECON). In 1989 and 1990, as one Eastern European communist government after another fell from grace and power, and as Gorbachev publicly renounced the Brezhnev Doctrine in order to release Eastern Europeans to political and economic self-determination, the basis of the Soviet-centered distribution and production system unraveled. Pursuant to the notion of "Europe whole and free," Eastern European governments turned to the United States and Western Europe for increased trade, development capital, debt relief, and direct investment. This signaled a turn from strict socialism to a transitional system of social capitalism, in which the welfare-state aspects of socialism would coexist with private enterprise, corporate ownership as contrasted with state ownership of the means of production, and reliance on the convertible currencies of the Western capitalist nations. Even the Soviet Union itself appealed to the United States for most-favored-nation treatment in trade (that is, terms of trade equal to the most favorable granted any trading partner of the United States) and for the withdrawal of American resistance to Soviet observership at (and subsequently membership in) the International Monetary Fund, from which it would be able to withdraw convertible Western currencies and development capital. Clearly, in the Gorbachev era full participation in the global economy is more important than a regional distribution and production system based on old and obsolete notions of capitalist encirclement, American aggressive imperialism, and the economic fight-to-the-finish of socialism and capitalism. Indeed, in early 1990, the Kremlin actually proposed to the COMECON governments that they begin to conduct their trade in goods at global market rates rather than at the artificial barter rates with which they have habitually traded with one another. Recognizing that a rapid shift to world market prices would raise the cost of imports even from the Soviet Union, they rejected this proposal and postponed Moscow's drive to change the financial basis of trade and its urge to make Eastern European national currencies fully convertible in the West.

The Chinese Perception of Integration

As with many aspects of China's foreign policy, the official view of international integration is evolving constantly. Prior to the 1980s, China looked upon Western Europe's progress toward economic unity principally as a means of reducing American economic hegemony and thus as one means of ensuring against Soviet-American domination of the world. As economic liberalism developed in China during the 1980s, however, China looked favorably toward European unity as a means of balancing its relations with the capitalist nations, with Western Europe, Japan, and the United States serving as separate trading partners. Toward the end of the decade, as China and the United States normalized numerous economic and even military ties, a strong American presence in Western Europe meant both assurances against ambitious Soviet military policies in the East and guarantees of brisk economic competition among the Atlantic allies. Vivid recollections of Japanese economic might, adventurism, and aggression stretching from the 1890s to the Second World War invariably lead the Chinese to find comfort in brisk economic competition between Japan and the West.

The forceful destruction of the democratization movement in China in 1989 introduced new complications to Beijing's economic foreign policy. On the one hand, the victory of domestic political forces that signaled the firing on thousands of unarmed civilians also indicated a reversal in the economic liberalization that had marked the 1980s. On the other hand, however, even the most hard-line communists in government recognized the importance of foreign-owned industry in China and of smooth international economic relations in the interest of China's continued modernization. This dilemma resulted in a policy in which severity in domestic policy was accompanied by intensified efforts to retain foreign investment. Hence, the Japan-Europe-America economic tripod remained important to China. But events in Eastern Europe quickly intervened to force yet another appraisal of global economic matters and their importance to China. With one communist government after another falling in Eastern Europe after mid-1989, and with the Soviet Union's active encouragement of self-determination throughout Eastern Europe, China's associations with the noncapitalist world were thrown into disarray. Its relations with only Albania and North Korea were undisturbed. Moreover, as aspirations mounted for the evolution of "Europe free and whole," including the remote possibility of German reunification, Beijing was faced with new questions about European economic integration. Preservation of domestic single-party order and encouragement of Westward-leaning political and economic liberalization in East Germany, Czechoslovakia, Hungary, and Romania was an impossible contradiction. To official China, then, an economically unified Western Europe was economically desirable and politically acceptable, but the spread of European unification to the East was politically unacceptable in the wake of China's own 1989 events.

The Third World Perception of Integration

Although there is considerable regional organizational activity in the Third World, progress toward integration is beset by a peculiar dilemma. The governments are confronted simultaneously by a need for rapid development and by the careful nurturing of nationalist spirits required by modernization. Although integration of the economic sectors might increase the pace of modernization, the need for nationalism prevents such progress. In the older regions of Central and South America, the dilemma has been bridged, with the resulting Central American Common Market, the Latin American Free Trade Association, and the Andean Pact. But in the new independent areas, only the East African Common Market (EACM) has achieved much integrative progress. The merger of Tanganyika and Zanzibar into Tanzania has had little external effect, and the Arab states have not successfully integrated either economically or politically. In Asia, a free trade arrangement was reached among Vietnam, Laos, and Cambodia in 1980. Moreover, the Preferential Trading Arrangement among the members of the Association of Southeast Asian Nations (ASEAN) has been credited with vast trade improvements in that area, as has the South Pacific Trade and Economic Cooperation Agreement in its region. These successes suggest once again that the functional imperative of cooperation in trade and economic policy, fundamental to the economic expansion of the EC, is spreading significantly to the developing areas.

Western Europe continues to be a focus of forward-looking Third World diplomats, both as a model of economic promise and as a symbol of the passing of bipolarity and of superpower imperialism. Virtually since the establishment of the EC, some Third World states, particularly the former colonial possessions of France, have enjoyed the status of associate members. This has always been a controversial status, for it required the less developed participants to offer tariff preferences to the EC members in return for selling their exports at low tariff prices within the community. More recently, through the Yaoundé and Lomé Conventions, the EC has tied itself economically to more than 100 developing countries with trade preferences and concessions that favor European trade with these nations, in contrast with the trade of these nations with other industrialized economies.

There is one aspect of the EC that is of undeniable benefit to the Third World. In recent years, the members of the community, acting in a coordinated but nonintegrated way, have become major providers of development funds. By 1970, the total foreign assistance offered by the Six exceeded the annual foreign aid budget of the United States for the first time. Generally, however, such lending is limited to associate members and to former colonial possessions of the members. Thus, it is enjoyed only selectively by the Third World.

Transnational Participation

Every structure of world order that we have thus far considered presumes as its central feature the nation-state, intergovernmental organization, or the integration of states into higher political units. Sovereignty, power, and official diplomacy lie at the heart of each of these systems. All of them are considered to be state-centric models of world order. Yet every traveler, every student of other cultures, every devotee of the creative arts, and every businessperson is aware that many transactions of the international system do not involve governments alone, and that much of what happens across international boundaries is removed from sovereignty and intergovernmental negotiations. Despite the omnipresence of governments and official regulations, many international transactions occur on a people-to-people basis or between one government and the corporations of another state. This process, referred to as transnational participation, has become the focus of new forms of research and observation in international relations.

Transnational interaction is defined as "the movement of tangible or intangible items across state boundaries when at least one actor is not an agent of a government or an intergovernmental organization."[45] It may involve contact between two or more nongovernmental actors or between one official actor and one or more private actors. The nongovernmental participants may be corporations, social organizations, interest groups, political parties, elite structures, or formally instituted organizations designed to facilitate private relations. An agreement between an oil company and a foreign government falls into this

---

[45]Robert O. Keohane and Joseph S. Nye, "Transnational Relations and World Politics: An Introduction," *International Organization*, vol. 25, 1971, pp. 329–349. This section borrows extensively from this article.

category, as does contact between the International Red Cross and the government of Cuba. An International Youth Conference, involving no governments, is also transnational.[46]

Goals of Transnational Participation

Although these forms of international contact have always taken place, their impact has traditionally been minimized because of state domination of the global system. Now it is acknowledged, however, that such contacts contribute to the quality of coexistence, either directly (by improving perceptions and tolerances) or indirectly (by affecting intergovernmental relations). With increasing private contact, ubiquitous international trade, and social communication, transnational participation can no longer be overlooked as a major aspect of international stability or integration.

These interactions have six kinds of prospective impact. First, transnational contact is assumed to promote changes in attitude among the actors. Contact may break down perceptions, erase social and cultural barriers, enlighten outlooks, and dissipate animosities. In general, such attitudinal changes may help transform the international system by raising levels of tolerance among peoples, especially elites.

The second identifiable impact is the promotion of international pluralism. More and more linkages will be developed between domestic political processes and the international system. More interests will come to be involved in decision making; more national elites will gain contact with their counterparts abroad; and more services will be provided for more people.

The creation of new avenues of dependence and interdependence is the third expectation. Transnational contact illuminates mutual needs, and in the long run it may obviate some causes of intersocietal conflict. In addition, reliance will be built on other societies, on their productivity, and on their unique forms of creativity. In this manner, transnational contact may assist in "denationalizing" the energies of national peoples, thus taking governments out of the center of international transactions.[47]

Fourth, increases in transnationalism may create beneficial side effects for those aspects of the international system that remain state centered. Specifically, stabilization of relations among peoples, with increasing intersocietal dependence, may enlarge the peaceful contacts of governments and actually create for them new avenues of influence. A dramatic and unusual example of this impact was President Richard M. Nixon's historic trip to the People's

---

[46]The Summer 1971 edition of *International Organization* is devoted to the subject "Transnational Relations and World Politics," Robert O. Keohane and Joseph S. Nye, Jr., eds. Among its many papers it considers the Ford Foundation, the Roman Catholic church, airlines flying international routes, labor unions, and scientific societies as transnational actors. Although these papers are not specifically cited here, the reader is alerted to this edition of the journal as the best single source of papers on the theory and illustrative studies of the transnational phenomenon.

[47]These first three features of transnationalism are especially well illustrated in the study of Robert C. Angell, *Peace on the March: Transnational Participation* (New York: Van Nostrand Reinhold, 1969).

Republic of China in 1972, a trip that, in American public opinion, was made possible by the prior amicable visit of a table-tennis team. Following the president's sojourn, informal contact was utilized further to break down long-standing barriers by exchanges of scientists, physicians, and surgeons. This feature of transnationalism led one observer to describe the process as "transactions which bypass the institutions of government but strongly affect their margin of maneuver."[48]

Fifth, transnational participation, when institutionalized, may create new influential autonomous or quasi-autonomous actors in the international system. Among these are scores of nongovernmental organizations (NGOs) and informal institutional arrangements through which transnational interactions are regulated. The International Red Cross is the best known of these, one that not only conducts its own relief operations but also to which governments frequently turn to arrange official contacts. Another important NGO is the International Chamber of Commerce, which has already contributed to international stability and amicable exchange by formulating norms of international business relations.[49]

The sixth possible effect of transnationalism is the gradual institutionalization of intersocietal transactions that may become the private counterpart of functional international organizations. Although public single-purpose organizations go about formulating international norms in their respective fields, transnational groups may proceed to develop the norms of their own relations. Furthermore, the national elites that direct functional organizations will be identical in some instances to those that regulate transnational contact. Such a process would maximize the linkages between national and international decision-making processes.

Types of Transnational Participation

Having noted the functional characteristics of transnational research, we may now classify and exemplify types of transnational participation. Most informal among them are the sociocultural activities, of which there are thousands annually. Most common is individual travel, which has some cumulative effect on international attitudes. Other sociocultural activities of significance are international visits of symphony orchestras, touring exhibits, lecture series, touring dance companies, and so on. International athletic events, particularly the Olympics, the Pan-American Games, and the Soviet-American games, also are in this category.

Political transnational activity is another. The earliest events were the International Peace Congresses of the nineteenth century, which met to formulate treaties for world peace. These were returned to national societies and national governments, with the Congress members serving as interest groups. At

---

[48]Karl Kaiser, "Transnational Politics: Toward a Theory of Multinational Politics," *International Organization*, vol. 24, 1971, pp. 790–817.

[49]Percy E. Corbett, *From International to World Law* (Bethlehem, Pa.: Lehigh University Department of International Relations, research monograph no. 1, 1969).

Source: Martin, © 1990, Cartoonists & Writers Syndicate

present, the World Peace Through Law movement does much the same thing. Other political transnationalism involves the international communications and meetings of some political parties, such as the socialist parties of Western Europe, national communist parties, and the several National Liberation Fronts. The International Youth Conferences sponsored periodically by the United Nations and other organizations are also examples of political transnationalism, because they present and discuss the political attitudes of young people from different lands.

By far the most important transnational activities are in the economic realm. Although many aspects of the international political economy are conducted by governments and although most are regulated by official norms, much of the modern international economy is privately regulated. At present, the transnational actor with the greatest power to affect national economies and the flow of international transactions is the transnational (or multinational) corporation (TNC). Its center of operations is in one country, but it has subsidiaries in several others that have major effects on international economics and the host economies. At present there are more than 4000 corporations with tentacles that reach out in this manner, many of them American. In 1988, of the 20 largest industrial corporations in the world, excluding, of course, the state-owned enterprises of the socialist states, 9 were American (down from 12 in 1985), and 39 American corporations ranked in the largest 100. Among the 500 largest non-American transnational corporations, the dominant ownership nations were as follows:

Japan	159
Britain	73
West Germany	53
France	38
Canada	27
Sweden	18
Switzerland	14
Australia	11
Finland	11
Netherlands	11
South Korea	11
Spain	8
Italy	7

And just as Japan heads the list of ownership among the industrial corporations, so too does it among the world's largest commercial banks. In 1988, 23 of the largest 50 were based in Japan, controlling about 60 percent of the total assets of $8.2 trillion, larger than the combined gross national products of the United States, Britain, France, West Germany, and Brazil! There are but five North American banks on the list, four in the United States and one in Canada. The Bank of China and one Hong Kong bank bring the Asian total to 25, with the remaining based in Western Europe.[50]

Table 17–2 lists the top 20 industrial transnational corporations in 1989, their countries of origin, their total world sales, and their net profits. One dramatic indicator of their influence on the international system is that their gross sales totaled no less than $1 trillion, more than the gross national products of all but three nations in the world and more than the combined gross national products of the majority of the underindustrialized nations. And their combined profits of almost $50 billion competes nicely with many a GNP. So large and powerful are these corporations that in 1972, when the domestic and overseas operations of ITT came under fire, the Solicitor-General of the United States remarked that the company was beyond the laws even of the United States!

Looked at from the viewpoint of a host government, the power of these corporations is equally great. An anecdote may suffice to illustrate. The British Ford subsidiary manufactures approximately 650,000 automobiles per year, slightly fewer than the Belgian and German subsidiaries. In 1971, when corporation president Henry Ford II arrived in Britain during a strike, he warned that unless the British economy presented less threat to productivity, Ford would consider closing the British operations and expanding productivity on the continent. Although labor reacted with a "we're-not-afraid" attitude, Ford was generally "treated more like a visiting head of state than an ordinary industrialist."[51] The story illustrates the immense power held by these corporations.

---

[50]"The World's Biggest Industrial Corporations," *Fortune,* July 31, 1989, pp. 282–283; also "The World's Biggest Commercial Banks," p. 286.

[51]As related in Christopher Tugendhat, "Transnational Enterprise: Tying Down Gulliver," *Atlantic Community Quarterly,* vol. 9, 1971/72, pp. 499–508.

Table 17–2 Twenty leading transnational corporations, 1988, measured by total world sales and net earnings, in billions of US dollars.

Corporation	National Base	World Sales (US$, billions)	Net Income (US$, billions)
General Motors	US	121.1	4.9
Ford Motor Company	US	92.5	5.3
Exxon	US	79.6	5.3
Royal Dutch/Shell Group	Netherlands/Britain	78.4	5.2
IBM	US	59.7	5.8
Toyota	Japan	50.8	2.3
General Electric	US	49.4	3.4
Mobil Oil	US	48.2	2.1
British Petroleum	Britain	46.2	2.2
IRI	Italy	45.5	0.9
Daimler-Benz	W. Germany	41.8	1.0
Hitachi	Japan	41.3	1.0
Chrysler Motors	US	35.5	1.0
Siemens	W. Germany	34.1	0.8
Fiat	Italy	34.0	2.3
Matsushita Electric	Japan	33.9	1.2
Volkswagen	W. Germany	33.7	0.4
Texaco	US	33.5	1.3
E. I. duPont deNemours	US	32.5	2.2
Unilever	Netherlands/Britain	30.5	1.5

Source: Fortune, July 31, 1989, p. 282.

What about the relations of the transnational company to the parent government—that is, the government of the state where the corporation is based? American-owned TNCs produce abroad goods amounting to three times the total annual American exports, and these companies are growing at an average rate of twice that of the world's most vigorous national economies. By the year 2000, it is estimated that the transnationals will produce upwards of one-half of the gross world product.[52]

These companies have had another effect on the world economy. Many of them, if not most, do not produce a commodity from start to finish at a single site. Instead, they build some parts in some areas and export them to second subsidiaries, where they are joined to other parts of the whole and then exported to yet a third place. It is not at all unusual for an automobile made by

[52]Similar data are explored by Raymond Vernon, *Sovereignty at Bay: The Multinational Spread of U.S. Enterprises* (New York: Basic Books, 1971). The estimates used here are summarized in Elliot R. Goodman, "The Impact of the Multinational Enterprise upon the Atlantic Community," *Atlantic Community Quarterly*, vol. 10, Fall 1972, pp. 357–367. For a comparative review of the book-length literature on the multinational corporation, see Robert O. Keohane and Van Doorn Ooms, "The Multinational Enterprise and World Political Economy," *International Organization*, vol. 26, 1972, pp. 84–120. The literature has grown substantially since this was published.

an American-owned corporation to consist of a transmission made in one country, a motor made in a second, a body made in a third, and tires and fixtures made in a fourth. Twenty-five percent of all American exports are to the overseas subsidiaries of American-based TNCs.

More than merely uncloaking the enormity of these corporations, these characteristics reveal the extent to which they—largely unregulated by governments or by international agreement—are able to control the world economy and the economies of the host states. Often their operations lead to political controversy, as in de Gaulle's insistence on "de-Americanizing" Europe, ITT's CIA-assisted coup d'état in Chile, and rampant scandals resulting from corrupt business practices abroad. In both developed and less developed economies, TNCs are able to penetrate fiscal policy and labor relations; they are able to profit by dispersing earnings and losses among subsidiaries without regard for the host economy; and they are able to remove their economic activity to the detriment of the host. Although they are able to contribute to economic development, they are also able to globalize such injurious phenomena as inflation and to use their economic might for political intervention. As a result, many governments have experimented with restrictions on foreign ownership of production, and the governments of the Third World have heightened their demand for international regulation of multinational corporate activity. Both the United Nations and the Organization for Economic Cooperation and Development (OECD) have labored long over this issue, and in 1976 the OECD adopted a series of declarations comprising guidelines for the behavior of multinational enterprises.[53] Despite this progress and despite the annual review of performance under the guidelines by the OECD, the Group of Seventy-Seven continues to consider this a major area of need.

The capital-lending institutions also affect the world economy and the domestic economies of the host states. Although no one disputes the need for operating capital in industrial modernization, some would argue that the rapid growth of branch banks overseas is an instrument of neoimperialism. If American capital is the only available source of funds, then American banks and American fiscal policy actually regulate interest rates and growth rates overseas. Furthermore, both in the banking business and in commodity industries, profits are siphoned off and returned with minimal reinvestment, with the result that the principal gains from the multinational enterprise accrue solely to the country of origin.[54]

---

[53]The OECD guidelines and the review documents for 1979 can be found in "Review of the 1976 Declaration and Decisions on Guidelines for Multinational Enterprises, National Treatment, International Investment Incentives and Disincentives, and Consultation Procedures," OECD, 1979. For background information, see particularly Robert O. Keohane and Van Doorn Ooms, "The Multinational Firm and International Regulation," *International Organization,* vol. 29, 1975, pp. 169–212; and Paul A. Tharp, Jr., "Transnational Enterprises and International Regulation: A Survey of Various Approaches in International Organization," *International Organization,* vol. 30, 1976, pp. 47–74.

[54]The most incisive critique of the political-economic effects is found in Harry Magdoff, *The Age of Imperialism: The Economics of U.S. Foreign Policy* (New York: Monthly Review Press, 1969). For a critical but less bleak European view, see J. J. Servan-Schreiber, *The American Challenge*

Considered from political and economic perspectives, the multinational corporation is a mixed blessing.[55] But what is it when viewed from the perspective of transnationalism? What is its value as a nongovernmental actor capable of creating new intersocietal communications?

At present, the transnational corporation may contribute to integration through its ability to forge shared values among participating elites. There is a growing consensus that the managers of overseas subsidiaries must subordinate nationalistic attitudes to corporate profit, regardless of the country of central operations. Because the principal decisions are economic rather than political, and because the function of capitalist business is to achieve profit in competitive markets, the tendency in these corporations is to minimize national feelings.

Yet it is also probable that this attitude does not filter down very far within the company. Below uppermost management, few employees are aware of the full meaning of their participation in a multinational enterprise. Their objective in most cases is to progress in the plant rather than in the corporation, or in the industry rather than in the conglomerate. Furthermore, at the consumer level, few in Britain, for example, who eat cornflakes realize that the company that made the product is a wholly owned American subsidiary.

The multinational business enterprise has not had a deep overall impact on national economic attitudes. There are many who feel that such organization is vital to efficiency in a technological world, and there are those who insist that regional supranationalism is dependent on multinational business.[56] But there is little evidence to suggest its positive effect on international stability through attitudinal change at the mass level. The opposite may be quite the case, in fact, because these huge operations tend to be exploitative and ready to use their considerable political weight. Often, they make themselves unwelcome guests by aggravating existing tensions. Although there is considerable evidence that the TNCs are effective agents for the transfer of technology from the developed to the developing economies, the overall effects of national and international political economies remain controversial, as does the broader role of the TNCs in social change and in the emerging world order.

(New York, Atheneum, 1969). For a study of US banking abroad, particularly the growth of branch banks in other economies, see Table 1–1 of this book.

[55]Theodore H. Moran, ''Multinational Corporations and Dependency: A Dialogue for Dependentistas and non-Dependentistas,'' *International Organization*, Winter 1978, pp. 79–100. Moran attempts to clarify the debate between the advocates of the dependency theory of development and the role of the TNCs and the more liberal or traditional view. He categorizes the charges against the TNC in the Third World as made by the dependency theorists and develops each into a testable hypothesis for nondependency-theory inquiry. Although the paper is inconclusive, it offers a logical procedure by which to explore the controversy between the two bodies of interpretation.

[56]On the relation between the multinational corporation and the progress of European economic integration, see particularly Werner J. Feld, *Transnational Business Collaboration Among Common Market Countries* (New York: Praeger, 1970), and ''Political Aspects of Transnational Business Collaboration in the Common Market,'' *International Organization*, vol. 24, 1970, pp. 209–238. See also a discussion of ''The Multinational Corporation and World Economic Development,'' *Proceedings of the 66th Annual Meeting of the American Society of International Law*, September 1972, pp. 14–22, especially the remarks by Jack N. Behrman.

To whatever extent transnational participation contributes to world stability, then, its virtue must be found in less visible places. Most such progress at present is found in the sociocultural sector. At its roots, the transnational process is one of awareness; and the indications are that at the individual level, maximum attitudinal change through awareness occurs through sociocultural contact only.

Governments cautiously safeguard their prerogatives and prevent escape of political functions to external agencies. But the intersocietal linkages created by the movement of persons, information, goods, and capital across national boundaries challenge the purely state-centered model of international stability. They may ultimately alter the supremacy of the state as an actor in the international system, although to date such transformation is minimal. All in all, however, the several alternatives to absolute sovereignty that we have studied in this chapter and the preceding two (international law, international organization, supranationalism, and transnational participation) all press in upon the nation-state and challenge its ability to remain the paramount actor in international relations.

CHAPTER 18

The Future World Order

During the era of the Apollo moon probes, an American astronaut told mission control that the most remarkable thing about space travel is looking back on earth as a planet without boundaries. From his vantage point deep in space, temporarily removed from armed conflict and the rhetoric of enmity, he voiced the long-standing view of many people—if enduring peace is to dawn, the international system must first be substantially altered. If war is a product of the nation-state system, then the role of the state must be diminished and that of other governing and social processes increased. Disillusioned with the balance of power, the balance of terror, and all known power distributions, observers ranging from nineteenth-century utopians to contemporary futurist scholars have sought alternative worlds, all focusing on one problem: how to supplant the nation-state's capacity for disruption.

But war/peace issues no longer monopolize scholarly examination of the future. On an overcrowded planet nearing depletion of resources and extinction of species, the dynamics of the international system have come upon new emergencies. Stability relies not only on the willingness of goverments to put aside their arms but also on their ability to correct anarchical ways. Consider briefly a few areas in which the records of nation-states are dismal and which now cry for international regulation.

1. Ecology

First among them is ecological anarchy. States have exploited the earth's natural riches without regard for the problem of exhaustibility and with little consideration of future generations or the needs of others. Growing energy demands deplete fossil fuels; deposits of hard metals have been used up; and

"Because it's a new category, they haven't settled the details of what to do with those who have sinned against the planet."
Source: Drawing by D. Reilly; © 1990 The New Yorker Magazine, Inc.

supplies of fresh water are dangerously low. Meanwhile, we have poisoned the air, despoiled most of the major rivers of the world, toxified vast areas of the seas, made urban living a painful clatter, and outgrown designated dumping areas. These problems have become so nearly universal as to make clear that national regulation is too little and too late. Without new levels of cooperation and international regulation, we are bent upon ecological suicide.

Sadly, international cooperation on this issue has scarcely commenced, despite the best efforts of the United Nations. Under its auspices, after fully four years of preparation, the Global Conference on the Human Environment was convened at Stockholm in 1972. Fraught with politics over the seating of East Germany (not then a member of the United Nations) and over Chinese charges against the use of defoliants in Vietnam and beset by the insistence of the less developed states that environmental preservation is a luxury for the industrialized, the conference achieved but modest ends. It established the seeds of a global environmental monitoring system, promulgated an action program and a declaration, and established UN oversight machinery. But beyond dramatic recognition of the need for international cooperation and the establishment of functional machinery, the Stockholm meeting itself was a less compelling impetus to cooperation than were subsequent events.

The years that followed Stockholm saw a number of dramatic environmental calamities. French ports and wildlife were menaced by the cargo of a disintegrating supertanker. Nuclear fallout from a Chinese nuclear explosion was measured more than halfway around the world. Lakes in the northern United States and Canada became lifeless as the result of acid rain contamination. And the US government was obliged to commit funds to move hundreds of families away from the chemical-contaminated Love Canal in New York and from Times Beach, Missouri. Then there were the near-disasters. The Three Mile Island nuclear power station in Pennsylvania released radiation through its cooling station in amounts so high that the long-range consequences are still not known. Terrorists penetrated the security of a West German nuclear station, accentuating concern for the possibility of nuclear blackmail or terrorism. An American Titan ICBM exploded in an Arkansas silo, reportedly throwing its nuclear warhead several hundred yards but without exploding. In a space of less than two years, from 1984 to 1986, several of the world's worst disasters occurred: a gas storage facility outside of Mexico City exploded and burned, killing scores and leaving thousands homeless; a chemical leak in Bhopal, India, killed over 2500 people and left countless thousands ill with respiratory and eye burns; and a nuclear reactor at Chernobyl in the Soviet Union exploded, releasing its radioactive content into the air, water, and soil, killing dozens, exposing many thousands to cancer caused by radiation exposure, spreading nuclear contamination over all of East Europe and part of West Europe, and wiping out the reindeer herding industry of the Arctic because of dangerously irradiated animals. In 1989, the supertanker *Exxon Valdez* went aground in Alaska's Prince William Sound, spilling millions of gallons of crude oil. The oil slick killed thousands of animals, forced cancellation of an entire salmon season, and marred hundreds of miles of both sandy and rocky beaches. Exxon's controversial billion-dollar cleanup effort was generally regarded as insufficient to prevent long-term disastrous effects for wildlife.

Less dramatic but equally alarming are the quieter cumulative effects of environmental spoilation. In the industrialized state, the last years have seen considerable measures against industrial smoke discharge; in control of health hazards in mines; in diminished stripmining or, alternatively, stripmining followed by reconstitution of the landscape; and in reduction of waste release into rivers and bays. But these familiar evils have been overtaken by new revelations, such as the extreme long-term effects of toxification and irradiation of soil, air, and waterways. The Great Lakes, until recently one of the largest providers of fish, are now so contaminated with PCB chemical compounds that reduction in consumption is publicly advocated. And the Chesapeake Bay has suffered a vast reduction in both its crab and oyster yield owing to the toxic effects of synthetic fertilizers, pesticides, and herbicides washed from agricultural soil. Meanwhile, so much waste is circulating in space that both Washington and Moscow have expressed concern about the safety of astronauts.

In recent years scientists throughout the world have sounded alarms about three new, long-term environmental threats. The first is depletion of the ozone layer of the earth's atmosphere, the layer that screens out the most

Environmental crisis: A (former East) German river boiled with toxic industrial pollution, 1989.
Source: © 1990, Suau/Black Star

harmful of the sun's rays. Depletion results from a high concentration of chlorofluorocarbons emissions from industry and from household uses. The latter include domestic refrigeration (particularly when refrigerators are scrapped and their cooling elements rupture and free their liquid and gas contents), pressurized spray cans, and dry cleaning fluids. A major hole has already been detected over the south pole, and there is at least circumstantial evidence that ozone depletion is the cause of an alarming rise in cases of skin cancer among Americans.

The second is deforestation, and particularly the destruction of tropical rain forests. In Africa, starvation and draught result in large measure from interruption in natural rain cycles by forest destruction. Man-made deserts, created when farmers in search of land level giant trees, produce little or no nutrition, and at the cost of removing the natural circumstances that create atmospheric moisture. In the equatorial forests of the Amazon basin in South America, there is a major battle between environmentalists, determined to prevent recurrence of the African experience, and land-starved farmers, who see deforestation as their economic salvation. In 1989, for example, the leading advocate of the environment was assassinated as he sought legal controls on continued destruction of the forest.

The third of these long-term dangers is the warming of the earth. Each year, millions of tons of waste are released into the atmosphere, laying an increasingly dense chemical cloud over the planet. Industrial emissions such as sulfur are precipitated back to earth in the form of acid rain, but carbon dioxide and other chemical products of fuels and thousands of square miles of burning tropical forest hover permanently. This cloud alters the mechanisms by which the earth's temperature is regulated, principally by cumulatively reducing its capacity for radiational cooling. Consequently, the planetary temperature gradually rises. It is to this phenomenon to which scientists look when attempting to explain why almost all the warmest years in the twentieth century have been in the decade of the 1980s. For those who prefer warm climates to cold, this may seem a desirable trend. But geologists are concerned with possible long-term dangers, such as the possibility that ocean tides might rise markedly as a result of glacial and polar melting, endangering coastal cities, obliterating farming lands, driving major rivers over continents and salinating precious sources of fresh drinking water.

The long-range genetic consequences of chemical and radiological contamination are particularly threatening and inconclusively understood. Mutations brought on by these hazards have the capability of fundamentally altering species, including humans. The increased use of nuclear fuels to replace diminishing supplies of conventional fuels is fraught with distant implications. Although we continue to be concerned more with the immediate consequences of irradiation, the more serious risks may not be visible for generations. One centers on freshly demonstrated leaks of radiation from barrels of nuclear substances dumped in the Pacific Ocean over a period of 25 years. By 1980, the leaked radiation had gotten into the human food chain; edible fish tissues were shown to have radiation levels hundreds of times greater than normal. Scientists expect that the genetic consequences for humans as well as for lower animals will evolve in unpredictable fashions for thousands of years. Meanwhile, both irradiation and chemical contamination of the environment continue to cause a wide variety of cancers and other diseases.

Since Stockholm, rapid industrialization and increased dependence on synthetic fertilizers for agricultural advancement have brought about new concern for ecology in the Third World. The environmental consequences of unplanned urban growth, involving such things as industrial discharge, waste disposal and treatment, poor fresh water supplies, and the natural consequences of deforestation have stimulated this concern. Two decades ago, the Third World nations put such a premium on economic development as to regard environmental issues as a luxury of the developed, but they now recognize the urgency of addressing ecological matters. Table 18–1 compares the specific concerns of the Third World governments with those of the industrialized states; those in capital letters indicate specific priorities. The important conclusion, however, is that whether developed or less developed, socialist or market economy, all states now have urgent concern for ecological preservation. Yet because environmental pollution knows nothing of national boundaries, this rising awareness can do nothing more than underscore the fact that national solutions to environmental problems are inadequate.

Table 18–1 Environmental concerns of developing and industrialized countries.

Environmental Concerns	Developing Countries	Industrialized Countries
I. *Natural environment*		
A. Air	Air pollution in major cities	AIR POLLUTION
B. Land, soil, mineral resources (including energy)	SOIL EROSION AND DEGRADATION, DESERTIFICATION	Soil loss and deterioration; dumping of waste; risk of radioactive contamination from nuclear-power production
C. Water	FRESHWATER SHORTAGE; freshwater pollution (sewage, pesticides); pollution of coastal waters	Freshwater shortage; INLAND AND MARINE WATER POLLUTION
D. Fauna and flora	DEFORESTATION (especially of tropical forests); loss of genetic resources; endangered species	Loss of genetic resources; endangered species
E. Ecosystems	Pollution of coastal ecosystems (decreasing fish catch)	Disruption of mountain, wetland, freshwater (especially from acid rains and eutrophication) and coastal ecosystems
F. Natural disasters	FLOODS; DROUGHTS; STORMS; earthquakes, volcanic eruptions	Floods; earthquakes
II. *Man-made environment and living conditions*		
A. Bioproductive systems	LOSS AND DEGRADATION OF ARABLE LAND; pests and pest resistance, water shortage, pressures on fish population (over-fishing, pollution); IMPACTS OF FUELWOOD CONSUMPTION, food contamination, post-harvest losses	Loss of croplands to urban sprawl; pests and pest resistance; contamination of crops and fish; overexploitation of fishing grounds
B. Human settlements	MARGINAL SETTLEMENTS (RURAL-URBAN MIGRATION, URBAN GROWTH)	URBAN SPRAWL; NOISE
C. Health	MAL- AND UNDERNUTRITION; INFECTIOUS AND PARASITIC DISEASES	CANCER; cardiovascular diseases; genetic and long-term effects of POTENTIALLY TOXIC CHEMICALS

Source: Peter Bartlemus, *Environment and Development* (Boston: Allen and Unwin, 1986), p. 19. Reprinted with permission.

2. Population

It took until the year 1800 for the world population to reach 1 billion. From there the extraordinary growth began: The second billion was reached in 1925, the third in 1960, the fourth in 1976, and the fifth in 1987. It is estimated that by the turn of the century, the world's population will have reached nearly 7 billion. At an annual growth rate of 1.7 percent (currently that means an additional 83 million people per year), the total is expected to top off at approximately 10 billion shortly before 2100. Most alarming, the population density is the most stable in the industrialized areas, where many nations have actually achieved below-replacement reproduction (negative population growth) and is the least stable in the less developed areas. In sub-Saharan Africa, for example, the population is expected to grow by a billion people in the next four decades. Current projections suggest that by 2000, the population density of North America will have increased by only 4 persons per square kilometer, whereas in South Asia it will have increased by 140 persons in a similar space.[1]

The world order consequences of these projections are manifold but not entirely clear. We do know that under typical circumstances such as those of the Third World, mortality rates decline before birthrates do, with the result that the population grows simultaneously at both the upper and the lower ends of the age scale. At each end are individuals that are resource consumers and not economic contributors. We know also from recent experience that in many of the nonoil-producing Third World countries, the population rates far outrun the rates of economic growth, with the result that quality of living per capita is actually declining, even in the face of economic growth. It is also well established that there is a correlation between deprivation resulting from a declining quality of life and conflict. Further, the current circumstances, when accompanied by domestic violence, result in large population migrations that become international issues.[2]

International attention was addressed to the population crisis first in 1974 at the World Population Conference in Bucharest, a meeting that made little progress because of the Third World's overriding concern with economic growth and the New International Economic Order. But ten years later, when the United Nations held the Second International Population Conference at Mexico City, the mood had changed considerably. The final report of the conference called upon all governments to make available birth control information and devices as an urgent international matter. Together with the United Nations Economic Program, the conference's documents were drafted to emphasize the relationship between economic development and population control.[3]

By the mid-1980s, it was apparent that faith in endless economic progress had been tempered with the strong reality that economic growth cannot be considered apart from other important social phenomena. Until then, only a

---

[1]Not all scientific projections concur, but they all transmit the same message. See, as examples, Mihajlo Mesarovic and Eduard Pestel, *Mankind at the Turning Point: The Second Report to the Club of Rome* (New York: New American Library, 1974), chap. 6; Wassily Leontief et al., *The Future of the World Economy: A United Nations Study* (New York: Oxford University Press, 1977), summary conclusions on p. 4; and Thomas W. Merrick and the staff of the Population Reference Bureau, ''World Population in Transition,'' *Population Bulletin*, April 1986.

[2]Myron Wiener, ''On International Migrations and International Relations,'' *Population and Development Review*, September 1985, pp. 441–455.

[3]For the final report of the conference, see ''Report of the International Conference on Population, 1984, Mexico City, August 6–14, 1984,'' UN Document E/Conf. 76/19, 1984. For current country-by-country populations statistics, see United Nations *Statistical Papers*, Series A, vol. XLI, no. 3, *Population and Vital Statistics Report: Data Available as of 1 July 1989.*

few Third World countries had undertaken massive programs of population control. In India, for instance, a program was instituted in 1976 to apply coercive sanctions in the form of economic penalties for the failure of at least one spouse to be sterilized after the birth of a third child. And in China, which had run a historically constant birth ratio of six children per woman, the rate dropped to two in the 1970s and has essentially remained there. That is the most dramatic birthrate reduction ever recorded.[4] But as it is still not satisfied that the population will adjust to a level that its economy can sustain, the Chinese government has launched a campaign of one child per family, a policy engulfed in some international controversy because it reportedly involves involuntary abortion for excessively productive women.

3. Natural Resources

As recently as a quarter-century ago, economic growth throughout the world was predicated on faith that there would always be more where it came from. World leaders had scarcely begun to predict the exhaustion of the earth's natural riches and, in typical power fashion, were more concerned with the geopolitical location of natural resources than with their potential depletion. But the oil embargo of 1973–1974 and the global politics of oil that followed changed that thinking forever.

Mineral resources are at present being expended at record rates, even at a time of reduced economic activity throughout the West and declines in national productivity. That this is most popularly evidenced by the diminishing world supply of petroleum is because individuals are so directly dependent on petroleum to fuel their cars, heat their homes, and drive the industries that employ them. But the shortages are becoming critical in other areas as well, such as among the nonferrous metals. Although it is probable that in the long run the exhaustion of fossil fuel supplies will be compensated by a combination of energy from nuclear fuel, solar power, synthetic fuels, and ocean thermal energy, many of the basic elements may not be replaceable in manufacturing and other socially important processes.

It is important to stress that the deterioration of world mineral supplies may have potential consequences beyond national and international economics. These minerals are not found equally distributed about the globe any more than petroleum is. Although the United States, China, and the Soviet Union have been rich in both coal and petroleum (yet only China among them now appears to have significant untapped supplies of oil), Britain and the continental powers of Western Europe have been rich only in coal (until discovery of oil in the North Sea). Japan, in contrast, has until the advent of nuclear power been wholly dependent on foreign sources of fuel. Metals are also distributed unevenly about the planet, and many of the unutilized supplies are now limited

---

[4]John Bongaarts and Susan Greenhalgh, ''An Alternative to the One-Child Policy in China,'' *Population and Development Review,* December 1985, pp. 585–618.

to the territories of the Third World countries. And while rapid increases in the export of these materials has contributed to economic development, dependence on them has led to unbalanced exports and has raised the prospect of export paralysis upon their depletion.

Beyond these potential consequences, it is important that the external quest for raw materials have been one of the major causes of war in the industrial age and is generally understood to have been one of the principal causes of imperialism. We have seen that the modern efforts to integrate the economies of Western Europe were inspired in the first instance by the desire to eliminate the repeated Franco-German competition for coal and steel. Similarly, it has long been understood that Japan's imperialistic behavior from 1931 to its attack on Pearl Harbor in 1941 was provoked in large measure by the paucity of mineral resources in the Japanese territory.[5] More recently, it has been argued that the Americanization of the Vietnam War in 1964 and the general interventionist trend of American foreign policy in that era were driven mainly by the need to control political events in those areas that may still have abundant natural resources.[6]

To the extent that these observations are accurate, deterioration of the globe's mineral supply may portend more than fundamental changes in world economic productivity. Surely, the uneven distribution of oil has already brought a major transition to the world, measured both politically and economically, particularly with the rise of the oil-exporting countries as political-economic powers despite their social and industrial underdevelopment. But such changes may be little more than the first phases of major new alignments in world politics heralded, among other things, by the remarkably rapid reversal in Sino-American relations in the 1970s and 1980s, and the American urge to renew progress after the events of Tiananmen Square in 1989. Without rational control of the politics of declining resources, new forms of imperialism and conquest could emerge.

Oil and metals are not the only natural resources on which we depend daily. Gradual chemical contamination is reducing the world's supply of fresh water to the point that water and its preservation against spoilage are major international issues. So, too, is the preservation of the air against chemical and radiation contamination. An even more complicated problem is the gradual deterioration of the earth's ozone layer, without which the most deadly rays of the sun would have no barrier to entry into the atmosphere. And the oceans, once the earth's last frontier, are threatened with bacteriological contamination from the dumping of organic waste and from various forms of chemical contamination.

Because air and water are international public property, national efforts to safeguard them, although helpful, cannot be final. Nonetheless, most multilateral diplomacy regarding them centers on economic exploitation rather than preservation. It was not until 1986, for example, that the United States and

---

[5]Herbert Feis, *The Road to Pearl Harbor* (Princeton, N.J.: Princeton University Press, 1950).
[6]Gabriel Kolko, *The Roots of American Foreign Policy* (Boston: Beacon Press, 1969).

Canada agreed for the first time to enter into serious research and policymaking on the problems related to acid rain. Little more time can be wasted before comprehensive regimes to protect these properties are undertaken.

4. Food

Preoccupation with the world's mineral distribution serves only to obscure the global nutrition crisis. In November 1974, just one year after the first major petroleum crisis, the United Nations convened the World Food Conference at Rome to deal with the long-term threat of dwindling food production relative to need. The United Nations had projected that by 1985, an increase of production per year of 2.5 percent globally would barely offset the increased demand of the industrialized states, thus leaving none to contribute to the 3.6 percent increase in need from the industrializing states.[7] More recent UN estimates take into account the results of the Green Revolution and increased land yields resulting from modern agricultural techniques. The experts now seem confident that the available agricultural land can be increased by 30 percent during the remainder of the century and that yields can be improved by as much as 60 percent. With massive investment, the study concludes, major crop staples might be produced in amounts as much as twice to three times the current annual global yields.[8] Already, there has been progress. By 1977, for example, Bangladesh, once considered beyond hope with respect to staple-crop sufficiency, predicted that it would be self-sufficient in rice production within five years. In 1979, American agricultural scientists announced soybean hybrids capable of 15 percent increases in yield. And China announced in 1980 what it considered to be a realistic plan to double its rice production.

What the Green Revolution was to world food supplies in the 1960s, 1970s, and 1980s new agricultural applications of genetic science may be in the 1990s.[9] When applied to agriculture, the same research techniques used to produce new therapeutic agents may result in major advances in productivity. In one massive effort, for example, so large as to be compared with the war on cancer, scientists are trying to move a particular nitrogen fixation gene from a soybean into corn. Because nitrogen fixation is an essential step in plants' energy and photosynthetic cycles, successful transplantation of the gene, and the subsequent successful expression of its normal function in a new host, would have profound consequences for corn production worldwide.

Although closely tied to the problem of population growth, global food shortages also present problems of their own. Aside from the obvious conse-

---

[7]*Assessment of the World Food Situation: Present and Future*, Item 8 of the Provisional Agenda for the World Food Conference, p. 225.

[8]Leontief et al., *The Future of the World Economy*, pp. 4,5.

[9]For a general review of genetic applications in agriculture, see Jack Doyle, ''Biotechnology Research and Agricultural Stability,'' *Issues in Science and Technology*, Fall 1985, pp. 111–124. The author discusses both animal and vegetable applications and the genetic alteration of pests as a means of reducing the environmental consequences of synthetic herbicides and pesticides.

quences—such as starvation, squalor, retarded economic growth—maldistribution of food resources introduces other potential difficulties. At present is
the fear that those states enjoying plentiful food supplies will use them coer-
cively to ensure steady flows of mineral resources from the mineral-rich Third
World countries. The introduction of food into the global formula of competitive embargoes would represent a major change in the power resources of international politics, but with individually measurable human costs. In 1979,
the prospect of using food as a weapon became a reality. As part of the American reaction to the Soviet invasion of Afghanistan, the Carter administration
terminated unilaterally a trade agreement with the Kremlin and in so doing
discontinued bulk grain sales to the Soviet Union. At almost the same time, as
Americans became impatient with the Iranian government for holding American diplomatic personnel hostage in retaliation for permitting the deposed
shah to enter the United States for surgical treatment, there was a growing
demand to discontinue food shipments to Iran. As this became a more popular
thought, some political forces in the United States advanced food embargoes
as a general policy in dealing with the OPEC countries in response to petroleum embargoes or uncontrolled price increases of raw petroleum. Except in
the case with the Soviet Union over Afghanistan, however, no such policy has
been applied.[10]

Despite the efforts of the World Food Conference to establish an international food production program, the large producers have made it clear that
food production will remain a matter of national policy. Indeed, because food
comprises a large portion of international trade volume, national agricultural
policies are linked directly to the international problem. As recently as 1986,
for example, the United States publicly recognized the extent to which its international trade balance was deteriorating because of the very successful agricultural policies of the European Economic Community, and so Washington
requested that Western Europe reduce its agricultural production of such staples as grains and butter. Such nationalistic policies ensure that effective international planning of food production and distribution is a matter for the
future. Until such planning is feasible, the industrializing world will have to
depend on declining terms of trade, scientific development of synthetic pro-
tein, and other sources of nutrition and foreign assistance in developing crop
yields through soil programs and irrigation.

But here one of the great ironies of modern life intrudes: Although malnutrition and starvation are increasingly prevalent in the Third World, competition for agricultural exports among the states of North America and Western
Europe countinues to drive an economic assumption that production is too

---

[10]On the general subject of food export policy as an instrument of international diplomacy, see
Raymond F. Hopkins and Donald J. Puchala, *Global Food Interdependence: Challenge to American Foreign Policy* (New York: Columbia University Press, 1979).

It is difficult, perhaps futile, to assess the impact of the American grain embargo on Soviet
behavior. The American secretary of agriculture has gone only so far as to label it "a significant
inconvenience." For a critical assessment, see Robert L. Pearlberg, "Lessons of the Grain Embargo," *Foreign Affairs*, Fall 1980, pp. 144–162.

plentiful. Meanwhile, because of adverse terms of trade and mounting debt, the Third World states actually reduced their agricultural imports during the first half of the 1980s. Now, as new scientific techniques offer the promise of greater productivity, less attention is given to the ability to feed the starving than to the potential price reductions and ensuing economic consequences in the producing countries. Moreover, as many Third World countries have attempted to improve their self-sufficiency in food, they have embarked upon programs of deforestation in order to increase the acreage of farmlands, only to find that they have, instead, expanded deserts and greatly increased starvation. It is widely theorized that the massive starvation in Ethiopia and other northeast African countries—for which the "Live Aid" and "We Are the People" campaigns were mounted in 1985—was the result of deforestation and desertification.

Before continuing with the list of subjects that calls urgently for the world's multilateral attention, it is appropriate to pause to consider the interrelationships of the subjects considered so far. For many years, both in diplomacy and in the scholarly literature, economic development, population, environmental preservation, and population control were largely considered as separate issues. But during the last decade it has become apparent that they are closely related. In a world of rapidly expanding population and shrinking resources, in which the old promise of limitless capacity for economic growth has been exposed as vacuous, we are now faced with the problem of adjusting aspirations in both the industrialized world and the Third World to access to those resources necessary for our survival, with a limited population and a restrained standard of living.

In light of this realization, the economic and development programs of the United Nations have been partially redrawn to integrate consideration of population, resources, environment, and development—PRED.[11] The Second International Conference on Population at Mexico City in 1984 marked the first practical effort to recognize the inseparability of these issues in a comprehensive consideration of the world's economic future. Although only a beginning, it does at least represent a broad recognition of the complexity of the problem and the willingness of the Third World to reconsider the social foundations of economic development. But even if these efforts succeed, the stratification of national standards of living will continue unless the recent competitive urge for nationalistic advantage is once again replaced by an effective spirit and program of economic interdependence. A successful initiative of a PRED-oriented world development cannot overcome the problems and miseries of the Third World except with the reversal of the twilight of internationalism that is sweeping the industrialized peoples.[12]

---

[11]Branislav Gosovic, "Population–Resources–Environment–Development Relationships in the United Nations: In Search of an Approach," *CEPAL Review,* no. 23, August 1984, pp. 135–154. This is a publication of the United Nations Economic Commission for Latin America and the Caribbean.

[12]Thomas L. Hughes, "The Twilight of Internationalism" *Foreign Policy,* Winter 1985–1986,

5. Science and Technology

The dramatic improvements in standards of living that have characterized the current century are attributable in large measure to advances in science and technology. Particularly since World War II, scientific discovery and application have reached into every facet of life in new ways. Biomedical science and engineering have produced chemical compounds that prolong life and machinery that sustains the ill. Recombinant DNA techniques that produce new forms of microbial life will soon produce enzymes, hormones, and other chemical compounds that afflicted organs fail to produce. Supersonic aircraft have reduced the duration of intercontinental travel to a few hours. Communications have been revolutionized to a point that home computer terminals may eventually replace daily newspapers. New synthetic fertilizers and genetically manipulated seed stocks—notwithstanding their costly ecological effects—have enabled farmers to increase crop yields. And the genetic engineering of animal species has resulted in the production of greatly enlarged meat animals and milk cows of greatly increased capacity.

But these miracles of the modern age are not without their liabilities. In the industrialized countries in particular, disposal of chemical waste poses dangers to plant and animal life. Because dumped chemicals eventually find their way back into the human food chain through soil and water and ingestion by lower species, the long-range consequences of carelessly planned dumping may be catastrophic. In 1980, the Surgeon General of the United States declared for the first time that the uncontrolled consequences of scientific and technological development are multiplying the disease burden of the American people and the annual national cost of health care. But it is the long-term results of toxification that are most alarming. With the United States alone producing over 300 billion pounds of synthetic chemicals annually, and other nations producing amounts in proportion to their economies, it is certain that national solutions to these problems will be inadequate.

Not all the consequences of scientific and technological modernization are physical or physiological. In recent years, social scientists have begun to focus on their social and political consequences. For some time, futurists have attempted to postulate the characteristics of the postindustrial or technological societies. More recently, as some of the liabilities of the age have become so alarmingly apparent, they have begun to focus on mechanisms of social control and forms of decision making that will preserve philosophies of government rather than simply respond to technological change. Increasingly they argue that socially responsible decision making is falling prey to decisional reactions necessitated by the lure of scientific discovery.[13] The use of nuclear fuel, for

---

pp. 25–48. This is an American self-criticism based on the supposition that the "traditional internationalist themes are no longer significant outlets for political idealism in the United States." The concept has been expanded for its global application here.

[13]See particularly Langdon Winner, *Autonomous Technology: Technics-Out-of-Control as a Theme in Political Thought* (Cambridge, Mass.: MIT Press, 1977); and Roger Benjamin, *The Limits of Politics* (Chicago: University of Chicago Press, 1980).

example, was scarcely a topic of public debate until after its dangers became apparent. But by that time so many billions of dollars had been invested in it that rational decision making had no practical application. By the same token, international exchanges of nuclear fuel were licensed by governments largely as a form of commerical competition until controls were demanded after India used fuel provided by the United States for peaceful purposes to construct and explode a nuclear weapon. The prospect of nuclear fuel's falling into the hands of terrorists has further prompted demands for controls, yet these have been demanded only after nuclear fuel exchanges have become common and only after reprocessing plants and breeder reactors (which permit certain types of nuclear fuel to be rejuvenated for a second use) have been completed and put into use.

The dilemma becomes apparent: Science and technology are largely responsible for the rapid improvement in national standards of living in the current century and are major hopes for the improved economic competitiveness of the Third World; yet the cost of such progress is measured not just in economic terms but in human and social terms as well. We have grown deeply dependent on these advances; but unless we control their long-term physical and political consequences, their forces may be as destructive as they are progressive.

6. Autocratic Government and Human Rights

From a humanistic viewpoint, another problem looms just as large. Traditionally, each political system has determined its governing philosophy and has established the quality of relations between the government and the governed. Many political systems—if not most—have justified stern restrictions on human freedoms and rights. Autocratic politics has been history's rule rather than its exception. In an era of growing literacy, improved mass communications, national liberation, and domestic protest, can the peace of national peoples be preserved against the brutality of governments? At present, Taiwan and South Korea are enjoying economic growth rates of 10 percent, twice that of Japan and two and one-half times that of the United States, yet these are two of the world's most repressive regimes. At what price progress? Furthermore, can the world's peace be preserved in the face of government brutality, the ever-present danger of insurgency, or revolution followed by foreign intervention? What role is there for international politics in building a global regime of human rights and dignity in face of absolute state control over national subjects?

In the last decade, much of the world's political consciousness has been riveted on the question of human rights. This has resulted in part from the communications revolution, which has made public spectacles of brutality and political repression. *Apartheid* (the policy of racial separation practiced by South Africa), the Nobel Prize–winning revelations of Amnesty International regarding the practices of some governments in imprisoning political enemies, and worldwide sympathy for Soviet Jews who have been prevented by their government from emigrating to Israel—these have all been issues of popular attention, fanned by the news media.

There have been official stimulants to the world conscience also. The Vladivostok accords called on the United States and the Soviet Union to treat their nationals according to agreed international standards. A quarter-century after the passage by the United Nations General Assembly of the Universal Declaration of Human Rights, two international covenants (the International Covenant on Political and Economic Rights and the International Covenant on Social and Cultural Rights) finally secured enough signatories to come into effect. The 1978 Belgrade Conference on Human Rights, resulting from the Vladivostok Conference in 1978, was conducted amid much popular acclaim but produced little of significance. And finally, President Jimmy Carter's emphasis on human rights in American foreign policy (even to the extent of chilling Soviet-American relations) kept the general issue in the forefront of international news, even if more as a political matter than as a humanistic one.

But with what practical result? Despite the expansion of international standards for the protection of human rights, political imprisonment, denial of due process, unethical (and perhaps illegal) economic exploitation of minorities, and other violations of basic human rights abound. This is due in part to the variety of ideological interpretations given to international standards and in part to the impulse of powerful factions to defend their position against rising expectations of political freedom. Without international sanctioning authority competent to monitor the proliferation of declaratory international standards, the protection of human rights will continue to suffer from inconsistencies of national policy and the maldistribution of political power in national political systems.

7. World Economics

Yet another form of contemporary anarchy is the international economic system. Despite foreign aid and international development programs, a powerful few dominate the world economy. Self-serving autocracy of the economically powerful states and of their political elites, together with central planning and allocation, is the guidepost of world economics. Imperialism, neoimperialism, exploitation, discrimination, and manipulation—these are the instruments used by the powerful to subordinate the weak. Stability in economic relations cries out for international supervision and new modes of decision making.

Already new patterns are emerging. The dependence of the Western industrialized nations on the wealthy but socially and economically less developed petroleum exporters of the Third World changed the face of global economic relations between 1973 and 1983. But this reverse dependency is marked by forms of anarchy of its own: Manipulation, retaliation for a century of subordination, and decisions of global impact made as much out of competition within OPEC as out of cooperation. Only in 1979 and 1980 did there begin to emerge a rational pattern of decision making with respect to the quantity of oil production and its price, based at first on the general principle of trying to force the industrial states to control inflation and subjected later to efforts to establish complex formulae giving attention to inflation, declining values of currencies, anticipation of resource depletion, and correlation of the export trade with the rate of internal economic development. But this progress declined in 1982 and 1983 when internal disagreement among the OPEC members flared up, sparked by the radicals who wished to maximize profits and the moderates who wanted to stabilize the world petroleum market. As a result, prices dropped, and incentives for exploration of new sources of oil were removed. In 1985, OPEC's power virtually collapsed.

A second new pattern centers on the activities of the transnational corporations. Although they are chartered by states of origin and licensed to operate in host economies, the magnitude and complexity of their operations place them virtually outside the legal control of any government(s) and subject them only to regional controls to the extent of their operations within those regions that have attempted to apply controls.

A third pattern, although perhaps less new, pertains to the imperatives of the welfare state. As the welfare-state concept has spread throughout the industrial world, individual nation-states have strengthened the arsenal of public policies by which they control and maintain the loyalty of their nationals.[14] The political imperatives that follow from this observation ensure that the state's commitment to a more rational international economic order may be secondary.

A closely related phenomenon is the ''new protectionism.'' Although the interdependence of economies and the activities of transnational corporations have generally stimulated technology transfer and industrial productivity, they have had detrimental consequences for some developed economies. At a time when American industrial sales at home and abroad have been challenged by imports from Japan and the European Economic Community, rising imports and troubling balance-of-trade deficits with respect to the Third World (particularly the OPEC Third World) have led to new demands for protection of the American economy. And this pattern has been repeated elsewhere.

Superimposed on all these difficulties is the growing scarcity in the world of natural resources, investment capital, and economic leadership. The 1973–1974 oil embargo gave rise to the notion of an age of scarcity; and the dwindling wealth of the United States relative to that of the world has, since about 1971, produced the notion that the American Century was really more like 25 years in duration. These two phenomena—scarcity and leadership decline—have encouraged new thinking about the future of the world economy. One person in particular has called for a system of global economic management

---

[14]Melvyn B. Krauss, *The New Protectionism: The Welfare State and International Trade* (New York: New York University Press, 1978); and George R. Neumann, ''Adjustment Assistance for Trade-Displaced Workers,'' in David B. H. Denoon, ed., *The New International Economic Order: A U.S. Response* (New York: New York University Press, 1979), pp. 109–140. A different analysis found governments reacting to the breakdown of this kind of order. See James Rosenau, ''A Pre-Theory Revisited: World Politics in an Era of Cascading Interdependence,'' *International Studies Quarterly,* September 1984, pp. 245–305.

(GEM), under the aegis of international organizations, to establish and monitor global and regional growth rates that do not produce major resource constraints or inflation. The constituent organizations would have the authority to
forecast and establish growth rates, to control supplies of funds to nations, and
to negotiate bilaterally and multilaterally any structural economic changes
necessary to achieve the agreed rates.[15]

It is doubtful that governments will go so far as to institute such a global
process. It is clear, however, that in an age of scarcity and decline, states will
turn inward, with the result that the normal antagonism between internationalism and nationalism will intensify.[16] The outcome of the struggle on a global
basis will determine whether the next quarter-century will see the creation or
the decay of a new economic regime. The argument of this book, however, is
that the erosion of the international economic regime is an obstacle to effective interdependence and that only reform of basic attitudes, structures, and
patterns of interaction can transform the global economy for the next century.
Contemporary system dynamics are self-destructive, and any further retreat to
narrow national goals at the expense of interdependent solutions to economic
problems cannot contribute to stability.

8. International Public Goods and Property

When we speak of the international economy, we refer to trade, capital, labor,
and specific commodities. But there are other aspects of global economic life
that do not fall into these categories. These we distinguish as international
public goods and international public property, and we save them for special
treatment here.

International public goods are not tangible commodities, yet they are the
products of domestic manufacture in the sense that they are the products of
policy. They are social goods that are not traded in the market, but without
which effective global economic activity cannot occur. And although there is
no generally accepted list of these goods, there are some that stand out.

From the standpoint of all the social sciences, the most important of these is
peace. As contrasted with rights that are elucidated in law, any moral philosophy or political theory posits peace as a public good. In 1984, the General
Assembly of the United Nations promulgated its Declaration on the Rights of
Peoples to Peace, but it did so with little support from the Western governments that objected to the political subjectivity of the language.

From an economic standpoint, there are several other international public
goods, most of them related to an open system of exchange. These include
freedom of the seas, well-defined rights of property in host territories, standards of weights and measures for fair exchange, internationally accepted

---

[15]D. B. Steele, ''The Case for Global Economic Management and U.N. System Reform,'' *International Organization,* Summer 1985, pp. 561–578.
[16]Ted R. Gurr, ''On the Political Consequences of Scarcity and Economic Decline,'' *International
Studies Quarterly,* March 1985, pp. 51–75.

currencies and exchange rates, politically agreed-on trading systems, capital flow mechanisms, consistent macroeconomic systems during times of stability, and agreed-on sources of crisis management and emergency lending in times of need.[17]

For much of the time since the Second World War, the United States has contributed a leadership role to the global economic system, partly by its direct action (for example, making the dollar available as an international currency, providing a steady flow of capital to the Third World) or through its leadership in establishing an international regime of institutions to govern the international economy (for example, the International Monetary Fund and the International Bank for Reconstruction and Development). Now, however, because of scarcity and America's own economic decline, attention has been turned inward, and the United States no longer practices this leadership. As a result, the intangible international public goods necessary for an effective global economy are in jeopardy.

International public property differs in that it consists of specific commodities, but they occur in nature, they are not fixed to national territories, and they are not for the most part traded in the market. Principal among them are the air and fresh waters shared by two or more nation-states. The waters of the seas and oceans also fall into this category, although it has long been established (and reaffirmed by the Law of the Sea Treaty) that exploitation of the sea and the seabed results in tradable national goods.

Unlike international public goods that support and sustain the economic system, international public properties sustain life. As a result, nations have a shared obligation to protect them against spoilage and pollution, against irradiation, and against sequestration. In our earlier treatment of ecological issues, we saw the extent to which governments have failed to protect against the former two. Now let us look briefly at the last. Does a government have a right to divert a river that flows to or through more than one nation for its exclusive use? If a downstream riparian state depends on the river's flow for commerce or drinking water or any other ligitimate purpose, does its upstream neighbor have a right to divert the flow to its own exclusive irrigation purposes? The concept of international public property says that it does not.

The habit of nationalistic exploitation of international public properties, together with the failure of governments to recognize their joint responsibilities in this domain, has put those properties at considerable risk. Redoubled international efforts for regulation in this vital area of interdependent concern is thus one of the major issues for the future of world order.

Despite the remedial efforts of diplomats to overcome these vexing problems through organization, law, and integration, the magnitude of the problems and the antiquity of national solutions further highlight the dilemma of traditional international remedies. So long as the unique sovereign attributes of the

---

[17]This entire section on international public goods is fashioned after Charles P. Kindleberger, "International Public Goods Without International Government," *American Economic Review*, March 1986, pp. 1–13.

nation-state are preserved, the pace of deterioration will continue to outrun proposed solutions, rendering them always ideas after their times. Accordingly, research has centered on wholly new approaches, although they vary considerably in scope. Some, labeled maximalist proposals, seek a fully structured world government; the minimalist proposals advocate upgrading existing international machinery; and the reformist proposals would generally retain the current systemic features but would subject the nation-state to global law.

The Idea of World Order

Although two world wars and the nuclear arms race have prompted new interest in the world order movement, the idea is an ancient one. It has arisen repeatedly in history from peace groups, governments, philosophers, religious thinkers, imperialists, and nationalistic zealots. Until recently, the world order movement has been synonymous with the quest for world government. One of the earliest-known forms was that of ancient Rome, whose imperial quest sought to bring all the known world under Roman political control. Other imperial impulses to world domination have been grossly maniacal, such as that of Adolf Hitler, whose aim was to rule Europe and then the world on behalf of the Aryan race.

Several other sources of universalist sentiment have also emerged. Theologians have posited concepts of control, although not through governmental superiority. St. Thomas Aquinas propounded the concept of a universal Christian spirit forging a human community and supplying the ideals and benevolence of Christian rulers throughout the world. He distinguished the power of the state (*imperium*) from that of the church (*sacerdotium*), leaving room for separate governments in different lands, even though as a papist he viewed papal power as superior to secular power. Even in a Christian Europe, however, and writing a half-century later than Thomas (about 1310 A.D.), Dante saw the only hope for world peace (meaning essentially European peace) in the consolidation of all power in the Roman emperor. In the words of one eminent student of political philosophy, "Neither by birth nor breeding was Dante a partisan of the imperial cause. His imperialism was purely an idealization of universal peace." [18]

Thinkers in more modern times have frequently revived these ideas. The Spanish theologian Francisco Suarez, writing in the absolutist era bridging the sixteenth and seventeenth centuries and imbued with Jean Bodin's notions of sovereignty, moved from the concept of moral law to the hope of world government. Later in the seventeenth century, the English philosopher Thomas Hobbes wrote in *Leviathan* that the political nature of society is that of war of every man against every man and that through social contract, men form governments to which they entrust the security of all. Applied to

---

[18]George H. Sabine, *A History of Political Theory,* 3rd ed. (New York: Holt, Rinehart and Winston, 1961), pp. 257–258.

international relations, Hobbes's social contract extrapolates to a theory of world government.

The German thinker Georg Hegel, whose dialectical method formed the basis of Marx's arguments about class conflict, included in his theory of history the concept of a world spirit of the governing class. Although Hegel was a nationalist, he nevertheless found a universal morality in political leadership, freedom, and even the arts. Despite his nationalistic fervor, he saw every state falling to the universal logic of the world spirit. Marx not only adopted Hegel's system of argument; he also made similar historical predictions. Rather than concentrate on a governing class and a mystical world spirit, Marx looked to the working class and the eventual elimination of class conflict. When power resides in the hands of the proletariat, states will wither away, and all people will be ruled in classless harmony. In this utopian prediction, government becomes not state centered but spirit centered.

But visions of universal political morality and utopian harmony have not arisen exclusively in philosophical abstraction. Indeed, the popularity of world order schemes has paralleled certain events: the frequency of war, the destructiveness of modern industrialized warfare, imperial competition, and the irrationality of ideological fears, to name only a few. There is at least impressionistic evidence of a correlation between world order enthusiasm and warfare. The activity and popularity of such proposals seem highest toward the end of, and upon conclusion of, major wars; the longer and more tranquil postwar periods are, the more rapid will be the decline in popularity of world government ideals. This correlation seems guided by a simple ''rule'' of world politics: When states serve their functions satisfactorily and with minimal external disruption, only a handful of activists advocate world government; but when the nation-state system breaks down, more people share the world government sentiment.

It follows from this ''rule'' that the present century has been one of consistently high interest in world order. The destruction caused by the First World War was unprecedented, and the vision of the further industrialization of war potential forged a solid core of sentiment for some form of central government. In America, a group known as the League to Enforce Peace considered several alternative forms of international organization, with some of its adherents arguing for virtual international government. Intent on retaining their sovereign prerogatives, however, national governments were willing to do no more than subscribe to President Woodrow Wilson's League of Nations. Predecessor to the United Nations, the League of Nations (1) prescribed mechanisms for the peaceful settlement of international disputes, (2) called upon its members to guarantee the territorial integrity and political independence of all other members, (3) looked forward to general arms limitation, (4) authorized its council to undertake enforcement action against aggressors, and (5) mandated member states to impose sanctions against violators of the peace.

As an instrument of world order, the League of Nations was generally a disappointment to the advocates of world government. They viewed it as little more than a smokescreen for power politics. Its voting provisions, especially on matters of greatest interest to members of the council, restricted progress toward effective international decision making and encouraged great-power domination of policy. Although many saw in the assembly, where all member states were represented, an opportunity to sow and to germinate the seeds of international society, there was general discouragement over the decentralization of sanction procedures and over the great-power control of peace/war issues. But of major long-range interest was the network of functional organizations (single-purpose agencies with specific technical tasks), which seemed to promise greater person-to-person contact around the world and to offer an opportunity for the development of loyalty to a political entity outside nation-states. Ultimately, the problem of the nation-state system is not simply the existence of multiple sovereignties, but the ability of governments to monopolize the secular loyalties of individuals and to mobilize them for nationalistic rather than universalistic purposes. Any institutional structure that might erode this pattern is acceptable to the advocates of world government and to the proponents of most other doctrines of world order as well.

Some universalists viewed the League of Nations with even deeper suspicion, principally because of its collective security provisions. Collective security could not govern, they argued; it could maintain peace only by the threat of force. Thus, it was a negative approach to international stability, still built on nationalistic preferences. It did not address the causes of conflict; it was powerless to legislate preventative social, political, and economic changes; and it was impotent when international norms were violated, except by the unanimous consent of the council members. Hence, some saw the League not as a steppingstone between the nation-state system and world government but as a threat to world government.

Although the League of Nations failed to prevent war, its history was partly successful from a world order perspective. It made modest but positive contributions to self-determinism, previously little more than a platitude. Its social, scientific, and economic projects made inroads into problems of squalor and disease. Postwar relief programs, assistance to refugees, and the League's management of intellectual exchanges all earned for the organization a reputation as a helpful intermediary among governments in matters not directly related to national security. One of the celebrated events of the League was its acceptance in 1939 of the Bruce Committee Report, which advocated a broad reorganization of authority for social and economic development. Although the Second World War prevented its immediate application, the report formed the rationale for establishing the Economic and Social Council as a permanent organ of the United Nations.

Despite these League successes, the concept of intergovernmental organization was not generally popular with advocates of world government during the interwar period. Like other critics of the League, they found its failings more notable than its successes. But more than that, the Second World War was testimony to the intrinsic weaknesses of collective security in particular and of intergovernmental organization in general.

The war and its aftermath further heightened the vigor of the world order movement. While the State Department was planning, at first secretly, to revitalize collective security in an organization to be known as the United

Nations, the United World Federalists were organizing in support of world government. That the war had been global rather than continental demonstrated the need for universal regulation. The unprecedented devastation, including the use of atomic weapons, accentuated the need for world government before technical advances led to world domination and centralized imperialism. The polarization of world politics and the Soviet-American standoff, along with the growing reality of a balance of terror, convinced many people that this might be humanity's last half-century to achieve effective world order.

Vigorous advocacy was untimely. At the end of the Second World War, hopes were high for the United Nations, dedicated in part to the principle— the grand design—that the major powers, despite their differences, could cooperate in peacetime to preserve stability as they had cooperated during wartime to establish it. Remembering the problems of 1918, advocates of world government had to contest this sentiment. Their first major effort occurred in October 1945 at a conference in Dublin, New Hampshire. Attended by both "world federalists" and proponents of a "world law" movement, the Dublin Conference derogated the adequacy of the United Nations, called for a world federal government of limited powers, and urged that either the United Nations Charter be amended into federalist form or that a world constitutional convention be called. Only five months later, in March 1946, a second conference was held at Rollins College in Winter Park, Florida. There, delegates reaffirmed the necessity for world federal government but found the United Nations Charter the most practicable route.[19]

For the moment, the world government movement remained almost exclusively the province of a few committed activists. In the United States, especially, sentiment seemed to lean toward intergovernmental organization, with the specific hope that this time, with the backing of American power, the UN experiment might prevent cataclysmic war. But the promise collapsed with the onset of the Cold War and the desire of like-minded nations to cluster into defensive alliances outside the United Nations. A new threat to the concept of world order emerged: the willingness of states to entrust the preservation of their sovereignty to their most powerful allies.

One result was the movement for a union of the Western democracies, which frightened the proponents of world government by the threat of a regional central government that, because of ideological inspiration, would harden the polarity of the world and further delay the universalist dream. There was fear that the North Atlantic Treaty Organization (NATO) might form the base of such a movement.

Faced with two competing movements—intergovernmental organization (UN) and the possibility of counterproductive regional supranationalism (NATO)—the universalists took to the offensive. In pursuit of the findings of the Rollins College meeting, Cord Meyer, Jr., president of the United World

---

[19]For a review of early events, see Edward McN. Burns, "The Movement for World Government," *Science,* vol. 25, 1948, pp. 5–13.

Federalists, offered testimony before the House Foreign Relations Committee (May 1948) in which he called upon Congress to champion greater strength for the United Nations through Charter amendment, not to strengthen its intergovernmental quality, but to advance it toward world government. A year later (October 1949) Grenville Clark, a distinguished lawyer and later director of the World Peace Through Law Movement, sat before the same committee to testify on two bills: for the World Federation Resolution and against the Atlantic Union Resolution. The former called for an American initiative for the evolution of world government, and the latter for a union of Western democracies. In an eloquent plea, Clark argued that "the distinction is of basic importance. It marks, I believe, the difference between peaceful evolution and a probable or possible third world war." He concluded:

> We ought always to remember that there are only two ways for the West and the East to be brought into cooperation. One way is an enforced cooperation, following the conquest of one by the other. But we know that the West cannot be conquered in the foreseeable future. And we know that while the West might well completely subjugate the East, after unprecedented slaughter, the West has no wish to do so. We realize that, as Henry L. Stimson [former secretary of state in the Hoover administration and secretary of war to President Franklin Roosevelt] has said: "Americans as conquerors would be tragically miscast."
>
> The only other way is that of cooperation by the free consent of both sides, to be achieved, slowly perhaps but steadily, by mutual toleration and without requiring either the sacrifice of honor or principle. That can be done and when it is achieved, the basis will exist to create the universal world federation by fundamental amendment of the United Nations Charter.
>
> One other thing we should never forget—that however necessary our present policy under the Atlantic Treaty (NATO) may be, that policy can be no more than a stopgap. It embodies no element of world order under law. On the contrary, it is the essence of power politics. It may well be helpful in gaining time to seek the solution. It is in itself no stable solution at all.
>
> The world federalism resolution fully recognizes this in calling for a more fundamental objective of our foreign policy, namely, the development of the United Nations into a world federation open to all nations.[20]

As the US Congress entertained world government resolutions in its sessions of 1948 and 1949, private groups were busily drafting universal constitutions. Some of these, such as that of Grenville Clark, aimed at reordering the United Nations. Others started from scratch, constructing world constitutional models as though the experience of intergovernmental organization were not at hand.

It is one thing to propound the establishment of government but quite another to equip it to achieve the desired ends in a heterogeneous world. How much power should there be? How should it be divided among governmental

---

[20]Meyer's testimony is reprinted in Julia E. Johnson, ed., *Federal World Government* (New York: H. W. Wilson, 1948), pp. 86–94. Clark's can be found in app. B of his *Plan for Peace* (New York: Harper and Brothers, 1950), pp. 78–83.

organs? To what extent should authority be left to "local" government of the former nation-states? What limitations on power ought to be prescribed? How can these limitations be preserved? What sorts of incentives to compliance should be arranged, and what kinds of punishment for violations? Even more fundamental, what aims and values is world government to pursue? One contemporary observer, a well-known international law scholar deeply concerned with problems of world order, expressed his troubled feelings:

> I believe *that it is no longer a question as to whether or not there will be world government by the year 2000. The questions are rather, how will world government come into being and what form will it take?*[21]

Still, however, not all world order concepts embrace the idea of world government, although such a tendency is typical of maximalist proposals.

World Order: A Maximalist Proposal

Committed to the need to restructure international order, some students of the future have considered maximal alternatives. Inasmuch as many of the serious proposals have come from Americans, the federal model of government pervades most investigations. Harking back to US constitutional heritage, the federal model has gained wider popularity through the United World Federalists and through implementation elsewhere. This is a system of government in which the total sovereignty of the state is divided in such a way as to make the central government sovereign over some transactions, other smaller units sovereign over some other transactions, and the two cooperatively sovereign over still other matters. This system is designed primarily to prevent absolutism or a drift toward full centralization. Moving from this model, Vernon Nash, then the vice-president of the United World Federalists, wrote this disclaimer of absolute central world government:

> Conscious, sharp aversion to the idea of world government arises mainly from two false assumptions. The first is that national governments would be abolished, or entirely subordinated, in the creation of a world state. The second is that nationality would thereby be wiped out. Both fears are baseless. We do not need nationalism; *we need only modify the present absolute nature of national sovereignty.*[22]

Hence, the movement for world federalism draws a distinct line between world government and the formation of a world state.

But in addition to its frontal assault on absolute sovereignty, world federalism seeks to supervene strident nationalism. Effective peace through government requires more than changes on the political map. It means changing national

---

[21]Saul H. Mendlovitz, "Models of World Order," in Richard B. Gray, ed., *International Security Systems* (Itasca, Ill.: Peacock, 1969), pp. 178–192. Emphasis in the original.

[22]Vernon Nash, *The World Must be Governed*, 2nd ed. (New York: Harper and Brothers, 1949), p. 4. Emphasis added.

perceptions, enlightening national views of the ideals and expectations of other peoples, and so on. In a symposium on the world community in 1947, one observer expressed a vivid notion that typifies the attack on nationalism:

> The person I cannot get out of my mind these days is the young man who dropped the first atomic bomb. I suppose he is a nice young man. . . yet the odd thing is that, if he had been ordered to go and drop it on Milwaukee, he almost certainly would have refused. . . . Because he was asked to drop it on Hiroshima, he not only consented but he became something of a hero for it. . . . Of course, I don't quite see the distinction between dropping it on Milwaukee and dropping it on Hiroshima. The difference is a "we" difference. The people of Milwaukee, though we don't know any of them, are "we," and the people of Hiroshima are "they," and the great psychological problem is how to make everybody "we," at least in some small degree. The degree need be only extremely small. I don't think we have to love our neighbor with any degree of affection. All that is necessary to create the psychological foundations of a world society is that people in Maine should feel the same degree of responsibility toward the people of Japan or Chile or Indo-China as they feel toward California. That is pretty small, really, but it is apparently enough to create the United States.[23]

Although world federalists customarily place the formation of world government chronologically ahead of the formulation of a world society, their intention is to eradicate the nationalistic consequences of sovereignty as well as national sovereignty itself.

Separation of Powers

A second fundamental concept is also borrowed by the world federalists from the American constitutional model: the separation of powers. A concept traditionally ascribed to the French philosopher Montesquieu, the separation of powers divides the power of the federal government into three branches—legislative, executive, and judicial—in order to avert tyranny by a single political authority. As James Madison argued in *Federalist Paper No. 47*, a pamphlet written to argue for ratification of the American Constitution, "The accumulation of all powers, legislative, executive, and judiciary, in the same hands, whether of one, a few, or many, and whether hereditary, self-appointed, or elective, may justly be pronounced the very definition of tyranny." Imbued with this spirit, major proposals for world federation usually include separation of powers.

The first attempt at world constitution making emerged from the Committee to Frame a World Constitution, formed at the University of Chicago in 1945. Its chief author was an Italian émigré, G. A. Borgese. Equipped to reveal its work publicly through its publication *Common Cause* (in no way related to the

---

[23]Kenneth E. Boulding, "Discussion of World Economic Contacts," in Quincy Wright, ed., *The World Community* (Chicago: University of Chicago Press, 1948), pp. 101–112.

contemporary American populist movement), this committee announced in 1947 and 1948, in serial fashion, a preliminary draft of a world constitution for the Federal Republic of the World.

In addition to prescription of the organs of government, the preliminary draft specified the areas of substantive power. In normal federal fashion, the draft stipulated, after enumerating specific powers, that "the powers not delegated to the World Government in this Constitution, and not prohibited by it to the several members of the Federal World Republic, shall be reserved to the several states or nations or unions thereof." This provision was intended to guarantee within the federal scheme the integrity of traditional governmental units and political communities. A few years later, addressing the same point, another advocate of world federalism wrote:

> The crucial need is for an effective division of the internal and external sovereignty of all nations. This would leave to each nation its internal sovereignty while helping all nations to pool their separately held fragments of international sovereignty for transfer to world federal government. Generally speaking, any problem national governments are unable to solve acting separately, requires international solution and ought to become a responsibility of world government.[24]

Inis L. Claude, Jr., expressed this sentiment somewhat more succinctly when he wrote: "Federalism symbolizes functionally-limited centralization, but centralization nonetheless."[25]

Highly institutionalized maximalist schemes such as the Borgese proposal have been rather common in the history of the world order movement. Yet, in their ambition to restructure the international system, they have run afoul of the same criticisms time and again. Principally, there have been three attacks. One concerns the social practicability of these schemes. A second relates to the slender probability of successful implementation. The third deals with the issue of the philosophical desirability of world government.

The Social Practicability of World Government

The theologian and social observer Reinhold Niebuhr once wrote: "Virtually all arguments for world government rest upon the simple presupposition that the desirability of world order proves the attainability of world government."[26] Even if one accepts the desirability of world government, which we will examine subsequently, what is the link between desirability and attainability?

The critical issue in addressing this question is the relation between society and government. World federalists tend to argue that if people will look be-

[24]Edith Wynner, *World Federal Government in Maximum Terms* (Afton, N.Y.: Fedonat Press, 1954), p. 38.

[25]Inis L. Claude, Jr., *Power and International Relations* (New York: Random House, 1962), p. 207.

[26]Reinhold Niebuhr, *Christian Realism and Political Problems* (New York: Scribner's, 1949), as reprinted in Arend Lijphart, ed., *World Politics,* 2nd ed. (Boston: Allyn & Bacon, 1971), pp. 71–80, "The Illusion of World Government."

yond their governments, they will be able to shape a supranational government capable of maximizing social integration, effective compliance with law, and perpetual peace. Critics hold, on the contrary, that governments have little ability to integrate communities; rather, the merger of diverse value patterns and heritages is a sociopsychological process to which governments may give direction but which cannot be legislated into effectiveness, regardless of the type of government. Integration is a matter of will rather than of power.

Studies have been conducted in a number of countries on the images that national people have of one another. Two of these, undertaken 15 years apart, used essentially the same technique. Respondents to questions were asked to describe their feelings about their own nations and about people in other countries, by placing in order several adjectives. In the earlier study, the frequency of selection of particular descriptive words was reported in percentages. For example, when Americans were asked to rate themselves, only 2 percent chose the word "cruel" and only 2 percent the word "backward." But when the same people were asked to rate the Russian people, no fewer than 50 percent selected "cruel" and 40 percent "backward." By the same token, 39 percent of British questioned thought the Russians cruel, and 36 percent thought them backward. Only 12 percent of both British and Americans thought the Russian people intelligent. In the polling among people of eight different Western countries (Australia, Britain, Germany, France, Italy, the Netherlands, Norway, and the United States), positive adjectives were applied most frequently to the subject's own people. Consistently, the Soviet people and the Chinese people were assigned positive adjectives least frequently and negative adjectives most frequently.

But even among Western neighbors and allies there appeared to be social barriers to complete trust and mutual respect. Not surprisingly, given historical relations, the German people held the French in low regard. German respect for the French was only a fraction above that for the Russians and the Chinese, although Germans thought the French more intelligent, less cruel, and less backward than the Russians. Yet Germans thought the French less brave, less self-controlled, and less peace-loving than Russians, even though the polling was done during the Korean War.[27]

A similar questioning technique presents subjects with pairs of adjectives that have opposite meanings, such as cowardly and brave, stupid and intelligent, lazy and industrious. In a study in which people were asked to select preferable adjectives first to describe foreign peoples and then to depict their governments, both ethnic images (people) and national images (governments) were determined. Among Americans polled, the results were tabulated in decreasing order of preference (see Table 18–2).

Note that in the ethnic ratings all noncommunist peoples are ranked higher than all communist peoples with the exception of Nationalist Chinese, who rank behind the European communists but ahead of the mainland Chinese. By

---

[27]For a full tabular report of results, see William Buchanan and Hadley Cantril, *How Nations See Each Other* (Urbana: University of Illinois Press, 1953), pp. 46–47.

Table 18–2 Americans' ranking of ethnic and national images, in decreasing order of preference.

Ethnic (peoples)	National (governments)
Finnish	United States
West German	Finland
American	West Germany
Russian	Nationalist China
East German	Soviet Union
Nationalist Chinese (Taiwan)	East Germany
Chinese	China

Source: Adapted by permission from Richard H. Willis, ''Ethnic and National Images: People vs. Nations,'' *Public Opinion Quarterly*, vol. 32, 1968, p. 190.

contrast, in the national ratings there is no exception. All noncommunist governments rate higher than do all communist governments. The Soviet people and the Soviet government both rate consistently above the peoples and governments of the other communist states about which questions were asked.[28]

Results concerning images and trust among allies were substantiated even more recently. In a study reported by NATO in 1973, Europeans have the highest trust for the Swiss, with the United States ranking second. Although the polling was conducted prior to British entry into the European Economic Community, trust for Britain ranked third among people questioned in Belgium, France, Germany, Italy, and the Netherlands. Although engaged in the process of economic integration, none of the Common Market members on the list received a majority expression of trust in all four other countries.[29]

These data, old as they may be, underscore the fact that governments are not alone in their resistance to world government. Among allies as well as among enemies, there are still barriers to mass perceptions that are sufficient to rebut the assumption that if national governments were subordinated to a world government, antipathies among the peoples would fade and that an integrated world society would result. We thus must be cautious in presuming the social practicability of world government.

Probable Success upon Implementation

What if the social and political barriers to the implementation of a world government were superable? Would the maturation of a world society be sure to deter further warfare? Most critics of the world government ideal argue that on the national level, central government has not invariably deterred civil war. Even in a world state, to say nothing of a global federation, occasional warfare will erupt.

[28]For a full report of findings, see Richard H. Willis, ''Ethnic and National Images: People vs. Nations,'' *Public Opinion Quarterly*, vol. 32, 1968, pp. 186–201.
[29]For a full summary of findings, see ''Swiss, Then Americans Most Trusted by Europeans,'' *Atlantic Community News*, March–April 1973, p. 2.

Advocates respond to this objection in a utopian way. On the assumption that an effective federation would achieve universal justice (but by what value standards?) and adequate distribution of authority and goods, they insist that the contemporary causes of war would be eradicated. They assume that the absolute centralization of military force will provide adequate deterrence to the use of force by members. But this blanket assumption overlooks that hostilities often involve the use of power at other levels—that the ability of force to deter force is not absolute but relative to conditions, situations, and perceptions. Furthermore, these assumptions trip upon the same snares as does collective security: Those who threaten the peace are not always identifiable; self-defense may justify the use of force, just as it may be used as camouflage for aggressive intentions; and states sympathize with one another's interests and perceptions, thus minimizing the efficiency of global decision making. The expectation that world government might invariably avert war is untenable in light of these observations. On this subject Claude concludes, "The hard fact is that the record does not support the generalization that the establishment of government, within a social unit of whatever dimensions, infallibly brings about a highly dependable state of peace and order."[30] The skeptics agree that world government and monopoly of force would not ensure perpetual peace.

Philosophical Desirability

Not all observers concur that world government is desirable. Some begin with the expectation that central government will gradually erode even the beneficial effects of different nation-states and of systems of government, leading to a dreary, uncompetitive, and dull political community. More acutely, however, they differ with the universalist assumption that world government is necessarily good government, either in efficiency or in quality. In the American federal system, the delicate balance between executive and legislative prerogatives has undergone fundamental change; why might not the same occur in a world federal system? If political conflict is capable of turning even ideal democracy into tyranny or constitutional authoritarianism, is there any prospect that global problems might produce a world government of universal tyranny? How would coalitions of like-minded states utilize their share of political power in a world system? Does world government necessarily eradicate the threat of worldwide absolutism?

These and scores of other related questions plague the theoretical integrity of the world government philosophy, just as does the claim that there is virtue in peaceful diversity. The critics of world government concepts agree that the idea carries an interpretation of Hobbes's social contract to logical absurdity. Inis Claude has observed, for example:

> Hobbes was right; when a community is so poorly developed that its pre-
> governmental condition is one of intolerable warfare, and its urge to establish

---

[30]Claude, *Power and International Relations*, p. 220.

government rests on no other foundation than a desperate desire to escape the perils of anarchy, the only theoretically adequate government is Leviathan, an omnipotent dictatorship. Locke, too, was right; when a community is held together by strong bonds of agreement concerning what is right and just, and common life is reasonably satisfactory, a limited and mild kind of government, based mainly upon consent, may suffice to supply its needs. World governmentalists describe the world's situation in Hobbesian terms, with a view of emphasizing the urgent need for a global social contract, but they depict the resultant government in Lockean terms, with a view of making the social contract palatable. It would be better to recognize that in so far as this is a Hobbesian world, it is likely to require a Hobbesian government.[31]

Yet there are many who hold that supranational world order short of total world government is both desirable and feasible. One such movement is that of World Peace Through World Law, and the other is the growing sentiment of globalism in the United States. We turn now to those alternatives of the future world order.

World Order: A Minimalist Proposal

The objective of the world order movement is the centralization of political authority for avoidance of war. However, because of the practical barriers to federation, other movements have proposed partial centralization of authority addressed to the specific problems of arms in international politics. The best known among these is the World Peace Through World Law movement, founded by Grenville Clark and assisted by Professor Louis B. Sohn of the Harvard Law School. The student is cautioned, however, that "world law" is not synonymous with "international law." International law purports to interpose norms of behavior between states; the world law movement, in contrast, is concerned explicitly with the removal of arms from international politics, and the establishment of collective security. In the words of Saul Mendlovitz:

> World law . . . ties together two very important notions; disarmament and a collective security system. It argues that the present system of international relations . . . [is] based on unilateral decision-making sanctioned by armaments, and maintains that this situation results in a spiralling arms race that may very well set off a cataclysmic war. The world law model therefore posits the need for complete and general disarmament of all the states in the world down to the level of police forces, and proposes the establishment of a transnational police force that can maintain the territorial integrity and political independence of each state.[32]

The emphasis is on the elimination of arms, rather than their mere limitation.

---

[31]Inis L. Claude, Jr., *Swords into Plowshares,* 4th ed. (New York: Random House, 1971), p. 429.
[32]Saul H. Mendlovitz, "Models of World Order," in Richard B. Gray, ed., *International Security Systems* (Itasca, Ill.: Peacock, 1969), p. 191.

The structural plans for the world law movement are found in the well-known volume *World Peace Through World Law,* prepared by Clark and Sohn.[33] The plan involves two steps. First, it calls for revision of the United Nations Charter to grant the General Assembly full authority of overseeing total disarmament, and with full power of enforcement through weighted voting. Thereafter, the General Assembly would establish an inspection commission that would begin by taking a world census on quality, quantity, and deployment patterns of national arms. The inspection would be accompanied by a truce on further arms production. Upon completion of this preliminary stage, the actual disarmament would consist of a decade in which each state would reduce its national arms stockpile by 10 percent annually, all reductions being distributed evenly among the several military services so that all are reduced at the same rate. Verification of compliance both during and after the actual disarmament stage would be conducted by the United Nations Inspection Service, operating in national territories without governmental barriers. An alternative plan calls for the establishment of a special World Disarmament and World Development Agency with powers similar to those of the other plan.

Although the Clark-Sohn proposals would impinge only on states' freedom to prepare for war, the plans run into several insuperable barriers. Can there be security without arms? Is international inspection trustworthy in a technological age? What are the possible political consequences of secret unilateral violations that result in clear military superiority, even monopoly? And there are still other problems. National armaments are the special possessions of arms manufacturers and certain elites in society, such as rival armed services. What are the prospects of weakening these groups to levels sufficient to make world disarmament proposals attractive to national governments? Do domestic political relationships bode well for the future of total disarmament? The skeptics—and they are legion—see little hope in current national perceptions. Thus, the Clark-Sohn proposals, although humane, remain futuristic, persuading diplomats to concentrate their efforts on international law rather than world law, and on arms limitation rather than arms abolition. The piecemeal attack on sovereignty remains the method of practical choice, despite the increasingly urgent need for major transformation of the international system.

World Order: A Reformist Proposal

In addition to the maximalist and minimalist proposals for world order, there have arisen other reformist ideas, each of which concentrates on adaptation of existing national and international machinery. The prevailing idea at the moment is globalism, a movement tied to the United Nations by virtue of the United Nations's growing role as a center of international planning. Although

---

[33]Grenville Clark and Louis B. Sohn, *World Peace Through World Law,* 3rd ed., enlarged (Cambridge, Mass.: Harvard University Press, 1966).

the United Nations has not achieved the level of authority proposed by Clark and Sohn and it has had little effect on the world's armaments, its record as an innovator and a clearinghouse for planning and activity on other issues has been modestly good. The United Nations has been most successful in economic development, through its Development Program (UNDP). Other areas to which globalism might spread are the allocation and preservation of national resources and the distribution of the world's produce.

But there is another dimension to globalism. As societies develop, they overcome problems; but at the same time, they create new ones. Industry, the prime aim of less developed states, is a case in point. Although industrialization may eradicate poverty, disease, starvation, and lack of the conveniences of life, it also causes environmental degradation, marked economic disparities of domestic social groups, problems of urbanization, depletion of natural resources, and scores of other potentially critical problems. The philosophy of globalism attempts to transform concern for these issues from the national level to the global level.[34] The United Nations began to tackle these problems in the Stockholm Conference on the Human Environment (1972), which was to coordinate a global attack on ecological problems. Outside the United Nations, the only coordinated attempts are regional, the most important among them being the NATO Committee on the Challenges of Modern Society (CCMS). The CCMS already has done significant work toward improving urban transportation and is working on methods to contain and clean maritime oil spills.

One globalist philosopher, Lester R. Brown, holds that the need for global planning is evident in a five-item ''inventory of mankind's problems'': environmental crisis, the widening gap between rich and poor, unemployment, urbanization, and malnutrition.

> Given the scale and complexity of these problems, the remainder of the twentieth century will at best be a traumatic period for mankind, even with a frontal attack on the principal threats of human well-being. At worst it will be catastrophic. At issue is whether we can grasp the nature and dimensions of the emerging threats to our well-being, whether we can create an integrated global economy and a workable world order, and whether we can reorder global priorities so that the quality of life will improve rather than deteriorate.[35]

Although Brown sees the solution to this problem in part as one for supranational institutions (agencies that exercise the sovereignty of governments), he is principally concerned with the development of global planning that is acceptable to governments and that does not alter their status as the principal actors in world politics. He looks ultimately to the creation of a globally planned economy and of a global infrastructure consisting of transport and communications systems. These, he suggests, will improve the quality of life

---

[34]For an eloquent plea for development of a globalist philosophy, see Philippe de Seynes, ''Prospects for a Future Whole World,'' *International Organization*, vol. 26, 1972, pp. 1–17.

[35]Lester R. Brown, *World Without Borders* (New York: Random House, 1972), pp. 11–12.

through central planning and will usher in a new world order—not through fear of threat but through universal satisfaction.

Others who accept the philosophy of globalism have given more attention to its institutional needs. One well known British author, for example, enumerates some of the social requisites to this globalist world order.[36] In fields of human rights, labor standards, and monetary controls, in particular, UN coordination is crucial to the implementation of the philosophy. It seems, therefore, that the development of globalism is tied to the future of some universal organization, most likely the United Nations. It is agreed that if the philosophy is to rise above futuristic platitudes regarding the human instinct for survival, then institutionalization is essential.

All the proposals thus far studied have one thing in common: They all are political-structural concepts of world order; that is, each deals with international anarchy by adjusting the system's structural characteristics and by prescribing mechanisms for addressing existing evils. More recent research, however, focuses on the universal cultural aspects of international relations, recognizing that international events are often nongovernmentally motivated. It assumes that there are universal cultural similarities and, further, that cultural imperatives underlie many international events. Richard Falk characterizes the cultural perspective in this manner:

> The creation of a new system of world order must draw its animating vision from the long and widespread affirmation that all men are part of a single human family, that a oneness lies buried beneath the manifold diversities and dissensions of the present fractionated world, and that this latent oneness alone can give life and fire to a new political program of transformation.[37]

Contemporary research into the future of the international system rests on the concept of universal culture as a basis for effective political cooperation.

The World Order Models Project (WOMP) typifies this new concern. To restore a humanistic view of the international system, WOMP focuses not only on peace and disarmament but also on social justice and welfare. One participant argues that "[i]n a sense, social justice is prior to economic welfare and minimization of violence. Welfare will not be equitably distributed nor violence averted unless justice is done or is in prospect."[38]

Even if one accepts the need for conscious international transformation to achieve peace, justice, welfare, and ecological restoration, many troubling questions remain about transactions in a world without sovereign states. Historically, values have been allocated by power, conflict, and war. How will

---

[36]C. Wilfred Jenks, *The World Beyond the Charter* (London: Allen and Unwin, 1969), especially chap. 4.

[37]Richard A. Falk, *This Endangered Planet* (New York: Random House, 1971), p. 296.

[38]Ali A. Mazrui, "World Order Through World Culture," *Proceedings,* American Society of International Law (1972), pp. 252–253. A comprehensive study of the traditions and contemporary ideas of futuristic research, especially with the universal cultural orientation, appears in Louis René Beres and Harry R. Targ, *Reordering the Planet: Constructing Alternative World Futures* (Boston: Allyn & Bacon, 1974).

these values be achieved in a warless world? Will merely eliminating absolute sovereignty necessarily be more effective for allocating global values? How will crucial value decisions be made? Will such a world be better than the one we have now?

The Problem of Sovereign Transfer

Whether by structural change or universal culture, the creation of world order requires the fundamental alteration of individual states, especially the more powerful. The state, after all, serves many functions, both internally and externally. And whereas the international law of a nation-state system strives to regulate at least the external functions of statehood, effective world order may have to deprive the state of control over those functions. If contemporary international law is only modestly successful in its quest, the drive for comprehensive world order will face the same problems in far greater magnitude. Whereas international law seeks to intrude in the exercise of functions with the consent of states, comprehensive world order attempts to abridge the absoluteness of states' sovereignty. And because this requires new institutional arrangements, world order schemes share with the world federalist notion the problem of transfer of loyalties away from the state to a culturally and politically heterogeneous entity.

But the picture need not be altogether bleak. Because world order ideas imply a rejection of world government, the transfer of loyalties, along with the readjustment of states' sovereignty, need only be both gradual and united. In this sense, the world order idea is consistent with the philosophy of functionalism, except that the reassignment of public tasks and the redirecting of individual loyalties are determined not by the political innocuousness of issues but by (1) the importance of the subject matter as a potential cause of war or as a preventative of war and (2) public and governmental support attainable for transfer away from the nation-state.[39] Even so, unanimity on such issues is unlikely. If issues of transfer are decided by international conventions, it will make little difference whether delegates are appointed by governments or elected by publics. Sentiment to alter fundamental attributes of statehood is not rampant. In addition, delegates are likely to differ on whether or not certain issues cause war.

Mechanisms of Sanction

Under institutionalized world order, by what means will the cooperation among nations be ensured? It is assumed that punishment of violators is the responsibility of all members of the community through both centralized and decentralized means. Besides the use of force by legitimized military control,

---

[39]Norman L. Hill, "The National State and Federation," in Howard O. Eaton, ed., *Federation: The Coming Structure of World Government* (Norman: University of Oklahoma Press, 1944), p. 131. This world order standard is part of the world federalist intellectual tradition.

however, the world order advocates prescribe various lesser sanctions. Foremost among these is the age-old technique of ostracism—economic boycott, censure, cultural isolation, and so on.

Power and Justice

There is probably universal agreement that power and war, the mechanisms by which international decisions have traditionally been made, have resulted in many unjust decisions. But what guarantee have we that some other mechanism will not occasionally be unjust? Presumably, the core values of different national peoples will continue to collide. In the absence of war and traditional power struggles, what standards of justice are to be used? Whose concept of justice ought to prevail in a political process without coercion? International decision making may require a functional equivalent to war, because we know that war has settled fundamental questions at critical historical moments. This is not to suggest that victory is the equivalent of justice; it suggests, rather, that war has been a prime instrument of making decisions and allocating values. Without it, states will require a functional equivalent, or they may be prompted to desert cooperative world order in favor of their individual abilities to coerce.

Furthermore, if states sacrifice their warmaking ability by vesting central coercing authority in some supranational agency, we will be confronted with the problem of that agency's capacity for justice. Might not such an authority be dictatorial and thus prone to injustice? Alternatively, could it fall under the command of an influential minority of states? Or the converse, could it succumb to the avarice of a tyrannical majority of states that disdain the values and interests of others? These problems especially plague maximalist proposals for world order, but they are only relatively less critical to minimalist and reformist views.

Value Standards and Value Objectives

Underlying all other problems and questions is the matter of what standards are to be used and what objectives pursued in a comprehensive world order. Order requires more than simple institutional mechanics; it reflects the value patterns that create it, and it is expected to perform in accordance with some values. The feasibility of world order depends largely on the pertinence of the larger values to their particular political and social cultures, their economic systems and expectations, and their philosophies regarding rights, freedoms, and other elements of public life. Proposals of world order cannot ignore the sociological imperatives of the international community.

Despite lingering sentiment for a world republic, most formal proposals have been products of the early Cold War—an age of extreme ideological sensitivity. As a result, most of them lean heavily on the philosophy of government that is broadly characterized as the Western liberal tradition, with emphasis on civil liberties and economic individualism. At the same time, however, they attempt to attract socialist attention by including collective responsibility for economic development, allocation of natural resources, and distribution of wealth. Nevertheless, there is a distinct Western tone to them, with patent leanings toward an idyllic Western model. Proposals that call for upgrading the United Nations as an instrument of world order, on the other hand, are more realistic in accepting diverse domestic ideologies and political heritages. This realism has been imposed on the Western world largely by the growing solidarity of the left-leaning Third World on economic issues at the United Nations.

The Problem of Internal War

Traditionally, students of international relations have distinguished sharply between international war and internal war, and a body of international law has arisen regulating each. In more recent years, especially in the revolutionary international system of the past half century, the sharpness of the distinction has faded because of the tendency for internal wars to become international wars through intervention and third-party belligerency. It is by now evident that internal wars are a major threat to international peace and security. Can effective world order instruments avert this threat by resolving internal problems? How much authority should be vested in the international community to intervene for such a purpose? Would the authority of centralized enforcement be tantamount to a dictatorial world state or a menace of the majority?

A related problem—and from the viewpoints of justice and welfare perhaps a larger one—is the relation of world order to insurgent groups in strife-torn countries. If insurgency threatens world or regional peace, and if international agents have authority to intervene, are they bound to intervene on behalf of incumbents? Or ought they to act on their judgment as to the relative merits of conflicting claims for social justice? What ideological and philosophical standards ought to be invoked? Who ought to create them? Furthermore, in internal situations, what will be the mechanisms for determining and executing value standards in the absence of unchallenged national authority?

Conclusion

In this section of the book, we considered several approaches to world order, and we concluded by exploring some existing proposals for alternative world futures. Despite the contributions made to international peace and stability by intergovernmental organization, international law, transnational participation, and regional integration, it is apparent that the international system presently points toward self-destruction. This is not due entirely to the potential for war in a balance-of-terror system. It is also attributable partly to the widening gap between the wealthy countries and the poor, with resulting social and political antipathies. Moreover, the presence of egalitarian ideals in the minds of virtually all peoples has heightened the demand for international protection of human rights in light of the failure of national governments in this matter. While all this political demand burgeons, the delicate balance of the human environment is deteriorating at an alarming rate. It is abundantly clear that the international system is in jeopardy unless diplomats and those whom they represent accept the critical need to rise above the narrow psychology of nation-states and nationalism.

In deciding among alternative world futures, we are faced with several choices. We may proceed in the traditional political-structural manner, through maximalist, minimalist, or reformist means. But the social imperatives, the problems of loyalty transfer, and fears about life in the future retard progress on these choices even while the need becomes clearer. Our choice, it now appears, is not between perpetuation of the present structure and vague alternatives but between world order based on piecemeal erosions of states' sovereignty, and highly institutionalized and expansionist world government. The longer the choice is delayed, the more the alternatives will narrow to two: expansionist world government or systemic destruction. As neither is desirable, the wise use of precious time is essential.

Index